To Taff.

All my love ~xxx

x.

Christmas 2000.

STOKE CITY
The Modern Era
– A Complete Record –

Stoke City: The Modern Era – A Complete Record   1-874287-39-2
West Ham: The Elite Era – A Complete Record   1-874287-31-7
Bristol City: The Modern Era – A Complete Record   1-874287-28-7
Colchester Utd: Graham to Whitton – A Complete Record   1-874287-27-9
Halifax Town: From Ball to Lillis – A Complete Record   1-874287-26-0
Portsmouth: From Tindall to Ball – A Complete Record   1-874287-25-2
Portsmouth: Champions of England – 1948-49 & 1949-50   1-874287-38-4
Coventry City: The Elite Era – A Complete Record   1-874287-03-1
Coventry City: An Illustrated History   1-874287-36-8
Luton Town: The Modern Era – A Complete Record   1-874287-05-8
Luton Town: An Illustrated History   1-874287-37-6
Hereford United: The League Era – A Complete Record   1-874287-18-X
Cambridge United: The League Era – A Complete Record   1-874287-32-5
Peterborough United: The Modern Era – A Complete Record 1-874287-33-3
Wimbledon: From Southern League to Premiership   1-874287-09-0
Wimbledon: From Wembley to Selhurst   1-874287-20-1
Wimbledon: The Premiership Years   1-874287-40-6
Aberdeen: The European Era – A Complete Record   1-874287-11-2
The Story of the Rangers 1873-1923   1-874287-16-3
The Story of the Celtic 1888-1938   1-874287-15-5
History of the Everton Football Club 1878-1928   1-874287-14-7
The Romance of the Wednesday 1867-1926   1-874287-17-1
Red Dragons in Europe – A Complete Record   1-874287-01-5
The Book of Football: A History to 1905-06   1-874287-13-9
England: The Quest for the World Cup – A Complete Record 1-897850-40-9
Scotland: The Quest for the World Cup – A Complete Record 1-897850-50-6
Ireland: The Quest for the World Cup – A Complete Record 1-897850-80-8

STOKE CITY
THE MODERN ERA
— A Complete Record —

Series Editor: Clive Leatherdale

Simon Lowe

DESERT ISLAND BOOKS

First Published in 2000

DESERT ISLAND BOOKS LIMITED
89 Park Street, Westcliff-on-Sea, Essex SS0 7PD
United Kingdom
www.desertislandbooks.com

© 2000 Simon Lowe

The right of Simon Lowe to be identified as author of this work has been
asserted under The Copyright Designs and Patents Act 1988

British Library Cataloguing-in-Publication Data
A catalogue record for this book is available from the British Library

ISBN   1-874287-39-2

Printed in Great Britain
by
Biddles Ltd, Guildford

Photographs in this book are reproduced by kind permission of:
Huston Spratt, Andy Peck, Central Office of Information,
Sporting Pictures UK, Action Images, Anthony Brown

CONTENTS

4. DECLINE AND FALL – 1985-91

5. SKIP TO MY LOU MACARI – 1991-97

6. RULE BRITANNIA – 1997-2000

PREFACE

The red and white colours of Stoke City have been graced by many great players over the years. When you think of Matthews, Franklin, Steele and, during my time, Banks, Greenhoff and Hudson, you can see the type of club Stoke is. The fans have been educated by players who performed at the very highest level. I joined the club in 1967 and never regretted my decision to choose the Potters ahead of Fulham.

Tony Waddington was the manager who signed me from Glentoran and it took him all of ten minutes to convince me that my footballing future lay at Stoke City. On joining the club I found myself in dreamland. I was barely twenty and had left my homeland and a big family behind me. I was greeted with great enthusiasm by Harry Gregg, hero of the Munich air crash, which nearly wiped out Matt Busby's Manchester United. Peter Dobing sat quietly in the corner smoking his pipe chatting with Roy Vernon of Wales, and Tony Allen and Gordon Banks, both of England. I had wanted since the age of five to become a professional footballer and here I was sitting in the company of players whose pictures had decorated my bedroom wall back in Dublin. That was fantasy football indeed.

Waddo gathered players of pure skill and encouraged them to express themselves. Very rarely did team-talks or tactics interfere with how the players wanted to play. I believe that the team of 1970 to '74 was the best the club has ever had. Winning the League Cup in 1972, losing two FA Cup semi-finals and coming so close to winning the championship in 1974 had every emotion you can think of – both for players and supporters, and I am proud to have been part of it.

The club's fall from grace was brought about by a combination of factors and is largely the subject of this book. However, the future is bright. Since the Icelandic takeover in November 1999, with Gudjon Thordarsson in charge, there is huge optimism surrounding the brand new Britannia Stadium. Stoke City has always been a big club. The mind just about remembers 49,000 at the Victoria Ground to see us beat Man U 2-1 in an FA Cup-tie. That's what potential is all about. Promotion in 2001 would settle the nerves and then – who knows what the club is actually capable of achieving.

TERRY CONROY
Stoke City and Republic of Ireland

AUTHOR'S NOTE

In December 1999 the quarterly record of the Association of Football Statisticians contained a Desert Island Books catalogue. It sought new football projects, and in due course this book was born. I have been fascinated by football facts and figures for as long as I can remember and accumulated them for almost as long. This book is the outcome of my two loves, statistics and Stoke City. My aim is to produce a definitive account of the most turbulent period in Stoke's history. In keeping with the 'complete record' format of Desert Island Football Histories, the book comprises two distinct sections. The first is a season-by-season narrative that analyses the changing fortunes of the club. The second presents a statistical game-by-game chronology, incorporating every fact that could possibly be fitted in and quite a few more besides. In an undertaking of such immensity there are bound to be errors and for those I apologise unreservedly. Every effort has been made to ensure that these are kept to the absolute minimum. Establishing the accuracy of previous research has seen me spend many hours leafing through the reports in the *Sentinel* at Newcastle-under-Lyme library, where cross-referencing has revealed many discrepancies, the most prevalent involving attendances. As the club's own figures were often rounded up, I have preferred those recorded in the *Sentinel*.

Such a book is never the result of just one person's endeavours. Clive Leatherdale and Gayle Newman at Desert Island Books have supported and guided me in my first venture into serious factual writing. Regarding the provision of photographs, I would like to express heartfelt thanks to the following: Huston Spratt, for many years the Stoke City photographer for the *Sentinel*; Andy Peck, photographer for the Stoke City Southern Supporters Club; and Julian Boodell, an avid collector. Each has provided invaluable help. Julian has also assisted in completing gaps in the statistical section through allowing me access to his programme collection. I would also like to thank my fellow Desert Island Books author Jim Brown – whose tome on Coventry City is superb – for his assistance and support.

Although forewarned about the size of the task when accepting this undertaking, nothing could truly prepare me for the time-consuming research required for such a detailed book. I would therefore like to thank my girlfriend, Kath, for her understanding and support, and the Thomas branch of my family for putting me up – and putting up with me – when researching in Staffordshire.

SIMON LOWE

INTRODUCTION

The origins of Stoke City Football Club have, in the recent past, been the matter of some dispute. For years, the club's crest bore the legend 'Founded 1863'. Being the second oldest League club, after Notts County, carried a certain kudos. However this date has been thrown into doubt by the research of Wade Martin, whose evidence points to a later year – 1868 – when Henry John Almond, an Old Carthusian, formed a team amongst his fellow apprentices at the North Staffordshire Railway Works.

Known initially as 'the Ramblers' and later as Stoke FC, the team played local friendlies, the most remarkable of which was a 26-0 victory over Mow Cop in the first round of the inaugural Staffordshire Cup in 1878. The club, having merged with the Stoke Victoria Athletics Club, settled into new premises, the athletics stadium, which became known as the Victoria Ground, taking its name from the nearby Victoria Hotel.

Turning professional in 1885, the club were founder members of the Football League in 1888, unfortunately finishing bottom for the first two seasons and losing their place – there being at the time no Second Division. Stoke returned in 1891-92, when the League was expanded from twelve clubs to fourteen. The Potters reached the semi-final of the FA Cup in 1899, beating Sheffield Wednesday and Tottenham on the way, before losing 1-3 to Derby. In 1906-07 they finished bottom of the First Division again, and the following year finished their first season in Division Two with a crippling £1,100 deficit, as a result of which they folded.

A new club rose out of the ashes. AJ Barker, the new secretary-manager, moulded a team which competed in the Birmingham and District League and the Southern League before rejoining the Football League's Division Two at the end of the Great War. Promotion to Division One in 1922 was followed by relegation in 1923 and then again in 1926. The club spent 1926-27 in Division Three (North), but at least their stay was brief: they finished the season as champions.

Renamed Stoke City FC in 1925, when Stoke-on-Trent was granted city status, the club did not return to the top flight until 1932-33, when they unleashed one of the greatest footballing talents the world has ever seen – Stanley Matthews. This time the club blossomed in the big time. Home attendances trebled. England international Matthews was the focus of attention throughout the land. Ground records were regularly broken when Stoke – and Matthews – visited. The largest crowd ever to attend an English domestic match outside Wembley, 84,569, saw Manchester City beat Stoke 1-0 at Maine Road in an FA Cup quarter-final in 1933.

Under the stewardship of manager Bob McGrory, Stoke achieved their highest ever finish in Division One, fourth, in 1935-36. West Brom were thrashed 10-3 at the Victoria Ground in February 1937 with centre-forward Freddie Steele scoring four. These halcyon days saw the club provide three of England's forwards for a game at Hampden Park in 1937 – Matthews, Steele and Joe Johnson. A record crowd at the Victoria Ground, 51,373, saw Stoke draw 0-0 with Arsenal on Easter Monday.

But trouble was never far away. A row was brewing, stemming from the dropping of McGrory's best friend, Bobby Liddle, when Matthews first broke into the team. Matthews refused to play when an improved signing-on fee was not forthcoming for the 1938-39 season. Eventually, Matthews got his money but lost out on being paid over the summer. The onset of World War II postponed the next instalment of the saga.

In the war years Stoke played in the League North, with players such as Frank Bowyer, Tommy Sale, Frank Mountford and Frank Soo losing the best part of their careers to the conflict. The War also saw the instigation of what became a great tradition of the club. Stoke President Sir Francis Joseph commissioned local potters to make 22 Loving Cups, 21 of which were distributed to the chairmen of the other First Division clubs. To this day, the Stoke board cele-brate the first home match of the New Year by drinking from the remaining cup with the directors of the visiting team.

The introduction of a two-leg FA Cup in 1945-46 saw Stoke travel to Bolton after a goalless first-leg quarter-final. A crowd of 65,419 saw the action with an estimated 20,000 locked outside. An influx of spectators just before kick-off led to two crush barriers collapsing behind the goal which Stoke were defending. It became necessary for the referee to take the players off the pitch as people spilled on to it. The crush claimed 33 lives and 520 injured in what became known as the Burnden Park disaster.

The 1946-47 season saw Stoke mount their first serious challenge for the championship. The icy winter extended the fixtures into early summer. City's last game was at Sheffield United on 14 June, when a win would bring the title to Stoke. At this inopportune moment tension between Matthews and McGrory erupted again.

This time the split was irrevocable. Matthews was dropped and asked to 'prove his fitness in the reserves'. He responded by demanding a transfer. Having settled in Blackpool, where he had been stationed during the War, Matthews was immediately subject to a bid by Joe Smith, the Blackpool manager. Ignoring the pleas of Stoke fans, Matthews, despite being a veteran of 32, was sold in May for £11,500 (at the time the record fee was £14,000). Without their star turn, Stoke went down at Bramall Lane 1-2. Who knows, Matthews might have made all the difference.

Next to leave the Victoria Ground was England centre-half Neil Franklin. Having made a record 27 consecutive appearances for his country, his name was among the first on selectors' team-sheets. Deluded with the lifestyle that the maximum wage of £12 could finance, Franklin decided to join a group of British professionals headed for Colombia, where he signed for Independiente Santa Fe, along with fellow Stoke player George Mountford. Reports indicate that the financial 'inducements' amounted to some £3,500 per year. But money wasn't everything, and inside two months the naive Franklin was back in England, banned from international football – as Colombia were not affiliated to FIFA – and ignominiously sold to Hull for £22,500. Although Franklin never played for Stoke again, Mountford completed the season in Colombia and, once he had served a suspension, carried on playing for Stoke.

Bob McGrory severed his connections with the club in 1952, resigning over policy differences with the board. The bluff Scot had played as a right-back for Stoke from 1921 to 1935, making a club record 511 appearances, before taking over as manager. McGrory had wanted to replace the departed Freddie Steele, as his side was shot-shy in attack. The board preferred to develop local talent and were reluctant to dip into their purses. McGrory was replaced by the former Wolves full-back and fitness fanatic, Frank Taylor, but, handicapped by a parsimonious board and an ageing squad, Stoke were relegated the following season after losing to doomed Derby in the last match, even missing a penalty.

Eight years in the doldrums followed. With few exceptions, Stoke failed to mount any serious challenge for promotion. A record 8-0 victory over Lincoln in February 1957, with winger Tim Coleman bagging seven goals, did little to disguise the wider problems. New chairman Albert Henshall decided to find another manager.

Coach Tony Waddington was promoted into the hot seat in June 1960 and he immediately set about building his own team. Despite the signings of Jimmy O'Neill, Jackie Mudie and Tommy Thompson the crowds continued to dwindle. Attendances in 1960-61 slumped below an average of 10,000 for the first time since 1908.

It took a simple masterstroke to transform the club. Waddington bought back Matthews, at the princely age of 46, from Blackpool. The maestro signed in front of BBC Television's Sportsview cameras and made his second Stoke debut at home to Huddersfield on 28 October 1961. The 35,974 crowd quadrupled that of City's previous home game and more than repaid Stan's £3,000 transfer fee. The club was on the up. In 1962-63 Stoke won promotion as Second Division champions with a sprightly 48-year-old Matthews scoring the championship-clinching goal at home to Luton.

City's players were employed over the summer to lay concrete on the Boothen Stand paddock. They were paid a shilling an hour for their labour. The previously atrocious pitch was injected with special sand to prevent waterlogging. This did not stop Waddington having the pitch watered before home matches by the local fire brigade, as his players had become accustomed to wet turf!

1963-64 saw Stoke reach the League Cup final, a two-legged affair against Leicester. Following a 1-1 draw at home, the away leg was lost 2-3 in a tight and dramatic contest. On 21 March 1964 Stoke racked up a 9-1 win against Ipswich, which still stands as the club's biggest ever margin of victory.

Stoke's centenary was celebrated (prematurely as it now appears) in 1963 with a prestigious friendly against European Champions Real Madrid. In February 1965 Stanley Matthews finally retired at the age of 50. He bade farewell to Stoke City with a celebratory game against a World XI, starring Puskas, Di Stefano, Masopust and Yashin, at the Victoria Ground.

Waddington had cannily signed several other experienced players to complement Matthews. Dennis Viollet (from Manchester United), George Eastham (Newcastle), and Jimmy McIlroy (Burnley) were all 30-plus when putting pen to paper. These old-stagers proved useful foils to the promising younger players, such as John Ritchie, Alan Bloor and Denis Smith, who were establishing themselves in what was becoming a redoubtable team.

The manager pulled off another coup when signing the goal-keeper widely acclaimed as the world's best. Gordon Banks arrived in 1967, after the emerging Peter Shilton had seized his place in the Leicester side. Playing behind a home-grown back four of Smith, Bloor, Jackie Marsh and Mike Pejic, Banks provided the last line of a resolute defence.

In 1969-70 Stoke finished ninth in the League. Despite being knocked out of the FA Cup by Second Division Watford, a wave of optimism surrounded the club. The fans had faith in Waddington. A challenge for domestic honours and a European place was expected.

## 1

LAND OF SMOKE AND GLORY
1970-1976

LEAGUE DIVISION 1   **1970-71**
League Division 1   13th
League Cup   2nd Round
FA Cup   3rd Place

After completing a decade in the manager's seat, Tony Waddington *was* Mr Stoke City. Shrewd in the transfer market, Waddington had invested heavily in experience. The likes of Stanley Matthews, Jimmy McIlroy, Jackie Mudie and Harry Gregg were all into the twilight of their careers when signing for the club, but their experience ensured that Stoke became a fixture in Division One. During the mid-1960s the manager had instituted what became known as 'Waddington Wall' – two midfielders sitting back to ensure safety in numbers should the opposition break away. The downside was that there was often not enough support for the forwards. The system was, however, effective, bringing a modicum of success through a first ever final appearance in the 1964 League Cup. The veteran players, however, only had two or three seasons in them and Stoke began to struggle for both continuity and goals, earning a reputation as a defensive, sometimes boring side, finishing just above the relegation zone in 1967-68 and 1968-69.

With this in mind, Waddington changed tack, turning to young, home-grown talent as the backbone of his team. In defence, Alan Bloor and Denis Smith forged a formidable centre-half partnership, while Jackie Marsh and Mike Pejic were overlapping full-backs in the mould of England's Armfield and Cohen. Each was capable of rugged challenges at a time when English football was plagued by the likes of Ron 'Chopper' Harris at Chelsea and Norman 'Bites yer legs' Hunter at Leeds, the tip of a violent iceberg.

Stoke also possessed grit in midfield, characterised by Mike Bernard, who powered through the Victoria Ground mud, biting into tackles alongside Welsh international John Mahoney. Neither were angels, but with such a rugged defensive unit Waddington no longer required the extra bodies to defend in depth. Stoke adopted a 4-4-2 passing game, dictated by veterans George Eastham and Peter Dobing and skilful forward Jimmy Greenhoff, the club's record signing at £100,000 from Birmingham in 1969. All three would have been termed inside-forwards in the era preceding Ramsey's 1966 'wingless wonders'. They provided the ammunition for John Ritchie, a powerful centre-forward whose skill with the ball at his feet belied his 6ft 2in frame. In 1969-70 City totalled 56 League goals, a marked improvement on the 40 scored during the previous season's relegation battle.

Waddington's coup de grace had come in 1967 when he signed the world's best goalkeeper, Gordon Banks. Leicester manager Matt Gillies could no longer keep young prodigy Peter Shilton out of the side and Waddington swooped for England's World Cup winning keeper. The signings of Banks and Greenhoff were major factors in the club's rise to ninth in 1969-70, and, with the balance of the team shifting towards youth, the future looked bright. On their day Stoke could beat anyone; Waddington just needed to instil consistency.

Banks was the only Stoke player to go to the 1970 World Cup in Mexico. The sickness that denied him a place in England's quarter-final with West Germany has sunk deep into the English football psyche, particularly as the lapses of his replacement, Peter Bonetti, contributed to England's 2-3 defeat. With Banks having made what is considered one of football's greatest ever saves during the group match with Brazil, to lose in the quarter-finals was a national disaster. Ironically, Banks succumbing to 'Montezuma's Revenge' enhanced his standing with the football public: he was now seen as indispensable to England's cause. How he fared for Stoke during the new season could prove crucial to England's chances in the forthcoming European Nations Cup (European Championships).

Stoke suffered a shaky start. Injuries exposed the lack of strength in depth and left the team short of goals. Denis Smith was never shy of throwing himself into dangerous challenges – dangerous as much to himself as to opponents. Throughout his career Smith's wholehearted approach meant he spent months on the treatment table rather than the pitch, where his influence was always missed. Marsh, Greenhoff and Dobing were also injured by the time City, with the only eleven fit players, drew 0-0 at home to Forest.

To add insult to injuries, Stoke were dumped out of the League Cup by Second Division Millwall and Mike Bernard earned himself the dubious distinction of becoming the first Stoke player to be shown a red card after the system had been introduced for the World Cup finals. To rub salt into the wounds, City were beaten by Motherwell in the inaugural Anglo-Scottish Cup. This tournament grew out of Celtic's European Cup success in 1967 and speculation about how Celtic would fare against the likes of Liverpool. In fact, this bastardised competition omitted clubs who had qualified for Europe – so the point was never put to the test – and acted as a distraction, not to say irrelevance, to everyone else.

As for Banks, he was not having the best of times. He conceded five at West Brom and four at Manchester City and was rested from the England team for the first international of the season. To make matters worse it was his nemesis, Peter Shilton, who was blooded by Ramsey as England beat East Germany 3-1. Banks even missed Stoke's best performance, the 5-0 thrashing of Bertie Mee's title-chasing Arsenal. But just two wins in the next twelve games put City in trouble.

Stoke's form was not helped by the worsening injury situation. Peter Dobing, although stylish enough to have won seven England Under-23 caps in the mid-1960s, was not afraid to mix it with the no-nonsense defenders with whom he was faced on a weekly basis. His disciplinary record was poor, culminating in a record nine-week suspension handed down by a despairing League commission. In his last game before the ban commenced Dobing broke his leg badly in a crunching challenge with Ipswich's Mick Mills. The following Saturday, Willie Stevenson also broke his leg, ending his season. Three weeks later Ritchie badly damaged his knee against Everton. He would be out for four months. By late November, as the crisis – a direct result of Stoke's belligerent style – deepened, City were struggling, woefully short of goals.

It was the players' spirit that saw City embark upon a run of seventeen games with only two defeats in League and Cup. The run took them clear of relegation and into the furthest reaches of the FA Cup. Nineteen-year-old Sean Haslegrave was given his opportunity, inspiring Stoke to a 1-0 win over Derby on his debut. Left-winger Harry Burrows, a £27,000 signing from Villa in 1965, also produced some of the finest football of his career, giving City an extra dimension on the left and contributing vital goals with his cannonball left foot. Another youngster, Stewart Jump, emerged from the reserves to cover in midfield. He also filled in at centre-half and even played as a striker. The injury crisis threatened the gargantuan FA Cup run, which came close to ending at both Ipswich and Second Division Hull, but Stoke's combative nature, so suited to cup football, allowed City to reach their first FA Cup semi-final for 71 years.

The catalyst was the return to form of Greenhoff and Terry Conroy. Of the 21 Cup goals City scored during the unbeaten run, Greenhoff netted six and Conroy, deputising for Ritchie at centre-forward, seven. Dubliner Conroy had arrived from Northern Irish side Glentoran, a well known nursery for talent from both sides of the Irish border for the English League. Waddington had tried to sign him as an 18-year-old after Conroy starred in a friendly against Stoke in 1964, but he opted to complete his printing apprenticeship. Waddington finally got his man for £10,000 in March 1967. The mere sight of Conroy – flowing red hair, enormous sideburns and waif-like, white legs – brought taunts from opposing fans. Often he would have the last laugh with his dramatic changes of direction, enabling him to skip past tackles and get to the byline or shoot. It had been thought by the more superstitious Stoke fans that the No 7 shirt was jinxed when worn by anyone other than Stan Matthews. Conroy's form soon laid that particular ghost to rest.

Defeat in the FA Cup semi-final (see Match of the Season) was bound to hit morale. League form slumped. Even with Ritchie back in the fold the goals dried up, particularly after Conroy injured his knee at home against Wolves, ending his season. Gates collapsed after the Cup exit as the euphoria, which so often attends the club in times of success, dissipated astonishingly quickly.

In the final match of the season Stoke became only the second club to finish third in the FA Cup. The FA experimented with the two beaten semi-finalists playing off for third place as a Friday-night prelude to the final. Traditionalists declared it a 'nothing' game and the gate of just over 5,000 enforced this view, but City fought back from 0-2 down to beat Everton. 'Watch out for us in the cups next year!' vowed man of the match Mike Bernard.

Match of the Season 1970-71

Arsenal 2   Stoke 2

FA Cup, Semi-final, 27 March 1971

Soothsayers had predicted that a team in red and white would lift the FA Cup in 1971. Arsenal also sported those colours, but the euphoria which greeted Stoke's quarter-final victory was tempered little by the thought of playing Bertie Mee's men. After all, City had put five past them earlier in the season. Being one game away from a first Wembley final meant that Stoke's allocation of 27,000 tickets sold out in under four hours as fans queued overnight in the rain to secure a place at Hillsborough.

The Gunners were chasing Leeds at the top of the table and aiming for the elusive double which only their rivals Tottenham had completed in the 20th Century. In the middle of a tremendous run of fourteen League wins out of sixteen, Arsenal had, however, gone out of the Fairs Cup on the away-goals rule to Cologne in midweek.

DID YOU KNOW?

The most matches Stoke have ever played in a season is 67 in 1971-72 – 42 League, 12 League Cup, 9 FA Cup, and 4 Anglo-Scottish Cup. Jackie Marsh played in 65.

Ironically both Stoke and Arsenal wore their change kits, so there was no red to be seen on the pitch.

Straight from the kick-off Stoke tore into Arsenal with Greenhoff outstanding. As one press report put it: 'You could have fired a cannonball at him and he would have nodded it down to Ritchie's feet.' Arsenal played as if they knew their season hung in the balance and City took a deserved lead with a rather fortuitous goal. From a corner, Smith blocked Peter Storey's clearance and the ball rocketed past Bob Wilson into the roof of the net. On 29 minutes Charlie George gifted a back-pass to John Ritchie, who calmly waltzed around Wilson to put Stoke 2-0 up. Another goal would surely have killed Arsenal off, but when Greenhoff found himself in the clear he lost his nerve and shot high and wide.

Arsenal were made of stern stuff. Just after half-time a half-cleared cross was rammed home by Peter Storey. The tide was turning inexorably towards the Gunners. Stoke's back four looked increasingly ill at ease and the nerves even spread to Banks, who shuffled uneasily around his penalty area, allowing himself to get worked up by volubly contesting every decision which went against Stoke.

In injury-time a corner was conceded after Banks appeared to be fouled when claiming a cross. Referee Pat Partridge waved away Stoke's massed protests and City paid for their indiscipline when a quick corner was nodded goalwards by Frank McLintock, who had escaped his marker, Smith. As the ball arrowed towards the corner of the net Mahoney threw himself full-length to punch it away. A penalty was inevitable and the City players visibly wilted. Banks, livid after what he felt were a succession of refereeing decisions favouring Arsenal, was wrong-footed by Storey's rather poor kick. The clock on the main stand at Hillsborough showed 4.44pm. Four minutes of injury-time had been played.

The result rankles to this day with many members of the team, of whom only Greenhoff ever played in an FA Cup final. Arsenal won the replay easily, going on to claim a famous double. City won just three more games all season.

LEAGUE DIVISION 1   **1971-72**
League Division 1   17th
League Cup   Winners
FA Cup   4th place

Perhaps influenced by the return to fitness of the majority of the squad, Waddo indulged in no transfer activity over the summer. Long-term broken-leg victim Peter Dobing was recovering match fitness in the reserves. Only Conroy was unavailable as he continued his rehabilitation following summer cartilage surgery. A 2-1 pre-season victory in Greece against Greek Cup holders Olympiakos added to the speculation that Stoke might challenge for the title, but within the opening week the title talk was dashed. A feeble draw at Coventry was followed by a 1-3 defeat at Southampton.

Waddington risked a half-fit Dobing in place of Willie Stevenson and everything clicked into place. The skipper's probing passing encouraged the team's momentum to flow. A 1-0 victory at Arsenal partly avenged the Cup semi-final defeat, and after a 0-0 draw at Nottingham Forest, Stoke were up to fifth. But a 0-4 hammering at Derby reiterated Stoke's inconsistency. This time it was suspension rather than injury which disrupted the team pattern. Smith and Bloor reached the points limit by mid-September. Pejic, Conroy and Dobing, yet again, would all miss games later in the season due to ill-discipline. City's small squad was once again being stretched to the limit by over-zealousness.

In the Anglo-Scottish Cup, now renamed the Texaco Cup, Stoke this time got the better of Motherwell. A 5-1 victory over two legs erased the previous season's embarrassment. In the next round a combined 45,000 people saw the two legs, as Stoke lost 3-4 overall to Derby. Those figures suggested that the competition was not such a dead duck after all, but the League killed it off following complaints of too much football for too little reward.

The upturn in the team's fortunes coincided with the return of veteran midfielder George Eastham from South Africa, where he was spending his summers coaching the Hellenic club in Cape Town. Eastham was a respected figure in the game, having been largely responsible for the lifting of the maximum wage in the early 1960s. He had gone on strike over Newcastle's refusal to either release him or offer improved terms upon the expiry of his contract. Supported by PFA Chairman Jimmy Hill, Eastham took the club to court and won, paving the way for the modern millionaire stars of today, who name their price. At the age of 36, Eastham was looking to the future, but his subtle touch-play meant that his influence on younger players around him was enormous.

The cups proved the happiest hunting grounds for Stoke. The epic League cup semi-final clashes against Ron Greenwood's West Ham have entered the folklore of both clubs. After going in front through Dobing in the home leg, Stoke wilted. Banks was beaten by England colleague Geoff Hurst's penalty and Clyde Best scored a second to make the second leg a formality. Or so it seemed. Stoke's resolve at Upton Park saw Ritchie level the tie and, with no away goals rule in operation, a nail-biting extra-time period ensued. With three minutes remaining, Hammers winger Harry Redknapp chased a through-ball on the right hand side of Stoke's penalty area. Banks called for the ball, believing that full-back Mike Pejic would leave it. Pejic lifted his foot as if to clear. Banks halted, only to see Pejic allow it to run under his foot and, as he thought, through to the keeper. Redknapp nipped in, and the desperate Banks wrapped his arms around his legs, bringing him down. A penalty was given and Banks, increasing tetchy in his 'mature' years, lost his rag. He ranted at referee Walker, and even at Redknapp, before taking his place on the goal-line. He later admitted that he was so incensed with himself for giving the penalty away that he was doing all he could think of to redress the balance. Geoff Hurst blasted this spot-kick just as fiercely as at the Vic, but not so accurately. The ball flew at shoulder height just to Banks' right, and the keeper diverted the thunderbolt over the bar. If any moment summed up Stoke's will to win a first trophy it was that. The save took the breath away and had a spectacular influence on the outcome of the tie. The balance had shifted crucially in favour of Stoke.

The third match, at Hillsborough, finished goalless, necessitating a fourth, at rain-soaked Old Trafford. Bobby Moore, deputising for injured keeper Bobby Ferguson, saved a Mike Bernard penalty, but the ball rebounded to Bernard, who scored. Stoke showed greater desire, and in monsoon conditions Conroy belted the winner past the restored Ferguson to send Stoke to Wembley for the first time in their history.

In the FA Cup, the quarter-finals saw Stoke draw at Old Trafford to bring Manchester United back to the Vic. There, Denis Smith wrote himself into club folklore by turning up injured, persuading Waddington he was fit, then scoring. In extra-time Stoke clinched a third semi-final appearance in two seasons.

The sense of excitement at a first Wembley final exceeded that experienced during the previous season's FA Cup semi. The largest crowd ever to watch Stoke assembled on 4 March to see a famous victory (see Match of the Season). City were even finding success in the Pop charts. *We'll Be With You*, penned by local songwriters Tony Hatch and Jackie Trent and recorded by the squad, reached No 34.

The music-writers of the *Crossroads* and *Neighbours* soaps produced a memorable terrace chant, still recited on a regular basis today.

We'll be with you, be with you, be with you / Every step along the way
We'll be with you, be with you, be with you / By your side we'll always stay
City, City / Tell the lads in red and white / Everything will be all right
City, City / You're the pride of all of us today

The celebrations as the team paraded the club's first trophy from Barlaston to Stoke Town Hall on an open-top bus reflected the long years bereft of success which had forced even the most ardent Stoke fans to doubt whether the club would ever win a major prize. Waddington had proved them wrong. It was he who, over a dozen years, had – on a shoestring budget – turned a club going nowhere into a team capable of challenging for honours.

The jubilation disguised Stoke's dreadful League form. City won only two games after 6 November and lost as many as they drew. Everything appeared overshadowed by the need to consummate the Wembley dream, as if the pain of the previous year's FA Cup semi-final needed to be expurgated, and quickly. The week before the FA Cup semi-final, City risked censure by the League for fielding a side with only two first-team regulars against doomed Forest, who duly won 2-0.

Their second successive FA Cup semi-final saw Stoke take on Arsenal once again, desperate to set the record straight. There was no shortage of drama this time, either. With Arsenal 1-0 up, Bob Wilson strained a cartilage trying to collect a hanging cross. He was soon beaten – by his own player. Peter Simpson, under pressure from Smith, turned a cross past his immobile keeper when in normal circumstances he would have left the ball for Wilson. Striker John Radford went in goal for the final fifteen minutes. Stoke piled on the pressure but failed to break down that famous defence.

Stoke went into the replay at Goodison Park full of confidence. But there was to be no fairytale repeat of the West Ham saga. City looked comfortable at 1-0 up, but then Peter Dobing mysteriously fouled George Armstrong and Charlie George rattled in the penalty. The match was settled by one of the most controversial incidents in Stoke City's history. Linesman Bob Mathewson mistook one of Everton's white-coated programme sellers on the far side of the ground for the change-kit shirt of a Stoke defender, thereby reckoning John Radford to be onside when in fact he was off. He kept his flag down as Radford raced clear to plant the winner past Banks. For his troubles, Mr Mathewson earned himself a statue of a horse's backside, presented to him by the Supporters Club.

DID YOU KNOW?

Playing for City, Denis Smith suffered 5 broken legs, 4 noses, 1 ankle, 1 collar-bone, 1 chipped spine, 1 ricked back, over 100 facial stitches and countless broken fingers.

Before the final game of the season Waddington offloaded a key player for the first time in nearly three years when selling midfielder Mike Bernard to Everton for £125,000, funds which would enable him to buy. Bernard's edgy performance in the League Cup final had singled him out as a player unsuited to the big occasion. Waddington envisaged Stoke being involved in more such games, and needed men who could handle the pressure. Rumours of new signings abounded but Waddington's message to the fans was that he would wait for the right players to become available.

Undoubtedly, with a first trophy adorning the boardroom, Stoke were now a team to be reckoned with, but if League success is the yardstick by which great teams are judged, they had fallen short. Waddington had to address this problem by improving the squad. He knew perfectly well that his team was prone to suspension and injury caused by over-exuberant tackling. To have a squad of only fifteen senior professionals was woefully short of the mark. Even with all the players fit, the side had yet to fully discover the killer instinct to win vital matches. Yet Stoke's success was reflected in the end-of-season polls. Gordon Banks was voted Footballer of the Year, with George Eastham finishing third. Banks was also voted Sportsman of the Year, a mark of his importance to the nation, a talisman rather than just a footballer.

Match of the Season 1971-72

Stoke 2 Chelsea 1

League Cup final, 4 March 1972

Dave Sexton's Blues could throw their weight around as well as any English side of the time. In Ron 'Chopper' Harris and David Webb they possessed two of the most uncompromising players of the era. Pitched against Stoke's rugged defence, this meant that the first final in City's history was never going to be a classic. Chelsea's recent cup pedigree – having won the FA Cup in 1970 and the Cup-Winners' Cup in 1971 – was second to none. The match also presented a contest between the two keepers vying for the England jersey, Gordon Banks and Peter 'the Cat' Bonetti. Chelsea had beaten Tottenham 5-4 in the semi-final to reach Wembley, but had been shocked in the FA Cup by Orient, 2-3 the previous week.

Stoke took the game to Chelsea from the start. Conroy had one effort saved by Bonetti before Eastham crossed to the far post where the Irish winger challenged for a header. The ball looped over the onrushing Bonetti and into the net. Chelsea needed to hit back quickly, and, as the tackles flew in, Bloor and Pejic were booked by referee Norman Burtenshaw. Peter Osgood returned the compliment, flattening first Greenhoff and then Smith to earn himself a booking.

City coped well with Chelsea's pressure until just before half-time, when Bloor made a hash of a clearance and the ball dropped into the path of Osgood. He initially miskicked and fell over, but recovered to hook the ball past a startled Banks whilst lying prone on the ground.

Chelsea were forced to reshuffle when Paddy Mulligan limped off at half-time with a knee injury. With their side unbalanced by having to move Peter Houseman to left-back, Stoke took advantage, feeding Conroy at every opportunity. City had the ball in the net again but Ritchie was offside as he headed home.

The breakthrough arrived on 73 minutes. Conroy now had the beating of Harris, who had swapped wings with Houseman. His cross found Ritchie at the far post where he cushioned the ball back to Greenhoff to unleash a volley. Bonetti parried, but only into the path of George Eastham, who prodded home left-footed from four yards. It was his first goal of the season.

With memories of the previous season's injury-time heartache in the FA Cup still fresh in everyone's minds, hearts were in mouths as Bernard tried a back-pass from the halfway line which fell short of Banks. Baldwin fastened onto the ball but the England keeper's presence outside his area ensured that the Chelsea player didn't get a clean contact with his attempted shot.

At the end the celebrations of a first trophy on a first visit to Wembley were loud and raucous. A Wembley spokesman went on record to say that he had never heard such fantastic vocal support.

LEAGUE DIVISION 1   **1972-73**
League Division 1   15th
League Cup   4th Round
FA Cup   3rd Round
UEFA Cup   1st Round

In June, Stoke competed in the Anglo-Italian Cup. The tournament, another attempt to discover whether English teams were 'better' than Johnny Foreigner, stemmed from 1969 when Swindon won the League Cup, but were denied entry to the Fairs Cup as they were not in the First Division. Swindon organised a game against Roma, the Italian League Cup winners, with a trophy as a prize, and the fully fledged competition, featuring sides from both countries who had not qualified for Europe, was born the following season. Stoke were drawn in a group with Blackpool, Roma and Cantanzaro, playing both Italian sides home and away. Under a blazing sun, the match in Rome boiled over and three players were sent off as Stoke lost 0-2. City beat Cantanzaro twice, but Roma secured a 2-1 win in the Potteries to knock Stoke out. The tournament generally failed to excite and was discontinued after just two years.

As promised, the money from Mike Bernard's sale was spent on quality. Winger Jimmy Robertson came from Ipswich for £80,000 and Geoff Hurst was recruited from West Ham for £70,000. The 28-year-old Robertson had won a Scottish cap with Tottenham and was a skilful player whose speciality was whipping crosses and corners across at pace.

Hurst, the only man to score a hat-trick in a World Cup final, was seen as a huge catch. His arrival was directly responsible for boosting season ticket sales to record six-figure levels. He had scored 252 goals in 502 appearances for West Ham, with whom he had won the FA Cup in 1964 and the European Cup-Winners' Cup in 1965. Now 31, Hurst's recent seasons had not been so successful. His England career had been terminated by a one-sided 1-3 defeat by West Germany in the European Nations Cup quarter-final. The fact that West Ham were prepared to part with such a talismanic figure could be viewed as good business for Stoke or good riddance by the Hammers, for it was known that manager Ron Greenwood had had his difficulties with his famous striker. When asked why he had signed for Stoke, Hurst replied drily, 'Firstly, so I don't have to play against Denis Smith and, secondly, so I don't have to take penalties against Gordon Banks!' Only time would tell if Waddington had pulled off another coup. With Hurst on board, the more excitable elements in the sporting press tagged Stoke as the 'Team of the Seventies'.

In the third and fourth place FA Cup play-off, held over as a curtain raiser for the new season, Birmingham and Stoke played out a goalless draw. The Blues won 4-3 on penalties, whereupon the idea of such a play-off was consigned to oblivion. The league season opened with Stoke's first home league win for seven months, but five defeats in the next eight followed. Hurst struggled to find his feet alongside Ritchie, scoring only twice in his first nine games. He became frustrated and, after missing a sitter at Ipswich, vented his spleen at the referee and was sent off for the first time in his career. A 0-2 defeat left City in twentieth place.

Stoke had qualified for the UEFA Cup (previously known as the Inter Cities Fairs Cup), a competition for the 'nearly' clubs of Europe. Those winning the League entered the European Cup, as it was then known, and those winning the national cup took part (until its recent demise) in the Cup-Winners' Cup. Those occupying the next few positions in their respective leagues made up the bulk of UEFA Cup entrants, but there were anomalies. The English League, for example, granted a place to the winners of the League Cup, by which route Stoke found themselves competing in Europe for the first time.

Stoke's first round opponents were the West German outfit Kaiserslautern, also tasting Europe for the first time. Kaiserslautern had 'qualified' by virtue of reaching their own cup final. The fact that they had been thrashed 0-5 by Schalke encouraged Stoke fans greatly. Little was known about their opponents, though Waddington and trainer Frank Mountford undertook fact-finding missions abroad. Kaiserslautern boasted just one international, the balding Yugoslav midfielder Idriz Hosic, and a seventh place finish in the Bundesliga suggested they were a capable, if hardly fearsome side.

Stoke stumbled into Europe somewhat blindly, knowing little about how to approach two-leg international football. At the Vic, City were three goals up and subconsciously thinking ahead to round two, when Hosic headed home a costly away goal. The second leg started badly and got progressively worse. Outplayed from the off, Stoke were 0-3 down just after the hour and on their way out. Waddington sent on Ritchie, who had been displaced by Eric Skeels in a more defensive line-up, just as Stoke were about to take a free-kick. Ritchie ran on, tussled with Hosic, who fell prone. Before the kick could be taken the Hungarian referee brandished a red card in Ritchie's direction. He had been sent off after spending just nine seconds on the pitch! Overall, Stoke were out-manoeuvred and paid for their earlier complacency with a humiliating defeat. Kaiserslautern progressed to the quarter-finals, where they lost 2-9 to eventual losing finalists Borussia Moenchengladbach.

With the defence leaking goals, the importance of Banks to the team was never more apparent. While still blessed with superior shot-stopping ability, psychologically Banks was not coping well with what was the twilight of an illustrious career, showing flashes of temper that would put his side in jeopardy. Following Stoke's visit to Anfield (see Match of the Season), with press criticism of his behaviour still ringing in his ears, Banks crashed his car when returning home from receiving treatment at the Victoria Ground, receiving career-threatening eye injuries. Such was his stature that the BBC interrupted its schedules to relay the news. What would England do without Gordon Banks, the nation wondered?

Reserve keeper John Farmer, who had waited for five years as Banks' understudy, also happened to be injured. Waddington had no alternative but to buy. He wanted Scottish international keeper Bobby Clark from Aberdeen. However, after a deal appeared to have been struck, Stoke's board pulled out at the last minute, plumping instead for the promising young Mike McDonald from Clydebank, who cost £20,000. The move did not work out. The defence of the League Cup took Stoke to Third Division Notts County in round four. Having beaten Southampton away 3-1 to reach this stage, County were a side Stoke were advised to respect. But Jimmy Sirrel's men swarmed all over City to win 3-1. McDonald's personal nightmare saw him dropped in favour of a fit-again Farmer.

Stoke were denied a repeat of the FA Cup heroics of the past two seasons when beaten 2-3 at Manchester City. The 56 League goals Stoke conceded was indicative of an over-reliance on Banks' organisation and ability to pull errant defenders out of the mire. Farmer was not in the same class as his famous predecessor. He was, however, something of a poet and penned his feelings:

Reserving at your will / the promise of my skills
shining stars treated with such contempt.

Feeling hard done by, maybe, but with Banks struggling for clear vision in his right eye, Farmer was given a run by Waddington which offered him the opportunity to prove his worth.

Match of the Season 1972-73

Liverpool 2 Stoke 1

Division 1, 21 October 1972

Liverpool were maturing into the side that would dominate English football for years to come. Stars such as Ian Callaghan, Emlyn Hughes

---

DID YOU KNOW?

Stoke's League Cup semi-final with West Ham in 1971-72 was the longest in duration in League Cup history. It began on 8 December and ended on 26 January.

---

and Steve Heighway were establishing big reputations and in Kevin Keegan and John Toshack, manager Bill Shankly had unearthed a potent strike-force.

Stoke had scored thirteen goals in four games. Unfortunately the defence had conceded five in losing at Wolves and four in defeat at Tottenham, but with Gordon Banks back in goal, City had won the previous game 2-0 against Newcastle.

Stoke started brightly, playing neat football. On 34 minutes, amidst a mad scramble, Ritchie fired against the bar. The rebound fell awkwardly to Greenhoff but he showed commendable agility to fire the ball in. City led at Anfield.

Marshalled by Denis Smith, Stoke's defence held the Red tide at bay. Just when City thought they had done enough, Banks took too many steps inside his area and referee Roger Kirkpatrick awarded an indirect free-kick to Liverpool. Banks was incandescent. After all, keepers across the country took too many steps all the time, why should he be penalised now? Once the hullabaloo had died down Hughes belted in a short free-kick via the underside of the bar.

Banks' lapses in concentration when a decision went against him had cost Stoke dear again. Liverpool attacked with renewed vigour, but City, with nine men behind the ball, clung on. In injury-time the Reds mounted one last attack. Heighway jinked past Marsh and Skeels, retaining his balance when both fouled him. The ref waved play on, but pulled the game back when Heighway's pass went astray. While City's players protested that the laws of the game did not permit him to bring play back once advantage had been awarded, Liverpool took the free-kick quickly and Callaghan drove a deflected shot past the immobile Banks.

The full-time whistle went immediately. Banks charged after the referee, who had justifiably added time for the huge amount City had wasted in a bid to run the clock down. An enraged Banks felt it was more a case of 'We'll play until Liverpool score'. He had to be dragged away by his opposite number, Ray Clemence, and would surely have faced an FA charge had fate not intervened.

Banks' car crash the following morning left him with injuries to both eyes, which sadly put paid to his career in England. Despite playing on in America – where he felt that people came to see him because he only had one eye – Banks' top-flight career was over.

LEAGUE DIVISION 1   **1973-74**
League Division 1   13th
League Cup   4th Round
FA Cup   3rd

By virtue of their scoring feats the previous season, Stoke qualified for the Watney Cup. This pre-season kickabout featured the two highest scoring teams in each division that did not either qualify for Europe or achieve promotion. In many ways it was a booby prize for those clubs who were not actually successful – except of course if you won it, which Stoke did, beating Plymouth 1-0, Bristol City 4-1 and Hull 2-0 in the final. The win was greeted enthusiastically in the Potteries, though in truth the tournament, which disappeared after a few seasons, meant little. The very fact that the win is still referred to today as one of Stoke's triumphs is a mark of just how far the club has sunk in the past 25 years.

After so many disappointing League campaigns, disguised by the euphoria of the Cup runs, the fans needed to be shown that the club meant business and yet, with another summer of inactivity in the transfer market, Waddington was testing their patience. Once again Stoke started badly in the League. Haslegrave's conversion to the play-making role from his natural wing position was not a success and in attack Greenhoff and Hurst were not gelling. Only when Ritchie returned from a knee injury did the scoring rate pick up. Waddington felt compelled to field Hurst as he was the 'name' player, but he was not performing to the heights which had made him an England and West Ham legend. Around Christmas, form picked up and the flow of goals conceded dwindled when Waddo restored veteran defender Eric Skeels, but Stoke still lay seventeenth at the turn of the year.

Alan Dodd cemented his place in the side, filling in for the injured Alan Bloor and forming a keen understanding with Denis Smith. When Bloor returned, Dodd's versatility allowed Waddington to switch him to right-back as cover for the injured Jackie Marsh. Dodd was only twenty and oozed class both in the air and with the ball at his feet. His distribution into midfield made him stand out in a First Division devoid of such talent and he was soon rewarded by England at Under-21 level. His two-footedness allowed him to be used all across the back four, and in a holding role in midfield, but also meant that he had yet to make one position his own. Crucially he lacked a forceful personality and seemed happy to be treated as a utility player rather than a permanent fixture.

George Eastham bade farewell to the Victoria Ground crowd in September. His 239th game for the club was against West Ham and, typically, he supplied the cross for Hurst's clinching goal in a 2-0 win, the first of the season. Eastham was 37 years and six days old, the fifth oldest player to play for Stoke and had received an OBE in the summer for his services to football. Wanting to harness the coaching skills Eastham had honed in South Africa, Waddington made him assistant manager.

Gordon Banks admitted defeat in his battle to regain full vision in his right eye and announced his retirement on 18 August, having tried to make a comeback in reserve games and a specially arranged friendly in Greece. Banks was granted a testimonial, and on 12 December a Stoke team, including Eusebio and Bobby Charlton, lost 1-2 to Manchester United in front of 20,664 who had turned out to honour one of the greats of the game. John Farmer, his successor, wrote a short elegy about his esteemed colleague.

All down the days and thro' the years / that now must be,
Your magic moments of inspiration / will serve me well
For in the cheers and in the air / I now must breathe,
Your winding spell will never fade / Or die.

Banks bade farewell just six weeks after England's catastrophic draw with Poland which denied them a place in World Cup '74. English football was at its lowest ebb since the 3-6 Wembley defeat by Hungary in 1953. To lose a hero of Banks' stature merely darkened the mood of the footballing nation.

The footballing mood reflected wider problems in society. The oil crisis and industrial strikes during the winter of 1973 bit hard into clubs' and supporters' resources alike. Stoke coped with the energy crisis as did many clubs, bringing forward Saturday kick-off times to 2pm, so as to obviate the need for floodlights.

There was little relief from the torpor of the League campaign in the cups. City went out of the Texaco (Anglo-Scottish) Cup following two goalless draws with Birmingham – to whom they lost again on penalties – while in the League Cup Stoke lost 1-2 at Coventry. The FA Cup offered no solace either. To the disquiet of traditionalists and some church-going quarters, Stoke took part in the first British football match played on a Sunday, losing 2-3 at Bolton. The sizeable crowd and exciting game ensured a positive press reaction. Sunday football was here to stay. With just a relegation battle to fight, Waddington boosted Stoke's coffers by selling Stewart Jump to Crystal Palace for £75,000. The deal brought howls of protest as Jump had appeared a good prospect.

But the wise Waddington pulled off a coup to rival that of his signing of Banks, when he lured midfielder Alan Hudson to Stoke from Chelsea for a club record £240,000. Renowned as a playboy, prone to giving his manager, Dave Sexton, problems, Hudson was convinced by Waddo that by moving to Stoke he would have the football world at his feet. There was a team in need of a playmaker of his ability and a public waiting to adore him. Waddington tried to sign Peter Osgood too and agreed a fee with Chelsea of £260,000. The England striker chose higher-placed Southampton instead, but ironically ended up relegated with them.

Hudson proved to be exactly the midfield force that Stoke had been lacking. His greatest asset was his footballing vision, which enabled him to make passes earlier and more accurately than those around him. He soon became a lynchpin around which the whole Stoke team revolved.

'Land of Smoke and Glory / Home of Stoke City
Higher, higher and higher / On to victory'

sang the Boothen End as City rocketed up the table, putting paid to runaway leaders, Leeds', record-breaking run along the way (see Match of the Season).

Peter Osgood, ever seeking the limelight, unwisely commented in the press before Southampton's visit to fortress Victoria that he doubted John Ritchie's ability to score goals with his head. This only served to wind up Ritchie, and Osgood stood and watched as the big striker completed his hat-trick by rounding keeper Eric Martin, stopping the ball on the line, kneeling down and heading the ball into the net. Osgood ate humble pie.

Stoke became a match for any team in the country and it was not just Hudson who was earning plaudits. Denis Smith's commanding form led to renewed calls for his inclusion in the England squad. Unfortunately for him the best form of his career coincided with the dying embers of Sir Alf Ramsey's reign. His chance would not come under Mercer or Revie either. Although Smith was overlooked, Mike Pejic was selected for England. He made his first appearance against Portugal in an experimental line-up, after Leeds, Liverpool, and Manchester United withdrew their players from the friendly, which proved to be the last team Ramsey selected. Pejic was one of only two of the six debutants retained for the next game, against Wales, under the caretaker-managership of Joe Mercer. He started four consecutive England games but lost his place as Terry Cooper of Leeds became the first choice left-back of Ramsey's permanent successor, former Leeds boss Don Revie.

City rounded off the season with three straight wins, including a final day victory over Manchester United, already condemned to playing Second Division football the following season. The rivalry between Stoke and Man U had built up during the recent FA Cup clashes and there were sizeable hooligan elements in both sets of fans eager to exploit it. There was trouble in Stoke town centre and on the terraces as United fans vented their disgust at relegation by burning banners and programmes. Sadly it was not an isolated incident. The spectre of hooliganism had blighted Potteries football since the turn of the century. It is a predominantly working class area which sees no more or less trouble of one kind or another than any comparable area, but Stoke City and Port Vale attracted more than their fair share of thuggish fans. Too often their 'passionate' support boiled over into disgraceful scenes in town centres across the country. Stoke, not wishing to put off paying customers, rarely acknowledged the problem even existed. At least, after the visit of United the club provided more match-day policing, and a distinct 'Away' enclosure was created at the Stoke End of the ground. It made little difference to those intent on causing trouble.

On the pitch, Stoke had hit championship form. Of the eighteen games in which Hudson played, City lost only two, and only two goals were conceded in the final nine games. The team charged up the table to finish in a creditable fifth place, qualifying for the UEFA Cup once more. Next season it would be time for Stoke again to test themselves against the best in Europe.

Match of the Season 1973-74

Stoke 3 Leeds 2

Division 1, 23 February 1974

Don Revie's Leeds were the most feared and hated team in England in the 1960s and early 70s. They had a reputation as marvellous footballers with a hard, dirty streak. Their aggression was aimed at one objective. Success. And yet they had little silverware to show for it. In seven of the previous nine seasons Leeds had finished in the top three, once losing the championship on goal-difference and twice by a single point. Their only title success had come in 1968-69. A single win in each of the FA and League Cups disguised the three FA Cup finals they had lost, including the previous season's shock defeat by Second Division Sunderland. That loss had made Leeds determined that this would be their year. Their star-spangled side boasted a record unbeaten run of 29 games from the start of the season which had carried them nine points clear at the top. The country was waiting with baited breath to see which side would end the run. Not many gave City much of a chance.

DID YOU KNOW?

Eric Skeels, Carl Saunders, and Paul Ware have worn every outfield shirt for Stoke City. Alan Dodd wore all but No 9.

Stoke were enjoying a run of their own – a more modest nine games unbeaten. With the Potteries still alight after Alan Hudson's arrival, a crowd of just under 40,000 packed the Vic to the rafters.

Leeds took the initiative from the off and Denis Smith committed a bad lunging foul on Bremner, who went down in seeming agony. As soon as a free-kick was awarded up sprang the cheeky Bremner to float a shot past John Farmer before Stoke had finished lining up the wall. The goal stood, despite vehement protests. Leeds swept forward again. This time Johnny Giles fed Allan Clarke, who had freed himself from the attentions of Alan Dodd. While City claimed offside, Clarke made it 0-2.

The substitution of Giles – injured executing that pass to Clarke – transformed the match. Hudson grabbed the game by the scruff of the neck, pinging passes across-field to Robertson, who switched flanks at will. His cross found Hurst, who looped a shot over David Harvey onto the top of the crossbar. In attempting to save, Harvey collided with the post, hurting his stomach. He was unable to kick for the rest of the game, forcing Leeds to defend deeper, which in turn allowed Hudson and Mahoney more room in midfield, which they revelled in.

Pejic rattled a free-kick in off the post to pull one back and City poured forward. Ritchie nodded down a Robertson cross into the path of the onrushing Hudson. Huddy dragged the ball out from underneath his feet in the mud on the edge of the six-yard box to poke Stoke level. His first goal for the club.

City piled on the pressure in the second half. Ritchie had a goal disallowed, but on 66 minutes Robertson's right-wing corner found the head of Denis Smith at the far post. Smith knocked the ball back across goal and continued his run forward. Hurst nodded the ball back to him and Smith powered a header into the net.

At the final whistle Stoke's players jigged around the pitch in delight. Revie's men had the last laugh, however, going on to win the title with a record 62 points (in the two points for a win era).

LEAGUE DIVISION 1   **1974-75**
League Division 1   5th
League Cup   4th Round
FA Cup   3rd Round
UEFA Cup   1st Round

Along with the rest of the country Stoke went metric, and, like almost everybody else, the club saw an opportunity to mask a price-hike when doing so. The new 60p terrace admission charge was, in reality, a twenty percent increase.

Waddington replaced the retired George Eastham by splashing out £160,000 on Sheffield United's Geoff Salmons, another left-sided midfielder. In the light of a team that had swept all before them in the latter stages of 1973-74, there was talk of a championship challenge and a prolonged European run. On City's books was a clutch of players in their prime and thirsting for glory. In his Bramall Lane days Salmons had been renowned for dressing room pranks. He now became Huddy's drinking pal and bosom buddy – which did not augur quite so well.

For once the season started with a bang. The visitors on the opening day were champions Leeds, now under the (brief) steward-ship of Brian Clough. The televised 3-0 victory served as a warning that Stoke meant business. City lost only one of their first seven games, before facing two tricky fixtures in back-to-back visits to Anfield and Portman Road.

When it came to the crunch, Stoke still came off second best. Liverpool won 3-0 – without Kevin Keegan, still suspended for his fisticuffs with Billy Bremner during the Charity Shield. Worse was to follow at Ipswich. Kevin Beattie's challenge broke John Ritchie's leg. The injury stirred City passions. Alan Dodd was sent off for a second caution and Ipswich romped to a 3-1 win. To make matters worse, the break proved bad enough to end Ritchie's career as a top-flight striker.

European giants Ajax of Amsterdam were City's opponents in the UEFA Cup first round. A fiercely contested tie saw Ajax progress at Stoke's expense, but only on the away-goals rule (see Match of the Season).

Stoke also fared poorly in the two domestic cup competitions. In the League Cup, the 6-2 second replay win over Chelsea – Stoke's best ever win in the competition – was the highlight of a campaign that ended at Ipswich in the fourth round. Stoke succumbed at the first hurdle in the FA Cup too, 0-2 at Liverpool.

Stoke reserved their brightest form for the League. Hudson often seemed to skim across the mud of the awful Victoria Ground pitch.

On his own he was majestic, in combination with Salmons, Mahoney and Haslegrave the team simply purred. 'Alan Hudson walks on water,' sang the fans on the Boothen End. 'The Working Man's Ballet,' Tony Waddington called it, a description of which Hudson approved, using it as the title of his 1997 autobiography. He felt at home in Stoke, warming to a people who had taken him to their hearts, and was enjoying the social life in the Potteries too. He and Hurst both invested money in pubs in the area and loved nothing more than to while away the hours, glass in hand, often with other players, such as Salmons and Marsh. It was Hudson's perfect lifestyle and his inner contentment was reflected on the field.

There were downsides, however. The subject of alcohol in professional football was not such a hot potato in the 1970s as it is today. To sink five or six pints after a game, or even the night before, was commonplace, to the extent that Waddington himself – whom Hudson considered a father figure – condoned his players' behaviour by joining in for late-night drinking sessions. In an era that boasted Southampton's 'Ale House Lads' and Chelsea's Kings Road 'Swingers', Stoke players were no better, and no worse, than anyone else.

Whether or not the team would have played better if peopled by teetotallers is a question without an answer. In any case, by mid-November Stoke were sixth, and Waddington's main worry was the up and down form of goalkeeper John Farmer, typified by his horrendous error which gifted a late equaliser at Chelsea. Within a week Waddington had paid £325,000 to Leicester for the services of England's Peter Shilton, a world record fee for a goalkeeper. Waddo hoped that Shilton's appetite for winning would rub off on others, making them hungry for success too. Shilton had lost the England jersey in the summer to Liverpool's Ray Clemence, who was clearly Revie's first choice. Shilton, blaming his exclusion on playing in a Leicester side content to finish clear of relegation, craved success to put him back into the limelight, and Waddington persuaded him of Stoke's ambitions. Shilton became the club's record signing and the board, prepared to send the club into debt to fund Stoke City's push for the championship, took a calculated gamble. Should his signing not prove successful, the club still had a marketable asset on their hands.

It was no surprise when John Farmer announced that he had decided to quit the club. He had played second fiddle once before to the world's best goalkeeper – Banks – and thought it a bit rich to be asked to do so again. His decision to quit football altogether was more surprising. Announcing his retirement, aged just 27, he penned these lines – once again in his favoured verse:

DID YOU KNOW?

Gordon Banks is Stoke City's most capped player with 36 for England. He earned 73
England caps in total, the other 37 with Leicester.

Often / looking back / along the wide expanse
we conquered I see / the dizzy heights we scaled,
feel the pain of losing / and hear the common bonds
and sounds / of a language never needing voices.
No things to come / can dull my feelings now
or erase from my memory / the better days.

But Waddington was proved right in signing Shilton. Within ten
days of his arrival, on the back of three clean sheets, including two
world-class saves beyond Farmer's capabilities, Stoke sat proudly
atop the First Division for the first time since 1938. The only part of
the team now under-strength was the front line. Club record scorer
Ritchie was missed badly. In previous seasons, goals had proved
rare in his absence. It was no different this time. Buying a top-rank
striker was out of the question, given the outlay on transfers over
the previous year. But matters were exacerbated by the fact that the
man who so often had come up trumps before, Conroy, was also
sidelined with cartilage problems that had dogged him for the past
two years. Perhaps the outlay on Shilton might have been better
spent on a proven goalscorer. Would a risky investment in a player
such as Stuart Pearson, Brian Little or Ted MacDougall, who had set
the Second Division alight, have been sounder? With just four goals
in the next six games, Stoke's sojourn at the top lasted just two
weeks, although they remained handily placed in third place at
Christmas.

The injury hoodoo again affected City badly, threatening their
title challenge. Greenhoff broke his nose at Birmingham. Jimmy
Robertson broke a leg in the first minute of a 0-2 defeat at Coventry.
Mike Pejic broke his leg against Wolves, and in the next home game
Denis Smith fractured a leg in another stormy contest with Ipswich.
Bobby Robson's second-placed team crucially won that game 2-1,
leaving Stoke in sixth.

With the squad stretched to breaking point, Stoke's spirit alone
enabled them to keep pace with the leading pack. Former leaders
Manchester City were brushed aside 4-0. Stoke briefly hit the top
again, taking advantage of their rivals' extended involvement in the
cups. A last-minute win at Derby proved the team's championship
credentials. Conroy, back to his sparkling best after recovering from
his knee problem, scored nine goals in five games, including both in

a 2-0 defeat of leaders Liverpool. City appeared to have acquired the temperament to win vital games. Could this be Stoke's year?

Alan Hudson was finally rewarded for his searing form over the past year by being picked for England. He made a starring debut in a 2-0 'friendly' win over West Germany and ran the show again as England thrashed Cyprus 5-0 in a European Nations Cup qualifier. Hudson would have grabbed the headlines but for Newcastle's Malcolm Macdonald scoring all five goals. Yet outspoken Hudson clashed with Revie over the England manager's famous dossiers on opposing players, which were considered essential reading by Revie. The outcome was that Hudson was dropped (as Alan Ball and Frank Worthington had previously been) in favour of QPR's Dave Thomas.

With three games remaining, the championship was there for the taking. City were level on 47 points with Liverpool, Ipswich and Derby, two points behind clear leaders Everton. Crucially, the long injury list proved too high a hurdle and Stoke's fluidity deserted them. They were not helped by an iffy penalty awarded against Shilton early on at Sheffield United. That goal forced City to chase the game, but, with another goal on the break, the Blades killed off Stoke's title hopes.

The other contenders slipped up as well, over the closing days, handing Derby, who only drew their final two matches, the title with the lowest points total since 1955. What hurt Stoke most was that they would have lifted the championship had they won their last three games.

As if to kick Stoke when they were down, UEFA changed the rules for admission into the UEFA Cup. City missed out on the place that finishing fifth would normally have earned, despite the intervention of the Football League on their behalf. Just one more point would have seen Stoke into Europe at Everton's expense.

Match of the Season 1974-75

Ajax 0 Stoke 0

UEFA Cup, 1st Round, 2nd leg, 2 October 1974

Now in the fourth year of its existence, the UEFA Cup was proving more competitive than its predecessor, the Inter Cities Fairs Cup. This season's entrants included Juventus, Inter Milan and Borussia Moenchengladbach. Stoke's second sojourn into Europe saw them handed a plum first round tie. Ajax were the European team of the early 1970s. Renowned as the inventors of 'total football', they won the European Cup in three successive years, 1971-1973. That treble was masterminded by master-tactician Rinus Michels. He had subsequently become Dutch national team manager and in his absence the Ajax side had begun to break up. Johann Cruyff's £1 million transfer to Barcelona was the beginning of the brain drain of Dutch talent that would see their best players scattered to the leagues of Spain, Italy and, latterly, England. That Ajax had been beaten by Feyenoord to the Dutch title in 1974 suggested the team was undergoing a transition. But youngsters like Arnold Muhren were still emerging through Ajax's famous youth system, stepping into a side that boasted Dutch World Cup finalists Arie Haan, Jonny Rep and Ruud Krol.

Ajax were currently fourth in the Dutch League and their first-leg visit was so eagerly anticipated in the Potteries that over 37,000 packed into the Victoria Ground. The previous week Alan Hudson had crashed his car after a late-night binge with Waddington and Hurst, breaking his hand, and he admitted that he was still dazed when he took the field. His penchant for a pint cost City dear as Ajax stroked the ball around, silenced the crowd and took the lead when Ruud Krol's shot beat Farmer just before half-time. Hudson accepted responsibility for not closing Krol down; not only had his drinking weakened Stoke's attacking prowess, but it had cost them a crucial away goal. Later in life Hudson would wistfully claim, 'If I hadn't had that crash we would have beaten Ajax.' But football is about what happens, not what might have been.

As it was, Stoke battled back with Denis Smith heading in at the near post to earn a draw. The fans were content, defeat had been avoided, even if Stoke had been palpably outplayed. Nobody seriously thought they would win in the Stadion de Meer.

Stoke started the second leg brightly. The left-hand side proved particularly profitable, and time and again Mike Pejic overlapped. Salmons' weighted balls fell perfectly into his path, to be whipped across goal. Had a fit Ritchie been available, Stoke might have won. Piet Schrijvers had a fine match in goal for Ajax, plucking countless crosses from the air. On the one occasion he flapped, the ball fell to Greenhoff, whose first-time chip narrowly cleared the crossbar. In the dying seconds Pejic crossed from the by-line and Robertson shot on the turn from six yards. Schrijvers' left boot deflected the ball wide to avert what would have been only the second home defeat Ajax had suffered in European competition.

Stoke's display imbued them with the confidence to mount a sustained title challenge. Sadly, their fifth-place finish would not allow them to test their mettle against European opposition again. Ajax fell victim to Juventus on away-goals in round three and would not challenge again for over a decade.

LEAGUE DIVISION 1   **1975-76**
League Division 1   12th
League Cup   2nd Round
FA Cup   5th Round

The enormous transfer outlay of the previous season brought a loss on the balance sheet of £448,342. The gamble on qualifying for Europe had not paid off. There would be no new signings over the summer and Waddington was left hoping that the three broken legs would mend, enabling their owners to return as good as new. Pejic and Smith, indeed, were fit to start the season, but Robertson was having complications and struggled for fitness until late October.

Geoff Hurst's departure to West Brom for £20,000 amounted to a confession by Waddington that the hero of '66 had failed to live up to his reputation. Bought to score goals, Hurst's record of 30 strikes in 108 League appearances was not what one expected of a World Cup winning striker. Some critics suggested he had been content to play out his remaining years without risking life or limb for the Stoke cause. In any event, Hurst lasted less than a season at the Hawthorns before quitting the game.

Having gone so close, it was expected that Stoke would go even closer this time, but another poor start left the team languishing in eighteenth place in mid-September. Morale was low. Division Four Lincoln provided the opposition in the second round of the League Cup. Stoke contrived to lose 1-2, in a performance that proved too much for the travelling support to bear. Several hundred Stoke fans tried to invade areas housing Lincoln supporters. In the ensuing mayhem a wall collapsed and people were hurt, some seriously. It was the single worst incident of hooligan-related disorder in Stoke City's history. For reasons that are not entirely clear, the matter merited little more than a passing word on the back page of the Stoke local newspaper, the *Evening Sentinel* – when it might have drawn severe editorial comment, but the events at Sincil Bank were nevertheless a severe embarrassment to the club.

On the field, Stoke belied the Lincoln debacle by winning eight out of the next twelve games, among them a 1-0 defeat of defending champions Derby. City established themselves in the top ten, but had developed a tendency to drop points from winning positions. Newcastle equalised in the last minute at the Vic and Dave Webb scored an injury-time winner for high-flying QPR after Stoke had led 2-1. On their day Stoke produced good approach play, but it was seldom converted into goals. Greenhoff was partnered in attack by beanpole striker Ian Moores, recently capped by England at Under-23 level. Moores totalled only twelve goals, being cursed by the knack of missing easy chances whilst taking more difficult ones. It was the misses that fans remembered. Terry Conroy returned from a recurrence of his knee injury for the Boxing Day visit of leaders Liverpool and crowned a fine performance by supplying the cross for Salmons' equaliser. Whilst 1-1 with Liverpool was fair enough, Stoke repeated the score in their next game, against lowly Birmingham, which was not. The patchy form frustrated the fans. How could a team which had come so close to winning the League make such a ham fist of the following season?

Peter Shilton was also performing beneath his full potential. He appeared depressed at failing to regain his England shirt from Ray Clemence. His only recent cap had been for the home match with Cyprus. Since England had won 5-0, it hardly presented him with an opportunity to shine. When Revie selected a squad to tour the United States during the summer, Shilton asked not to be considered. In other circumstances such 'unavailability' might have terminated his international career. As it was, he did not appear in the England team until the dying embers of Revie's reign a year hence. Shilton's frustration was reflected in his club form. Stoke conceded 50 goals during the season, but Waddington could hardly drop Shilton. He had signed the world's most expensive goalkeeper and had no ready-made replacement to hand.

The FA Cup was Stoke's last opportunity to inject some buzz into what was turning into an anti-climatic season. Drawn away at Tottenham, the Stoke party travelled down to London by rail the day before the game. The players had just settled into their seats when the train passed the Victoria Ground. The stadium looked as if a bomb had hit it. The wooden roof of the Butler Street stand, on the side of the ground backing onto the railway, had been stripped away in the storms that had whipped across the country over the New Year. Within a few days stories began circulating that the club was having difficulties in claiming from the insurers in respect of the damage. After initial denials, Stoke finally admitted that the cost of erecting a new roof would be in excess of £250,000. Their insurance cover amounted to less than a third of that sum. As the roof could not be ignored, its repair imposed another financial burden upon an already overstretched bank account. With crowds already down on the previous season, Stoke City were entering a period of severe financial difficulty.

The immediate problem was where to play. Work to shore up the storm-damaged roof precipitated a further collapse, in which three workmen were hurt, whereupon the Victoria Ground was declared unsafe. Neighbours Port Vale offered the use of their ground and Stoke won their first 'home' League match outside the

Victoria Ground 1-0 against Middlesbrough on 17 January. Tottenham were beaten in the FA Cup replay 2-1 at a reopened Vic, but
the fall-out over the club's financial woes was coming to a head.
Sensing problems ahead, both Hudson and Pejic slapped in transfer
requests, claiming that Stoke lacked the ambition to match theirs.
This was hardly the right frame of mind in which to take on
Sunderland in the fifth round of the Cup, and Stoke bowed out 1-2
in a replay.

In March England manager Don Revie bowed to popular opinion
and picked both Jimmy Greenhoff and Alan Hudson for his squad
to play Wales. They were set to be Stoke's first two outfield players
to be capped in the same England side since Stanley Matthews and
Neil Franklin faced Scotland in April 1947. Alas, City rearranged a
League game with Derby for the same night. Clubs had first call on
players so Greenhoff and Hudson played at the Baseball Ground
rather than Wrexham that night, and to cap it all Hudson broke his
leg. Neither was selected for England again, while both Pejic and
Smith had also fallen out of favour. There was disgust at Revie's
treatment of Stoke's star players, when those from other unfashion-
able clubs – Viljoen, Johnson and Mills of Ipswich, Clement, Francis
and Bowles of QPR, and Whitworth of Leicester – were given more
than a fair crack of the whip. Especially so as, in truth, only two,
Mills and Gerry Francis, could be said to be international class. The
major criticism of Revie was that he spread caps, which under
Ramsey had been treasured possessions, like confetti, thus diluting
the honour of playing for England. That none came the way of a
club that had finished in the top five in successive seasons seemed
remarkable. Stoke folk had an easy answer; Revie still bore a grudge
against City for ending Leeds' unbeaten run two years earlier.

The season ended poorly, with Stoke winning only two of the
last eleven games. That was relegation form and it prompted much
disquiet amongst the fans. Only 15,598 turned up to see Stoke lose
the final game, 0-2 at home to Norwich. The match marked an end
of an era. Eric Skeels, 36, made his record 606th Stoke appearance in
all competitions and bade farewell before moving to Port Vale on a
free transfer.

Stoke's fortunes had taken a fatal twist in the winds of early
January. The short period of champagne football had raised hopes
but the board had made themselves hostages to fortune to chase the
dream of winning the League. As close as the team had come, it
would matter little once it was realised that acute financial hardship –
brought about by the collapse of the roof of the Butler Street stand –
would threaten the club's fortunes on and off the field for many
years to come.

Match of the Season 1975-76
Stoke 3 Leeds 2

Division 1, 13 September 1975

Stoke were languishing in nineteenth place after a poor start to the season. The previous week they had been overturned 0-3 by Jack Charlton's newly promoted Middlesbrough. Returning to the side after injury were Jackie Marsh and Alan Bloor, both missing since the opening game. Leeds were no longer the dominant force of the late 1960s and early 70s. Since the departure of Don Revie for the England job, they had lost their cutting edge, but under new manager Jimmy Armfield had reached the European Cup final, where a 0-2 defeat by all-conquering Bayern Munich in Paris had sparked disgraceful scenes from their notorious fans. Armfield's team was packed with British internationals and lay sixth in the League.

Stoke set off briskly with Hudson swaggering through midfield in the sunshine. It seemed only a matter of time before City made their superiority tell. The breakthrough came on 32 minutes when, from a Hudson cross, Conroy tapped in from close range. Five minutes later Hudson skipped down the right and picked out Pejic at the near post in a crowded penalty area. 2-0.

No Leeds side of that era turned over easily. Peter Lorimer, who had been the subject of Waddington's interest over the summer, pulled a goal back after 53 minutes and two minutes later converted a penalty, awarded for Dodd's trip on Allan Clarke. City's mettle was being severely tested. On 73 minutes Moores got the better of McQueen in the air, flicked the ball on and Greenhoff lashed it beyond David Harvey. Stoke held on for a victory that kick-started a run of eight wins in twelve games, sparking pipedreams of another championship challenge. Leeds' star was fading. They would finish only fifth in the League and lost at home to lower division opposition in both cups. It would be fifteen years before they would challenge for major honours again.

Gordon Banks at full stretch at home to Manchester United (February 1970)

City came so close to beating Ajax in Amsterdam (October 1974)

The 1977-78 squad, featuring a young Garth Crooks, bottom right

Crooks beats Blackpool's Paul Gardner to the ball but heads over (November 1977)

Mike Doyle and Sheffield United's John Flood in the Bramall Lane mud (March 1979)

Former Stoke keepers Shilton and Banks support Denis Smith's testimonial (1980)

O'Callaghan beats Manchester United's Joe Jordan to bury a header (October 1980)

Loek Ursem puts the boot into Southampton keeper Ivan Katalinic (October 1980)

## 2

STEADYING THE SHIP
1976-1981

LEAGUE DIVISION 1	**1976-77**
League Division 1	21st (Relegated)
League Cup	3rd Round
FA Cup	3rd Round

There was nothing but trouble on the horizon. The directors made it clear to Waddington that the gleaming new steel roof adorning the Butler Street Stand would have to be funded by the sale of players. To give them credit, they initially tried to recoup the outlay by cashing in on younger, less experienced players. Sean Haslegrave departed for Nottingham Forest for £35,000, while Ian Moores was snapped up by Spurs for £75,000. Waddington was clearly unhappy about this, but his hands were tied. The loss of revenue from the failure to qualify for Europe meant that, when all was said and done, his purchases had not brought success. He was now paying the price. Supporters wrote complaining to the *Sentinel*, but there were more departures to come.

The season started steadily, but injuries soon began to mount. Denis Smith had been in dominant form, but a strained hamstring while warming-up for Stoke's League Cup-tie with Leeds left him sidelined for twelve games. City squeaked past Leeds 2-1, but fell at the next hurdle, outplayed at Newcastle 0-3. Waddington reverted Alan Dodd to his preferred centre-half role to cover for Smith, with the added aim of preparing Dodd to take over from Smith's partner of seven years, Alan Bloor, who, at 34, was beginning to creak. A knee injury to John Mahoney forced him out for seventeen games and Waddo papered over the cracks by blooding youngster Brian Bithell in midfield. With teenagers Garth Crooks and Ian Bowers featuring regularly, City's line-up lacked experience and class.

Problems were mounting off the pitch too. Crowds were below the 20,000 mark and Stoke faced a growing overdraft and impatient creditors, who demanded crippling interest repayments be met on time. The only way out of the vicious circle was to sell the club's crown jewels. Jimmy Greenhoff was the first to go. He was sold to Manchester United for a paltry £120,000. The fans were up in arms: the club had not only lost one of the most talented players in its history, but to cap it all he had joined the arch enemy. They also felt that the board had sold Greenhoff behind their, and Tony Wadding-ton's backs. The situation even strained the bond between the manager and Alan Hudson. Huddy, frustrated at the obvious back-ward steps the club was taking, wanted Waddington to face up to the board, and could not stand by and see the team ripped apart. He was also unhappy at being forced to play when he felt that he was still not fully recovered from his broken leg. The upshot was a transfer demand. Hudson then railed at the press when a £350,000 price tag (high in those days) was slapped on him. His form suffered badly. Objectively, the board's valuation seemed fair enough. Still only 25, Hudson had been turned into one of the best midfielders in the country and was now a full England cap. Within three weeks he was gone, another body blow for the fans. The fee paid by Arsenal, just £200,000, was £40,000 less than Stoke had paid Chelsea for Hudson three years earlier. Not only were the board selling the club's best players; they were leaving at knockdown prices. The hurried sales smacked of panic.

The creative heart had been ripped out of the team and, not surprisingly, defeats piled up. Even though Smith, who replaced Greenhoff as club captain, returned, City went eight games without a win. The immediate replacements for Greenhoff and Hudson were John Tudor (from Newcastle £25,000) and Alan Suddick (from Blackpool £12,000). They brought with them a wealth of experience and over 100 League goals apiece, but neither gelled with the team. By early February, with the bank knocking on the door once again, Waddington was forced to sell Mike Pejic to Everton for £140,000. The team was almost decimated. The fans, dazed and confused at the sudden turn of events, sought a scapegoat.

The FA Cup offered no relief. Stoke lost 0-2 to Everton with only Shilton able to hold his head high. A gutless goalless draw with Newcastle was followed by a 0-1 home defeat by Leicester. The fans, who for so long had worshipped Waddington, turned on him with a vengeance. Cries of 'Waddington Out!' tumbled down from the Boothen End. He was the easy target, of course, but the chants cut him to the quick and he obliged, tendering his resignation. The board accepted. If the manager was seen to take the blame then perhaps less vitriol would be hurled in their direction. The club, which had been on the crest of a wave just twelve months earlier, was now reduced to petty politicking as factions fought to maintain their positions. The manner of Waddington's departure tarnished his seventeen-year reign as manager. Stoke had won 241, lost 263, and drawn 197 of his 701 League games in charge and had established themselves in the First Division for the first time since the 1930s. He had also won the club its first trophy.

Assistant manager George Eastham took charge temporarily, aided by coach Alan A'Court, and a mini-recovery ensued, but City were still woefully short of goals, scoring a meagre 30 all season. Stoke failed to win any of the next five games, including crunch relegation battles with Bristol City, Coventry and Tottenham, and were teetering in nineteenth place when Manchester United visited the Victoria Ground (see Match of the Season). Other results went against them and the 3-3 draw proved insufficient. With just two away fixtures remaining, Division Two beckoned.

Stoke got off to the best possible start at West Brom, thanks to an Alan Suddick free-kick, but once Albion equalised City's spirit drained and the Baggies ran out 3-1 winners. There was still hope. Stoke travelled to Villa Park two days later knowing their fate was out of their hands, but that a point might be enough. Rivals Bristol City and West Ham faced, on paper, tough games with Liverpool and Manchester United respectively. What Stoke had not taken into account was that those two giants were shortly going to contest the FA Cup final and would not wish to bust a gut in an otherwise bothersome League fixture. Bristol City and West Ham won, while Stoke lost 0-1 to Villa and were relegated.

The only bright note was struck when Peter Shilton was finally picked by Revie for England's Home International Championship matches against Northern Ireland and Wales. It would take another year before he re-established himself as a regular England keeper, but which time he too had gone.

Match of the Season 1976-77

Stoke 3   Manchester United 3

Division 1, 11 May 1977

Early May saw Stoke embroiled in a desperate fight to stay in the First Division, where they had belonged for fourteen years. Despite having been outside the drop-zone all season, it now looked like Stoke had to win this game, the last at home, to stand a chance of staying up. That Manchester United were the visitors was a cruel twist. Only three years previously Stoke had sent United crashing out of the top flight with a 1-0 win on the final day of the season. That game had been marred by ugly scenes. More trouble was expected this time, with so much riding on the outcome.

Stoke's line-up bore little resemblance to that which had come within striking distance of the championship only twelve months before, featuring four players under twenty and an attack, in Crooks and Suddick, which had scored only four goals all season. United, warming up for the FA Cup final, fielded former Stoke idol Jimmy Greenhoff and a strikeforce including Macari, Pearson, Coppell and Hill that had collectively found the net more than 70 times.

A frenetic start saw Stoke pushing forward, but United hit back on the break. Gordon Hill raced through to beat Shilton with Stoke claiming offside. The tension on the terraces mounted as United broke through again. Stoke's defence again stopped, arms raised, as McCreery broke away and rounded Shilton. City were down, but not quite out. Crooks turned the ball home from close range and, amidst an ugly atmosphere as fans baited each other, Bloor poked in the equaliser in a scramble just after the break.

At 2-2 City looked more confident, but on the hour Smith, under pressure, knocked the ball back to Shilton. It fell short and Hill nipped in to score. The distraught Stoke skipper rallied his troops for another push. As United conceded ground, Crooks gathered the ball just outside the area, wove past three defenders and fired past Alex Stepney, sparking uproar around the ground. Another goal might keep City alive.

United shut up shop, knowing a draw was no good to Stoke, and played on the break. Lacking the creative guile of Hudson and Greenhoff, City failed to penetrate United's stubborn defence. The only real chance fell the way of Garth Crooks. He raced clear and beat Stepney, but a linesman had his flag raised for offside. It was a crushing blow.

There was trouble inside and outside the ground as Stoke fans reacted angrily to the decision, which they felt had cost City the chance to stay up. In truth, the blame for Stoke's demise lay firmly at the club's own door. Just as United had bid goodbye to the top flight with an orgy of violence, now Stoke's hooligan element took out the frustration of their team's failure on opposing supporters.

United went on to win the FA Cup, Jimmy Greenhoff scoring the winning goal. That hurt City fans all the more.

LEAGUE DIVISION 2   **1977-78**
League Division 2   7th
League Cup   2nd Round
FA Cup   4th Round

The financial problems at the root of the team's collapse were finally beginning to abate. Indeed, Stoke City announced a trading profit for the previous season of £476,766. This hardly pleased the fans. Neither did the fact that nearly all the money disappeared into a void to pay off the debt incurred for replacing the roof on the Butler Street Stand. Outgoing players had brought in more than £600,000 but the club were left without a squad of players with the necessary experience to mount a serious promotion challenge. The lack of quality throughout the side had been cruelly exposed in the top flight. George Eastham, officially confirmed as manager after the board flirted with the idea of bringing in Derek Dougan, needed to act fast to replenish his resources.

To generate income for team-building, Eastham sold Mahoney to Middlesbrough for £90,000, Tudor to Ghent (£10,000) and Ruggiero to Brighton (£30,000). Incoming were England international left-back Alec Lindsay (from Liverpool £25,000), experienced midfielders Howard Kendall (from Birmingham £40,000) and Paul Richardson (£50,000 Chester), plus promising striker David Gregory (£50,000 Peterborough). It was obvious that neither Salmons nor Shilton had any appetite for the Second Division and both were quickly off-loaded. Salmons joined Leicester for £42,500, while Shilton left for Nottingham Forest, and a hatful of trophies under Brian Clough, for £270,000. Shilton called his time at the Victoria Ground 'the lost years of my career'. He had lost his international place and become disillusioned with club football. He was looking for a manager who could provide a platform for him to display his undoubted talent to the full. Brian Clough proved to be that man.

Any thoughts that Stoke would hop back to the top flight at the first attempt were cruelly exposed on the opening day at newly promoted Mansfield. The 1-2 defeat went down as one of the worst results in the club's history and the disgraceful scenes at Field Mill, sparked by Stoke fans, only served to enhance the club's unwanted reputation for violence. Showing some semblance of character, City won three of the next four games, with Garth Crooks looking a cut above the standard of defenders he was now facing. His first three goals of the season clinched wins over Southampton, Burnley and Sheffield United. His reputation spread as far as Hull where a brutal reception greeted him from Gordon Nisbet, who was sent off for persistent fouling. Yet Stoke failed to beat Hull's ten men and won only one of the next eight games, despite either taking the lead or having an opponent sent off in six of them. It was patently clear that this would be a season of rehabilitation at best.

Stoke put in another lacklustre performance to lose 0-1 at Bristol City in the League Cup. With goals elusive and confidence low, Eastham turned to two players he had groomed at Hellenic of Cape Town, the club he had coached in the early 1970s. Strikers Jeff Cook, signed from Hellenic, and Des Backos, via Los Angeles Aztecs, made their debuts at Ninian Park in early November. The new strike-force failed dismally. Cardiff won 2-0 and within a month Backos, clearly out of his depth, was back in South Africa with the Highlands Park club.

Roger Jones had replaced Shilton as Stoke's custodian. He had arrived from Newcastle on a free transfer in the February of the previous season, with Waddington taking a risk on the recurring knee injury which had prompted Bill McGarry to release him. He took time to settle at Stoke, but once given his chance responded with some fine displays, proving to be an excellent shot-stopper. His weakness was crosses. At 6ft he was not the tallest of keepers and his handling was sometimes questionable.

Doubts were cast over Eastham's managerial acumen, particularly in the transfer market. Of his seven purchases, only Kendall, who was productive in midfield, and Richardson, industrious down the left-hand side, could be called successes. His only other acquisition, Norwich forward Viv Busby (£50,000), hardly set the world alight either. Known during his playing career as 'Gentleman' George, Eastham lacked Waddington's forceful personality and – having so recently quit playing – was unable to distance himself from players who had been team-mates. Not surprisingly, Eastham experienced difficulties in man-management.

The turn of the year saw two encouraging 4-0 wins. Expectations rose, but Stoke failed to win again until March, by which time Eastham had resigned and City had suffered numbing defeat at the hands of minnows Blyth Spartans in the fourth round of the FA Cup (See Match of the Season).

The end of Eastham's reign came in the wake of a dreadful 1-1 home draw with bottom of the table Mansfield, who had won just two of their previous fifteen games. Eastham threw in the towel and left for his beloved South Africa, admitting he was not cut out for the pressures of management. He would spend over twenty years in Cape Town coaching black youngsters, thirsty for football, to which his temperament was better suited. As the board sought a new manager, first team coach Alan A'Court was handed the reigns as caretaker for two games, including the traumatic defeat by Blyth.

After being accused of trying to poach Newcastle boss Bill McGarry, their choice was 36-year-old Shrewsbury manager Alan Durban, a member of Derby's 1972 championship winning side. He arrived at the Vic with morale at rock bottom.

Form picked up immediately. Durban's belief in his players was visible from the start. Those whom he didn't rate were soon out of the door. Alec Lindsay, having lost his place to reserve Geoff Scott, departed to Oakland Stompers in the NASL for £7,000. The numerous fringe players that Eastham had tried out – Busby, Cook, Gregory, Paul Johnson and Jim McGroarty – were dumped into the reserves. Durban dipped just once into the transfer market – in March – when he signed burly centre-forward Brendan O'Callaghan from Doncaster Rovers for £15,000. Call it luck or judgement, but O'Callaghan scored with a header after just eleven seconds of his debut as a substitute against Hull. He later claimed that he didn't see his most famous goal hit the net as he had been clattered by one of his own players. No matter. In one fell swoop O'Callaghan acquired hero status, and Durban was commended for working the transfer market as astutely as had Tony Waddington.

Stoke won six out of the next nine games. A 1-3 away defeat by runaway leaders Tottenham indicated that the team had some way to go before becoming genuine promotion contenders, but goals were proving easier to come by. Garth Crooks became the youngest player ever to score a League hat-trick for Stoke, aged twenty years and eight days in a 4-2 win over Blackburn. O'Callaghan was fitting well into the team pattern. He was a willing target man and Crooks played in the space around him, using his lightning pace to beat defenders. The balding Kendall had one of his best ever seasons, scoring seven goals from midfield to finish as second highest scorer. His sharp passing and energetic running kept the side ticking as he enjoyed something of a renaissance at the age of nearly 32. The fans took him to their hearts and Kendall's displays earned him the first ever 'Player of the Season' award from the Supporters Club.

Match of the Season 1977-78

Stoke 2 Blyth Spartans 3

FA Cup, 4th Round, 6 February 1978

After thrashing Tilbury 4-0 in round three, Stoke were odds on to dispose of Northern Premier League side Blyth Spartans. Blyth's team was composed of local part-timers and amateurs, although 33-year old skipper Ron Guthrie had played for Sunderland in their famous win over Leeds in the 1974 Cup final and 38-year-old Terry

DID YOU KNOW?

Eric Skeels holds the club record for League appearances at 507, the FA Cup record at 44, and the joint second (behind Peter Dobing) record in the League Cup at 40.

Johnson had enjoyed a long League career with Southend and Brentford. Stoke were playing their second game under the stewardship of Alan A'Court after the resignation three weeks earlier of George Eastham.

Crucially, Stoke were missing skipper Denis Smith, injured against Mansfield. On an atrocious surface at the Victoria Ground, over 18,500 fans turned up expecting Blyth to become ritual lambs to the slaughter. How wrong they were. Brian Slane's spirited team took the game by the scruff of the neck and in the eleventh minute a deep corner put Roger Jones in trouble. He failed to gather the ball, which dropped obligingly for veteran striker Johnson to tap in. The Spartans' fans went wild, as might be imagined. Stoke failed to wake up for the rest of the half.

Booed off at the break, City set about getting a grip on the game. Blyth held on grimly, inspired by the monumental Guthrie. Stoke applied heavy pressure until finally they broke Spartans' resistance. In the 56th minute Viv Busby scored and two minutes later Crooks netted a second. Blyth's Robert Carney later admitted to thinking to himself 'Uh-oh, this is going to be a 6-1 job'. Crucially, City relaxed, reckoning without Blyth's spirit. It proved fatal. On 75 minutes Guthrie's free-kick deflected off the wall. The ball thudded against the left-hand post, was headed against the other by Alan Shoulder and then slotted home by Steve Carney. City teetered, and with two minutes remaining the Spartans swung over another cross and Stoke dithered again. The defence failed to clear and Terry Johnson pounced with a shot that took a wicked deflection to beat Jones. The Boothen End emptied almost instantaneously.

Spartans became only the third non-league side in the last 50 years to reach the fifth round, where they surpassed themselves again, drawing 1-1 at Wrexham. For the replay Blyth hired St James' Park, Newcastle, and were rewarded with a gate of nearly 45,000. Wrexham squeaked into the quarter-finals 2-1.

Arguably the worst result in Stoke's history forced the board into promptly appointing a permanent replacement for Eastham. Within ten days Alan Durban was named as new manager. There would be no such embarrassments during his reign!

LEAGUE DIVISION 2   **1978-79**
League Division 2   3rd (Promoted)
League Cup   Quarter-finals
FA Cup   3rd Round

Despite the good form shown at the tail end of the previous season, Durban felt his squad lacked solidity at the back and vigour in midfield. He paid £50,000 for centre-half Mike Doyle from Manchester City, and £60,000 for Sammy Irvine, an attacking midfielder from his old club, Shrewsbury. He also pursued Bristol Rovers' free-scoring forward Paul Randall, who had consistently impressed him, but was rebuffed. Late the previous season Durban had signed 21-year-old goalkeeper Peter Fox from Sheffield Wednesday, a snip at £15,000.

After seventeen years as a professional with the club, Alan Bloor was given a free transfer. Known as 'Bluto', after the ruffian foe in the Popeye cartoons, Bloor had established a reputation as a tough-tackling centre-half. He went on to have a short spell as manager at Port Vale, before retiring from the professional game to run a news-agents in Longton, one of the six towns which comprise the city of Stoke-on-Trent. Howard Kendall was appointed chief coach. He replaced Alan A'Court who, having served Stoke since 1969, joined Crewe as assistant manager. Durban had spotted Kendall's credentials – which, as an industrious, scheming midfielder with championship-winning experience, were not dissimilar to his own – and earmarked him as a coach/manager of the future. Kendall relished his new responsibilities, although he was still required to combine his coaching duties with anchoring the midfield. Durban's stated aim was to instil a professional approach into the club from top to bottom, something he felt had been lacking during the dramatic fall from grace. This meant apprentices were now required to sweep the corridors after training!

Durban's new broom swept away the cobwebs to pay immediate dividends. Stoke won five of the first six games to leap to the top of the division. City then faced successive matches against the three teams immediately below them – and failed to win any. Late equal-isers were conceded against Brighton and Crystal Palace, while City were outplayed at Fulham. Despite the stutter, Durban earned a second successive Manager of the Month award. Doyle's arrival released Alan Dodd to play alongside Kendall. In an early indication of his tactical caution, Durban preferred to use Dodd's tackling and distribution skills to add solidity in central midfield

Stoke also made their presence felt in the League Cup. A 3-2 win at fellow promotion challengers Charlton put City through to face

Third Division Watford in the quarter-finals. The Hornets, guided by another young manager, Graham Taylor, were the League's form team, renowned for their physical presence and dreaded 'route one' tactics. The press decried them as not pretty to watch, but history records that Watford would soon finish second in the First Division and reach a Wembley Cup final. After a 0-0 draw at the Vic, Stoke visited Vicarage Road for the replay knowing that victory would earn a semi-final against European Champions Nottingham Forest. The fans expected to win. They reckoned without the hustle and bustle of the Hornets, who deservedly won 3-1 in extra-time.

An FA Cup run also beckoned when Stoke led Oldham 2-0 early in the second half, only for fog to force an abandonment. Oldham won the replay 1-0, to Durban's disgust.

In December, Durban finally got his man when he signed prolific striker Paul Randall from Bristol Rovers for £150,000. The big-money signing, who had scored an impressive 33 goals in 49 starts for the Pirates, was always going to be in Durban's starting line-up, which was bad news for Garth Crooks, who was moved out onto the left wing. Crooks was unhappy at this turn of events, preferring a central role, and was not afraid to say so. The switch affected his form and he scored only four goals after the arrival of Randall, who himself only found the back of the net on five occasions. Randall and Crooks failed to click, unlike Crooks and O'Callaghan. Crooks' barren run was disguised by goals scored by others. Sammy Irvine notched seven in the League, while Busby and Richardson weighed in with six. Added to O'Callaghan's fifteen and Crooks' total of twelve, it was a true team effort.

Stoke enjoyed a thirteen-match unbeaten run which propelled them into the promotion frame. This time they were unbeaten in dog-eat-dog games against promotion rivals, forcing 1-1 draws at third-placed Brighton and one-time leaders Crystal Palace. Fourth-placed West Ham, featuring the world's most expensive goalkeeper, Phil Parkes, were swept aside 2-0 at the Vic.

City's success was based upon a rock-solid defence. Mike Doyle had proved yet another astute signing by Durban. Despite having played for England – albeit during the reign of Revie, who seemed to cap almost anything that moved – only two seasons previously, Manchester City had released him at a bargain price and Durban had snapped him up. Stoke conceded just eight goals during their unbeaten run and only twice fell behind in matches. Durban's style attracted criticism for lacking flair and excitement. His contention was that promotion was the over-riding objective, and grinding out results was more important than simple entertainment. Flair and dynamism can mean the difference between winning and losing games at the top level of football, but lower down it can sometimes be a luxury. Often it is pragmatism, organisation and making fewer mistakes which wins promotion. Durban knew that if City were tight at the back, then his potent strike-force and goalscoring midfield would, more often than not, find a way past any opposition in the division.

Durban was still looking to improve his squad before the transfer deadline. The experienced Brian Kidd, of Everton, and Cardiff's centre-half, Phil Dwyer, were top of his list, but, with the board still shy of spending speculatively, no more transfers went through. It was at this point that Stoke hit a sticky patch. Sunderland, chasing the top three, stole a 1-0 win at the Vic, despite Stoke dominating for 85 minutes. The next home game saw a defeat by next-to-bottom Blackburn. Suddenly Stoke were back down to fourth, with teams above them having precious games in hand.

Durban refused to tinker with his line-up, insisting that he was sending out his best team. The players responded in fine style with three wins and a draw. Exemplifying Durban's desire, courageous skipper Denis Smith played at Wrexham with eight stitches in his forehead, leading Stoke back to the top with just two games left.

The last game at the Vic was against Newcastle, Sunderland's bitter rivals, but Bill McGarry's men did their neighbours a huge favour by clinging on for a 0-0 draw. A nervy Stoke were down to second, but Cardiff's unexpected 2-1 win at Roker Park threw the Potters a lifeline.

Three up and three down between the top two divisions had been introduced in 1973, giving Stoke an extra place to aim for. They entered the last match knowing victory against Notts County would ensure promotion (see Match of the Season). Midfielder Paul Richardson's late goal clinched a famous victory. Durban's pragmatic team had battled their way back into the top flight. Whether they had the ability to stay there was another matter.

Match of the Season 1978-79

Notts County 0 Stoke 1

Division 2, 5 May 1979

Stoke went into the last game of the season knowing that a win would see them promoted. Anything less and they would be at the mercy of Crystal Palace, Brighton and Sunderland, all of whom had easier games left, on paper. In the only change to what had become Durban's preferred line-up, Garth Crooks started in place of Viv Busby, who had disappointed in the 0-0 draw with Newcastle.

Notts County, managed by Jimmy Sirrel, had finished the season strongly and were guaranteed to finish sixth – missing promotion in those pre play-off years. Encouragingly for Stoke, County's Achilles heel was their modest home record, which had seen them draw more than they had won at Meadow Lane. Their predominantly young side featured the experienced former Coventry and England centre-half, Jeff Blockley, and Scottish international midfielder Don Masson, who had played in the 1978 World Cup.

Meadow Lane was bedecked in red and white, with an estimated 16,000 of the 21,579 crowd willing the Potters to victory. The game started cagily. As was typical under Durban, Stoke were determined to give nothing away, which would force them to chase the game, and the first half passed largely without incident. Only Brighton, of the other promotion contenders, were leading at half-time. Early in the second half Stoke's bench learnt that Crystal Palace had taken the lead at Orient, and that Sunderland now were 2-1 up at Wrexham. With all of their promotion rivals now leading, the message went out that a goal was essential if all the season's hard work was not to go to waste.

The team responded by picking up the tempo. Denis Smith added his physical presence to the attack and Crooks and O'Callaghan both went close. With just two minutes remaining, the promotion prize appeared to be slipping from Stoke's grasp. Durban was on his feet urging his players forward. As the pressure rose towards boiling point, the Magpies buckled. Irvine crossed and O'Callaghan knocked the ball back for Richardson to head home, sending the hordes of Stoke fans wild with delight.

Stoke reserve Adrian Heath, watching in the Away End, had his leather jacket ripped in the frenzy that greeted the goal. The restart was delayed by encroaching fans, and by the time the game kicked off, the results from the other matches were known. City had to hang on to secure promotion. With nine men behind the ball there was little problem in keeping the Magpies at bay. The final whistle sparked ecstatic celebrations. It was almost like being at the Vic.

LEAGUE DIVISION 1   **1979-80**
League Division 1   18th
League Cup   3rd Round
FA Cup   3rd Round

Durban's only aim for the 1979-80 season was for Stoke to stay up. With that in mind, he signed Fulham's experienced right-back Ray Evans for £100,000. Evans was renowned as a battler with a short fuse, but also a player who could overlap and cross the ball at pace. Evans replaced Jackie Marsh who, along with Terry Conroy, was given a free transfer, leaving Denis Smith as the last remaining Stoke player to have tasted Wembley glory in 1972. Goalkeeping cover was provided by Eric McManus (£85,000 from Notts County). Durban also purchased Stoke's first overseas signing, Loek Ursem. The Dutch Under-23 international midfielder arrived for £58,000 from AZ67 Alkmaar and soon proved to be a firm favourite with the fans.

The Victoria Ground also saw the completion of the new Stoke End stand, which had a seating capacity of 4,250, rising above a paddock which held 2,500 standing spectators. It replaced the antiquated Town End terrace, which was little more than shored up concrete, open to the elements, and, more to the point, had been almost impossible to police. The new stand could be sectioned off to provide areas for both home and away supporters. The development was funded by the hugely successful lottery operations which commercial manager Dudley Kernick had instituted. This suggested that the board had finally got to grips with the financial problems which had seen two years in the Second Division wilderness.

The club nearly lost their manager before the new season even kicked off. Derby, having parted with the flamboyant Tommy Docherty, hoped to acquire the services of the highly regarded Durban, a former player of theirs. Fortunately for Stoke he decided to stay and finish the job he had started at the Victoria Ground. City did lose their coach, though. Howard Kendall was released to take charge as player-manager at Blackburn, which would mark the start of a notable managerial career, in which he won two League championships, an FA Cup and the European Cup-Winners' Cup – all with his next club, Everton. Durban appointed the experienced Cyril Lea as his new assistant. Lea had been coach under Bobby Robson for eleven years during Ipswich's emergence as a First Division force.

Kendall's replacement on the pitch was 19-year old Adrian 'Inchy' Heath, so called because of his lack of them. Heath went on to win eight England Under-21 caps after impressing in Durban's workaholic midfield. Kendall had taken the young midfielder under his wing during his season as player-coach and Heath was emerging as a player very much in the image of his mentor.

Once the gloves came off, City were soon struggling against the classier teams in the top flight, failing to win in ten games. Ipswich and Manchester United both taught Stoke a thing or two about the art of finishing. In both games Stoke wasted early chances, whereas the two title challengers took their opportunities clinically. More worryingly, City were also failing to finish off lesser opponents, including those promoted alongside them. Crystal Palace won 2-1 at the Vic after Stoke had led at half-time. All of which raised the hard question: were Stoke good enough to stay up?

Things weren't much better in the League Cup. In the third round Stoke received what appeared to be a kind draw – Third Division Swindon at home. After drawing a mite fortuitously, Stoke folded embarrassingly in the replay (see Match of the Season).

After Mike Doyle had been injured against Swindon, Durban asked Alan Dodd to partner Denis Smith at centre-half. Dodd shone in his favoured position and played a major role as Stoke conceded only eleven goals between 7 October and 1 March. City were suddenly much harder to beat and pulled away from the relegation zone, looking more comfortable in the company of most average Division One teams.

City's lengthening list of embarrassing cup exits was extended when Second Division strugglers Burnley triumphed 1-0 in the third round at Turf Moor, with Evans and Smith both sent off in a stormy last ten minutes. There were ructions off the pitch too. Cyril Lea was not proving to be a success as first team coach. He refused to move house to the Potteries, as had apparently been agreed, and the daily travelling from his Suffolk home consumed too much of his time. He parted company with the club by mutual consent early in the New Year. Durban sought to promote from within. Reserve team coach Wally Gould, who, along with Tony Lacey had been responsible for the talented crop of youngsters breaking into the first team, was asked to replace Lea.

At the end of February midfielder Sammy Irvine was involved in a horrific car crash. Sadly, he failed to recover fully from his injuries and his football career was terminated at the age of 24. He became a publican. Irvine had never been the most popular of players with the Stoke faithful, who saw him as a bulldozer rather than a rapier. His style was symptomatic of Durban's grinding, aggressive tactics. Brought up to appreciate the skills of Hudson or Greenhoff, having a player of Irvine's limited range rankled with Stoke's fickler fans. Nevertheless, he had only missed three games in two seasons, and

City missed his attacking verve. 'Inchy' Heath was handed the task of replacing Irvine as an attacking midfielder, while apprentice Paul Bracewell emerged as Durban's first choice as the holding player. City's line-up was looking ever more youthful, and in late December Durban felt able to sell Viv Busby to Tulsa Roughnecks in the NASL for £30,000.

Stoke hardly seemed to be helping themselves in the battle to avoid the drop. Garth Crooks missed one penalty and his successor, Paul Richardson, missed three successive spot-kicks. Ray Evans assumed responsibility, netting his first penalty in a 2-0 win over Aston Villa. Fortunately none of the other relegation candidates enjoyed particularly good runs either. Stoke only fell two places to eighteenth. With three points needed from the last two games to be sure of avoiding relegation, successive 1-0 wins, with Heath grabbing both goals, ensured safety.

Durban's achievement cannot be underestimated. No matter that the sides he put out were not entertaining: by first winning promotion and then avoiding relegation he had allowed the club to rediscover its belief in itself. He also encouraged the flourishing youth programme by blooding a number of youngsters. Compared with the modern era, when simple survival in a higher division is seen as an achievement in itself, even by teams who bandy around millions of pounds, Durban had achieved relative success on a veritable shoestring.

Garth Crooks, with fifteen goals in his first full season among the elite, was one of the success stories, but the striker felt that the club did not fully appreciate his talents. Not one to let sleeping dogs lie, he still bridled over Durban's demand that he play wide on the left during the promotion season and openly courted transfer speculation. This made him less than popular with the fans, who prize nothing higher than loyalty to the cause, not to mention the manager, who had dropped him yet again during the end of season run in. Crooks' good performances put himself in the shop window and it was obvious that his departure was imminent. The question was – where would the goals come from when he had gone?

Match of the Season 1979-80

Swindon 2 Stoke 1

League Cup, 3rd Round replay, 2 October 1979

In the midst of a poor League run, Stoke looked to the League Cup to provide relief. Despite leading 2-0 at home to Third Division Swindon, complacent City ended up desperately clinging on for a draw. Stoke travelled nervously to the County Ground for the replay. Recent cup form had been poor and the club was garnering a reputation for being suckers to lower division opposition.

Swindon, moreover, were riding a crest of a wave. Having spent most of their existence in the lower divisions, under manager Bobby Smith they were challenging for promotion to the Second. Andy Rowland and Alan Mayes, later to sign for Chelsea, formed a useful strike-force, which had accounted for the comeback goals at the Vic.

Durban sprang a surprise by naming 20-year-old Lee Chapman in the starting line-up. The tall, fair-haired striker – whose father, Roy, had been an inside-forward, scoring over 200 goals in a career with Port Vale, Lincoln and Mansfield – debuted as a replacement for the injured O'Callaghan.

Denis Smith, far from being 'Mr Dependable', suffered a game he would rather forget, failing to get to grips with Mayes. Roger Jones pulled off two sharp saves before Swindon broke through, Ray McHale lashing a 25-yarder into the top corner. City, lacking balance and confidence, could barely muster a shot as Crooks and Chapman failed to produce an instant rapport.

Swindon continued to play the better football after the break and it was no surprise when Mayes, slipping Smith again, made it two. Despite the fact that Doyle was slowed by a leg injury, Durban withdrew Smith, throwing on Busby in an attempt to retrieve the game. With four forwards on the pitch, City could do nothing but attack. Eventually Chapman scored, but the Robins held on. They would claim Arsenal's scalp, before losing narrowly on aggregate to Wolves in the semi-finals.

After losing to lowly Second Division Burnley in the FA Cup later in the season, Stoke's cup record against lower division opposition stood at two wins out of ten. City's cup record since has been no less shocking. Why do Stoke City struggle in cup-ties? It can only be put down to temperament. Successive managers and players have failed consistently to produce the goods on big occasions. Even in crunch League games Stoke always seemed nervous. The situation is often not helped by the fans, with fear of impending humiliation bred into them, who communicate their fears to the players from the stands. Perhaps if the club feared failure less and embraced winning more, these crucial games would be won.

LEAGUE DIVISION 1   **1980-81**
League Division 1   11th
League Cup   2nd Round
FA Cup   3rd Round

Renegade Garth Crooks got his dream move when Stoke agreed a £650,000 (record outgoing transfer) fee with Tottenham. The quick-silver striker would go on to win successive FA Cups with Spurs, scoring in the 1981 final replay win over Manchester City. Also leaving the Victoria Ground was Roger Jones, sold to Derby for £25,000. Having successfully negotiated the first season back in the First Division, helped by a trading-profit in the transfer market, Durban had got the club into a position whereby it had surplus to spend. He strengthened the squad by signing Peter Hampton, a left-back from Leeds for £170,000. Hampton's opportunities had been limited by living in the shadow of England's Terry Cooper. Finally, after a prolonged on-off saga that involved a failed medical at Everton – who also wanted him – goalscoring winger Paul Maguire was acquired for £262,000 from Shrewsbury.

The pre-season games saw Stoke pick up a glut of injuries. Denis Smith broke a leg, putting him out of action for a year, while both O'Callaghan and Randall picked up calf injuries on the club's tour of the Caribbean. Consequently, the season got off to an appalling start. On the opening day Stoke were thrashed by John Bond's Norwich, with teenage prodigy Justin Fashanu scoring a hat-trick. To add to the trauma Stoke lost Dodd (knee) and Heath (groin). With the heart of the team ripped out and Maguire yet to make his debut – due to the back injury that had scuppered his move to Goodison – Durban had to field 17-year-old Dave McAughtrie and reserve Dennis Thorley at centre-half at European Champions Nottingham Forest. City were duly thrashed 0-5.

One reason Durban had plumped for Maguire was his reputation as a dead-ball specialist. He scored a beauty when he finally made his debut at home to Leeds in a 3-0 win. Unfortunately, his back problem flared up again, denying him an opportunity to establish himself for a further six months. Faced with a desperate player-shortage for the next game, at Arsenal, Durban formulated a 3-5-2 defensive strategy which earned stinging press criticism for its negativity. 'Get a bunch of clowns if you just want entertainment,' scorned Durban. Arsenal won 2-0.

The situation required action. Rather than panic buy, Durban found a solution from within. A fit O'Callaghan was switched from centre-forward to central defence and in a 2-1 win at Manchester City looked as if he had played in that role all his life. Lee Chapman spearheaded the attack that day, with Heath and Ursem supporting him. The change of tactics paid immediate dividends. Stoke beat Middlesbrough and then won at Southampton for the first time since 1968. That match featured a debut goal from the Scot, Iain Munro, purchased for £165,000 from St Mirren. Although predominantly a left-back, Durban envisaged him fitting into the left side of midfield, where the veteran Paul Richardson lacked cover. In fact, Munro eventually displaced Loek Ursem, whom the fans loved for his flair, but whose inconsistency Durban distrusted.

The scouting network also came up trumps. Peter Griffiths was spotted playing for Bideford Town in the Western League and was snapped up for £15,000. With the arrival of Griffiths and the form of the maturing Chapman, Paul Randall was permitted to return to Bristol Rovers for just £55,000. Having paid out £150,000 for him, Durban had championed the bushy haired striker and given him his chance. But Randall's return of just eight goals in 51 games was not enough to justify the manager's faith. It was one of the few transfers that failed Durban, whose record bears comparison with any of Stoke's modern managers. Bristol Rovers fans rated Randall so highly that they raised much of the fee in a public appeal.

Stoke's good run included a revenge 3-1 win over Norwich. Lee Chapman scored all three to become the second youngest player to net a Stoke hat-trick, twenty days before his 21st birthday. Two months later he bagged a treble at Leeds. Stoke lost only two of the intervening League games and the early season relegation gloom seemed but a distant memory.

It was, however, the same old story in the cups. Stoke bowed out of the League Cup to Manchester City. In the FA Cup, a home thriller with Wolverhampton ended 2-2 (see Match of the Season), with Wanderers winning the replay 2-1. If consolation was required, at least Stoke had lost to teams from their own division this time!

Durban's no-nonsense style ensured that Stoke's disciplinary record was – to put it mildly – awful. Ray Evans collected yellow cards like they were going out of fashion – which in fact they were. The League had abandoned the use of coloured cards, fearing that referees were too keen to use them and thus sent more players off than they needed to. They were also thought to inflame the crowd. Paul Richardson became the last player of any club to be shown a red card when sent off for two cautions in the last minute at Crystal Palace. The FA eventually turned turtle on the matter. Players did not know if they had been booked, or sent off, and the cards were reinstated after eighteen months. Meanwhile, Paul A Johnson was sent off for fouling a histrionic Garth Crooks at Spurs in March. Crooks was now firmly the No 1 hate figure for Stoke fans.

DID YOU KNOW?

In the 1970s, when asked for his opinion of Sunday soccer, John Ritchie replied:
'Of course I'm against Sunday football. It'll spoil my Saturday nights.'

The form of Chapman and Heath earned them England Under-21 caps and the attention of managers of bigger clubs. Chapman finished the season with seventeen goals, while Heath, along with O'Callaghan and Loek Ursem, scored seven. Heath was now playing alongside Chapman as a supporting striker and revelled in his new position, using his low centre of gravity to turn more cumbersome opponents who populated First Division defences at the time. His understanding with Lee Chapman was akin to that which O'Callaghan and Crooks had developed. Durban's method suited this combination of players and, injury worries now behind him, Maguire was emerging as a key creative force on the right. His pace and trickery established him in the side toward the end of the season and allowed him to provide the ammunition for the new strikeforce. Stoke became a solid mid-table side, losing only once in the last nine matches – at champions Liverpool – to finish eleventh, a pleasant improvement on the hair-raising finish to the previous season.

The improvement in the team, if unspectacular, was clear to see. Durban's master-stroke of switching O'Callaghan, who still retained his ability to score goals from set-pieces, to defence, had done the trick. In just over three years he had turned the club from one sliding towards the Third Division into one which finished above the likes of Everton, Wolves and Sunderland in the First. Durban's taciturnity and dour tactics won him few friends, but where it counted, on the pitch, he had worked wonders for Stoke City. He was, however, growing restless. Disappointed at the lack of support, both on the terraces and from the boardroom – where his relationship with new chairman Percy Axon had deteriorated – Durban felt the time was right to move on. He declined a new contract and, lured by the prospect of funds to spend, never an option at Stoke, accepted the top job at Sunderland, whose potential clearly exceeded City's. Durban had argued for funds to invest in developing Stoke's squad, but the board, understandably wary perhaps after the 1976 debacle, were not prepared to risk a repetition. Moreover, in this respect Durban was his own worst enemy. He had proved he could build a reasonably successful side without funds to buy. Now he needed the challenge of managing one with money to spare. He left saying: 'I wish to manage a bigger club.' It spoke volumes about the board's ambition.

Match of the Season 1980-81

Stoke 2 Wolverhampton 2

FA Cup, 3rd Round, 3 January 1981

Stoke's FA Cup form was summed up by the 1978 Blyth Spartans debacle, and it was five years since they had last beaten League opponents. Drawn at home to John Barnwell's struggling Wolves, there was every prospect of this being Stoke's year for a good run. Despite wearing No 5, Brendan O'Callaghan partnered Lee Chapman in attack, with Heath assuming a more conventional midfield role. Dodd and Doyle formed the central defensive pairing.

Wolves were Stoke's bogey team of late. It was nine games and seven years since Stoke had beaten them. Wanderers' record scorer, John Richards, was joined by Mel Eves in a threatening forward line, supported by Kenny Hibbitt in midfield. In defence, the experienced George Berry, Geoff Palmer and Colin Brazier formed an overtly physical barrier in front of the underrated goalkeeper, Paul Bradshaw.

The game proved to be an all-action thriller. Wolves came out of the starting blocks the stronger and scored on 26 minutes, when Mel Eves headed past Fox. Stoke hit back instantly when Chapman stuck out a foot to deflect home Richardson's shot. Almost before anyone could draw breath, Fox saved from Richards and Hibbitt's shot was deflected in. Wolves ended a breathless first half 2-1 ahead.

Stoke started the second half with renewed vigour. O'Callaghan and Richardson both had shots saved by Bradshaw. Then, during a prolonged siege of the Wolves goal, the ball fell to Paul Bracewell on the edge of the box. He controlled it, turned and lashed a rapier-like shot into the far corner to equalise. Both keepers produced fine saves in the closing minutes and at the final whistle the teams were treated to a standing ovation, both sets of supporters recognising the superb entertainment and commitment they had witnessed.

The replay was won 2-1 by Wolverhampton, who went on to beat Watford, Wrexham and Middlesbrough on their way to losing controversially to eventual winners Tottenham in the semi-final. Stoke would have to wait another two years before finally winning an FA Cup-tie.

Paul Bradshaw saves on the line for Wolves in a titanic FA Cup-tie (January 1981)

Swansea's future Stoke star Robbie James and Brendan O'Callaghan (October 1981)

Peter Fox holds the club record appearances for a goalkeeper - 477

Adrian Heath in action at Brighton's Goldstone Ground (October 1981)

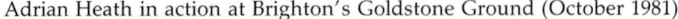

Lee Chapman and Paul A Johnson with Kevin Moran of Man Utd (January 1982)

Griffiths and Watson deal with Southampton's Mark Whitlock (March 1982)

The 1982 arrivals from neighbours Port Vale – Mark Harrison and Mark Chamberlain

Mischievous Mickey Thomas celebrates scoring against West Ham (October 1982)

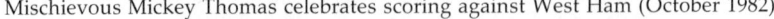

## 3

MAXIMUM OPPORTUNITY
1981-1985

LEAGUE DIVISION 1   **1981-82**
League Division 1   18th
League Cup   2nd Round
FA Cup   3rd Round

Alan Durban's legacy to Stoke City was to insist that his successor be his former assistant at Shrewsbury, Richie Barker, who was enjoying a growing reputation in coaching circles and was currently assistant to John Barnwell at Wolves. Needing to generate cash to bring in new players, Barker offloaded Paul Johnson (to Shrewsbury) and Paul Richardson (Sheffield United). Each earned a £20,000 fee, while Iain Munro followed Durban to Roker Park for £160,000.

Stoke's coffers were also boosted by a sponsorship deal with Telford-based company Ricoh. Sponsorship invited much debate within football at the time. Television was not allowed to show shirt advertising, forcing clubs to use kit without sponsors' names for televised games. This threatened lucrative deals with multinational companies, big business for leading clubs and a lifeline for smaller ones, such as Stoke. 'After all,' said Barker, 'I don't think they [Ricoh] will be too happy if we're top of the league and on TV every week, because then we won't be able to wear their name on our shirts.' The impact of television money on football was becoming ever more apparent. Glamour attracted viewers. Greg Dyke, now Director General of the BBC, but then in charge of ITV Sport, once reminded his commentators: 'It may be a 0-0 draw out there, but as far as the TV audience is concerned it's the best 0-0 draw there has ever been.' Effective though Durban's reign was, it had earned the club a reputation as boring. It was hard to imagine Stoke pulling in the viewers in their millions.

Without yet investing in new signings, Barker's team started the season in a whirlwind, pinching a 1-0 win at Arsenal before burying Coventry 4-0. With three points now awarded for a win, Stoke had six in the bag already. The main architects of those early wins were the midfield quartet of Griffiths, Dodd, Bracewell and Maguire. Any fantasies of a championship challenge fell to earth in the next game, at home to Manchester City, with double million pound transfer man Trevor Francis making his debut. He scored twice in a 3-1 win. Barker blamed Doyle for Francis's goals and as soon as Denis Smith had recovered from his year-long lay-off with a broken leg, the club captain was back in the team at Doyle's expense.

Stoke won only one of the next eight games as Barker's attacking philosophy left gaping holes at the back. O'Callaghan failed to dovetail with Smith as well as he had with Doyle. They coped with airborne attacks easily, but as a pair they were too alike and lacked mobility on the ground. Smith was also finding that an injury-blighted career was taking its toll on his body. First Division strikers were quick to take advantage.

With money burning a hole in his pocket, Barker looked for new players. Leeds' Welsh international Brian Flynn and Swedish mid-fielder Robert Prytz both interested him. Prytz agreed to sign, but, after much to-ing and fro-ing, the Department of Employment refused to grant him a work permit as he did not meet the criteria for international clearance. Within a year he had signed for Rangers, amid rumours that their influence at the Scottish Football Association had been decisive. Sour grapes or no, it strongly hinted at Stoke's 'small club' status.

In view of his early season form, Adrian Heath was coveted by a number of top clubs. It was Everton's Howard Kendall, Heath's mentor during Kendall's season as player-coach at the Vic, who secured the England Under-21 international's signature for £700,000 (a record outgoing transfer fee) in early January. With the aftermath of the Butler Street Stand crisis still fresh in their minds, supporters feared that Stoke were once again selling their best players. Their views were reinforced by events on the pitch. After Stoke lost 0-3 at home to Manchester United, Barker fell out with Doyle and Evans, blaming them for defensive lapses. Within a fortnight Doyle had moved to Bolton for £20,000. Evans was suspended by the club for two weeks after a training ground fracas involving coach Wally Gould. The incident soured both men's relationship with the club. Gould left in March after differences with senior players, who felt his affinities lay with the younger lads, having been responsible for their development. With quality players proving difficult to attract to the Potteries, Barker was forced to field reserves Steve Bould, Steve Ford, John Lumsden, Steve Kirk and Eric McManus.

The FA Cup provided no solace. Second Division Norwich won 1-0 at the Victoria Ground as Stoke extended their losing cup streak against League teams to six. Murmurs of relegation, reinforced by

---

DID YOU KNOW?

Some players love scoring against Stoke. Peter Withe scored 9 (with Villa, Newcastle, and Sheff U) and Frank Worthington 7 (with Huddersfield, Bolton and Birmingham).

---

dressing room shenanigans, were ringing louder. Barker had to act and acquired 35-year-old former England centre-half Dave Watson for £50,000 from Southampton. His signing proved inspired, and within two months Watson had been recalled to the England side, playing in a 4-0 win over Northern Ireland. Wearing the Irish green that day was a new team-mate, Barker having paid a club record £350,000 for Sammy McIlroy (27) of Manchester United. McIlroy had captained Northern Ireland to the World Cup finals, which they would contest for the first time in 24 years. He scored on his Stoke debut in a 2-0 win at Alan Durban's Sunderland, who were also having a poor season. Barker's audacious swoop enabled Stoke to restore shape in midfield.

Just as things seemed to be fitting into place, the fixture list handed Stoke a run of games against top teams. City lost eight out of nine to plummet back into the relegation dog-fight. For the visit of Bob Paisley's Liverpool, Ray Evans was given one last chance to redeem himself. The Reds, however, were in their pomp and hammered Stoke 5-1. Evans was soon on his way, moving to Seattle Sounders in the NASL on a free transfer.

Trailing 0-3 at leaders Southampton in their next game, Stoke fought back to 3-3, only to lose to a late goal. That knocked the stuffing out of the team, and three successive defeats saw the relegation trapdoor creak open. Belated transfer activity saved the day. Deadline-day signing Derek Parkin, from Barker's old club Wolves, replaced young Kirk at right-back and provided experience and solidity down a flank that had proved vulnerable. Barker also signed striker Alan Biley on loan from Everton. City eked out wins over Wolves and Aston Villa, then drew a vital relegation clash at Leeds 0-0. Safety was within reach, but another draw, this time at home against Notts County, threw Stoke back into the melting pot (see Match of the Season).

Stoke now had 41 points, one fewer than Allan Clarke's Leeds, each with one game left. Both would face Ronnie Allen's West Brom, who were level on points with Stoke. Albion beat Leeds 2-0. The result favoured Stoke as, two days later, exhausted after their efforts against Leeds, the Baggies fell apart at the Victoria Ground. Stoke won easily 3-0 and were safe. Barker knew he might not be so fortunate if it came to the crunch next time around. Fresh faces were imperative.

Match of the Season 1981-82

Stoke 2 Notts County 2

Division 1, 8 May 1982

The introduction of three points for a win had made winning all the more vital. Correspondingly, draws were no longer neutral results, but bad ones – any team drawing all its matches was likely to get relegated. Stoke now needed three points to ensure survival. They knew that of their remaining three fixtures, the one at home to mid-table Notts County provided the best opportunity to collect them. Barker kept the same team for the third game running, a luxury he had not enjoyed since February.

Jimmy Sirrel's Notts County were consolidating after promotion. Their uncompromising line-up included the bearded Brian Kilcline at centre-half and the tricky John Chiedozie on the right wing. Just twelve days previously they had come from behind to beat Stoke at Meadow Lane 3-1, a match in which Dave Watson endured a personal nightmare. He had gifted the Magpies a penalty for a silly foul on Mark Goodwin and, unusually, misjudged a header to allow Gordon Mair to lob the advancing Fox.

On a sunny afternoon Stoke started well and went close through Chapman and Biley. Watson, determined to atone for his errors at Meadow Lane, powered in a header. Within a minute it was 2-0. Maguire intercepted a lazy Pedro Richards back-pass to round the keeper and slot home. Survival beckoned. Stoke eased off, happy to sit on their lead, allowing County back into the game. With half-time approaching Chiedozie wriggled into the area where O'Callaghan brought him down. Trevor Christie dispatched the resultant spot-kick past Fox.

Stoke started the second half tentatively. Fox collected numerous back-passes – this was long before FIFA's decision to penalise them – as City chose to eat up the minutes. Tension mounted as the team retreated in a bid to preserve their precious lead. The last minutes seemed an eternity. Stoke, penned into their own half, appeared to have survived, but in injury-time Gordon Mair's shot was deflected into the path of Pedro Richards, who, making up for his earlier error, slammed the ball into the net for the equaliser. There was just time for Alan Biley to try an audacious shot direct from the kick-off before the referee blew for full-time. From being seconds from safety, Stoke had left themselves deep in trouble.

LEAGUE DIVISION 1   **1982-83**
League Division 1   13th
Milk Cup   2nd Round
FA Cup   4th Round

Barker spent £200,000 of the £700,000 received for Adrian Heath on Brighton's Welsh international midfielder Mickey Thomas, who bore a reputation as a disruptive talent. Rumour had it that he had been sold by Manchester United because a director's wife disapproved of his cheeky wink in the title sequence to Match of the Day! Barker's Wolves connection came up trumps again when he signed 25-year-old Afro-haired central defender George Berry, on a free transfer. Also arriving were two Marks – Chamberlain and Harrison – from local rivals Port Vale for a joint fee of £150,000. After the elder Chamberlain brother, Neville, signed – also from Vale – two months later, Barker quipped, 'We're getting Port Vale into the First Division – one at a time!'

Outgoing players included Lee Chapman. Barker accepted Arsenal's £500,000 offer for the burly centre-forward who appeared to crave the bright lights of the capital. Although his move to Highbury would not work out, he went on to score 253 goals in 679 appearances with a number of clubs, including Sunderland, Niort in France, Nottingham Forest, Leeds and West Ham.

Denis Smith was given a free transfer after serving the club for fourteen years. His unquestionable commitment to Stoke had led to him suffering an astonishing number of serious injuries, including four broken legs. At his testimonial the previous summer, he was supported by many of the players whom he had appeared alongside in Stoke's colours, including Peter Shilton and Gordon Banks. Smith left for York, where he had been on a month's loan the previous season. He would later become boss at Bootham Crescent, the start of a managerial career that took him to Sunderland, Bristol City, West Brom and Oxford, although his apparent destiny of becoming manager of Stoke City has, at the time of writing, yet to materialise.

The day before Stoke's League opener, at home to Arsenal, Barker asked Mark Chamberlain whether he would prefer to play through the middle, replacing Chapman, or on the right. Chamberlain replied 'on the right', provided he saw enough of the ball. In that short conversation, a plan to devastate the best defences in the country had been formed.

Chamberlain's debut was little short of sensational. The winger ripped apart Kenny Sansom, England's left-back, as McIlroy and Bracewell fed him pass after pass and set up both goals in a 2-1 win.

Stoke's day was completed when Chapman's instant return to the Vic ended in a booking, as the frustration got to him.

Nor was that win a flash in the pan. Defenders appeared to have little idea how to cope with Chamberlain's speed and panache. 4-1 victories over Birmingham and Swansea preceded a 3-2 triumph at Ipswich. This time Chamberlain's victim was former England captain Mick Mills.

Dave Watson returned from a summer 'rebel' tour to South Africa. Fearing reprisals by the authorities, Stoke had cancelled his registration with the Football League as South Africa was subject to anti-Apartheid restrictions. Those participating in an English cricket touring party of South Africa had recently received international bans for up to three years. At the heart of City's defence, Watson's partnership with Berry gave the team a solid base from which to build flowing attacking moves.

Goalkeeper Peter Fox also started the season in excellent form, and was touted by Barker as an England possible. When Luton visited in late September (see Match of the Season), Fox found himself at the centre of a controversial sending off incident, as a result of which he was suspended. His deputy, Mark Harrison, coped admirably with being thrown in at the deep end, performing heroics as Stoke lost 0-1 at Old Trafford and keeping City in the game against the champions, Liverpool. Now able to compete with the best teams in the country, Stoke were able to teach those lesser mortals a footballing lesson. City overwhelmed West Ham 5-2, avenging an early League Cup exit at the hands of the Hammers. Paul Maguire's near-post corner routine with O'Callaghan was also working wonders. It was proving almost impossible to defend against and produced a number of goals for players arriving late into the penalty area. City rose to seventh, scoring 28 goals in thirteen games.

A leg muscle injury, sustained against Manchester United, kept Berry out for six weeks and Stoke missed his influence at the back. City lacked defensive cover after Barker had taken the decision in October to sell Alan Dodd to Wolves. Still only 28, Dodd had made 400 appearances for the club over eleven seasons and Wolves were happy to meet Barker's low asking price of £10,000. The scoring touch started to desert Stoke too, as defences wised up to the threat posed by Chamberlain and often man-marked him. When at last Berry returned he became error-prone. It was his mistake that led to Coventry's opener in a 0-2 defeat at Highfield Road and, in Stoke's worst display of the season, he allowed Ian McCulloch to score twice as Notts County hammered City 4-0. By the turn of the year Stoke were back down to fifteenth.

DID YOU KNOW?

Paul Peschisolido's surname is the longest ever to represent Stoke City.
It equals Harry Crossthwaite (12 letters).

Early in the season Stoke had instituted a scheme called Match-mates, encouraging young Potters fans, aged 7-11, to play fans of similar ages of the visiting clubs on the morning of the games, then sit together to watch the seniors in the afternoon. Matchmates helped to foster understanding between young supporters and was pioneered by Dougie Brown, a former physio at the club in the 1960s, whose brother Roy had played for Stoke during the 1940s. Dougie had become mayor of Stoke and is still a much-admired dignitary in the city. The scheme was adopted by a number of other First Division clubs and ran for two further seasons.

In December, Mark Chamberlain was named by new England manager Bobby Robson in his squad to play Luxembourg at Wembley. He made his debut as a substitute, becoming the first Stoke player to be capped by England since Peter Shilton in 1977, and scored with a flying header. Former Ipswich boss Robson, more mindful of the talents which lurk in the less fashionable clubs than some of his predecessors, gave the likes of Luton's Hill and Stein, Brighton's Steve Foster and Norwich's Mark Barham the opportunity to prove themselves. Chamberlain enjoyed a longer career with Robson's England than most, as he fitted into the 4-2-4 pattern which allowed Robson to accommodate the two in-form wingers in the First Division, Chamberlain on the right and John Barnes of Watford on the left. The experience re-energised Chamberlain, and back at Stoke he recaptured his early season form, sparking the team into life.

City even won an FA Cup-tie! Their 3-2 replay victory over Sheffield United meant a place in round four for the first time in six years. There they were paired with Liverpool at Anfield, and went out 0-2. Liverpool also put a stop to Stoke's winning ways in the League, dishing out a 5-1 hiding. A poor home defeat to Sunderland followed and, to make matters worse, Derek Parkin badly injured his leg. This allowed Steve Parkin, no relation, to become the fifth youngest player ever to appear for Stoke, aged seventeen years, 120 days, when Nottingham Forest visited in March. Mickey Thomas scored the only goal. Thomas had become the fans' favourite after declaring that he was playing the best football of his career and loved being at Stoke. City fans admired his impish spirit and never say-die attitude. His obvious desire to stay on the pitch when badly gashing his shin against Luton had been just one example of his commitment. Thomas also found the net regularly, finishing as top scorer with twelve goals, and was an overwhelming choice as Player of the Season. After hammering second-placed Watford 4-0, Stoke were riding high in fifth place. The fans talked of Europe and a title challenge the following year.

Influential skipper Dave Watson had hoped to continue playing over the coming summer for Vancouver Whitecaps in the NASL. At nearly 37, he felt he needed to retain match fitness over the English close season. He planned to return to Stoke as soon as possible, but a League rule, designed to stop clubs from circumventing loan deal quotas (five per season), meant that he was refused permission to re-sign for Stoke within a year of leaving. Nearing the end of his career, he moved to Canada for £5,000 and bade farewell to the Vic in April. He did return to England in September, joining Derby, for whom he completed a full season.

Watson's departure left a gaping hole at the back and the team's form declined alarmingly, not helped by the persistent hamstring problems plaguing Chamberlain. Stoke failed to win any of the last six games and faded out of contention for European places. They finished a disappointing thirteenth. Thomas, described by Richie Barker as 'irresponsible off the field and irresponsible on it', was aggrieved at the manager's choice of George Berry as captain after Watson's departure. Thomas craved the job, despite his colourful image. It was the beginning of his disillusionment with Barker.

On the bright side, the financial woes that had dogged Stoke for the last seven years had been assuaged. In two years at the helm, Barker had made a trading profit of £500,000 in the transfer market, at the same time attracting international stars and unearthing local talent. Stoke had enjoyed their best season since 1975-76. The future looked good. What could possibly go wrong?

Match of the Season 1982-83

Stoke 4 Luton 4

Division 1, 25 September 1982

Every once in a while a game comes along which has everything. Great goals, superb attacking play and wonderful cameo performances, with the odd controversial decision thrown in. This was such a match.

Under David Pleat (tactical motto: 'attack and be damned'), Luton had become one of the most attractive teams in the country. Promoted as Second Division champions in 1981-82, the Hatters had begun the season with a string of fine performances, culminating in a 5-0 thrashing of Brighton the previous weekend. Their potent strikeforce of Brian Stein and highly rated Paul Walsh was supplied from midfield by classy Ricky Hill and dashing right-winger David Moss. Luton's defence, however, was leaky.

Stoke scored first on ten minutes through a Berry header, but Walsh equalised spectacularly from 25 yards. There was no let-up as both teams poured forward. Chamberlain wove his way down the right-hand side of the area towards the by-line. Confronted by two defenders, he turned his back to goal, then spun on a sixpence to whip a cross to the near post. Luton's defence stood transfixed and Berry stole in to score a second.

Ricky Hill then played Walsh in behind the defence. Fox raced out of his goal and smothered the ball outside his area. Realising he could be sent off, under a new FA directive, for deliberate handball, Fox attempted to keep his hands by his sides. Walsh nicked the ball from under his body and swept it into the net. But referee Gilbert Napthine had already blown for handball against Fox and, to the dismay of Luton awarded them nothing more than a direct free-kick just outside the box. He then angered Stoke by sending off Fox for handball. Paul Bracewell donned Fox's gloves and it was not long before he was beaten by Stein's flying header. 2-2.

The pace did not slacken after the break. Barker switched Derek Parkin to play in goal, and, as Luton pressed, Stoke broke out on the right. Bracewell flung himself to nod the ball home after Luton keeper Judge spilled Chamberlain's cross.

Almost immediately Stein waltzed around two defenders to drive past Parkin. At 3-3 Luton stepped up the pressure and Stoke cracked. Mal Donaghy stole in on the blind side to loop a header over the stranded Parkin. Luton did not expect City's ten men to retrieve the game, but with ten minutes left Brendan O'Callaghan drove into the far corner of the net from twenty yards. 4-4.

Yet the drama was far from over. Bracewell tripped Stein in the box. Moss, Luton's renowned penalty taker, stepped up to take the kick against stand-in keeper Parkin. Somehow he scuffed his shot against the foot of the post, sending the Boothen End wild. The 4-4 draw was made even more memorable on account of being televised the following day to a national audience.

Fox seriously considered quitting the game after his sending off. The hundreds of letters he received in support changed his mind. Within a month the League had withdrawn the instruction that had made deliberate handball an automatic dismissal, although FIFA enshrined it within the laws of the game for the 1990 World Cup.

LEAGUE DIVISION 1   **1983-84**
Canon Division 1   18th
Milk Cup   4th Round
FA Cup   3rd Round

Despite Richie Barker's best efforts, Paul Bracewell – capped by England at Under-21 level at the end of the previous season – left to join his mentor, and former boss, Alan Durban at Sunderland. Strapped for cash again, Barker bit the bullet and agreed a miserly £250,000 for a player who would go on to win two championships and a European Cup-Winners' Cup under another former Stoke employee, Howard Kendall, at Everton.

Another loss was the death of industrious chairman Percy Axon. He was succeeded by Frank Edwards. The new chairman's first act was to increase the size of the board, the intention being to attract new investment. Average home gates had dropped below 17,000, and the consequent drop in income impinged upon Barker's preparations. Stoke scraped together enough money to buy Robbie James from Swansea for £160,000 and Paul Dyson for £150,000 – replacing Bracewell and Watson respectively. Without the sale of Bracewell there would have been no money to buy anyone.

The barrel-chested James was a Welsh international midfielder with eleven caps to his name. At 27, he was in his prime, having been instrumental in the success of John Toshack's Swansea side that had briefly headed the First Division in 1981. He possessed a fierce right-footed shot and Stoke fans grew to love his pot-shots from distance. When he got it right, as in a Milk Cup-tie at Peterborough, the ball would rocket into the net before the goalkeeper could move. The balding Dyson was a 6ft 3in central defender who arrived with a physical reputation. He lacked Watson's dominance in the middle of the back four and failed to partner George Berry successfully.

Barker was well-known for subscribing to coaching theory and often attended seminars and courses on the subject. During the summer he had attended a course at the National Sports Centre at Lilleshall, where FA coach Charles Hughes expounded the theory of 'Position of Maximum Opportunity', or POMO for short. The system involved the defence hitting long balls into the penalty area at the earliest opportunity for big strikers to challenge for, and smaller players to pick up the scraps from. It was an extension of the 'scientific kick and rush' theory employed by Stan Cullis's successful Wolves of the 1940s and 50s. Watford, under Graham Taylor – who summed up the system as 'goals come from mistakes, not possession' – had successfully utilised POMO in the previous campaign, finishing second in the League behind Liverpool, but had been condemned by football purists for ruining the 'beautiful game'. The tactics could even be expressed in a mathematical equation! $S=R/Nxn$, although nobody ever explained to Stoke fans what the letters stood for.

Barker believed that the long-ball system could bring success to a club such as Stoke, which was struggling to keep pace with the bigger glamour clubs, who had money to burn. His argument was this: he could not hope to attract the quality of player that Manchester United, Liverpool or Tottenham might sign, therefore his inferior quality team had to play the long ball game to stand any chance of competing. The logic seemed flawed, given that his squad featured a ball-playing midfield and two strikers, in Painter and Maguire, under 5ft 10in.

Barker's decision to implement POMO was unpopular with his players. McIlroy and Thomas were particularly vocal dissenters, but on a pre-season Scandinavian tour City scored 38 goals in six games and Barker felt vindicated. The players still didn't like it. Back home, a 0-3 friendly defeat at Third Division Bournemouth was dismissed as a blip. It was, in fact, a more accurate assessment of the season that lay ahead than the thrashings of largely second-rate teams in Scandinavia.

Another innovation was a hideous pin-striped kit, introduced by Tactics, a PR company employed by the newly expanded board to enhance the club's image. The new kit was detested from the moment Stoke emerged from the tunnel in their first home game, against West Brom. City steamrollered the Baggies 3-1, through three close-range strikes after long balls had induced mayhem in the visitors' penalty area. Perhaps POMO was going to be good for Stoke after all.

One win in the next sixteen games suggested otherwise. There were dreadful defeats along the way. City were hammered 0-5 at Ipswich and 0-4 at home to a Watford team employing the same tactics as Barker, but with the right personnel. The likes of beanpole strikers George Reilly and Jimmy Gilligan, players not fit to lace the boots of Stoke's international midfield, were made to look world beaters by playing to a system which suited them. An abysmal 0-0 draw with Fourth Division Peterborough in the Milk Cup at the Vic prompted heaps of letters to the local paper, the *Evening Sentinel*, complaining at the 'appalling style of football', even though Stoke squeezed through in the second leg.

The likes of Chamberlain and Thomas barely saw the ball, and simply scurried from one box to another with it whizzing over their heads. When Paul Dyson was injured in a 1-3 defeat at home to

Coventry, Barker was forced to revert O'Callaghan to centre-half, leaving no target man at all. Stoke were simply awful and the last straw was defeat in the Milk Cup by Second Division Sheffield Wednesday. That the outcome came as no surprise said everything. Something had to give.

Barker was sacked, on his wife's birthday as it turned out, with Stoke next to bottom on a paltry twelve points. His profit on transfers was more than £600,000, a tidy sum that had helped to keep the club afloat. Barker had become obsessed with POMO, missing the glaringly obvious point that the long-ball game simply didn't suit the players he had. More than that, they did not want to be a part of it.

Assistant manager Bill Asprey, a former Stoke full-back who had coached at Coventry, Wolves and West Brom and been manager at Oxford, was put in temporary charge and, after an abject 2-4 home thrashing by Luton, acted to stem the run of defeats. He axed George Berry from the team, stripped him of the club captaincy and made him train with the youth squad. Quite what Berry had done to justify such action remains a mystery to him today. The pair never spoke again. Despite Barker's departure, Mickey Thomas was anxious to get away. Stoke finally got the price they were looking for and Thomas joined Chelsea for £275,000. Playing without confidence, Stoke were hammered 0-6 by newly promoted QPR on their controversial plastic pitch.

On the bright side, Tony Lacey's promising youth team made it to the final of the FA Youth Cup, after a 6-2 win on aggregate over Arsenal in the semi-final. Following a 2-2 draw at Everton, where Howells and Sutton scored Stoke's goals, City were favourites for the second leg. Everton proved too strong for the junior Potters, however, scoring twice without reply to win 4-2 on aggregate. Nevertheless, with players such as Chris Hemming and Phil Heath breaking through into the first team, there were good portents for the future.

At the end of January, with Stoke still languishing in 21st place, Asprey pulled off a coup that transformed the season. He secured the signature of Alan Hudson, now 32, from Chelsea for a nominal £22,500. Nominal or not, it cleaned out Stoke's kitty and on his purchase rode the club's First Division future. Hudson thereby became a statistical rarity, having played twice for two different clubs in the same division, and even rarer in having gone from the same club to the other on both occasions. Hudson signed on one condition; that he be allowed to dictate the way the team played. Asprey let him have his head. The master playmaker's promptings released Chamberlain down the wing and, in tandem with McIlroy, happier to be playing with the ball rather than craning his neck to the sky to spot it, Hudson prompted Stoke to win seven out of ten games, hauling themselves out of the relegation zone. The run included Stoke's best performance of the season, a 2-0 defeat of Liverpool (see Match of the Season). City now looked likely to avoid the drop.

Once again Stoke contrived to put their supporters through the agonies of a prolonged battle for survival. City won just one of the next five games to drop to twentieth position, level on points with Birmingham and Coventry, with just one match left. Remarkably, there were still five sides in danger of filling the final relegation position.

Fortuitously, the fixture list provided Stoke with a home fixture against Wolves, who had been cannon fodder all season and would finish twelve points adrift at the bottom. Hopes ran high along the Boothen Old Road as supporters gathered at the Vic. They were not to be disappointed. Stoke's hero in a 4-0 win was Paul Maguire, who scored all four goals to become the first player since John Ritchie in February 1966 to notch four in a game. His second was a spectacular bicycle-kick. His third and fourth were both penalties. Rumour, possibly fanciful, had it that Alan Dodd, who had left Stoke the previous season, purposefully gave away a penalty to help his beloved City stay in the First Division.

The win proved just enough. Three of Stoke's rivals won, but the unlucky team was Birmingham, who could only manage a 0-0 home draw with Southampton and went down. City's remarkable escape did not, however, stop one of Stoke's longest serving employees, Dudley Kernick, the commercial manager, nipping into his local bookmakers and placing a judicious £1,000 at 6-1 on Stoke being relegated the following season.

Match of the Season 1983-84

Stoke 2 Liverpool 0

Division 1, 14 April 1984

Stoke were riding high after the return of the prodigal son, Alan Hudson, who had been instrumental in turning the fortunes of the club on their head. But City still needed every point they could muster in the battle to avoid the drop. Many fans felt that getting even one point out of this match would be a moral victory.

Liverpool had all but mathematically won their third successive Championship. The previous weekend they had murdered West Ham 6-0 at Anfield. In Dalglish and Rush they had the best striking

---

DID YOU KNOW?

In the late '80s a craze for inflatables swept English football. Grimsby had haddocks.
Stoke plumped for Pink Panthers, and ran out to Henry Mancini's theme tune.

---

partnership of the 1980s and the midfield of Whelan, Souness and Lee were without par in Britain. Goalkeeper Bruce Grobbelaar was only weeks away from writing himself into football legend with his wobbly knees routine in the European Cup final penalty shoot-out.

On a sunny afternoon Stoke started well. McIlroy and Hudson prompted Chamberlain forward. He twice outpaced Alan Kennedy before striking a vital blow. Collecting the ball near the halfway line, Chamberlain set off on a run that carried him 50 yards into the Liverpool penalty area, where he shot low and hard. Grobbelaar made an instinctive save, but the ball fell to Ian Painter, who drove it exultantly home.

Stoke's midfield looked in control. Liverpool found it hard to get out of second gear. Rush was almost anonymous and the supply line to Dalglish, so often the instigator of dangerous Liverpool moves, was cut by Robbie James.

Five minutes into the second half McIlroy enticed Phil Neal into conceding a free-kick just outside the box. Stoke threw O'Callaghan and Dyson forward to keep Liverpool's defence occupied at the far post and McIlroy cunningly whipped the free-kick low towards the near. The ball was glanced delicately past a transfixed Grobbelaar by on-loan striker Colin Russell. The Vic erupted.

City were enjoying themselves and, such was their dominance, that O'Callaghan even found time to dabble in a spot of baiting, standing on the edge of the penalty area, his foot on the ball inviting a challenge. It took thirty seconds or so for anyone to take it up, but as soon as O'Callaghan saw them coming he simply back-heeled the ball to the waiting Fox to thunderous applause.

Stoke had outplayed the champions – and not just any old champions at that. This Liverpool team had already won one European Cup and would be Champions of Europe again within six weeks, completing a first ever treble (European Cup, League championship and League Cup). The Reds did not take kindly to the defeat and captain Graeme Souness stormed off the pitch, putting his fist through a window on the way to the dressing room.

LEAGUE DIVISION 1   **1984-85**
Canon Division 1   22nd (Relegated)
Milk Cup   2nd Round
FA Cup   3rd Round

The improbable escape from relegation had served only to paper over the cracks that were appearing all over the club. A drop in average attendances of seventeen per cent caused more financial hardship, to the extent that the experienced Peter Hampton and four-goal hero Paul Maguire were released on free transfers to ease the burden of the wage bill. Bill Asprey, aside from being confirmed as manager on a permanent basis, was coach and stand-in physiotherapist. One of his first decisions was to revert training to the antiquated facilities at the Victoria Ground. The club had been using Keele University's superb sports facilities, but Asprey felt he needed to be near the stadium to fulfil his onerous duties. It was also cheaper to train at the Vic, which pleased the board.

Asprey spoke of new signings but talk proved cheap. Youngsters Maskery, Heath, Parkin, Bould and Painter started the season at Luton. Nine months later there would be six teenagers in the side, hardly an improvement. Asprey did not believe the youngsters were ready for the First Division. He was right, but with no funds forthcoming from the newly expanded board, City had little choice but to start the new season with a thin squad.

It soon became apparent that the squad was painfully inadequate for First Division football. Five players were tried at left-back, where opponents were causing Stoke endless problems. The midfield, for so long the strongest department, was now looking long in the tooth. McIlroy's industry could not compensate for his loss of pace, while Chamberlain's lack of confidence would have warranted him being dropped – except that there was no one to replace him. An embarrassing home defeat by Third Division Rotherham in the Milk Cup provoked the first protests from fans. The club was falling apart.

Chairman Frank Edwards was trying to raise funds by selling the car park and training pitches – covering a huge area between the stadium and the A500 artery through Stoke – to supermarket chain Asda, but the deal fell through. Planning permission was refused in early 1985 and an appeal rejected after more than twelve months of wrangling. Much hope had been placed upon the £3 million that Stoke expected to receive for the land. Rejection meant there was nowhere else to look for funds. The board could hardly expect to cash in on the players, not when they were associated with such an appalling team.

DID YOU KNOW?

The Stoke anthem 'Delilah' originated with City fan Anton 'TJ' Booth. Following a bad
display at Derby in 1987 he was asked to sing something 'clean' at a Derby pub!

With the club hamstrung financially, there was no possibility of
bringing in new players, as had happened in previous seasons, to
stop the rot. Nor was there an Alan Hudson to effect a dramatic
escape, as injury restricted him to just seventeen appearances. In
desperation Asprey sold the one player who had been performing
to anywhere like his potential, Robbie James, for £100,00 to QPR in
mid-October to finance the £80,000 purchase of Keith Bertschin, a
striker, who had become surplus to requirements at Norwich. The
transactions smacked of desperation. Bertschin had only appeared
in five of Norwich's games, scoring just twice to add to his poor
return of seven the previous season, but, with the transfer market
spiralling higher in line with inflation in Britain as a whole, Stoke
could not afford a top-drawer striker.

With stalwart keeper Peter Fox injured, Welsh Youth International Stuart Roberts, aged seventeen years 258 days, became the
youngest goalkeeper ever to play for Stoke – a record he holds at
the time of writing – when he started against Ipswich. His appearance was brought about by desperation, rather than ability. Playing
behind a porous back four, Roberts let in eight goals in three games
and was traumatised to such an extent that he never played league
football again.

From the team that had beaten Liverpool in April to the rabble
that picked up only eight points before Christmas was but a blink of
the eye. The side showed little imagination going forward and
downright confusion at the back. The frustration turned to ill-
discipline as Dyson, Hudson, Berry and loanee Tony Spearing were
all sent off in the space of a few weeks. Each was for dissent, or
aggressive behaviour towards the referee or opponents, rather than
dangerous challenges. City also gave away five own-goals and nine
penalties over the season, a sign that the constant pressure on the
defence was too much to withstand. An insurance assessor would
have made Stoke a write-off.

After a 2-3 home defeat by Luton in an FA Cup replay in early
January Stoke's season was effectively over. Asprey was reduced to
talk of 'building for next year', while Chairman Edwards was
subjected to much personal abuse as the club lumbered through its
most disastrous season ever. There were more calls for his resignation than Asprey's, as it was obvious that it was the dire state of
the club that needed addressing rather than any coaching issue.

Stoke's decline was a microcosm of the sea change which football was undergoing during the 1970s and 80s. Gone was the pre-eminence of the northern traditional football region. The likes of Blackpool, Burnley, Blackburn and Derby had all fallen down the divisions. Wolves and Sheffield United both sank as low as Division Four. A new order was developing. Watford and Oxford, clubs with small support bases, but backed by sizeable investment by distant sugar daddies from the media and pop music world, were now challenging the established elite of Liverpool, Manchester United, Everton, Tottenham and Arsenal.

But there was no Robert Maxwell or Elton John waiting in the wings to ease Stoke's pain. The board, inexcusably, blamed the humiliations on the pitch on the manager and Asprey, who had suffered ill-health and depression over the preceding months, was relieved of his duties after another abject home defeat – this time by Luton. Tony Lacey, the only other coach employed by Stoke, took charge and was faced with the thankless task of trying to get a team predominantly populated with his youth team players to survive in the First Division. It was, of course, impossible. That it took until Easter for City's relegation to be confirmed was the only surprising aspect of their demise. Dudley Kernick's nous was rewarded by collecting £6,000 from the bookmaker and his P45 from the board, becoming another victim of the internal feuding which riddled the entire club.

By curtain fall Stoke had run up a host of unwanted records for a 42-game season in the Football League. Most defeats in a season (31), most home defeats (fifteen), fewest points (seventeen), and fewest goals scored (24). Stoke also set club records for most goals conceded (91), worst goal difference (–67) and fewest home wins (three). The average attendance had fallen to below 11,000. The club was in such a parlous state that another relegation the following season seemed more probable than possible.

Match of the Season 1984-85

Stoke 0 Coventry 1

Division 1, 17 May 1985

At the end of the worst season in not only their own, but of any club's, history, Stoke faced one final match, postponed until after the conclusion of the regular season due to illness in their opponents' camp earlier in the campaign. Wearied by a run of ten successive defeats, the last thing Stoke needed was one more game, particularly against a team who would come out with their sleeves rolled up. Having narrowly avoided relegation the previous season, Coventry faced an even deeper crisis this time. Perennial bookies' favourites for the drop, the Sky Blues were eight points adrift and faced three games in nine days, all of which had to be won, to avoid joining Stoke in the Second Division.

Coventry had parted with manager Bobby Gould at Christmas following a run of nine wins in 42 games. His replacement was assistant manager Don Mackay. Form had hardly improved and Coventry entered this match having won only two of their previous nine. Brian 'Killer' Kilcline, a muscular centre-half who sported a beard that lent him a gladiatorial air, had joined Coventry earlier in the season from Notts County. Along with left-back Stuart Pearce, completing his first full season in professional football after signing from non-league Wealdstone, and the powerful Cyrille Regis in attack, he formed the backbone of a physical Coventry side.

The game was desperate. Coventry were up-tight, Stoke merely going through the motions. The first half passed without incident. In the second period Coventry began to exert pressure as the lively Dave Bennett had the beating of Chris Hemming down Stoke's left. As usual Stoke wilted. From a corner, Regis headed goalward only for the ball to strike Berry's hand. Referee Neil Midgley blew for a penalty. Stoke protested but the decision stood and new skipper Stuart Pearce nervelessly slotted the spot-kick.

To give Stoke their due, they roused themselves for one final fling at First Division football. A draw would enable them to equal the all-time lowest points total in a 42-game season of eighteen, set by QPR in 1969, rather than set a new record of seventeen. With Coventry falling back to protect their precious lead, Stoke found space to attack for the first time in months. On 83 minutes Paul Dyson jogged forward to attempt to get his head to another corner but as he jumped he was nudged by Regis and another penalty was awarded. Ian Painter, who had already scored four penalties during the season, cracked the ball against the underside of the bar, from where it rebounded to safety. Coventry breathed a collective sigh of relief. They were off the hook.

Coventry went on to win both their remaining games – including an improbable 4-1 victory over Everton – champions and European Cup-Winners' Cup winners – to stay up, sending Norwich down. Within two years the Sky Blues would be celebrating a Wembley FA Cup triumph with Ogrizovic, Regis and Kilcline becoming heroes. Stoke's players were consigned to posterity for different reasons.

Mark Chamberlain taps in the second goal against Brighton (October 1982)

Villa's Gary Williams cannot believe Ian Painter's winning goal for City (March 1984)

Barry Siddall claims the ball at The Dell as City clinch a rare away point (March 1985)

Tony 'Zico' Kelly holds off Derby's Phil Gee (November 1986)

Steve Bould scores the first as Stoke hammer Sheffield United 5-2 (December 1986)

The men who made Stoke City – Waddington and Matthews (March 1987)

Steve Parkin won five England Under-21 caps whilst at Stoke (October 1987)

Gary Gillespie nets for Liverpool but fouls George Berry (January 1988)

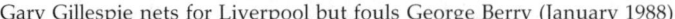

## 4

DECLINE AND FALL
1985-1991

LEAGUE DIVISION 2   **1985-86**
Canon Division 2   10th
Milk Cup   3rd Round
FA Cup   3rd Round

Brendan O'Callaghan had gone to Oldham for £30,000 in February and Sammy McIlroy was freed in the summer. Their departure eased the wage bill but left the squad short of experience. Chairman Frank Edwards died in June, having come under pressure from supporters during the relegation season. Sandy Clubb replaced him. Clubb's first task was to seek a manager capable of putting a club on its knees back on its feet.

Due to the change in the chair, the managerial question was not settled until late June. Clubb plumped for the first player-manager in the club's history. Mick Mills was a former international full-back who had captained England (in the absence of the injured Kevin Keegan) during the 1982 World Cup. He had just been released by Southampton. Stoke hoped that, having worked with the likes of Bobby Robson, Lawrie McMenemy and Ron Greenwood, he would have much to give, and his arrival also filled the problem left-back position. Mills' choice as coach was Cyril 'Sammy' Chung, who had top-flight managerial experience with Wolves. Mills hoped Chung's tactical brain, combined with his own motivational skills, would halt the club's slide. But with an atmosphere of deep gloom permeating the club, that would not be easy.

Clubb also identified a need for improved public relations with the fans. Firstly, the pin-striped kit, now indelibly associated with the club's worst ever season, was ditched, along with the PR people who had introduced it. The club also instituted the 'Lifeline Society' – an appeal for funds to allow Stoke to continue to develop its own youngsters and, it was hoped, keep them. Admission prices rose slightly, to £2.50 for the Boothen End and £5 for a seat. These compared well with the cost of seeing First Division football across the country, especially in London where the average price was £4 to stand on the terrace. A Stoke season ticket cost £50 on the terraces and £100 to sit down.

The prevarication over Mills' appointment meant he had little opportunity to add to the playing staff, even with free transfers. Every chance to liquidise cash had to be taken. The beginning of the season saw Mark Chamberlain return to something like the form which had seen him win the last of his eight full England caps just eleven months earlier. He starred in a 6-2 thrashing of Leeds and was suddenly marketable again. Surprisingly, his dribbling skills caught the eye of Howard Wilkinson, whose Sheffield Wednesday side were renowned as the most physical, long-ball team in the First Division. Wilkinson tempted Chamberlain, but as the clubs could not agree a fee it went to a tribunal. Stoke were aggrieved to receive only £300,000 for a player who a year earlier would have been worth almost a million. Worse, the bank sought to reduce Stoke's over-draft rather than allow reinvestment in new players. The outlook was bleak. Stoke were deep in the bottom half and – the 6-2 win aside – scored just four goals in the opening ten games.

Supporters deserted the club in droves. Football was no longer the drug which had seen attendances hit the 40 million mark in the immediate post-war years. 1985-86 saw audiences dip below seven-teen million for the first time. There is no telling how many were put off by the yob element. Trouble had been commonplace inside and outside Britain's grounds since the 1960s. Stoke were one of the worst offenders. The Boothen End had a reputation for vociferous support, but those same fans enjoyed nothing more than baiting the opposition team and supporters. At times, this could spill over into violence which ordinary folk wanted no part of. With better trans-port and higher disposable incomes, the average working man could look elsewhere for his Saturday entertainment. Even in such a predominantly working class area as the Potteries, attractions such as Alton Towers and the new Festival Park, with its cinema complex and bowling alleys, ensured that football slipped down the pecking order. The more so, now that City were in the Second Division. Stoke's average gates hit their lowest for 78 years.

The return of Peter Fox from long-term injury put an end to the goalkeeping torments that marred the previous campaign. Under Mills, George Berry also found himself back in favour. The popular centre-half was reinstated as captain and provided solidity in the middle of the back four. Neil Adams, an 18-year-old apprentice, was the next player to emerge from the youth system. He replaced Chamberlain on the right wing, using his body swerve and pace to beat defenders, while his accurate crossing created chances for the new strikeforce of Bertschin and 18-year-old Graham Shaw. The youngsters, outclassed last season, were finding their feet.

Alan Hudson retired through injury in November. Mills replaced him with Norwich's John Devine on a free transfer. Devine was tempted by the chance of teaming up again with Keith Bertschin and proved an inspired signing. He had played for Arsenal in an FA Cup final and in a memorable European Cup-Winners' Cup semi-final at Juventus, which the Gunners won 1-0. Principally a full-back at Highbury, he converted to midfield during a three-year spell at Carrow Road, but had fallen out of favour the previous season, when the Canaries were relegated alongside Stoke. Devine's debut coincided with a 4-2 win at Oldham (see Match of the Season) which began a run of four straight wins that propelled Stoke from eighteenth to tenth. His neat passing released Heath and Adams down the wings. City only lost three matches of the fifteen which Devine started, but a hideous tackle by Brighton's Eric Young at the Goldstone Ground ended his career in March and Stoke lost a major midfield influence just as their momentum was mounting.

Mills' full-back partner was Steve Bould, but Mills and Chung, being flank players themselves, believed that the lanky defender was actually better suited to the centre-half role. Bould had a good awareness, a strong physique and was dominant in the air. With a ready-made replacement in Bould, Mills sold the unpopular Paul Dyson to West Brom for £60,000 in March. The cash was earmarked for a playmaker to replace Hudson and Devine.

Mills plumped for Tony Kelly of Wigan for £80,000. Popularly known as 'Zico', Kelly was a portly midfielder, prone to flashes of brilliance, renowned for being among the best free-kick specialists outside the top flight, but with an Achilles heel of food and beer. Clearly unfit, having been dropped by Wigan boss Bryan Hamilton, Kelly still controlled the game on his debut, a 2-0 win over Oldham, providing killer passes for both goals. With the summer in which to get fit, Kelly was seen as the great hope of the future, personifying Mills' positive approach. It had needed a fresh face, from outside the club, to replace Asprey, and Mills' perceived value to the club was such that his contract was extended to the summer of 1989.

Match of the Season 1985-86
Oldham 2 Stoke 4

Division 2, 23 November 1985

Joe Royle's Oldham were one of the best sides outside the top flight throughout the late 1980s. They had vied for promotion each season from 1985-86, bar one, until that goal was finally achieved in 1991. In Micky Quinn and Roger Palmer they had goalscorers who could win any game. They were virtually unbeatable at home, having lost only one game all season.

There were signs that City's confidence was returning after the nightmare of the previous season, but Mills recognised the lack of craft in midfield. Constrained by the dire financial situation, Mills had signed Norwich's experienced midfielder John Devine on a free transfer in midweek. Sometimes new signings take time to settle in. This one made an immediate impact.

Devine pulled on the No 4 shirt, which had already seen five occupants this season as Mills searched for an answer to his creative problem in midfield. Hudson had retired, and Williams, Parkin, Hemming and Beeston were too young to be able to dictate a game. On a freezing cold day, Devine showed them exactly how it should be done as he pulled the strings and Stoke tore Oldham apart. He set up Bertschin for a coolly taken goal, and once Phil Heath had rounded off a run from the halfway line with a superb strike, Stoke played the ball around confidently on the uneven surface.

After the break Chris Maskery and Bertschin both capitalised on Devine's short passes to put Stoke 4-0 ahead away from home. No one could quite believe what was happening. Oldham were finally stirred and managed to score twice, one a penalty, but their two goals flattered them. City killed the game, with Devine now acting as a midfield spoiler. His all-round performance, as that of the team, had been outstanding.

The game marked the first sign that Stoke were starting the long road to recovery, sparking a run of one defeat in ten games. Sadly John Devine was not able to share in the team's success further than March, when his leg was broken in five places at Brighton. His career in British football was over, but he played on in Norway, for IK Start, and later in India, where he also coached.

Oldham's form slumped and they dropped out of the promotion running, finishing just three points ahead of Stoke in eighth place.

LEAGUE DIVISION 2   **1986-87**
Today Division 2   8th
Littlewoods Cup   2nd Round
FA Cup   5th Round

Central to Stoke's preparations for 1986-87 was the announcement of a sponsorship deal with local ceramics company H & R Johnson. The brand name that adorned the players' shirts was 'Cristal Tiles'. To that £200,000 deal was added the sale of Neil Adams, who had impressed Everton manager Howard Kendall to the extent that he paid £150,000 for a player who had only completed one year as a professional. By the end of the season Adams had won a League championship medal. The decision to sell the young winger upset many Stoke fans who had contributed to the 'Lifeline' appeal in the hope that Stoke would be able to hold onto its young stars, but at least the money allowed Mills to venture into the transfer market for the first time. He proceeded to bring in 22-year-old Lee Dixon from Bury for £50,000 – to fill Bould's place at right-back – and experienced right-sided midfielder Tony Ford from his hometown club, Grimsby, to replace Adams.

There was tentative talk that Stoke might achieve one of the play-off spots, which had been introduced. The teams finishing third, fourth and fifth in the Second Division, together with the side finishing third from bottom of the First, would fight it out for the right to play in the top flight. Despite his pledge to get fit over the summer, Tony Kelly returned to the club palpably overweight and was immediately put on a vigorous training programme. Without Kelly firing on all cylinders, Stoke won just one of their first nine games. Bertschin and Shaw were missing the crosses that Adams once provided, and each managed only one goal from open play, although Shaw did find the net from a penalty. Confidence was so low that both he and Bertschin managed to miss one spot-kick each. Following a 0-1 defeat at Brighton, Stoke were firmly rooted to the bottom of the table and had been dumped out of the Littlewoods Cup by Shrewsbury.

With things going awry, Peter Coates took over from Sandy Clubb as chairman. Coates was a self-made millionaire who ran catering company Stadia Catering. He promised much in providing funds for the redevelopment of the squad. His backing allowed Mills to invest a modest £25,000 in his old Ipswich team-mate, Brian Talbot, who signed from Watford. At 33, Talbot was a combative midfielder who had become the first player to win the FA Cup in consecutive seasons with different clubs, after leaving Ipswich for Arsenal. He was also chairman of the Professional Footballers'

Association, the Players' Union. Talbot's arrival provided a stable base in midfield, allowing Mills to persist with the experiment of playing midfielder Carl Saunders as a striker. Saunders used his pace to make inroads into opposing defences, revelling in the spaces opened up by a fit Kelly's through-passes.

Next to arrive was Nicky Morgan, a striker who had fallen out of favour with Alan Ball at Portsmouth and cost Stoke just £40,000. Although only 5ft 10in, Morgan was an excellent shielder of the ball, allowing the midfield time to support him and take return passes. Morgan proved the perfect foil for the quicksilver Saunders. Stoke embarked upon an unbeaten run of eleven games, racking up 24 goals in eight games in the period around Christmas. Bertschin, Morgan and Saunders all scored hat-tricks. At the height of the run City thrashed Grimsby 6-0 to win only their second FA Cup-tie since 1978. By the end of January Stoke were up to fourth. The fans talked of automatic promotion now. Mills was named Manager of the Month for December and, with City the form team in the division, confidence was sky-high.

Not only were Stoke scoring goals, they had stopped conceding them. Steve Bould adapted well to his switch to centre-half and was improving visibly with every match. At 6ft 3in, and over thirteen stone, his was an imposing bulk for opposing forwards to pass. His presence led to him becoming widely recognised as the best centre-half outside the First Division. George Graham, Arsenal's manager, made no secret of his admiration for Bould. However, a back injury sustained during a defeat by Blackburn truncated his season and quelled the transfer speculation, for now.

George Berry had found a new lease of life after his exclusion from first-team affairs under Bill Asprey. He relished the challenge of pulling together a young, growing team and was a demonstrative captain. Mills respected Berry, relying on him to lift the dressing room when results did not go Stoke's way with his irrepressible sense of humour. He had a distinctive 'Afro' hairstyle which often brought him abuse from opposition fans, but Berry revealed that it was actually a tactic! He deliberately grew his hair so that when he stood at the near post for a corner in the opponents' area, nobody could see past him. If the ball was directed to the near post, as was a favourite ploy at Stoke, the first time the defence and goalkeeper would be able to catch sight of it was when Berry had flicked it on, causing confusion which often led to Stoke goals.

The FA Cup run carried Stoke into the fifth round, where First Division Coventry were waiting. It was a mark of how far the side had come under Mills that there was a real feeling in the Potteries that Stoke could beat their higher-ranked opponents. In the event,

DID YOU KNOW?

Until he resigned in February 1977, Tony Waddington was the longest serving
First Division manager at 16 years and 8 months.

Stoke pushed Coventry to the limit, but lost to a Mickey Gynn goal, despite having a good penalty shout turned down when Lee Dixon was felled in the area. On such decisions seasons turn. Coventry went on to Wembley glory, Stoke embarked on a run of one win in ten games to drop out of the play-off picture entirely. But the Cup run confirmed the enormous potential deep within Stoke City FC. The crowds had flocked back: indeed Stoke were one of only six Second Division clubs to record improved gates, including the promoted teams from Division Three and those sides that were challenging for promotion.

No sooner were they out of the Cup than Stoke's form slumped, primarily due to Bould's injury, which cost the team stability at the back and possibly the play-offs. The crowds tapered off once it was clear that City would not make the play-off shake-up. Kelly's form had also dipped as his weight increased. To spice things up, Mills bought veteran midfielder Gerry Daly, who had been instrumental in dumping Stoke out of the Littlewoods Cup, for £15,000 from Shrewsbury. He injured his thigh on his debut and did not play again until the following season. Hindsight is a wonderful thing but, at 32, the gamble on Daly was possibly not worth the risk.

It was a season of three distinct thirds, with a successful spell in the middle sandwiched by periods of relegation form. These directly coincided with the periods when Tony Kelly had been in and out of form. His fitness was the key and he, and his twin Achilles heels of food and alcohol, had proved too frustrating for Mills to deal with. Before the final match Kelly was told he would be leaving and in July Mills took a small loss by selling him to West Brom for £60,000. The question was, could Mills produce the necessary consistency over a whole season to enable what was undoubtedly a talented squad to challenge for promotion?

Match of the Season 1986-87
Stoke 7 Leeds 2

Division 2, 21 December 1986

Eighth-placed Leeds were managed by former midfield firebrand Billy Bremner. Unsurprisingly, he had fashioned a team in his own image. Centre-backs Peter Swan and Jack Ashurst, midfielder David

Rennie and centre-forward Ian Baird were all hard, physical players, who liked to get amongst opponents.

Stoke were in a rich vein of form which had dragged them up from bottom to mid-table inside six weeks, and Mills was able to field an unchanged team for the fourth consecutive game. Despite the recent good form, Mills believed the goals-to-chances ratio could be improved and he asked the team to prove that they had the killer instinct. Leeds, the biggest club in the Second Division, were seen as the litmus test for Stoke's promotion credentials.

Despite it being the weekend before Christmas, the crowd was the biggest of the season so far. As the teams emerged, Stoke fans taunted Leeds' keeper Mervyn Day with the result of the previous season's game – 6-2 to Stoke. He had vowed in the press that no way he was going to concede six this time!

Stoke swarmed forward with accurate and clinical passing and scored three goals in the first twenty minutes, through Morgan, Saunders and a Lee Dixon bicycle-kick. Morgan bagged his second as Leeds were forced back in the face of wave upon wave of attacks. The perfect first half, as far as Stoke fans were concerned, was completed by a cheeky Kelly free-kick. After pointing to Day to tell him that he was going to aim for the right side of the goal, he proceeded to beat the keeper with a delicate chip exactly where he had indicated.

Leeds got among the goals themselves, without ever threatening to match Stoke's scoring spree. Baird and Sheridan, the latter from the penalty spot, found the net, but City also scored twice through Tony Ford and Morgan, who completed his hat-trick with a neat turn and shot from twelve yards. Mills was delighted that Stoke had finally shown what he had always believed they were capable of. The 7-2 win was City's best since Ipswich had been thrashed 9-1 in 1964. Everything seemed to be falling into place for a serious promotion challenge. The turnaround in the eighteen months in which Mills had been in charge was remarkable.

Leeds reached the FA Cup semi-final and the promotion play-off final, losing to Coventry and Charlton respectively. Unlike Stoke, they found the consistency over the season, and it nearly took them into the top flight.

LEAGUE DIVISION 2   **1987-88**
Barclays Division 2   11th
Littlewoods Cup   4th Round
FA Cup   3rd Round

There was huge anticipation that this would finally be Stoke's year. It was misplaced. City conceded the first goal of the new season in the first minute in a 0-2 defeat by Birmingham. Mills was worried about the defence. The unit were separated from the rest of the squad and given an intensive defensive clinic at Keele University. It improved matters little. Cliff Carr, a £45,000 signing from Fulham, had not had the best of starts and was the target of the Boothen End's boo-boys. He benefited from Mills' influence, but the chunky left-back never won over the cynics in the crowd who scorned his one-footedness and poor distribution. Bould's return, following his back problems, added solidity to the centre of the back four, but Mills was reduced to describing the general standard of defending as 'unprofessional'. 24-year-old keeper Scott Barrett was brought in from Wolves, initially on loan, before signing for £10,000. Mills gave him an extended run in the team due to a knee injury to Fox, the first of several opportunities, but Barrett lacked consistency and each time Fox returned to reclaim his place.

Despite the obvious shortcomings in defence, Mills appeared to have misread the situation. It was in attack where Stoke were really struggling. A paltry nine goals in the first sixteen league games told its own story. Carl Saunders, the previous season's goalscoring hero, had his confidence dented by a series of bad misses and he scored only three times all season. Instead of persevering with the talented player, Mills dropped him. His replacement, Graham Shaw, fared little better, finding the net only twice in the League before Christmas.

The problem stemmed from the lack of a credible replacement for Tony Kelly. Mills had signed Ian Allinson, a predominantly left-footed player who had been on the fringes of an average Arsenal side. Allinson had been freed as part of George Graham's summer clear-out, but he proved a flop, losing his place to Phil Heath after only seven starts. It emerged that Allinson did not particularly relish the idea of moving to the north and as a result he was sold to Luton, much nearer to his Hertfordshire home, for £15,000 in October. To cap it all, Nicky Morgan dislocated his collarbone in the 'dead' second round, second leg Littlewoods Cup-tie at Gillingham, as a result of which Mills, with barely enough fit professionals available, was forced to use a palpably unfit Gerry Daly as a make-shift striker for six weeks.

DID YOU KNOW?

The Stoke fanzine 'The Oatcake' is named after a Staffordshire delicacy made of oats and cooked on a griddle. It is best eaten hot with cheese or with a cooked breakfast.

Occasionally, to Mills' frustration, Stoke would get it right. City were drawn at home to struggling First Division Norwich in the third round of the Littlewoods Cup. Stoke thoroughly outplayed the Canaries to win 2-1, with even Daly managing to find the net. In the Simod Cup (a filler competition, designed to compensate clubs denied European competition in the wake of the Heysel ban on English clubs), Stoke were drawn at Alan Ball's Portsmouth, headed for promotion to Division One. City's 3-0 win was described by Mills as 'the best in my time here as manager'. Stoke picked up the Barclays Team of the Week Award for their efforts.

With the squad stretched to the limit, Mills was even forced to pick himself – becoming the third oldest player ever to appear for the club, aged 38 years, 289 days – when filling in for the injured Cliff Carr against Swindon in October. The game was a microcosm of Stoke's season, culminating in Talbot's sending off for retaliation. Frustration was setting in. Mills was on the defensive, both on the field and in the press. He threatened to put the whole team up for sale if results did not improve. If this was intended as shock tactics, it failed. Stoke won only two of the next eight games and went out of the Littlewoods Cup at Arsenal. A dire display at Crystal Palace forced Mills to belatedly dip into the transfer market.

Mills signed Oldham midfielder Tony Henry for £40,000 and QPR's Simon Stainrod for £90,000, believing that they would spark City's sluggish attack into life. He was wrong. Stainrod failed to score until the end of April, and Henry proved to be a one-paced player in an increasingly anonymous midfield. In a bid to inject flair, Mills signed Shrewsbury winger Gary Hackett, splashing out a further £110,000 to bring his total spending for the season to over £300,000. The experienced Hackett was not short on commitment, which had brought him his share of injuries. He made his Stoke debut with a pain-killing injection for a groin injury, broke down within twenty minutes, and did not reappear until the following season.

Mills had proved to be fallible in the transfer market. Perhaps his failure to transform Tony Kelly's career had affected his judgment. He no longer trusted 'flair' players, preferring to rely on consistent ones. The downside was that the team lacked spark and drive. It also lacked personalities, becoming bland, methodical and unin-spiring. The club was slipping towards terminal torpor.

The only excitement in a tortuous second half of the season was provided by the visit of Liverpool in the FA Cup (see Match of the Season). Once again the club's potential was shown by the sell-out 31,979 crowd but average league gates were still below 10,000. It seemed to many that the board was happy for the club to idle along in the lower reaches of the Second Division, and there were isolated incidents of protests by groups of concerned supporters. The board rejected the criticism, citing the transfer expenditure as an example of their efforts to turn the club around.

The board's self-espoused philanthropy proved false. Their true colours were revealed in February when they redressed the season's transfer deficit by selling Lee Dixon to Arsenal for £375,000. The financial reality of running a football club in the late 1980s was that players such as Dixon would be groomed by Stoke for elite clubs to enjoy the pick of the crop. Steve Bould had been catching Graham's eye for the past two seasons and it seemed that it was only a matter of time – back-injury permitting – before he would be joining Dixon at Highbury. Brian Talbot also left, signing for West Brom for a nominal £10,000. He joined the Baggies as player-coach to Ron Atkinson, although by the end of the season he would find himself manager at the Hawthorns. With no money to replace the departed players Mills turned to the youth squad. In April, defender Lee Fowler became the third youngest player ever to appear for Stoke, aged sixteen years and 247 days. Paul Ware wasn't far behind, in May, aged just seventeen. Ian Gibbons, Andy Holmes and Kevin Lewis also helped to plug the gaps.

No sooner was the season over than Bould was sold to Arsenal. The fee, set by a tribunal at £390,000, was a travesty for a player who had proved to be the best centre-half outside the First Division for three seasons. That he, alongside Dixon, would form part of Arsenal's most successful defence, playing for eleven seasons for the club, proved that his true value was far higher. Stoke had failed to cash in on one of the few successes of an altogether forgettable season. Some sections of the crowd had begun to call for Mills' head. Such drastic action seemed premature to the majority, and Mills promised improvements for the following season.

Match of the Season 1987-88
Stoke 0 Liverpool 0

FA Cup, 3rd Round, 9 January 1988

Stoke reserved some of their best performances in this season of underachievement for the cup competitions. The third round draw paired them with an all-conquering Liverpool side featuring the creative talents of Peter Beardsley and John Barnes. Many observers felt this to be the best of the Liverpool sides that had dominated English, and European, football over the previous twenty years. The Heysel Stadium disaster of 1985 and the subsequent banning of English clubs from European competition meant that they were denied the opportunity to pit their talents against the best that the continent had to offer, and so prove the pundits right. Liverpool had started the season in blistering form, and were on a run which would see them equal Leeds' feat of 29 games unbeaten from the start of the season.

The cup-tie was a sell-out and there was enormous anticipation that Stoke might just be able to sneak a result. After all, with form as erratic as theirs, wouldn't it be typical for the team to go and win. There was just the smallest chink in Liverpool's armour: with Bruce Grobbelaar injured, second-choice keeper Mike Hooper was in goal.

On a dreadful surface Liverpool struggled to make their passing game tell. Steve Bould policed John Aldridge expertly, barely allowing the First Division's leading scorer a sight of the ball, while Talbot and Henry kept Ronnie Whelan and Ray Houghton quiet. Liverpool held a territorial advantage, while Stoke looked for opportunities to hit them on the break. It was absorbing stuff, but there seemed little chance of a goal at either end until, with under five minutes remaining, Graham Shaw, on as a substitute for Stainrod, was sent clear by Henry's pass from the halfway line. Crucially the young forward stuttered, and glanced across to the linesman to see if he was onside. This delayed his run onto the ball, which allowed Hooper to race out of his goal to block. A chance to win the game and cause the biggest cup upset in years was wasted.

Stoke had played above themselves and fared well in the replay, losing to Beardsley's goal at Anfield. To Mills' eternal frustration City could not reproduce the same form in the League. Liverpool walked away with the League title and also reached the FA Cup final. Strong favourites to beat Wimbledon, their limp performance on the day allowed the Dons to sneak a famous victory and deny Liverpool a second double in three years.

LEAGUE DIVISION 2   **1988-89**
Barclays Division 2   13th
Littlewoods Cup   2nd Round
FA Cup   4th Round

With Bould gone, Mills had to find a centre-half capable of replacing him. The team would undoubtedly miss one of its few quality players. The manager prevaricated, hoping to sign no-nonsense Kevin Moran of Manchester United, who asked for time to consider his options after being freed by Alex Ferguson. Moran eventually decided to chance his luck with Spanish club Sporting Gijon, where the lifestyle and pay packet better suited his idea of winding down his career than three years in Stoke.

The season started with Mills desperately seeking an alternative. He eventually plumped for Bury's Mark Higgins who cost £150,000. Higgins, at nearly 30, was an experienced defender, who had also proved to be injury prone, having been forced to quit Everton due to persistent groin problems. After his experience with the now fit Gary Hackett, for Mills to risk such a sum on yet another injury-plagued player was risky in the extreme. Higgins never approached the form expected of a capable centre-half and, predictably, his injury problems recurred. Was the manager losing his grip?

Two of Mills' other signings adapted better. Chris Kamara was a combative midfielder who was signed from Swindon for £27,500. The nominal fee reflected Swindon's wish to rid themselves of a player whose disciplinary record was little short of disgraceful. The last straw for the Robins came at Shrewsbury, when Kamara had been involved in a fracas which led to a court appearance and heavy fine. Mills wanted him to instil grit into a shambolic midfield. Flair would be provided by Peter Beagrie, recruited from Sheffield United for £215,000. The moustachioed winger was viewed by many as the best creative force outside the First Division and there was surprise that the Blades were prepared to let him go. He replaced Phil Heath on the left, whom Mills had sold to Oxford for £80,000. Beagrie had a trick that allowed him to flummox full-backs. It was a variation of the 'Cruyff turn', which saw him speed down the wing and shape to cross before dragging the ball inside the defender. He then either crossed with his other foot, or took the ball on into the penalty area. Beagrie also scored spectacular goals, evidenced by a superb match winner against Bournemouth, which allowed the fans a first sight of his trademark backflip somersault celebration.

With the new arrivals failing to gel, Stoke found themselves next to bottom with just three points after six games. To make matters worse, City lost at home on penalties to Fourth Division Leyton

Orient in the Littlewoods Cup (see Match of the Season). Things could not get much worse than that. Mills was floundering and the board inactive. The supporters could not stand by and see their beloved club fall apart so humiliatingly. Those dissenting voices of the previous season rallied themselves into groups campaigning to keep the club alive. Several 'fanzines' emerged. Most were one-offs, but one, The Oatcake, the brainchild of Martin Smith – a disaffected supporter who believed the club was headed for a fall – proved so popular that its circulation grew from a few hundred at games in the autumn of 1988 to over 3,000. It soon became the most widely read fanzine in the country. So influential was it that The Oatcake began to dictate the debate over the club's future. For anyone who wanted to know what was happening at Stoke City, it – rather than the club programme – became required reading.

Mills was also finding that discipline was a problem. Stainrod and Ford got themselves stupidly sent off, Stainrod against Chelsea and Ford, uncharacteristically, in a 0-6 mauling at West Brom. Indeed, Stoke ended the season with the second worst disciplinary record in the League. Mills needed to act, and he brought in John Butler, a full-back, from Wigan for £75,000, and Dave Bamber from Watford for £190,000, touting the new arrivals as 'the missing link'. Butler's arrival meant Mills allowed Ford to move to West Brom for £50,000, despite the player believing he was playing the best football of his career. That he earned England B honours as a 30-year-old, proved Mills' judgment was questionable.

Dave Bamber was a lumbering centre-forward with the look and demeanour of Frankenstein's monster. His goalscoring record had never been particularly good, showing that he had only managed double figures in two of his ten seasons in League football. He had only found the net three times in eighteen games for Watford, but Mills now saw him as a player who could capitalise on Beagrie's crosses, previously aimed at the height-impaired Shaw-Stainrod partnership. Bamber proved to be slow, awkward on the ground and prone to missing the easiest of opportunities. He scored just nine goals, despite being provided with a succession of crosses from the boots of Beagrie and Hackett. Part of the problem was that Beagrie liked to over-indulge, loving nothing better than beating his man twice or three times before crossing. This made it hard to judge the timing of runs into the box and often resulted in players – having committed themselves too early – being caught offside, or having the ball fly over their heads. Mills urged Beagrie to be more consistent in his delivery: Beagrie replied that he would have no hold over a full-back if the defender knew that he was always going to try to cross.

Kamara was also proving to be something of a poisoned chalice. The fans loved his commitment, but bridled when Kamara went looking for revenge after being fouled. Too often his heart ruled his head and a silly challenge would lead to a yellow or red card. He missed eight games through suspension, of which Stoke won only two.

Though City skirted around the edges of the play-off pack, there were early exits to Barnsley in the FA Cup and Southampton in the Simod Cup. A dreadful run of one win in the final fourteen League matches meant Stoke's season was effectively over by Easter. Five successive defeats thereafter meant a paltry crowd of 5,841 paid to watch the last game of the season. The life was slowly being strangled out of the club.

The date 15 April 1989 saw a football tragedy that transcended everything. The Hillsborough disaster, which saw the death of 96 fans at an FA Cup semi-final, stunned the nation. Its aftermath had profound implications throughout the football world. Lord Justice Taylor's report into the management of crowds at grounds ushered in a new era of all-seater stadia. For Stoke City, whose antiquated stadium – aside from the relatively new Stoke End Stand – had for years been the butt of complaints from visiting fans, the report spelt the end of an era. Within three years, all grounds in the top two divisions would have to become all-seating. The 'standing terrace culture' was to be eradicated. The intention was to provide a stable environment where football could become a family spectator sport. Football had historically been a sport watched predominantly by white, working-class males, but it was now time for it to grow up and open its arms to women, children and ethnic minorities. Stoke were amongst the worst offenders. Women and, particularly, black people had never felt welcome at the Victoria Ground. The debate commenced about transforming the Vic into an all-seated stadium, suitable for top division football, where the club hoped to be in twelve months' time.

Match of the Season 1988-89

Stoke 1 Leyton Orient 2
> Littlewoods Cup, 2nd Round, 2nd leg, 11 October 1988

Leyton Orient were a club going nowhere in the autumn of 1988. A poor start in the League saw them 21st in the Fourth Division, some fifty places below City. Frank Clark, Orient's manager for six years, was under increasing pressure. His team had been expected to be among the promotion challengers after missing out on the play-offs

---

DID YOU KNOW?

Six players have played 100 consecutive League games for Stoke – Tony Allen, Arthur Turner, Tom Holford, Alan Dodd, Bob McGrory, and Nigel Gleghorn.

---

by a point the previous season. Stoke were expected to dispose of them easily, but there were signs in the first leg at Orient that all was not going to plan. The O's had applied early pressure and deservedly went ahead thanks to Ian Juryeff's 30-yard strike. Mills read the riot act at half-time and City came out stoked up for the second half. Kamara was in a particularly fiery mood. His goal, coupled with Morgan's header, gave Stoke a 2-1 win.

By the second leg, two weeks later, City's form had improved slightly. They had recovered from two goals down at Oldham to draw 2-2, securing the club's first ever point on an artificial pitch. Orient's away form was atrocious: they had picked up one point and scored one goal on their travels thus far. It looked an obvious home banker, but football is never quite that straightforward. The match turned into a freakish penalty competition, beginning in the first half when Kevin Hales scored from the spot for Orient. Beagrie then skied a penalty over the bar for Stoke, before Stainrod made amends from yet another spot-kick. City, thinking the tie was as good as won, went to sleep and failed to close down Alan Comfort, who lashed in a 30-yarder to send the game into extra-time.

Stoke's dreadful performance got no better in the extra half-hour and the tie went to penalties, an outcome which not even the most diehard O's fan could possibly have contemplated before kick-off. Peter Wells saved two of Stoke's kicks and Simon Stainrod missed a third to hand Orient a morale-boosting victory. While their players celebrated, Stoke's fans reacted angrily, calling for Mills' head. For Stoke to have lost to Orient was unforgivable.

The O's win sent them for the first time in twelve years into the third round, where they lost 0-2 to Ipswich. Buoyed by their win over Stoke, they promptly thrashed Colchester 8-0, a result which sparked a run that saw them scrape into the play-offs by finishing sixth. They duly beat Scarborough and Wrexham to win promotion. The next time they faced Stoke would be in the Third Division.

LEAGUE DIVISION 2   **1989-90**
Barclays Division 2   24th (Relegated)
Littlewoods Cup   2nd Round
FA Cup   3rd Round

Mick Mills' contract with Stoke expired in June and there was doubt about whether he should be offered a new one. He had worked hard to rebuild the club after the trauma of relegation, but the lack of progress over the past two years raised questions about Mills' ability to make an impact on his players. Opinions were divided, but finally his contract was renewed. Simon Stainrod left for Rouen in France for £70,000. More surprisingly, Steve Parkin was also allowed to leave, joining his former midfield mentor, Brian Talbot, at West Brom for £190,000. Having won six England Under-21 caps whilst at Stoke, many were surprised at Mills' decision to let the popular 'Billy' go.

The reason soon became apparent. Having decided that Mills was still their man, the directors produced over £1 million for him to spend to finance a push for promotion. Mills had proved that he sometimes had an eye for a bargain in the transfer market. What could he do now with money to burn? When Ian Cranson arrived from Sheffield Wednesday for £450,000, he became the club's record signing. Mills had played alongside Cranson at Ipswich during the central defender's formative years. Dominant in the air, Cranson sported a headband that added to his imposing appearance. Bolstering the forward line was Wayne 'Bertie' Biggins, a £240,000 signing from Manchester City. Midfielder Ian Scott also arrived from Maine Road for £175,000. Mills was so determined that Scott should join Stoke that he met the player at Manchester Airport on his return from holiday in order to secure his signature. Derek Statham arrived from West Brom for £60,000, with a further £40,000 payable after 40 appearances. Mills' million had all been spent. The board now demanded success to recoup it. The consequences of failure were unimaginable.

Sadly, Mills once again fell victim to signing injured players. Cranson's knee had required surgery whilst at Wednesday and in consequence he had lost pace on the turn. Furthermore, the injury now recurred, at Bournemouth. After just seventeen games for Stoke, Cranson was forced to go under the surgeon's knife and would not re-appear for nearly a year. Statham was also carrying a knee injury, which had been common knowledge, as it had caused the curtailment of both Rangers' and Liverpool's interest in him two seasons earlier. He made only 21 appearances for Stoke before the injury flared up again. The other summer signings did not produce the goods either. Biggins lacked pace and scored just ten goals – although that was enough to make him top scorer – while Scott made just fourteen starts. City failed to win any of their first eleven League games and went out of the Littlewoods Cup at the first hurdle to Millwall. They also lost in the FA Cup at the first time of asking, though their conquerors were the defending champions, Arsenal. In the Full Members' Cup (the Simod Cup had lost its sponsorship and had only two more years to run) Stoke lost on penalties to Leeds in the second round after a 2-2 draw. The early cup exits served to focus attention on Stoke's dreadful League form. Following a 1-1 draw with bottom club Hull, there were demands by supporters for Mills' head. Confidence in the manager, players and the board was zero.

In a bid to bolster players' self-belief, Alan Ball was appointed as first-team coach. He had previously managed Portsmouth for four years before becoming assistant manager at Colchester, and was persuaded by his former England colleague, Mills, that a move to Stoke could bring about a change in fortunes for both himself and the club. It was tantamount to Mills signing his own death warrant. The board now had a ready-made replacement. It was surely a matter of time before Mills was shown the door.

Mills' last desperate act was to sell Peter Beagrie to Everton for £750,000 in October. Beagrie's departure had been on the cards for some time, but it left the side bereft of its one star player. Mills was also victim of the success of near neighbours Port Vale. Stoke fans could not stomach the sight of 'the Fail' – as they are not so affectionately known – rising above them in the League. After decades of languishing in the lower reaches of the League, Vale, under the astute management of John Rudge, had risen through the ranks, joining Stoke in the Second Division this season. To be below Vale in the table confirmed how low Stoke had sunk. Mills' first two seasons had, on the whole, been positive, but since the failed 1986-87 promotion campaign, City had won only 37 out of 122 League games. With only one win in sixteen this term, the club was headed for the abyss. Still the board dithered, and it took a 0-6 thrashing at Swindon to force their hand. Mills was sacked.

There was considerable hope that caretaker manager Ball might be the right man to inject much-needed passion and commitment into Stoke's players. He had been the youngest of England's World Cup winning side of 1966 and as recently as 1982 had finished a highly successful playing career, which had seen him win 72 caps and a League championship medal with Everton. Since moving into management his record was patchy. His first match in charge of Stoke brought a much-needed win over Brighton (see Match of the

Season). Carl Beeston's first-minute goal seemed to signal a change of fortune and perhaps a change of luck under the now permanently appointed new manager.

Ball's first-team coach, Graham Paddon, struggled to make an impact on a constantly changing team as, in a bid to halt the slide, Ball wheeled and dealed to bring in new players. Many wondered if this was wise, as common sense told the average fan that one of the reasons for the team's wretched form was the influx of new players who had yet to gel.

Nonetheless Ball was determined to bring in players he trusted, which meant those that had brought him success at Portsmouth. The board backed his judgment and in came Lee Sandford, Vince Hilaire (on loan) and Chris Male, all recruited from Portsmouth for a combined fee of £140,000. Noel Blake, a hardman centre-half who had also been with Ball on the south coast, arrived from Leeds for £160,000. Ball also signed forwards Nyrere 'Tony' Kelly from non-league St Albans City for £20,000 and Tony Ellis from Preston, who cost £250,000 with Graham Shaw going in the other direction. Dave Kevan and Paul Barnes joined from Notts County for a combined fee of £105,000. To balance the books, Kamara was sold for £150,000 to Leeds, whom he would help to gain promotion. Bamber went to Hull for £130,000 and Hackett joined West Brom for £70,000. Morgan joined Bristol City for £30,000, while his erstwhile partner, Saunders, was sold to the other Bristol club, Rovers, for £70,000. The sale of those strikers left a bitter aftertaste, for both rediscovered their form in teams that came up as Stoke went down.

Such a huge turnover of players ensured there was hardly any understanding in the team. Twenty games with only one win shut the door on Stoke's chances of avoiding the drop. The fans vented their spleen on the manager. Indeed, Ball proved more unpopular than Mills had ever been. Ball retaliated, openly criticising fans for not getting behind the team. He had a point but he had not been at Stoke long enough to realise that they were more worried about the long-term structural decline of the club, rather than any specific games lost. The spirit had vanished from the side well before a 0-3 defeat at Newcastle confirmed relegation.

The board's £1 million gamble had failed catastrophically. Mills should have gone earlier and the choice of Ball as his belated successor was ill-conceived. Stoke would play in the Third Division for only the second time. Their previous experience at that level, in 1926-27, had seen them promoted as Third Division (North) champions at the first attempt. The current financial plight, as the club announced a trading deficit of £377,000 for the year, suggested that any hopes of a repetition were clutching at straws.

Match of the Season 1989-90

Stoke 3 Brighton 2

Division 2, 11 November 1989

After Mick Mills' sacking, Alan Ball, who had been first-team coach for six weeks, took charge of the team for the first time – against Brighton. It was understood that improved performances would lead to his position being made permanent. It was crucial that City find some form as they were in danger of being marooned at the foot of the table. Ball was confident, predicting good things.

Barry Lloyd's Brighton were mid-table, although they had lost consecutive home games 1-2 against Blackburn and Swindon. The Seagulls' side was made up of journeyman players who functioned well as a team. Alan Curbishley and Dean Wilkins, brother of England's Ray, formed the engine room in midfield, while Paul Wood and Kevin Bremner provided the firepower in attack.

Ball's managerial career at the Victoria Ground started in stirring fashion. In the first minute Carl Beeston skirted over two tackles to crash the ball past John Keeley. By half-time Stoke led 3-1, Bamber netting a header and Kamara haring in to convert Beeston's cross. Brighton's reply came from Robert Codner but City were dominating a game for the first time in the season.

On the hour Stoke were awarded a penalty for a trip on debutant Vince Hilaire. George Berry, reinstated by Ball in a bid to add some pride to the side, cracked the kick against the post. The confidence visibly drained out of Stoke. The more so, when Kevin Bremner pulled a second goal back. City were on the ropes for the final twenty minutes but somehow clung on. The celebrations at the final whistle were more akin to those surrounding a vital promotion win, indicating the depth of the despair which many fans felt about the club's plight.

The win proved a false dawn. Despite Ball's media bluster that he would lead Stoke clear of the relegation mire, City would win just four more games all season and be ignominiously relegated.

LEAGUE DIVISION 3   **1990-91**
Barclays Division 3   14th
Rumbelows Cup   2nd Round
FA Cup   2nd Round

If last season's horror show had tested Stoke fans' patience to the limit, then this year would see it snap. City considered themselves far too big a club to be languishing in the Third Division. Ball felt he had a squad of players able to climb out of the division at the first attempt. His only summer signing was another former Portsmouth player, Mick Kennedy, who signed from Luton for £180,000 and a reported £70,000 a year in wages, making him the highest paid player in Stoke's history. Kennedy was a well-known midfield hardman who had assisted Luton in their successful battle to avoid relegation from the top flight. Ball appointed him captain, expecting him to add much-needed steel in midfield. Guile would be provided by the return of veteran Mickey Thomas, whose loan period from Leeds was made permanent on a free transfer.

Despite relegation, the board thought it necessary to increase admission prices. To stand on the Boothen End now cost £4.50, an increase of 50p, while seats also went up by 50p to £7.50. The rise sparked protests, spearheaded by The Oatcake, rightly claiming that it was the financial mismanagement of the board that had saddled the club not only with Division Three, but also with another hefty overdraft. To pass on the cost of their malpractice was yet another indignity that could only drive supporters away. It was vital that the club make a quick return to Division Two.

Ball's promises of a quick return seemed to have some foundation when David Webb's table-topping Southend were thrashed 4-0 and, following a 2-0 win over Wigan in early November, Stoke sat comfortably in third place.

But there were signs that all was not well. A 1-3 home defeat by Shrewsbury saw Lee Sandford contrive to score an own-goal and he was targeted by more vocal sections of the fans as a player to abuse. He was seen as 'Ball's man', and his form suffered under a barrage of invective. Poor displays against Grimsby and Cambridge, who were charging up the divisions under the maniacal management of John Beck, rocked the boat further. The fans were not taking to life in Division Three and the defeat at Blundell Park was the cue for demonstrations which quickly turned into fisticuffs with Mariners fans. There would in consequence be bad blood between the clubs for years to come.

Ball's team were starting to be shown up for what they really were, a collection of ill-disciplined cloggers. From Noel Blake, who had been exposed as a limited, if wholehearted centre-half, even at this level, through Mick Kennedy to Tony Ellis, the team lacked skill and mobility. Paul Ware, who had risen through the ranks of the youth team to become a regular in midfield under Ball, had learnt a number of dirty tricks from Kennedy and contributed to getting two opponents sent off before finally being rumbled and dismissed himself. Kennedy was also red-carded and was fortunate that his appalling disciplinary record did not bring him a more hefty suspension than the four games handed down by the League. In attack the team was one-dimensional and the goals dried up for Biggins and Ellis. Seven goals in thirteen games from the pairing was hardly promotion form. Ball had persisted with his favourites and they had failed him. The crowd were not slow in vocalising their feelings, but that did not help steady the ship. Noel Blake was an immensely proud man and disliked the treatment he got from some sections of the crowd. Abuse relating to his colour was rightly derided by everyone at the club.

Stoke lost to West Ham in the Rumbelows Cup second round, having edged past Swansea 1-0 on aggregate in the first, and only squeezed past non-league Telford 1-0 after an FA Cup first-round replay. The second round brought more humiliation in the shape of defeat by Fourth Division Burnley. Mansfield, bottom of the Third, beat Stoke 3-0 in the preliminary round of the Leyland DAF Cup, as the Associate Members Cup was now known. That defeat meant Stoke failed to qualify from a group of three teams, having drawn against Fourth Division Northampton 1-1 at the Vic. A puny crowd of just over 4,000 demonstrated both the low regard with which the competition was held, and also how faith had been sapped in the manager's ability to lead Stoke to promotion.

The supporters no longer trusted Ball's judgment and a stream of vitriol was poured upon the manager, much of it unseemly. He was hounded by angry fans, not just after matches but also arriving at and leaving the ground after training. Ball stuck to his guns, insisting that 'his' players were the right ones for the job. He was plainly wrong. City won two out of thirteen games, which included defeats by Chester, Exeter and Southend. Ball's position was untenable and following an embarrassing 0-4 defeat by Wigan (see Match of the Season) he resigned, claiming that abuse he received from a young fan in the aftermath of the defeat at Springfield Park was the final straw. He left the club in its worst ever position in the Football League, having called upon 42 players in fifteen months. Ball went on to manage Exeter and act as coach and advisor to Graham Taylor during his abortive tenure as England manager. In truth, his record as a manager is indefensible. He has been relegated with each of the five clubs he has managed, aside from Southampton, whom he guided to a creditable tenth-place in the Premiership. Many football fans believe that certain managers suit certain clubs. Ball found his place on the south coast with Pompey and the Saints. It most certainly was not in Stoke.

Graham Paddon was handed the task of seeing Stoke through to the end of the season. The board wished to wait till then before appointing a new manager, when they would have a wider range of options. The truth was that they couldn't afford to lure a contracted manager from another club at this stage of the season and wanted to wait to see who would be out of contract come the summer. Just eighteen months earlier they had lavished £1 million in spending money on a manager whose contract they had nearly decided not to renew. Two ill-judged decisions relating to successive managers had contributed enormously to the plight in which Stoke City now found itself.

A cloud hung over the Victoria Ground and no matter where the dwindling numbers of Stoke fans looked, it was hard to see a silver lining. The club was all but broke, had no manager and a playing staff of run-of-the-mill professionals and barely blooded youngsters. The Oatcake made representations to the board that the situation must be dealt with or there was a danger that the club would actually go under. There had been talk for many years that smaller clubs would start to disappear once television money enhanced the power of the elite. Within a year Aldershot would fold. To suggest that Stoke City might go the same way was almost heretical, but did not go unwhispered in many quarters. It would take something or someone outstanding to lift the club out of its seemingly terminal malaise.

Match of the Season 1990-91
Wigan 4   Stoke 0

Division 3, 23 February 1991

Alan Ball's last match in charge of Stoke City was a desperate affair. Having won only eighteen out of the 67 games in which he was in charge, he was under intolerable pressure from supporters to quit. Stoke's first ever League visit to Springfield Park was an indication of just how far the club had sunk. The ground itself was falling to bits, with the away fans housed under a leaking roof on the top of a grassy bank behind one of the goals. The pouring rain did not help Stoke fans' humour. The mood was black. The supporters wanted heads to roll. Starting with Ball's.

Under Bryan Hamilton, Wigan were having the most successful period in their history. Hamilton had first joined the Latics in 1985 and taken them to within a point of promotion to the Second Division. He had moved on to manage Leicester, returning to Springfield Park after the club had finished in mid-table under Ray Mathias. Hamilton had failed to make the same impact second time around and Wigan lay one position below Stoke, although they had taken First Division Coventry to an FA Cup replay the previous month.

The game started badly for Stoke and got progressively worse. Cliff Carr and Wayne Biggins both missed golden opportunities to open the scoring. Wigan, on the other hand, were not so profligate. Phil Daley put them ahead with a glancing header. It all seemed depressingly familiar and triggered torrents of abuse aimed towards the Stoke dug-out from the outraged fans.

If the team had been poor in the first half, they appeared to lie down and die in the second. Daley chipped Fox from the edge of the area and Darren Patterson and Don Page both rose above City's supposed giant defence to nod home. Stoke's players were happy to wait for the final whistle and disappear from the pitch before the inevitable vitriol-charged invasion by hordes of angry fans baying for Ball's blood.

The news that Ball had finally thrown in the towel came as a relief. However, some of the inflammatory personal abuse hurled in his direction was unforgivable. Ball's departure, although essential, did not divert attention from the appalling state of Stoke City in general. Sixteen years to the day that Stoke had last topped the Football League, the club was at its lowest ebb since 1908, when it had gone out of existence, only to be re-formed by AJ Barker, a local businessman. There were no local millionaires in the 1990s stepping forward to place wads of cash at City's disposal. The next managerial appointment could prove vital to the club's continued existence.

Graham Shaw scores from the spot against Orient (October 1988)

... but Peter Beagrie misses as Stoke lose to Orient on penalties

Cliff Carr celebrates Berry's goal against Manchester City (December 1988)

Gary Hackett in full flow (March 1989)

Peter Beagrie slots the second goal against Sunderland (March 1989)

Gary Hackett takes on Sunderland's Reuben Agboola (March 1989)

Dave Bamber beats Walsall's Andy Saville to a header (April 1989)

Wayne Biggins cracks in a shot against Sheffield United (March 1990)

## 5

SKIP TO MY LOU MACARI
1991-1997

LEAGUE DIVISION 3	**1991-92**
Barclays Division 3	4th
Rumbelows Cup	2nd Round
FA Cup	1st Round

Lou Macari was the man the board chose as the next manager. He had quit Birmingham following a dispute with the Kumar brothers, who had taken control of the club, over money for team-building. Indeed, Macari had not been far from controversy throughout his career. As a 24-year-old forward he was a hot property and chose Manchester United ahead of Liverpool when leaving Celtic, thus becoming one of the few men ever to say no to Bill Shankly. After 311 League games for United, and 24 Scotland caps, Macari became player-manager at Fourth Division Swindon. Sacked by chairman Harry Gregg, he was reinstated six days later after supporters – believing that he cared passionately about their club – petitioned the board. Swindon thrived under his stewardship, winning consecutive promotions. Having achieved success on a shoestring, Macari was then offered the chance to manage West Ham, an altogether different kind of club, who had been relegated to Division Two. After just seven months at Upton Park he became embroiled in a scandal from his Swindon days, relating to non-payment of tax. Macari resigned from West Ham, to prevent his new club being dragged into the affairs of his old. Swindon were eventually denied the place in the First Division they had secured by winning the 1990 play-offs. The threat of legal action still hung over Macari, his chairman, Brian Hillier, and several other Swindon directors.

Macari promised nothing other than to instil an appetite to win into the Stoke team. His frankness endeared him to the fans, who sensed that here was no blustering Ball or meek Mills. He was also a disciplinarian, expecting players to be fit enough to put in 100 per cent effort throughout the 90 minutes of a game. His teams often scored vital goals in the closing stages of matches.

DID YOU KNOW?

When Old Trafford was closed in 1973-74 as punishment for hooliganism,
Manchester United played one of their 'home' games at the Victoria Ground.

Macari's choice of No 2 was former Shrewsbury manager Chic
Bates, who had been his assistant at Swindon and Birmingham.
Macari's appointment convinced a new sponsor, Ansells, to commit
£100,000 to the club over a period of two years.

Renowned for a direct style of play, Macari described his system
as 'a power game to get the ball into the final third of the pitch.
Once there to play incisive, attacking football'. But after a sticky
start, which had some fans wondering if Stoke needed 'route one'
football at the Vic again, sorting out the ramshackle defence became
Macari's priority. Ian Cranson, Stoke's record signing, had finally
recovered from injury. Having to cut his cloth, Macari offered the
out-of-contract player reduced terms, entitling him to a free transfer.
Cranson thought long and hard, weighed up an offer from Hearts,
but finally put pen to paper. He had a superb season, showing why
Mills had risked nearly half a million pounds on him.

Macari's first buy was Vince Overson, a towering man-mountain
of a centre-half, from Birmingham for a tribunal-set fee of £55,000. It
proved money well spent. Overson was made captain, as he had
been under Macari at St Andrews, and marshalled the new system
of three big centre-backs, Overson, Cranson and either Blake or
Sandford.

The first sign that Stoke meant business came when Tony Kelly
nutmegged Liverpool goalkeeper Bruce Grobbelaar at Anfield to
earn City a 2-2 draw in the Rumbelows Cup. The second leg was
lost 2-3, but Stoke conceded only eight goals in nine games before
Christmas, winning six to find themselves handily placed in fourth
position.

Wayne Biggins was having his best season. He was a head-
down-and-go type of striker, lacking any pretence at finesse, but
possessing a good shot and a cool head from the penalty spot. He
also appeared obsessed with his appearance, sporting a perma-tan
that belied the weather in the Potteries. Macari's system played to
his strengths, but he needed to secure Biggins the right partner.
Having toyed with signing Bournemouth's Jimmy Quinn, but
lacked the £300,000 fee, Macari unearthed another gem in the tiny
form of Mark Stein, who was acquired on loan from Oxford. Stein
provided finesse and lightning speed around the box, combining
well with Biggins. Stein was signed permanently for £100,000 and
repaid Macari's faith by scoring regularly. He had a rapier-like right-

foot shot and Macari made him practice with his left so that he became comfortable when shooting with either foot. Stein outscored Biggins over the second half of the season.

The new strike partnership was unable to save Stoke from further FA Cup humiliation. City drew Telford in the first round for the second year running and the 1-2 defeat prompted Macari to seek a new goalkeeper. He chose Ronnie Sinclair from Bristol City, who was initially taken on loan and asked to prove his worth. At only 5ft 9in, Sinclair was short for a keeper and consequently often struggled in the air. The bulky defenders in front of him often took care of matters, but Sinclair was prone to the odd rush of blood, coming for crosses he was never going to reach. Despite this, he convinced Macari that he was worth the £25,000 that Bristol City were asking. Signing permanently boosted his confidence and he was an integral part of a defence which conceded only eight goals in twelve games after Boxing Day.

The system Macari had adopted often meant that the side played straight up and down the pitch in a rather narrow fashion. A 0-2 defeat at promotion rivals Brentford in January prompted Macari to look for more width to boost the team for a final promotion push. He signed right-sided Steve Foley for £50,000, a highly experienced midfielder whom he had previously signed for Swindon, left-winger Kevin Russell from Leicester on loan, and Ashley Grimes, a left-sided midfielder, who was looking to return to this country after a two-year spell with Osasuna in Spain. Grimes was also made coach of the club's youth set-up.

With the season coming to the boil, there were signs that things were getting tense. In February, the game at Birmingham, Macari's old club, boiled over after Paul Barnes scored an injury-time equaliser, precipitating a pitch invasion by angry Blues fans. Referee Roger Wiseman took the players off the pitch and the stadium was cleared, allowing the teams to play out the final 90 seconds of the game at walking pace behind closed doors. The riot made headlines around the world, but, although not initiated by Stoke fans, other incidents were. There was a sizeable element amongst Stoke fans who would just not let Ball's failure at the Vic drop and the former manager was disgracefully spat at and abused, describing his visit to the Vic as Exeter's manager as 'the most harrowing experience of my career'. Despite all this the crowds were streaming back through the turnstiles. No matter that it was the Third Division; City fans had something to sing about. Adapting the old school playground chant the Boothen End's mantra now became 'Lou, Lou, skip to my Lou, Skip to my Lou Macari!' Gates were up by 12.5 per cent and nearly 24,000 saw Stoke knock West Brom off the top on a chilly

February night. Macari was being hailed a hero and a genius in the transfer market.

Added to City's promotion push was a second Wembley final. Stoke beat Walsall and Birmingham in the Autoglass Trophy (as the Leyland DAF Cup was now called) preliminary round group, from which two teams qualified, allowing Stoke the privilege of beating Walsall again in the second round, before defeating Peterborough in a two leg semi-final to earn a place at Wembley.

With eight games to go, Stoke sat atop the League, favourites for promotion. At this crucial stage their form deserted them, failing to beat some of the also-rans of the division. Hull and Bury, both just above the relegation zone, won at the Vic in consecutive matches, before City lost at Torquay, who were next to bottom. The team exposed its old Achilles heel – ill-discipline. Seven players received suspensions during the season, five in April, and Stoke finished bottom of the Third Division fair-play league, devised to assess disciplinary records across the divisions. A pitiful home defeat by another relegation candidate, Chester, condemned Stoke to the end of season play-offs for the first time.

Stockport were City's play-off semi-final opponents. The first leg, at Edgeley Park, was an unmitigated disaster. Carl Beeston was sent off and Stoke lost 0-1 to a Peter Ward free-kick. The second leg did not start much better. Chris Beaumont headed Stockport into a first-minute lead which Stoke never looked likely to retrieve, despite exerting heavy pressure. Stein finally broke through to set up a frantic last ten minutes, but Stoke went out. The club was devastated at missing promotion, though they would be permitted an early opportunity for revenge, as Stockport were their opponents in the Autoglass Trophy final (see Match of the Season).

Macari's arrival had sparked renewed life into the club. The turnaround in the space of a season was testament to his, and the players', hard work. It was an all-round good year for Stoke as the reserves, under Peter Henderson, won the Pontin's League Second Division, often attracting crowds of over 2,000 during their run in. The club was also improving its public relations, having finally constructed a permanent stand for wheelchair-bound supporters in the Butler Street stand. The development was paid for by a £5,000 grant from the Football Trust, a body dedicated to the improvement of football grounds, which had been set up in the aftermath of the Taylor Report. There was also a new, larger club shop, housed in the bottom of the Stoke End stand. To encourage fans to buy its merchandise a club-sponsored credit card was launched, with City receiving a small percentage of each transaction. New life had been breathed into Stoke City.

Match of the Season 1991-92

Stoke 1 Stockport 0

Autoglass Trophy final, 16 May 1992

Danny Bergara's Stockport appeared to be hewn out of rock. Up front they boasted 6ft 7in Kevin Francis, the League's tallest player. He was partnered by 6ft 1in Andy Preece, who had joined County midway through the season from Wrexham and provided thirteen goals in their promotion push. Jim Gannon, a rugged centre-back, had found a new lease of life as a goalscoring midfielder, finishing as leading scorer with 21 goals. This was County's first appearance at Wembley.

The local public had barely responded. Stockport's average gate was below 5,000 and they had only 13,000 fans at Wembley. Stoke had sold more than 34,000 of their 45,000 allocation at the tunnel end. Basic ticket prices were £11 for the lower tier, rising to £21 for the Olympic Gallery. Stoke fans did not mind paying these prices. It meant a modicum of success had come their way and they were going to enjoy it.

Stoke's line-up featured veteran keeper Peter Fox in goal. He had appeared in most of the Autoglass games, as Ronnie Sinclair was cup-tied after appearing on loan for Walsall in the preliminary round, ironically against Stoke.

After two combative League games and the play-off semi-finals, there was sufficient tension between the two teams to ensure that this was no showpiece final. The expected succession of long balls aimed at Francis was capably dealt with by Overson and Cranson. In an untidy first half there were few chances and it was well into the second before Stein and Biggins made inroads into County's defence. On 65 minutes a long ball fell to Stein, who turned sharply on the edge of the area, let the ball drop and whacked a half-volley past Neil Edwards in the County goal. Stoke hung on, as, once Andy Preece was substituted, County's threat subsided.

There was jubilation at the final whistle. It mattered little that it was only the Autoglass Trophy, a competition contemptuously dismissed as the Nissan Cherry Brake Line Fluid Wotsit Cup until Stoke actually won it! The win signalled a change of fortunes of the kind that had hardly been imaginable just twelve months earlier.

Stockport were left to concentrate on winning the promotion play-off final, but lost in the last minute to Peterborough. Stoke toured the Potteries in an open topped bus in glorious sunshine, proudly displaying the first trophy the club had won in twenty years. Promotion was next on the bill.

LEAGUE DIVISION 2	1992-93
Barclays Division 2	1st (Champions)
Coca-Cola Cup	2nd Round
FA Cup	1st Round

Even without winning promotion Stoke were back in the Second Division. After the formation of the breakaway Premier League, the Football League had been re-constituted and what had been the Third Division was now renamed the Second. The formation of the FA Premiership seemed just the first step on the way to an inevitable European Super league, which the likes of Manchester United, Barcelona, AC Milan and Bayern Munich craved. That the breakaway coincided with the arrival on the British media scene of Rupert Murdoch's Sky Television Corporation was no accident. Sky's deal, which brought live Premier League football to subscribers on a weekly basis, brought sponsorship money swilling into the game at the top level, changing the face of football forever. For clubs like Stoke, the revolution meant the probability of further financial hardship as the media homed in on the Premier League at the expense of the lower divisions. The change in football's financial climate had already claimed its first victim. Aldershot of the Fourth Division had gone to the wall at the end of the previous season and Barnet had only survived by the skin of their teeth. Maidstone would perish within weeks. It was perverse that, while clubs struggled to stay alive, record transfer fees were being set almost monthly. Duncan Ferguson was the latest to bear the tag of Britain's most expensive player, having signed for Rangers for £4 million. Stoke were still £1.9 million in debt and, to the supporters, the crazy figures commanded by these players was pie in the sky. The only possible means of paying off the overdraft was to win promotion.

In June Lou Macari had been acquitted of all complicity in the tax scandal which had rocked his former club, Swindon. His former chairman was not so fortunate. In October, Macari also stood trial on charges of illegal operation of a bookmakers, in which he held a stake. He was acquitted by magistrates in Devizes, whereupon City fans breathed a huge sigh of relief.

Keeping the players that had taken Stoke so close to promotion was proving tricky. Seven of the squad rejected new contracts and, with trouble brewing, Macari issued an ultimatum: either sign or leave. Most signed, although Cranson procrastinated, refusing until November to sign anything other than a weekly contract. Kevin 'Rooster' Russell signed permanently from Leicester for a tribunal-fixed fee of £95,000, and Macari managed to finally rid himself of Tony Ellis, with whom he had fallen out. Ellis objected to a £100,000

SKIP TO MY LOU MACARI – SEASON 1992-93

price tag the manager had placed on him, whereupon Macari swapped him for former Stoke forward Graham Shaw, now with Preston, plus £50,000. This reversed the transfer of some two years earlier.

The sense of expectation was intense. Stoke were favourites to win the championship, at 6-1 with Corals. This was to be City's year, but initially the players found the pressures difficult to cope with and won only one of the first seven games, also going out of the Coca-Cola Cup to First Division Cambridge, despite drawing 2-2 at the Abbey Stadium. In the League, a 1-1 draw with Brighton saw City ahead after only 45 seconds, but they failed to win. The team appeared to be losing the winning momentum instilled the previous season. The next visitors were West Brom who, conversely, had shot out of the starting stalls and were top of the table (see Match of the Season). The manner of Stoke's victory spoke volumes about the determination of the team to put matters right. These were now Macari's players, singing from his hymnbook.

Macari reasoned that City's sluggish start was partly down to the unsettling influence of 'Bertie' Biggins, who hankered after a bigger club. Macari also believed that Biggins, who had amassed six cautions in the previous campaign for dissent-related incidents, was a disruptive influence on the pitch. Before the start of the season the club introduced a new disciplinary code aimed at reducing the number of suspensions which had disrupted the team at a crucial stage. Biggins' 'dream' move to Barnsley was completed in October, costing the Tykes a tribunal-fixed fee of £200,000, £100,000 short of Stoke's valuation. Despite scoring on his debut, within a month Biggins was on the phone to Macari asking to return to Stoke. There is no record of the manager's response!

With cash in hand Macari was on the lookout for quality players, not only for this season's promotion bid, but also to establish a firm footing in the First Division the following year. He returned to his former club Birmingham to sign Nigel Gleghorn, a stylish midfielder whose vision and distribution gave the team an added dimension. Gleghorn's fee was a paltry £100,000, with Macari taking advantage of the fact that he knew Birmingham were in serious financial difficulties.

Mark Stein, who by now was known to the fans as 'the golden one', found the net 33 times, earning himself a place in the hearts of Potters fans and acquisitive glances from Newcastle boss Kevin Keegan. Macari was concerned that Stein's pocket-sized partnership with Shaw lacked the necessary muscle to compete over a whole season in a physical league. After enquiring about Blackburn's Steve Livingstone and Notts County's Tony Agana, in October Macari bought 28-year-old Dave Regis from Plymouth for £130,000. At 6ft 3in, Regis – brother of former West Brom, Coventry and England centre-forward Cyrille – was a combative player who was capable of providing more chances for Stein with his knockdowns than could be created with Shaw in the side.

Armed with their new signings, Stoke were head and shoulders above the rest of the Second Division. 25 games separated the 0-0 draw with Bolton on 25 September and the 0-1 defeat at Leyton Orient on 27 February – a club record. Stoke hit the top with a win over Blackpool during a run of seven successive victories. Macari was named manager of the month for October and December amid press rumours that Liverpool and Celtic were keeping tabs on him – incumbents Graeme Souness and Liam Brady were under intense pressure. Macari scotched the gossip by claiming that he would never want to work in 'goldfish bowl environments where every move is examined'.

The season was given added spice by the duels with local rivals Port Vale, relegated from Division One, but now neck and neck with Stoke at the top of Division Two. The season saw five sell-out clashes, with Stoke winning both League meetings. The 2-0 victory at Vale Park in late March was City's most complete performance of the season and all but guaranteed promotion. Vale exacted revenge in the Cups. The clubs were paired in the FA Cup for the first time since 1951, and such was the interest generated that it was switched to a Monday night for Television coverage. With the intense focus on the match it was no surprise that it turned out to be a scrappy affair, necessitating a replay. In diabolical conditions Vale clinched a place in the second round after Dave Regis's shot stuck in the mud on the line, with Stoke trailing 1-2. Vale also won the Autoglass Trophy Southern Area semi-final, when Stein's missed penalty saw Stoke relinquish their hold on the Trophy.

Continuing the previous season's PR initiative under new director Paul Wright, Stoke restricted half of the Boothen Paddock to a Family Membership area, with entrance for adults only if accompanied by at least one child. The 'Lifeline' initiative, launched on City's relegation from the First Division in 1985, was relaunched as the Executive Society, with the promise that half of the weekly £2 members' contribution would go towards purchasing players. The rest was put into a pot, from which cash prizes were handed out via a lucky dip. With the club on a crest of a wave, prizes often totalled over £1,000. One innovation, that proved not so popular, was a ghastly new away kit, featuring two bright shades of purple.

Back on the pitch, battle was rejoined with Stockport, who were also challenging for promotion. Stein and County's Jim Gannon, who had been involved in Carl Beeston's dismissal in the previous season's play-off semi-final, grappled on the pitch after the latter's allegedly racial abuse. The case ended in court, with Stein bound over to keep the peace. For his part, Gannon became a favourite hate victim of the Boothen End, and consequently reserved his best form for visits to the Vic. Stoke had the last laugh, winning at home and drawing away to put County out of the automatic promotion picture.

Slight promotion jitters were not helped by a cruciate ligament injury sustained by goalkeeper Ronnie Sinclair at Bournemouth. Macari brought in 35-year-old Liverpool keeper Bruce Grobbelaar on loan, but when he was recalled to Anfield turned to veteran Peter Fox. His brilliant double save from Plymouth's Steve Castle allowed Stoke to register the vital win that saw them claim promotion and the championship in one fell swoop.

Macari had triumphed in bringing the fans what they most craved – promotion. He was rightly made manager of the season for the Second Division. The difference he had made to the club in the two years of his reign was quite astonishing. It was built on hard work, commitment and self-belief. Simple qualities, but difficult ones to instil in a motley assortment of players who had seemed so disparate under Ball. There was a growing tendency for promoted clubs to return immediately whence they came. This season had seen Brentford make a rapid return to Division Two, having gone up as champions, while fellow promoted club Birmingham only avoided the drop with a last-day win. Getting to the First Division was one thing; staying there quite another. Stoke fans did not care. They had Lou Macari.

Match of the Season 1992-93

Stoke 4   West Brom 3

Division 2, 19 September 1992

Ossie Ardiles' West Brom held an early lead at the top of the Second Division, three points clear of second placed Leyton Orient and twelve ahead of Stoke. In a division dominated by physical, route-one teams, Albion stood out by playing a neat, incisive, short-passing game.

Rivalry between the two clubs was becoming something of a millstone for Albion. Since beating City 6-0 in December 1988, they had not repeated the feat in seven attempts. Stoke, for their part, were finding the burden of expectation weighing heavily on them. One win in seven games meant that the pressure was on.

DID YOU KNOW?

When Stoke played in a 1976 pre-season tournament in Madrid against Atletico and Cruzeiro (Brazil), it was sandwiched between friendlies against Rhyl and Buxton.

Albion dominated the game from the off, with their four-man midfield running rings round City's three. The pitch was greasy from early morning rain and suited the Baggies' neat-passing style. Stoke's goalkeeper, Tony Parks, on loan from West Ham, had been brought in as last-minute cover for Sinclair, who had strained his hamstring in training. Parks was still getting acclimatised when he lost his footing in the process of taking a goal-kick. The ball rolled to Bob Taylor who waltzed around Parks to deservedly give Albion the lead.

That goal acted as an alarm-call to Stoke. Driven forward by Steve Foley, the midfield began to take a hold on the game. Just on half-time Foley broke clear on the left edge of the box to equalise. The balance was swinging towards Stoke, and immediately after the restart City went 2-1 up through Russell. Stoke's three centre-backs were not used to facing strikers as skilled with the ball at their feet as Taylor and Garner. In combination with Hamilton they fashioned two openings in quick succession and scored from both. The game then swung back towards Stoke. Russell carved his way past three players before rounding Stuart Naylor to level the score at 3-3.

City's midfield proved decisive. They ground Albion down and on 83 minutes the Baggies cracked. A right-wing corner was swung across and Ian Cranson crashed a header in off the underside of the bar. He later said that the emotion of that goal in that game was one of the highlights of his career.

Football is not just about talent, it is about application and heart. Stoke proved that they had those qualities in abundance and the result launched a run which took the team to the Second Division title. They were fortunate that they did not face many teams of Albion's class that season. West Brom also made it into the First Division, but by a more circuitous route. Finishing fourth meant they had to endure the agonies of the play-offs where they beat Port Vale 3-0 in the final.

LEAGUE DIVISION 1   **1993-94**
Endsleigh Division 1   10th
Coca-Cola Cup   2nd Round
FA Cup   4th Round

Promotion meant a financial bonanza. Record season-ticket sales of over 8,000 resulted in almost £1 million being banked before a ball was kicked. Supporters carped about the 10 per cent hike in admission prices and the cost of the new replica kit (£48) but, reacting to the first positive season at the club for a decade, Stoke fans happily spent record amounts in the club shop too.

Macari wanted to recruit experienced, quality players and was linked with Leeds' Gordon Strachan, Blackburn's Gordon Cowans and Graeme Hogg of Hearts. Despite the improved financial situation, resources were not available to fund the wages of players who expected Premiership levels of pay. Instead, Macari raided Premier League reserve sides. Striker Martin Carruthers, 21, signed from Aston Villa: he had been top scorer as Villa's reserves won the Pontins League. Icelandic midfielder Thorvaldur 'Toddy' Orlygsson arrived from Nottingham Forest on a free transfer, and Macari swooped for the Birmingham duo, right-back Ian Clarkson, £50,000, and striker Simon Sturridge, £75,000. Goalkeeper Ronnie Sinclair would be out with his cruciate ligament injury until after Christmas, so Macari signed Mark Prudhoe, £120,000 from Darlington and Carl Muggleton, on loan from Leicester.

Stoke started steadily and, following a 3-2 win at Frank Clark's Nottingham Forest, lay seventh, but a 1-4 defeat at early leaders Crystal Palace indicated that City still had some way to go if they wanted to make their mark. Promotion also meant an opportunity to compete in the Anglo-Italian Cup after a gap of 21 years. The competition, now exclusively for teams in the second division of each country, involved initial round-robins of three teams, with the winner of each group progressing. Despite being viewed very much as an early season kick-about, Stoke progressed to the second stage. At the Vic they beat Cosenza 2-1 and drew 0-0 with Fiorentina. But they lost both games in Italy and failed to make it to the semi-final stage.

There was more excitement generated by City's pairing with Manchester United in the second round of the Coca-Cola Cup (see Match of the Season). Stoke matched United for spirit and endeavour, indicating just how far the club had come under Macari in just two years, and held their heads high after narrow defeat.

Macari was losing patience with the lack of money available to him for transfers. This had recently denied him the opportunity of signing Newcastle's Gavin Peacock and Derby's Paul Williams. The fees wanted were around £750,000, and Macari declared publicly that his spending limit had been capped by the board at £500,000. Stoke could not compete in this market. Despite the recent success, the club was still saddled with an overdraft in excess of £2 million. The board were keen to improve the club's footing with the bank and the sale of Kevin Russell, for £140,000, realising a £45,000 profit, hinted at the club's priorities.

Rumours that began circulating back in March were confirmed when Celtic – whose supremo David Smith wanted Lou Macari to spearhead the Bhoys' attempt to knock Rangers from their perch – were given permission to speak to Stoke's manager, provided 'suitable compensation' could be agreed should he decide to leave. Coincidentally, with a profit of over £1.4 million beckoning, the board accepted a £1.5 million bid for hot property Mark Stein from Glenn Hoddle's Chelsea. Within two days Macari had accepted Celtic's offer, explaining his decision to Stoke's distraught fans: 'If you are in any walk of life and *the* job comes up, wouldn't you want it?' But it was the sale of Stein that convinced Macari that his long-term future lay away from the Victoria Ground.

Stoke's backroom staff all resigned to join Macari at Parkhead, while Director Robert Lee also resigned, citing differences of opinion over the appointment of the new manager. Lee required the repayment of a loan that he had made to the club, the effect of which was to compromise financial stability once again. It emerged that each of the remaining four directors had loaned sizeable amounts and that it was only this which had kept the club afloat, despite the record season ticket sales.

Macari's replacement was Joe Jordan, formerly Liam Brady's assistant at Celtic. As an indication of the quicksands which were to beset Macari's reign, 42-year-old Jordan had quit Parkhead after just one day as caretaker manager. He protested that the club had been pursuing other managers while he was taking a training session in the belief that he was a candidate for the job. Jordan brought in former Scotland midfielder Asa Hartford as his assistant and former Leicester and Chelsea full-back Denis Rofe as reserve-team coach. Brian Caswell, a former Walsall and Leeds full-back, was appointed as Youth Team Coach.

Jordan's dour exterior did not endear him to Stoke's fans, although it was a two-way thing. Quite simply Joe Jordan was not Lou Macari – their hero. Abortive terms with Hearts (as manager) and Celtic (as Brady's assistant), meant that Jordan was inclined to take a safety-first approach, and without Stein's firepower Stoke scored only nine goals in fifteen games. Jordan's team produced stale, boring football and the crowd were quick to protest. Jordan's loanee keeper, Gordon Marshall, had a nightmare debut in Stoke's 2-6 hammering by Luton, raising questions about the manager's judgement, but the question which vexed most Stoke fans was why did Jordan not replace Stein?

The reason lay in the board paying off much of the overdraft. By March, Stoke were only £500,000 in debt, having reduced the deficit by £2 million in twelve months. The decision was intended to reduce interest repayments totalling £187,000 in the previous year. The price for this financial prudence was lack of investment in the team, a risky business in the first season after promotion. Jordan did contrive to win an FA Cup-tie for Stoke, the first for four years, albeit against Conference side Bath. Premiership Oldham proved too strong in the next round, winning 1-0 in a Vic replay.

On 29 January the death was announced of former manager Tony Waddington after a short illness. His funeral cortege began its journey from the Victoria Ground and thousands lined the streets to say farewell, braving atrocious weather. His departure did not help the mood of defeatism enveloping the club.

After weeks of begging for time to find new players, a flurry of activity marked deadline day. For £170,000 Jordan signed 'Bertie' Biggins, who returned from unhappy sojourns at Oakwell and Celtic Park, where he had joined Macari. Defender Mickey Adams signed on a free transfer from Southampton. Terms were agreed with Swindon for £250,000 striker Andy Mutch, but his suspect knee killed the deal. The new arrivals made little impact and, after a 2-4 defeat at Derby, the first calls for the manager's head were heard. There was terrace talk that ex-Stoke player Steve Bould was being lined up as player-manager, having been spotted attending several Stoke home games.

Jordan's position was also under threat by director Bob Kenyon's bid to buy out majority shareholders Peter Coates and Keith Humphreys, with the aim of reinstating Macari as manager. Coates and Humphreys refused what would have been a sizeable injection of capital into the club, not wanting to relinquish control.

Over the course of the season rumours had circulated about the viability of redeveloping the ground. This was now becoming a burning issue, as Stoke had only three years to turn the Victoria ground into an all-seated arena compliant with the Taylor Report. Other options included moving to a site a mile from the ground, known as Sideway or Trentham Lakes. This was earmarked for possible development should rebuilding of the Vic prove too expensive. The idea of leaving the Victoria Ground, home to Stoke City since 1878, provoked much heated debate.

DID YOU KNOW?

In September 1975, Lincoln City became the lowest placed opponents ever to knock Stoke out of the League Cup. Lincoln were 9th in Division 4 at the time.

Match of the Season 1993-94

Stoke 2 Manchester United 1

Coca-Cola Cup, 2nd Round, 1st leg, 22 September 1993

Under Alex Ferguson, United were patently the best team in the country, having won the inaugural Premier League with ten points to spare. Their customary line-up featured Frenchman Eric Cantona, whose arrival from Leeds had inspired the Red Devils to their first title since 1967. Cantona, though, was absent as United fielded an 'understrength' side which still included ten full internationals! Heavily involved in Europe, United had made noises about fielding their second team in the Coca-Cola Cup and, when threatened with sanctions by the League, declared several of their first team 'unfit' instead.

United started the better and it took the force of Vince Overson's tackling to bring Stoke into the game. Following his lead was Toddy Orlygsson, who proved a thorn in United's left flank and gave Republic of Ireland international full-back Denis Irwin a torrid night. Orlygsson set up Stein to hammer a shot high past Peter Schmeichel. Once ahead City dominated. Stoke's midfield had such a grip on the game that former England captain Bryan Robson was substituted for winger Lee Sharpe, whose arrival sparked a United fightback. Dion Dublin, starting in place of Cantona, rose to nod home his cross.

Stoke attacked again and Stein wriggled free of three defenders to shoot past Schmeichel. Understandably the ground went berserk, and Stein was booked for celebrating with fans who had encroached onto the pitch. Stoke hung on to record a famous victory. As Macari put it: 'Two years ago we were struggling to beat teams like Wigan. Now we have beaten Manchester United and that's a credit to the players.'

United won the second leg 2-0, scoring the winner three minutes from time. They reached the final of the Coca-Cola Cup, where they lost 1-3 to Aston Villa. United retained the Premier League title and completed the first double in the club's history thanks to a 4-0 hammering of Chelsea, including Mark Stein, in the FA Cup final.

LEAGUE DIVISION 1   **1994-95**
Endsleigh Division 1   11th
Coca-Cola Cup   3rd Round
FA Cup   3rd Round

After the boardroom shenanigans of the spring, City fans were frustrated by a summer of silence. The apparent inability of Chairman Coates to communicate with fans had the effect of casting him in the role of villain. There were demonstrations outside the ground by angry fans demanding a boycott of Stoke's opening games. The objective was to oust Coates and Humphreys and allow Bob Kenyon to take over and inject fresh capital. Coates' blunt response was to call the protests 'absolute nonsense'. Kenyon wanted his fellow directors to match his proposed injection of £500,000 into the club, but Coates refused to comply and Kenyon, along with Paul Wright, was voted off the Board at an EGM in early September. In response, the pair apparently demanded repayment of the interest free loans they had made to the club, as a consequence of which the overdraft was back over £1 million again. Stoke's terrible public image impeded season-ticket sales. It also took a turn for the worse when the club overturned its stated policy of only changing shirts every two years and introduced new Home and Away kits simultaneously. Commercial Manager Mick Cullerton cryptically countered criticism by saying: 'We get more complaints if we don't change the kit than if we do.'

As for the team, signing a proven striker was paramount, but Jordan received a pointed rebuff from Nottingham Forest striker Lee Glover, who chose to sign for Port Vale rather than Stoke, believing Vale had the better prospects of success! Jordan eventually signed £400,000 Paul Peschisolido, who arrived from Birmingham. Pesch, as he became known, was a 5ft 8in forward in the mould of Mark Stein, although not yet as prolific. One of the major reasons for his departure from St Andrews was his relationship with managing director Karren Brady; indeed the couple would wed at the end of the season. The two-way deal included £200,000-rated Dave Regis joining Birmingham and was the largest transfer package that Stoke had ever put together to bring a player to the club. It also allowed the board to crow about the money they were investing in players. Midfielders Ray Wallace from Leeds, Keith Downing from Birmingham, and Luton central defender John Dreyer joined the club on free transfers, a truer indication of the lack of cash Jordan had to contend with.

Jordan did not help his own position by informing club captain Vince Overson that he was surplus to requirements, stripping him of the captaincy and handing the job to Nigel Gleghorn. The rift became public. Now it seemed Jordan had lost the players' respect. Sandford, Ware and Butler all rejected new terms. Ware eventually joined Stockport for £40,000, while Butler and Sandford grumpily re-signed after receiving slightly improved offers. Confidence was hardly improved when the manager declared his aim to be to collect enough points to avoid the drop.

Stoke won just one of their first five League games. With Jordan coming under severe pressure, his resignation was announced on 8 September, after only ten months in the job. His undemonstrative style, defensive tactics, and insistence on using striker Peschisolido wide on the right had cost him dear. The following day Jordan sensationally revealed that he had not quit but had been told to go. 'I was the victim of politics,' he said, hinting that he had been jettisoned to save the hides of certain unnamed directors. Asa Hartford took control for seven games – which saw a dramatic improvement in form – giving time for the board to decide who the next man in the hot seat would be.

It turned out to be a familiar face. Lou Macari had been sacked by new Celtic Chairman Fergus McCann and was only too pleased to accept Stoke's offer to return, filing a £400,000 suit for wrongful dismissal against Celtic in the process. Rumours had been rife that his return would be confirmed over the summer, but it was typical of the board's intransigence that it took consecutive 0-4 defeats and two red cards to prompt Jordan's inevitable departure.

Returning alongside Macari was first-team coach Chic Bates. The players responded well to the restoration of the old order, winning Macari's first match in charge, against West Brom, 4-1 (see Match of the Season). But City struggled to make any impression thereafter. Qualification for the semi-finals of the Anglo-Italian cup – courtesy of beating Udinese 3-1 away and Piacenza 4-0 at the Vic – appeared to affect League form. Stoke twice lost on Saturdays following Anglo-Italian matches. The same quandary faced British clubs in the major European competitions and led to the belief that a rotational squad system was the answer to twice-a-week football. That option was not open to a club in Stoke's position. City lost in the semi-final of the Anglo-Italian Cup 2-3 on penalties after two tedious 0-0 draws with Notts County.

A 1-2 defeat at Liverpool in the Coca-Cola Cup hinted that there was still some spirit left, but defeat by Bristol City in the FA Cup – now managed by a certain Joe Jordan – was hard to take. Over the winter Macari introduced several new faces as he sought to breathe life back into the team. Larus Sigurdsson, signed from Icelandic side Thor Akuyeri, was the cousin of Toddy Orlygsson. He impressed at

---

DID YOU KNOW?

**In 1993 the club had to upgrade the Victoria Ground's floodlights
to meet new League standards. Each new bulb cost £850!**

---

centre-half in place of Vince Overson, whose lack of mobility was being exposed at First Division level. New strikers Keith Scott, from Swindon for £300,000, and John Gayle, from Burnley for £70,000, both looked cumbersome players. Gayle proved better in the air for a big man than Scott, who soon became a target for the boo-boys. The jury was out on Macari's other signings – £300,000 midfielder Kevin Keen from Wolves, and centre-half Justin Whittle (bought out of the Army when Macari was at Celtic) on a free transfer. Perhaps Macari was losing his touch in the transfer market. Physiotherapist Richard Gray had also left the club after Jordan's departure and the vacant position had not been filled. When, inevitably, Stoke lost several players through injury, the lack of professional treatment available to them spoke volumes about the deterioration at the club since Macari's departure.

By Easter the situation was becoming a worry. A 2-4 defeat at Southend left Stoke just one place above the relegation zone. There was genuine fear that this might be one crisis too far for Macari. A last bid to inject much-needed goals was dashed when Macari's £450,000 bid for Wolves striker David Kelly was rejected and the board refused to sanction the £650,000 asking price. A few gutsy displays meant relegation was narrowly averted, but the fans' mood was not helped by the AGM announcement that Stoke had made a profit of over £1.5 million in the past year. As ever, the economics of football proved maddening, and, rather than spending the money on improving the team, it had to be reserved to fund Stoke's compliance with the Taylor Report.

The debate raged over whether Stoke should remain at the Victoria Ground or move to a new, purpose-built stadium. The sum needed to revamp the Vic was put at £5 million. Plans were drawn up, but the fact that the canal ran under the south-eastern corner of the ground made the club think again. Port Vale Chairman Bill Bell threw in his tuppence ha'penny, suggesting that a new stadium could be shared between both clubs. Unsurprisingly, a telephone poll in the *Sentinel* revealed that a massive 88 per cent of supporters of *both* clubs were against the move. Stoke's board were not in favour either. They were leaning towards the new stadium option, which although more costly than developing the Vic, would attract more outside investment, particularly from the Football Trust and the City council, whose leader, Ted Smith, was an advocate of the project. Supporters were angry that they had been omitted from the decision-making process. One letter to the *Sentinel* read: 'The most important decision the club have possibly ever faced is in the hands of a board who seem contemptuous of the views of supporters as both stakeholders and as customers – this is no way to run a business.' With the decision all but reached, the board moved to put in place a man to oversee the operation. Jez Moxey, 31, was recruited from Scottish club Partick Thistle to become the club's first Chief Executive. His brief included responsibility for the new stadium and negotiating players' contracts. With the divide between planning for the new ground and investing in players, his job was going to require the finest of balancing acts.

Match of the Season 1994-95
Stoke 4 West Brom 1

Division 1, 2 October 1994

The icing on the cake of Lou Macari's triumphant return to the Victoria Ground was this rout of rivals West Brom. The popular Scot had been confirmed as Stoke manager three days previously, after sorting out legal wrangles over his sacking from Celtic. Albion were struggling, one place off the bottom of the table as they adjusted to life under new boss Alan Buckley, their ninth manager in ten years.

It rained all day until just before kick-off, when as Lou Macari appeared from the tunnel, the skies, as if in reverence, cleared to reveal glorious sunshine. Stoke were clearly wound up from the start, putting Albion under heavy pressure which finally took its toll when Gary Strodder slipped and allowed Martin Carruthers to score. Carl Muggleton returned the compliment six minutes later, when he dropped a cross at the feet of Bob Taylor, who gratefully equalised, but Stoke tore into Albion once again. Five minutes later Ray Wallace played a neat one-two and blasted home his first goal for the club.

Orlygsson kept City on the offensive. Midway through the second period Peschisolido applied the finishing touch in a goalmouth scramble and Carruthers, having his best game for the club so far, scored the fourth as Stoke cruised to victory. Despite the win, Macari knew there was much work to do in regenerating an ageing squad which had suffered a crisis of confidence under the ineffective Jordan.

LEAGUE DIVISION 1   **1995-96**
Endsleigh Division 1   4th
Coca-Cola Cup   3rd Round
FA Cup   3rd Round

Relegation avoided, Macari conducted major surgery on his squad, letting numerous players go. Wayne Biggins and Keith Downing were released on frees, joining Oxford and Hereford respectively, while John Butler was offered the same terms in the knowledge that that entitled him to a free transfer, as he had been at the club for more than five years. He returned to his former club Wigan. Nigel Gleghorn and Martin Carruthers were offered pay-as-you-play deals, a type of contract Stoke had pioneered the previous season, which allowed players to put themselves in the shop window. Despite the departures, Macari still had no money to spend. He hoped to buy Lee Martin of Celtic, Alan McLoughlin of Portsmouth and Mark Walters of Liverpool, but as their combined fees topped £1 million the moves were not sanctioned.

The reason for the directors' parsimony was the continuing saga over relocation. The decision to press ahead with plans for a new stadium had been taken over the summer and fans now voiced concerns about the design of Stoke's new home. One of the biggest advantages of the Vic was that it was an intimidating place to visit and the testimony of City players through the ages proved how the Boothen End was, in effect, a twelfth man. After an open meeting, where one director's remark that 'fans like big bowls like Old Trafford' brought howls of derision, the worry was that the new ground would be a concrete cavern, devoid of atmosphere. Given the lack of investment in the team, it could even be hosting Second Division football.

More intrigue was afoot when it was revealed that Independent Supporters organisation, SCISA, led by Lester Hughes, had made a bid to invest funds on behalf of Staffordshire businessman Keith Sutherland. Chairman Coates rejected the offer, saying, 'We live within our overdraft and within our means. We can manage our finances and are currently looking at ways to improve our income.' Why then were Sutherland's advances rejected?

Joining the coaching staff was Mike Pejic, Stoke's former left-back of the 1970s. Renowned as a disciplinarian, Pejic replaced Asa Hartford, who departed to Manchester City to partner Alan Ball. Stoke finally filled the vacant physiotherapist's position with Ian Liversage, who had been at Oldham for ten years.

The team was slow to get going. Ian Cranson began the season recovering from a snapped cruciate ligament, which kept him out until late November. Toddy Orlygsson was left in the cold after announcing that he wanted to leave the club. He would eventually sign for Oldham, with the tribunal setting the fee at £180,000. He departed amid much flak, accusing the club of trying to stifle his career. Keith Scott had proved immobile and lackadaisical and was dropped after remonstrating with some Boothen Stand Paddockers as he trudged off after a home defeat by Oldham. He would not last much longer. Poor early form, coming to a head in a dreadful defeat at Watford, was turned around after City were paired with Chelsea in the Coca-Cola Cup. A 0-0 draw at the Vic restored much of the faith of both players and fans. When Stoke returned from Stamford Bridge with a place in the third round draw, the season took off (see Match of the Season).

League form picked up, helped by a 4-1 victory at promotion favourites Wolves. Mark Prudhoe seized his first opportunity in over a year for senior football, turning in a series of consistent displays that added stability at the back. When Peschisolido injured his knee against Luton, Simon Sturridge grabbed his chance, scoring twice as a substitute versus Luton and, working well with John Gayle, notched a hat-trick at Southend the following week. A run of six wins in seven took Stoke into the play-off zone.

Stoke's three draws in the group phase of the Anglo-Italian Cup meant that as the final game, against Reggiana, could not affect qualification, it was cancelled. The competition itself was scrapped, a reflection of public apathy and an unsavoury incident involving Birmingham in Ancona, whose coach, Masimo Cacciatori, was accused of attacking the referee and starting a mass brawl. Macari suggested an Anglo-Scottish Cup might be a better idea!

In November Macari signed striker Mike Sheron from Norwich. He had cost the Canaries £850,000 from Manchester City fifteen months earlier, but two changes of manager inside a year had seen Sheron rusting away in the reserves. At 23, he needed the challenge of regular first-team football and he arrived in a straight swap for Keith Scott, although Stoke were committed to paying £150,000 once Sheron played 30 games. There were rumours that Norwich manager Martin O'Neill, in the midst of an acrimonious parting of the ways with Chairman Robert Chase to join Leicester, sold Sheron in a fit of pique, deliberately lumbering Norwich with misfit striker Scott. Sheron and Sturridge soon struck up a formidable partnership. Once fit, Sheron's close control and expert finishing brought him media attention, but Sturridge contributed greatly to the team's success. His unselfish running and passing provided Sheron with a number of goals, while 'Studger' finished only one behind his partner in the scoring stakes, with fourteen.

DID YOU KNOW?

Lee Sandford's sale to Sheffield United in 1996 for £450,000 realised the only profit on any player that Alan Ball brought to Stoke City.

Stoke outplayed Premier League Nottingham Forest in the FA Cup, but Forest sneaked a draw and won the replay 2-0. Graham Potter, a Joe Jordan signing from Birmingham, shone at the City Ground. Potter was a boyish 20-year-old whose ability to beat full-backs for pace gave Stoke an added dimension on the left wing. His emergence allowed Macari to switch Nigel Gleghorn inside. At 33, Gleghorn relished the role as playmaker, prompting the team forward from midfield. His passing ability benefited the strikers, who liked the ball to feet on the ground, or played into space ahead of them. Alongside Gleghorn, Kevin Keen was proving a shrewd acquisition. Standing only 5ft 7in, the blond midfielder's diminutive stature belied his committed approach to the game. Completing the midfield quartet was Ray Wallace, who worked hard to cover the ground between both penalty areas, regularly winning the ball back outside Stoke's box and feeding either Gleghorn or Keen. At the back, Larus Sigurdsson was proving almost impossible to pass. His positioning allowed him to pull off tackles which he seemed to have no chance of making. His form brought him to the attention of Icelandic national manager Gudjon Thordarsson, and he played for Iceland 'A' against Slovenia in February. With Stoke riding high in fourth, after a 2-0 win over play-off rivals Barnsley in early March, it appeared that Macari had once again made a silken purse from a sow's ear.

On transfer deadline day Peschisolido was controversially sold back to Birmingham for £475,000. Macari claimed he knew nothing of the deal – being on the training pitch when it was struck – and expressed anger at it. But Pesch's contribution had dwindled, partly due to international commitments with Canada. He had not started a Stoke game since the turn of the year. Even so, it seemed a low price to pay for an international forward. Attention was diverted by Mike Sheron's club record run of seven goals in seven League games, one of which was a last-gasp winner as City won their first away match in four months, at Luton. Five wins out of the last seven games put Stoke into the play-offs.

The board finally sought fans' opinion when they took members of the Oatcake's editorial team on a fact-finding mission to Middlesbrough's new Cellnet stadium, upon which Stoke's new ground was to be based. There was debate about a name for the stadium. Many suggested the Stanley Matthews Stadium, in honour of the

Life President, but Stan, as ever, bashfully declined the honour. Permission was granted by the football licensing authority to play at the Vic for one more year, even though Stoke had exceeded the three-year limit on their non all-seated arena.

The new stadium was to be built and owned by the Stoke-on-Trent Regeneration Company, in which both the club and council owned shares, and would cost in the region of £19 million. The council agreed to plough in £4.5 million, £3 million came from the Football Trust, £1 million from the brewers McEwans, which included sponsorship of the main stand, and £2.6 million was raised from a number of banks. This still left Stoke City to find £6 million. The move was officially approved by National Heritage Secretary Virginia Bottomley on 13 May, as City were embroiled in the end of season play-offs against Martin O'Neill's Leicester, whom they had beaten twice in the League. Stoke had the better of a tense 0-0 draw at Filbert Street, but when it came to the crunch Stoke turned in their worst home performance of the season and the Foxes won 1-0. The fact that Leicester made it into the Premiership, where they have remained ever since, rubbed salt into the wounds.

The rewards of winning the play-offs were huge. The difference between just one season in the Premiership (as is the fate of most First Division play-off winners) and another in Division Two was put at £4 million – enough to clear Stoke's debts as the club announced a £1.89 million loss on the financial year. City fans could not understand why, with such riches at the end of a fairly short rainbow, the board did not speculate, investing in quality talent to push for promotion. Furthermore, the Potteries was an area in structural decline, with the traditional pottery and coal-mining industries mere shadows of their former selves. These factors explained why, despite the most successful season in a decade, Stoke's crowds dipped by 10 per cent. Those fans who did turn up made it quite clear that they were supporting the team in spite of the increasingly remote board.

Match of the Season 1995-96
Chelsea 0 Stoke 1
Coca-Cola Cup, 2nd Round, 2nd leg, 4 October 1995

Stoke's poor start to the season saw them languishing two places off the bottom when they were paired with Glenn Hoddle's Chelsea in the Coca-Cola Cup. Just a week earlier Macari had replaced want-away midfielder Orlygsson with inexperienced left-winger Graham Potter, while reinstating Mark Prudhoe in goal in place of Carl

Muggleton. These changes had prompted an improved performance to hold Tranmere to a draw. Chelsea were resurgent under Glenn Hoddle, having reached the semi-finals of the European Cup-Winners' Cup and an FA Cup final. Their lynchpin was former Dutch international midfielder Ruud Gullit, who had started the season impressively as a sweeper in Hoddle's new system.

Stoke had the better of the first leg at the Vic. Vince Overson headed against the bar and Carruthers twice wasted chances to score. Chelsea emerged unscathed with a goalless draw. Between the two legs Stoke's form continued to improve as they beat West Brom and drew at high-flying Crystal Palace. Chelsea beat Arsenal 1-0 but the Blues were still short of goals. Their principal source was veteran Welsh international striker Mark Hughes, whose tally was three in nine games. Former Stoke golden boy Mark Stein rarely got a look in, although he was named as a substitute for the second game.

Stamford Bridge was undergoing huge changes in the mid-1990s and Stoke's fans were housed in a temporary stand at what had been the Shed End, where the new Chelsea Village hotel complex was being built. On a balmy evening all the attacking was done by Chelsea. Their measured, constructive approach created numerous half chances and it only seemed a matter of time before they scored. Stoke's new-found resilience, founded on Vince Overson, allowed the Potters back into the game. A series of crunching tackles cut the supply to strikers Hughes and Paul Furlong. Chelsea's frustration began to show and, with fifteen minutes to go, Hughes, foraging deep to receive the ball, was harried by Wallace into presenting the ball to Peschisolido. Pesch raced into the area, received a lucky bounce off Sinclair and gleefully swept the ball home.

Chelsea poured forward, missing chance after chance. Stein, on for the final few minutes, poked a glorious opportunity wide when, as they say, it seemed easier to score. Sandford headed off the line the one shot to defeat Prudhoe and the final whistle blew on the shock of the round.

The win was Stoke's first against a team from a higher division since Norwich in the Littlewoods Cup in 1987. Lightning could not be expected to strike twice and a 0-4 defeat at home to Kevin Keegan's Premier League leaders Newcastle in the next round was only to be expected.

LEAGUE DIVISION 1   **1996-97**
Nationwide Division 1   12th
Coca-Cola Cup   3rd Round
FA Cup   3rd Round

The valedictory season at the Victoria Ground was one of preparing for the biggest upheaval in the club's history. The all-consuming ground move swallowed cash, severely affecting the team's fortunes on the field. By early October the foundation piles of the steel superstructure had been driven into the soil high on the hill looking down on the city. The project had just ten months to be completed, giving rise to a nervous year for chief executive Jez Moxey and developers St Modwen's. The construction company, Mowlem's, were given a deadline of 1 July, which would then allow six weeks for the start of the new season. Supporters, divided on the issue, either saw the ground as a new start, or a millstone around the club's neck, or both.

The first ramifications of the move became clear in the summer of 1996. Eleven players refused to sign the initial contracts on offer, of which Cranson, Whittle, Keen, Overson and Gleghorn were the highest profile. The latter pair left for Burnley, and Gleghorn, in particular, was outspoken in his criticism of the club, revealing that the difference between what he asked and what he was offered was a mere £50 per week. Cranson, Keen and Whittle eventually re-signed. Funds were generated by the sale of Graham Potter to Southampton for £300,000 and Lee Sandford to Sheffield United for £450,000. The board did permit Macari to spend £200,000 on Birmingham midfielder Richard Forsyth, who became the first signing to cost money since Keith Scott in 1994. Coventry right-back Ally Pickering signed for a tribunal-fixed fee of £300,000. The only other arrival, Leeds' experienced left-back, Nigel Worthington, came on a free. Stoke also bade farewell to Tony Lacey after 24 years' involvement with the youth set-up which had seen him develop the likes of Garth Crooks, Adrian Heath and Paul Bracewell.

With the team losing three of its most consistent performers of recent years, two of them club captains, supporters were downbeat about the club's prospects, so an opening five-match unbeaten run took many by surprise and Stoke to the top of the League. Macari was manager of the month and talk was of starting the following season with a brand new stadium in the Premiership. A 0-3 defeat at Barnsley pulled the wool from the eyes and prompted Macari to sign Spurs' Northern Ireland international winger Gerry McMahon for £250,000 and midfielder Graham Kavanagh, after an initial loan spell, from Middlesbrough, also for £250,000. The chairman claimed that these signings, and Sheron's acceptance of a two-year contract extension, 'demonstrates we are an ambitious club and anxious for Premier League football.' For a moment even some of the sceptics were taken in, until ever-present central defender John Dreyer, in the best form of his career, was sold to Bradford City for £25,000.

The huge upsurge of football fever that accompanied England's performances as hosts of Euro '96 prompted BSkyB to pay a record £674 million over five years for the rights to show live Premiership football. The gap between the haves and have-nots was now a yawning chasm, although Sky also purchased the rights to show Nationwide League football, guaranteeing each First Division club £1 million per season. None of this would be much help to cash-strapped Stoke if they slipped back into the Second. The club's turnover of £5 million was lower than that of many 'smaller' clubs, including Norwich, West Brom, QPR and Bolton. It begged the question of where would Stoke find their share of the money, amounting to £6 million, for the new stadium. Part of the answer came when the Britannia Building Society confirmed a £1.3 million sponsorship deal. The stadium was to be called the Britannia Stadium and the logo would adorn the team's shirts. It was the biggest deal in the club's history, but over a ten-year period it was not as generous as initially thought. The lion's share would still have to be raised in Stoke's traditional manner, the sale of their best players. Prime contender to bring in a sizeable fee was Mike Sheron. He finished as runner-up in the Nationwide Player of the Year awards to Derby's Igor Stimac and was now the most predatory striker in the division. His strikes at Ipswich and Charlton were international class and a bidding war developed, which the club fanned openly, between Harry Redknapp's West Ham, Trevor Francis' Birmingham and QPR's Stewart Houston.

Behind the scenes yet more shenanigans leaked out from time to time, which did the club no credit. Director Mike Moors offered to put funds into the club and resigned when he was rebuffed 'so the board could pursue alternative arrangements'. These proved to be a link-up with Stan Clarke, the owner of developers St Modwen, who agreed to act as guarantor of the sums involved, in return for acquiring first option on buying shares in the club. It then emerged that Clarke, who had turned around the Staffordshire racecourse of Uttoxeter, had five years to decide whether to take up the shares option, putting Stoke in limbo once again. In an era when clubs of comparable size were going public to raise funds for team-building, Stoke were still in the hands of parochial businessmen. That the board then had the temerity to attack supporters in the press for not supporting a team that had gone from promotion contenders to mid-table also-rans under their stewardship merely served to drive more fans away. Average gates were a mere 12,748, a 21 per cent fall in just three years.

Stoke won one game in seven to drop into mid-table and defeats by Arsenal in the Coca-Cola Cup and Second Division Stockport in the FA Cup effectively ended the season.

Macari's squad, often depleted by international call-ups for Sigurdsson, Worthington and McMahon, proved exceptionally thin. Struggling for available players against Portsmouth, Macari blooded Neil Mackenzie and Andy Griffin, despite the two of them having played for the 'A' team four hours earlier. Worthington eventually lost his place at left-back to Griffin, who produced a string of confident performances, earning a call up for England Under-18s. Injury also deprived Stoke of Ian Cranson, who announced his retirement after having to undergo yet another knee operation. Simon Sturridge damaged ligaments at Barnsley, putting him out for the season.

Stoke's away form was appalling. They lost eight of their final nine away games scoring just one goal, an own-goal at that, in the process. Fortunately, home form held up as the landmark games came and went. Stoke won the last evening game and drew the last Saturday match, while Port Vale were soundly beaten 2-0 in the last Potteries derby at the Vic.

Ominously, on the eve of the Vale match, news came that Lou Macari would vacate his position as manager at the end of the season. He initially claimed it was to allow him to concentrate on his £400,000 litigation with Celtic, which was due to come to court early the following season, although prior to the final game Peter Coates announced that Macari had been 'stripped of his responsibilities'. Soon after leaving, Macari launched a lawsuit against Stoke for wrongful dismissal, claiming that 'as soon as I said I might be leaving people were coming up to me with their diaries saying "When are you going then?" I cannot work in an environment like that.' Less of a mystery was the departure of Mike Sheron who signed for QPR for £2.75 million at the end of the season. His fee conveniently matched the deficit required to complete the new stadium. The widely predicted impact on the team of the move to a new ground had struck its most damaging blow.

The season was kept alive by the nostalgia of the Vic, which hosted its last League match on 4 May 1997 (see Match of the Season). Chief Executive Jez Moxey predicted that the move to the Britannia Stadium would mark the beginning of a new, successful era, proving that the club had ambition. Not many shared his optimism.

> **DID YOU KNOW?**
>
> Stoke always lose replayed FA Cup-ties abandoned when they were ahead – Reading (home, 1913, fog), Doncaster (away, 1930, snow) and Oldham (home, 1979, fog).

Match of the Season 1996-97

Stoke 2   West Brom 1

Division 1, 4 May 1997

The last League game at the Victoria Ground was a stomach-churning occasion. The club had set up a special day for the fans. Alan Hudson, Gordon Banks, Eric Skeels and George Berry appeared in a pre-game celebrity kick-about against former West Brom players, among them Jeff Astle. There was also a parade of Stoke heroes from earlier eras, including the likes of Stan Matthews, Johnny King, Jimmy O'Neill and Dennis Wilshaw. To great cheers Sir Stan symbolically scored one last goal at the Boothen End. Fans also competed for prizes for the best fancy dress costume, which attracted a large number of entrants, and best banner.

After a downpour drenched the pitch, the two teams took to the field in blazing sunshine for a re-run of the first League game to be played at the ground, which West Brom had won 2-0 on 8 September 1888. But Stoke won this game thanks to a McMahon diving header and Kavanagh's lob over the advancing Alan Miller. With five minutes left Justin Whittle gave away a penalty, which Andy Hunt converted, to slightly dampen the occasion, but the scenes at the final whistle brought tears to the eyes of hardened supporters. Outpourings of emotion greeted the departing Macari and Sheron as they circled the pitch, but most of the capacity crowd were there to say goodbye to the Victoria Ground which had played such an important part in their lives. Fans lingered for hours after the game to sit quietly and reflect on their favourite matches and moments. Lou Macari bade farewell by saying, 'It has been a humbling experience to have this duty to discharge.'

The Vic was the oldest remaining League football ground in the world, second only to non-league Northwich Victoria's Drill Field, to be in continuous use since 1874. The Boothen End was the largest terrace left in Britain, holding a much reduced capacity of 9,000. The Victoria Ground was demolished at the end of 1997. The pitch's turf sold out in hours at £5 per square half-metre.

Boughey shoots wide with Blackburn keeper Terry Gennoe looking on (April 1990)

Alan Ball's 1990-91 squad, with coach Graham Paddon, extreme left (August 1990)

Noel Blake heads City's first goal of the 1990-91 season v Rotherham (August 1990)

'Bertie' Biggins fires past Swansea keeper Lee Bracey (December 1990)

Blake and Gallimore guide Cambridge's Steve Claridge away from goal (April 1991)

A second Wembley win, the Autoglass Trophy against Stockport (May 1992)

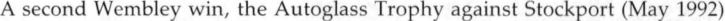

The 1991-92 squad proudly display the Autoglass Trophy (July 1992)

Skipper Vince Overson lifts the Second Division trophy (May 1993)

Lou Macari celebrates winning the Second Division championship (May 1993)

Party-time for two of the Stoke faithful as City win the Division Two title

## 6

RULE BRITANNIA
1997-2000

LEAGUE DIVISION 1	**1997-98**
Nationwide Division 1	23rd (Relegated)
Coca-Cola Cup	3rd Round
FA Cup	3rd Round

The dawn of the new era at the Britannia Stadium should have been full of hope, but the departure of Macari – still not fully explained – plus the farcical search for a replacement, left fans wondering exactly what was going on. Many felt the board's delay in naming Macari's successor was just a ruse to boost season ticket sales. Initially the board announced that an appointment would be made by the end of May, as the man they wanted – believed to be Sammy McIlroy, manager of League new boys Macclesfield – was under contract. The ensuing silence was deafening and Chic Bates, in his caretaker capacity, assumed responsibility for developing the squad. It became increasingly obvious that Bates would be named manager and after much prevarication, in late July, he was.

Bates had proved to be an excellent coach, but he was out of his depth in the hot seat. By early September former boss Alan Durban, who had given Bates his first chance in football at Shrewsbury, was invited back as assistant manager to take the weight off Bates' shoulders.

If Stoke had bade farewell to the Victoria Ground in a blaze of glory, then the fiasco surrounding the opening of the new stadium was a pit of despair. From the outset there were problems actually getting there. The plans catered for only one access road from the nearby A50. That meant that spectators arriving from the City and the motorway, the vast majority, had to travel up the A50 for over a mile to a roundabout, then double-back on themselves on the other side of the dual carriageway. This resulted in hideous tail-backs. Those on foot fared equally badly. The footbridge, allowing access from the canalside path that led to the city centre, was barely wide enough to carry the large number of supporters who chose to walk.

Problems emerged after matches, as the area became dangerously crowded. There was also congestion around the ticket office, as tickets could not be bought at turnstiles. With spectators already fed up with the effort of getting to the ground, to ask them to queue up for just seven booths was folly. Congestion was such that many fans missed much of the first half. Although tickets were soon made available on all gates around the stadium, visitors to the club shop discovered that for several months it was not even equipped to take its own credit cards.

The three open corners of the ground meant that the wind buffeted round the stadium, causing a nuisance for fans and the bizarre sight of the four corner flags blowing in different directions. For the opening fixture, against Swindon, pre-match ceremonies included a 'sing-alike' Tom Jones who led the crowd in a dreadfully out of time rendition of 'Delilah'. The crowning glory was to be Sir Stanley Matthews officially declaring the stadium open by scoring at the new 'Boothen End', the North Stand, just as he had done to close the Vic.

Stupidly, the ball was placed on the edge of the penalty area and 82-year-old Stan's 'shot' was whisked away by the wind, coming to rest just outside the six-yard box. This high farce symbolised Stoke's season. Stan declared that watching City at the Brit was 'like watching Stoke play away from home' and he attended only a handful of games at the new ground. While acknowledging the difficulties of a project the size and complexity of the Britannia Stadium, the club brought many of the problems on itself by not listening to supporters' concerns, particularly over the access issue, during the planning stage.

Before long the rumblings turned into actual dissent. In the third home game two fans invaded the pitch at half-time with a banner proclaiming 'Coates out', which precipitated chants of 'Stand up if you want Coates out' from around the ground.

At least Stoke had a new avenue to explore in their quest to find cheap players. Jean-Marc Bosman, a Belgian footballer, had won a test case in the European court of Human Rights which allowed him to leave a club for free at the end of his contract. Stoke took advantage as Paul Stewart (Sunderland), Dutchman Dick Schreuder from JC Roda, Zay Angola, formerly known as Jose Andrade, who had been at the club during the 1994-95 season, and Scottish central defender Steven Tweed, from Greek club Ionikos, all arrived on frees. The only signing to cost money was 24-year-old striker Peter Thorne. He had the onerous responsibility of following in Sheron's footsteps and would cost the club £550,000, after appearances were taken into consideration. Coates' justification of the club's failure to invest in the team – 'some clubs have spent money and failed' – had supporters scratching their heads in disbelief.

City were already in serious trouble. The team failed to adjust to playing at the 'Brit' as it did not feel like home to either players or fans. Visiting teams would be inspired by the superb facilities, including warm-up gymnasium, and the vast acres of empty home seats in the ground. In attack, Thorne and Stewart proved one-paced and lacking in finishing ability. Two goals in the first five games did not bode well, and around Christmas five successive losses, including a first ever defeat by Crewe, set the scene for the second half of the season.

The slump was brought to a head early in the New Year. Nine players discovered via the *Sentinel* that they were no longer required by the club – McMahon, McNally, Andrade, Birch, Woods, Devlin, Nyamah, and Mike and Paul Macari. Six of these faced Birmingham's reserves two days later and were hammered 0-4. Three days later the Blues' first team thrashed Stoke 0-7 at the Brit. The team were effectively striking in support of their unwanted colleagues. There were ugly scenes at the final whistle as 2,000 fans invaded the pitch with some climbing the McEwans stand in an attempt to stampede the directors box. The result was, after all, Stoke's worst ever home defeat, surpassing the 1-6 inflicted by Spurs in 1951.

Early exits in the League and FA Cup – a 1-3 loss at West Brom, which brought to an end Stoke's long unbeaten run against the Baggies stretching back nearly a decade – left morale at an all-time low. For the visit of Bradford City, Stoke fans organised a protest and the watching world, courtesy of Sky TV, saw 2,000 supporters enter fifteen minutes into the game bearing placards with the words 'Coates Out!' The protests stirred the board into action.

Coates resigned as chairman, handing over to Keith Humphreys. Their shareholding was unchanged. Although it was claimed that new investors were sought, the club's record of stone-walling any attempt to inject money, giving the appearance of denying outside interference in a closed-shop, meant that this was taken with a big pinch of salt. The sale of the Vic to St Modwen, the developers of the Britannia Stadium, for £1 million (half the asking price and £6 million less than the value of the stadium in the club's assets column) raised more questions. Once again, fans felt that their club had been undersold. In fact, Stan Clarke insisted he had no interest in taking control of the club, investing in Brighton racecourse in the same week. SCISA staged a meeting at the King's Hall in Stoke, at which motions of no confidence in the board and in chief executive Jez Moxey were carried by over 2,000 fans. They also decided to boycott the club shop, season tickets, and Stadia Catering's produce in an attempt to topple the board. It was felt that such extreme action was necessary to effect change, even though it was likely to damage the club in the short term. Relegation had already been accepted. The board's response was to demote Bates to first-team coach, replacing him with ex-Bradford City manager Chris Kamara. The sideways shuffle convinced no one of anything.

As a player, Kamara had been headstrong and reactionary, and his managerial style was no different. He arrived claiming, 'Stoke is a sleeping monster. We're going to build a squad for the Premier League,' but one of his first acts was to sell the only classy player the club had left. Andy Griffin left for Kenny Dalglish's Newcastle for £1.5 million. Kamara sacked coach Mike Pejic, replacing him with his former Bradford City coach Martin Hunter, and introduced a ghetto-blaster into the dressing room in an effort to pep up the team before games. This innovation had little effect other than to inspire cheeky letters to the *Sentinel*, suggesting that it play 'The Only Way is Up' and 'Heaven Knows I'm Miserable Now'. Kamara used 31 players in his thirteen games in charge and, after winning just once, resorted to slamming his players in the press. On deadline day, appropriately April Fool's Day, he put the entire squad up for sale. No club made an offer for any Stoke player. After a 0-3 home defeat by Tranmere, Kamara quit. His three-month tenure had seen City plummet into the relegation zone. Declaring Kamara's appointment as 'a nightmare for all concerned', Humphreys handed the reigns to Alan Durban, who was given the task of trying to pull Stoke clear of the relegation zone.

So despairing were Stoke fans that during the defeat by Huddersfield they began singing 'Bring on the Hippo', referring to the club mascot, Pottermus! The portly Hippo went on to finish seventh in the club's player of the season awards, won, astonishingly by bit-part player Justin Whittle.

Three wins in four home games gave Stoke hope but a heavy defeat by Manchester City on the last day (see Match of the Season) confirmed what had seemed inevitable all along. Relegation. The perceived arrogance of those at the helm, in the face of the club's total collapse, attracted even more condemnation. At the AGM, Jez Moxey claimed that the club's problems stemmed from the fans' protests which 'let the side down'. Shares in Stoke City traditionally changed hands for a £1. Those at the top were now apparently holding out for £15 per share, and when this became public knowledge there was uproar. A protest group called SOS (Save Our Stoke) was formed by an irate fan, Tim Gallimore, which demanded that the club's affairs be made more public. Stoke were £4.3 million in debt, had no manager, and were back in the Second Division.

DID YOU KNOW?

Peter Dobing, Stoke's skipper in the 1972 League Cup final, once appeared as 12th man for the Lancashire cricket team in a Roses county match against Yorkshire.

Match of the Season 1997-98
Stoke 2 Manchester City 5
Division 1, 3 May 1998

Both teams went into this game knowing that defeat spelled certain relegation and that even a win might not be enough. The other four relegation candidates – Port Vale, QPR, Bury and Portsmouth – had a mixed bag of fixtures. Six clubs were vying to avoid the last two relegation places, Reading being doomed, but Stoke and Man City filled them at start of play and needed favours from others if either was to escape. With their 4,000 allocation sold out, during the week Manchester City fans had driven south in droves to buy tickets from Stoke, despite the policy of strict segregation. This led to problems during the game, the first ever sell-out at the Brit.

Live on Sky, mainly due to the involvement of Man City, the Blues took the game by the scruff of the neck. Goater lobbed the portly Southall from 25 yards to put them 1-0 ahead at the break. Stoke rarely threatened.

The half-time scores were not encouraging, as each of the other four teams involved was winning. Man City scored early in the second half through an unmarked Dickov, before Thorne replied in similar fashion. By this stage it was clear that each of the other four relegation candidates would win easily, leaving Stoke and Man City to play out time. Stoke collapsed and allowed three more goals, while scoring what in other situations might be called a consolation themselves. The Man City fans supported their side to the death while Stoke's fans reacted angrily to another dreadful performance. There were numerous ejections and post-match scuffles as Stoke's hoodlum element chucked bricks at departing Manchester fans. In town that evening, Stoke and Port Vale fans clashed while the Valiants were celebrating their escape from relegation. After viewing closed-circuit TV camera footage, police arrested 28 fans in dawn raids on homes on the Potteries over the summer. Disgraced at all turns, Stoke City was now at its lowest ebb.

LEAGUE DIVISION 2   **1998-99**
Nationwide Division 2   8th
Worthington Cup   2nd Round
FA Cup   2nd Round

Jez Moxey predicted Stoke would lose around £1 million through being in Division Two for just *one* season. Such was the price the board paid for the mismanagement of the previous two years. In a bid to retain fans' interest, a freeze on ticket prices was announced with special deals for children and families introduced. During the summer Keith Humphreys apologised to fans for the 'bloody awful nine months' but pleaded that the season ticket and merchandise bans, spearheaded by Save Our Stoke, should be lifted. SOS leader Tim Gallimore pointed out that the intention was indeed to harry the current board to the point where they would have to sell the club to those prepared to breathe life and, more importantly, money into Stoke City. SOS appeared to hold sway. Just 4,500 season-ticket holders renewed, a drop of nearly 1,000.

It came as a welcome surprise when Humphreys announced that Brian Little would be Stoke's new manager. Little was an experienced manager, having resuscitated Darlington after their demotion from the Football League in 1989 and led them to two successive promotions before being lured to Leicester. The board believed that his record of wheeling and dealing during his time at Darlington made him perfectly suited to Stoke's current situation. Some detractors pointed to his subsequent record of having baled out of both the Leicester and Aston Villa jobs when the pressure mounted. Having walked out of Villa, Little had been recuperating in Mallorca when contacted by Stoke. For once the board had exceeded fans' expectations. Little assembled his own managerial team of assistant manager Tony McAndrew, Allan Evans as coach, and Ian Cranson as reserve-team coach. Durban and Bates were dispensed with, which seemed sensible, given the need for a complete change of direction. There were thirteen departures from the playing staff, including McMahon and Stewart, as Stoke cut its wage-bill, and a new physiotherapist arrived, Rob Ryles.

Accepting the fact that there was no money, Little exploited his knowledge of the lower divisions to sign some experienced players. He lured defenders Chris Short from Sheffield United, Bryan Small from Bury, and Phil Robinson from Notts County, plus midfielder David Oldfield from Luton, all on free transfers. He clung on to star midfielder Graham Kavanagh, despite Moxey confirming that 'every player is available at the right price'. Aberdeen's £450,000 bid was rejected as Stoke were holding out for £1 million.

DID YOU KNOW?

During Stoke's tour of Australasia in 1973, John Ritchie scored all 8 goals in the win over New Zealand side Otago. That remains an individual record for Stoke City.

Little's new-look side set off with a bang, winning seven League games on the trot, a club record from the start of the season, and a manager of the month award for Little in his first month in the job. The run was reward for a tactical switch to a 5-3-2 formation, with Small and Short operating as wing-backs. In attack Dean Crowe and Peter Thorne looked a cut above most Second Division defenders. A 4-3 win at Preston saw Stoke installed as 9-4 favourites for promotion. A rapid exit from the League Cup (now sponsored by Worthington) at the hands of Sammy McIlroy's Macclesfield put things into perspective. It was the first time Stoke had been knocked out in the first round of the competition in its 38-year history, and provided supporters with another glimpse of the behind-the-scenes workings of the club. Jez Moxey divulged that City had budgeted for three cup rounds and thereby lost some £125,000 in anticipated revenue. Given Stoke's appalling record in cup competitions this seemed a crass assumption to make.

As John Cleese's character in the film Clockwise said, 'It's not the despair. Despair I can handle. It's the hope. The hope I can't cope with.' Stoke's good start was too good to last. The reality was that it was impossible to turn around a shambolic club so quickly. Stoke's run came to an end at promotion favourites Fulham where, alarmingly, Chris Short was carried off the pitch having suffered a breathing problem. He was out of action for a month, disrupting the balance of the five-man defence. The mystery condition would eventually end his career. Up front, the goals started to dry up. £500,000 striker Kyle Lightbourne, signed by Kamara, but out for six months due to a blood disorder, was still not fully fit and Simon Sturridge's career had been ended by his cartilage problems. The injuries checked City's progress, while David Oldfield suffered loss of form and became the target of the boo-boys. The experienced midfielder possessed good passing ability but lacked pace and bite in the tackle. This gave an impression of lack of commitment, which Stoke fans will never tolerate.

Stoke won their first away FA Cup-tie in 26 years against League opponents. Their victims were Reading, 1-0, in the first round, but normal service was resumed in the second when Third Division Swansea won 1 0. There was no joy either in the Auto Windscreens Shield, with an embarrassing exit to Rochdale 1-2, which brought new levels of humiliation. Not only did the team muster just one shot against Third Division opposition, but the players were openly squabbling among themselves on the pitch. While promotion rivals Fulham were splashing out £2 million on Bristol Rovers striker Barry Hayles, whose goals would push them to the championship, City had to be content with blooding a number of reserves. Free transfer imports Ben Petty and Lee Collins came from Aston Villa, centre-half Greg Strong arrived on loan from Bolton, while midfielder James O'Connor was promoted from Stoke's second team.

Stoke won one game between Christmas and the beginning of March, dropping out of the play-off scene entirely. The knives were out, particularly after a humiliating 0-2 defeat by nine-man Millwall, about which Little said: 'That was the worst result in my twelve years in management.' During the game at Bloomfield Road, Stoke and Blackpool fans staged the first ever combined protest with 1,000 black balloons being released. At the next home game the Oatcake issued 5,000 red cards to be brandished towards the directors box. Moxey countered by saying that he only saw three cards waved. A 2-3 defeat by Notts County four days later prompted all 5,000 to be displayed simultaneously, as Stoke lost their sixth home game in a row. The board countered by offering seats at £5 per head and £1 for juniors for the game against Bristol Rovers. But in front of a bumper 17,500 crowd, Stoke lost 1-4 (see Match of the Season). The board were hoist by their own petard.

Little's final fling was to sign keeper Gavin Ward from Bolton and Nicky Mohan, a centre-half from Wycombe, on free transfers. They would be the last arrivals. In February the club declared that it had exceeded its overdraft limit and now lacked funds to pay the wages of any further loanees. The AGM revealed that the wage bill had risen to £3.3 million, up £1 million on 1996-97.

With the club seemingly disintegrating, Lester Hughes, chairman of the SCISA, attempted to put together a supporters' buy-out. Through the pages of the *Sentinel*, fans were invited to donate £200 to secure their place in the consortium. Hughes cited the recent example of Bournemouth, where a similar situation had led to a successful takeover and the saving of the club. Stoke replied to this initiative by publicly stating that it would listen to any serious offer. Hughes raised £250,000 in a week, with £6,000 being pledged by the Scandinavian supporters' branch, but the target of £2 million was never close to being achieved.

Brian Little had lost interest long before the season's end, and on his return from holiday he resigned, saying 'I have tried my best and the disappointment is very hard to take. I hope the supporters understand that it's the right time for me to go.' Eleven days before the start of the new season, he was installed as the new manager at

West Brom. That appointment led to Stoke receiving compensation to cover the costs of terminating the contracts of Little's backroom staff, Allan Evans and Tony McAndrew. Speculation about Little's successor started immediately. Among the names canvassed were Adrian Heath, Sammy McIlroy, John Rudge, Steve McMahon, and Tony Pulis.

Match of the Season 1998-99
Stoke 1   Bristol Rovers 4

Division 2, 22 August 1998

A large crowd of 17,823 responded to Stoke's ticket price-slashing for this game. There was still a glimmer of hope of a play-off place, if the team put together a good run, but there had been protests at each of the last five home matches and more were expected should City fail against Rovers. The visitors were angry that Stoke should reduce admission prices for home fans, but not theirs, and Rovers' directors joined Rovers' fans in the South Stand in protest. Stoke could not even get a gesture of goodwill right.

The Pirates, managed by Ian Holloway, enjoyed the blossoming partnership of Jason Roberts (nephew of former Stoke striker Dave Regis) and Jamie Cureton. Brian Little's line-up lacked width and struggled to make an impression from the start. With Robinson playing in midfield, and Strong having a nightmare at centre-half, Stoke fell back under Rovers' pressure. Roberts, in particular, had the beating of Bryan Small on the left. Yet Stoke went ahead against the run of play when Thorne nodded in Kavanagh's cross. A lucky lead at home! Could this be the turning point? Far from it. Rovers stormed forward after the interval and scored four times without reply. Stoke capitulated in the last ten minutes: Foster headed home unmarked and Cureton twice beat Muggleton. Stoke even managed to waste a penalty, when Kavanagh fired wide from the spot.

The manner and scale of defeat sparked noisy protests. Several hundred fans from the North Stand invaded the pitch and some of the players were manhandled, including striker Kyle Lightbourne, who, disgracefully, received a punch to the head. Sick of these humiliations heaped upon them by the board, supporters performed an hour-long sit-down protest on the pitch. There now appeared to be open warfare between supporters and the ruling regime. Stoke City were coming apart at the seams.

LEAGUE DIVISION 2   **1999-2000**
Nationwide Division 2   6th (lost in play-offs)
Worthington Cup   2nd Round
FA Cup   1st Round

For the third consecutive summer, Stoke were hunting for a new manager. This time the club's search took a new and humiliating twist when Tony Pulis, their first choice, joined Bristol City instead, openly admitting that he felt Stoke lacked ambition. Second choice was Gary Megson, a hard-working and honest manager who had previously been in charge at Norwich, his last club as a player, and Stockport. Megson accepted the challenge and brought in former Middlesbrough skipper Nigel Pearson as first-team coach. The final addition to the backroom staff was the surprise appointment as football executive of former Port Vale boss John Rudge. Rudge was renowned as one of the best managers outside the Premiership, but had been sacked five months previously as Vale struggled against relegation. Some Stoke fans felt that his appointment showed just how desperate City had become. In reality it was one of the best appointments the club has ever made. Rudge has always got the best from players he has worked with, allowing Robbie Earle, Mark Bright and Steve Guppy to enjoy careers in the Premiership, not to mention earning Vale a sizeable income in transfer fees. His role was to do precisely that for Stoke.

There was little expectation of anything other than a season of consolidation. A second round defeat by Sheffield Wednesday in the Worthington Cup at least gave Stoke the satisfaction of holding the Premiership's bottom side to a goalless draw at the Brit. There was steady, if unspectacular, progress, but as the team grew in confidence they put together a run of seven wins in nine matches to climb into third place.

As the financial situation grew ever more perilous, Megson was forced to sell Larus Sigurdsson to West Brom for £350,000. This seemed perverse, given that Stoke had rejected Aberdeen's £500,000 bid over the summer, but the club now reasoned that with his contract up the following year it was better to cash in than lose out entirely. It looked as though Kavanagh and Thorne would be the next to go to balance the books. To add to their woes, Stoke were knocked out of the FA Cup at Blackpool before the end of October and embarked upon an eternity of 368 minutes without a goal.

Into this arena stepped the club's saviours. An Icelandic-based consortium tabled a bid for Stoke City that could not be ignored. As details emerged it became clear that one of the provisos was the replacement of Megson with former Icelandic national team boss

Gudjon Thordarsson, who had led his team to within a whisker of qualification for Euro 2000 – no mean feat for a country that had never qualified for anything. Many fans bridled at this condition, arguing that Megson was doing a creditable job on scant resources. An orchestrated campaign ensued, fuelled by the media, that Megson should stay. It was only later that it emerged that the whole deal was in fact the brainchild of Thordarsson himself. He had regularly visited Stoke in his capacity as manager of Iceland to watch Toddy Orlygsson and Larus Sigurdsson, and had observed the potential of the club at first hand. Megson, it appeared, would become a casualty of circumstance.

The takeover was officially completed on 15 November, and at a press conference at the Britannia Stadium more details emerged. The consortium had acquired a 66 per cent holding in Stoke City, now owned by a company called Stoke Holding. The plan was to restructure the club's debts so that the crippling interest payments no longer impeded the club from signing new players. For the first time in years, the people in charge of Stoke City were speaking of how things could be achieved rather than why they couldn't. The new board members included Gunnar Thor Gislason, who became the youngest League club chairman at the age of 34 and 'Sigi' Sigurvinsson, an Icelandic international of the early 1980s, who, in 1984 had been voted Germany's Sportsman of the Year whilst with Stuttgart.

The residual misgivings relating to Megson's sacking were soon cast aside as the team, featuring two new signings brought in by Thordarsson, thrashed Wycombe 4-0 away from home in his first game in charge. 'It's just like watching Iceland!' sang the huge travelling support. One of the first actions of the new board was to institute a regular 'fans' forum', where supporters groups could send delegates to air their views about any issue involving the club. After the previous incumbents 'head in the sand' attitude towards supporters, this proved popular and extremely constructive, helping to deal with issues such as the proposed moving of season-ticket holders from their existing seats in the North Stand, which was scrapped after discussion at the forum.

On 23 February arguably the greatest footballer the world has seen, Sir Stanley Matthews, died at the age of 85. Stan's career had spanned a remarkable 33 years during which he had won 54 England caps, played in 734 League games and won the inaugural Footballer of the Year and European Footballer of the Year trophies. Stan's health had been causing concern for several years, but the death of his wife, six years his junior, had hit him hard. It seemed as if football's greatest survivor had died of a broken heart. Pele called him 'the Sport's greatest ambassador'. His pall-bearers included Bobby Charlton, Gordon Banks, Nat Lofthouse and Geoff Hurst. Flowers festooned his statue, which stands in Stoke city centre.

Three days after his death, at Wigan's new JJB Stadium, the club were once again disgraced by the antics of a minority of louts who reacted to the breaking by home fans of the minute's silence in Sir Stan's honour. Fighting spewed onto the pitch and the teams had to be taken off, returning after nine minutes once the huge police presence had restored order. It later emerged that challenges had been issued via the internet between rival factions which had stirred up the prospect of trouble well in advance. The club's stated intention of eradicating the hooligan element through indefinite bans must be strictly adhered to if there is to be any improvement in City's reputation. Figures released at the end of season showed Stoke as the club with the third highest number of fans in the country banned from attending matches. The thugs who besmirch Stoke's name with incessant regularity know no shame and should be added to this list.

This aspect of the season apart, the club went from strength to strength. City sailed through the early rounds of the Auto Windscreens Shield and a 4-1 aggregate victory over Rochdale in the Northern final sent Stoke back to Wembley to face Bristol City in the real final. A near sell-out crowd of 75,000 witnessed an exciting contest. Graham Kavanagh opened the scoring for Stoke with a mazy run and shot. Bristol City fought back, equalised from a corner-kick, and looked the more likely winners until Peter Thorne popped up to ensure Stoke maintained their 100 per cent record under the Twin Towers.

The excitement caused by the Wembley win was increased by an extraordinary run of form in the League. Stoke won nine and drew the other four of thirteen League games. The team was playing exhilarating football, utilising an attacking 5-3-2 formation under Thordarsson, whose arrival sparked an influx of other players from Arctic climes. Brynjar Gunnarsson, a 24-year-old Icelandic central defender – also at home in defensive midfield – arrived for £509,000 from Swedish club Orgryte, while Mikael Hansson, a right wing-back, arrived from Norkopping on a free. The manager brought in Leicester's Icelandic left-winger, Arnar Gunnlaugsson, on loan and even signed his own son, midfielder Bjarni Gudjonsson, from Genk of Belgium for £250,000.

While the team was on its winning roll, no one player deserved more acclaim than Peter Thorne. He had taken flak during his two years at the Vic for seeming aloof and disinterested. Thordarsson had fired him up and he scored sixteen goals in those thirteen League games, plus three more during the Auto Windscreen Shield triumph. He thrived on through balls provided by Kavanagh, who was released by Thordarsson's system to play a more advanced play-making role. The other revelation was 19-year-old James O'Connor in midfield. Nicknamed 'little hard man', the ginger-haired Irishman fought tooth and nail for every ball in the middle of the park, earning comparisons with countryman Roy Keane. His zeal often got him into trouble with referees, however, and he faced an FA commission for having accumulated fourteen bookings in the season. John Rudge won over any remaining sceptics by pleading the youngster's case, winning a reprieve, subject to further good behaviour.

Stoke qualified for the promotion play-offs on the back of their unbeaten run, losing out to Gillingham, who had lost their grip on an automatic promotion spot on the last day of the season (see Match of the Season).

Despite the play-off defeat, the club's fortunes were on a definite upturn. The longevity of the Icemen's involvement remains to be tested, but the new board have made it clear that they are *here to stay*. They have made a huge difference to Stoke City. There lurks enormous potential within the club, reflected in Stoke being made hot favourites to win the Second Division championship in the 2000-01 season. There is many a slip twixt cup and lip, but there is a belief around the Britannia Stadium that, should promotion be achieved, then the club can go onwards and upwards. It may be hard to return to the glory days of Waddington, Greenhoff, Hudson and Conroy but, after one of the most turbulent periods of the club's history, Mr G's red and white army are on the march.

Match of the Season 1999-2000

Gillingham 3 Stoke 0

Play-off, semi-final, 2nd leg, 17 May 2000

Stoke's fortunes in the play-offs had previously hinged on their making poor starts to the first leg. This time City could not have begun better. Two goals up after eight minutes, Stoke looked set for a quick return to Wembley. They were still two goals ahead, at 3-1, into the sixth minute of injury-time. The Gills, however, under the management of former England international Peter Taylor, were made of stern stuff and their inspirational captain, Andy Hessen-thaler, belted a 30-yard shot past the despairing Ward. At 3-2 the Gills were now favourites.

Stoke went into the second leg minus Peter Thorne, who took a knock to his knee during the tense last ten minutes at the Brit. The restricted capacity of Gillingham's Priestfield Stadium meant that only 1,800 tickets were available to Stoke fans. A further 7,500 watched the game on a big screen at the Brit.

The game soon deteriorated into a series of niggly fouls, which in many senses should have suited Stoke, who merely needed to keep a clean sheet to progress. Crucially, City's players reacted to provocation from their opponents. Clive Clarke, already booked, let his temper get the better of him as he challenged for a ball which went out for a throw in and petulantly threw it away, earning a second yellow inside a minute and an early bath. The players rallied to the cause and repelled waves of Gillingham attacks. Back at the Britannia Stadium, the tension became so great that the fans asked for the commentary over the tannoy to be switched off.

Early in the second half City were reduced to nine. Kavanagh, involved in an off-the-ball incident at a set-piece, was shown the red card, despite the fact that he was the one bleeding from his face. Still the nine men battled on, conceding only one goal in normal time.

Extra-time upped the ante even more. It took a further ten minutes before Gillingham made the vital breakthrough, Onoura's header putting them ahead in the tie. Stoke did not let their heads drop and substitute Paul Connor came agonisingly close to forcing penalties when he hit the inside of the post just before the Gills grabbed their third and clinching goal.

Gillingham went on to beat Wigan 3-2 in the final to earn the right to play in the First Division for the first time in their history. For Stoke, the inevitable talk was of being robbed by a biased refe-ree. True, he had only cautioned one Gillingham player, when a total of four or five may have been more appropriate, but the two dismissals were the result of a loss of cool on Stoke's part. The players had no one to blame but themselves.

A minute's silence for Bobby Moore at Brisbane Road, Orient v Stoke (February 1993)

The Victoria Ground, Stoke City's home for 119 years (1993)

Nigel Gleghorn fires home the winner against Tranmere (August 1994)

... and is buried by his jubilant team-mates

Gerry McMahon celebrates scoring in the last match at the Vic (May 1997)

Mark Stein in classic pose

Flags fly at half-mast after Stanley Matthews' death (February 2000)

The order of service for the funeral of Sir Stanley Matthews (March 2000)

GUIDE TO SEASONAL SUMMARIES

Col 1: Match number (for league fixtures); Round (for cup-ties).
         e.g.2:1 means 'Second round; first leg.'
         e.g.4R means 'Fourth round replay.'

Col 2: Date of the fixture and whether Home (H), Away (A), or Neutral (N).

Col 3: Opposition.

Col 4: Attendances. Home gates appear in roman; Away gates in *italics*.
         Figures in **bold** indicate the largest and smallest gates, at home and away.
         Average home and away attendances appear after the final league match.

Col 5: Respective league positions of Stoke and their opponents after the match.
         Stoke's position appears on the top line in roman.
         Their opponents' position appears on the second line in *italics*.
         For cup-ties, the division and position of opponents is provided.
         e.g.2:12 means the opposition are twelfth in Division 2.

Col 6: The top line shows the result: W(in), D(raw), or L(ose).
         The second line shows Stoke's cumulative points total.

Col 7: The match score, Stoke's given first.
         Scores in **bold** indicate Stoke's biggest league win and heaviest defeat.

Col 8: The half-time score, Stoke's given first.

Col 9: The top line shows Stoke's scorers and times of goals in roman.
         The second line shows opponents' scorers and times of goals in *italics*.
         A 'p' after the time of a goal denotes a penalty; 'og' an own-goal.
         The third line gives the name of the match referee.

Team line-ups: Stoke line-ups appear on the top line, irrespective of whether
         they are home or away. Opposition teams appear on the second line in *italics*.
         Players of either side who are sent off are marked !
         Stoke players making their league debuts are displayed in **bold**.

Substitutes: Names of substitutes appear only if they actually took the field.
         A player substituted is marked *
         A second player substituted is marked ^
         A third player substituted is marked "
         These marks do not indicate the sequence of substitutions.

N.B.   For clarity, all information appearing in *italics* relates to opposing teams.

LEAGUE DIVISION 1 — Manager: Tony Waddington — SEASON 1970-71

Match summary

No	Date	V	Opponent	Att	Pos	Pt	F-A	H-T	Scorers, Times	Referee
1	15/8	H	IPSWICH	17,099	1	1	0-0	0-0	—	C Nicholls
2	19/8	H	NEWCASTLE	15,197	—	3	3-0 W	2-0	Burrows 22, Ritchie 38, 89	K Styles
3	22/8	A	DERBY	35,461	10 / *5*	3	0-2 L	0-1	Hinton 20p, Wignall 48	A Bone
4	26/8	A	WEST BROM	22,607	13 / *8*	3	2-5 L	1-1	Ritchie 12, Conroy 55 / Astle 2, 90, Brown 47, 80, Reed 64	P Partridge
5	29/8	H	CRYSTAL PALACE	13,469	14 / *10*	4	0-0 D	0-0	—	C Thomas
6	2/9	H	NOTT'M FOREST	13,951	14 / *2*	5	0-0 D	0-0	—	R Matthewson
7	5/9	A	WOLVES	21,056	15 / *19*	6	1-1 D	1-1	Greenhoff 25 / Curran 13	V James
8	12/9	H	LEEDS	22,592	11 / *1*	8	3-0 W	1-0	Ritchie 20, 90, Burrows 47	G Hill
9	19/9	A	MANCHESTER C	35,473	14 / *2*	8	1-4 L	0-3	Bernard 80 / Book 15, Young 23, Lee 32, 68	J Hunting
10	26/9	H	ARSENAL	18,153	11 / *4*	10	5-0 W	2-0	Ritchie 28, 43, Con'y 62, G'nhoff 64, [Bloor 84]	G Jones

Line-ups (Stoke City listed first, opponents in italics)

No	Team	1	2	3	4	5	6	7	8	9	10	11	12 sub used
1	Stoke	Banks	Marsh	Pejic	Bernard	Bloor	Skeels	Conroy*	Greenhoff	Ritchie	Dobing	Burrows	Eastham
1	*Ipswich*	*Best*	*Carroll*	*Harper*	*Morris*	*Baxter*	*Jefferson*	*Robertson*	*Mills*	*Clarke*	*Woods*	*Lambert*	
2	Stoke	Banks	Marsh	Pejic	Bernard	Bloor	Skeels	Conroy	Greenhoff	Ritchie	Dobing	Burrows	
2	*Newcastle*	*McFaul*	*Craig*	*Gibb*	*McNamee*	*Moncur*	*Dyson*	*Robson*	*Davies*	*Smith*	*Foggon*		
3	Stoke	Banks	Marsh	Pejic	Bernard	Smith*	Bloor	Eastham	Greenhoff	Ritchie	Dobing	Burrows	Stevenson
3	*Derby*	*Green*	*Webster*	*Robson*	*Hennessey*	*McFarland*	*Mackay*	*McGovern*	*Carlin*	*O'Hare*	*Hector*	*Hinton*	*Wignall*
4	Stoke	Banks	Marsh	Pejic	Bernard	Bloor	Stevenson	Conroy	Greenhoff*	Ritchie	Dobing	Burrows	Eastham
4	*West Brom*	*Cumbes*	*Hughes*	*Wilson*	*Merrick*	*Talbut*	*Robertson*	*Cantello*	*Brown*	*Astle*	*Suggett*	*Hope**	*Reed*
5	Stoke	Banks	Marsh	Pejic	Skeels*	Smith	Bloor	Conroy	Bernard	Ritchie	Dobing	Burrows	Eastham
5	*Crystal Palace*	*Jackson*	*Sewell*	*Wall*	*Hoadley*	*McCormack*	*Blyth*	*Taylor*	*Kember**	*Queen*	*Birchenall*	*Tambling*	*Humphreys*
6	Stoke	Banks	Elder	Pejic	Bernard	Smith	Bloor	Conroy	Eastham	Ritchie	Stevenson	Burrows	
6	*Nott'm Forest*	*Barron*	*Hindley*	*Winfield*	*Chapman*	*O'Kane*	*Newton*	*Lyons*	*Rees*	*Ingram*	*Cormack*	*Moore**	*Richardson*
7	Stoke	Banks	Elder	Pejic	Bernard	Smith	Bloor	Conroy	Stevenson	Ritchie*	Eastham	Burrows	Greenhoff
7	*Wolves*	*Parkes*	*Taylor*	*Parkin*	*Wilson*	*Munro**	*McAlle*	*McCalliog*	*Hagan*	*Gould*	*Curran*	*Wagstaffe*	*Dougan*
8	Stoke	Banks	Skeels	Pejic	Bernard	Smith	Bloor	Conroy	Greenhoff	Ritchie	Dobing	Burrows	Eastham
8	*Leeds*	*Sprake*	*Madeley*	*Cooper*	*Bremner*	*Yorath*	*Hunter*	*Lorimer*	*Clarke*	*Jones*	*Bates*	*Gray*	
9	Stoke	Banks	Skeels	Pejic	Bernard	Smith	Bloor	Conroy	Greenhoff*	Ritchie	Dobing	Burrows	Marsh
9	*Manchester C*	*Corrigan*	*Book*	*Pardoe*	*Doyle*	*Booth*	*Oakes*	*Summerbee**	*Bell*	*Lee*	*Young*	*Towers*	
10	Stoke	Farmer	Marsh	Pejic	Bernard	Smith	Bloor	Conroy	Greenhoff	Ritchie	Dobing	Burrows	
10	*Arsenal*	*Wilson*	*Rice*	*McNab*	*Kelly*	*McLintock*	*Roberts*	*Armstrong*	*Storey*	*Radford*	*Kennedy*	*Graham*	

Match reports

1 — Ipswich. A small crowd see City struggle against Bobby Robson's defence-minded Ipswich. Eastham, Burrows and Ritchie all test keeper Dave Best with Greenhoff blazing the best chance over the bar.

2 — Newcastle. Clive Woods, playing up in attack with Mick Mills, forces Gordon Banks into a late save. Banks is a virtual spectator as City rip into the Toon. Burrows grabs the first with a sharp turn in the area. Ritchie's brace are gifts as first Bob Moncur and then Smith hit back-passes into his path. Mike Bernard treats the Boothen paddock to a striptease after Jim Smith rips his shorts.

3 — Derby. Denis Smith returns again as Derby out-fight Stoke in a bruising battle. Terry Hennessey is replaced as early as the 12th minute but substitute Frank Wignall blasts home the second after Bernard handles to give Derby an early penalty. Mackay and Carlin clear off the line.

4 — West Brom. In a night of high drama the Baggies run away with it after an even first half. Ritchie has a goal disallowed at 1-1. Brown's 25-yard free-kick is the pick of the goals. At 2-3 down City pour forward looking for the equaliser but Colin Suggett sets up two late goals on the break for Albion.

5 — Crystal Palace. A nine-man Palace defence stifles the Potters' attacking ideas. George Eastham enters the fray at half-time to improve City's passing game, but to no avail as Stoke resort to the long ball to John Ritchie late on. Clive Thomas turns down a penalty appeal as Burrows goes down in the box.

6 — Nott'm Forest. The injury crisis deepens as Stoke field the only 11 fit senior players but still outplay unbeaten Forest. The score-line remains blank as Ritchie has a personal nightmare and misses six clear-cut chances. Alex Elder flattens Ian Moore with a late tackle and is booed by the paddock fans.

7 — Wolves. Greenhoff returns from injury to replace Ritchie and equalises with a super solo goal. Banks saves brilliantly from Hugh Curran but can't stop the opener after Gould miskicks in front of goal. Derek Dougan replaces the injured Munro and plays at centre-half for Bill McGarry's men.

8 — Leeds. England manager Sir Alf Ramsey sees City rip table-toppers Leeds apart. The first two goals are opportunist strikes, while Ritchie looks offside for his second. Gary Sprake is injured and Lorimer goes in goal for eight minutes in the second half. Leeds miss Reaney, Charlton and Giles.

9 — Manchester C. Stoke are undone by City's early onslaught. The first three goals are all hit from the edge of the area. The fourth is down to Harry Burrows' mistake in the area. Bernard's header is no consolation. Man City play last 25 mins with only 10 men after Booth and Summerbee are injured.

10 — Arsenal. Match of the Day sees Stoke annihilate the Gunners, fresh from a 6-2 thrashing of WBA. Ritchie's second is a superb run and shot while Terry Conroy's strike is voted goal of the season. Bloor scores after Marsh's surging run and shot. City don't miss Banks, injured at Manchester City.

Stoke City — Match Log (matches 11–21)

#	V	Opponent	Date	Pos	Res	Score	HT	Att	League	Pts
11	A	BLACKPOOL	3/10	11	D	1-1	0-1	25,324	21	11
12	H	WEST HAM	10/10	9	W	2-1	1-1	23,035	19	13
13	A	IPSWICH	17/10	9	L	0-2	0-1	18,159	19	13
14	A	TOTTENHAM	24/10	11	L	0-3	0-3	36,238	3	13
15	H	HUDDERSFIELD	31/10	10	W	3-1	1-0	17,625	20	15
16	A	MANCHESTER U	7/11	10	D	2-2	1-1	47,451	14	16
17	H	EVERTON	14/11	10	D	1-1	1-0	26,240	11	17
18	A	LEEDS	18/11	10	L	1-4	1-1	25,004	11	17
19	A	CHELSEA	21/11	12	L	1-2	1-1	36,227	4	17
20	H	SOUTHAMPTON	28/11	12	D	0-0	0-0	18,848	9	18
21	A	COVENTRY	5/12	13	L	0-1	0-1	22,275	10	18

Scorers & Referees

#	Scorers	Ref
11	Dobing 56 / Burns 33	D Pugh
12	Greenhoff 36, Dobing 89 / Greaves 26	J Thacker
13	/ Clarke 45p, Hill 65	J Lewis
14	/ Chivers 4, 28, Gilzean 17	P Baldwin
15	Greenhoff 5, Conroy 54, 75 / Worthington 46	E Wallace
16	Conroy 1, Ritchie 72 / Law 29, Sadler 70	A Oliver
17	Ritchie 42 / Hurst 67	L Callaghan
18	Conroy 15 / Madeley 38, Clarke 63, Giles 85p, [Jones 90]	D Laing
19	Smith T 30 / Osgood 2, Bernard 83 (og)	R Kirkpatrick
20	—	P Baldwin
21	/ O'Rourke 19	R Challis

Line-ups (Stoke bold / opponent in italics)

11 Blackpool: Banks, Marsh, Pejic, Bernard, Bloor, Skeels, Conroy, Greenhoff, Ritchie, Dobing, Burrows
Thompson, Armfield, Mowbray, Hatton, James, Alcock, Burns, Suddick, Craven, Bentley, Hutchinson

12 West Ham: Banks, Marsh, Pejic, Bernard, Bloor, Smith, Conroy, Greenhoff, Ritchie, Dobing, Burrows
Grotier, Bonds, Lampard, Lindsay, Stephenson, Moore, Boyce, Best, Hurst, Brooking, Greaves, Eustace*

13 Ipswich: Banks, Marsh, Pejic, Bernard, Bloor, Smith, Conroy, Greenhoff, Ritchie, Dobing*, Burrows, Skeels
Sivell, Hammond, Mills, Morris, Baxter, McNeill, Robertson, Woods, Clarke, Hill, Collard

14 Tottenham: Banks, Marsh, Pejic, Bernard, Bloor, Smith, Conroy*, Greenhoff, Ritchie, Skeels, Burrows
Jennings, Kinnear, Knowles, Mullery, England, Beal, Gilzean, Perryman, Chivers, Peters, Neighbour, Stevenson*

15 Huddersfield: Banks, Marsh, Pejic, Bernard, Bloor, Smith, Conroy, Greenhoff, Ritchie, Eastham, Burrows
Poole, Jones, Hutt, Nicholson, Ellam, Clarke, Smith, Lawson, Worthington, McGill, Chapman, Dobson*

16 Manchester U: Banks, Marsh, Pejic, Bernard, Bloor, Smith, Conroy, Greenhoff, Ritchie, Eastham*, Burrows
Rimmer, Edwards, Burns, Fitzpatrick, James, Sadler, Law, Best, Charlton, Kidd, Aston

17 Everton: Banks, Marsh, Pejic, Bernard, Bloor, Smith, Conroy, Greenhoff, Ritchie*, Eastham, Burrows, Mahoney
Rankin, Wright, Brown, Kendall, Labone, Newton H, Whittle, Ball, Royle, Hurst, Morrissey

18 Leeds: Banks, Marsh, Pejic, Bernard, Bloor, Skeels, Conroy, Greenhoff, Ritchie*, Eastham*, Mahoney [Giles 85p.]
Sprake, Davey, Cooper, Bates, Charlton, Hunter, Lorimer, Clarke, Jones, Giles, Madeley, Belfitt*

19 Chelsea: Banks, Marsh, Pejic, Bernard, Smith D, Bloor, Conroy, Mahoney, Smith T, Eastham, Burrows
Bonetti, Boyle, Harris, Hollins, Hinton, Webb, Weller, Cooke, Osgood, Houseman, Baldwin

20 Southampton: Banks, Marsh, Pejic, Bernard, Smith, Bloor, Conroy, Mahoney, Greenhoff, Eastham, Burrows
Martin, Kirkup, Hollywood, Fisher, McGrath, Gabriel, Paine, Channon, Davies, O'Neill, Jenkins

21 Coventry: Banks, Marsh, Pejic, Bernard, Bloor, Smith D, Conroy, Greenhoff, Eastham, Burrows, Smith T
Glazier, Coop, Smith, Mortimer, Blockley, Parker, Hill, Carr, Mahoney, Martin, O'Rourke, Clements*

Match reports

11 Honours are even in an open game. Burns nets after ex-Stokie Bill Bentley's header is saved by Banks. Inspirational Dobing converts Bloor's header. Jimmy Armfield is at the hub of Blackpool's best attacks. Jackie Marsh clears off the line. Bernard is booked in a tough second half.

12 Against the run of play, veteran goalpoacher Jimmy Greaves curls in the first goal City have conceded at home in the League. Jimmy Greenhoff equalises with a first-time shot. The pressure builds in the second half. Ritchie hits the post, then Dobing races through to grab a late winner.

13 City have the upper hand against lowly Ipswich until a penalty is awarded for a Pejic tackle on Woods. Banks and Dobing are booked for their protests. Worse is to follow as Dobing, in the best form of his career, breaks his leg in a tackle with Mills. Laurie Sivell denies Ritchie late on.

14 Stoke wilt under early Spurs pressure. Chivers and Gilzean score in goalmouth scrambles. The third sees Stoke stop after an apparent foul on Smith, but Chivers nets and asks questions later. The injury hoodoo strikes again. Willie Stevenson, on for the injured Conroy, breaks his leg.

15 Stoke start brightly and Greenhoff's early goal is well deserved. Frank Worthington grabs an equaliser through a crowd of players. Burrows misses a 36th-minute penalty after he is felled by Dennis Clarke but his blushes are spared by Terry Conroy, who belts home two beauties.

16 Conroy's good form continues as his first-minute volley puts Stoke ahead. United fight back through Law and then go ahead when Sadler's header is adjudged to have crossed the line. Ritchie beats the offside trap to equalize but then gets himself booked for applauding the referee.

17 Defending champions Everton fight back in a tough, physical game. Ritchie, Conroy and Burrows are foiled in penalty box scrambles before Ritchie buries Conroy's cross. John Hurst heads home Alan Ball's cross for the equaliser. Ritchie is carried off with a badly damaged knee.

18 City dominate early on and are good value for Conroy's deflected volley. Then Leeds take over. Madeley and Clarke score from close in. City hold out under incessant pressure until Marsh pulls Johnny Giles down. Banks saves Johnny Giles' first effort but is adjudged to have moved.

19 Both England's World Cup keepers turn in good displays, despite being dropped by Sir Alf. Osgood heads in a Harris cross after hitting the bar in the 6th minute. Terry Smith scores on his debut as City are down to the bare bones again. Bernard diverts a cross past Banks for the decider.

20 A dull game with few chances. 10 goal Mick Channon is kept quiet by Smith. After five without a win, the Boothen End is restless, but cannot rouse City from their torpor. Ted Bates' Southampton leave with the point they wanted. Jackie Marsh reveals he wears contact lenses to play in.

21 Coventry's early goal is down to a Banks howler as he lets John O'Rourke's header through his legs. Alan Bloor has a header cleared off the line as the Sky Blues are put under severe pressure in the second half. Young Terry Smith makes no impression when he replaces Mahoney.

LEAGUE DIVISION 1 — Manager: Tony Waddington — SEASON 1970-71

No	Date	Att	Pos	Pt	F-A	H-T	Scorers, Times, and Referees	1	2	3	4	5	6	7	8	9	10	11	12 sub used
22	H BURNLEY 12/12	13,299	14 D	19	0-0	0-0	Ref: H Williams	Banks	Marsh	Pejic	Bernard	Smith	Skeels	Conroy	Mahoney	Greenhoff	Eastham	Burrows	
								Mellor	Angus	Nulty	Docherty	Waldron	Dobson	Thomas	Kindon*	Probert	Collins	West	James
23	H DERBY 19/12	21,906	13 W	21	1-0	0-0	Burrows 60 — Ref: P Nicholson	Banks	Marsh	Pejic	Smith	Skeels	Bloor	Haslegrave	Bernard	Conroy	Eastham	Burrows	
								Green	Webster	Robson	Hennessey	McFarland	MacKay	Butlin	Durban	O'Hare	Hector	Gemmill	
24	A LIVERPOOL 26/12	47,103	12 D	22	0-0	0-0	Ref: A Morrissey	Banks	Marsh	Pejic	Bernard	Smith	Bloor	Conroy	Greenhoff	Skeels	Eastham	Burrows	
								Clemence	Lawler	Boersma	Smith	Lloyd	Hughes	Callaghan	McLaughlin	Heighway	Toshack	Hall	
25	A NEWCASTLE 9/1	25,680	11 W	24	2-0	1-0	Greenhoff 1, Burrows 62 — Ref: W Johnson	Banks	Marsh	Pejic	Bernard	Bloor	Skeels	Haslegrave	Greenhoff	Conroy	Eastham	Burrows	
								McFaul	Craig	Clark	Gibb	McNamee	Moncur	Robson	Dyson	Davies	Young	Mitchell	
26	H WEST BROM 16/1	20,882	10 W	26	2-0	1-0	Conroy 23, 78 — Ref: J Homewood	Banks	Marsh	Pejic	Bernard	Bloor	Skeels	Haslegrave	Greenhoff	Conroy	Eastham	Burrows	
								Cumbes	Lovett	Wilson	Brown	Wile	Kaye	McVitie	Suggett	Astle	Hope	Hartford	
27	A SOUTHAMPTON 30/1	19,500	10 L	26	1-2	1-1	Greenhoff 20 / O'Neil 5, Davies 58 — Ref: J Finney	Banks	Marsh	Pejic	Bernard	Bloor	Skeels	Haslegrave*	Conroy	Greenhoff	Elder	Smith	Lees
								Martin	Kirkup	Hollywood	Fisher	McGrath	Gabriel	Paine	Channon	Davies	O'Neil	Jenkins	
28	H COVENTRY 6/2	17,208	10 W	28	2-1	1-1	Mortimer 45 (og), Greenhoff 50 / Alderson 39 — Ref: G Hartley	Farmer	Marsh	Pejic	Skeels	Smith	Jump	Haslegrave	Greenhoff	Conroy	Bernard	Eastham	
								Glazier	Smith	Clements	Machin	Blockley	Parker	Mortimer	Carr	Joicey	Hunt	Alderson	
29	H CHELSEA 20/2	26,595	11 L	28	1-2	0-0	Conroy 47 / Hutchinson 60, Smethurst 66 — Ref: T Davies	Banks	Marsh	Pejic	Jump	Smith D	Skeels	Haslegrave	Smith T	Conroy	Bernard*	Burrows	Lees
								Phillips	Harris	McCreadie	Hollins	Dempsey	Webb	Smethurst	Cooke	Hutchinson	Hudson	Weller	
30	A BURNLEY 23/2	12,209	9 D	29	1-1	1-0	Conroy 12 / Dobson 66 — Ref: A Morrissey	Banks	Marsh	Pejic	Skeels	Smith	Bloor	Haslegrave	Mahoney	Conroy	Jump	Burrows	
								Waiters	Angus	Latcham	Docherty	Waldron	Dobson	Thomas	Coates	Bellamy	Probert	Kindon	
31	A HUDDERSFIELD 27/2	15,626	9 W	31	1-0	0-0	Conroy 78p — Ref: S Kayley	Banks	Marsh	Pejic	Skeels	Smith	Bloor	Conroy	Mahoney	Ritchie	Jump	Haslegrave*	Burrows
								Lawson	Clarke	Hutt	Nicholson	Ellam	Cherry	Smith	Mahoney	Worthington	McGill	Hoy	

Match 22 (Burnley): At least Stoke City show some promise against struggling Burnley, having three goals disallowed in the first half. Terry Conroy is booked for protesting at the third. Colin Waldron is in dominant form for Burnley alongside ex-Stoke trainee Geoff Nulty. Seven games without a win.

Match 23 (Derby): A win at last! Inspired by the excellent debutant Sean Haslegrave, City sneak past the Rams. The winner is slightly fortuitous as Burrows scores direct from a corner. Banks saves from new-signing Archie Gemmill at the foot of the post near the end. Greenhoff's leg injury rules him out.

Match 24 (Liverpool): Stoke are defiant in the face of an Anfield onslaught. Gordon Banks is back in top form as he saves brilliantly from Toshack's header and Phil Boersma's rocket. City's only chance comes in the last minute as Burrows is clean through, but Clemence foils him. Goalless is a good result.

Match 25 (Newcastle): Injury-hit Stoke grab an early lead at St James' through Greenhoff's left-foot shot. Newcastle have a goal ruled out for offside. Gordon Banks is flattened by Wyn Davies and has blood pouring from his nose. A rare right-footed goal from Harry Burrows seals City's first away win.

Match 26 (West Brom): Unchanged Stoke attack from the off. Sean Haslegrave pressures the young John Wile into presenting the ball to Terry Conroy, who then beats Jim Cumbes. From Burrows' quick free-kick Conroy rounds the goalkeeper to ensure successive wins for Stoke for the first time this season.

Match 27 (Southampton): A makeshift Stoke side battle gamely at the Dell but lose to a Ron Davies header as he outjumps the returning Denis Smith. Their personal battle is decisive. Davies wins it and Smith is booked. Early on Brian O'Neil is put in by Davies and Conroy crosses for Greenhoff to equalize.

Match 28 (Coventry): Stoke fall behind to 20-year-old Brian Alderson's effort, but Mortimer turns Conroy's cross past the keeper under pressure from Bernard and City win at as Greenhoff strikes from TC's pass. Ernie Hunt tries one of his famous 'donkey' free-kicks but is foiled by debutant Stewart Jump.

Match 29 (Chelsea): Confident Chelsea are always in control despite falling behind to Conroy's finish to Haslegrave's pass. Hutchinson and Smethurst score from corners and Hudson has a goal disallowed on a six-minute purple patch. Haslegrave nearly finds a second but Stoke lose unbeaten home record.

Match 30 (Burnley): Conroy prods home to give City an early lead against relegation-threatened Burnley, but are pegged back when Dobson's shot is ruled to have crossed the line despite Pejic's clearance. The lack of any fit strikers shows as City probe for a winner but are thwarted by the spirited Clarets.

Match 31 (Huddersfield): After the tumultuous cup clashes, battle is resumed with the Terriers. John Ritchie returns to lead the line and Stoke hold the upper hand before Conroy calmly nets a penalty after Hutt handles a goalbound Jump header. Town press for an equaliser but resilient City hold out to the end.

Results

No	H/A	Opponent	Date	Att	Pos	Res	Score	(n)	Pts
32	A	EVERTON	13/3	38,924	12	L	0-2	9	31
33	H	MANCHESTER U	20/3	39,889	12	L	1-2	9	31
34	A	CRYSTAL PALACE	3/4	16,963	15	L	2-3	14	31
35	H	WOLVES	7/4	22,808	13	W	1-0	3	33
36	H	LIVERPOOL	10/4	28,810	14	L	0-1	6	33
37	H	BLACKPOOL	13/4	13,916	14	D	1-1	22	34
38	A	WEST HAM	17/4	26,269	15	L	0-1	20	34
39	H	MANCHESTER C	24/4	14,836	14	W	2-0	8	36
40	H	NOTT'M FOREST	27/4	13,502	13	D	0-0	16	37
41	A	ARSENAL	1/5	50,011	13	L	0-1	2	37
42	H	TOTTENHAM	5/5	14,319	13	L	0-1	3	37

No	Scorers (Stoke)	Scorers (Opponent)	Ref
32	—	Whittle 50, Royle 75	V Batty
33	Ritchie 77	Best 23, 34	W Dow
34	Ritchie 81, 90	Kember 17, Birchenall 37, Wharton 89	M Kerkhof
35	Burrows 61p	—	H New
36	—	Thompson 30	A Oliver
37	Jump 16	Hutchison 45	C Thomas
38	—	Hurst 56	E Merchant
39	Bernard 20, Ritchie 52	—	I Jones
40	—	—	H Williams
41	—	Kelly 65	R Matthewson
42	—	Peters 25	I Jones

Line-ups

No	Team	Banks	Marsh	Pejic	Skeels	Smith	Bloor	Greenhoff	Bernard	Ritchie	Conroy	Burrows	Mahoney
32	Stoke	Banks	Marsh	Pejic	Skeels	Smith	Bloor	Greenhoff	Bernard	Ritchie*	Conroy	Burrows	Mahoney
32	Everton	Rankin	Wright	Newton K	Kendall	Labone	Harvey	Whittle	Ball	Royle	Hurst	Johnson*	Kenyon
33	Stoke	Banks	Marsh	Pejic	Skeels	Smith	Bloor	Greenhoff	Bernard	Ritchie	Conroy	Burrows	Mahoney
33	Man U	Stepney	Fitzpatrick	Dunne	Crerand	Edwards	Sadler	Morgan	Best	Charlton	Law	Aston*	Burns
34	Stoke	Farmer	Marsh	Pejic	Jump	Smith	Bloor	Mahoney	Bernard	Ritchie	Conroy	Burrows	
34	Palace	Jackson	Payne*	Wall	Hoadley	McCormack	Taylor	Wharton	Kember	Tambling	Birchenall	Scott	Sewell
35	Stoke	Banks	Skeels	Pejic	Bernard	Smith	Bloor	Mahoney	Greenhoff	Ritchie	Conroy*	Burrows	Marsh
35	Wolves	Parkes	Shaw	Parkin	Bailey	Munro	McAlle	Hegan	Hibbitt	Gould	Wagstaffe	Curran	
36	Stoke	Banks	Skeels	Pejic	Bernard	Smith	Bloor	Haslegrave	Greenhoff	Ritchie	Mahoney	Burrows*	Jump
36	Liverpool	Clemence	Lawler	Lindsay	Smith	Lloyd	Hughes	Callaghan	Evans	Thompson	Toshack*	Hall	Heighway
37	Stoke	Banks	Marsh	Pejic	Skeels	Smith	Bloor	Mahoney	Bernard	Ritchie	Jump	Haslegrave*	Elder
37	Blackpool	Taylor	Alcock	Bentley	Nicholson	James	Suddaby	Kemp	Rowe	Craven	Johnston	Hutchison	
38	Stoke	Banks	Marsh	Pejic	Bernard	Smith	Bloor	Haslegrave	Greenhoff	Ritchie	Mahoney	Jump*	Lees
38	West Ham	Ferguson	Holland	Lampard	Stephenson	Taylor	Moore	Redknapp	Bonds	Hurst	Robson	Greaves	
39	Stoke	Banks	Skeels	Pejic	Bernard	Smith	Bloor	Haslegrave	Greenhoff	Ritchie	Mahoney	Jump	Lees
39	Man City	Corrigan	Book	Mann	Towers	Booth	Donachie	Johnson	Connor	Lee	Hill	Young	
40	Stoke	Banks	Marsh	Pejic	Skeels	Smith	Bloor	Mahoney	Bernard	Greenhoff	Jump	Haslegrave	
40	Nott'm Forest	Barron	Hindley	Winfield	Chapman	O'Kane	Fraser	Jackson*	Richardson	McKenzie	Cormack	Moore	Rees
41	Stoke	Banks	Marsh	Pejic	Skeels	Smith	Bloor	Mahoney	Skeels	Greenhoff	Jump*	Haslegrave	Elder
41	Arsenal	Wilson	Rice	McNab	Storey*	McLintock	Simpson	Armstrong	Graham	Radford	Kennedy	George	Kelly
42	Stoke	Banks	Marsh	Pejic	Bernard	Smith	Bloor	Mahoney	Greenhoff	Ritchie	Lees	Haslegrave	Jump
42	Tottenham	Jennings	Kinnear	Knowles	Mullery	Collins	Beal	Gilzean*	Perryman	Chivers	Peters	Neighbour	Pearce

Match reports

32 – Everton (A): City, under pressure throughout, succumb despite Bloor's fine display. Alan Whittle back-heads over Pejic and past an astonished Banks. Stoke pile on the pressure. Andy Rankin tips Ritchie's point-blank header over the bar but Royle forces the ball in during a scramble to seal the win.

33 – Manchester U (H): George Best scores two opportunist strikes for United, under the temporary charge of Sir Matt Busby after Wilf McGuinness' sacking. Ritchie fires home to set up a grandstand finish. City escape after Bernard blatantly handles in the box. Ill temper on the terraces as the police eject 30.

34 – Crystal Palace (A): The FA Cup hangover shows at Palace, who only have one point in eight games. The three goals come from crosses not cleared by City's out-of-sorts defence. The second half is much better. Ritchie's goals come too late to force a draw. Wharton's late 'offside goal' keeps Palace up.

35 – Wolves (H): A good performance is only crowned by a penalty after Bernard Shaw handles Ritchie's header on the line. Pejic, for the second time in three games, follows Francis Munro into the book as the tackles fly in. Conroy is injured (knee) after 20 minutes and will miss the rest of the season.

36 – Liverpool (H): Sean Haslegrave flies back from a youth tournament in Switzerland to shore up an injury-hit attack. Greenhoff and Ritchie miss badly as Stoke struggle up front. Toshack nods back for Peter Thompson to volley the winner. Burrows' shot from Bernard's 'donkey' free-kick just misses.

37 – Blackpool (H): City waste numerous chances, Mahoney twice when it is easier to score. He's lucky to escape with yellow when lashing out at Peter Suddaby. Jump's header is his first goal. Tommy Hutchison follows up Kemp's shot to equalise. The ref misses Bloor's effort being handled on the line.

38 – West Ham (A): Record signing Bryan Robson beats Banks but also the post as struggling Hammers start well. Smith is commanding as Stoke defend fiercely. City are better after the break but fail to a Hurst strike in a scramble after Skeels fails to clear. Ritchie cannot beat Ferguson when put clear.

39 – Manchester C (H): Inspired Mike Bernard harries Joe Mercer's much changed Man City to distraction. Joe Corrigan saves from Greenhoff, then Bernard volleys home a corner high into the net. Haslegrave finds Ritchie for the second and Greenhoff nearly grabs a third. Fred Hill hits the bar for the Blues.

40 – Nott'm Forest (H): A solid defensive display without a complete forward line. Greenhoff plays alone up front with Jump supporting. Stoke create the best chances. Banks saves a Duncan McKenzie scorcher. Jim Barron brilliantly saves a Mahoney header. Stoke work so hard even the referee gets cramp.

41 – Arsenal (A): Ritchie, Bloor, Burrows and Conroy all have knee injuries but a disciplined performance sees Stoke frustrate a tense Arsenal, who need the win to have a chance of the double. Jump and Haslegrave waste chances. Arsenal cling on after sub Kelly steals it in a frantic goalmouth scramble.

42 – Tottenham (H): Spurs cruise to victory and a third place finish after Martin Peters beats the offside trap from Alan Mullery's pass to skip round Gordon Banks. The goal kills off attack-minded Stoke. To rub salt into the wounds Phil Beal's last-minute handball is seen by everyone except referee Jones.

Home 19,952 Average Away 28,455

LEAGUE DIVISION 1 (CUP-TIES) Manager: Tony Waddington SEASON 1970-71

League Cup

Rd	Fixture	Date	Att		Pos	Res	F-A	H-T	1	2	3	4	5	6	7	8	9	10	11	12 sub used	Scorers, Times, and Referees
2	H MILLWALL	9/9	10,230	2:14	15	D	0-0	0-0	Banks	Marsh	Pejic	Bernard !	Smith	Bloor	Conroy	Dobing	Greenhoff	Stevenson*	Eastham	Ritchie	Ref: H Davey
									King	Brown B	Cripps	Dorney	Kitchener	Burnett	Brown S	Jacks	Bolland	Dunphy	Allder		
2R	A MILLWALL	21/9	12,789	2:19	14	L	1-2	0-0	Farmer	Marsh	Pejic	Skeels	Smith	Bloor	Conroy	Greenhoff	Ritchie	Dobing	Eastham*	Burrows	Conroy 57; Possee 61, Allder 70. Ref: M Kerkhof
									King	Brown B	Cripps	Dorney	Kitchener	Burnett	Brown S	Dunphy	Bolland	Possee	Allder		

Match 2 — Benny Fenton's men stand defiant at the Vic. Dobing has a goal disallowed in the 16th minute and a night of frustration culminates in Bernard's sending off (68 mins) for swinging at Eamon Dunphy. Marsh clears off the line with five mins to go. Willie Stevenson dislocates his collarbone.

Match 2R — City take the lead through Conroy's left-footed volley but relax and Millwall grab a deserved win. Bloor loses the ball to Dunphy, who releases Derek Possee for the first. Doug Allder curls an unstoppable shot past the shell-shocked Farmer to win it. Brian King defies Conroy late on.

FA Cup

Rd	Fixture	Date	Att		Pos	Res	F-A	H-T	1	2	3	4	5	6	7	8	9	10	11	12 sub used	Scorers, Times, and Referees
3	H MILLWALL	2/1	21,398	2:13	12	W	2-1	1-1	Banks	Marsh	Pejic	Bernard	Smith*	Bloor	Conroy	Greenhoff	Ritchie	Eastham	Burrows	Skeels	Ritchie 31, Greenhoff 77; Possee 1. Ref: A Fussey
									King	Brown B	Cripps	Dorney	Kitchener	Burnett	Possee	Boland	Bridges	Dunphy	Allder	Lees	
4	H HUDDERSFIELD	23/1	34,231	15	10	D	3-3	1-2	Banks	Marsh	Pejic	Bernard	Bloor	Skeels	Haslegrave	Greenhoff	Conroy	Eastham	Burrows*	Lees	Greenhoff 3, Burrows 65, Conroy 75; Worth' 33, Chap'n 37, Mahoney 49. Ref: D Laing
									Lawson	Clarke	Hutt	Nicholson	Ellam	Cherry	Smith S	Mahoney	Worthington	McGill	Chapman		
4R	A HUDDERSFIELD	26/1	40,363	15	10	D	0-0	0-0	Banks	Marsh	Pejic	Bernard	Bloor	Skeels	Haslegrave	Greenhoff	Conroy	Eastham	Smith*	Elder	Ref: D Laing
									Lawson	Clarke	Hutt	Nicholson	Ellam	Cherry	Smith S	Krzywicki*	Worthington	McGill	Chapman	Dobson	
4RR	N HUDDERSFIELD (at Old Trafford)	8/2	39,302	17	10	W	1-0	0-0	Banks	Marsh	Pejic	Bernard	Bloor*	Skeels	Haslegrave	Greenhoff	Conroy	Eastham	Smith	Elder	Greenhoff 68. Ref: D Laing
									Lawson	Jones	Hutt	Nicholson	Ellam	Cherry	Smith S	Greenhalgh	Worthington	McGill	Chapman		
5	H IPSWICH	13/2	36,809	18	10	D	0-0	0-0	Banks	Marsh	Pejic	Bernard	Smith	Skeels	Haslegrave	Greenhoff*	Conroy	Eastham	Burrows	Elder	Ref: E Wallace
									Sivell	Hammond	Mills	Morris	Bell	Jefferson	Robertson	Viljoen	Clarke	McNeil	Hill		
5R	A IPSWICH	16/2	30,232	18	10	W	1-0	0-0	Banks	Marsh	Pejic	Bernard	Smith	Bloor	Haslegrave	Skeels	Conroy	Eastham	Burrows		Smith 74. Ref: E Wallace
									Sivell	Hammond	Mills	Morris	Bell	McNeil	Robertson	Viljoen	Clarke	Collard*	Hill	Lambert	
QF	A HULL	6/3	41,452	2:4	9	W	3-2	1-2	Banks	Marsh	Pejic	Bernard	Smith	Bloor	Haslegrave*	Conroy	Ritchie	Skeels	Burrows	Mahoney	Conroy 45, Ritchie 70, 81; Wagstaff 15, 35. Ref: B Homewood
									McKechnie	Banks	De Vries	Wilkinson	Neill	Simpkin	Lord	Houghton	Chilton	Wagstaff	Butler		

Match 3 — Millwall upset Stoke once again as Derek Possee grabs a first-minute goal. Incessant Stoke pressure finally pays off when John Ritchie buries George Eastham's free-kick. Gallant Millwall hold out until 13 mins from time when Jimmy Greenhoff's left-foot volley goes in off the post.

Match 4 — Stoke's early lead is cancelled out by three opportunist strikes either side of half-time. A frantic fightback sees Burrows put clear by Eastham and Conroy find the net in a goalmouth scramble. A frenetic finale ensues with both sides having chances to win. Terry Lees makes his debut.

Match 4R — Stalemate on a rain-soaked night. Over 5,000 Stokies see a heroic effort by an injury-hit team led by Denis Smith. He loses half an ear-lobe in a challenge with namesake Steve. Extra-time is tough but Steve Smith's effort is disallowed for offside. Waddo wins toss to choose next venue.

Match 4RR — 'The eleven fittest players will play,' says Tony Waddington before the game as the injury crisis deepens. It is a grim struggle but Stoke finally emerge on top as the epic tie is decided by Jimmy Greenhoff, who flicks home Terry Conroy's cross. Gordon Banks is rarely troubled in goal.

Match 5 — Another stalemate as defensive Ipswich stand firm under intense pressure. Conroy comes closest in a game of few chances, while Banks saves from Peter Morris in a one on one. Derek Jefferson flattens Greenhoff as it gets physical towards the end. Another game is not what City need.

Match 5R — Denis Smith grabs the winner as Haslegrave's deep cross finds Smith 8in from goal. Burrows and Haslegrave are sharp on the wings throughout. Stoke's pressing is nearly undone by Ian Collard but Banks saves when he is clean through. Battle-hardened City march on.

Match QF — With snow swirling around Boothferry Park, Ken Wagstaff's goals seem to put Terry Neill's men in control. Conroy rounds the keeper right on the whistle. The winner is Ritchie's far-post header from a throw incorrectly given to Stoke. All hands to the pump at the end. Banks is superb.

Semi-final & Third-place matches

SF · 27/3 · ARSENAL · 12 · D · 2-2 · 2-0 — Smith 22, Ritchie 31 / Storey 49, 90p
Ref: P Partridge — 54,770 (2) (at Hillsborough)

Stoke	Banks	Skeels	Pejic	Greenhoff	Smith	Bloor	Mahoney	Bernard	Ritchie	Conroy	Burrows
Arsenal	*Wilson*	*Rice*	*McNab*	*Storey*	*McLintock*	*Simpson*	*Armstrong*	*Graham*	*Radford*	*Kennedy*	*George*

25,000 City fans are rewarded with a fantastic first half from Stoke. Smith prods home after a corner and Ritchie slots from Charlie George's suicidal back-pass. At 2-1 Stoke hang on until the 6th minute of injury-time. Mahoney handles a header on the line. Storey cruelly beats Banks.

R · 31/3 · ARSENAL · 12 · L · 0-2 · 0-1 — Graham 13, Kennedy 47
Ref: P Partridge — 62,356 (2) (a Villa Park)

Stoke	Banks	Skeels	Pejic	Greenhoff	Smith	Bloor	Mahoney	Bernard	Ritchie	Conroy	Burrows
Arsenal	*Wilson*	*Rice*	*McNab*	*Storey*	*McLintock*	*Simpson*	*Armstrong*	*Graham*	*Radford*	*Kennedy*	*George*

Disheartened Stoke are never in it after George Graham's early header. Charlie George lets the ball run through his legs to put Ray Kennedy in for the clincher shortly after the interval. Frank McLintock marshalls assured Arsenal through to Wembley and an appointment with history.

3P · 7/5 · EVERTON · 13 · W · 3-2 · 1-2 — Bernard 27, Ritchie 47, 80 / Whittle 8, Ball 17
Ref: B Homewood — 5,031 (14) (at Selhurst Park)

Stoke	Banks	Skeels	Pejic	Greenhoff	Smith	Lees	Haslegrave	Bernard	Ritchie	Mahoney	Burrows*
Everton	*Rankin*	*Wright*	*Newton H*	*Kendall*	*Labone*	*Harvey*	*Whittle*	*Ball*	*Johnson*	*Lyons*	*Morrissey*

Sub: Burrows* / Jump

A patched up City defence concedes two early goals and Pejic heads off the line. The comeback is begun by the battling Bernard. Ritchie wins it from Mahoney's pass. 'Watch out for us in the Cups next year!' says the exuberant Bernard. Stoke's 56th competitive match of the season!

Appearances & Goals

	Appearances						Goals			
	Lge	Sub	LC	Sub	FAC	Sub	Lge	LC	FAC	Tot
Banks, Gordon	39				10					
Bernard, Mike	40		1		10		2	1		3
Bloor, Alan	36		2		8		1			1
Burrows, Harry	33	1	1		8		5		1	6
Conroy, Terry	34		2		9		11	1	2	14
Dobing, Peter	11		2		2		2			2
Eastham, George	16	3	2		6	3				
Elder, Alex	3	2								
Farmer, John	3		1							
Greenhoff, Jimmy	33		2		8		7		3	10
Haslegrave, Sean	15				7					
Jump, Stewart	10	2				1	1			1
Lees, Terry	4	3			1					
Mahoney, John	15	3			3	1				
Marsh, Jackie	34		2		8					
Pejic, Mike	42		2		10					
Ritchie, John	26	1	1	1	5	1	13	1	5	19
Skeels, Eric	27	2	2		9	1				
Smith, Denis	36		2		8		2			2
Smith, Terry	2	1								
Stevenson, Willie	3	2	1							
(own-goals)							1			1
21 players used	462	22	22	2	110	7	44	1	15	60

League table

		P	Home					Away					Pts
			W	D	L	F	A	W	D	L	F	A	
1	Arsenal	42	18	3	0	41	6	11	4	6	30	23	65
2	Leeds	42	16	2	3	40	12	11	8	2	32	18	64
3	Tottenham	42	11	5	5	33	19	8	9	4	21	14	52
4	Wolves	42	13	3	5	33	22	9	5	7	31	32	52
5	Liverpool	42	11	10	0	30	10	6	7	8	12	14	51
6	Chelsea	42	12	6	3	34	21	6	9	6	18	21	51
7	Southampton	42	12	5	4	35	15	5	7	9	21	29	46
8	Manchester U	42	9	6	6	29	24	7	5	9	36	42	43
9	Derby	42	9	5	7	32	26	7	5	9	24	28	42
10	Coventry	42	12	4	5	24	12	4	6	11	13	26	42
11	Manchester C	42	7	9	5	30	22	5	8	8	17	20	41
12	Newcastle	42	9	9	3	27	16	5	4	12	17	30	41
13	STOKE	42	10	7	4	28	11	2	6	13	16	37	37
14	Everton	42	10	7	4	32	16	2	6	13	22	44	37
15	Huddersfield	42	7	8	6	19	16	4	6	11	21	33	36
16	Nott'm Forest	42	9	4	8	29	26	5	4	12	13	35	36
17	West Brom	42	9	8	4	34	25	1	7	13	24	50	35
18	Crys Palace	42	9	5	7	24	24	3	6	12	15	33	35
19	Ipswich	42	9	4	8	28	22	3	6	12	14	26	34
20	West Ham	42	6	8	7	28	30	4	6	11	19	30	34
21	Burnley	42	4	8	9	20	31	3	5	13	9	32	27
22	Blackpool	42	3	9	9	22	31	1	6	14	12	35	23
		924	215	135	112	652	437	112	135	215	437	652	924

Odds & ends

Double wins: (2) Huddersfield, Newcastle.
Double losses: (2) Chelsea, Tottenham.

Won from behind: (2) West Ham (h), Coventry (h).
Lost from in front: (2) Leeds (a), Chelsea (h).

High spots: Reaching the FA Cup semi-final for second time in the club's history.
The first-half display at Hillsborough.
Thrashing Arsenal 5-0 in the League.
Finishing third in the FA Cup!

Low spots: Storey's last-minute penalty that denied Stoke a Wembley appearance.
Losing the FA Cup semi-final replay.
The dreadful injury crisis which lasts all season.
Defeat by Millwall in the League Cup.
The slump in attendance at the end of the season.

Ever-presents: (1) Mike Pejic.
Hat-tricks: (0).
Leading scorer: (19) John Ritchie.

LEAGUE DIVISION 1 — Manager: Tony Waddington — SEASON 1971-72

No	Date	Team	Att	Pos	Pt	F-A	H-T	Scorers, Times, and Referees	1	2	3	4	5	6	7	8	9	10	11	12 sub used
1	A 14/8	COVENTRY	20,739		D 1	1-1	0-1	Ritchie 46 / Hunt 44 / Ref: V James	Banks	Marsh	Pejic	Bernard	Smith	Bloor	Mahoney*	Greenhoff	Ritchie	Stevenson	Haslegrave	Skeels
								Pre-season title talk is dashed as Stoke struggle against Noel Cantwell's Sky Blues. Ritchie turns Jeff Blockley to equalize Hunt's close-range header. Greenhoff has a penalty appeal turned down in the dying minutes. Willie Stevenson returns from his ten-month broken leg nightmare.	*Glazier*	*Smith*	*Cattlin*	*Machin*	*Blockley*	*Barry*	*Mortimer*	*Carr*	*Rafferty**	*Hunt*	*Clements*	*Alderson*
2	A 17/8	SOUTHAMPTON	18,382		L 1	1-3	0-2	Greenhoff 82 / Channon 8, Smith 35 (og), Stokes 46 / Ref: M Kerkhof	Banks	Martin	Pejic	Bernard*	Smith	Bloor	Mahoney	Greenhoff	Ritchie	Stevenson	Haslegrave	Skeels
								The FA's new 'get tough' refereeing policy sees Ritchie and Banks booked for protesting as Stoke go three down despite having most of the play. Channon scores a beauty and Smith's own-goal is a 30-yard lob over Banks' head. Marsh hits the post and Mahoney is denied a penalty.	*Martin*	*Kirkup*	*Hollywood*	*Fisher*	*McGrath*	*Gabriel*	*Paine*	*Channon*	*Stokes*	*O'Neil*	*Jenkins*	
3	H 21/8	CRYSTAL PALACE	18,958	11 / 19	W 3	3-1	2-0	Ritchie 20p, Mahoney 44, Greenhoff 52 / Tambling 50 / Ref: G Jones	Banks	Jackson	Pejic	Bernard	Smith	Bloor	Mahoney	Greenhoff	Ritchie	Dobing	Haslegrave	Hadley
								Stoke swarm all over Palace. Haslegrave's early effort is ruled out for offside. John Ritchie is bundled over for the penalty. Mahoney's goal is his first since 12 Oct 1968. Greenhoff nods in after Dobing's shot is tipped on to a post. Tambling has a late goal disallowed for fouling Banks.	*Jackson*	*Payne*	*Wall*	*Kember*	*McCormack*	*Blyth*	*Wharton*	*Tambling**	*Scott*	*Queen*	*Taylor*	*Hoadley*
4	H 25/8	LEICESTER	21,678	9 / 16	W 5	3-1	0-0	Ritchie 64, Bernard 78, Dobing 80 / Brown 63 / Ref: C Robinson	Banks	Shilton	Pejic	Bernard	Smith	Bloor	Mahoney	Greenhoff*	Ritchie	Dobing	Haslegrave	Skeels
								Newly promoted Leicester are dazzled by half an hour of all-out attacking football. Ritchie's header equalizes Ally Brown's effort. Bernard nets from Ritchie's pass and Dobing's shot goes in off Cross for his 200th career league goal. Shilton saves a penalty after Cross fouls Ritchie.	*Shilton*	*Whitworth*	*Nish*	*Kellard*	*Sjoberg*	*Cross*	*Farrington*	*Brown*	*Fern*	*Carlin*	*Sammels*	
5	A 28/8	ARSENAL	37,637	5 / 14	W 7	1-0	1-0	Ritchie 20 / Ref: J Thacker	Banks	Wilson	Pejic	Bernard*	Smith	Bloor	Mahoney	Greenhoff*	Ritchie	Dobing	Haslegrave	Stevenson
								Revenge for Stoke against the shaky champions. In blustery conditions Ritchie lashes a long through-ball past Bob Wilson. Smith and Bloor dominate for City. Gunners' dangerman Armstrong finds Ray Kennedy unmarked but he miskicks Arsenal's best chance. Smith booked again.	*Wilson*	*Rice**	*McNab*	*Storey*	*McLintock*	*Simpson*	*Armstrong*	*Kelly*	*Radford*	*Kennedy*	*Graham*	*Roberts*
6	A 31/8	NOTT'M FOREST	19,017	5 / 18	D 8	0-0	0-0	Ref: J Homewood	Banks	Barron	Pejic	Bernard	Smith	Bloor	Mahoney	Greenhoff	Ritchie	Dobing	Haslegrave*	Stevenson
								Stoke move into fifth spot after a grim battle at the City Ground. 4,000 away fans travel to see Ian Moore hit the bar from a free-kick and Jim Barron save pluckily from Sean Haslegrave. Gordon Banks' late dive keeps out John Winfield's effort. It is the fifth successive draw v Forest.	*Barron*	*Hindley*	*Winfield*	*Chapman*	*O'Kane*	*Fraser*	*Rees*	*McKenzie*	*Cormack*	*Jackson*	*Moore*	
7	H 4/9	WOLVES	29,026	12 / 5	L 8	0-1	0-0	Hegan 59 / Ref: C Nicholls	Banks	Parkes	Pejic	Bernard*	Smith	Bloor	Mahoney	Greenhoff*	Ritchie	Conroy	Haslegrave	Stevenson
								Conroy returns after a cartilage operation but it isn't Stoke's day as Ritchie puts a penalty over the bar on 27 mins after Bernard Shaw handles. Dan Hegan scores from Richards' pass. Sub Haslegrave nets with his first kick but it is ruled out for offside. Then skipper Dobing hits the post.	*Parkes*	*Shaw*	*Parkin*	*Bailey*	*Munro*	*McAlle*	*Hegan*	*Hibbitt*	*Richards*	*Dougan**	*Wagstaffe*	*Taylor*
8	A 11/9	DERBY	32,545	12 / 2	L 8	0-4	0-2	Todd 30, O'Hare 33, Hinton 50, [Gemmill 90] / Ref: E Wallace	Banks	Boulton	Pejic	Bernard*	Smith	Lees	Mahoney	Greenhoff	Ritchie	Dobing	Haslegrave	Stevenson
								Third-placed Derby pulverize City in a game of three bookings, the third for Smith who will now serve a suspension. Colin Todd's curling shot and John O'Hare's fine leap bring the Rams' best goals. Gemmill sweeps home the fourth after incessant pressure. Banks keeps it respectable.	*Boulton*	*Webster*	*Robson*	*Todd*	*McFarland*	*Gemmill*	*Durban*	*Wignall*	*O'Hare*	*Hector*	*Hinton*	
9	H 18/9	HUDDERSFIELD	16,463	10 / 21	W 10	1-0	1-0	Conroy 25 / Ref: A Hart	Banks	Lawson D	Pejic	Bernard	Smith	Jump	Haslegrave	Greenhoff*	Ritchie	Dobing	Conroy	Mahoney
								Conroy's first goal since his comeback from injury sneaks in at the near post as he beats Roy Ellam to the ball. The makeshift defence holds firm. Banks defies a disbelieving Jimmy Lawson and Worthington has a goal ruled out for offside. City fail to convert several late chances.	*Lawson D*	*Clarke*	*Hutt*	*McGill*	*Ellam*	*Cherry*	*Hoy*	*Smith S**	*Worthington*	*Lawson J*	*Chapman*	*Krzywicki*
10	A 25/9	WEST HAM	29,193	12 / 10	L 10	1-2	0-1	Ritchie 58 / Best 26, Moore 78 / Ref: C Thomas	Banks	Ferguson	Pejic	Bernard	Smith	Bloor	Mahoney	Greenhoff	Ritchie	Dobing	Conroy*	Stevenson
								The returning Smith and Bloor fail to snuff out Clyde Best's physical presence. His header eludes everyone for the opener. Ritchie bends in a left-footed equalizer but a rare goal from Bobby Moore, deflected past the luckless Banks, sinks Stoke. John Ritchie misses when well placed.	*Ferguson*	*McDowell*	*Lampard*	*Bonds*	*Taylor*	*Moore*	*Ayris**	*Best*	*Hurst*	*Brooking*	*Robson*	*Howe*
11	H 2/10	LIVERPOOL	28,698	11 / 8	D 11	0-0	0-0	Ref: H Davey	Banks	Marsh	Jump	Bernard	Smith	Bloor	Mahoney	Greenhoff	Conroy*	Dobing	Haslegrave	Mahoney
								In the dazzling sun ITV's cameras see a stalemate as Liverpool fail to find a way past City's dominant back four. Woeful shooting means both the goalkeepers have a quiet afternoon. Denis Smith heads Stoke's best chance straight at Ray Clemence. Stoke fans are by far the happier.	*Clemence*	*Lawler*	*Lindsay*	*Ross*	*Lloyd*	*Hughes*	*Hall*	*McLaughlin*	*Heighway*	*Graham*	*Callaghan*	

Football season match log (Stoke City) — matches 12–23

Match 12 (Sheffield United) — report
Super Stoke defeat league leaders United in a ding-dong battle. Alan Woodward's early penalty, after Jump and Dearden collide, is equalized by Ritchie with his injured left foot. Smith taps in from two yards and Terry Conroy grabs the winner after a thunderous Tony Currie equaliser.
Sheffield United: Hope | Badger | Hemsley | Flynn | Colquhoun | Hockey | Woodward | Salmons | Dearden* | Currie | Scullion | Reece
Ref: B Daniels

---

13 — H COVENTRY — 16/10 — W 1-0 (HT 0-0) — Att 20,040 — 9 12 15
Scorer: Smith 82
Ref: G Hill
Stoke: Banks | Marsh | Pejic | Smith | Bloor | Smith | Greenhoff | Conroy | Ritchie | Stevenson | Jump
Coventry: Glazier | Coop | Barry | Smith | Blackley | Parker | Young* | Carr | Chilton | St John | Hunt | Alderson
Report: Banks returns injured from England duty v Switzerland but plays with a strapped knee. Denis Smith heads the winner from Conroy's corner. Jump starts as sweeper, his seventh position so far. Waddington is watching Shrewsbury striker Alf Wood, the league's leading scorer with 14.

14 — A IPSWICH — 23/10 — L 1-2 (HT 1-2) — Att 17,678 — 10 13 15
Scorers: Bernard 33 / Hill 27, 36
Ref: R Raby
Stoke: Banks | Marsh | Pejic | Smith | Bloor | Smith | Greenhoff | Conroy | Mahoney | Dobing | Jump
Ipswich: Sivell | Mills | Harper | Viljoen | Hunter | Jefferson | Robertson | Collard* | Clarke | Hill | Miller | Lambert
Report: Against a weakened City team, Ipswich win only their second home game of the season. Stoke miss Smith's height as new Welsh cap Mick Hill outleaps Jump for both Town goals. Bernard scores after Sivell parries Mahoney's shot and Dobing has a late equalizer ruled out for pushing.

15 — H TOTTENHAM — 30/10 — W 2-0 (HT 0-0) — Att 28,343 — 10 8 17
Scorer: Mahoney 49, 55
Ref: S Kayley
Stoke: Banks | Marsh | Pejic | Smith | Bloor | Smith | Greenhoff | Conroy | Ritchie | Eastham | Jump
Tottenham: Jennings | Evans | Knowles | Mullery* | England | Beal | Pearce | Perryman | Chivers | Peters | Neighbour | Pratt
Report: In George Eastham's first league game since returning from South Africa two left-footed strikes from John Mahoney, cutting in from the wing, give Stoke victory over high-flying Spurs. Jump and Smith snuff out England's Martin Chivers. Jennings turns Conroy's shot around the post.

16 — A WEST BROM — 6/11 — W 1-0 (HT 1-0) — Att 19,207 — 8 17 19
Scorer: Greenhoff 42p
Ref: W Gow
Stoke: Banks | Marsh | Pejic | Smith | Bloor | Smith | Greenhoff | Conroy | Ritchie | Dobing | Mahoney
West Brom: Osborne | Minton | Wilson | Cantello | Wile | Robertson | Brown T | Glover | Johnson | Gould | Hope
Report: Ritchie has a penalty appeal turned down before he wins one for being upended by Osborne. Marsh heads off the line from John Wile but City are in control. Ritchie and Greenhoff miss when clean through. Stoke curb Tony Brown and Albion miss Asa Hartford, being sold to Leeds.

17 — H CHELSEA — 13/11 — D 0-1 (HT 0-1) — Att 22,190 — 8 11 19
Scorer: Osgood 43
Ref: C Howell
Stoke: Banks | Marsh | Pejic | Smith | Bloor | Smith | Greenhoff | Conroy | Ritchie | Dobing | Mahoney
Chelsea: Bonetti | Boyle | Harris | Hollins | Dempsey | Webb | Cooke | Baldwin | Osgood | Hudson | Houseman
Report: Glamour boys Chelsea snatch a win at the Vic thanks to Peter Osgood's strike from John Boyle's pass. Banks saves point blank from Tommy Baldwin before Stoke have two penalty appeals turned down. Banks is by far the busier keeper as Stoke leave their shooting boots at home.

18 — A LEEDS — 20/11 — L 0-1 (HT 0-1) — Att 32,012 — 10 4 19
Scorer: Lorimer 5
Ref: D Smith
Stoke: Banks | Marsh | Pejic | Smith | Bloor | Smith | Greenhoff | Conroy | Ritchie | Dobing | Eastham
Leeds: Sprake | Madeley | Cooper | Bremner | Charlton | Hunter | Lorimer | Clarke | Jones | Giles | Gray
Report: Jump's mistake lets in Lorimer for the only goal of a game that Leeds control. Gray and Bremner run midfield. Banks saves point blank from Lorimer and tips Bremner's bicycle kick over. Gary Sprake saves well from Greenhoff. Smith has a header ruled out but City are well beaten.

19 — H NEWCASTLE — 27/11 — D 3-3 (HT 1-1) — Att 16,815 — 11 19 20
Scorers: Ritchie 22, Conroy 65, 70 / MacDonald 15, 79, Craig 81
Ref: R Challis
Stoke: Banks | Marsh | Pejic | Smith | Bloor | Smith | Greenhoff | Conroy | Ritchie | Dobing | Mahoney
Newcastle: McFaul | Craig | Clark | Howard | Burton | Nattrass | Barrowclough* | Green | MacDonald | Tudor | Hibbitt | Reid
Report: A fabulous tussle in the mud sees Pejic cross for Ritchie to finish neatly for Stoke's opener. Conroy puts City 3-1 up and cruising with 20 mins left. Newcastle hit back through SuperMac and David Craig to force a draw. Craig's shot hits a bump in the goalmouth and flies past Banks.

20 — A EVERTON — 4/12 — D 0-0 (HT 0-0) — Att 35,469 — 11 15 21
Ref: M Sinclair
Stoke: Banks | Marsh | Pejic | Smith | Bloor | Smith | Greenhoff | Conroy | Ritchie | Dobing | Eastham
Everton: West | Wright | McLaughlin | Kendall | Kenyon | Harvey* | Johnson | Ball | Royle | Hurst | Whittle | Husband
Report: Stoke have a defensive look at Goodison against Everton, fresh from an 8-0 thrashing of Southampton. Denis Smith, in his last game before a three-week ban, stars in a fierce battle. Pejic is booked. Banks saves point blank from David Johnson and Dobing misses Stoke's best chance.

21 — H MANCHESTER U — 11/12 — D 1-1 (HT 1-1) — Att 33,807 — 11 1 22
Scorers: Mahoney 27 / Law 28
Ref: H New
Stoke: Banks | Marsh | Pejic | Smith | Bloor | Smith | Greenhoff | Conroy | Ritchie | Dobing | Mahoney
Manchester U: Stepney | O'Neil | Burns | Gowling | James | Sadler | Morgan | Kidd* | Charlton | Law | Best | McIlroy
Report: John Mahoney, playing up front, flicks home Ritchie's header to put City ahead against the league leaders. Denis Law's header a minute later restores parity. Stoke have the upper hand through Dobing and Eastham's probing but United have ten men behind the ball to ensure a point.

22 — A WOLVES — 18/12 — L 0-2 (HT 0-2) — Att 22,619 — 11 9 22
Scorers: Dougan 60, Bloor 89 (og)
Ref: H Williams
Stoke: Banks | Marsh | Pejic | Skeels | Bloor | Smith | Greenhoff | Conroy | Stevenson | Ritchie | Mahoney
Wolves: Parkes | Shaw | Parkin | Bailey | Munro | McAlle | Hibbitt | McCalliog | Richards | Dougan | Wagstaffe | Eastham
Report: Fussy referee Williams gives seven free-kicks in the opening five minutes of a scrappy affair which Wolves get the upper hand in through Jim McCalliog's industry. Derek Dougan heads home a Wagstaffe cross and Shaw's header deflects in off Bloor. Skeels battles well for Stoke.

23 — H MANCHESTER C — 27/12 — L 1-3 (HT 0-1) — Att 43,007 — 11 2 22
Scorers: Smith 90 / Towers 14, Book 83, Lee 85
Ref: K Burns
Stoke: Banks | Marsh | Pejic | Bernard | Bloor | Smith | Greenhoff* | Conroy | Jump | Dobing | Mahoney | Eastham*
Manchester C: Corrigan | Book | Donachie | Doyle | Booth | Oakes | Summerbee | Bell | Lee | Davies | Towers | Skeels
Report: Stoke's highest attendance for five years, with over 1,000 locked out, sees Man City keep up the championship challenge with a fine win. The pressure finally tells on Stoke's defence when Book and Lee drive home goals in scrambles just before time. Smith's tap-in is no consolation.

LEAGUE DIVISION 1 — Manager: Tony Waddington — SEASON 1971-72

No	Date	Att	Pos	Pt	F-A	H-T	Scorers, Times, and Referees	1	2	3	4	5	6	7	8	9	10	11	12 sub used
24	A 1/1 HUDDERSFIELD	12,665	12 / 19	D 23	0-0	0-0	Ref: D Laing	Banks	Marsh	Pejic	Bernard	Smith	Jump	Dobing	Skeels	Conroy	Jackson	Mahoney*	Eastham
								Lawson D	Clarke	Hutt	Smith S	Ellam	Cherry	Fairclough	Dolan	Worthington	Lawson J	Chapman	
	commentary						Banks is the star, flinging himself to the left to deny Chapman and to the right to save from Clarke. Struggling Town can't find a way past him. Stoke struggle for fluency in yet another goalless draw with the Terriers. George Jackson (20) has a happy New Year when given his debut.												
25	H 8/1 ARSENAL	18,965	11 / 8	D 24	0-0	0-0	Ref: E Jolly	Banks	Marsh	Pejic	Bernard	Smith	Bloor	Jackson	Mahoney	Conroy	Skeels	Eastham*	Jump
								Wilson	Rice	McNab	Kelly	McLintock	Simpson	Armstrong	Ball	Radford	Kennedy	Graham	
	commentary						Dobing and Bernard are flu victims while Arsenal field new record £220,000 signing Alan Ball. Eastham is captain in his 500th league game. Skeels shackles Ball as makeshift Stoke take a deserved point. Waddo is interested in signing Argentinian Babbington, on trial at the club.												
26	H 22/1 SOUTHAMPTON	17,480	11 / 18	W 26	3-1	1-0	Ritchie 12, Greenhoff 51, 82, Byrne 85 — Ref: R Matthewson	Banks	Marsh	Pejic	Bernard	Smith	Bloor	Conroy	Greenhoff	Ritchie	Dobing	Mahoney	
								Martin	McCafferty	Fry	Stokes	Gabriel	Byrne	Paine	Channon	Davies	O'Brien	Jenkins	
	commentary						City trounce Saints and could have had a hatful. Ritchie rounds Eric Martin for the opener. Jimmy Greenhoff's first is a 30-yarder cannoning in off the angle. He wraps it up when put through by Ritchie. Tony Byrne's late consolation is overshadowed by Stoke's superb attacking display.												
27	A 29/1 LEICESTER	26,931	11 / 12	L 26	1-2	1-2	Greenhoff 13, Glover 25, Farrington 28 — Ref: G Kew	Banks	Marsh	Pejic	Bernard	Smith	Bloor	Mahoney	Greenhoff	Ritchie	Dobing	Eastham	Fern
								Shilton	Whitworth	Nish	Cross	Sjoberg	Brown	Weller	Farrington	Birchenall*	Sammels	Glover	
	commentary						Ritchie flattens Shilton early on and Stoke snatch the lead when the keeper cannot reach a corner and Greenhoff fires in. Leicester roar back as Len Glover's 30-yard rocket scorches past Banks and John Farrington coolly slots home. Leicester run the second half. City cannot compete.												
28	H 12/2 IPSWICH	20,247	13 / 16	D 27	3-3	0-1	Ritchie 55, Greenhoff 75p, Smith 87, Lambert 14, 57, Miller 62 — Ref: H Hackney	Banks	Marsh	Skeels	Bernard*	Smith	Bloor	Conroy	Greenhoff	Ritchie	Dobing	Mahoney	Jackson
								Best	Mills	Harper	Morris	Hunter	Jefferson	Miller*	Viljoen	Belfitt	Clarke	Lambert	Woods
	commentary						A great comeback by City who look dead and buried after John Miller's soaring 22-yarder beats Banks. The penalty is given by the linesman – no-one knows what for! Smith's equalizer is a flying header at boot level. Another draw against Ipswich but much more entertaining this time.												
29	A 19/2 TOTTENHAM	32,841	13 / 5	L 27	0-2	0-1	Chivers 39, 90 — Ref: C Nicholls	Banks	Skeels	Pejic	Stevenson	Smith	Bloor	Haslegrave	Conroy	Greenhoff	Jackson	Burrows*	Mahoney
								Jennings	Evans	Knowles	Coates	England	Beal	Gilzean*	Perryman	Chivers	Morgan	Holder	
	commentary						Chivers poaches a brace against England team-mate Banks, the first from 16 yards and then nipping in after Banks spills a cross late on. Big spending Spurs dominate but Stoke have chances. Jennings saves from Stevenson. Harry Burrows is injured again after his long-term lay-off.												
30	H 11/3 SHEFFIELD UTD	31,667	14 / 9	D 28	2-2	0-0	Smith 65, Ritchie 85, Smith 75 (og), Scullion 89 — Ref: J Hunting	Farmer	Marsh	Pejic	Bernard	Smith	Bloor	Jackson*	Conroy	Ritchie	Dobing	Mahoney	Ogden
								Hope	Badger	Hemsley	Mackenzie	Colquhoun	Salmons	Woodward	Scullion	Dearden*	Currie	Ford	
	commentary						The League Cup is paraded before kick-off. Mahoney fills in for Eastham after turning down an offer from Millwall. Stoke concede at the death after looking to have won it with Ritchie's shot from Smith's flick on. Smith heads past Farmer diving full length to clear Salmons' cross.												
31	H 25/3 DERBY	33,592	15 / 2	D 29	1-1	0-0	Greenhoff 48p, Durban 62 — Ref: R Kirkpatrick	Banks	Marsh	Jump	Bernard	Smith	Bloor	Conroy	Greenhoff	Ritchie	Dobing	Burrows	
								Boulton	Webster	Robson	Durban	McFarland	Todd	McGovern	Gemmill	Hector	Hinton	Walker	
	commentary						Todd brings down the returning Harry Burrows for Stoke's penalty. Alan Durban equalizes with a glorious bending free-kick. Cloughie leaves the Vic in a huff after Hector's late goal is ruled out for kicking the ball from Banks' grasp. New England cap Roy McFarland quells Ritchie.												
32	A 28/3 LIVERPOOL	42,489	15 / 4	L 29	1-2	1-1	Ritchie 35, Callaghan 41, Keegan 54 — Ref: W Gow	Banks	Marsh	Jump	Stevenson	Smith	Bloor	Conroy	Greenhoff	Ritchie	Eastham*	Burrows	Skeels
								Clemence	Lawler	Lindsay	Smith	Lloyd	Hughes	Keegan	Hall	Heighway	Toshack	Callaghan	
	commentary						Gordon Banks nearly silences the Kop with a fabulous performance. Ritchie nods in the opener. Stoke look in charge until Callaghan belts one from 25 yards and Keegan beats Jump to the ball to force in the winner. Clemence saves from Greenhoff. Banks' display earns him an ovation.												
33	A 1/4 MANCHESTER C	49,392	15 / 1	W 31	2-1	1-1	Doyle 35 (og), Ritchie 53, Lee 37 — Ref: T Reynolds	Banks	Marsh	Elder	Bernard	Smith	Bloor	Conroy	Greenhoff	Ritchie	Dobing*	Burrows	Skeels
								Healey	Book	Donachie	Doyle	Booth	Oakes	Summerbee	Bell	Davies	Lee	Hill	
	commentary						Stoke grab a win in their third game in a week against a top-four team. Ritchie's shot rebounds off Healey onto Mike Doyle for the opener. Lee fires home after Marsh lets the ball run through his legs but Ritchie rounds the keeper to win it. City's defence frustrates the Blues' title hopes.												
34	H 4/4 WEST HAM	24,688	14 / 12	D 32	0-0	0-0	Ref: E Wallace	Banks	Marsh	Elder	Bernard	Bloor	Skeels	Conroy	Greenhoff	Ritchie	Dobing	Eastham	
								Grotier	McDowell	Lampard	Bonds	Taylor	Moore	Redknapp	Best	Hurst	Brooking	Robson	
	commentary						Patched up Stoke withstand heavy pressure. Skeels clears dramatically from Best's shot on 14 mins with Banks beaten. Brooking is denied by unsighted Banks' wonder save low to his right and Stoke cling on. Grotier, in for the injured Ferguson, denies Eastham, who also hits the post.												

#		Date	Opponent	Pos	W/L/D	Score	Att		
				35,123	4	32			
36	H	10/4	N'TT'M FOREST	15	L	0-1	13,920	22	32
37	H	22/4	EVERTON	16	D	1-1	16,796	15	33
38	A	24/4	CHELSEA	16	L	0-2	23,443	7	33
39	A	26/4	CRYSTAL PALACE	17	L	0-2	24,550	20	33
40	A	29/4	MANCHESTER U	17	L	0-3	34,959	7	33
41	H	5/5	WEST BROM	17	D	1-1	16,206	16	34
42	A	8/5	NEWCASTLE	17	D	0-0	21,350	11	35

Home 24,235 Away 28,098 — Average 28,098

(continuation of Match 35 — Leeds lineup at head of page)

Leeds: Harvey, Madeley, Cooper*, Bremner, Charlton, Hunter, Lorimer, Clarke, Jones, Giles, Gray, Reaney

Jones 39, 86, Lorimer 66 bb. Ref: K Walker

Smith plays through the pain barrier but to no avail as Leeds outplay Stoke. Black armbands are worn for ex-Stoke hero Bobby Liddle who has died. Jones twice buries long through-balls past Banks while Lorimer scores a typical right-foot belter. Terry Cooper breaks his leg at the close.

---

36 — N'TT'M FOREST (H)
Gemmell 34, McIntosh 48. Ref: P Partridge

Stoke: Farmer, Marsh, Pejic, Bernard, Skeels, Bloor, Jackson, Stevenson, Mahoney, Jump, Haslegrave, Lees
Forest: Barron, Hindley, Gemmell, Serella, Cottam, Fraser, Richardson, Martin, Cormack, McKenzie, McIntosh, Burrows

Stoke, lacking 11 first teamers, can't compete with doomed Forest. Driving rain makes conditions tricky and Farmer's nightmare sees Tommy Gemmell's free-kick leave him standing and McKenzie's cross squirm from his hands to McIntosh. Possible League enquiry into a weak team.

---

37 — EVERTON (H)
Lyons 30 (og), Kendall 88. Ref: P Oliver

Stoke: Banks, Marsh, Pejic, Bernard, Skeels, Bloor, Greenhoff, Dobing, Ritchie, Haslegrave, Burrows
Everton: West, Wright, McLaughlin, Kendall, Kenyon, Newton H, Husband, Buckley, Royle, Johnson, Lyons

Stoke find the resilience after their FA Cup exit to outplay Everton. Skeels, despite lack of height, contains Joe Royle well. Mick Lyons' own-goal is a comical header past Gordon West. Howard Kendall's late shot breaks stern resistance after Greenhoff, Ritchie and Burrows go close.

---

38 — CHELSEA (A)
Hudson 9, Garland 79. Ref: N Paget

Stoke: Farmer, Marsh, Pejic, Bernard, Smith, Bloor, Greenhoff, Dobing, Ritchie, Walker, Eastham, Haslegrave
Chelsea: Bonetti, Mulligan, Harris, Hollins, Droy, Webb, Garland, Baldwin, Hudson, Kember, Cooke

Pejic returns after a five-week ban and shows remarkable self control amidst severe provocation. He is punched by Mulligan who only receives a ticking off. Alan Hudson hits a scorching free-kick and Garland notches from close-in. Pejic also clears off the line as Stoke are well beaten.

---

39 — CRYSTAL PALACE (A)
Kellard 46p, Queen 79. Ref: C Thomas

Stoke: Farmer, Marsh, Pejic, Bernard, Smith, Bloor, Greenhoff, Dobing, Ritchie, Jackson, Haslegrave, Burrows
Palace: Jackson, Payne, Wall, Kellard, Blyth, McCormack, Craven, Queen, Wallace, Taylor, Tambling

City have a £150,000 bid for Burnley winger Dave Thomas rejected. Manager Bert Head's pledge to attack condemns Huddersfield and Forest to the drop. Waddo wants to reinforce an attack which hasn't scored in six. A bumpy pitch leads to the ball hitting Bernard's hand for the pen.

---

40 — MANCHESTER U (A)
Charlton 1, Moore 15, Best 45p. Ref: J Yates

Stoke: Farmer, Marsh, Pejic, Bernard, Skeels, Bloor, Stevenson, Greenhoff, Ritchie, Walker, Jackson, Lees
Man U: Stepney, O'Neil, Dunne, Buchan, James, Young, Best, McIlroy, Charlton*, Law, Moore, Gowling

United clinch it early on as Bobby Charlton scores before a City player touches the ball and then Moore rams home. Best's penalty comes after Pejic's magnificent two-handed save from Law's header. George Jackson goes close to scoring his first senior goal but Charlton runs the show.

---

41 — WEST BROM (H)
Burrows 68, Gould 29. Ref: G Hartley

Stoke: Banks, Marsh, Pejic, Bernard, Skeels, Bloor, Jump, Mahoney, Ritchie, Greenhoff, Burrows
WBA: Osborne, Nisbet, Wilson, Cantello*, Robertson, Wile, Hope, Suggett, Brown A, Hartford, Hughes

The club slashes prices to a blanket 30p for the last home game, on a Friday night to avoid a clashing with the Cup Final. Gould scores on the break as Stoke pile on the pressure at the other end. Osborne saves miraculously three times before Burrows' piledriver, his first goal in a year.

---

42 — NEWCASTLE (A)
Ref: E Jolly

Stoke: Farmer, Marsh, Pejic, Jump, Bloor, Smith, Mahoney, Greenhoff, Ritchie, Conroy, Haslegrave, Stevenson, Burrows
Newcastle: McFaul, Craig, Clark, Gibb, Howard, Moncur, Reid*, Green, MacDonald, Tudor, Hibbitt, Nattrass

Mike Bernard is sold to Everton for £125,000 as Stoke look to purchase new talent. An absorbing if uneventful match is dominated by the midfield tussle between Jump, Bernard's replacement, and Green. Pejic fires Stoke's best chance over as City's attack dries up once more.

League Cup

#		Date	Opponent	Pos	W/L/D	Score	Att	
2	A	8/9	SOUTHPORT	12	W	2-1	10,223	4:2
3	A	6/10	OXFORD	11	D	1-1	15,024	2:14
3R	H	18/10	OXFORD	9	W	2-0	11,767	2:10
4	A	26/10	MANCHESTER U	10	D	1-1	27,062	1
4R	H	8/11	MANCHESTER U	8	D	0-0 aet	41,829	1

2 — SOUTHPORT (A)
Bloor 10, Greenhoff 70; Dunleavy 16. Ref: H Hackney

Stoke: Farmer, Marsh, Pejic, Bernard, Smith, Bloor, Mahoney, Greenhoff, Ritchie, Dobing, Haslegrave
Southport: Taylor, Turner, Sibbald, McPhee, Peat, Lee, Sloan, Clayton, Dunleavy, Redrobe*, Hartle, Lloyd

Stoke are given an early penalty, but then the ref changes his mind and awards Southport a free-kick. Greenhoff wins it from Ritchie's cross.

---

3 — OXFORD (A)
Greenhoff 13; Evanson 78. Ref: K Walker

Stoke: Banks, Marsh, Pejic, Bernard, Smith, Bloor, Conroy, Greenhoff, Ritchie, Dobing, Haslegrave
Oxford: Kearns, Way, Shuker, Roberts, Clarke C, Evanson, Sloan, Skeen, Atkinson, Cassidy, Clayton

With £20,000 record signing Nigel Cassidy, Oxford control the game. Greenhoff nets after keeper Mick Kearns rolls the ball straight to Ritchie.

3R — OXFORD (H)
Ritchie 30, Haslegrave 86. Ref: K Walker

Stoke: Banks, Marsh, Pejic, Bernard, Smith, Bloor, Conroy, Greenhoff, Ritchie, Dobing, Haslegrave
Oxford: Kearns, Lucas, Shuker, Roberts, Clarke C, Evanson, Sloan, Skeen, Clayton D, Atkinson, Skeen

A tough affair is settled by Haslegrave's volley. Oxford create little until Roy Clayton heads against a post. Greenhoff injures his groin again.

---

4 — MANCHESTER U (A)
Ritchie 72; Gowling 84. Ref: V Jones

Stoke: Banks, Marsh, Pejic, Bernard, Smith, Bloor, Mahoney, Conroy, Ritchie, Greenhoff, Haslegrave
Man U: Stepney, O'Neil, Burns, Morgan, Sadler, James, Kidd, Charlton, Law, Best, Gowling

Man U are happy to draw. Ritchie has a header ruled out before scoring. Alan Gowling's late header flatters United. The crowd rise to Stoke.

4R — MANCHESTER U (H)
Ref: V James

Stoke: Banks, Marsh, Pejic, Bernard, Bloor, Smith, Mahoney, Greenhoff*, Ritchie, Conroy, Haslegrave, Lloyd
Man U: Stepney, O'Neil, Burns, Gowling, James, Sadler, Morgan, McIlroy, Charlton, Sartori, Best, Eastham

Few chances are created in normal time. Greenhoff injures his stomach and Bernard a wrist. The replay is put back, both sides are worn out.

League Cup (cont) — Match summary

Tie	Date	V	Opponents	Att	Pos	Res	F-A	H-T	Scorers, Times, and Referees
4 RR	15/11	H	MANCHESTER U	42,233 (1)	8	W	2-1	0-1	Dobing 70, Ritchie 88 / *Best 37* / Ref: B Homewood
5	23/11	A	BRISTOL ROV	33,626 (3:10)	10	W	4-2	2-0	Greenhoff 7, Smith 20, Bernard 61, Stubbs 75, Godfrey 90p, [Conroy 64] / Ref: R Nicholson
SF 1	8/12	H	WEST HAM	36,407 (13)	11	L	1-2	1-1	Dobing 14 / *Hurst 26p, Best 63* / Ref: A Morrissey
SF 2	15/12	A	WEST HAM	38,771 (12)	11	W	1-0	0-0	Ritchie 72 / Ref: K Walker
SF R	5/1	N	WEST HAM (at Hillsborough)	46,916 (11)	12	D	0-0	0-0	Ref: R Matthewson
SF RR	26/1	N	WEST HAM (at Old Trafford)	49,247 (12)	11	W	3-2	2-2	Bernard 32, Dobing 45, Conroy 49 / *Smith 34 (og), Brooking 45* / Ref: P Partridge
F	4/3	N	CHELSEA (at Wembley)	97,852 (10)	13	W	2-1	1-1	Conroy 5, Eastham 73 / *Osgood 45* / Ref: N Burtenshaw

FA Cup — Match summary

Tie	Date	V	Opponents	Att	Pos	Res	F-A	H-T	Scorers, Times, and Referees
3	15/1	H	CHESTERFIELD	26,559 (3:9)	11	W	2-1	1-1	Conroy 15, Dobing 67 / *Randall 39* / Ref: N Burtenshaw
4	5/2	A	TRANMERE	24,426 (3:17)	11	D	2-2	0-0	Conroy 68, Ritchie 75 / *Yeats 80, Ritchie 87* / Ref: H Davey
4R	9/2	H	TRANMERE	35,352 (3:17)	11	W	2-0	1-0	Bernard 31, Greenhoff 70p / Ref: H Davey
5	26/2	H	HULL	34,558 (2:20)	13	W	4-1	2-0	Greenhoff 44, 45, Conroy 79, Ritchie 87 / *Wagstaffe 82* / Ref: G Hill
QF	18/3	A	MANCHESTER U	53,620 (6)	14	D	1-1	0-0	Greenhoff 58 / *Best 83* / Ref: B Homewood

Line-ups (1–11, 12 = sub used; * = player substituted)

Tie	Team	1	2	3	4	5	6	7	8	9	10	11	12
4 RR	Stoke	Banks	Marsh	Pejic	Bernard	Smith	Bloor	Conroy	Greenhoff	Ritchie	Dobing	Mahoney*	Eastham
4 RR	Man U	Stepney	O'Neil	Burns	Gowling	James	Sadler	Morgan	McIlroy	Charlton	Sartori	Best	
5	Stoke	Banks	Marsh	Pejic	Bernard	Smith	Bloor	Conroy	Greenhoff	Ritchie	Dobing	Eastham	
5	Bristol Rov	Sheppard	Roberts	Parsons	Godfrey	Taylor	Prince	Stephens	Jones W	Jones R	Stubbs	Jarman	
SF 1	Stoke	Banks	Ferguson	Pejic	Bernard	Bloor	Jump	Conroy	Greenhoff	Ritchie	Dobing	Eastham	
SF 1	West Ham	Ferguson	McDowell	Lampard	Bonds	Taylor	Moore	Redknapp	Best	Hurst	Brooking	Robson	
SF 2	Stoke	Banks	Marsh	Pejic	Bernard	Bloor	Skeels	Conroy	Greenhoff	Ritchie	Dobing	Eastham*	Mahoney
SF 2	West Ham	Ferguson	McDowell	Lampard	Bonds	Moore	Taylor	Redknapp	Best	Hurst	Brooking	Robson	
SF R	Stoke	Banks	Ferguson	Pejic	Bernard	Bloor	Jump	Conroy	Greenhoff*	Ritchie	Dobing	Eastham	Skeels
SF R	West Ham	Ferguson	McDowell	Lampard	Bonds	Moore	Taylor	Redknapp	Best	Hurst	Brooking	Robson	
SF RR	Stoke	Banks	Marsh	Pejic	Bernard	Smith	Bloor	Conroy	Greenhoff	Ritchie	Dobing	Eastham	
SF RR	West Ham	Ferguson	McDowell	Lampard	Bonds	Moore	Taylor	Redknapp*	Best	Hurst	Brooking	Robson	Eustace
F	Stoke	Banks	Marsh	Pejic	Bernard	Smith	Bloor	Conroy	Greenhoff*	Ritchie	Dobing	Eastham	Mahoney
F	Chelsea	Bonetti	Mulligan*	Harris	Hollins	Dempsey	Webb	Cooke	Garland	Osgood	Hudson	Houseman	Baldwin
FA 3	Stoke	Banks	Marsh	Pejic	Bernard	Smith	Bloor	Conroy	Mahoney	Ritchie	Dobing	Eastham	
FA 3	Chesterfield	Stevenson	Holmes	Tiler	Bell	Statt	Pugh	Wilson	Moss	Randall	Phelan	McHale	
FA 4	Stoke	Banks	Skeels	Jump	Bernard	Smith	Bloor	Conroy	Mahoney	Ritchie	Dobing	Eastham	
FA 4	Tranmere	Lawrence	Mathias	Farrimond	Molyneux	Yeats	Fagan	Russell	Beamish	Crossley	Moore	Storton	
FA 4R	Stoke	Banks	Marsh	Skeels	Bernard	Smith	Jump	Conroy	Greenhoff	Ritchie	Dobing	Eastham	
FA 4R	Tranmere	Lawrence	Mathias	Farrimond	Molyneux	Yeats !	Fagan	Russell	Beamish	Moore	Storton	Crossley	
FA 5	Stoke	Banks	Marsh	Pejic	Bernard	Smith	Bloor	Conroy	Greenhoff	Ritchie	Dobing	Eastham	
FA 5	Hull	McKechnie	Banks	De Vries	Wilkinson	Neill	Baxter*	McGill	Lord	Kaye	Wagstaff	Butler	O'Riley
FA QF	Stoke	Banks	Marsh	Pejic	Bernard	Smith	Bloor	Conroy	Greenhoff	Ritchie	Dobing	Eastham	
FA QF	Man U	Stepney	O'Neil	Dunne	Buchan	James	Sadler*	Morgan	Kidd	Charlton	Law	Best	Gowling

Match reports

4 RR — Manchester U (H): Drama as the injured Ritchie heads City into the last eight. Behind for the first time in the tie to a George Best special, City slowly claw it back with Eastham's half-time introduction the turning point. He provides the cross for the winner. Clear chances at both ends but Stoke cling on.

5 — Bristol Rov (A): On a tricky surface Stoke steamroller Rovers. Greenhoff slots a superb opener, Denis Smith breaks two fingers heading the second, and only Dick Sheppard stands between Ritchie and a hatful. Banks stops Harry Jarman's piledriver but Stoke relax and concede two in the last 15 mins.

SF 1 — West Ham (H): Stoke's aim of a two-goal lead to take to Upton Park looks realistic when Dobing slots home after Greenhoff hits the post. Then Clyde Best earns a penalty for West Ham before belting home a goal good enough to win any game. City slip out of their stride and nearly out of the Cup.

SF 2 — West Ham (A): Sheer drama at Upton Park as Ritchie's goal seems to have taken it to a replay when Banks and Pejic get mixed up and Banks fells Redknapp. Pandemonium lets loose as Banks saves the penalty, blasted high to his right by fellow '66 hero Geoff Hurst. Away goals don't count double.

SF R — West Ham (at Hillsborough): Best misses two good chances for West Ham, but Stoke have most of the pressure. Bobby Ferguson denies Smith, Ritchie and Greenhoff, then Tommy Taylor clears Pejic's cross off the line. Extra-time cannot separate them, but City have the upper hand as Waddington wins the toss.

SF RR — West Ham (at Old Trafford): Bobby Moore, in goal for the injured Ferguson, saves Bernard's penalty but not the follow up. Conroy cracks home the winner after Brooking lashes in for the Irons to make it 1-2. Jubilation at wind-swept Old Trafford as City earn the first Wembley appearance in the club's history.

F — Chelsea (at Wembley): Conroy's close-range header is levelled by Peter Osgood's grounded finish. City gradually get on top and veteran George Eastham pokes home from three yards after Bonetti fails to hold Greenhoff's volley. Bernard's back-pass nearly lets in Garland but City cling on to win a Cup at last.

FA 3 — Chesterfield (H): City squeeze past Jimmy McGuigan's Spireites. Conroy beats Alan Stevenson but Chesterfield strike back. McHale almost claiming a replay.

FA 4 — Tranmere (A): While Hereford are beating Newcastle, City nearly lose at Tranmere. Their lead, doubled by Ritchie's header, is destroyed when Beamish nets.

FA 4R — Tranmere (H): Yeats is sent off when he appears to punch Bernard, who still nets despite a swollen cheek. With 10 men behind the ball, Rovers never threaten.

FA 5 — Hull (H): Stoke outclass Hull, who cannot repeat last season's heroics. Greenhoff coolly slots two in a minute to put City in control. Conroy's goal is a 25-yard right footer. Talk is of Wembley in both FA and League Cups. Greenhoff is denied a treble by the bar but Ritchie prods home the fourth.

FA QF — Manchester U (A): Stoke are at full strength for once and have the better of an open game. Greenhoff scores after Alex Stepney parries his initial shot. City defend stoutly with Marsh and Pejic booked as United pour forward. Bernard nearly seals it before George Best pounces home to force yet another replay.

									Stepney	*O'Neil*	*Dunne*	*Gowling*	*James*	*Buchan*	*Morgan**	*Kidd*	*Charlton*	*Law*	*Best*	*McIlroy*
							Ref: B Homewood	Denis Smith unricks his back getting out of his car and declares himself fit! In a frenetic match Gowling hits the bar and Stepney saves from Ritchie before Best scores. Hero Smith equalizes from Eastham's corner. Conroy's half-volley wins it, but only after Banks' two reflex saves.											
SF	N	ARSENAL	15	D	1-1	0-0	Simpson 65 (og)	Banks	Marsh	Elder	Bernard*	Smith	Bloor	Skeels	Greenhoff	Ritchie	Dobing	Eastham	Burrows
	15/4	56,570	6				*Armstrong 47*	*Wilson*	*Rice*	*McNab*	*Storey*	*McLintock*	*Simpson*	*Armstrong*	*Ball*	*George*	*Radford**	*Graham*	*Kennedy*
		(at Hillsborough)					Ref: K Walker	Stoke are out for revenge but Armstrong fires home for Arsenal after Bloor's weak clearance. Bob Wilson is injured collecting a cross and City immediately equalize as Smith challenges Simpson and the ball flies in. Dobing hits the inside of the post with stand-in keeper Radford beaten.											
SF	N	ARSENAL	17	L	1-2	1-0	Greenhoff 19p	Banks	Marsh	Elder	Bernard	Smith	Bloor	Skeels*	Greenhoff	Ritchie	Dobing	Eastham	Burrows
R	19/4	35,976	6				*George 55p, Radford 76*	*Barnett*	*Rice*	*McNab*	*Storey*	*McLintock*	*Simpson*	*Armstrong*	*Ball*	*Radford*	*George*	*Graham*	
		(at Goodison Park)					Ref: K Walker	City lead after Greenhoff is flattened by McLintock. Arsenal's penalty is for Dobing's push on Armstrong – highly contentious. Linesman Bob Matthewson mistakes a white-coated programme seller for a Stoke defender on the far side of the pitch allowing Radford to fire in the winner.											
3P	A	BIRMINGHAM		D	0-0	0-0		Farmer	Marsh	Pejic	Skeels	Smith	Bloor	**Robertson**	Greenhoff	Ritchie	**Hurst**	Dobing	
	5/8	23,841						*Cooper*	*Carroll*	*Pendrey*	*Smith*	*Hynd*	*Harland*	*Campbell*	*Francis*	*Latchford*	*Hatton*	*Taylor*	
							Ref: V James (City lost 3-4 on penalties)	Played as a pre-season kick-about, a dull game is only enlivened by the fierce contest between Denis Smith and Bob Latchford. Extra-time is plain boring. Dobing's kick is saved by Paul Cooper to earn the Blues the dubious distinction of being the last club to finish 3rd in the FA Cup.											

			Home					Away					
	P	W	D	L	F	A	W	D	L	F	A	Pts
1 Derby	42	16	4	1	43	10	8	6	7	26	23	58
2 Leeds	42	17	4	0	54	10	7	5	9	19	21	57
3 Liverpool	42	17	3	1	48	16	7	6	8	16	14	57
4 Manchester C	42	16	3	2	48	15	7	8	6	29	30	57
5 Arsenal	42	15	2	4	36	13	7	6	8	22	27	52
6 Tottenham	42	16	3	2	45	13	3	10	8	18	29	51
7 Chelsea	42	12	7	2	41	20	6	5	10	17	29	48
8 Manchester U	42	13	2	6	39	26	6	8	7	30	35	48
9 Wolves	42	10	7	4	35	23	8	4	9	30	34	47
10 Sheffield Utd	42	10	8	3	39	26	7	4	10	22	34	46
11 Newcastle	42	10	6	5	30	18	5	5	11	19	34	41
12 Leicester	42	9	6	6	18	11	4	7	10	23	35	39
13 Ipswich	42	7	8	6	19	19	4	8	9	20	34	38
14 West Ham	42	10	6	5	31	19	2	6	13	16	32	36
15 Everton	42	8	9	4	28	17	1	9	11	9	31	36
16 West Brom	42	6	7	8	22	23	6	4	11	20	31	35
17 STOKE	42	6	10	5	26	25	4	5	12	13	31	35
18 Coventry	42	7	10	4	27	23	2	5	14	17	44	33
19 Southampton	42	8	5	8	31	28	4	2	15	21	52	31
20 Crys Palace	42	4	8	9	26	31	4	5	12	13	34	29
21 Nott'm Forest	42	6	4	11	25	29	2	5	14	22	52	25
22 Huddersfield	42	4	7	10	12	22	2	6	13	15	37	25
	924	227	129	106	723	437	106	129	227	437	723	924

Odds & ends

Double wins: (0).
Double losses: (3) Chelsea, Leeds, Wolves.

Won from behind: (2) Leicester (h), Sheffield U (a).
Lost from in front: (2) Leicester (a), Liverpool (a).

High spots: Winning the first trophy in the club's history.
Beating Manchester U twice in the Cups.
The marathon semi-final versus West Ham.
Winning at Highbury for the first time since 1950.

Low spots: League form suffering due to the Cup runs.
The lowest League goals scored total since 1924-25.
No win in the last 9 league games.
The linesman's decision in the FA Cup semi-final replay.

Ever-presents: (0).
Hat-tricks: (0).
Leading scorer: (18) John Ritchie.

	Appearances						Goals			
	Lge	*Sub*	LC	*Sub*	FAC	*Sub*	Lge	LC	FAC	Tot
Banks, Gordon	36		11		8					
Bernard, Mike	36		12		8		2	2	1	5
Bloor, Alan	35		11		9			1		1
Burrows, Harry	10					*2*	1			1
Conroy, Terry	27		11		6		4	3	4	11
Dobing, Peter	27	*1*	10		9		1	3	1	5
Eastham, George	13	*1*	6	*2*	8			1		1
Elder, Alex	6				2					
Farmer, John	6		1		1					
Greenhoff, Jimmy	35		12		7		8	3	5	16
Haslegrave, Sean	17	*1*	2	*1*				1		1
Hurst, Geoff					1					
Jackson, George	8	*1*								
Jump, Stewart	17	*2*	5		2					
Lees, Terry	3	*2*								
Mahoney, John	25	*4*	4	*2*	2		4			4
Marsh, Jackie	41		12		8					
Pejic, Mike	32		12		4					
Robertson, Jimmy					1					
Ritchie, John	32		12		9		12	4	2	18
Skeels, Eric	13	*6*	1	*1*	5					
Smith, Denis	28		9		9		5	1	1	7
Smith, Terry	1									
Stevenson, Willie	12	*5*	1							
Walker, Tommy	2									
(own-goals)							2		1	3
25 players used	**462**	***23***	**132**	***6***	**99**	***2***	**39**	**19**	**15**	**73**

LEAGUE DIVISION 1

Manager: Tony Waddington — SEASON 1972-73

Match details

No	Venue	Opponent	Date	F-A	H-T	Att	Pos	Pt	Scorers, Times, and Referees
1	H	CRYSTAL PALACE	12/8	W 2-0	1-0	22,564		2	Smith 32, Ritchie 64. Ref: H Williams
2	A	SOUTHAMPTON	15/8	L 0-1	0-1	18,292		2	Channon 25. Ref: C Nicholls
3	A	ARSENAL	19/8	L 0-2	0-1	42,164	15	2	Kennedy 25, 46. Ref: J Thacker
4	H	SHEFFIELD UTD	23/8	D 2-2	0-1	20,402	14	3	Smith 55, Hurst 68. Reece 10, 78. Ref: D Smith
5	H	EVERTON	26/8	D 1-1	1-0	26,360	14	4	Ritchie 12. Royle 75. Ref: G Hill
6	A	NORWICH	30/8	L 0-2	0-2	30,269	19	4	Paddon 32, Stringer 43. Ref: A Hart
7	A	COVENTRY	2/9	L 1-2	0-2	14,317	20	4	Pejic 85. Carr 25, 43. Ref: N Burtenshaw
8	H	LEEDS	9/9	D 2-2	0-1	26,709	20	5	Hurst 59, Conroy 80. Lorimer 33, Clarke 53. Ref: J Homewood
9	A	IPSWICH	16/9	L 0-2	0-1	17,810	20	5	Belfitt 24, 53. Ref: K Sweet
10	H	MANCHESTER C	23/9	W 5-1	2-0	26,448	18	7	Conroy 6, Greenhoff 13, 68, 82, [Hurst 57]. Lee 74p. Ref: B Daniels

Line-ups (Stoke rows in roman; opponents in italic)

No	Team	1	2	3	4	5	6	7	8	9	10	11	12 sub used
1	Stoke	Farmer	Marsh	Pejic	Skeels	Smith	Bloor	Robertson	Greenhoff	Ritchie	**Hurst**	Dobing	
1	*Crystal Palace*	*Jackson*	*Payne*	*Wall*	*Pinkney*	*McCormick*	*Blyth*	*Craven*	*Wallace*	*Jenkins*	*Kellard*	*Taylor*	*Lees*
2	Stoke	Farmer	Marsh	Pejic	Skeels	Smith	Lees	Robertson	Greenhoff	Ritchie	Hurst	Dobing	
2	*Southampton*	*Martin*	*McCarthy*	*Burns*	*Fisher*	*McGrath*	*Steele*	*O'Brien*	*Channon*	*Davies*	*O'Neil*	*Jenkins*	
3	Stoke	Farmer	Marsh	Pejic	Skeels	Smith	Lees	Robertson	Greenhoff	Ritchie	Hurst	Dobing*	Stevenson
3	*Arsenal*	*Barnett*	*Rice*	*McNab*	*Storey*	*McLintock*	*Roberts*	*Armstrong*	*Ball*	*Radford*	*Kennedy*	*Graham*	
4	Stoke	Farmer	Marsh	Pejic	Lees	Smith	Skeels	Robertson	Greenhoff	Ritchie	Hurst	Dobing	
4	*Sheffield Utd*	*McAllister*	*Goulding*	*Hemsley*	*Flynn*	*Colquhoun*	*Hockey*	*Woodward*	*Salmons*	*Cammack*	*Currie*	*Reece*	
5	Stoke	Banks	Marsh	Pejic	Lees	Smith	Skeels	Robertson	Greenhoff*	Ritchie	Hurst	Dobing	Burrows
5	*Everton*	*Lawson*	*Wright*	*Newton*	*Kendall*	*Kenyon*	*Lyons*	*Johnson*	*Bernard*	*Royle*	*Harvey*	*Connolly*	
6	Stoke	Banks	Marsh	Pejic	Lees	Smith	Skeels	Robertson	Greenhoff	Ritchie	Hurst*	Dobing	Conroy
6	*Norwich*	*Keelan*	*Payne*	*Butler*	*Stringer*	*Forbes*	*Briggs*	*Livermore*	*Bone*	*Cross*	*Paddon*	*Anderson*	
7	Stoke	Banks	Marsh	Pejic	Lees	Smith	Skeels	Robertson	Greenhoff	Hurst	Conroy	Dobing*	Jump
7	*Coventry*	*Glazier*	*Coop*	*Cattlin*	*Machin*	*Blockley*	*Barry*	*Mortimer*	*Young*	*Hunt**	*Carr*	*Smith*	*McGuire*
8	Stoke	Banks	Marsh	Pejic	Lees	Stevenson	Skeels	Robertson	Mahoney	Ritchie	Hurst	Conroy	
8	*Leeds*	*Harvey*	*Madeley*	*Cherry*	*Bremner*	*Charlton*	*Hunter*	*Lorimer*	*Clarke*	*Jordan*	*Giles*	*Gray*	
9	Stoke	Banks	Marsh	Pejic	Mahoney*	Smith	Bloor	Robertson	Greenhoff	Ritchie	Hurst !	Conroy	Skeels
9	*Ipswich*	*Best*	*Mills*	*Harper*	*Collard*	*Hunter*	*Jefferson*	*Hamilton*	*Morris*	*Belfitt*	*Whymark*	*Lambert*	
10	Stoke	Farmer	Marsh	Pejic	Lees	Smith	Bloor	Robertson	Greenhoff	Hurst	Mahoney	Conroy	Skeels
10	*Manchester C*	*Corrigan*	*Jeffries**	*Donachie*	*Doyle*	*Booth*	*Oakes*	*Mellor*	*Bell*	*Marsh*	*Lee*	*Towers*	*Carrodus*

Match reports

1. Crystal Palace — Stoke grab their first home league win for nearly seven months. Denis Smith pokes home Ritchie's pass and then Geoff Hurst, on his league debut, flicks on for Ritchie to bury the second. Blyth's effort is ruled offside with the score 1-0. Robertson tortures Peter Wall on Palace's left.

2. Southampton — Sir Alf Ramsey watches Saints overrun City. Channon swerves past Marsh and buries a screamer into the net. Lees replaces Jump (38 mins) to help stiffen the defence. Marsh and Smith are booked as Stoke dig in against the onslaught. A mini-fightback sees Hurst net but he is offside.

3. Arsenal — John Farmer, who has West Brom chasing him, shines but Stoke succumb to two fine Ray Kennedy goals. The second, a free-kick, enters the net before a City player has touched it in the second half. As City battle hard, Denis Smith is given his 20th stitch of the season after the game.

4. Sheffield Utd — Stoke have plenty of pressure but are hit by a sucker punch for the opener. Geoff Hurst's first goal for Stoke is a splendid 20-yard drive. Smith buries a header from a Robertson cross, but Gilbert Reece notches his second and forces Smith to bring him down when clean through late on.

5. Everton — Close-season departure Mike Bernard returns to the Vic and forces Banks to fly to his left to save. The high-flying Toffees struggle to contain Hurst. Ritchie prods home the rebound after Lawson parries his initial shot but Stoke can't hang on and Royle's close-range header squares it.

6. Norwich — Terry Conroy is back from a long-term cartilage injury but his belated introduction cannot help sad Stoke. Graham Paddon and Dave Stringer crack home from outside the area, and after Terry Lees has a goal disallowed (41 mins), heads drop. Newly promoted Norwich out-run Stoke.

7. Coventry — In front of Coventry's lowest ever Division One gate Stoke score their first away goal of the season through Pejic's fabulous shot. Jump is inches away from the equaliser as City almost complete an undeserved but dramatic late fightback. This is Coventry's first win of the season.

8. Leeds — In a fabulous game Stoke fight back after once more conceding first. Allan Clarke misses a sitter before heading Leeds two goals to the good. Hurst's header and Conroy's fizzing drive are nearly added to by John Mahoney, who hits one against the bar in the last minute. City are 20th.

9. Ipswich — Stoke City's abysmal away run continues at in-form Ipswich. A grim performance is capped by Hurst missing a sitter and then being sent off for arguing with the ref. Rodney Belfitt lobs Banks for the first of his brace to round off Jimmy Robertson's nightmare return to Portman Road.

10. Manchester C — City burst into life. Jimmy Greenhoff's hat-trick is the first by a City player for four years. He rounds it off by burying a left-wing cross after starting the move himself. He also sets up Conroy for the opener. Lee is pushed by Terry Conroy for the penalty but Stoke annihilate the Blues.

No.	Venue	Opponent	Date	Att.	Pos	Res	Opp Pos	Pts	FT	HT	Scorers (Stoke / Opponent)	Ref
11	A	WOLVES	30/9	24,133	20	L	5	7	3-5	2-2	Hurst 3p, Greenhoff 24, Bloor 75 / R'hards 13, 67, 90, D'gan 23, H'gan 82	P Walters
12	A	TOTTENHAM	7/10	31,951	21	L	3	7	3-4	1-3	Ritchie 32, 51, Bloor 82 / Pratt 22, 33, Gilzean 25, Peters 75	I Jones
13	H	NEWCASTLE	14/10	21,205	18	W	12	9	2-0	0-0	Hurst 77, Robertson 90	W Gow
14	A	LIVERPOOL	21/10	43,604	20	L	1	9	1-2	1-0	Greenhoff 34 / Hughes 66, Callaghan 90	R Kirkpatrick
15	H	LEICESTER	28/10	24,421	18	W	20	11	1-0	1-0	Hurst 9	T Morrissey
16	A	SHEFFIELD UTD	4/11	19,322	17	D	13	12	0-0	0-0		R Matthewson
17	H	SOUTHAMPTON	11/11	17,772	17	D	11	13	3-3	2-2	Smith 5, Ritchie 45, Conroy 50 / Channon 15p, Davies 44, Stokes 83	D Howell
18	H	BIRMINGHAM	18/11	23,046	18	L	17	13	1-2	1-1	Greenhoff 3 / Latchford R 5, 60	W Hall
19	A	WEST BROM	25/11	23,316	21	L	18	13	1-2	1-1	Hurst 38 / Brown T 28, 84p	J Hunting
20	H	CHELSEA	2/12	20,274	20	D	5	14	1-1	0-1	Conroy 65 / Osgood 4	N Burtenshaw
21	A	MANCHESTER U	9/12	44,247	18	W	20	16	2-0	2-0	Pejic 17, Ritchie 42	G Kew

11 — A WOLVES
Stoke: Farmer, Marsh, Pejic, Skeels, Smith, Bloor, Robertson, Greenhoff, Hurst, Mahoney, Conroy (Robertson)
Wolves: Parkes, Shaw, Taylor, Bailey, Munro, McAlle, Hegan, Hibbitt, Richards, Dougan, Wagstaffe

Stoke grab an early lead after Hurst is brought down by Shaw and nets the penalty himself. Greenhoff taps in to make it 2-2 and Alan Bloor maintains parity with a low shot. But John Richards' treble outguns Stoke. Dougan, Wagstaffe and Hegan have the Potters' defence in a tangle.

12 — A TOTTENHAM
Stoke: Banks, Marsh, Pejic, Skeels, Smith, Bloor, Robertson, Greenhoff, Hurst, Mahoney*, Conroy (Ritchie)
Tottenham: Jennings, Kinnear, Knowles, Pratt, England, Beal, Gilzean, Perryman, Ritchie, Peters, Chivers (Coates)

Another free-scoring game sees John Pratt have a hand in all three of Spurs' first-half goals. Ritchie's brace gives Stoke hope. His first is from Martin Peters' mis-hit back-pass, but Peters makes amends in a goalmouth scramble to put the game out of reach despite Bloor's late effort.

13 — H NEWCASTLE
Stoke: Banks, Marsh, Pejic, Jump*, Smith, Bloor, Robertson, Greenhoff, Hurst, Mahoney, Conroy (Dobing)
Newcastle: McFaul, Craig, Guthrie, Gibb, Howard, Clark, Barrowclough, Smith, Tudor, Hodgson, Hibbitt

Stoke leave it late after dominating against a very defensive Newcastle line-up. Terry Conroy is back to his best and crosses for Greenhoff who sets Hurst up for the first. Jimmy Robertson fires home his first goal for the club after Conroy goes on a decoy run to open up oceans of space.

14 — A LIVERPOOL
Stoke: Banks, Marsh, Pejic, Skeels, Smith, Bloor, Dobing, Greenhoff, Hurst, Mahoney, Conroy* (Robertson)
Liverpool: Clemence, Lawler, Lindsay, Smith, Lloyd, Hughes, Keegan, Cormack, Heighway, Boersma, Callaghan

On a day of passion at Anfield, Stoke concede a hotly disputed goal when the referee brings back play after applying advantage and Callaghan fires in a deflected free-kick. Emlyn Hughes equalises Greenhoff's headed goal to put it in the melting pot as Liverpool chase the League title.

15 — H LEICESTER
Stoke: McDonald, Marsh, Pejic, Skeels, Smith, Bloor, Robertson, Greenhoff, Hurst, Mahoney, Conroy* (Dobing)
Leicester: Shilton, Whitworth, Woollett, Sammels, Munro, Cross, Farrington, Worthington, Birchenall, Partridge* (Glover, Manley)

A muted game between Gordon Banks' last two clubs is won by Hurst, beating Shilton to a Robertson lob. With Banks out for at least a year and Farmer also injured, Mike McDonald, a £20,000 signing from Clydebank, starts in goal. City are linked to Aberdeen keeper Bobby Clark.

16 — A SHEFFIELD UTD
Stoke: Farmer, Marsh, Pejic, Skeels, Smith, Bloor, Greenhoff, Greenhoff, Dodd, Mahoney, Conroy* (Jump)
Sheffield Utd: McAlister, Badger, Hemsley, Flynn, Colquhoun, Hockey, Woodward, Staniforth, Dearden, Currie, Warboys

Waddo gives Alan Dodd his debut in midfield as Peter Dobing goes into hospital for surgery on his nagging knee injury. Defence-minded City withstand incessant pressure. Tony Currie finally nets but is offside. John Mahoney brings the best save of the game from Thomas McAlister.

17 — H SOUTHAMPTON
Stoke: Farmer, Marsh*, Pejic, Skeels, Smith, Dodd, Mahoney, Greenhoff, Hurst, Hurst, Conroy (Stokes)
Southampton: Martin, McCarthy, Kirkup, Fisher, Bennett, Steele, Paine, Channon, Davies, O'Neil, Stokes

City are buoyed by the news of Banks' decision to attempt a comeback. In a rumbustious game John Ritchie's 20-yarder is Stoke's best effort. Greenhoff hits his 10th-minute penalty at Eric Martin. Mick Channon buries his. Bobby Stokes' equaliser dashes hopes of rising up the league.

18 — A BIRMINGHAM
Stoke: Farmer, Lewis*, Pejic, Skeels, Smith, Bloor, Robertson, Greenhoff, Hurst, Mahoney, Conroy (Ritchie)
Birmingham: Latchford D, Martin, Want, Pendrey, Hynd, Harland, Hope, Calderwood, Latchford R, Hatton, Taylor

Jimmy Greenhoff nets against his old club with a neat trap and finish from Hurst's flick. Freddie Goodwin's men battle their way to victory as Mahoney is flattened leaving Stoke's 10 men to battle on. The best of Latchford's brace is the winner as he buries Hatton's cross on the run.

19 — A WEST BROM
Stoke: Farmer, Jump, Pejic, Dodd*, Smith, Bloor, Skeels, Greenhoff, Hurst, Mahoney, Mahoney (Robertson)
West Brom: Latchford P, Nisbet, Wilson, Cantello, Robertson, Merrick, Brown A, Brown T, Gould, Hartford, McLean

Farmer, in splendid form, foils Tony Brown three times before he opens the scoring. City, playing in a new Claret & Blue away kit, fight back through Hurst's powerful run and shot. Referee Hunting awards Albion's penalty for Smith's handball. Greenhoff miskicks a last gasp chance.

20 — H CHELSEA
Stoke: Farmer, Marsh, Pejic, Dodd*, Smith, Bloor, Robertson, Greenhoff, Hurst, Conroy, Conroy (Ritchie)
Chelsea: Phillips, Harris, McCreadie, Hollins, Droy, Webb, Garner, Kember, Osgood, Hudson, Houseman

George Eastham is appointed Assistant Manager and returns to the Stoke line up after 6 months in South Africa. Conroy's dipping shot sails in to equalise Osgood's opener from Houseman's cross. Smith is booked again and will face a ban. Greenhoff and Conroy are foiled by Phillips.

21 — A MANCHESTER U
Stoke: Farmer, Marsh, Pejic, Mahoney, Smith, Skeels, Conroy, Greenhoff, Hurst, Ritchie, Eastham (Hurst)
Manchester U: Stepney, O'Neil, Dunne, Young*, Sadler, Buchan, Morgan, MacDougall, Chatton, Davies, Moore (Law)

A win at last! Pejic starts and ends a neat move for the opener. Ritchie stabs home Hurst's far-post knock back as Frank O'Farrell's men are in trouble from the off. Farmer keeps the Red Devils' new signing, Ted MacDougall, at bay. The second half starts late due to floodlight failure.

No	Date		Att	Pos	Pt	F-A	H-T	Scorers, Times, and Referees	1	2	3	4	5	6	7	8	9	10	11	12 sub used
22	A	WEST HAM		18	L	2-3	1-2	Hurst 8, Ritchie 89	Farmer	Lees	Elder	Mahoney	Smith	Skeels	Conroy	Greenhoff	Ritchie	Hurst	Eastham*	Robertson
	16/12		*23,269*	*7*	16			*Robson 32, 35, Best 76*	*Ferguson*	*McDowell*	*Lampard*	*Bonds*	*Taylor*	*Moore*	*Ayris*	*Best*	*Holland*	*Brooking*	*Robson*	
								Ref: R Toseland	City, hit by flu, have Alex Elder and Terry Lees in. Hurst makes it the best possible start by back-heading Ritchie's flick into the net. Bryan Robson scores from two fine Trevor Brooking crosses. Ritchie's close-range effort, after Ferguson fumbles Mahoney's high cross, is too late.											
23	H	DERBY		17	W	4-0	3-0	Ritchie 10, 58, Hurst 30, Greenhoff 36	Farmer	Marsh	Pejic	Mahoney	Smith	Skeels	Conroy	Greenhoff	Ritchie	Hurst	Eastham	
	23/12		23,084	*10*	18				*Boulton*	*Webster*	*Nish**	*O'Hare*	*McFarland*	*Todd*	*McGovern*	*Gemmill*	*Davies*	*Hector*	*Hinton*	*Sims*
								Ref: A Oliver	Stoke thrash the Champions. George Eastham is at the hub of each goal. Ritchie and Hurst bury headers then Greenhoff nips in to touch past Boulton. Eastham then threads an inch-perfect ball through to Ritchie for the fourth. Derby miss a penalty (32 mins) when Hinton hits the post.											
24	A	MANCHESTER C		19	D	1-1	0-1	Mahoney 65	Farmer	Marsh	Pejic	Mahoney	Smith	Jump	Conroy	Greenhoff	Ritchie	Hurst	Eastham	
	26/12		*36,334*	*12*	19			*Mellor 16*	*Corrigan*	*Jeffries*	*Pardoe*	*Doyle*	*Booth*	*Barrett*	*Summerbee*	*Hill*	*Marsh*	*Mellor*	*Towers*	
								Ref: V Batty	Stoke are pummelled as City force 15 corners but Mahoney's 25-yard rocket leaves Joe Corrigan helpless. Farmer's heroics keeps City at bay. Stoke's battling results in four bookings but knocks City out of their stride. A frustrated Rod Marsh receives Blues' 26th booking of the season.											
25	H	ARSENAL		16	D	0-0	0-0		Farmer	Marsh	Pejic	Mahoney	Smith	Skeels	Robertson	Greenhoff	Ritchie	Hurst	Conroy	
	30/12		24,586	*2*	20				*Wilson*	*Rice*	*McNab*	*Storey*	*Blockley*	*Roberts*	*Armstrong*	*Ball*	*Radford*	*Kennedy*	*Kelly*	
								Ref: E Jolly	Fog keeps the anticipated bumper Christmas crowd down as Arsenal, fresh from a 0-5 thrashing at Derby, hold the upper hand. Conroy shoots just wide and Ritchie's effort is blocked on the line. Arsenal have an effort disallowed following a scramble, but neither side deserves to win.											
26	A	EVERTON		17	L	0-2	0-0		Farmer	Marsh	Pejic	Mahoney	Smith	Skeels	Robertson	Greenhoff	Ritchie	Eastham	Conroy	
	6/1		*26,818*	*13*	20			*Buckley 55, Connolly 82*	*Lawson*	*Wright*	*Styles*	*Kendall*	*Kenyon*	*Hurst*	*Harper*	*Bernard*	*Belfitt*	*Buckley*	*Connolly*	
								Ref: C Thomas	Stoke cling on with John Farmer acrobatically saving Mike Bernard's penalty after Skeels fouls Wright. Then Buckley scrambles the ball past him from two yards. Harry Catterick's men clinch it when Connolly buries Smith's weak clearance. Smith gets his 6th booking of the season.											
27	A	LEEDS		18	L	0-1	0-0		Farmer	Lees	Pejic !	Mahoney	Bloor	Skeels	Robertson	Greenhoff	Ritchie	Eastham*	Conroy	Jump
	27/1		*33,487*	*3*	20			*Clarke 55*	*Harvey*	*Reaney*	*Cherry*	*Bremner*	*Madeley*	*Hunter*	*Lorimer*	*Clarke*	*Jordan**	*Giles*	*Bates*	*Yorath*
								Ref: H Davey	Denis Smith is banned for two matches, but Alan Bloor makes his first start for 2 months. Pejic is sent off for fouling keeper David Harvey and receiving his second yellow card in the last minute. Allan Clarke's winner inevitably is a header from Yorath's cross. Stoke never get a grip.											
28	A	DERBY		18	W	3-0	2-0	Mahoney 19, Robertson 44, [Greenhoff 80]	Farmer	Marsh	Pejic	Mahoney	Bloor	Skeels	Robertson	Greenhoff	Ritchie	Eastham	Conroy	
	14/2		*22,106*	*6*	22				*Boulton*	*Webster*	*Nish*	*Durban*	*Daniel*	*Todd*	*Sime*	*Gemmill*	*Davies*	*Hector*	*Walker**	*Parry*
								Ref: V James	Stoke's first win at the Baseball Ground since 1955. Mahoney takes a return ball from Eastham to beat Boulton. Robertson breaks clear from Peter Daniel and curls in. A high bouncing Farmer kick puts Greenhoff in to finish things off nicely. Stoke fans chanting 'Easy' by the end.											
29	A	CRYSTAL PALACE		20	L	2-3	0-2	Greenhoff 56, Smith 68	Farmer	Marsh	Pejic	Mahoney	Bloor	Skeels	Robertson	Greenhoff	Ritchie*	Eastham	Conroy	Smith
	17/2		*32,099*	*17*	22			*Possee 37, Whittle 41, Rogers 59*	*Jackson*	*Mulligan*	*Taylor*	*Philip*	*Bell*	*Blyth*	*Possee*	*Hinshelwood*	*Whittle*	*Cooke*	*Rogers*	
								Ref: T Reynolds	Stoke start brightly, but Paddy Mulligan is in control at the back for Palace. Despite Greenhoff's wonderful left-foot volley City are never quite up with the pace. Palace force City back and look comfortable until Smith, playing at centre-forward, heads home Jackie Marsh's cross.											
30	H	WEST HAM		17	W	2-0	2-0	Greenhoff 4, Robertson 15	Farmer	Marsh	Pejic	Mahoney	Smith	Bloor	Robertson	Greenhoff	Hurst	Eastham	Conroy	
	24/2		21,885	*7*	24				*Ferguson*	*McDowell*	*Lampard*	*Bonds*	*Taylor*	*Moore*	*Ayris**	*Best*	*Holland*	*Brooking*	*Robson*	*Lock*
								Ref: R Raby	Geoff Hurst is back after pneumonia to face his old team and is made captain for the day. Greenhoff strikes after the ref awards a free-kick in the area for handball. Robertson whips in a 15-yard left-footer and then Hurst nearly takes advantage of Tommy Taylor's misplaced back-pass.											
31	A	NEWCASTLE		19	L	0-1	0-0		Farmer	Marsh	Jump	Mahoney	Smith	Bloor	Robertson	Greenhoff	Hurst*	Eastham	Skeels	Conroy
	10/3		*23,570*	*5*	24			*MacDonald 86*	*Burleigh*	*Craig*	*Kennedy*	*Nattrass*	*Howard*	*Clark*	*Barrowcl'gh*	*Smith*	*MacDonald*	*Tudor*	*Hibbitt*	
								Ref: G Hartley	Stoke nearly escape with a point but Malcolm MacDonald's hooked shot steals it. SuperMac also has a goal disallowed when play is brought back for an earlier free-kick awarded to him. Greenhoff also nets twice but is offside both times. City are outraged. George Eastham sparkles.											

No	Opponent	Date	Venue	Res	FT	HT	Pos		Pts	Att
32	TOTTENHAM	14/3	A	D	1-1	0-0	18	8	25	23,351
33	LIVERPOOL	17/3	H	L	0-1	0-0	19	1	25	33,540
34	LEICESTER	24/3	A	L	0-2	0-2	19	13	25	18,473
35	COVENTRY	26/3	H	W	2-1	0-1	18	11	27	20,218
36	WEST BROM	31/3	H	W	2-0	0-0	18	22	29	21,296
37	IPSWICH	4/4	H	W	1-0	1-0	15	4	31	18,319
38	CHELSEA	7/4	A	W	3-1	2-1	14	12	33	19,706
39	MANCHESTER U	14/4	H	D	2-2	0-0	14	16	34	37,051
40	BIRMINGHAM	21/4	A	L	1-3	0-2	19	11	34	22,513
41	WOLVES	24/4	H	W	2-0	1-0	16	6	36	25,251
42	NORWICH	28/4	H	W	2-0	1-0	14	20	38	9,350

32. TOTTENHAM (14/3) — Stoke: Farmer, Marsh, Jump, Skeels*, Smith, Bloor, Robertson, Mahoney, Hurst, Greenhoff, Eastham, Conroy. Tottenham: Jennings, Kinnear, Knowles, Coates, Collins, Beal, Neighbour, Perryman, Chivers, Peters, Pearce.
Greenhoff 84 / Pearce 84. Ref: H New.
Despite heavy pressure and having two penalty appeals turned down Spurs grab the lead after Conroy loses possession to Kinnear and he finds Pearce. Captain courageous, Jimmy Greenhoff, saves Stoke with a right-foot shot from 12 yards when all seems lost. A frenetic finale ensues.

33. LIVERPOOL (17/3, H) — Stoke: Farmer, Marsh, Jump, Skeels, Smith, Bloor, Robertson, Mahoney, Hurst*, Greenhoff, Eastham, Conroy. Liverpool: Clemence, Lawler, Lindsay, Smith, Lloyd, Hughes, Keegan, Cormack, Boersma*, Heighway, Callaghan, Hall.
Mahoney 68 (og). Ref: M Sinclair.
Tension mounts as Champions elect Liverpool win without playing well. Mahoney attempts a strange lofted back-pass but beats Farmer to find the corner of his own net. Seeking to redress the balance Mahoney forces Clemence to save, who also tips over Robertson's close-range header.

34. LEICESTER (24/3, A) — Stoke: Farmer, Marsh, Pejic, Mahoney, Smith, Bloor, Robertson, Greenhoff, Hurst, Greenhoff, Eastham, Conroy. Leicester: Shilton, Whitworth, Rofe, Cross, Manley, Sammels, Farrington, Worthington, Weller, Birchenall, Glover*, Tomlin.
Tomlin 52, Birchenall 84. Ref: H Hackney.
Hurst puts a penalty wide (43 minutes) after Weller pulls down Mahoney. Smith and Len Glover are both hurt in a collision and it is Glover's replacement, Tomlin, who scores with a close-range header. Birchenall's breakaway goal denies City after a furious attacking spell at the end.

35. COVENTRY (26/3, H) — Stoke: Farmer, Marsh, Pejic, Greenhoff, Smith, Bloor, Haslegrave, Hurst, Ritchie, Eastham, Conroy. Coventry: Glazier, Coop, Cattlin, McGuire, Barry, Dugdale, Mortimer, Alderson, Stein, Carr, Hutchison.
Ritchie 47, Haslegrave 64 / Stein 5. Ref: R Tinkler.
Stein pounces on Farmer's mistake to prod Coventry ahead. Smith characteristically bundles Bill Glazier and the ball into the net as City battle back. Ritchie's header squares it and Haslegrave blasts home a thunderous 20-yard left-footer. Hutchison causes problems as Stoke cling on.

36. WEST BROM (31/3, H) — Stoke: Farmer, Marsh, Pejic, Greenhoff, Smith, Bloor, Haslegrave, Hurst, Ritchie, Eastham, Conroy, Mahoney. West Brom: Osborne, Cantello, Wilson, Shaw, Wile, Robertson, Merrick, Brown T*, Astle, Hartford, Johnston, Glover.
Greenhoff 68, Hurst 70. Ref: R Matthewson.
Both sides attack from the off, Farmer touches over Astle's header and Osborne keeps Haslegrave out for the Baggies who have no wins in six. Greenhoff finally breaks the deadlock after Osborne parries Bloor's shot. Hurst then sidefoots home Conroy's cross and the relief is tangible.

37. IPSWICH (4/4, H) — Stoke: Farmer, Marsh, Pejic, Mahoney, Smith, Bloor, Haslegrave, Hurst, Ritchie, Greenhoff, Eastham, Conroy. Ipswich: Best, Mills, Harper, Morris, Hunter, Beattie, Hamilton, Viljoen, Johnson, Whymark, Lambert.
Ritchie 13. Ref: A Jones.
Both sides have goals disallowed for offside but City are worthy winners. The goal has a touch of fortune about it as Sean Haslegrave tries a 35-yard shot that deflects off Ritchie's thigh leaving David Best hopelessly wrong footed. Best then saves brilliantly from Geoff Hurst's header.

38. CHELSEA (7/4, A) — Stoke: Farmer, Marsh, Pejic, Mahoney, Smith, Bloor, Haslegrave, Hurst, Ritchie, Greenhoff, Eastham, Conroy. Chelsea: Bonetti, Harris, McCreadie, Hollins, Dempsey, Hinton, Britton, Osgood, Boyle, Ord, Brolly.
Greenhoff 23, Ritchie 39, Ord 22 [Haslegrave 78]. Ref: R Grabb.
Injury-hit Chelsea grab the lead through Tommy Ord on his debut but defiant City hit back with Greenhoff and Ritchie notching from close in. Haslegrave's screamer leaves Bonetti helpless and Stoke could have more as Greenhoff plays in Eastham's 'scheming' role behind the attack.

39. MANCHESTER U (14/4, H) — Stoke: Farmer, Marsh, Pejic, Mahoney, Smith, Bloor, Haslegrave*, Hurst, Ritchie, Greenhoff*, Eastham, Conroy. Manchester U: Stepney, Young, Buchan, Graham, Holton, James, Morgan, Charlton, Anderson*, Macari, Martin, Fletcher.
Greenhoff 75, Ritchie 82 / Macari 65, Smith 87 (og). Ref: K Styles.
City are on top but behind to Macari's strike. Pejic's 35-yard shot is only palmed out by Stepney and Greenhoff nets to level. Ritchie races onto Eastham's pass to seemingly clinch it. A bizarre own-goal, as Pejic hacks a clearance against Smith's legs, leaves the Potters with only a point.

40. BIRMINGHAM (21/4, A) — Stoke: Farmer, Marsh, Pejic, Mahoney, Smith, Bloor, Robertson, Hurst, Ritchie, Greenhoff, Eastham, Haslegrave. Birmingham: Latchford D, Martin, Pendrey, Page, Hynd, Roberts, Campbell, Francis, Latchford R, Hatton, Taylor.
Robertson 85 / Page 10, Francis 42, Hatton 53. Ref: P Baldwin.
Stoke's defence only wake up at half time after Malcolm Page and teenager Trevor Francis are both left unmarked to bury easy chances. Bob Hatton and Stoke, missing Eastham, are never really in it despite Robertson's lob over the advancing Dave Latchford.

41. WOLVES (24/4, H) — Stoke: Farmer, Marsh, Pejic, Mahoney, Smith, Bloor, Robertson, Hurst, Ritchie, Greenhoff, Eastham, Daley. Wolves: Parkes, Taylor, Parkin, Bailey, McAlle, Jefferson, Powell, Sunderland, Richards, Dougan*, Kindon.
Robertson 29, Greenhoff 87. Ref: W Johnson.
Denis Smith wins his fierce battle with Derek Dougan, who is booked. Robertson neatly chips home the first at the far post and Greenhoff nets from Ritchie's flick from a corner. Bailey drives Bill McGarry's Wolves forward but Alan Sunderland hits the bar and Farmer foils Kindon.

42. NORWICH (28/4, H) — Stoke: Farmer, Marsh, Pejic, Mahoney, Smith, Bloor, Robertson, Hurst, Ritchie, Greenhoff, Eastham*, Burrows. Norwich: Keelan, Payne, Black, Stringer, Forbes, Hackey, Livermore, Suggett, Cross, Briggs, Mellor.
Greenhoff 25, Ritchie 58. Ref: J Wrennall.
Stoke clinch a Watney Cup place by finishing as a high scoring team in the Division. Greenhoff finishes off an intricate move between himself and Hurst. Ritchie prods Pejic's cross past Kevin Keelan to round off a good afternoon's football by a City team free of the spectre of the drop.

Home 23,751 Away 2?,?90 Average 23,751

LEAGUE DIVISION 1 (CUP-TIES)

Manager: Tony Waddington

SEASON 1972-73

League Cup

		Att		F-A	H-T	1	2	3	4	5	6	7	8	9	10	11	12 sub used	Scorers, Times, and Referees
2	H SUNDERLAND 6/9	16,706	20 W 2:8	3-0	1-0	Banks	Marsh	Pejic	Lees	Stevenson	Jump	Robertson	Greenhoff	Ritchie	Hurst	Conroy	Hughes	Greenhoff 8, 70, Hurst 90
						Montgomery	*Malone*	*Coleman*	*Horswill*	*Pitt*	*Porterfield*	*McGiven*	*Kerr*	*Watson*	*Lathan**	*Tueart*		Ref: G Hartley

Stoke cruise past Sunderland, despite fielding an injury-hit team. Willie Stevenson makes a rare appearance at centre-half. Greenhoff scores twice from Conroy's incisive passes and Hurst heads home a Conroy cross. Stand-in skipper John Ritchie blazes over with the goal gaping.

		Att		F-A	H-T	1	2	3	4	5	6	7	8	9	10	11	12 sub used	Scorers, Times, and Referees
3	A IPSWICH 3/10	14,602	20 W 8	2-1	0-1	Banks	Marsh	Pejic	Skeels	Smith	Bloor	Robertson*	Greenhoff	Ritchie	Hurst	Mahoney	Conroy	Hurst 64, Ritchie 88
						Best	*Mills*	*Harper*	*Collard*	*Hunter*	*Beattie*	*Hamilton*	*Viljoen*	*Hill*	*Whymark*	*Lambert*		Viljoen 38
																		Ref: R Tinkler

City wipe out the memories of their recent league visit by beating in-form Ipswich. After Waddo takes Robertson off and allows the full-backs to overlap, Hurst equalises from Mike Pejic's deep cross. John Ritchie beats both Allan Hunter and Kevin Beattie to belt home the late winner.

		Att		F-A	H-T	1	2	3	4	5	6	7	8	9	10	11	12 sub used	Scorers, Times, and Referees
4	A NOTTS CO 31/10	20,297	18 L 3:13	1-3	0-2	McDonald	Marsh	Pejic	Skeels*	Smith	Bloor	Robertson	Mahoney	Hurst	Ritchie	Conroy	Dobing	Bloor 80
						Brown	*Brindley*	*Worthington*	*Carlin*	*Needham*	*Stubbs*	*Nixon*	*Randall*	*Bradd*	*Masson*	*Mann*		Randall 4p, Bradd 31, Stubbs 62
																		Ref: J Yates

Humiliation for City. Mike McDonald is in goal after the signing of Aberdeen keeper Bobby Clark is aborted. Jimmy Sirrel's men swarm all over Stoke, the penalty is awarded for Conroy's handball. Bradd and Stubbs both notch headers and Bloor's left foot strike is no consolation.

FA Cup

		Att		F-A	H-T	1	2	3	4	5	6	7	8	9	10	11	12 sub used	Scorers, Times, and Referees
3	A MANCHESTER C 13/1	38,648	17 L 11	2-3	1-2	Farmer	Marsh	Pejic	Mahoney	Smith	Bloor	Robertson	Greenhoff	Ritchie	Eastham	Conroy		Greenhoff 25, 55
						Corrigan	*Book*	*Donachie*	*Doyle*	*Booth*	*Jeffries*	*Summerbee*	*Bell*	*Marsh*	*Lee*	*Mellor*		Bell 2, Marsh 15, Summerbee 68
																		Ref: E Wallace

Stoke fight back after a torrid start and Greenhoff's equaliser from Conroy's cross is a peach. Rod Marsh's effort stands out and Summerbee's winner knocks the fight out of Stoke. Ritchie and Francis Lee hit the post at either end in a topsy-turvy match which Man City deserve to win.

UEFA Cup

		Att		F-A	H-T	1	2	3	4	5	6	7	8	9	10	11	12 sub used	Scorers, Times, and Referees
1:1	H KAISERSLAUTERN 13/9 (West Germany)	22,182	18 W 7	3-1	0-0	Banks	Marsh	Pejic	Mahoney	Smith	Bloor	Robertson	Greenhoff	Ritchie	Hurst	Conroy	Rade'i/Pirr'g	Conroy 51, Hurst 72, Ritchie 85
						Elting	*Huber**	*Schwager*	*Blitz*	*Fuchs*	*Friedrich*	*Diehl*	*Seel^*	*Vogt*	*Hosic*	*Achermann*		Hosic 78
																		Ref: K Wahler

Keeper Josef Elting keeps the West Germans in it, saving seven times in the five minutes before the break. Conroy scores City's first European goal. Hurst scores at the second attempt. Ritchie has a header ruled out before he equals. Yugoslav Hosic's header skids past Banks.

		Att		F-A	H-T	1	2	3	4	5	6	7	8	9	10	11	12 sub used	Scorers, Times, and Referees
1:2	A KAISERSLAUTERN 27/9	18,000	18 L 8	0-4	0-2	Farmer	Marsh	Pejic	Skeels	Smith	Bloor*	Robertson	Greenhoff	Mahoney	Hurst	Conroy	Ritchie!	*[Hosic 80]*
						Elting	*Reinders*	*Schwager*	*Diehl^*	*Fuchs^*	*Friedrich*	*Blitz*	*Pirrung*	*Toppmullot*	*Hosic*	*Seel*	H'tkes/Huber	Huber 20, Friedrich 45, Bitz 64,
																		Ref: R Eksztazn
																		(Stoke lose 3-5 on aggregate)

It all goes horribly wrong for City. At 0-3 down and on their way out, Waddo sends on John Ritchie to try and grab a goal back. Instead he is sent off before the game restarts for hitting Hosic who had pushed him. The fourth, a Hosic free-kick in off Farmer's shoulder, really rubs it in.

League Table

		P		Home						Away				Pts
			W	D	L	F	A	W	D	L	F	A		
1	Liverpool	42	17	3	1	45	19	8	7	6	27	23		60
2	Arsenal	42	14	5	2	31	14	9	6	6	26	29		57
3	Leeds	42	15	4	2	45	13	6	7	8	26	32		53
4	Ipswich	42	10	7	4	34	20	7	7	7	21	25		48
5	Wolves	42	13	3	5	43	23	5	8	8	23	31		47
6	West Ham	42	12	5	4	45	25	5	7	9	22	28		46
7	Derby	42	15	3	3	43	18	4	5	12	13	36		46
8	Tottenham	42	10	5	6	33	23	6	8	7	25	25		45
9	Newcastle	42	12	6	3	35	19	4	7	10	25	32		45
10	Birmingham	42	11	7	3	39	22	4	5	12	14	32		42
11	Manchester C	42	12	4	5	36	20	3	7	11	21	40		41
12	Chelsea	42	9	6	6	30	22	4	8	9	19	29		40
13	Southampton	42	8	11	2	26	17	3	7	11	21	35		40
14	Sheffield U	42	11	4	6	28	18	4	6	11	23	41		40
15	STOKE	42	11	8	2	38	17	3	2	16	23	39		38
16	Leicester	42	7	9	5	23	18	3	8	10	17	28		37
17	Everton	42	9	5	7	27	21	4	6	11	14	28		37
18	Manchester U	42	9	7	5	24	19	3	6	12	20	41		37
19	Coventry	42	9	5	7	27	24	4	4	13	13	31		35
20	Norwich	42	7	9	5	22	19	4	1	16	14	44		32
21	Crys Palace	42	7	7	7	25	21	2	5	14	16	37		30
22	West Brom	42	8	7	6	25	24	1	3	17	13	38		28
		924	236	130	96	724	436	96	130	236	436	724		924

Appearances and Goals

Player	Appearances								Goals					
	Lge	Sub	LC	Sub	FAC	Sub	Eur	Sub	Lge	Sub	LC	FAC	Eur	Tot
Banks, Gordon	8		2				2							
Bloor, Alan	28		2		1		2		2		1			3
Burrows, Harry							2							
Conroy, Terry	29	4	2	1	1		2		4				1	5
Dobing, Peter	9	2	2				2							
Dodd, Alan	3													
Eastham, George	17	1			1				2					2
Elder, Alex	1													
Farmer, John	33		1		1									
Greenhoff, Jimmy	41		2	1			2		16		2	2		20
Haslegrave, Sean	6						2		2					2
Hurst, Geoff	38		3				2		10		2		1	13
Jump, Stewart	7	3	1		1									
Lees, Terry	7	1	1											
Lewis, Kevin	1													
Marsh, Jackie	38		3	1	1		2							
Mahoney, John	33	1	2	1			2		2					2
McDonald, Mike	1													
Pejic, Mike	38		3		1		2							
Ritchie, John	29	2	3	1	1		2		14	1	1		1	16
Robertson, Jimmy	27	4	3	1			2		5					5
Skeels, Eric	30	1	2				1							
Smith, Denis	37	1	2	1	1		2		4					4
Stevenson, Willie	1	1	1		1		1							
24 players used	462	23	33	2	11		22		61	1	6	2	3	72

Odds & ends

Double wins: (1) Derby.

Double losses: (2) Birmingham, Liverpool.

Won from behind: (2) Coventry (h), Chelsea (a).

Lost from in front: (4) Birmingham (h), Liverpool (a), West Ham (a), Wolves (a).

High spots: The free-scoring forwards: Greenhoff, Ritchie and Hurst. Thrashing Manchester City 5-1. Beating Champions Derby by 7-0 over the two league games. Winning six out of the last eight games to stave off relegation. Winning the club's first-ever European match.

Low spots: Not picking up an away point until November. Gordon Banks' horrific career-ending car crash. Being dumped out of Europe by Kaiserslautern. John Ritchie's sending off in Germany.

Ever-presents: (0).

Hat-tricks: (1) Jimmy Greenhoff.

Leading scorer: (20) Jimmy Greenhoff.

Results

No	Date	Venue	Opponent	Att	Pos	Pt	F-A	H-T	Scorers, Times, and Referees
1	25/8	A	LIVERPOOL	52,938	—	L 0	0-1	0-1	Highway 6 — Ref: R Tinkler
2	29/8	A	MANCHESTER U	43,614	—	L 0	0-1	0-1	James 22 — Ref: J Hunting
3	1/9	H	MANCHESTER C	22,436	21 / 9	D 1	1-1	1-0	Greenhoff 21; Law 86 — Ref: H Davey
4	5/9	H	EVERTON	22,435	21 / 11	D 2	0-0	0-0	Ref: G Hill
5	8/9	A	QP RANGERS	18,118	19 / 12	D 3	3-3	1-1	Hurst 26, 67, Smith 64; Leach 15, Venables 47p, Mancini 78 — Ref: W Gow
6	11/9	A	EVERTON	20,242	16 / 11	D 4	1-1	0-1	Greenhoff 65; Harper 38 — Ref: K Styles
7	15/9	H	IPSWICH	17,096	16 / 19	D 5	1-1	0-0	Hurst 72; Woods 48 — Ref: A Jones
8	22/9	A	ARSENAL	30,578	17 / 10	L 5	1-2	1-1	Greenhoff 35; Radford 2, Ball 73 — Ref: V James
9	29/9	H	WEST HAM	16,395	17 / 21	W 7	2-0	1-0	Goodwin 40, Hurst 68 — Ref: W Johnson
10	6/10	A	LEEDS	36,562	16 / 1	D 8	1-1	0-1	Smith 89; Jones 41 — Ref: M Sinclair

Line-ups

No	Team	1	2	3	4	5	6	7	8	9	10	11	12 sub used
1	Stoke	Farmer	Lees	Pejic	Mahoney	Smith	Bloor	Robertson	Greenhoff	Hurst	Conroy	Haslegrave	
1	Liverpool	Clemence	Lawler	Lindsay	Thompson	Lloyd	Hughes	Keegan	Cormack	Heighway	Boersma	Callaghan	
2	Stoke	Farmer	Lees	Pejic	Mahoney	Smith	Bloor	Robertson	Greenhoff	Hurst	Eastham*	Haslegrave	Conroy
2	Man U	Stepney	Young	Buchan	Martin	Holton	James*	Morgan	Anderson	Macari	Graham	McIlroy	Fletcher
3	Stoke	Farmer	Marsh	Pejic	Mahoney	Smith	Bloor	Robertson	Greenhoff	Ritchie	Hurst	Haslegrave	
3	Man C	Corrigan	Pardoe	Donachie	Doyle	Booth	Oakes	Summerbee	Bell	Law	Lee*	Marsh	Carrodus
4	Stoke	Farmer	Marsh	Pejic	Mahoney	Smith	Bloor	Robertson	Greenhoff	Ritchie	Hurst	Haslegrave	
4	Everton	Lawson	Darracott	Newton	Kendall	Kenyon	Hurst	Harvery	Bernard	Lyons	Harper	Connolly	
5	Stoke	Farmer	Pejic	Marsh	Mahoney	Smith	Bloor	Robertson	Greenhoff	Ritchie*	Hurst	Haslegrave	Conroy
5	QPR	Parkes	Clement	Watson	Venables	Mancini	Hazell	Thomas	Francis	Leach	Bowles	Givens	
6	Stoke	Farmer	Marsh	Pejic	Mahoney	Smith	Bloor	Robertson	Greenhoff	Ritchie*	Hurst	Haslegrave	Conroy
6	Everton	Lawson	Darracott	McLaughlin	Bernard	Kenyon	Hurst	Newton	Lyons	Royle	Harper	Connolly	
7	Stoke	Farmer	Marsh	Pejic	Mahoney	Smith	Bloor	Robertson*	Greenhoff	Hurst	Conroy	Haslegrave	Ritchie
7	Ipswich	Best	Mills	Harper	Collard	Miller	Beattie	Hamilton	Viljoen	Johnson	Woods	Lambert	
8	Stoke	Farmer	Marsh	Pejic	Mahoney	Smith	Bloor	Ritchie	Greenhoff	Hurst	Conroy	Haslegrave*	Jump
8	Arsenal	Wilson	Rice	McNab	Storey	Blockley	Simpson	Armstrong	Ball	Radford	Kennedy	George*	Kelly
9	Stoke	Farmer	Marsh	Pejic	Dodd	Smith	Bloor*	Conroy	Greenhoff	Hurst	Goodwin	Eastham	Jump
9	West Ham	Ferguson	McDowell	Lampard	Bonds	Taylor	Moore	Tyler	Lock	MacDougall	Brooking	Robson	Ritchie
10	Stoke	Farmer	Marsh	Pejic	Mahoney	Smith	Dodd	Conroy	Greenhoff	Hurst	Goodwin*	Haslegrave	Lees
10	Leeds	Harvey	Reaney	Cherry	Bremner	Madeley	Hunter	Lorimer*	Clarke	Jones	Giles	Yorath	Bates

Match reports

1. Liverpool are on the rampage from the off as Cormack's back-header almost sneaks in after 45 seconds. Heighway nips in to head a bouncing ball from Hughes past Farmer. Stoke fight back with Mahoney prominent. Pejic hits a post and Robertson rounds Clemence but cannot finish.

2. Stoke malfunction in attack despite the promptings of golden oldie George Eastham. He is booked for the first time in his career for taking a free-kick before the referee is ready! Steve James nods in McIlroy's cross and Stoke cannot find a way past big Jim Holton in the pouring rain.

3. Sean Haslegrave revels in his new midfield role as both Ritchie and Greenhoff are kept out by Joe Corrigan. Greenhoff pounces after Corrigan palms away Hurst's thunderbolt. The Blues fight back and snatch a draw when Denis Law finishes neatly after John Mahoney loses possession.

4. A drab affair ends with honours even after John Hurst and Roger Kenyon snuff out the threat of City's frontline. Everton, under new boss Billy Bingham, keep Farmer on his toes with Harper and Connolly going close late on. Ritchie pokes Stoke's best chance straight at David Lawson.

5. City nearly snatch that elusive win. Geoff Hurst's goals both come from long balls over the top. Smith heads home a Greenhoff cross. Referee Gow awards a harsh penalty for Pejic's tackle on Givens. Farmer saves Givens' initial effort but is adjudged to have moved. Venables scores.

6. John Farmer is the hero saving Joe Harper's injury-time penalty awarded by the linesman. In a tetchy affair Denis Smith is booked once again. Greenhoff's equaliser is fortunate as Jimmy Robertson's swirling cross evades Lawson and hits him on the head before dropping into the net.

7. The Boothen End is restless as City again struggle for rhythm. Clive Woods buries Johnson's pass and Ipswich are comfortable with nine men in defence until Hurst side-foots home Greenhoff's cross. Stoke lack the guile to create further openings. A midfield general is what's needed.

8. Stoke succumb after a brave fight at Highbury. Greenhoff converts Hurst's cross to equalize. Alan Dodd battles gamely in midfield and Terry Conroy has a penalty appeal turned down. Arsenal win it with Ball's scorching drive after Bloor misses Radford's cross in the bright sunshine.

9. Dave Goodwin scores on debut from Greenhoff's nod back and Stoke are in the ascendancy. Geoff Hurst relishes the tussle with old pal Bobby Moore and finishes on top, heading Eastham's curling cross home. Ferguson foils Hurst and Marsh to keep the score down. City back on track.

10. Pejic and Hurst are booked inside the first minute. Jones fires home from Bremner's free-kick and Don Revie's Leeds seem to be holding firm, even hitting the bar through Bates, until Smith outjumps David Harvey to head home Conroy's cross. City's first point at Elland Rd for 8 years.

Stoke City — match-by-match (continued)

13/10 (match 11) — SHEFFIELD UNITED — 1-2 — L — att 17,975 — Pts 8
Colquhoun 30 (og) / Woodward 52, Scullion 87
Ref: E Jolly

Stoke: McDonald, Marsh, Pejic, Mahoney, Smith, Dodd, Haslegrave, Greenhoff, Hurst, Ritchie, Goodwin
Sheffield United: McAllister, Badger, Hemsley, Flynn, Colquhoun, Speight, Woodward, Salmons, Dearden, Scullion, Staniforth

John Harris' Blades snatch victory from a shell-shocked Stoke. Eddie Colquhoun puts a header past his own keeper, but United battle back and Scullion breaks away to score after a mix up between Hurst and Goodwin. City waste chances, with Hurst and Ritchie thwarted by McAllister.

---

12 A SOUTHAMPTON — 20/10 — 0-3 — L — Pos 18 / Opp 9 — att 15,521 — Pts 8
Paine 2, Stokes 7, 45
Ref: T Dawes

Stoke: McDonald, Marsh, Pejic, Mahoney, Smith, Dodd, Robertson, Greenhoff, Hurst, Ritchie, Haslegrave* (Conroy)
Southampton: Martin, McCarthy, Mills, Fisher, Bennett, Steele, Paine, Channon*, Gilchrist, O'Neil, Stokes (O'Brien)

A makeshift Stoke team are sunk in the first seven mins. Mike McDonald misjudges Terry Paine's corner and can only help it into the net, then Bobby Stokes' header slips through the embarrassed keeper's hands. Waddo brings on Conroy after just 23 minutes but to no avail. Very poor.

---

13 H COVENTRY — 27/10 — 1-0 — W — Pos 18 / Opp 7 — att 17,421 — Pts 10
Greenhoff 6, 75, Hurst 72p
Ref: P Baldwin

Stoke: Farmer, Marsh, Pejic, Mahoney, Smith, Dodd, Robertson, Greenhoff, Hurst, Ritchie, Haslegrave
Coventry: Glazier, Coop, Holmes, Mortimer, Philpotts, Dugdale, Smith, Alderson, Stein, Cartwright, Hutchison

Stoke take Coventry apart with John Ritchie giving debutant David Philpotts a tough time. Greenhoff converts Robertson's cutback. Robertson hits the bar with a penalty but Hurst buries one after Holmes handles and Greenhoff slides in Robertson's cross to complete a deserved victory.

---

14 A NEWCASTLE — 3/11 — 1-2 — L — Pos 18 / Opp 2 — att 27,941 — Pts 10
Ritchie 52 / McDermott 35, Gibb 72
Ref: H Williams

Stoke: Farmer, Marsh, Pejic, Mahoney, Smith, Dodd, Haslegrave, Greenhoff, Hurst, Ritchie, Skeels
Newcastle: McFaul, Craig, Clark, McDermott*, Howard, Moncur, Gibb, Smith, Hibbitt, Cassidy, Barrowclough (Hudson)

Stoke battle gamely at high-flying Newcastle, but the Toon profit from Smith's underhit back-pass which Gibb slots home. Ritchie's cracking left-foot shot, his first goal this season, equalises McDermott's crashing drive. Tommy Gibb nearly makes it three for Joe Harvey's Magpies.

---

15 H NORWICH — 10/11 — 2-0 — W — Pos 17 / Opp 19 — att 5,363 — Pts 12
Ritchie 33, Goodwin 87
Ref: G Kew

Stoke: Farmer, Marsh, Pejic, Mahoney, Smith*, Dodd, Robertson, Greenhoff, Hurst, Ritchie, Goodwin
Norwich: Keelan, Prophett, Black, Stringer, Forbes, Briggs*, Livermore, Suggett, Cross, Paddon, Howard (Mellor)

Stoke outclass hapless Norwich. Kevin Keelan saves point blank from Hurst. Greenhoff has a goal controversially ruled out for offside. Black clears off the line from Ritchie who returns to something like his best form. He bags the opener from Pejic's free-kick. Goodwin finishes it off.

---

16 H BIRMINGHAM — 17/11 — 5-2 — W — Pos 16 / Opp 22 — att 13,179 — Pts 14
Ritchie 10, 83, Robertson 25, Hurst 60, Hynd 50, Latchford 55 [Mah'ly 70]
Ref: D Hippard

Stoke: Farmer, Marsh, Pejic, Mahoney, Smith, Dodd, Robertson, Greenhoff, Hurst, Ritchie, Goodwin
Birmingham: Sprake, Clarke, Want, Campbell, Hynd, Pendrey, Jenkins, Francis, Latchford, Hatton, Taylor

Stoke stuff Birmingham despite having a makeshift central defence. Having tried to sign Liverpool's Tommy Smith on loan City simply attack all game. Mahoney's first-time drive and Ritchie's running header to round it off are the pick of the goals. Francis hits the bar for Birmingham.

---

17 A BURNLEY — 24/11 — 0-1 — L — Pos 17 / Opp 3 — att 12,478 — Pts 14
Fletcher 4
Ref: I Jones

Stoke: Farmer, Marsh!, Pejic, Mahoney, Smith, Dodd, Robertson, Greenhoff, Hurst, Goodwin, Haslegrave
Burnley: Stevenson, Nulty, Newton, Dobson, Waldron, Thomson, Noble, Hankin, Fletcher, Collins, James

High-flying Burnley surprisingly only have one goal to show for their domination. Leighton James torments Jackie Marsh and his aggressive tackles earn him an early bath for two cautions. Only Hurst's rocket, which hits the underside of the bar, troubles Jimmy Adamson's Clarets.

---

18 A TOTTENHAM — 8/12 — 1-2 — L — Pos 17 / Opp 15 — att 4,034 — Pts 14
Ritchie 62 / Evans 70, Pratt 72
Ref: P Walters

Stoke: Farmer, Marsh*, Dodd, Mahoney, Smith, Bloor, Robertson, Greenhoff, Hurst, Ritchie, Haslegrave
Tottenham: Jennings, Evans, Knowles*, Pratt, England, Beal, McGrath, Perryman, Chivers, Neighbour, Coates (Naylor)

The lowest crowd of the season sees Spurs in charge as Stoke toil without creating much. Ritchie scores with a tap in. Alan Bloor returns after 10 weeks out but cannot stave off the Spurs comeback. Ray Evans' equaliser is a stunner and the defence goes to sleep for John Pratt's header.

---

19 H WOLVES — 15/12 — 2-3 — L — Pos 18 / Opp 17 — att 13,343 — Pts 14
Smith 63, Robertson 65 / Munro 27, Richards 30, Hibbitt 69
Ref: H New

Stoke: Farmer, Dodd, Pejic, Mahoney, Smith, Bloor, Robertson, Greenhoff, Hurst, Ritchie, Haslegrave
Wolves: Parkes, Sunderland, Taylor, Bailey, Munro, McAlle, Powell, Hibbitt, Richards, Dougan, Wagstaffe* (Jefferson)

The lack of power available to run the lights due to the national strike means a 2pm start. City don't switch on until Smith finishes Greenhoff's overhead kick and then Robertson fires in. Then Stoke relax and Hibbit converts Dougan's cross. Wolves hang on despite a late penalty appeal.

---

20 A WEST HAM — 22/12 — 2-0 — W — Pos 18 / Opp 22 — att 12,513 — Pts 16
Robertson 49, Greenhoff 84
Ref: W Castle

Stoke: Farmer, Dodd, Pejic, Mahoney, Smith, Bloor, Robertson, Greenhoff, Hurst, Ritchie, Haslegrave
West Ham: Day, McDowell, Lampard, Holland, Taylor, McGiven, Ayris*, Paddon, Gould, Coleman, Best (Wooler)

A tough basement battle brings Stoke's first away win. Robertson pounces after Day palms away Hurst's shot. Greenhoff clinches it with a 20-yard first time volley after tremendous pressure on the City goal. Dodd and McDonald both deny West Ham on the line as the Potters cling on.

---

21 H DERBY — 26/12 — 0-0 — D — Pos 18 / Opp 5 — att 24,435 — Pts 17
Ref: C Thomas

Stoke: Farmer, Dodd, Pejic, Skeels, Smith, Bloor, Robertson, Greenhoff, Hurst, Mahoney, Haslegrave
Derby: Boulton, Webster, Nish, Newton, McFarland, Todd, McGovern, Gemmill, Davies*, Hector, Hinton (Thomas)

Dave Mackay's men are happy to sit back as Stoke buzz in attack, but for all the effort City lack the guile to open up the resolute Rams. Even when Geoff Hurst shrugs off Colin Todd to score he is brought back by the referee who gives Stoke a free-kick and books the Derby defender!

LEAGUE DIVISION 1

Manager: Tony Waddington

SEASON 1973-74

No	Date	V	Opponent	Att	Pos	Opp	F-A	Res	Pt	H-T	Scorers, Times, and Referees	1	2	3	4	5	6	7	8	9	10	11	12 sub used
22	29/12	H	QP RANGERS	18,910	16	10	4-1	W	19	0-1	Mahoney 49, Pejic 60, Ritchie 79, [Greenhoff 85] Leach 27 Ref: R Armstrong	Farmer	Dodd	Pejic	Skeels	Smith	Bloor	Robertson	Greenhoff	Hurst	Mahoney	Haslegrave*	Ritchie
			QP RANGERS									Parkes	Clement	Abbott	Venables*	Evans	McLintock	Thomas	Francis	Leach	Bowles	Givens	Beck
23	1/1	A	MANCHESTER C	35,009	17	14	0-0	D	20	0-0	Ref: V James	Farmer	Dodd	Pejic	Skeels	Smith	Bloor	Robertson	Greenhoff	Ritchie	Mahoney	Haslegrave	
			MANCHESTER C									Corrigan	Barrett	Donachie	Doyle	Booth	Towers	Summerbee	Bell	Marsh	Law	Leman	
24	12/1	A	IPSWICH	18,581	17	6	1-1	D	21	0-0	Hurst 70 Johnson 63 Ref: R Toseland	Farmer	Marsh	Pejic	Skeels	Smith	Bloor	Robertson	Greenhoff	Hurst	Dodd	Mahoney	
			IPSWICH									Best	Burley	Mills	Collard	Keeley	Beattie	Hamilton	Viljoen	Johnson	Whymark*	Lambert	Woods
25	19/1	H	LIVERPOOL	32,789	17	2	1-1	D	22	0-0	Hurst 67 Smith 90 Ref: D Biddle	Farmer	Marsh	Pejic	Dodd	Smith	Bloor	Robertson	Greenhoff	Hurst	Hudson	Mahoney	
			LIVERPOOL									Clemence	Smith	Lindsay	Thompson	Lloyd	Hughes	Keegan	Cormack	Waddle	Heighway*	Callaghan	Boersma
26	27/1	H	CHELSEA	31,985	16	18	1-0	W	24	0-0	Hurst 80p Ref: I Smith	Farmer	Marsh	Pejic	Dodd	Smith	Bloor	Robertson	Greenhoff	Hurst	Hudson	Mahoney	
			CHELSEA									Phillips	Locke	Harris	Hollins	Droy	Webb	Britton	Garland	Kember	Garner	Cooke	
27	2/2	A	WOLVES	30,128	15	15	1-1	D	25	0-0	Ritchie 68 Pejic 55 (og) Ref: P Hackney	Farmer	Marsh	Pejic	Dodd*	Smith	Bloor	Robertson	Greenhoff	Hurst	Hudson	Mahoney	Ritchie
			WOLVES									Pierce	Palmer	Parkin	Bailey	Munro!	Taylor	Sunderland	Hibbitt	Richards	Dougan	Wagstaffe	
28	16/2	A	SHEFFIELD UTD	19,972	17	10	0-0	D	26	0-0	Ref: F Reeves	Farmer	Marsh	Pejic	Dodd	Smith	Skeels	Robertson	Greenhoff	Ritchie	Hudson	Mahoney	
			SHEFFIELD UTD									Hope	Badger	Hemsley	Flynn	Colquhoun	Eddy	Woodward	Speight!	Garbett	Cammack*	Salmons	Nicholl
29	23/2	H	LEEDS	39,958	13	1	3-2	W	28	2-2	Pejic 27, Hudson 35, Smith 68 Bremner 7, Clarke 17 Ref: B Homewood	Farmer	Marsh	Pejic	Dodd	Smith	Bloor	Robertson	Greenhoff	Hurst	Hudson	Mahoney	
			LEEDS									Harvey	Yorath	Cherry	Bremner	Ellam	Hunter	Lorimer	Clarke	Jordan	Giles*	Madeley	Cooper
30	2/3	A	DERBY	28,176	13	3	1-1	D	29	0-1	Ritchie 55 Bourne 2 Ref: T Spencer	Farmer	Marsh	Pejic	Dodd	Smith	Mahoney	Robertson	Greenhoff	Hurst	Hudson	Ritchie	
			DERBY									Boulton	Webster	Nish	Rioch	McFarland	Todd	Powell	Gemmill	Davies	Hector	Bourne	
31	9/3	A	COVENTRY	28,176	15	10	0-2	L	29	0-0	Hutchison 49, Cross 74 Ref: L Hayes	McDonald	Marsh	Pejic	Dodd	Smith	Mahoney	Robertson	Greenhoff	Hurst	Hudson	Ritchie	
			COVENTRY									Glazier	Smith	Holmes	Mortimer	Cattlin	Dugdale	Green	Alderson*	Cross	Carr	Hutchison	Cartwright

22 — QP Rangers: City pummel the R's into submission with a whirlwind second-half display. True to form Rangers grab a half-time lead against the run of play, but Stoke hit back with sub Ritchie making the difference. His cross-shot and Greenhoff's flying header are the pick of rampant City's efforts.

23 — Manchester C: City mount a rearguard action after John Farmer is injured and is hindered on his right-hand side. He saves from Summerbee and Marsh as Ron Saunders' men pile forward in frozen temperatures. Pejic heads off the line. Ritchie sets up Robertson to score but the ball is out of play earlier.

24 — Ipswich: Ipswich put Stoke under intense pressure early on but Farmer is equal to Hamilton and Johnson when both are clean through. Jimmy Robertson produces a fabulous display against his old team and all but scores the equaliser. Hurst follows the ball in to make sure. A valuable away point.

25 — Liverpool: Alan Hudson, a record £240,000 signing from Chelsea, shines on his debut as Stoke outplay the Champions in their best display of the season. Time and again Clemence thwarts Greenhoff and Hurst. City seem to be home and dry until a cross is dropped by Farmer and Smith prods in.

26 — Chelsea: Hudson is the captain and runs the show against his former club, eventually being tripped by Gary Locke to give City a penalty, taken by Hurst who thumps it home in triumph. Huddy nearly loses it for Stoke when his back-pass falls to Garner who hits the post but City are worth the win.

27 — Wolves: Pejic's unlucky own-goal is slightly against the run of play but Wolves actually dominate after Munro is sent off for an off-the-ball incident on the hour. Richards and Hibbitt go close. After turning down a £30,000 move to Preston, Ritchie comes off the bench to ram home Pejic's cross.

28 — Sheffield Utd: Long serving defender Eric Skeels replaces the injured Alan Bloor as City battle it out in a fierce game at Bramall Lane. Micky Speight is sent off for kicking Pejic after 53 mins and the game overheats. Smith gets his third caution of the season. Hurst nods agonisingly wide at the death.

29 — Leeds: Stoke put Leeds' 29-match unbeaten run to the sword. Bremner's cheeky quick free-kick and Clarke's 'offside' goal put Leeds ahead but Pejic cracks home from 25 yards and Huddy neatly levels. Then Denis Smith rises at the far post to majestically head the winner of a fantastic game.

30 — Derby: Stoke's 11th game unbeaten despite a bad start as debutant Bruce Rioch crosses for Jeff Bourne to head home. Hudson sets up Ritchie superbly to fire in the equaliser. Then tempers flare and Marsh is booked again. Farmer saves point blank from Davies and injures himself saving again.

31 — Coventry: The unbeaten run ends unceremoniously at Highfield Road. Hutchison scores from close in and Cross hounds McDonald into a mistake from Dodd's back-pass. Hurst fires home, but the referee gives a foul on Bill Glazier. As an experiment both linesmen wear black and white hoops!

(This page is a rotated statistical season-record grid. Top of the page is cut off. Match no. 32 is partly visible at the top.)

Match record

No.	Date	Venue	Opponent	Pos	Res	Score	HT	Att	Opp Pos	Pts	Scorers (Stoke / opposition)	Ref
32	16/3	H	SOUTHAMPTON	—	W	4-1	—	20,415	19	31	Hurst 13, Ritchie 30, 75, 80 / Dodd 36 (og) *(top cut off)*	A Jones
33	23/3	A	NORWICH	15	L	0-4	0-0	19,924	21	31	— / Sissons 56, 75, MacDougall 59, [Suggett 87]	R Challis
34	30/3	H	ARSENAL	16	D	0-0	0-0	13,532	12	32	—	J Rice
35	3/4	H	NEWCASTLE	11	W	2-1	1-1	13,437	13	34	Greenhoff 23, Mahoney 57 / Tudor 9	M Lowe
36	6/4	H	BURNLEY	8	W	4-0	2-0	14,253	7	36	Ritchie 28p, 80p, Greenhoff 31, [Hudson 77]	R Toseland
37	13/4	A	BIRMINGHAM	8	D	0-0	0-0	29,467	20	37	—	K Styles
38	15/4	H	LEICESTER	8	W	1-0	0-0	27,468	9	39	Hurst 87	H Williams
39	16/4	A	LEICESTER	8	D	1-1	1-1	21,682	9	40	Hurst 40 / Worthington 14	T Dawes
40	20/4	H	TOTTENHAM	6	W	1-0	1-0	20,139	16	42	Haslegrave 44	P Willis
41	27/4	A	CHELSEA	6	W	1-0	0-0	17,150	17	44	Hudson 50	R Crabb
42	29/4	H	MANCHESTER U	5	W	1-0	1-0	27,332	21	46	Ritchie 30	G Hill

Average: Home 21,579 — Away 25,553

Line-ups

(Stoke players in roman; opposition players in italics as printed.)

v Southampton: Farmer, Marsh, Pejic, Dodd, Smith, Mahoney, Robertson, Greenhoff, Hurst, Hudson, Ritchie / *Martin, McCarthy, Peach, Fisher, Bennett, Steele, Paine, Channon, Osgood, Gilchrist, Stokes*

v Norwich: Farmer, Marsh, Pejic, Dodd, Smith, Mahoney, Robertson, Greenhoff, Hurst, Hudson, Ritchie / *Keelan, Machin, Benson, Stringer, Forbes, Howard*, Prophett, MacDougall, Suggett, Boyer, Sissons, (Grapes)*

v Arsenal: Farmer, Marsh, Pejic, Dodd, Smith, Mahoney, Robertson, Greenhoff, Hurst, Hudson, Ritchie / *Wilson, Rice, Nelson, Storey, Blockley, Kelly*, Armstrong, Ball, Radford, Kennedy, George, (Simpson)*

v Newcastle: Farmer, Marsh, Pejic, Dodd, Smith, Mahoney, Robertson, Greenhoff, Hurst, Hudson, Ritchie / *McFaul, Craig, Clark, McDermott, Howard, Moncur, Bruce, Cassidy, Tudor, Hope, Kennedy*

v Burnley: Farmer, Marsh, Pejic, Dodd, Smith, Mahoney, Robertson, Greenhoff, Hurst, Hudson, Ritchie / *Stevenson, Noble, Brennan, Dobson, Waldron, Thomson, Nulty, Hankin, Fletcher, Collins, James*

v Birmingham: Farmer, Marsh, Pejic, Dodd, Smith, Skeels, Robertson, Greenhoff, Hurst, Hudson, Ritchie / *Latchford, Martin, Pendrey, Kendall, Hynd, Roberts, Campbell, Francis, Gallagher, Hatton, Taylor*

v Leicester (H): Farmer, Marsh, Pejic, Dodd, Smith, Skeels, Robertson, Hurst, Ritchie, Hudson, Mahoney / *Shilton, Whitworth, Rofe, Earle, Munro, Cross, Weller*, Sammels, Worthington, Waters, Glover, (Yates)*

v Leicester (A): Farmer, Marsh, Pejic, Dodd, Smith, Skeels, Robertson*, Hurst, Ritchie, Hudson, Bloor / *Shilton, Whitworth, Rofe, Earle, Munro, Cross, Weller, Sammels, Worthington, Waters, Glover, (Conroy)*

v Tottenham: Farmer, Marsh, Pejic, Dodd, Smith, Skeels, Haslegrave, Greenhoff, Ritchie, Hudson, Hurst / *Jennings, Kinnear, Naylor, Pratt*, England, Beal, Coates, Perryman, Chivers, Dillon, Neighbour, (Holder)*

v Chelsea: Farmer, Marsh, Pejic, Dodd, Smith, Skeels, Haslegrave, Greenhoff, Ritchie, Hudson, Hurst / *Phillips, Wilkins G, Sparrow, Hollins, Droy, Webb, Garland, Wilkins R, Hutchinson, Swain, Houseman*

v Manchester U: Farmer, Marsh, Pejic, Dodd, Smith, Skeels, Haslegrave, Greenhoff, Ritchie, Hudson, Hurst / *Stepney, Forsyth, Houston, Greenhoff, Holton, Buchan, Morgan, Macari, McIlroy, McCalliog, Martin*

Match reports

Southampton — Saints, with one win in 12, cannot compete with rampant Stoke. Ritchie's hat-trick are all from moves begun by the superb Mahoney and Alan Hudson. For his third he stops the ball on the line, kneels down and heads it in. Hurst's header through Martin's fingers is his 200th league goal.

Norwich — Stoke are hammered by John Bonds' struggling Canaries. Sissons' unstoppable drive sparks an avalanche. City's attacking policy is punished as Norwich pick off the stranded defenders, left to mark one on one, with ease. The coup de grace is Colin Suggett's flick over Farmer's head.

Arsenal — Arsenal blunt Stoke's attacking ambitions. Hudson is thwarted by Bob Wilson and Ritchie has two efforts whistle past the post. Sound defence by the Gunners reduces City to long-range efforts. Towards the end Mike Pejic nearly buries one and Bertie Mee's men are happy with a point.

Newcastle — Joe Harvey's Wembley-bound Magpies have a makeshift attack but snatch the lead through Tudor's shot. Greenhoff heads in Hudson's quick free-kick for his first goal of the year. Willie McFaul lets Mahoney's 35-yarder through his fingers. A late Toon goal is disallowed for offside.

Burnley — City see off Burnley with a superb attacking display. Huddy is at the crux of everything. New England cap Pejic and then Robertson are fouled for the two penalties. Hudson's volley from 22 yards out is sheer class. Greenhoff lobs Alan Stevenson cheekily and it's party time at the Vic.

Birmingham — Birmingham force 21 corners to Stoke's two but cannot find a way past the injured John Farmer and his battered defence. Denis Smith is at the heart of the new resolution which has appeared at the back. Bob Hatton has the Blues' clearest chances but the inspired Farmer foils him twice.

Leicester (H) — City steal the points with Hurst's fine 25-yard left-footed piledriver right at the death. Stoke remain on course for Europe. Jimmy Bloomfield's Foxes deserve a draw after a battling display but Peter Shilton is the busier of the two goalkeepers. Bloor clears Sammels' header off the line.

Leicester (A) — Stoke show their grit to earn a draw at Filbert Street after Frank Worthington's classy left-footed free-kick. Marsh heads off the line then City break away and Hurst volleys into the roof of the net. Farmer saves Alan Dodd's blushes by smothering Len Glover's effort from his back-pass.

Tottenham — Stoke are different class but can only score once thanks to Pat Jennings. Haslegrave's header from Greenhoff's cross is scant reward as Bloor, Hudson, Pejic, Robertson and Ritchie are all denied. Spurs can't compete with City's passing and movement. Europe is certainly possible now.

Chelsea — Alan Hudson once again proves to be the match winner as he fires home Smith's knockback for the only goal of a drab game played in swirling winds. Chelsea's youthful team struggle but Ray Wilkins forces one good save from Farmer. Eric Skeels goes closest to adding to Stoke's lead.

Manchester U — United's hooligan element express their disgust at relegation by running riot around the ground. Hudson's class shows as he torments the Red Devils' defence. In an ugly atmosphere banners burn as Ritchie's strike from Haslegrave's pass seals it. United just try to keep the score down.

LEAGUE DIVISION 1 (CUP-TIES) Manager: Tony Waddington SEASON 1973-74

League Cup

League Cup	Att	Pos	Opp	R	F-A	H-T	Scorers, Times, and Referees	1	2	3	4	5	6	7	8	9	10	11	12 sub used
2 H CHELSEA 8/10	17,281	16	15	W	1-0	0-0	Smith 48 — Ref: J Yates	McDonald	Marsh	Pejic	Mahoney	Smith	Dodd	Haslegrave	Greenhoff	Hurst	Ritchie	Goodwin	
								Bonetti	*Locke*	*Harris*	*Hollins*	*Droy*	*Webb*	*Baldwin*	*Hudson*	*Osgood*	*Kember*	*Garland*	
3 H MIDDLESBROUGH 31/10	19,194	18	2:1	D	1-1	0-0	Pejic 50 — Brine 55 — Ref: J Rice	Farmer	Marsh	Pejic	Mahoney	Smith	Dodd	Robertson	Greenhoff	Ritchie	Hurst	Haslegrave	
								Platt	*Craggs*	*Spraggon*	*Souness*	*Boam*	*Maddren*	*Murdoch*	*Brine*	*Smith*	*Foggon*	*Armstrong*	
3R A MIDDLESBROUGH 6/11	26,063	18	2:1	W	2-1	1-0	Greenhoff 39, Pejic 106 — Foggon 80 — aet — Ref: J Rice	Platt	Marsh	Pejic	Mahoney	Smith	Dodd	Skeels	Greenhoff	Ritchie	Hurst	Haslegrave	
								Platt	*Craggs*	*Spraggon*	*Gates*	*Boam*	*Maddren*	*Murdoch*	*Mills*	*Hickton*	*Foggon*	*Armstrong*	
4 A COVENTRY 20/11	17,483	17	15	L	1-2	1-1	Hurst 35 — Green 41, Stein 68 — Ref: R Challis	Farmer	Marsh	Pejic	Mahoney	Dodd	Jump	Robertson	Greenhoff	Ritchie	Hurst	Haslegrave	
								Glazier	*Coop*	*Holmes*	*McGuire*	*Parker*	*Dugdale*	*Cartwright*	*Alderson*	*Stein*	*Green*	*Hutchison*	

2 H CHELSEA — John Mahoney's industry lays the foundations of the win. Jimmy Greenhoff knocks Haslegrave's corner back in to the middle and Denis Smith dives full length to plant the ball in Bonetti's net for his second goal in three days. Mike McDonald defies Peter Osgood as Chelsea battle back.

3 H MIDDLESBROUGH — Jack Charlton's Second Division table-toppers defend in depth until Pejic's drive puts City ahead. Boro level when four defenders converge on David Armstrong who puts the unmarked Peter Brine in to finish. Stoke have mountains of pressure but cannot find the finish to a tense finale.

3R A MIDDLESBROUGH — Mike Pejic hits the post and Greenhoff turns in the rebound. Boro huff and puff, but City seem to have it in the bag, until Alan Foggon pops up to bury a ricochet from Murdoch's shot. Extra-time is tense but Pejic's left-foot rocket settles it in front of Ayresome's biggest gate of the year.

4 A COVENTRY — The windscreen on Stoke's coach smashes on the way to the game – a sign of things to come. City should have more than Geoff Hurst's strike, after Ritchie steps over a cross, to show for early dominance. Bill Glazier keeps the Sky Blues in it until Green nods in and Coventry take over.

FA Cup

FA Cup	Att	Pos	Opp	R	F-A	H-T	Scorers, Times, and Referees	1	2	3	4	5	6	7	8	9	10	11	12 sub used
3 A BOLTON 6/1	39,138	17	2:18	L	2-3	0-1	Ritchie 65, Haslegrave 84p — Byrom 23, 46, 63 — Ref: H Hackney	Farmer	Dodd	Pejic	Skeels	Smith	Bloor	Robertson	Greenhoff	Ritchie	Hurst*	Mahoney	Haslegrave
								Siddall	*Ritson*	*Nicholson*	*Rimmer**	*Jones P*	*Waldron*	*Byram*	*Jones G*	*Greaves*	*Whatmore*	*Thompson*	*Lee*

3 A BOLTON — Sunday soccer is introduced to the nation and a bumper crowd sees John Byrom plunder a hat-trick for Jimmy Armfield's men. He beats three defenders to fire in his second. Ritchie's left-foot shot and Haslegrave's penalty, for a foul on Ritchie, make it tense but City can't find a third.

Football League Division One — Final Table

Pos	Team	P	W	D	L	F	A	W	D	L	F	A	Pts
			Home					Away					
1	Leeds	42	12	8	1	38	18	12	6	3	28	13	62
2	Liverpool	42	18	2	1	34	11	4	11	6	18	20	57
3	Derby	42	13	7	1	40	16	4	7	10	12	26	48
4	Ipswich	42	10	7	4	38	21	8	4	9	29	37	47
5	STOKE	42	13	6	2	39	15	2	10	9	15	27	46
6	Burnley	42	10	9	2	29	16	6	5	10	27	37	46
7	Everton	42	12	7	2	29	14	4	5	12	21	34	44
8	QP Rangers	42	8	10	3	30	17	5	7	9	26	35	43
9	Leicester	42	10	7	4	35	17	3	9	9	16	24	42
10	Arsenal	42	9	7	5	23	16	5	7	9	26	35	42
11	Tottenham	42	9	4	8	26	27	5	10	6	19	23	42
12	Wolves	42	11	6	4	30	18	2	9	10	19	31	41
13	Sheffield Utd	42	7	7	7	25	22	7	5	9	19	27	40
14	Manchester C	42	10	7	4	25	17	4	5	12	14	29	40
15	Newcastle	42	9	6	6	28	21	4	6	11	21	27	38
16	Coventry	42	10	5	6	25	18	4	5	12	18	36	38
17	Chelsea	42	9	4	8	36	29	3	9	9	20	31	37
18	West Ham	42	7	7	7	36	32	4	8	9	19	28	37
19	Birmingham	42	10	7	4	30	21	2	6	13	22	43	37
20	Southampton	42	8	10	3	30	20	3	4	14	17	48	36
21	Manchester U	42	7	7	7	23	20	3	5	13	15	28	32
22	Norwich	42	6	9	6	25	27	1	6	14	12	35	29
		924	218	149	95	674	433	95	149	218	433	674	924

Odds & ends

Double wins: (2) West Ham, Chelsea.
Double losses: (0).

Won from behind: (3) Leeds (h), Newcastle (h), QP Rangers (h).
Lost from in front: (2) Sheffield Utd (h), Tottenham (a).

High spots: Second highest-ever final League placing.
Most League points since returning to First Division in 1963.
Fantastic form after the signing of Alan Hudson.
Only 2 goals conceded in the final 9 matches.
Putting an end to Leeds' record unbeaten run.
Winning the Watney Cup.

Low spots: The dreadful start with only two wins before November.
Losing in the FA Cup to Bolton.
Being thrashed 0-4 by bottom club Norwich.

Ever-presents: (0).
Hat-tricks: (1) John Ritchie.
Leading scorer: (15) John Ritchie.

Appearances & Goals

Player	Lge	Sub	LC	Sub	FAC	Sub	Lge	LC	FAC	Tot
	Appearances						Goals			
Bloor, Alan	27									
Conroy, Terry	5	3					2	2		4
Dodd, Alan	31		4		1					
Eastham, George	2									
Farmer, John	38		3		1					
Goodwin, Dave	4	1	1				2			2
Greenhoff, Jimmy	39		4		1		9		1	10
Haslegrave, Sean			4	1			1	1		2
Hudson, Alan	18						3			3
Hurst, Geoff	35		4		1		12	1		13
Jump, Stewart	2	1	1							
Lees, Terry	3	1	1							
Mahoney, John	35		4		1		3			3
Marsh, Jackie	31		4		1					
McDonald, Mike	4		1							
Moores, Ian	1									
Pejic, Mike	41		4		1					
Ritchie, John	26	4	4		1		14		1	15
Robertson, Jimmy	37		2		1		3			3
Skeels, Eric	15		1		1					
Smith, Denis	41		3		1		4	1		5
(own-goals)							1			1
21 players used	462	10	44	1	11	1	54	5	2	61

LEAGUE DIVISION 1   Manager: Tony Waddington   SEASON 1974-75

No		Date	Opponent	Att	Pos	W/D/L	Pt	F-A	H-T	Scorers, Times, and Referees
1	H	17/8	LEEDS	33,534		W	2	3-0	0-0	Mahoney 50, Greenhoff 85, Ritchie 87 — Ref: J Burns
2	A	20/8	EVERTON	35,817		L	2	1-2	1-1	Salmons 17; Royle 30p, 73 — Ref: K Baker
3	A	24/8	QP RANGERS	21,117	8 12	W	4	1-0	0-0	Hurst 86 — Ref: R Toseland
4	H	28/8	EVERTON	27,594	7 4	D	5	1-1	0-0	Mahoney 75; Latchford 53 — Ref: M Lowe
5	H	31/8	MIDDLESBROUGH	23,484	6 7	D	6	1-1	1-1	Ritchie 17p; Souness 20 — Ref: W Gow
6	A	7/9	CARLISLE	14,507	4 7	W	8	2-0	1-0	Hudson 5, Ritchie 58 — Ref: E Garner
7	H	14/9	COVENTRY	22,482	4 21	W	10	2-0	0-0	Mahoney 59, Ritchie 84 — Ref: H Hackney
8	A	21/9	LIVERPOOL	51,423	4 2	L	10	0-3	0-2	[Heighway 55] Ritchie 42 (og), Boersma 45, — Ref: G Hill
9	A	24/9	IPSWICH	24,470	6 1	L	10	1-3	0-0	Salmons 90; Viljoen 59, Hamilton 70, Whymark 75 — Ref: B Daniels
10	H	28/9	DERBY	23,589	9 8	D	11	1-1	1-0	Hurst 28; Lee 75 — Ref: A Jones

Line-ups

No	Team	1	2	3	4	5	6	7	8	9	10	11	12 sub used
1	Stoke	Farmer	Marsh	Pejic	Dodd	Smith	Mahoney	Haslegrave	Greenhoff	Ritchie	Hudson	Salmons	
1	Leeds	Harvey	Reaney	Cooper	Bremner	McQueen	Cherry	Lorimer	Madeley	Jordan	Giles	McKenzie	
2	Stoke	Farmer	Marsh	Pejic	Mahoney	Smith	Dodd	Haslegrave	Greenhoff*	Hurst	Hudson	Salmons	Conroy
2	Everton	Lawson	Darracott	Seargeant	Clements	Kenyon	Hurst	Buckley	Harvey*	Royle	Latchford	Lyons	
3	Stoke	Farmer	Marsh	Pejic	Mahoney	Smith	Dodd	Haslegrave	Greenhoff	Hurst*	Hudson	Salmons	Conroy
3	QP Rangers	Parkes	Clement	Gillard	Busby	Mancini	Webb	Thomas	Francis	Beck	Bowles*	Givens	Leach
4	Stoke	Farmer	Marsh	Pejic	Mahoney	Smith	Dodd	Haslegrave	Greenhoff	Hurst*	Hudson	Salmons	Conroy
4	Everton	Lawson	Darracott	Seargeant	Clements	Kenyon	Hurst*	Buckley	Dobson	Royle	Latchford	Lyons	Connolly
5	Stoke	Farmer	Marsh	Pejic	Mahoney	Smith	Dodd	Haslegrave	Greenhoff	Ritchie	Hudson	Salmons	
5	Middlesbrough	Platt	Craggs	Spraggon	Souness*	Boam	Maddren	Murdoch	Mills	Hickton	Foggon	Armstrong	Brine
6	Stoke	Farmer	Marsh	Pejic	Mahoney	Smith	Dodd	Haslegrave	Greenhoff	Ritchie	Hudson	Salmons	
6	Carlisle	Ross	Carr	Gorman	O'Neill	Green	Parker	Barry*	Train	McIlmoyle	Balderstone	Laidlaw	Owen
7	Stoke	Farmer	Marsh	Pejic	Mahoney	Smith	Dodd	Haslegrave	Greenhoff	Ritchie	Hudson	Salmons*	Conroy
7	Coventry	Ramsbottom	Oakey	Cattlin	Mortimer	Lloyd	Hindley	McGuire	Alderson	Cross	Holmes	Hutchison	
8	Stoke	Farmer	Marsh	Pejic	Mahoney	Smith	Dodd	Haslegrave*	Greenhoff	Ritchie*	Hudson	Salmons	Robertson
8	Liverpool	Clemence	Smith	Lindsay	Thompson*	Cormack	Hughes	Boersma	Hall	Heighway	Kennedy	Callaghan	Waddle
9	Stoke	Farmer	Marsh	Pejic	Mahoney	Smith	Dodd!	Haslegrave	Greenhoff	Ritchie*	Hudson	Salmons	Robertson
9	Ipswich	Sivell	Burley	Mills	Talbot	Hunter	Beattie	Hamilton	Viljoen	Johnson	Whymark	Woods	
10	Stoke	Farmer	Marsh	Pejic	Mahoney	Smith	Dodd	Haslegrave	Greenhoff	Hurst*	Hudson	Salmons	Robertson
10	Derby	Boulton	Webster	Nish	Rioch*	Todd	Daniel	Newton	Gemmill	Davies	Hector	Lee	Powell

Match reports

1. City field £160,000 signing Geoff Salmons from Sheffield United. He and Hudson combine to set up Mahoney for a 25-yard screamer past the motionless David Harvey. Clough's Leeds have no answer. Clever strikes by Greenhoff and Ritchie round off an impressive opening day win.

2. Stoke gift Everton the points after taking the lead through Salmons' diving header, his first for the club. The penalty is given against Hudson in a melee of players. Then Pejic sells Farmer short with a back-pass and Joe Royle mops up. Lawson brilliantly saves Conroy and Smith's efforts.

3. City edge a close game with some splendid passing movements involving Hudson, Salmons, Francis and Bowles. Denis Smith heads just over in his 200th league game. Geoff Hurst volleys home a near-post Salmons cross to win it. Greenhoff shoots straight at Phil Parkes when through.

4. In front of new England manager Don Revie, Alan Hudson plays another blinder. Despite the midfield flair the Potters find Everton's ten-man defence difficult to break down. Latchford buries a powerful header and City are in trouble. Finally Mahoney's diving header rescues a point.

5. In a crunching game four players are booked. Stuart Boam handles for the penalty and Ritchie sends Jim Platt the wrong way. Graeme Souness equalizes with a snap shot from the edge of the box and then limps off. Foggon and Hudson waste good chances in an entertaining encounter.

6. Salmons and Hudson on the rampage again as Stoke bring Ron Ashman's Carlisle back down to earth. Ritchie steps over Salmons cross to give Hudson a tap in. Huddy tees up Greenhoff whose shot rebounds to the prowling Ritchie. Pejic's screamer is tipped on to the post by Alan Ross.

7. Hudson returns with a broken hand after crashing his car during the week and missing the win over Halifax. Haslegrave sets up Mahoney for an easy opener as Coventry flood midfield, keeping nine men behind the ball. John Ritchie's unstoppable volley flies past Neil Ramsbottom.

8. Liverpool miss Keegan, suspended after shirt throwing at Wembley. City hold up well in the usual Anfield pressure cooker but Ritchie cruelly deflects a corner home to end the resistance. The other strikes are great individual goals. City sport a new white away kit with diagonal stripes.

9. John Ritchie is causing havoc in Town's defence but his left leg is badly broken by Kevin Beattie's 55th-min hefty challenge as the night turns sour for Stoke. Three goals in 16 mins is bad but Alan Dodd is dismissed for his second yellow card (handball) and City's misery is complete.

10. Geoff Hurst ably fills the gap left by Ritchie's injury as he flicks home Mike Pejic's free-kick. City make all the running until Archie Gemmill fires past the post. Franny Lee latches on to his cross to fire home. Stoke react, forcing three corners in injury-time, but cannot find the winner.

No		Opp	Date	Pos	W/D/L	Score	HT	OppPos	Pts	Att
11	H	SHEFFIELD UTD	5/10	6	W	3:2	2-0	8	13	21,726

SHEFFIELD UTD — Hurst 15, Greenhoff 38, Smith 57 / Eddy 65p, Field 79. Ref: I Smith

Stoke: Farmer, Marsh, Pejic, Mahoney, Smith, Dodd, Robertson, Greenhoff, Hurst, Hudson, Salmons
Sheffield Utd: Brown, Badger!, Hemsley, Eddy, Colquhoun, Franks, Woodward, Speight*, Dearden, Currie, Field, Bradford

Another bruising encounter. Hurst follows up his own penalty, saved by Brown for the opener. Greenhoff nets from close in despite stumbling and Smith taps in when Robertson's effort is blocked. Badger is sent off for fouling Pejic and Utd's spot-kick is for Smith's clumsy late tackle.

12	A	NEWCASTLE	12/10	6	D	2:2	1-2	7	14	38,228

NEWCASTLE — Salmons 25, Mahoney 63 / Keeley 5, Tudor 31. Ref: J Goggins

Stoke: Farmer, Marsh, Pejic*, Mahoney, Smith, Dodd, Haslegrave, Greenhoff, Hurst*, Hudson, Salmons
Newcastle: McFaul, Nattrass, Kennedy, McDermott, Keeley, Howard, Burns*, Gibb, MacDonald, Tudor, Hibbitt, Barrowcl'gh

Stoke gamely fight back twice with Hudson's promptings lead to Salmons' long-range header and Mahoney's 20-yarder. SuperMac again hits the bar as City battle to hold on. MacDonald hits the bar, then City fail to deal with another corner which Tudor converts.

13	H	BURNLEY	19/10	6	W	2:0	2-0	8	16	23,466

BURNLEY — Marsh 13, Hurst 30. Ref: R Tinkler

Stoke: Farmer, Marsh, Pejic, Mahoney, Smith, Dodd, Haslegrave, Greenhoff, Hurst, Hudson, Salmons
Burnley: Stevenson, Newton, Brennan, Flynn, Waldron, Rodaway, Noble, Hankin, Fletcher, Collins, James

Jackie Marsh blasts home a rare left-footed goal to set City on their way. Hurst's predatory instincts allow him to nip in and finish off Hudson's free-kick. City cruise the second half without looking to add to the score. The crowd are impatient but Stoke tire after the recent run of games.

14	A	CHELSEA	26/10	6	D	3:3	1-1	17	17	24,718

CHELSEA — Gr'nhoff 13, Hasle' 60, Rob'tson 85 / Dray 28, Garland 61, Hutchinson 90. Ref: D Nippard

Stoke: Farmer, Marsh, Pejic, Mahoney, Smith, Dodd, Haslegrave, Greenhoff, Hurst*, Hudson, Salmons
Chelsea: Phillips, Locke, Harris, Hollins, Droy, Dempsey, Britton, Garland, Cooke, Hutchinson, Kember

Feuding Chelsea want revenge for their midweek League Cup humiliation. In a titanic struggle Robertson's tap in seems to have clinched it but Chelsea force Huddy to head off the line and Farmer to tip over, then he spills the ball to Ian Hutchinson who nets. Two floodlight bulbs blow.

15	H	TOTTENHAM	2/11	5	D	2:2	2-2	20	18	24,668

TOTTENHAM — Salmons 8, Greenhoff 35 / Duncan 25, 30. Ref: J Rice

Stoke: Farmer, Marsh, Pejic, Mahoney*, Smith, Dodd, Haslegrave, Greenhoff, Hurst, Hudson, Salmons
Tottenham: Jennings, Evans, Beal, Pratt, England, Naylor, Coates, Perryman, Chivers, Peters, Duncan, Robertson

City make it 10 without loss against an attacking Spurs side. Huddy's body swerve defeats the entire Spurs defence as he puts Salmons through for the first. Greenhoff's shot on the turn levels things after John Duncan's first goals for Spurs. The second-half stalemate frustrates the fans.

16	A	MANCHESTER C	9/11	8	L	0:1	0-1	1	18	36,966

MANCHESTER C — Marsh 20. Ref: J Bent

Stoke: Farmer, Marsh, Pejic, Mahoney, Smith, Dodd, Haslegrave*, Greenhoff, Hurst, Hudson, Salmons
Man City: MacRae, Hammond, Donachie, Doyle, Barrett, Oakes, Summerbee, Bell, Marsh, Hartford, Tueart, Conroy

Man City go top thanks to Rodney Marsh's strike after Smith and Mahoney fail to clear. The fiery Marsh goes close with two dribbles through City's defence and then is booked. City fail to muster any more than long-range efforts until Keith MacRae turns away Hurst's far-post header.

17	H	LUTON	16/11	6	W	4:2	1-1	22	20	20,646

LUTON — Hud'3, R'bertson 60, Gr'nhoff 62, 68 / Anderson 30, Garner 73. Ref: H New

Stoke: Farmer, Marsh, Pejic, Mahoney, Smith, Dodd, Robertson, Greenhoff, Hurst*, Hudson, Salmons
Luton: Barber, Ryan John, Thomson, Anderson, Faulkner, Garner, Ryan Jim, Husband, Alston, West, Spring, Moores

Stoke outclass strugglers Luton after being frustrated in the first half. Hudson buries a half chance but City allow Anderson a sight of goal and he threads one past Farmer. Robertson's header opens the floodgates and Greenhoff's brace of well-taken goals finishes the Hatters off nicely.

18	A	WOLVES	23/11	7	D	2:2	2-2	13	21	28,216

WOLVES — Salmons 10, Robertson 58 / Powell 33, Hibbitt 90p. Ref: P Willis

Stoke: Shilton, Marsh, Pejic, Bowers, Smith, Dodd, Robertson, Greenhoff, Hurst*, Hudson, Salmons
Wolves: Parkes, Palmer, Parkin, Bailey, Munro, McAlle, Hibbitt, Powell, Richards, Kindon, Wagstaffe

Stoke unveil record signing Peter Shilton who keeps City in the game with a string of world class saves. His punt leads to Salmons' 25-yarder. Shilts is finally beaten by a left-foot volley off the post. Greenhoff squares for Robertson before Smith fouls Richards for the last gasp penalty.

19	H	QP RANGERS	27/11	3	W	1:0	1-0	14	23	22,403

QP RANGERS — Hurst 9. Ref: T Spencer

Stoke: Shilton, Marsh, Pejic, Bowers, Smith, Dodd, Robertson, Greenhoff, Hurst*, Hudson, Salmons
QPR: Parkes, Clement, Gillard, Leach, McLintock, Hazell, Thomas, Francis, Rogers, Bowles, Givens, Moores

Stoke hold out under pressure from Rangers, inspired by new England captain Gerry Francis. Hudson's classy flick sets Hurst up for a left-foot finish. Shilton's aura of calmness sees Stoke through the danger period. Youngster Ian Bowers handles Dave Thomas' tricky wing play well.

20	H	LEICESTER	30/11	1	W	1:0	0-0	19	25	21,293

LEICESTER — Smith 86. Ref: I Jones

Stoke: Shilton, Marsh, Pejic, Bowers, Smith, Dodd, Robertson, Greenhoff, Hurst*, Hudson, Salmons
Leicester: Jayes, Whitworth, Yates, Sammels, Munro, Cross, Weller, Earle, Worthington, Birchenall, Glover, Moores

Thanks to Liverpool's draw at Coventry, Stoke sit atop Div 1 for the first time in 37 years. Huddy's probing sets up chances for Hurst, Moores and Greenhoff as Carl Jayes covers himself in glory. Denis Smith buries a tremendous left footer for the winner to replace frustration with joy.

21	A	BIRMINGHAM	7/12	1	W	3:0	3-0	13	27	35,999

BIRMINGHAM — Greenhoff 14, 36, Moores 29. Ref: G Kew

Stoke: Shilton, Marsh, Pejic, Mahoney, Smith, Dodd, Robertson, Greenhoff*, Moores, Hudson, Salmons
Birmingham: Latchford, Martin*, Styles, Kendall, Gallagher, Page, Campbell, Taylor, Burns, Hatton, Calderwood, Hendrie

Jimmy Greenhoff fires home a spectacular volley to open the scoring at St Andrews. Hudson slots through for Moores to notch his first senior goal and then Greenhoff glances a header past Latchford before his nose is broken in a challenge with Joe Gallagher. Stoke always in control.

LEAGUE DIVISION 1

Manager: Tony Waddington — SEASON 1974-75

No	Date	Venue / Opp	Att	Pos	Pt	Res	F-A	H-T	1	2	3	4	5	6	7	8	9	10	11	12 sub used
22	14/12	A LEEDS	34,685	3	27	L	1-3	0-1	Shilton	Marsh	Pejic	Mahoney*	Smith	Dodd	Robertson	Skeels	Moores	Hudson	Salmons	Hurst
		Leeds		*10*					*Harvey*	*Reaney*	*Cherry*	*Bremner*	*McQueen*	*Madeley*	*McKenzie*	*Clarke*	*Jordan*	*Lorimer*	*Yorath**	*Giles*
23	21/12	H ARSENAL	23,292	7	27	L	0-2	0-2	Shilton	Marsh	Pejic	Mahoney	Smith	Dodd	Robertson	Hurst	Moores*	Hudson	Salmons	Skeels
		Arsenal		*17*					*Rimmer*	*Rice*	*McNab*	*Kelly*	*Mancini*	*Simpson*	*Storey*	*Ball*	*Radford*	*Kidd*	*Cropley*	
24	26/12	A COVENTRY	22,345	7	27	L	0-2	0-0	Shilton	Dodd	Pejic	Mahoney	Smith	Skeels	Robertson*	Greenhoff	Hurst	Hudson	Salmons	Marsh
		Coventry		*16*					*Ramsbottom*	*Smith*	*Cattlin*	*Mortimer*	*Lloyd*	*Dugdale*	*Carr*	*Alderson*	*Stein*	*Cross*	*Hutchison*	
25	28/12	H WEST HAM	33,498	5	29	W	2-1	0-0	Shilton	Marsh	Pejic	Mahoney	Smith	Dodd	Conroy	Greenhoff	Hurst	Hudson	Salmons	
		West Ham		*6*					*Day*	*Coleman*	*Lampard*	*Holland*	*Taylor T*	*Lock*	*Taylor A**	*Paddon*	*Gould*	*McDowell*	*Best*	*Ayris*
26	11/1	H BIRMINGHAM	26,157	4	30	D	0-0	0-0	Shilton	Marsh	Pejic	Mahoney	Smith	Dodd	Haslegrave	Greenhoff	Hurst*	Hudson	Salmons	Moores
		Birmingham		*17*					*Latchford*	*Page*	*Styles*	*Kendall*	*Gallagher*	*Pendrey*	*Emmanuel*	*Taylor*	*Burns*	*Hatton**	*Calderwood*	*Hynd*
27	18/1	A LEICESTER	21,734	7	31	D	1-1	0-0	Shilton	Marsh	Pejic	Mahoney	Smith	Skeels	Haslegrave	Greenhoff	Hurst	Hudson	Salmons	
		Leicester		*21*					*Wallington*	*Whitworth*	*Rofe*	*Earle*	*Munro*	*Cross*	*Weller*	*Sammels*	*Worthington*	*Birchenall*	*Glover*	
28	1/2	H MANCHESTER C	32,007	3	33	W	4-0	1-0	Shilton	Marsh	Pejic	Mahoney	Smith	Skeels	Moores	Greenhoff	Hurst	Hudson	Salmons	
		Manchester C		*9*					*MacRae*	*Hammond*	*Donachie*	*Doyle*	*Booth*	*Oakes*	*Summerbee*	*Bell*	*Royle*	*Hartford*	*Tueart*	
29	8/2	A TOTTENHAM	22,941	2	35	W	2-0	2-0	Shilton	Lewis	Pejic	Mahoney	Smith	Skeels	Moores	Greenhoff	Hurst	Hudson	Salmons	
		Tottenham		*19*					*Daines*	*Pratt*	*Knowles*	*Beal*	*England*	*Naylor*	*Conn*	*Perryman*	*Chivers*	*Peters**	*Duncan*	*Coates*
30	15/2	H WOLVES	30,611	1	36	D	2-2	0-1	Shilton	Marsh	Pejic	Mahoney	Smith	Dodd	Moores	Greenhoff*	Hurst	Hudson	Salmons	Conroy
		Wolves		*14*					*Pierce*	*Williams*	*Parkin*	*Bailey*	*Munro*	*Jefferson*	*Hibbitt*	*Daley*	*Richards*	*Kindon*	*Farley*	
31	22/2	A LUTON	19,894	1	37	D	0-0	0-0	Shilton	Marsh	Lewis	Mahoney	Dodd	Skeels	Moores*	Greenhoff	Conroy	Hudson	Salmons	Hurst
		Luton		*20*					*Horn*	*Ryan John*	*Buckley*	*Anderson*	*Faulkner*	*Futcher P*	*Ryan Jim*	*Husband*	*Futcher R*	*West*	*Aston*	

Scorers, Times, and Referees

22 — A LEEDS: Moores 89 / McQueen 21, Lorimer 50, Yorath 80. Ref: P Reeves.
City, without an entire forward line, battle hard but succumb to the lively Champions. Gordon McQueen's towering header sets things moving. Lorimer and Yorath both hit unstoppable shots past Shilton. Ian Moores taps in for a consolation but Stoke are well beaten by a forceful Leeds.

23 — H ARSENAL: Kidd 5, 38. Ref: K Styles.
City are shocked by a lowly Arsenal team who score twice on the break and shut up shop. Smith moves into attack in the second half as Stoke pound away but Mahoney, Hudson and Smith all have shots blocked. Even when Rimmer gives away a free-kick for steps Hudson fires over.

24 — A COVENTRY: Cross 65, Hutchison 73. Ref: N Riley.
Jimmy Robertson is stretchered off with a broken leg after just a minute. After considerable pressure from Coventry, Stoke finally concede and Tommy Hutchison's volley beats Shilton all ends up to clinch it. Smith clears off the line as the wheels come off the championship challenge.

25 — H WEST HAM: Salmons 70p, Hurst 76 / Holland 53. Ref: D Richardson.
Stoke show great resolve to recover from Pat Holland's header to defeat the resolute Hammers. Smith is fouled for the penalty. Mahoney rides two tackles to force Mervyn Day to parry his shot only for Hurst to pounce. Shilton makes a world class save from Frank Lampard's free-kick.

26 — H BIRMINGHAM: Ref: D Biddle.
Despite having most of the play Stoke's chances are few and far between. Hurst hits the side netting from Hudson's pass but little else troubles Latchford. City nearly lose to Page's shot from a poor clearance. Kendall hits the bar and Burns turns the rebound in only to be flagged offside.

27 — A LEICESTER: Hurst 57 / Glover 87. Ref: M Sinclair.
Shils produces a wonder save from Alan Birchenall's flying header to keep Stoke ahead after Hurst bursts through to fire home against the run of play past Mark Wallington. The Foxes press City back throughout and then grab a point with Len Glover's header past the helpless Shilton.

28 — H MANCHESTER C: Moores 44, 84, Hudson 68, Hurst 87. Ref: B Homewood.
Stoke adapt well to Waddo's 4-3-3 attacking formation and overrun Man City. Hudson is outstanding, turning the defence inside and out to lay on both of Moores' brace and also fire home on the run himself. Geoff Hurst converts Moores' cutback to complete a comprehensive victory.

29 — A TOTTENHAM: Greenhoff 23, Hudson 32. Ref: G Hill.
Stoke win at White Hart Lane for the first time ever. The result is never in doubt against a weakened Spurs side after Greenhoff nets from close range and then Hudson plays a one-two with Moores and fires home from 15 yards. City are in control with Skeels impressive alongside Smith.

30 — H WOLVES: Conroy 87, Skeels 88 / Hibbitt 25p, Munro 47. Ref: E Jolly.
City's late comeback steals a point as trouble flares on the terraces. Play is stopped twice as fans encroach on the pitch. Conroy and Skeels both convert crosses in goalmouth scrambles as Stoke pile forward. Wolves cannot believe it. Mike Pejic breaks his leg in a challenge with Kindon.

31 — A LUTON: Ref: T Reynolds.
Stoke are frustrated by Paul Futcher and Graham Horn who hold out resolutely. Geoff Salmons puts a penalty wide after Conroy is fouled by Faulkner. Mike Pejic breaks his leg in a challenge with Kindon. Horn tips round Greenhoff's running header. Shilton palms away Aston's effort. Hudson's shot is ruled not to have crossed the line.

Stoke City — Match Record (Matches 32–42)

No		Date	Opponent	Att	Pos	Res	Pts	Opp Pos	Score	Scorers	Referee
32	A	1/3	MIDDLESBROUGH	25,766	3	L	37	9	0-2	Hickton 18, Foggon 25	Ref: J Goggins
33	A	15/3	DERBY	29,985	3	W	39	6	2-1	Greenhoff 75, 89 / Hector 49	Ref: R Toseland
34	H	18/3	IPSWICH	28,589	6	L	39	2	1-2	Greenhoff 67 / Whymark 50, Mills 65	Ref: W Gow
35	H	22/3	CARLISLE	20,525	5	W	41	22	5-2	Conroy 8, 65, 73, Greenhoff 66 / Laidlaw 20, Carr 78 [Salmons 88]	Ref: R Tinkler
36	A	28/3	WEST HAM	29,811	3	D	42	12	2-2	Conroy 40, 49 / Brooking 39, Jennings 69	Ref: H Davey
37	A	29/3	ARSENAL	23,852	5	D	43	17	1-1	Salmons 33 / Kelly 82	Ref: A Grey
38	H	31/3	LIVERPOOL	32,954	5	W	45	4	2-0	Conroy 20p, 50	Ref: I Jones
39	H	5/4	CHELSEA	32,375	3	W	47	19	3-0	Conroy 28, 87, Greenhoff 63	Ref: D Richardson
40	A	12/4	SHEFFIELD UTD	23,255	5	L	47	8	0-2	Eddy 25p, Field 57	Ref: P Reeves
41	H	19/4	NEWCASTLE	25,284	5	D	48	15	0-0		Ref: R Matthewson
42	A	26/4	BURNLEY	13,791	5	D	49	10	0-0		Ref: M Lowe

Home Average 26,961 · Away 25,377

Stoke City line-ups

No	1	2	3	4	5	6	7	8	9	10	11	Sub
32	Shilton	Dodd	Lewis	Mahoney	Smith	Skeels	Conroy	Greenhoff	Hurst*	Hudson	Salmons	Moores
33	Shilton	Marsh	Lewis*	Mahoney	Smith	Skeels	Conroy	Greenhoff	Moores	Hudson	Salmons	Hurst
34	Shilton	Marsh	Dodd	Mahoney	Smith*	Skeels	Lewis	Greenhoff	Hurst	Hudson	Salmons	
35	Shilton	Marsh	Bowers	Mahoney	Dodd	Skeels	Conroy	Greenhoff	Hurst*	Hudson	Salmons	Moores
36	Shilton	Bloor	Bowers	Mahoney	Dodd	Skeels	Conroy	Greenhoff	Hurst*	Hudson	Salmons	Moores
37	Shilton	Bloor	Bowers	Mahoney	Dodd	Skeels	Conroy	Greenhoff	Hurst	Hudson	Salmons	
38	Shilton	Marsh	Bowers	Mahoney	Dodd	Skeels	Conroy	Greenhoff	Hurst	Hudson	Salmons*	
39	Shilton	Marsh	Bowers	Mahoney	Dodd	Skeels	Conroy	Greenhoff	Hurst	Hudson	Salmons	
40	Shilton	Marsh	Bowers	Mahoney	Dodd	Skeels	Conroy	Greenhoff	Hurst	Hudson	Salmons	
41	Shilton	Marsh	Bowers	Mahoney	Dodd	Skeels	Conroy	Greenhoff	Hurst	Hudson	Salmons	
42	Shilton	Marsh	Bowers	Mahoney	Dodd	Skeels	Conroy	Greenhoff	Hurst	Hudson	Salmons	

Opponents' line-ups

No	Opponent	Players
32	Middlesbrough	Craggs, Spraggon, Cooper, Souness, Boam, Maddren, Murdoch, Hickton, Mills, Foggon*, Armstrong (Willey)
33	Derby	Boulton, Thomas, Nish, Rioch, Daniel, Todd, Newton, Gemmill, Davies, Hector, Hinton
34	Ipswich	Sivell, Burley, Mills, Talbot, Hunter, Beattie, Hamilton, Osborne, Johnson, Whymark, Lambert* (Woods)
35	Carlisle	Ross, Carr, Spearritt, O'Neill*, Green, Parker, Martin, Train, Owen, Laidlaw, Clarke (Balderstone)
36	West Ham	Day, Coleman, Lampard*, McDowell, Taylor T, Lock, Jennings, Paddon, Taylor A, Brooking, Gould (Ayris)
37	Arsenal	Rimmer, Rice, McNab, Storey, Kelly, Simpson, Matthews, Ball, Stapleton*, Rostron, Hornsby (Brady)
38	Liverpool	Clemence, Smith, Neal, Thompson, Cormack, Hughes, Keegan, Hall, Highway*, Kennedy, McDermott (Toshack)
39	Chelsea	Phillips, Locke, Harris, Hollins, Dray, Hinton, Kember, Hay, Wilkins G, Finnieston*, Houseman* (Garner)
40	Sheffield Utd	Brown, Badger, Bradford, Eddy, Colquhoun, Flynn, Woodward, Speight, Dearden, Currie, Field
41	Newcastle	Mahoney, Craig D*, Kennedy, Hibbitt, Keeley, Clark, Barrowclough, Nulty, MacDonald, Craig T, Bruce (Howard)
42	Burnley	Stevenson, Scott, Brennan, Ingham, Waldron, Rodaway, Flynn, Hankin, Noble, Collins, James

Match reports

32 — Middlesbrough (A) 0-2. Boro haven't won in seven but put Stoke under heavy pressure which pays off when Hickton finishes off a good move. Then Foggon pounces on a poor clearance. City are faced by a wall of defenders as Jack Charlton's men settle for a two-goal lead and never look in any real danger.

33 — Derby (A) 2-1. Stoke steal the points with a gritty display in the mud. Dave MacKay bemoans Rod Thomas's suicidal back-pass which Greenhoff nips in to fire past Boulton. His first is from Salmons' cross. The tackles fly in with the game level and the mood transmits to the terraces where scuffles start.

34 — Ipswich (H) 1-2. Bobby Robson's Ipswich foil City yet again. Greenhoff needs attention after lunging in to score, but Town are already two up with Mick Mills' screamer a worthy winner of this vital game. Denis Smith breaks a leg for the fifth time in his career in a fierce challenge with Mick Lambert.

35 — Carlisle (H) 5-2. City overcome a determined Carlisle side with Salmons exploiting long balls over the top for Conroy to run on to. TC's first two are headers, the third a deflection of Moores' shot. Greenhoff nods home from a corner and Salmons claims a deserved fifth as TC repays the compliment.

36 — West Ham (A) 2-2. Stoke have Alan Bloor in for his first start of the season. West Ham warm up for next week's FA Cup semi v Ipswich rounding Shilton to score. Conroy's two strikes both leave Mervyn Day helpless. Jennings scores a super solo goal after a 35-yard swerving run to level.

37 — Arsenal (A) 1-1. City score against the run of play when Geoff Salmons fires home Hudson's short free-kick. The defence stands firm only allowing long-range efforts from Rice and Hornsby. Stoke finally succumb to Arsenal's incessant pressure when Kelly knocks in the rebound from Storey's effort.

38 — Liverpool (H) 2-0. City knock Bob Paisley's Reds off the top of the table with a display of flowing football topped off by two Conroy strikes. The penalty is for Phil Thompson's foul on John Mahoney. Then TC breaks clear to slot in at the second attempt. Ian Bowers snuffs out the threat of Kevin Keegan.

39 — Chelsea (H) 3-0. A hammer blow to Chelsea's survival chances as Stoke move equal on points with the top two. Conroy plunders goals from passes by Salmons and Mahoney. Jimmy Greenhoff pounces on a poor back-pass from Micky Droy to put City well out of reach. Youthful Chelsea rarely threaten.

40 — Sheffield Utd (A) 0-2. Stoke have a penalty appeal turned down when Colquhoun appears to handle. Then the referee awards Utd a pen when Shilton upends Dearden which Keith Eddy coolly slots. Stoke press forward but Anthony Field turns past Dodd and Skeels to fire in and City's title hopes are in tatters.

41 — Newcastle (H) 0-0. City cannot find a way past Keeley and Clark in their bid for Europe. Conroy and Marsh come close. A tumultuous ending sees all the players bar Shilton in Newcastle's half for the last five mins. SuperMac nearly steals it for Joe Harvey's Toon but misses the target when put through.

42 — Burnley (A) 0-0. City fail to qualify for Europe after a tame game in which they hold the upper hand. The Clarets hold firm as Hurst brings the best out of Alan Stevenson. He also tips Salmons' free-kick round the post. When Shilts saves point blank from Ray Hankin even the Burnley players applaud!

LEAGUE DIVISION 1 (CUP-TIES)

Manager: Tony Waddington

SEASON 1974-75

League Cup

		Att	F-A	H-T	Scorers, Times, and Referees	1	2	3	4	5	6	7	8	9	10	11	12 sub used
2 H HALIFAX 11/9	W	17,805 *3:8*	3-0	1-0	Conroy 42, 67, 71p Ref: P Reeves	Farmer *Smith A*	Marsh *Quinn*	Pejic *Collins*	Mahoney *Mair*	Smith *Rhodes*	Dodd *Lowe*	Haslegrave *Jones*	Greenhoff *Shanahan**	Hurst *Downes*	Conroy *Gwyther*	Salmons* *Ford*	Robertson *Smith P*

City overwhelm Halifax with Haslegrave outstanding and Terry Conroy scoring his first hat-trick in his first start for 11 months. Conroy scores two headers and then is fouled for the penalty which he lashes high into the net. Robertson heads against the keeper as City threaten to run riot.

		Att	F-A	H-T	Scorers, Times, and Referees	1	2	3	4	5	6	7	8	9	10	11	12 sub used
3 A CHELSEA 9/10	D	19,953 *20*	2-2	1-1	Robertson 6, Hurst 47 Hutchinson 22, 52 Ref: L Hayes	Farmer *Phillips*	Marsh *Locke*	Pejic *Harris*	Mahoney *Hollins**	Smith *Droy*	Dodd *Dempsey*	Robertson* *Kember*	Greenhoff *Garner*	Hurst *Cooke*	Hudson *Hutchinson*	Salmons *Houseman*	Haslegrave *Wilkins*

Chelsea offer stern resistance after Dave Sexton's departure. Robertson and Hurst pounce for opportunist goals as City are on top. In a bruising encounter Hutchinson kicks John Farmer in the throat in the act of scoring the second equaliser. Pejic is booked for lunging at Charlie Cooke.

		Att	F-A	H-T	Scorers, Times, and Referees	1	2	3	4	5	6	7	8	9	10	11	12 sub used
3R H CHELSEA 16/10	D	24,376 *16*	1-1	0-1	Greenhoff 80 Britton 21 Ref: L Hayes	Farmer *Phillips*	Marsh *Locke*	Pejic *Harris*	Mahoney* *Hollins*	Smith *Droy*	Dodd *Dempsey*	Robertson *Britton*	Greenhoff *Garland**	Hurst *Cooke*	Hudson *Hutchinson*	Salmons *Houseman*	Conroy *Garner*

Jimmy Greenhoff darts in to power a header past John Phillips to keep City alive. Ian Britton's close-range effort seems to have seen Chelsea through but Stoke lay siege in the second half. Hudson, Robertson twice and Conroy all come mighty close. Waddo wins the toss for venue.

		Att	F-A	H-T	Scorers, Times, and Referees	1	2	3	4	5	6	7	8	9	10	11	12 sub used
3RR H CHELSEA 22/10	W	26,271 *17*	6-2	4-0	Hurst 2, 67, Smith 10, Droy 37 (og), Hollins 80, Baldwin 84 [Harris 44 (og), Salmons 62] Ref: R Toseland	Farmer *Phillips*	Marsh *Locke*	Pejic *Harris*	Mahoney *Hollins*	Smith *Droy*	Dodd *Dempsey*	Haslegrave *Britton*	Greenhoff *Garner*	Hurst *Cooke*	Hudson *Hutchinson*	Salmons *Houseman**	Salmons *Baldwin*

Stoke on the rampage as everything goes right for once. Salmons has his best game yet and his glorious free-kick crowns his display. The own-goals are both headed past the disbelieving Phillips. After the sixth City call a halt and play possession football, allowing Chelsea to score two.

		Att	F-A	H-T	Scorers, Times, and Referees	1	2	3	4	5	6	7	8	9	10	11	12 sub used
4 A IPSWICH 12/11	L	20,677 *4*	1-2	0-0	Robertson 90 Hamilton 59, Johnson 72 Ref: R Challis	Farmer *Sivell*	Lewis *Mills*	Pejic *Harper*	Mahoney *Talbot*	Smith *Hunter*	Dodd *Beattie*	Robertson *Hamilton*	Greenhoff *Viljoen*	Moores *Johnson*	Hudson *Whymark*	Salmons *Woods*	

A titanic struggle which Ipswich edge. Stoke try young Ian Moores up front and have the edge in a fiery first half, but Ipswich go ahead. Smith is up in attack looking for the equaliser when David Johnson surges through to beat Farmer. Robertson's header never threatens Ipswich's lead.

FA Cup

		Att	F-A	H-T	Scorers, Times, and Referees	1	2	3	4	5	6	7	8	9	10	11	12 sub used
3 A LIVERPOOL 4/1	L	48,723 *1*	0-2	0-0	Heighway 75, Keegan 89 Ref: T Reynolds	Shilton *Clemence*	Marsh *Neal*	Pejic *Lindsay*	Mahoney *Thompson*	Smith *Cormack*	Dodd *Hughes*	Conroy *Keegan*	Greenhoff *Hall*	Hurst *Heighway*	Hudson *Toshack*	Salmons *Callaghan*	

The deadlock in a titanic cup-tie is broken by Heighway's strike after Shilton's punch lands at his feet. That aside Shilton is immaculate as the Reds raid down both wings. Hall's cross provides Keegan with the clincher, but Stoke hold their heads high against the reigning Cup holders.

UEFA Cup

		Att	F-A	H-T	Scorers, Times, and Referees	1	2	3	4	5	6	7	8	9	10	11	12 sub used
1:1 H AJAX 18/9 (Holland)	D	37,398	1-1	0-1	Smith 76 Krol 38 Ref: A Michelotti (Italy)	Farmer *Schrijvers*	Marsh *Van Doord*	Pejic *Blankenburg*	Mahoney *Dusvaba*	Smith *Krol*	Dodd *Van Santen*	Haslegrave *Haan*	Greenhoff *Geels*	Conroy *Muhren G*	Hudson *Rep*	Salmons* *Keizer*	Robertson *R'tson/Conroy*

Hans Kraay's clinical Ajax play the perfect European away leg, gaining a vital goal through Rudi Krol's bullet from 20 yards. City change the formation, introducing Robertson's speed after 72 minutes. Denis Smith flings himself to head home the equaliser with aplomb at the near post.

		Att	F-A	H-T	Scorers, Times, and Referees	1	2	3	4	5	6	7	8	9	10	11	12 sub used
1:2 A AJAX 2/10	D	29,000	0-0	0-0	Ref: N Raines (Romania)	Farmer *Schrijvers*	Marsh *Van Santen*	Pejic *Blankenburg*	Mahoney *Dusvaba*	Smith *Krol*	Dodd *Haan*	Haslegrave* *Muhren G*	Greenhoff *Keizer**	Hurst *Geels^*	Hudson *Rep*	Salmons *Mulder*	R'tson/Conroy *M'hr'n A/Steff'*

Stoke go out on away goals despite having the better of things in Holland. 1,500 Stokies roar the team on as City silence the home fans. Ajax, having won every league game so far, are complacent and only Piet Schrijvers' outstretched left boot saves them when Robertson goes clear.

Final League Table

Pos	Team	P	Home W	D	L	F	A	Away W	D	L	F	A	Pts
1	Derby	42	14	4	3	41	18	7	7	7	26	31	53
2	Liverpool	42	14	5	2	44	17	6	6	9	16	22	51
3	Ipswich	42	17	2	2	47	14	6	3	12	19	30	51
4	Everton	42	10	9	2	33	19	6	9	6	23	23	50
5	STOKE	42	12	7	2	40	18	5	8	8	24	30	49
6	Sheffield Utd	42	12	7	2	35	20	6	6	9	23	31	49
7	Middlesbro	42	11	7	3	33	14	7	5	9	21	26	48
8	Manchester C	42	16	3	2	40	15	2	7	12	14	39	46
9	Leeds	42	10	8	3	34	20	6	5	10	23	29	45
10	Burnley	42	11	6	4	40	29	6	5	10	28	38	45
11	QP Rangers	42	10	4	7	25	17	6	6	9	29	37	42
12	Wolves	42	12	5	4	43	21	2	7	13	14	33	39
13	West Ham	42	10	6	5	38	22	3	7	11	20	37	39
14	Coventry	42	8	9	4	31	27	4	6	11	20	35	39
15	Newcastle	42	12	4	5	39	23	3	5	13	20	49	39
16	Arsenal	42	10	6	5	31	16	3	5	13	16	33	37
17	Birmingham	42	10	4	7	34	28	4	5	12	19	33	37
18	Leicester	42	8	7	6	25	17	4	5	12	21	43	36
19	Tottenham	42	8	4	9	29	27	5	4	12	23	36	34
20	Luton	42	8	6	7	27	26	3	5	13	20	39	33
21	Chelsea	42	4	9	8	22	31	5	6	10	20	41	33
22	Carlisle	42	8	2	11	22	21	4	3	14	21	38	29
		924	235	124	103	753	460	103	124	235	460	753	924

Player Appearances & Goals

Player	Appearances Lge	Sub	LC	Sub	FAC	Sub	Eur	Sub	Goals Lge	Sub	LC	FAC	Eur	Tot
Bloor, Alan	2													
Bowers, Ian	10													
Conroy, Terry	11	5	1	1	1	1	1		10	1	3			13
Dodd, Alan	39		5		1		2							
Farmer, John	17		5				2							
Greenhoff, Jimmy	39		5		1		2	2	14		1			15
Haslegrave, Sean	18	1	2	1	1		2		1					1
Hudson, Alan	42		4		1		2		4					4
Hurst, Geoff	30	5	4		1		1		8		3			11
Lewis, Kevin	5				1									
Mahoney, John	39		5		1		2		4					4
Marsh, Jackie	37	1	4	1	1		2		1					1
Moores, Ian	10	7	1						4					4
Pejic, Mike	28		5				2							
Ritchie, John	7	5							4					4
Robertson, Jimmy	9	5	3	1	1				3	2	2			5
Salmons, Geoff	42		5				2		8		1			9
Shilton, Peter	25													
Skeels, Eric	22	1												
Smith, Denis	30		5		1		2		2		2	1		4
(own-goals)														2
20 players used	462	25	55	3	11		22	3	64	3	13		1	78

Odds & ends

- Double wins: (2) QP Rangers, Carlisle.
- Double losses: (1) Ipswich.
- Won from behind: (2) West Ham (h), Derby (a).
- Lost from in front: (1) Everton (a).
- High spots: Winning away at eventual Champions Derby.
- Second consecutive top-five finish.
- No home attendance under 20,000.
- Unbeaten in Europe.
- Breaking the world record fee for a goalkeeper.
- Low spots: Two points from last three games when three wins would have won the League title.
- John Ritchie's career ended by a broken leg.
- Mike Pejic also a victim of a broken limb.
- Yet to win a European tie.
- Ever-Presents: (2) Alan Hudson, Geoff Salmons.
- Hat-tricks: (2) Terry Conroy (twice).
- Leading scorer: (15) Jimmy Greenhoff.

LEAGUE DIVISION 1 — Manager: Tony Waddington — SEASON 1975-76

No	Date	1	2	3	4	5	6	7	8	9	10	11	12 sub used
1	H WEST HAM 16/8	Shilton	Dodd	Pejic	Mahoney	Smith	Bloor	Skeels*	Moores	Conroy	Hudson	Salmons	Haslegrave
		Day	*McDowell*	*Lampard*	*Holland*	*Taylor T*	*Lock*	*Taylor A*	*Paddon*	*Gould*	*Brooking*	*Robson*	
2	H WOLVES 20/8	Shilton	Marsh	Pejic	Mahoney	Smith	Dodd	Mahoney*	Greenhoff	Conroy	Hudson	Salmons	Moores
		Parkes	*Parkin*	*McNab*	*Bailey*	*Munro*	*McAlle*	*Hibbitt**	*Carr*	*Richards*	*Kindon*	*Farley*	*Sunderland*
3	A ARSENAL 23/8	Shilton	Marsh	Pejic	Mahoney	Smith	Dodd	Bowers	Greenhoff	Conroy	Hudson	Salmons	
		Rimmer	*Rice*	*Nelson*	*Kelly*	*Mancini*	*O'Leary*	*Armstrong*	*Cropley*	*Hornsby*	*Kidd*	*Brady*	
4	A LEICESTER 27/8	Shilton	Marsh	Pejic	Mahoney	Smith	Dodd	Bowers	Greenhoff	Conroy*	Hudson	Salmons	Moores
		Wallington	*Whitworth*	*Rofe*	*Kember*	*Sims*	*Birchenall*	*Weller*	*Lee*	*Worthington Sammels*	*Garland*		
5	H MANCHESTER U 30/8	Shilton	Marsh	Pejic	Mahoney	Dodd	Skeels	Bowers	Greenhoff	Conroy	Hudson	Salmons*	Moores
		Stepney	*Forsyth*	*Houston*	*Jackson*	*Greenhoff*	*Buchan*	*Cappell*	*McIlroy*	*Pearson*	*Macari*	*Daly*	
6	A MIDDLESBROUGH 6/9	Shilton	Lewis	Pejic	Mahoney	Dodd	Skeels	Haslegrave	Greenhoff	Conroy	Hudson	Salmons	
		Platt	*Craggs*	*Cooper*	*Souness*	*Boam*	*Maddren*	*Murdoch*	*Mills*	*Hickton*	*Willey**	*Armstrong Foggon*	
7	H LEEDS 13/9	Shilton	Marsh	Pejic	Mahoney	Dodd	Bloor	Haslegrave	Greenhoff	Conroy	Hudson	Salmons	
		Harvey	*Cherry*	*Gray F*	*Bremner*	*McQueen*	*Hunter*	*Lorimer*	*Clarke*	*McKenzie**	*Yorath*	*Madeley Harris*	
8	A COVENTRY 20/9	Shilton	Marsh	Pejic	Mahoney	Dodd	Bloor	Haslegrave	Greenhoff	Moores	Hudson	Salmons	
		King	*Coop*	*Brogan*	*Craven*	*Dugdale*	*Holmes*	*Powell**	*Mortimer*	*Cross*	*Green*	*Hutchison Ferguson*	
9	A MANCHESTER C 24/9	Shilton	Marsh	Pejic	Mahoney*	Dodd	Bloor	Haslegrave	Greenhoff	Moores	Hudson	Salmons	
		Corrigan	*Clements*	*Donachie*	*Doyle*	*Watson*	*Oakes*	*Hartford*	*Bell*	*Royle*	*Marsh*	*Tueart*	
10	H DERBY 27/9	Shilton	Marsh	Pejic	Dodd	Smith	Bloor	Haslegrave	Greenhoff	Moores	Hudson	Salmons	
		Boulton	*Thomas*	*Nish*	*Rioch*	*MacFarland Todd*		*Newton*	*Gemmill*	*Bourne*	*Hector*	*George*	

No	Att	Pos	Pt	F-A	H-T	Scorers, Times, and Referees
1	23,744		0	L 1-2	0-2	Moores 89 / Gould 26, Taylor A 44 — Ref: L Hayes
2	22,551		1	D 2-2	0-1	Bowers 53, Conroy 57p / Carr 41, Richards 55 — Ref: A Jones
3	28,025	7	3	W 1-0	1-0	Hudson 42 — Ref: H Davey
4	22,878	17	4	D 1-1	1-0	Hudson 3, Garland 49 — Ref: J Bent
5	23,337	1	4	L 0-1	0-1	Dodd 15 (og) — Ref: K Styles
6	20,975	9	4	L 0-3	0-1	Hickton 11, Mills 47, 89 — Ref: A Porter
7	23,139	6	6	W 3-2	2-0	Conroy 32, Pejic 40, Greenhoff 73 / Lorimer 53, 55p — Ref: R Toseland
8	18,965	9	8	W 3-0	1-0	Greenhoff 44, Moores 47, 77 — Ref: H Hackney
9	28,915	9	8	L 0-1	0-0	Marsh 67 — Ref: J Yates
10	25,097	6	10	W 1-0	1-0	Greenhoff 11 — Ref: R Matthewson

1. West Ham — City are off the pace as the Hammers breeze into a half-time lead. Only Eric Skeels' shot against the bar threatens until Salmons comes into the game. New England U-23 cap Ian Moores finally bundles in a corner but West Ham aren't troubled. The Potters miss the departed Geoff Hurst.

2. Wolves — Tony Waddington's half-time dressing down sparks City into action after dominating but trailing to Carr's unstoppable drive. In a frenetic spell Ian Bowers notches his first goal and then TC's pen, after Kindon handles, equalises Richards' strike. Stoke struggle to create further chances.

3. Arsenal — As Arsenal press forward, Stoke mop up the pressure with Smith dominant and Bowers doing a holding job in midfield. Alan Hudson nets after Greenhoff's challenge on Rimmer is allowed by the ref. George Armstrong wastes the Gunners' best chance when he shoots tamely at Shilton.

4. Leicester — In a punishing encounter Huddy's third-minute boomerang shot deceives Mark Wallington. Shilton produces two world-class saves to deny Jon Sammels but cannot keep out Garland's far-post header. Moores nearly settles it but the humidity catches up with both teams towards the end.

5. Manchester U — United steal the points to go top as trouble brews at the Vic. Numerous supporters are ejected after Pearson deflects Daly's shot onto Dodd and past Shilts. City put Stepney under pressure but the ball will not run for t'em and United, full of running, snuff out the threat of Terry Conroy.

6. Middlesbrough — Stoke fall to a splendid Boro team who never stop running. Hickton's unmarked header starts them off. Shilton keeps City in it, but eventually can only parry Craggs' shot back to David Mills. Greenhoff and Pejic both test Platt. Alan Dodd's slip lets in Mills who casually lobs Shilton.

7. Leeds — Stoke seem in control as Hudson swaggers through midfield to set up Conroy and Pejic for close-range goals. Lorimer's brace stuns City. The penalty comes from Dodd's trip on Allan Clarke but Jimmy Greenhoff fixes it by getting onto Moores' flick and Stoke run out worthy winners.

8. Coventry — Coventry begin brightly but Green and Cross fail to hit the target. Then Greenhoff heads in Pejic's swinging cross and Moores flicks Salmons' cross home. Moores then fires past Brian King from Greenhoff's pass. Confident City swarm forward with Hudson and Pejic both going close.

9. Manchester C — City have a patched up Shilton in goal but take the game to Man City. Tony Book's team pick up the pace after the interval and Rodney Marsh prods home when Shilts cannot hold Tueart's header. Hudson, back to h's best, provides two good chances for Ian Moores who fails to convert.

10. Derby — Stoke rock the Champions as Greenhoff's fabulous left-footed volley sends the Boothen End into raptures. Smith and Bloor resume their tried and tested partnership and Alan Dodd plays the anchor role in midfield. Shilton saves Bruce Rioch's scorcher late on to keep the Rams at bay.

#				Pos		FT	HT	Att		
11	A	NORWICH	4/10	10	W	1-0	0-0	22,318	12	12
12	H	IPSWICH	11/10	11	L	0-1	0-1	21,978	15	12
13	A	SHEFFIELD UTD	18/10	10	W	2-0	0-0	23,410	22	14
14	H	NEWCASTLE	25/10	10	D	1-1	0-0	24,057	12	15
15	A	BURNLEY	1/11	8	W	1-0	0-0	19,269	18	17
16	H	EVERTON	8/11	7	W	3-2	1-0	23,651	10	19
17	A	TOTTENHAM	15/11	7	D	1-1	0-0	25,698	14	20
18	H	SHEFFIELD UTD	22/11	7	W	2-1	2-0	21,959	22	22
19	A	QP RANGERS	29/11	8	L	2-3	0-1	23,328	2	22
20	H	ASTON VILLA	6/12	8	D	1-1	1-1	28,492	14	23
21	A	ARSENAL	13/12	8	W	2-1	0-0	19,328	18	25

11 — A NORWICH, 4/10 — Haslegrave 73 — Ref: B Homewood

Stoke: Shilton, Marsh, Pejic, Mahoney, Dodd, Bloor, Haslegrave, Greenhoff, Moores, Hudson, Salmons
Norwich: Keelan, Machin, Sullivan, McGuire, Forbes, Powell, Miller*, MacDougall, Boyer, Suggett, Peters, Steele; Austin

Sean Haslegrave's strike from Moores' cross puts the finishing touch to a super Stoke display. Confident City lack the killer instinct in front of goal despite Hudson, Greenhoff and Haslegrave all having efforts cleared off the line. John Bonds' team cannot match Stoke's classy display.

12 — H IPSWICH, 11/10 — Hamilton 31 — Ref: J Hunting

Stoke: Shilton, Marsh, Pejic, Mahoney, Dodd, Bloor, Haslegrave, Greenhoff, Moores, Hudson, Salmons*
Ipswich: Cooper, Burley, Mills, Osborne*, Hunter, Beattie, Hamilton, Viljoen, Johnson, Whymark, Woods, Austin

City are shocked by Brian Hamilton's neat right-foot finish against the run of play. Paul Cooper performs wonderfully, saving three times from Moores. Anxiety soon sets in and Stoke rush their passing, allowing Ipswich to break up play, with Kevin Beattie and Mick Mills outstanding.

13 — A SHEFFIELD UTD, 18/10 — Greenhoff 75, 84 — Ref: C White

Stoke: Shilton, Marsh, Pejic, Mahoney, Dodd, Bloor, Haslegrave, Greenhoff, Moores, Hudson, Salmons
Sheffield Utd: Brown, Badger, Hemsley*, Eddy, Colquhoun, Franks, Garbett, Cammack, Guthrie, Currie, Dearden, Field

Stoke once again perform better away from home, always holding the upper hand against managerless United. Greenhoff's strikes are thanks to brave runs by Salmons and Hudson. United fling bodies forward but Stoke mop up the pressure and Alan Bloor blocks well from Tony Currie.

14 — H NEWCASTLE, 25/10 — Greenhoff 60, Gowling 90 — Ref: A Lees

Stoke: Shilton, Marsh, Pejic, Mahoney, Dodd, Bloor, Haslegrave, Greenhoff, Moores, Hudson, Salmons
Newcastle: Mahoney, Craig D, Kennedy, Nattrass, Howard, Nulty, Burns*, Barrowclough, MacDonald, Gowling, Craig T, Bird

New Toon manager Gordon Lee sees Jimmy Greenhoff have one disallowed before striking from Salmons' corner. It's nearly added to by both Mahoney and Pejic. Stoke seem to have things under wraps until Alan Gowling's late burst through the middle to poke past a helpless Shilton.

15 — A BURNLEY, 1/11 — Moores 55 — Ref: W Gow

Stoke: Shilton, Marsh, Pejic, Mahoney, Dodd, Bloor, Haslegrave, Greenhoff, Moores, Hudson, Salmons
Burnley: Stevenson, Docherty, Newton, Noble, Waldron, Thomson, Summerbee, Casper, Fletcher, Flynn, James

City win away again. This time against the run of play as Shilton dominates. Casper, James and Fletcher are all denied. Even when Peter Noble nets, the linesman has his flag up. In a last-minute scramble Shilton and Dodd block three times as the Clarets search for that elusive equaliser.

16 — H EVERTON, 8/11 — Salmons 12, Robertson 80, Moores 81; Telfer 57, Pearson 68 — Ref: G Seel

Stoke: Shilton, Marsh, Pejic, Mahoney, Dodd, Bloor, Haslegrave*, Greenhoff*, Moores, Hudson, Salmons
Everton: Davies, Darracott, Seargeant, Hurst, Lyons, McNaught, Buckley*, Dobson, Pearson, Irving, Smallman, Telfer, Robertson

Jimmy Robertson, in his first appearance since breaking his leg, inspires City's first win over Everton since 1968. Coming on after 65 minutes he fires home the equaliser from Hurst's flick and then crosses for Moores to finish in a devastating two-minute spell. The Toffees are stunned.

17 — A TOTTENHAM, 15/11 — Moores 71; Jones 57 — Ref: R Tinkler

Stoke: Shilton, Lumsdon, Pejic, Mahoney, Dodd, Bloor, Haslegrave*, Greenhoff*, Moores, Hudson, Salmons
Tottenham: Jennings, Naylor, McAllister*, Pratt, Young, Osgood, Coates, Perryman, Conn, Jones, Duncan, McGrath, Robertson

Stoke deserve a draw after falling behind when Jones swivels to half-volley home a Coates corner. Salmons roams down the wing and has one effort cleared off the line before his centre finds Moores who heads past Pat Jennings. Dodd is superb at the back as Spurs mount a late flurry.

18 — H SHEFFIELD UTD, 22/11 — Salmons 20, 28p, Woodward 61 — Ref: J Goggins

Stoke: Shilton, Lewis, Pejic, Mahoney, Dodd, Bloor, Robertson, Greenhoff, Moores, Hudson, Salmons
Sheffield Utd: Brown, Badger, Garner, Speight, Colquhoun, Franks, Johnstone*, Dearden, Cammack, Bradford, Woodward, Guthrie

Geoff Salmons revels in the limelight against his old club. He hits a corking left-footed drive past Brown for the opener and then puts a penalty in off the post after having his own shot handled on the line. United net through Jimmy Johnstone for the first time but Stoke don't look like losing.

19 — A QP RANGERS, 29/11 — Moores 46, Bloor 55; Masson 31, Clement 61, Webb 90 — Ref: K Baker

Stoke: Shilton, Lewis, Pejic, Mahoney, Dodd, Bloor, Robertson*, Greenhoff*, Moores, Hudson, Salmons
QP Rangers: Parkes, Clement, Gillard, Hollins, McLintock, Webb, Thomas, Beck, Masson, Bowles, Leach*, Nutt, Haslegrave

In a see-saw thriller Stoke fightback with Moores' looping header and Bloor's tap in after Parkes drops a Robertson free-kick. As four players are booked Clement slams the equaliser past Shilton before Webb wins it for Dave Sexton's team with the last kick of the match in a scramble.

20 — H ASTON VILLA, 6/12 — Greenhoff 22, Graydon 17 — Ref: M Lowe

Stoke: Shilton, Lewis, Pejic, Mahoney, Dodd, Bloor, Robertson, Greenhoff, Moores, Hudson, Salmons
Aston Villa: Burridge, Gidman, Robson, Ross, Nicholl, Pimblett, Graydon, Deehan, Carrodus, Phillips, Hamilton

City struggle for rhythm against dogged opponents. Ray Graydon latches on to Deehan's flick to finish. City's quick riposte is from Robertson who hits the inside of the post with Greenhoff following in to score. Chris Nicholl and Ian Ross cope well with Moores as the game peters out.

21 — A ARSENAL, 13/12 — Salmons 73, Greenhoff 80; Armstrong 63 — Ref: K Burns

Stoke: Shilton, Marsh, Pejic, Mahoney, Dodd, Bloor, Robertson, Greenhoff, Moores, Hudson, Salmons
Arsenal: Barnett, Rice, Nelson*, Storey!, O'Leary, Powling, Armstrong, Ball, Stapleton, Kidd, Brady, Simpson

Arsenal have Stapleton and Kidd funnelling back for extra cover. Finally Salmons forces his way through to beat Barnett and then provides the cross for Greenhoff's angled header. Feelings then boil over. Peter Storey kicks Mahoney and is dismissed. Rice, Brady and Bloor are booked.

LEAGUE DIVISION 1

Manager: Tony Waddington — SEASON 1975-76

No	Date		Team	Att	Pos	(Opp Pos)	Pt	Res	F-A	H-T
22	20/12	A	WEST HAM	21,135	8	6	25	L	1-3	1-2
23	26/12	H	LIVERPOOL	32,092	8	1	26	D	1-1	0-1
24	27/12	A	BIRMINGHAM	37,166	8	19	27	D	1-1	1-1
25	10/1	A	LEEDS	36,909	10	2	27	L	0-2	0-2
26	17/1	H	MIDDLESBROUGH (at Vale Park)	21,009	7	9	29	W	1-0	0-0
27	31/1	A	WOLVES	24,190	9	19	29	L	1-2	0-1
28	7/2	H	LEICESTER	21,001	11	13	29	L	1-2	1-1
29	21/2	H	TOTTENHAM	17,113	13	14	29	L	1-2	1-2
30	3/3	A	NEWCASTLE	37,459	11	14	31	W	1-0	1-0
31	6/3	H	BURNLEY	16,065	9	20	33	W	4-1	3-1

Line-ups (positions 1–11, and 12th sub used)

No	1	2	3	4	5	6	7	8	9	10	11	12 sub used
22	Shilton	Marsh	Pejic	Mahoney	Dodd	Bloor	Robertson	Greenhoff	Moores*	Hudson	Salmons	Haslegrave
22 *(opp)*	*Day*	*Coleman*	*Lampard*	*McDowell*	*Taylor T*	*Lock*	*Taylor A*	*Paddon*	*Holland*	*Jennings*	*Robson*	
23	Shilton	Marsh	Pejic	Mahoney	Lewis	Bloor	Robertson	Greenhoff	Conroy	Hudson	Salmons	
23 *(opp)*	*Clemence*	*Smith*	*Neal*	*Thompson*	*Cormack**	*Hughes*	*Keegan*	*Case*	*Heighway*	*Toshack*	*Callaghan*	*Kennedy*
24	Shilton	Marsh	Pejic	Mahoney	Lewis	Bloor	Robertson	Greenhoff	Moores	Hudson	Salmons	
24 *(opp)*	*Latchford*	*Osborne*	*Want*	*Kendall*	*Gallagher*	*Burns*	*Bryant*	*Francis*	*White*	*Hatton*	*Hibbitt*	
25	Shilton	Lewis	Pejic	Mahoney	Dodd	Bloor	Haslegrave*	Greenhoff*	Moores	Hudson	Salmons	Robertson
25 *(opp)*	*Harvey*	*Reaney*	*Gray F**	*Bremner*	*Madeley*	*Hunter*	*Lorimer*	*Clarke*	*McKenzie*	*Yorath*	*Cherry*	*Gray E*
26	Shilton	Dodd	Pejic*	Mahoney	Smith	Bloor	Robertson	Greenhoff	Moores	Hudson	Salmons	Lumsdon
26 *(opp)*	*Platt*	*Craggs*	*Cooper*	*Souness*	*Boam*	*Madren*	*Brine*	*Spraggon*	*Willey*	*Hickton*	*Armstrong*	
27	Shilton	Marsh	Bowers	Mahoney	Dodd	Bloor	Robertson	Conroy*	Moores	Hudson	Salmons	Haslegrave
27 *(opp)*	*Parkes*	*Williams*	*Parkin*	*O'Hara*	*Munro*	*McAlle*	*Sunderland*	*Carr*	*Bell*	*Gould*	*Richards*	
28	Shilton	Marsh	Pejic	Mahoney	Dodd	Bloor	Conroy*	Greenhoff	Moores	Hudson	Salmons	Robertson
28 *(opp)*	*Wallington*	*Whitworth*	*Rofe*	*Kember*	*Blockley*	*Woollett*	*Lee*	*Sammels*	*Garland*	*Alderson*	*Worthington*	
29	Shilton	Lumsdon	Dodd	Mahoney	Skeels	Bloor	Robertson	Greenhoff	Moores	Hudson	Haslegrave*	Salmons
29 *(opp)*	*Jennings*	*Stead*	*McAllister*	*Pratt*	*Young*	*Osgood*	*Hoddle*	*Perryman*	*Duncan**	*Chivers*	*Neighbour*	*Jones*
30	Shilton	Marsh	Pejic	Mahoney	Smith	Dodd	Bloor	Greenhoff	Moores	Hudson	Salmons	
30 *(opp)*	*Mahoney*	*Blackhall*	*Kennedy*	*Barrowcl'gh*	*Craig D*	*Howard*	*Burns*	*Cassidy*	*MacDonald**	*Cannell*	*Craig T*	*Hudson*
31	Shilton	Marsh	Pejic	Mahoney	Smith	Bloor	Dodd	Greenhoff	Moores	Hudson	Salmons	
31 *(opp)*	*Peyton*	*Scott*	*Newton*	*Rodaway**	*Waldron*	*Thomson*	*Morris*	*Hankin*	*Fletcher*	*Flynn*	*Summerbee*	*Morley*

Scorers, Times, and Referees

22 — Bloor 34 / Holland 30, Jennings 35, 60 / Ref: D Nippard
Stoke's London bogey strikes again as they struggle against Ron Greenwood's men. Bloor heads home Huddy's free-kick for the equaliser but defensive lapses allow Jennings two chances which he coolly places past Shilton. Lampard and Lock have things under control for West Ham.

23 — Salmons 52 / Toshack 8 / Ref: R Lee
Terry Conroy returns surprisingly after a long layoff to provide Salmons with a great equaliser against Bob Paisley's men. John Toshack heads home unmarked as Stoke's reshuffled defence look out of sorts. Jimmy Robertson then nearly scores twice with delicate flicks. A great point.

24 — Moores 40 / Hatton 33 / Ref: R Kirkpatrick
Ian Moores plays despite a septic throat and scores with a cheeky back header past Dave Latchford. Hudson mis-kicks in the penalty area to let in Bob Hatton after a frantic opening. Peter Shilton saves Joe Gallagher's point-blank header before Greenhoff brings the best out of Latchford.

25 — McKenzie 27, Bremner 44 / Ref: J Homewood
Stoke yield to Leeds' attacking display with Duncan McKenzie at the forefront. He nets from Clarke's flick on and then Bremner knocks in the rebound after Lorimer's shot is saved by Shilton. David Harvey saves with his legs when Hudson is clean through. Bremner clears off the line.

26 — Moores 87 / Ref: A Gray
After the wind blows the roof off the Butler Street stand Stoke are forced to hire Vale Park. Moores steers home Boam's weak back-pass after having had one effort ruled out. Mike Pejic is taken to hospital at half-time with a stomach upset. Shilton tips round Maddren's bullet header.

27 — Conroy 72 / Carr 16p, Bell 74 / Ref: M Taylor
Stoke struggle in farcical conditions and concede an early penalty when Robertson is adjudged to have handled. Sure-footed Wanderers press forward and are stunned when Conroy nips in to head home Salmons' cross. They retaliate with Bell's back header and have another ruled out.

28 — Moores 3 / Worthington 15, Lee 49 / Ref: C Thomas
Moores' early header should be added to by Salmons who misses from the spot after Kember handles. Shilton cannot do anything about Frank Worthington's snapshot and lax defending allows Alderson to hit the bar and Rob Lee follows up. Leicester's first win at the Vic for 38 years.

29 — Greenhoff 6 / Duncan 29, Hoddle 42 / Ref: P Willis
City, decimated by injuries, take a miraculous lead against Spurs. Greenhoff finishes Robertson's pass for the opener. But Stoke are beaten by Duncan's finish from Neighbour's pass and a Glenn Hoddle fire-cracker. Rumours are rife of financial problems caused by the storm damage.

30 — Burns (og) 37 / Ref: H Hackney
Micky Burns turns Pejic's cross past Mahoney for the only goal of a dour game. Ray Hudson's introduction sparks Newcastle's best period but Shilton makes two superb saves. John Mahoney clears off the line in the last minute. Pejic is back after being dropped for requesting a transfer.

31 — Smith 18, 30, Gr'nhoff 25, Mah'ney 75 / Hankin 37 / Ref: T Spencer
Stoke put lowly Burnley to the sword. Smith pops up twice in the Burnley area to bury Hudson's passes. Greenhoff angles in a header and John Mahoney applies the finish after Peyton saves Moores' shot. Ray Hankin's goal comes when Shilton and Smith collide going for the same ball.

No	V	Date	Opponent	Att	Pos	Res	Score	HT		Pts
32	A	13/3	IPSWICH	22,812	10	D	1-1	0-0	9	34
33	H	20/3	QP RANGERS	22,848	11	L	0-1	0-1	7	34
34	A	24/3	DERBY	30,156	11	D	1-1	1-1	4	35
35	A	27/3	ASTON VILLA	32,359	11	D	0-0	0-0	18	36
36	H	2/4	MANCHESTER C	18,798	11	D	0-0	0-0	7	37
37	A	7/4	EVERTON	15,974	12	L	1-2	0-1	14	37
38	H	10/4	COVENTRY	13,059	12	L	0-1	0-0	15	37
39	A	17/4	LIVERPOOL	44,069	14	L	3-5	1-2	1	37
40	A	19/4	BIRMINGHAM	15,918	12	W	1-0	1-0	19	39
41	A	21/4	MANCHESTER U	53,879	11	W	1-0	1-0	3	41
42	H	24/4	NORWICH	15,598	12	L	0-2	0-0	10	41

Average: Home 21,816 Away 25,042

Match 32 — IPSWICH (A)
Stoke: Shilton, Marsh, Pejic, Mahoney, Smith, Dodd, Haslegrave, Greenhoff, Moores, Hudson, Salmons; Robertson
Ipswich: Cooper, Burley, Mills, Sharkey, Hunter, Peddelty, Woods*, Osborne, Johnson, Whymark, Lambert; Austin
Smith 53; Osborne 82. Ref: D Biddle
Stoke nearly plunder both points against bogey team Ipswich, but Roger Osborne fires past Shilton at the death to rescue Bobby Robson's men. Denis Smith scores again from Salmons' deep cross. Hudson runs the Town midfield ragged. Cooper is the busier keeper as Stoke take charge.

Match 33 — QP RANGERS (H)
Stoke: Shilton, Marsh, Pejic, Mahoney, Smith, Dodd, Haslegrave, Greenhoff, Moores, Hudson, Salmons*; Robertson
QPR: Parkes, Clement, Gillard, Hollins, McLintock, Webb, Thomas, Leach, Masson, Bowles, Givens
Webb 32. Ref: G Courtney
Table-toppers Rangers deny a sprightly Stoke side. Webb nets after Masson's quick free-kick is helped on by Leach and City cannot find a way past Phil Parkes. Parkes tips over a wicked Hudson shot and in a tremendous scramble the ball is cleared off the line twice as Rangers cling on.

Match 34 — DERBY (A)
Stoke: Shilton, Marsh, Pejic, Mahoney, Smith, Bloor, Dodd, Haslegrave, Greenhoff, Moores, Hudson*; Salmons
Derby: Moseley, Thomas, Nish, Rioch, MacFarland, Todd, Powell, Gemmill, Hector, George*, James; Davies
Bloor 2; Rioch 16p. Ref: K Burns
Greenhoff and Hudson are withdrawn from the England squad as they are needed against Derby. Huddy fractures his leg but Charlie George's dislocated shoulder redresses the balance. Even the referee gets injured! Bloor nets from close range, but fouls Leighton James for the penalty.

Match 35 — ASTON VILLA (A)
Stoke: Shilton, Lumsdon, Pejic, Mahoney, Smith, Dodd, Haslegrave, Greenhoff, Moores, Hudson, Salmons*; Robertson
Villa: Burridge, Gidman, Robson, Ross, Nichol, Mortimer, Graydon, Little, Gray, Hamilton, Carrodus
Ref: H Davey
Shilton foils a lively Villa attack. He has a personal battle with Andy Gray who barges him to the ground early on and then forces him to save point blank. Little fizzes one just over and Shilton tips round from Carrodus. Bloor is in tremendous form, blocking shots from Gray and Little.

Match 36 — MANCHESTER C (H)
Stoke: Shilton, Lumsdon, Pejic, Mahoney, Smith, Dodd, Haslegrave, Greenhoff, Moores, Hudson, Salmons
Man C: Corrigan, Hammond, Donachie, Doyle, Booth, Oakes, Barnes, Keegan, Royle, Power, Tueart
Ref: K Styles
City easily contain the Blues but with only one goal in 270 mins the strikers are struggling. Against youthful opponents Sean Haslegrave twists and turns to force Joe Corrigan to save and then Moores freezes when clean through. Stoke miss Huddy's flair and cannot find the extra spark.

Match 37 — EVERTON (A)
Stoke: Shilton, Lumsdon, Pejic, Mahoney, Smith*, Dodd, Robertson, Greenhoff, Conroy, Haslegrave, Salmons
Everton: Davies, Bernard, Jones D, Lyons, McNaught, Kenyon, Hamilton, Dobson, Pearson, Connolly, Telfer
Greenhoff 59p; Hamilton 20, Bernard 80p. Ref: W Johnson
Everton's lowest post-war crowd sees Stoke struggle with the midfield sitting far too deep. Mahoney is tripped by Dobson and Greenhoff fires in the equaliser. Late controversy as Pearson falls over himself and the referee gives a spot-kick. The home fans chuckle as Bernard tucks it in.

Match 38 — COVENTRY (H)
Stoke: Shilton, Lumsdon, Pejic, Mahoney, Smith*, Bloor, Conroy, Greenhoff, Moores, Haslegrave, Salmons; Crooks
Coventry: Blyth, Oakey, Cattlin, Craven, Holmes, Coop, Cartwright, Green, Ferguson, Powell, Hutchison; Dodd
Powell 53. Ref: R Tinkler
Garth Crooks makes his debut one month after signing professional. Barry Powell fires home Hutchison's free-kick for the only goal. Shilton changes direction in mid-air to save Mike Ferguson's deflected shot and Stoke only have Crooks' shot, saved by Blyth, on target.

Match 39 — LIVERPOOL (A)
Stoke: Shilton, Marsh, Pejic, Mahoney, Dodd, Bloor, Robertson, Greenhoff, Conroy, Moores*, Salmons; Crooks
Liverpool: Clemence, Smith, Neal, Thompson, Kennedy, Hughes, Case*, Keegan, Heighway, Toshack, Callaghan; Fairclough
C'roy 30, M'res 60, Bloor 89 (Fair 79); Neal 37p, Tos' 44, Ken' 51, Hugh' 75. Ref: R Toseland
City's defence is taken apart after snatching the lead through Conroy's 30-yarder. Emlyn Hughes and Ray Kennedy grab the Reds' best goals as they march inexorably on to the title. Ian Moores nods home from point-blank range. Neal mis-hits the penalty in after Marsh fouls Keegan.

Match 40 — BIRMINGHAM (A)
Stoke: Shilton, Marsh, Pejic, Mahoney, Dodd, Bloor, Conroy, Greenhoff, Crooks, Moores*, Salmons; **Sheldon**
Birmingham: Latchford, Calderwood, Styles, Page, Gallagher, Want, Emmanuel, Francis, Burns, White, Bryant; Haslegrave
Gallagher 6 (og). Ref: K McNally
Kevin Sheldon announces his arrival by forcing Joe Gallagher to turn a cross past his own keeper. Conroy also looks sharp. Birmingham seem content to keep the score down as they bid to avoid the drop. Greenhoff's shot hits the inside of the post and Pejic's class keeps Francis quiet.

Match 41 — MANCHESTER U (A)
Stoke: Shilton, Lumsdon, Pejic, Dodd, Smith, Bloor, Conroy, Greenhoff, Crooks, Moores, Salmons; Haslegrave
Man U: Stepney, Forsyth, Houston, Daly, Greenhoff, Buchan, Jackson*, McIlroy, McCreery, Macari, Hill; Nicholl
Bloor 87. Ref: C White
A young City team soak up United's pressure and hit back on the break. Alex Stepney makes a superb reflex save from Greenhoff's header just before Bloor swoops to head home Sheldon's cross. The battling Smith and Bloor dominate the diminutive Lou Macari and David McCreery.

Match 42 — NORWICH (H)
Stoke: Shilton, Lumsdon, Pejic, Dodd, Smith*, Bloor, Conroy, Greenhoff, Moores, Haslegrave, Salmons; Bowers
Norwich: Keelan, Jones, Morris, McGuire, Forbes, Powell, Steele, MacDougall, Boyer, Suggett, Peters; Bowers
MacDougall 47, Suggett 65. Ref: E Read
Eric Skeels waves goodbye to the Boothen End after 592 appearances. Stokies also bid farewell to Freddie Steele who died in the night. Keelan saves well from Greenhoff. Norwich score when Dodd's mistake allows Ted MacDougall a free run on goal and Suggett powers in a 25-yarder.

LEAGUE DIVISION 1 (CUP-TIES)   Manager: Tony Waddington   SEASON 1975-76

League Cup

			Date	Att				F-A	H-T	Scorers, Times, and Referees	1	2	3	4	5	6	7	8	9	10	11	12 sub used
2	A	LINCOLN	10/9	13,472	4:9	19	L	1-2	1-1	Greenhoff 18 / Harding 19, Booth 68 / Ref: P Reeves	Shilton	Marsh	Pejic	Mahoney	Dodd	Bloor	Haslegrave	Greenhoff	Conroy	Hudson	Moores	
											Grotier	*Branfoot*	*Leigh*	*Booth*	*Ellis*	*Cooper*	*Fleming*	*Ward*	*Freeman*	*Smith*	*Harding*	

One of the most humiliating nights in the club's history. Not only do Stoke lose to the lowly Imps but fighting fans cause a wall to collapse and injure 18. Greenhoff's run and shot is cancelled out by Alan Harding's drive. Booth dives headlong to grab the winner. Moores misses a sitter.

FA Cup

			Date	Att				F-A	H-T	Scorers, Times, and Referees	1	2	3	4	5	6	7	8	9	10	11	12 sub used
3	A	TOTTENHAM	3/1	26,715	16	8	D	1-1	1-0	Mahoney 31 / Duncan 52 / Ref: R Matthewson	Shilton	Marsh	Pejic	Mahoney	Dodd	Bloor	Robertson	Greenhoff	Moores	Hudson	Salmons	
											Jennings	*Naylor*	*McAllister*	*Pratt*	*Young*	*Osgood*	*Coates**	*Perryman*	*Chivers*	*Duncan*	*Neighbour*	*Jones*

In a dour game Stoke take the lead through Mahoney's rocket and then sit back. Spurs mount intense pressure after the break and John Duncan out-jumps Salmons to bury a header from Willie Young's flick on. Shilton saves well from Duncan who also shoots wide when clean through.

3R	H	TOTTENHAM	24/1	29,520	16	7	W	2-1	1-1	Moores 35, Salmons 88p / Perryman 27 / Ref: R Matthewson	Shilton	Dodd	Bowers	Mahoney	Smith	Bloor	Robertson	Greenhoff	Moores	Hudson	Salmons	
											Jennings	*Naylor*	*McAllister*	*Pratt*	*Young*	*Osgood*	*Coates*	*Perryman*	*Duncan*	*Jones*	*Neighbour*	

The game bursts into life after Steve Perryman's deflected goal. Stoke reply straight away when Pat Jennings drops the ball for Moores to prod home. Greenhoff heads just wide and then Moores' shot is punched over by Naylor and Salmons sends the wrong way from the spot.

4	H	MANCHESTER C	27/1	38,073	7	9	W	1-0	0-0	Greenhoff 81 / Ref: P Partridge	Shilton	Marsh	Pejic !	Mahoney	Dodd	Bloor	Robertson	Greenhoff	Moores	Hudson	Salmons	
											Corrigan	*Barrett*	*Donachie !*	*Doyle*	*Booth*	*Oakes*	*Barnes**	*Power*	*Royle*	*Hartford*	*Tueart*	*Keegan*

In a turbulent affair Stoke grab victory through Greenhoff's shot after Corrigan saves Moores' initial effort. Pejic is dismissed for head-butting Tueart, Donachie for two bookings after lunging challenges on Robertson. He doesn't even wait for the red card but just trots down the tunnel.

5	H	SUNDERLAND	14/2	41,171	2:3	11	D	0-0	0-0	/ Ref: T Reynolds	Shilton	Marsh	Dodd	Mahoney	Smith	Bloor	Robertson	Greenhoff	Moores	Hudson	Salmons	
											Montgomery	*Malone*	*Bolton*	*Towers*	*Clarke*	*Moncur*	*Kerr*	*Ashurst*	*Holden*	*Robson*	*Finney*	

Sunderland weather the early storm and then contain City ably. Montgomery is outstanding as he foils Hudson and Dodd. Greenhoff does beat Monty but Towers clears off the line. Stoke, rocked by Hudson and Pejic's transfer requests, cannot find their usual attacking flair and rhythm.

5R	A	SUNDERLAND	17/2	47,583	2:3	11	L	1-2	0-2	Smith 77 / Holden 76, Robson 80 / Ref: T Reynolds	Shilton	Marsh	Dodd	Mahoney	Smith	Bloor	Robertson	Greenhoff	Conroy	Hudson	Salmons*	Moores
											Montgomery	*Malone*	*Bolton*	*Towers*	*Clarke*	*Moncur*	*Kerr*	*Ashurst*	*Holden*	*Robson*	*Finney**	*Halom*

Bob Stokoe's men hound City out of the Cup in a passionate match. Shilton tips over Holden's acrobatic effort then Sunderland have two goals ruled out. Holden nets a header but Bloor hits the post and Smith nets the rebound from the kick-off. Robson beats the offside trap to clinch it.

Home / Away League Table

#	Team	P	Home W	D	L	F	A	Away W	D	L	F	A	Pts	Odds & ends
1	Liverpool	42	14	5	2	41	21	9	9	3	25	10	60	Double wins: (2) Arsenal, Sheffield Utd.
2	QP Rangers	42	17	4	0	42	13	7	7	7	25	20	59	Double losses: (2) West Ham, QP Rangers.
3	Manchester U	42	16	4	1	40	13	7	6	8	28	29	56	
4	Derby	42	15	3	3	45	30	6	8	7	30	28	53	Won from behind: (2) Arsenal (a), Everton (h).
5	Leeds	42	13	3	5	37	19	8	6	7	28	27	51	Lost from in front: (4) Leicester (h), Liverpool (a), QP Rangers (a),
6	Ipswich	42	11	6	4	36	23	5	8	8	18	25	46	Tottenham (h).
7	Leicester	42	9	9	3	29	24	4	10	7	19	27	45	
8	Manchester C	42	14	5	2	46	18	2	6	13	18	28	43	High spots: Best away record for 18 years.
9	Tottenham	42	6	10	5	33	32	8	5	8	30	31	43	First double over Arsenal since 1950-51.
10	Norwich	42	10	5	6	33	26	6	5	10	25	32	42	Beating Leeds 3-2 at the Vic.
11	Everton	42	10	7	4	37	24	5	5	11	23	42	42	Excellent early season form hints at a title tilt.
12	STOKE	42	8	5	8	25	24	7	6	8	23	26	41	
13	Middlesbro	42	9	7	5	23	11	6	3	12	23	34	40	Low spots: The Butler Street roof crashes down, bringing huge
14	Coventry	42	6	9	6	22	22	7	5	9	25	35	40	financial problems.
15	Newcastle	42	11	4	6	51	26	4	5	12	20	36	39	Appalling home form – worst record for 16 years.
16	Aston Villa	42	11	8	2	32	17	0	9	12	19	42	39	Knocked out of the League Cup by Division 4 Lincoln.
17	Arsenal	42	11	4	6	33	19	2	6	13	14	34	36	Poor late season form sees championship challenge fade.
18	West Ham	42	10	5	6	26	23	3	5	13	22	48	36	Alan Hudson's broken leg at Derby.
19	Birmingham	42	11	5	5	36	26	2	2	17	21	49	33	
20	Wolves	42	7	6	8	27	25	3	4	14	24	43	30	Ever-presents: (1) Peter Shilton.
21	Burnley	42	6	6	9	23	26	3	4	14	20	40	28	Hat-tricks: (0).
22	Sheffield Utd	42	4	7	10	19	32	2	3	16	14	50	22	Leading scorer: (13) Jimmy Greenhoff.
		924	229	127	106	736	494	106	127	229	494	736	924	

Appearances and Goals

Name	App Lge	Sub	LC	Sub	FAC	Sub	Goals Lge	LC	FAC	Tot
Bloor, Alan	32		1		4		5			5
Bowers, Ian	6	1			2		1			1
Conroy, Terry	16		1		1		4			4
Crooks, Garth	2									
Dodd, Alan	39		1		5					
Goodwin, Dave	2	2								
Greenhoff, Jimmy	40		1		5		11	1	1	13
Haslegrave, Sean	23	5					1			1
Hudson, Alan	34	1	1		5		2			2
Lewis, Kevin	9									
Lumsdon, John	9	1								
Mahoney, John	38		1		5		1		1	2
Marsh, Jackie	25	1	1		4					
Moores, Ian	29	3	1		4	1	11		1	12
Pejic, Mike	39		1		2		1			1
Robertson, Jimmy	12	6			5		1			1
Salmons, Geoff	39	1	1		5		5		1	6
Sheldon, Kevin	3									
Shilton, Peter	42		1		5					
Skeels, Eric	4									
Smith, Denis	19				3		3		1	4
(own-goals)							2			2
21 players used	462	21	11		55	1	48	1	5	54

LEAGUE DIVISION 1

Manager: Waddington ⇨ George Eastham

SEASON 1976-77

No		Date		Att	Pos	Pt	F-A	H-T	Scorers, Times, and Referees	1	2	3	4	5	6	7	8	9	10	11	12 sub used
1	H	21/8	SUNDERLAND	27,530		1	D 0-0	0-0	Ref: A. Jones	Shilton	Dodd	Pejic	Mahoney	Smith	Bloor	Salmons*	Greenhoff	Conroy	Hudson	Crooks	Bowers
										Montgomery	*Malone*	*Bolton*	*Towers*	*Clarke*	*Moncur*	*Kerr*	*Ashurst*	*Hughes*	*Robson*	*Train*	
2	A	24/8	BRISTOL CITY	25,316		2	D 1-1	0-0	Smith 86 / Gillies 50 — Ref: D Lloyd	Shilton	Dodd	Pejic	Mahoney	Smith	Bloor	Salmons	Greenhoff	Conroy	Hudson	Crooks*	Bowers
										Cashley	*Sweeney*	*Drysdale*	*Gow*	*Collier*	*Merrick*	*Tainton*	*Ritchie*	*Mann*	*Cheesley* *	*Whitehead*	*Gillies*
3	A	28/8	MANCHESTER C	39,878	15/3	3	D 0-0	0-0	Ref: J Rice	Shilton	Dodd	Pejic	Mahoney	Smith	Bloor	Salmons	Greenhoff	Conroy	Hudson	Bowers	
										Corrigan	*Docherty*	*Donachie*	*Doyle*	*Watson*	*Power*	*Conway*	*Hartford*	*Barnes*	*Royle*	*Tueart*	
4	H	4/9	WEST HAM	19,131	6/20	5	W 2-1	1-0	Crooks 32, Conroy 52 / Taylor A 70 — Ref: W Dow	Shilton	Marsh	Pejic	Mahoney	Dodd	Bloor	Salmons	Greenhoff	Conroy	Hudson	Crooks	
										Day	*Coleman*	*Lampard*	*Bonds*	*Green*	*McGiven*	*Taylor T* *	*Paddon*	*Taylor A*	*Brooking*	*Holland*	*Jennings*
5	A	11/9	EVERTON	22,277	13/5	5	L 0-3	0-0	Telfer 62, 67, Latchford 77 — Ref: A Porter	Shilton	Marsh	Pejic	Mahoney	Dodd	Bowers	Salmons	Greenhoff	Conroy	Hudson	Crooks*	Sheldon
										Davies	*Bernard*	*Jones*	*Lyons*	*McNaught*	*Kenyon*	*King*	*Dobson*	*Latchford*	*Goodlass*	*Telfer*	
6	H	18/9	IPSWICH	20,171	7/17	7	W 2-1	2-0	Tudor 2, 19 / Whymark 53 — Ref: G Flint	Shilton	Marsh	Pejic	Greenhoff	Dodd	Bloor	Salmons	Tudor	Conroy	Hudson	Crooks	Tibbatt
										Sivell	*Burley*	*Mills*	*Talbot*	*Hunter*	*Peddelty*	*Turner* *	*Gates*	*Bertschin*	*Whymark*	*Lambert*	
7	A	25/9	QP RANGERS	21,621	14/9	7	L 0-2	0-1	Bowles 8, Givens 80 — Ref: E Read	Shilton	Marsh	Pejic	Bithell	Dodd	Bloor	Salmons	Greenhoff	Conroy*	Hudson	Tudor	Sheldon
										Parkes	*Clement*	*Gillard*	*Hollins*	*McLintock*	*Webb*	*Thomas*	*Kelly*	*Masson*	*Bowles*	*Givens*	
8	A	29/9	LEICESTER	15,391	15/9	7	L 0-1	0-1	Worthington 24 — Ref: J Yates	Shilton	Lumsdon	Pejic	Bithell	Dodd	Bloor	Salmons	Greenhoff	Conroy	Tudor	Sheldon	
										Wallington	*Whitworth*	*Rofe*	*Kember*	*Blockley*	*Woollett*	*Weller*	*Birchenall* *	*Worthington*	*Sammels*	*Garland*	*Earle*
9	H	2/10	ASTON VILLA	29,652	10/11	9	W 1-0	1-0	Conroy 37 — Ref: J Wrennall	Shilton	Lumsdon	Pejic	Bithell	Dodd	Bloor	Salmons	Greenhoff	Conroy	Tudor	Sheldon	
										Burridge	*Gidman*	*Smith*	*Phillips*	*Nicholl*	*Mortimer*	*Graydon*	*Little*	*Gray*	*Cropley*	*Carrodus*	
10	A	16/10	ARSENAL	28,057	16/4	9	L 0-2	0-1	Rice 12, MacDonald 48 — Ref: D Nippard	Shilton	Lumsdon	Pejic	Bithell	Dodd	Bloor	Salmons	Greenhoff	Conroy	Hudson	Sheldon	
										Rimmer	*Rice*	*Storey*	*Ross*	*O'Leary*	*Howard*	*Ball*	*Brady*	*MacDonald*	*Stapleton* *	*Armstrong*	*Ratford*

Match commentaries

1. Bob Stokoe has just Bryan Robson up front as Sunderland leave with their point intact. Conroy forces Jim Montgomery to save from two long-range efforts and then hits a post. Mike Pejic blazes over from a corner as City make no impression on Jack Ashurst's well-marshalled defence.

2. Derek Lloyd, once an amateur on Stoke's books, cautions three City players as the Potters struggle for form. Greenhoff sears a volley wide and then Bowers gifts Don Gillies the opener (Bristol's only shot on goal). In a late flurry Denis Smith towers above the defence to ensure parity.

3. Conroy mis-hits a glorious chance and Hudson shows signs of his class but City still struggle in front of goal. Stoke enjoy more of the play after the interval as Asa Hartford hits the post for Tony Book's Blues as the game fizzles out. Waddington is interested in Peter Lorimer of Leeds.

4. Marsh and Conroy create havoc down the flanks and force Day into several great saves. Garth Crooks grabs his first goal when he follows up Marsh's shot. Conroy hits the bar and has another shot superbly saved before blasting home from the edge of the area as Stoke win at a canter.

5. City look sharp in the first half. Conroy holds his head after missing a 24th-minute penalty, slicing it wide. Hudson and Salmons fire straight at Dai Davies then Stoke wilt under intense pressure. Telfer's brace are both close-range finishes while Latchford nets a trademark diving header.

6. A dream debut from on-loan John Tudor who nets after Sivell palms away Salmons' shot and then buries Pejic's delicate cross to put Stoke in charge. Crooks dives full length to head wide. Ipswich hit back with Whymark's header and have a goal ruled out for offside but City cling on.

7. City are unlucky as Greenhoff hits the bar (6 mins) before Stan Bowles beats three defenders to plant the ball past Shilton. Salmons blasts over, as does debutant Brian Bithell. Tudor twice heads wide during intense City pressure. Don Givens nets on the break for Dave Sexton's Rangers.

8. Conroy misses a first-half trio of chances as Kevin Sheldon torments Denis Rofe on the right. Foxes boss Jimmy Bloomfield sees Wallington deny Pejic and Greenhoff. Dodd heads over from three yards out as City fail to take advantage and lose to Frank Worthington's 30-yard effort.

9. The cost of rebuilding the Butler Street stand mounts as the unsettled, outspoken Alan Hudson is told he can leave. He is left out but Conroy's finish to Greenhoff's flick still bags City the points. Shilton saves Ray Graydon's 51st-minute penalty, awarded after Dodd handles on the line.

10. Hudson plays but is unhappy at having a £350,000 price tag slapped on him. City are never in a game which is won by a rare Pat Rice goal and MacDonald's clinical finish to Brady's pass. Shilton prevents a third by flinging himself across his goal to save Stapleton's point-blank header.

League results 11–21

No.	Venue	Opponent	Date	Att.	Pos.	Res.	Pts	FT	HT	Scorers	Referee
11	H	DERBY	23/10	20,916	14	W	11	1-0	0-0	Tudor 70	Ref: G Nolan
12	A	NEWCASTLE	30/10	32,339	16	L	11	0-1	0-0	Cannell 64	Ref: L Hayes
13	H	MIDDLESBROUGH	6/11	16,068	13	W	13	3-1	1-1	Waddington 20, Greenhoff 47, 54 / Armstrong 5	Ref: D Civil
14	A	LEEDS	10/11	29,199	14	D	14	1-1	0-0	Dodd 86 / Lorimer 73p	Ref: P Richardson
15	H	BIRMINGHAM	20/11	21,488	9	W	16	1-0	0-0	Crooks 70	Ref: C Thomas
16	A	TOTTENHAM	27/11	22,230	11	L	16	0-2	0-0	Osgood 49, 67p	Ref: J Homewood
17	H	WEST BROM	18/12	13,006	14	L	16	0-2	0-1	Statham 44, Trewick 75	Ref: K Ridden
18	A	LIVERPOOL	27/12	50,371	17	L	16	0-4	0-1	Thompson 4, Neal 57p, Keegan 63, Johnson 81	Ref: K Walmsley
19	A	MIDDLESBROUGH	1/1	24,140	16	D	17	0-0	0-0	—	Ref: P Richardson
20	A	SUNDERLAND	22/1	22,901	17	D	18	0-0	0-0	—	Ref: P Morris
21	A	NORWICH	29/1	8,408	15	D	19	1-1	0-1	Salmons 48 / Reeves 2	Ref: R Lewis

11. H DERBY — Tudor 70
Stoke: Shilton, Lumsden, Pejic, Bithell, Dodd, Bloor, Salmons, Greenhoff, Tudor, Hudson, Sheldon; sub **Waddington**
Derby: *Moseley, Thomas, Nish, Macken*, MacFarland, Todd, Powell, King, Rioch, George, James; sub Daniel*

In a dynamic match Hudson prompts City forward at every opportunity. City harass the Rams out of their stride and the breakthrough arrives when Tudor nods in Greenhoff's cross. David Nish drives just past the post and Bruce Rioch's curling shot is well dealt with by Peter Shilton.

12. A NEWCASTLE — Cannell 64
Stoke: Shilton, Lumsden, Pejic, Bithell, Dodd, Bloor, Sheldon, Greenhoff, Tudor, Hudson, Salmons*; sub **Craig T**
Newcastle: *Mahoney, Nattrass, Kennedy, Cassidy, McCaffrey, Nulty, Barrowcl'gh, Cannell, Burns, Guy*

City, in a Yellow and Sky Blue change kit, seem in control until Shilton's uncharacteristic error gifts the Toon the match. He punches the ball straight to Paul Cannell who scores easily. Stoke struggle to find a way back. Tudor, back at his old club, has two snap shots blocked late on.

13. H MIDDLESBROUGH — Waddington 20, Greenhoff 47, 54 / Armstrong 5
Stoke: Shilton, Lumsden, Pejic, Bithell, Dodd, Bloor, Sheldon, Greenhoff, Tudor, Conroy, Waddington
Middlesbrough: *Platt, Craggs, Cooper, Souness, Boam, Madden, McAndrew, Mills, Wood, Brine*, Armstrong; sub Hickton*

Boro have the best defensive record in the Division but Steve Waddington heads home on his full debut and Greenhoff bags from a tight angle and then from Pejic's neat reverse pass. In dismal conditions Conroy heads just wide and Greenhoff is inches away from grabbing a hat-trick.

14. A LEEDS — Dodd 86 / Lorimer 73p
Stoke: Shilton, Lumsden, Pejic, Bithell, Dodd, Bloor, Waddington, Greenhoff, Tudor, Conroy, Sheldon*; sub **Salmons**
Leeds: *Harvey, Reaney, Hampton, Cherry, McQueen, Gray F, Lorimer, Hankin, Jordan, Currie, Gray E*

Kevin Sheldon breaks his leg after 13 minutes when sandwiched between Reaney and Jordan. The penalty is for Tudor's push on McQueen but Dodd grabs his first goal with a far-post header and Conroy nearly wins it. After the game Jimmy Greenhoff is sold to Man Utd for £120,000.

15. H BIRMINGHAM — Crooks 70
Stoke: Shilton, Lumsden, Pejic!, Dodd, Smith, Bloor, Waddington, Conroy, Tudor, Hudson, Bithell; sub **Crooks**
Birmingham: *Latchford, Page, Styles, Pendrey, Gallagher, Want, Jones*, Francis, Burns, Hibbitt, Connolly; sub Calderwood*

Stoke, led by new club captain Denis Smith, ride their luck as Trevor Francis misses a 72nd-minute penalty. Garth Crooks nets the winner after Bithell's short free-kick before Pejic is sent off for a knee-high challenge on Jim Calderwood and Willie Bell's Blues have a goal disallowed.

16. A TOTTENHAM — Osgood 49, 67p
Stoke: Shilton, Lumsden, Pejic, Dodd, Smith, Bloor, Waddington, Conroy, Tudor, Hudson, Bithell
Tottenham: *Jennings, Naylor, Gorman, Haddle, Young, Osgood, Conn, Perryman, Moores, Coates, Taylor*

City are under pressure from the off as Young hits the underside of the bar and Ian Moores, playing against his former colleagues, misses two open goals. Keith Osgood's brace includes a penalty for Conroy's challenge on Young. After the game Hudson is sold to Arsenal for £200,000.

17. H WEST BROM — Statham 44, Trewick 75
Stoke: Shilton, Lumsden, Pejic, Dodd, Smith, Salmons, Waddington, Conroy, Tudor*, Bithell, Robertson
West Brom: *Ward, Mulligan!, Statham, Brown T, Wile, Robertson, Martin, Treacy, Cross, Trewick, Johnston*

Derek Statham scores after a fine run and shot on his debut for Albion. John Trewick hammers home and then Lumsdon misses when standing on the line. Paddy Mulligan is sent off with 8 mins to go but by then it is too late. City are a shambles. Waddo pursues an interest in Alan Ball.

18. A LIVERPOOL — Thompson 4, Neal 57p, Keegan 63, Johnson 81
Stoke: Shilton, Marsh, Pejic, Smith!, Bloor, Dodd, Waddington, Bithell, Tudor*, Salmons, Crooks
Liverpool: *Clemence, Neal, Jones, Thompson, Kennedy, Hughes, Keegan, McDermott, Heighway, Toshack, Callaghan*; subs Callaghan*, Johnson 81*

The referee plays Scrooge as Denis Smith is sent off (55 minutes) for a second booking. Conroy is already serving a ban for reaching 20 points. City are under the cosh from then on. Marsh trips Toshack for the penalty before Keegan's clinical finish and Johnson's header wrap things up.

19. A MIDDLESBROUGH
Stoke: Shilton, Marsh, Pejic, Dodd, Smith, Dodd, Waddington, Robertson, Tudor, Bithell, Salmons
Middlesbrough: *Cuff, Craggs, Cooper, Souness, Boam, Madden*, McAndrew, Mills, Brine, Wood, Armstrong; sub Boersma*

City have Pejic, Smith and Dodd defiant to earn a good point. Mills' shot is miraculously held by Shilton and Alf Wood's effort is disallowed for handball. Both sides earn praise for providing an entertaining match on a very muddy pitch from Harold Sheperdson, the England trainer.

20. A SUNDERLAND
Stoke: Shilton, Marsh, Pejic, Bithell, Smith, Dodd, Robertson, Suddick, Tudor, Conroy, Salmons
Sunderland: *Siddall, Elliott, Bolton, Towers, Clarke, Ashurst, Kerr, Arnott, Lee, Holden, Rowell*; sub Brown*

In a grim affair Dodd tames Gary Rowell and Smith restricts Mel Holden to only one chance, a header which deflects wide off Pejic. Salmons provides Bithell with Stoke's best chance, but he blazes over. Allan Suddick makes his debut after his New Year's Eve move from Blackpool.

21. A NORWICH — Salmons 48 / Reeves 2
Stoke: Shilton, Marsh, Pejic, Mahoney, Smith, Dodd, Bloor, Suddick, Tudor, Conroy, Salmons
Norwich: *Keelan, Ryan, Sullivan, Machin, Forbes, Powell, Neighbour, Reeves, Gibbins, Boyer, Peters*

After six blank scoresheets City finally receive some luck in front of goal when Forbes' attempted clearance cannons off Salmons and past the astonished Keelan. John Bond's Norwich lead when Kevin Reeves robs Bloor to score. Salmons' 40-yard effort whistles past. A point will do.

LEAGUE DIVISION 1   Manager: Waddington ➪ George Eastham   SEASON 1976-77

Match details

No	Date	V	Opponent	Att	Pos	OppPos	Pt	Res	F-A	H-T	Scorers, Times, and Referees
22	5/2	H	MANCHESTER C	27,141	15	3	19	L	0-2	0-1	*Tueart 39, Royle 89* — Ref: G Flint
23	12/2	A	WEST HAM	20,106	16	21	19	L	0-1	0-1	*Robson B 7* — Ref: E Robinson
24	16/2	H	COVENTRY	12,255	14	15	21	W	2-0	1-0	Conroy 1, 55p — Ref: J Taylor
25	19/2	H	EVERTON	19,586	15	16	21	L	0-1	0-0	Ref: A Morrissey
26	26/2	A	IPSWICH	25,865	15	2	23	W	1-0	1-0	Goodwin 37 — Ref: D Reeves
27	5/3	H	QP RANGERS	15,454	14	17	25	W	1-0	0-0	Bowers 47 — Ref: G Kew
28	15/3	H	NEWCASTLE	12,708	14	5	26	D	0-0	0-0	Ref: W Johnson
29	19/3	H	LEICESTER	14,087	14	6	26	L	0-1	0-0	*Worthington 89* — Ref: T Reynolds
30	23/3	H	ARSENAL	13,951	14	11	27	D	1-1	0-1	Conroy 7; *Price 1* — Ref: T Mills
31	2/4	A	DERBY	23,161	15	19	27	L	0-2	0-1	*Daly 42p, James 53* — Ref: K McNally

Line-ups (Stoke = roman, opponents = italic)

No	1	2	3	4	5	6	7	8	9	10	11	12 sub used
22	Shilton	Dodd	Pejic	Mahoney	Smith	Bloor	**Ruggiero**	Suddick	Goodwin	Conroy	Salmons	
22	*Corrigan*	*Clements*	*Donachie*	*Doyle*	*Watson*	*Power*	*Owen*	*Kidd*	*Royle*	*Hartford*	*Tueart*	*Marsh*
23	Shilton	Dodd	Bowers	Mahoney	Smith	Bloor	Crooks	Suddick*	Goodwin	Conroy	Salmons	
23	*Day*	*Bonds*	*Lampard*	*Otulakowski*	*Green*	*Lock*	*Taylor A*	*Radford*	*Devonshire*	*Brooking*	*Robson B**	*Robson K*
24	Shilton	Dodd	Bowers	Mahoney	Smith	Bloor	Tudor	Suddick	Goodwin	Conroy	Salmons	
24	*Blyth*	*Coop*	*McDonald*	*Yorath*	*Dugdale**	*Holmes*	*Beck*	*Green*	*Roberts*	*Powell*	*Hutchison*	*Wallace*
25	Shilton	Dodd	Bowers	Mahoney	Smith	Bloor	Tudor	Suddick*	Goodwin	Conroy	Salmons	
25	*Lawson*	*Jones*	*Pejic*	*Lyons*	*McNaught*	*Rioch*	*Hamilton*	*Dobson*	*Latchford*	*McKenzie*	*Goodlass*	*Crooks*
26	Shilton	Dodd	Bowers	**Johnson PA**	Smith	Bloor	Tudor	Robertson	Goodwin	Conroy	Salmons	
26	*Sivell*	*Burley*	*Mills*	*Talbot*	*Hunter*	*Beattie*	*Osborne*	*Wark*	*Mariner*	*Whymark*	*Woods**	*Bertschin*
27	Shilton	Dodd	Bowers	**Johnson PA**	Smith	Bloor	Tudor	Robertson	Goodwin	Conroy	Salmons	
27	*Parkes*	*Hollins*	*Gillard*	*Kelly*	*McLintock*	*Webb*	*Thomas*	*Richardson*	*Masson*	*Bowles*	*Givens**	*Clement*
28	Shilton	Dodd	Bowers	**Johnson PA**	Smith	Bloor	Tudor	Robertson	Goodwin	Conroy	Salmons	
28	*Mahoney*	*Nattrass*	*Kennedy*	*Cassidy*	*McCaffery*	*Nulty*	*Barrowcl'gh*	*Oates*	*Burns*	*Gowling*	*Craig T*	
29	Shilton	Dodd	Bowers	**Johnson PA**	Smith	Bloor	Tudor	Robertson	Goodwin	Mahoney	Salmons	
29	*Wallington*	*Whitworth*	*Rofe*	*Kember**	*Woollett*	*Sims*	*White*	*Birchenall*	*Worthington*	*Alderson*	*Earle*	*Yates*
30	Shilton	Lumsdon	Bowers	**Johnson PA**	Smith	Dodd	Waddington	Crooks	Goodwin	Conroy	Salmons	
30	*Rimmer*	*Rice*	*Nelson*	*Powling*	*Young*	*O'Leary*	*Brady !*	*Hudson*	*MacDonald*	*Price*	*Armstrong*	
31	Shilton	Lumsdon	Bowers	Bloor	Smith	Dodd	Robertson	Waddington	Goodwin	Conroy	Salmons	
31	*Boulton*	*Langan*	*Webster*	*Daly*	*MacFarland*	*Powell*	*Newton*	*Hector*	*James*	*Gemmill*	*James*	

Match reports

22 — Stoke's first home game for 6 weeks due to the bad weather and they are second best throughout. An injury and suspension-hit line-up features Ruggiero and Goodwin in attack. Man City dominate but only beat Shilton after he saves twice before rebounds are knocked in for each goal.

23 — Mike Pejic is sold to Everton for £150,000 and his place is taken by Bowers. Conroy's header shaves the post and Goodwin hits Day from two yards out. Robson turns home Taylor's cross for the winner. Bonds misses a penalty after Smith handles (64 mins). A much better performance.

24 — In front of the lowest league gate for 7 years Stoke score through TC's back header on 38 seconds. He then picks himself up to score from the spot after being fouled by Dugdale. George Eastham is in charge while Waddo travels to Scotland to check out Rangers' striker Derek Parlane.

25 — Mike Pejic returns to mark Conroy out of the game as Everton steal the points. Looking to impress new Manager Gordon Lee, Rioch heads just wide before Goodwin hits the post for City and Tudor nods wide when well placed. Shilton cannot prevent Dobson's half-hit shot creeping in.

26 — Fabulous win at 2nd place Town. Dave Goodwin places a left-foot shot wide of Laurie Sivell to notch his first of the season. The much-vaunted Mariner/Whymark combination are defied by Alan Dodd and some fine Shilton saves. Paul Johnson makes his debut. Not out of the woods yet

27 — Ian Bowers spectacularly wins City the game with a whiplash left-foot shot, leaving Phil Parkes rooted to the spot. Shilton saves Mick Thomas' shot and then defies Dave Webb. Stoke clamp down in midfield and coast to full-time without further danger to put QPR in relegation trouble.

28 — City are unlucky as John Tudor has what would have been his 200th career goal ruled out for Conroy's offside. Goodwin has an effort saved by Mahoney and Robertson is deliberately tripped by Burns when clean through. Magpies, under caretaker Richard Dinnis, are happy with a point.

29 — Stoke concede in the last minute of a game they should have won when Worthington hammers home Yates' cross. City's build-up play is better but there is little on offer inside the box. Salmons stumbles in the act of shooting and Goodwin shoots straight at the keeper. Not good enough.

30 — City, fuelled by Waddo's resignation, equalise when Conroy bursts through to score left footed. All hell breaks loose with Steve Waddington's thigh-high tackle brings him a yellow and Brady a red for retaliation. Stoke cannot take advantage as Arsenal only leave MacDonald up front.

31 — Stoke struggle from the moment Dodd trips Leighton James. James then adds a second after Shilton parries Daly's shot out to him. City fail to match Derby's industrious midfield. Smith heads City's best chance wide. Robertson shows everyone's frustration as he is booked for dissent.

Stoke City — League Results (matches 32–42)

No.	Venue	Opponent	Date	Att.	Pos	Res	—	Pts	Score	Goalscorers	Referee
32	A	MANCHESTER U	9/4	53,102	16	L	5	27	0-3	Houston 52, Macari 60, Pearson 82	Ref: L Hayes
33	H	LIVERPOOL	11/4	29,905	16	D	2	28	0-0	—	Ref: M Lowe
34	H	LEEDS	12/4	17,960	14	W	9	30	2-1	Crooks 67, 76 / Jordan 90	Ref: E Garner
35	A	BIRMINGHAM	16/4	19,554	15	L	12	30	0-2	Francis 79, Burns 88	Ref: A Jones
36	H	BRISTOL CITY	20/4	12,277	15	D	22	31	2-2	Smith 56, Bloor 70 / Ritchie 40, Garland 67	Ref: K Styles
37	H	TOTTENHAM	23/4	16,641	15	D	19	32	0-0	—	Ref: R Matthewson
38	A	COVENTRY	30/4	15,720	17	L	16	32	2-5	Ruggiero 40, 66p / Beck 5, Wallace 7, 10, 85, Powell 29	Ref: C White
39	H	NORWICH	7/5	13,202	18	D	12	33	0-0	—	Ref: W Gow
40	H	MANCHESTER U	11/5	24,632	19	D	6	34	3-3	Crooks 40, 65, Bloor 49 / Hill 21, 59, McCreery 23	Ref: B Martin
41	A	WEST BROM	14/5	22,772	20	L	7	34	1-3	Suddick 22 / Martin 44, Cunningham 80, Cross 85	Ref: T Burns
42	A	ASTON VILLA	16/5	28,931	21	L	5	34	0-1	Gray 10p	Ref: J Bent

Average — Home 18,893 | Away 2?,?88

Line-ups (Stoke / opponent in italic)

32 v Manchester Utd — Stoke: Shilton, Dodd, Bowers, Mahoney, Smith, Bloor, Robertson, Johnson PA*, Conroy, Goodwin, Tudor (sub Lumsden). Manchester Utd: *Stepney, Nicholl, Houston, McIlroy, Greenhoff B, Buchan, Coppell, Greenhoff J*, Macari, Hill, McCreery* (sub *Pearson*).

33 v Liverpool — Stoke: Jones, Dodd, Marsh, Mahoney, Smith, Bloor, Robertson, Salmons, Crooks, Conroy, Ruggiero. Liverpool: *Clemence, Neal, Jones, Smith, Kennedy, Hughes, Keegan, Case, Heighway, Fairclough*, McDermott* (sub *Johnson*).

34 v Leeds — Stoke: Jones, Dodd, Marsh, Mahoney, Smith, Bloor, Robertson, Waddington*, Crooks, Ruggiero, Tudor (sub Conroy). Leeds: *Stewart, Reaney, Hampton, Cherry, McQueen, Madeley, Gray F, Lorimer, Jordan, Currie, Harris*.

35 v Birmingham — Stoke: Shilton, Dodd, Marsh, Mahoney, Smith, Bloor, Robertson*, Ruggiero, Crooks, Conroy, Salmons. Birmingham: *Montgomery, Calderwood, Pendrey, Kendall, Gallagher, Want, Jones, Francis, Burns, Hibbitt, Connolly*.

36 v Bristol City — Stoke: Shilton, Dodd, Marsh, Mahoney, Smith, Bloor, Robertson, Salmons, Crooks, Ruggiero, Tudor. Bristol City: *Shaw, Sweeney, Merrick, Gow, Collier, Hunter, Tainton, Ritchie*, Garland, Cormack, Whitehead* (sub *Fear*).

37 v Tottenham — Stoke: Shilton, Dodd, Marsh, Mahoney, Smith, Bloor, Robertson*, Salmons, Crooks, Ruggiero, Tudor (sub Conroy). Tottenham: *Jennings, Naylor, Stead, Hoddle, Osgood, Perryman, Holmes, Coates, Moores, Pratt, Armstrong*.

38 v Coventry — Stoke: Shilton, Dodd, Marsh, Mahoney, Smith!, Bloor, Conroy, Salmons, Crooks, Ruggiero, Tudor. Coventry: *Sealey, Oakey, McDonald, Beck, Holton, Coop, Cartwright, Wallace, Ferguson, Powell, Hutchison*.

39 v Norwich — Stoke: Shilton, Dodd, Marsh*, Mahoney, Smith, Bloor, Ruggiero, Salmons, Crooks, Conroy, Bithell. Norwich: *Hansbury, Ryan, Sullivan, Suggett, Forbes, Powell, Neighbour, Reeves, Gibbins, Busby, Peters*.

40 v Manchester U — Stoke: Shilton, Dodd, Bithell, Mahoney, Smith, Bloor, Johnson PA, Suddick, Crooks, Conroy, Salmons. Manchester Utd: *Stepney, Nicholl, Albiston, McIlroy, Greenhoff B, Buchan, Coppell, Greenhoff J*, Pearson, Macari, Hill, McCreery*.

41 v West Brom — Stoke: Shilton, Dodd, Bowers*, Mahoney, Smith, Bloor, Johnson PA, Suddick, Crooks, Conroy, Salmons; Bithell!. West Brom: *Osborne, Mulligan, Statham, Wile, Robertson, Martin, Cunningham, Cross, Giles, Johnston...*

42 v Aston Villa — Stoke: Shilton, Dodd, Marsh, Mahoney, Smith, Bloor, Ruggiero*, Salmons, Crooks, Conroy, Suddick (sub Goodwin). Aston Villa: *Burridge, Smith, Robson, Phillips, Nicholl, Mortimer, Deehan, Little, Gray*, Cropley, Carrodus* (sub *Linton*).

Match reports

32. Jimmy Greenhoff faces his old team but Eastham drops Salmons, who reacts angrily. Stoke have their backs to the wall. Finally Houston buries a loose ball before Lou Macari's 25-yard volley catches Shilton off his line. Lumsdon's back-pass lets in Pearson and City finish a ragged team.

33. City put tremendous effort into containing Liverpool. Bloor marks Keegan out of the game and Ruggiero stars in a midfield role. Clemence tips a Crooks volley round the post. Shilts misses his first game in 106 (stomach upset) but Roger Jones deals well with Highway's dashing runs.

34. Garth Crooks finishes off good crosses by Conroy and Robertson to take vital points for City. Jones saves 14 on-target shots as Leeds dominate but Joe Jordan's swooping header is too late. Two goals for the first time in two months. George Eastham applies for manager's job full-time.

35. In the first of five vital relegation battles Stoke rely on Shilton to show his England form, finger tipping Gallagher's header round the post. The Blues win a dour game through Francis' header and Burns' cool strike. The fact that City don't test Montgomery until 86 mins speaks volumes.

36. Stoke fail to get a grip of left winger Clive Whitehead. He provides the crosses for both of Alan Dicks' Robins' goals. City bring up the trusty rearguard of Smith and Bloor and their height poses problems. Bloor's header slips from Shaw's grasp to trickle over the line for a point saver.

37. Stoke are in control with Shilton a spectator but Spurs hold out. Crooks has an effort ruled out on 68 as the 10-man defence sways slightly. Ian Moores, on the eve of his wedding, captains Spurs against his old team. Terry Conroy's introduction sparks City's best spell. A win is needed.

38. City are never in the game. Conroy misses a penalty after Sealey fouls Crooks (42 mins). Denis Smith walks after a second caution for fouling Hutchison (66 mins). Wallace earns his hat-trick with an angled drive. Ruggiero's first is a 30-yard belter. His penalty is for a foul on Salmons.

39. Stoke provide all the huff and puff but cannot defeat Roger Hansbury. With Bithell and Salmons both denied by the keeper desperation sets in towards the finish. Conroy's work-rate keeps City attacking but Ruggiero's 30-yard shot is their best effort. Eastham will be the new manager.

40. Tension as City go two down through offside-looking goals. Crooks' first is turned in from three yards. Bloor pokes home in a scramble before Smith's back-pass allows Hill in to make it 2-3. Crooks weaves past three defenders to equalise and nearly wins it, but an offside flag is raised.

41. City lead through Suddick's first goal for the club as he curls a free-kick beyond Osborne. Martin's nods home just before the break. Bithell is the 100th player sent off this season. In going for the win Stoke concede two sucker-punch goals and their First Division life hangs by a thread.

42. City fail when Dodd's push on Gray is spotted by the ref and Gray tucks away the pen. Ron Saunders' men send Stoke spiralling into Division Two for the first time since 1963. West Ham guarantee their status by beating Man Utd 4-2. Eastham's 13th game in charge – unlucky for City.

LEAGUE DIVISION 1 (CUP-TIES)　　Manager: Waddington ⇨ George Eastham　　SEASON 1976-77

League Cup			Att		F-A	H-T	Scorers, Times, and Referees	1	2	3	4	5	6	7	8	9	10	11	12 sub used
2	H	LEEDS	22,631	15	W 2-1	0-1	Conroy 75, Greenhoff 89	Shilton	Marsh	Pejic	Mahoney	Dodd	Bloor	Salmons	Greenhoff	Conroy	Hudson	Bowers*	Crooks
1/9				19			*Currie 28*	*Stewart*	*Reaney*	*Gray F*	*Bremner*	*Madeley*	*Hunter*	*Cherry*	*Clarke*	*Jordan*	*Currie*	*Harris*
							Ref: K Burns												

Jackie Marsh steps into Denis Smith's boots after he is injured warming up. Leeds seem in control through Tony Currie's unstoppable shot but Hudson is in rampant mood. In a frenetic finale Conroy buries Greenhoff's flick and then Greenhoff flies in to head home Hudson's fine cross.

			Att		F-A	H-T	Scorers, Times, and Referees	1	2	3	4	5	6	7	8	9	10	11	12 sub used
3	A	NEWCASTLE	25,129	7	L 0-3	0-2		Shilton	Marsh	Pejic	Mahoney	Dodd	Bloor	Salmons	Greenhoff	Conroy	Hudson	Rooks*	Bowers
22/9				10			Nattrass 16, Craig T 37p, Burns 83	*Mahoney*	*Nattrass*	*Kennedy*	*Cassidy**	*McCaffrey*	*Nutty*	*Barrowcl'gh*	*Cannell*	*Burns*	*Oates*	*Craig T*	*Craig D*
							Ref: C Seel												

City confirm they will buy on-loan John Tudor but Newcastle boss Gordon Lee does not allow him to play. Stoke's defence wilts after Nattrass blasts home a rebound. Pejic trips Craig for the penalty. Shilton saves wonderfully from Oates's header before Burns nets after a breakaway.

FA Cup			Att		F-A	H-T	Scorers, Times, and Referees	1	2	3	4	5	6	7	8	9	10	11	12 sub used
3	A	EVERTON	32,952	16	L 0-2	0-1		Shilton	Marsh	Bowers	Dodd	Smith	Bloor	Waddington	Salmons	Tudor	Bithell*	Robertson	Crooks
8/1				14			Lyons 20, McKenzie 50p	*Lawson*	*Robinson*	*Jones*	*Lyons*	*McNaught*	*Rioch*	*King*	*Dobson*	*Latchford*	*McKenzie*	*Goodlass*	
							Ref: G Kew												

City fall to Billy Bingham's men's attacking flair. Duncan McKenzie makes Mick Lyons' opener and then nets a penalty after Bloor trips him. Stoke have little to offer in return. Shilton defies Bob Latchford from close in three times, then spectacularly tips Bruce Rioch's free-kick over.

Home / Away League Table

Pos	Team	P	Home					Away					Pts
			W	D	L	F	A	W	D	L	F	A	
1	Liverpool	42	18	3	0	47	11	5	8	8	15	22	57
2	Manchester C	42	15	5	1	38	13	6	9	6	22	21	56
3	Ipswich	42	15	4	2	41	11	7	4	10	25	28	52
4	Aston Villa	42	17	3	1	55	17	5	4	12	21	33	51
5	Newcastle	42	14	6	1	40	15	4	7	10	24	34	49
6	Manchester U	42	12	6	3	41	22	6	5	10	30	40	47
7	West Brom	42	10	6	5	38	22	6	7	8	24	34	45
8	Arsenal	42	11	6	4	37	20	5	5	11	27	39	43
9	Everton	42	9	7	5	35	24	5	7	9	27	40	42
10	Leeds	42	8	8	5	28	26	7	4	10	20	25	42
11	Leicester	42	8	9	4	30	28	4	9	8	17	32	42
12	Middlesbro	42	11	6	4	25	14	3	7	11	15	31	41
13	Birmingham	42	10	6	5	38	25	3	6	12	25	36	38
14	QP Rangers	42	10	7	4	31	21	3	5	13	16	31	38
15	Derby	42	9	9	3	36	18	0	10	11	14	37	37
16	Norwich	42	12	4	5	30	23	2	5	14	17	41	37
17	West Ham	42	9	6	6	28	23	2	8	11	18	42	36
18	Bristol City	42	8	7	6	25	19	3	6	12	13	29	35
19	Coventry	42	7	9	5	34	26	3	6	12	14	33	35
20	Sunderland	42	9	5	7	29	16	2	7	12	17	38	34
21	STOKE	42	9	8	4	21	16	1	6	14	7	35	34
22	Tottenham	42	9	7	5	26	20	3	2	16	22	52	33
		924	240	137	85	753	430	85	137	240	430	753	924

Appearances / Goals

Player	Appearances						Goals			
	Lge	Sub	LC	Sub	FAC	Sub	Lge	LC	FAC	Tot
Bithell, Brian	16	1					2			2
Bloor, Alan	37		2		1		1			1
Bowers, Ian	13	2	1	1	1		1			1
Conroy, Terry	34	2	2				5		1	6
Crooks, Garth	20	3	1		1	1	6			6
Dodd, Alan	42		2		1		1			1
Goodwin, Dave	12	1					1			1
Greenhoff, Jimmy	14						2		1	3
Hudson, Alan	11		2		2					
Johnson, Paul A	8									
Jones, Roger	2									
Lumsdon, John	11	1								
Mahoney, John	22		2							
Marsh, Jackie	16		2		1					
Pejic, Mike	21		2							
Robertson, Jimmy	9				1					
Ruggiero, John	12	1					2			2
Salmons, Geoff	33		2		2		1			1
Sheldon, Kevin	7		2		2					
Shilton, Peter	40		2		1					
Smith, Denis	30		2		1		2			2
Suddick, Alan	9						1			1
Thorley, Dennis	1									
Tudor, John	28	2			1		3			3
Waddington, Steve	14				1	1	1			1
25 players used	462	18	22	2	11	1	28		2	30

Odds & ends

Double wins: (1) Ipswich.

Double losses: (3) West Brom, Everton, Leicester.

Won from behind: (1) Middlesbro (h).

Lost from in front: (1) West Brom (a).

High spots: Doing the double over title contenders Ipswich.

The emergence of Garth Crooks.

Beating Leeds twice in League and Cup.

An improved home record on last season.

Low spots: Relegation.

Failing to win any of the five vital relegation battles late in the season.

Finishing only one point from safety.

Lowest goals scored total since 1890.

Lowest home league gate for 7 years v Coventry.

Ever-presents: (1) Dodd.

Hat-tricks: (0).

Leading scorer: (6) Terry Conroy, Garth Crooks.

No	Date		Att	Pos	Pt	F-A	H-T	Scorers, Times, and Referees	1	2	3	4	5	6	7	8	9	10	11	12 sub used
1	A	MANSFIELD			L	1-2	0-0	Lindsay 88p	Shilton	Lumsdon	**Lindsay**	**Kendall**	Smith	Dodd	Salmons	**Richardson**	**Gregory**	Conroy*	Crooks	Bloor
	20/8		*14,077*		0			*Syrett 50, Sharkey 55p*	*Arnold*	*Bird*	*Wood*	*McEwan*	*Mackenzie*	*Foster*	*Sharkey*	*Moss*	*Syrett*	*Hodgson*	*Miller*	
								Ref: K Burns	Crowd trouble before the game sets a nightmare scenario for City. Peter Morris' Promoted Stags have the tall Syrett giving Smith a torrid time. He nets after Dodd's miscontrol and Smith handles for the penalty. Crooks is tripped for Stoke's spot-kick which £40,000 Alec Lindsay scores.											
2	H	SOUTHAMPTON			W	1-0	0-0	Crooks 77	Shilton	Marsh	Lindsay	Kendall	Smith	Dodd	Goodwin	Richardson	Gregory	Waddington	Crooks	
	24/8		13,867		2				*Turner*	*Andr'szewski*	*Peach*	*Williams*	*Nichol*	*Pickering*	*Ball*	*Boyer*	*Osgood*	*Holmes*	*MacDougall*	
								Ref: M Peck	Stoke face up to a wall of Saints defenders. Howard Kendall's free-kick looks to have crossed the line, at least according to the Boothen End, but referee Peck waves play on. Crooks skips past three defenders and rounds Chris Turner to net the winner. Stoke are well worth the victory.											
3	H	BURNLEY		7	W	2-1	1-0	Lindsay 10p, Crooks 80	Shilton	Marsh	Lindsay	Kendall	Smith	Dodd	Goodwin	Richardson	Gregory	Waddington	Crooks	
	27/8		12,835	*22*	4			*Burke 82*	*Stevenson*	*Scott*	*Brennan*	*Noble*	*Robinson*	*Rodaway*	*Cochrane*	*Ingham*	*Smith**	*Flynn*	*Morley*	*Burke*
								Ref: W Gow	Stoke could have a hatful but are content just to win as Crooks stabs home the clincher when Stevenson spills Waddington's fierce drive. Paul Richardson produces a fine performance in midfield. Billy Rodaway fells Crooks for the penalty and Burke's header is against the run of play.											
4	A	MILLWALL		10	D	0-0	0-0		Jones	Marsh	Lindsay	Kendall	Smith	Dodd	Goodwin	Richardson	Gregory	Waddington	Crooks	
	3/9		*9,679*	*21*	5				*Johns*	*Donaldson*	*Walker*	*Brisley*	*Kitchener*	*Hazell*	*Hamilton*	*Seasman*	*Pearson*	*Lee*	*Chambers*	
								Ref: A Robinson	Shilton has a groin strain which may be related to Brian Clough's reported bid for him. Defences rule. Stoke's best efforts are from Dodd, who fires straight at Nicky Johns, and Gregory's fine 50-yard run and shot. Crooks hits the bar and Lee the inside of a post for Gordon Jago's men.											
5	H	SHEFFIELD UTD		3	W	4-0	3-0	Gregory 28, Kendall 30, Lindsay 43p, [Crooks 60]	Jones	Marsh	Lindsay	Kendall	Smith	Dodd	Waddington	Richardson	Gregory	Conroy	Crooks	
	10/9		14,217	*20*	7				*Brown*	*Franks*	*Calvert*	*Longhorn*	*Speight*	*Kenworthy*	*Cutbush*	*Campbell*	*Edwards*	*Hamson*	*Hamilton**	*Colquhoun*
								Ref: R Chadwick	Shilton is sold to Forest for £270,000 and City produce a fine performance to destroy United. Gregory heads his first for the club and is tripped for the penalty. Kendall curls home a free-kick while Crooks heads home. After Conroy is felled Lindsay wastes a second pen as Brown saves.											
6	A	HULL		4	D	0-0	0-0		Jones	Marsh	Lindsay	Kendall	Smith	Dodd	Richardson	Gregory	Conroy	Waddington	Crooks	
	17/9		*9,126*	*10*	8				*Wealands*	*Nisbet !*	*De Vries*	*Bremner*	*Croft*	*Roberts*	*Haigh*	*Galvin*	*Warboys*	*Bannister*	*Stewart*	
								Ref: P Willis	In a tetchy game four are booked and Nisbet walks (68 mins), after a second card for felling Crooks. Despite dominating City have few sights of goal. Richardson shoots over and Gregory hammers wide. Conroy has more trouble evading rogue Hull fans than defenders out on the wing.											
7	H	SUNDERLAND		5	D	0-0	0-0		Jones	Marsh	Lindsay	Kendall	Smith	Dodd	Waddington	Richardson	Gregory	Conroy	Crooks	
	24/9		18,820	*15*	9				*Siddall*	*Docherty*	*Bolton*	*Rowell*	*Waldron*	*Ashurst*	*Rostron*	*Elliott*	*Holden*	*Lee*	*Collins**	*Kerr*
								Ref: A Hughes	Waddington, Kendall, Richardson and Crooks are all guilty of wasting good chances as Stoke are on top in midfield against Jimmy Adamson's physical Rokerites. Bob Lee nets but the referee sees his fist not head connect. Stoke continue to press but Barry Siddall saves from Gregory.											
8	A	BOLTON		6	D	1-1	1-1	Kendall 20	Jones	Lumsdon	Lindsay	Kendall	Smith	Dodd	Waddington	Richardson*	Gregory	Conroy	Crooks	Johnson PA
	1/10		*20,799*	*3*	10			*Worthington 22*	*McDonagh*	*Nicholson*	*Dunne*	*Greaves*	*Walsh*	*Allardyce*	*Morgan*	*Whatmore*	*Worthington*	*Reid*	*Train*	
								Ref: J Hough	A physical game played against a backdrop of running battles between Police and Supporters on the terraces. Smith dominates at the back but Frank Worthington scores against City again. Kendall fires home from Crooks' pass. Crooks' floated effort is disallowed for Gregory's offside.											
9	A	OLDHAM		6	D	1-1	1-1	Smith 6	Jones	Lumsdon	Lindsay	Kendall	Smith	Dodd	Waddington	Johnson PA	Gregory	**McGroarty**	Crooks	
	4/10		*8,458*	*14*	11			*Halom 37*	*Ogden*	*Hoolickin*	*Holt*	*Bell*	*Edwards*	*Hurst*	*Valentine*	*Wood*	*Halom*	*Chapman*	*Young*	
								Ref: T Challinor	Stoke only draw despite Smith's early diving header. Ogden keeps out a repeat effort and also Crooks' low shot. Oldham find City's pace hard to deal with but McGroarty, Crooks and Gregory all have efforts blocked and Gregory has a goal disallowed as Jimmy Frizzell's men cling on.											
10	H	CRYSTAL PALACE		9	L	0-2	0-1		Jones	Lumsdon	Lindsay	Kendall	Smith	Dodd	Waddington	Richardson	Gregory	McGroarty*	Crooks	Johnson PA
	8/10		17,749	*7*	11			*Chatterton 38, Perrin 72*	*Burns*	*Hinshelwood*	*Sansom*	*Graham !*	*Cannon*	*Wall*	*Chatterton*	*Hilaire*	*Perrin*	*Bourne*	*Swindlehurst*	
								Ref: B Martin	City are shocked by Terry Venables' 10-man Palace who have Graham dismissed (66 mins) for persistently fouling Kendall. Chatterton touches home Bourne's cross. Perrin drives a fierce shot into the roof of Jones' net as bewildered City are left to rue misses by McGroarty and Crooks.											

No	Venue/Date	Att	Pos	Res	HT	Stoke Scorers	Opp Scorers	Referee
11	A BRIGHTON 15/10	13,290	7 5 13	W 1-0	0-0	Gregory 52		Ref: D Richardson
12	A BLACKBURN 22/10	12,221	9 7 13	L 1-2	1-0	Hird 31 (og)	Round 54, 65	Ref: C Seel
13	H TOTTENHAM 29/10	21,012	10 2 13	L 1-3	0-1	Crooks 75	Armstrong 29, 62, Pratt 77	Ref: J Hunting
14	A CARDIFF 5/11	8,428	13 18 13	L 0-2	0-1		Dwyer 42, Sayer 60	Ref: D Nippard
15	H FULHAM 12/11	14,155	12 16 15	W 2-0	2-0	Waddington 25, Crooks 40		Ref: K Hackett
16	A LUTON 19/11	5,384	9 10 17	W 2-1	2-0	Kendall 26, Crooks 38	Buckley 72	Ref: J Sewell
17	H BLACKPOOL 26/11	5132	10 6 17	L 1-2	0-1	Cook 90	Walsh 7, 75	Ref: K Styles
18	A NOTTS CO 3/12	9,309	13 6 17	L 0-2	0-1		Vinter 4, Hooks 76	Ref: A Jenkins
19	H BRISTOL ROV 10/12	10,513	11 19 19	W 3-2	1-2	Richardson 2, Crooks 74, Kendall 82p	Staniforth 25, Gould 35	Ref: A McDonald
20	A FULHAM 17/12	8,914	12 11 19	L 0-3	0-2		Evanson 2, Evans 3, Bullivant 54	Ref: A Robinson
21	H CHARLTON 26/12	14,345	11 16 21	W 4-0	0-0	Busby 68, Crooks 72, Scott 73, [Conroy 80]		Ref: N Midgley

11 — BRIGHTON
Stoke: Jones, Marsh*, Lindsay, Kendall, Smith, Waddington, Richardson, Gregory, Goodwin, Crooks, Bowers
Brighton: Steele, Cattlin, Williams, Horton, Winstanley, Lawrenson, Potts*, Ward, Mellor, Piper, O'Sullivan, Ruggiero / Scott, Wagstaffe
Ex-Stokie John Ruggiero plays for high-flying Brighton but an insipid game is won by Dave Gregory's superb volley. Goodwin and Crooks go close before Alan Mullery's Seagulls put Stoke under heavy pressure. Alan Dodd tackles both Mark Lawrenson and Stephen Piper at the death.

12 — BLACKBURN
Stoke: Jones, Lumsdon, Lindsay, Kendall, Smith, Waddington, Richardson, Gregory, Goodwin, Crooks, Scott
Blackburn: Butcher, Hird, Bailey, Metcalfe, Hird, Fazackerley, Lewis, Round*, Parkes, Taylor, Wagstaffe
City press from the off as Gregory and Crooks force Butcher into superb saves. Hird is hit on the back by a Conroy cross which flies in. Stoke sit back and Paul Round grabs two close-range strikes for Jim Smith's Rovers. Smith and Gregory go close as Stoke try to rectify the situation.

13 — TOTTENHAM
Stoke: Jones, Marsh, Lindsay, Kendall, Smith, Waddington, Richardson, Gregory, Goodwin, Crooks, Crooks
Tottenham: Daines, Naylor, Holmes, Hoddle, McAllister, Perryman, Pratt, McNab, Moores, Armstrong, Taylor
Lindsay's mis-hit back-pass gifts Spurs, fresh from beating Bristol Rov 9-0, the lead. Crooks' header makes a game of it. City waste two close-range chances. 45 are arrested as trouble flares when a Stoke penalty appeal is turned down at 1-2. Pratt heads home a Hoddle corner to seal it.

14 — CARDIFF
Stoke: Jones, Marsh, Lindsay, Kendall, Smith, Bloor, Richardson, Cook, Backus*, Crooks, Conroy
Cardiff: Irwin, Thomas, Pethard, Campbell, Went, Pontin, Dwyer, Grapes, Robson, Sayer, Giles
Stoke field two debutants, but come unstuck at Ninian Park. Dwyer scores from Cardiff's first real attack and the midfield goes to pieces. Sayer exposes City's lack of mobility in defence to round Jones for No 2. Marsh fires past the post with Stoke's only real chance of the second half.

15 — FULHAM
Stoke: Jones, Marsh, Lindsay, Kendall, Smith, Waddington, Bowers, Gregory, Busby, Crooks, Crooks
Fulham: Peyton, Evans, Strong, Bullivant, Lacy, Howe, Margerrison, Mitchell, Maybank, Evanson
Sir Stanley Matthews returns to the Vic for the first time since 1965 to see Stoke punish Bobby Campbell's weak Fulham. Debutant Viv Busby is in the thick of things, setting up Waddington. Then Crooks chips Gerry Peyton. Busby has a shot cleared off the line and Marsh hits the post.

16 — LUTON
Stoke: Jones, Marsh, Lindsay, Kendall, Smith, Waddington, Bowers*, Gregory, Busby, Crooks, Richardson
Luton: Aleksic, Price, Buckley, West, Faulkner, McNichol, Husband, Futcher R, Fuccillo, Heale*, Stein
Stoke sell Geoff Salmons to Leicester and Dave Goodwin to Mansfield to pay for the recent signings. Plenty of action at Luton where each side has a goal disallowed before Kendall rounds off a neat move. Crooks shoots beyond Milja Aleksic to seal City's first away win in 13 attempts.

17 — BLACKPOOL
Stoke: Jones, Marsh, Lindsay, Kendall, Smith, Waddington, Bowers, Gregory*, Busby, Crooks, Cook
Blackpool: Ward, Gardner, Harrison, Hart, Suddaby, McEwan, Ainscow, Weston, Walsh, Hatton, Groves
Stoke are beaten by Allan Brown's Blackpool, who go ahead through Walsh's long-range piledriver and then seal it as he pokes a Hatton cross home. Cook's late left-footed finish doesn't disguise Stoke's lack of promotion credentials as they continue to struggle against top eight teams.

18 — NOTTS CO
Stoke: Jones, Marsh, Lindsay, Kendall, Smith, Waddington, Richardson, Cook, Busby, Crooks, Busby
Notts Co: McManus, Richards, O'Brien, Chapman, Stubbs, McVay, Carter, Hooks, Vinter, Birchenall, Mann
City sport an unfamiliar orange and sky blue kit but end the day frustrated. Mick Vinter's close-range finish and Paul Hooks' superb effort seal the points for Ron Fenton's men. Busby has a goal disallowed, O'Brien clears off the line, then McManus dives full length to save from Marsh.

19 — BRISTOL ROV
Stoke: Jones, Marsh, Scott, Kendall, Smith, Dodd, Johnson PA, Richardson, Busby, Conroy, Busby
Bristol Rov: Thomas, Aitken, Bater, Day, Taylor, Prince, Gould, Williams, Powell*, Staniforth, Barry, Hendrie
City are shocked by Rovers' breakaway goals after Richardson angles past Thomas for an early lead. Profligate Stoke get lucky when the ref spots a handball and Kendall converts. Geoff Scott, starting a game for the first time, sets up Crooks' headed goal before hitting the bar himself.

20 — FULHAM
Stoke: Jones, Marsh, Scott, Kendall, Smith, Dodd, Gregory, Richardson, Busby, Conroy, Busby
Fulham: Peyton, Evans, Strong, Money, Hatter, Lacy, Greenaway* Gale, Mitchell, Evanson, Margerrison, Bullivant
Fulham strike early as Scott's clearance falls to Evanson and then Ray Evans bends in a free-kick. Bullivant buries Gale's knockdown as Stoke wilt under heavy pressure. Marsh and Richardson test Gerry Peyton from long range and Crooks nets but is given offside. City are second best.

21 — CHARLTON
Stoke: Jones, Dodd, Lindsay, Kendall, Smith, Bloor, Waddington, Gregory, Busby, Scott, Crooks
Charlton: Wood, Berry, Shaw, Tydeman, Campbell, Dugdale, Powell, Gritt, Flanagan, Peacock, Abrahams
City seem out of luck against Andy Nelson's Charlton until Alan Bloor, on his return, sparks a goal rush. His 25-yarder is parried by Wood but only out to Busby. Crooks heads Conroy's cross home and Scott hits a scorcher into the roof of the net. Conroy bursts through to make it four.

LEAGUE DIVISION 2

Manager: Eastham ⇒ Alan Durban — SEASON 1977-78

Match summary

No	Date		Att	Pos	Pt	Res	F-A	H-T	Scorers, Times, and Referees
22	A	ORIENT 27/12	6,192	14 *14*	21	L	0-2	0-0	Kitchen 78, 89 — Ref: R Challis
23	A	SOUTHAMPTON 31/12	23,460	15 *3*	21	L	0-1	0-1	Boyer 26 — Ref: A Gunn
24	H	MANSFIELD 2/1	13,834	14 *20*	22	D	1-1	1-1	McGroarty 26 / Goodwin 30 — Ref: K Walmsley
25	A	BURNLEY 14/1	11,282	15 *21*	22	L	0-1	0-0	Kindon 71 — Ref: G Owen
26	H	BOLTON 25/2	19,280	18 *2*	23	D	0-0	0-0	Ref: T Mills
27	A	CRYSTAL PALACE 4/3	14,702	15 *8*	25	W	1-0	0-0	Busby 55 — Ref: A Glasson
28	H	HULL 8/3	13,890	14 *19*	27	W	1-0	0-0	O'Callaghan 78 — Ref: J Butcher
29	A	BRIGHTON 11/3	24,797	15 *4*	27	L	1-2	0-2	Richardson 60 / Potts 2, Sayer 5 — Ref: E Hughes
30	A	SHEFFIELD UTD 14/3	12,950	13 *14*	29	W	2-1	1-0	Kendall 39, Crooks 72 / Franks 88 — Ref: J Sewell
31	H	BLACKBURN 18/3	18,989	12 *5*	31	W	4-2	0-0	Scott 55, Crooks 66, 67, 90p / Radford 65, Lewis 85 — Ref: G Nolan / R Pearson

Line-ups (top row = Stoke; italic row = opponents)

No	1	2	3	4	5	6	7	8	9	10	11	12 sub used
22	Jones	Dodd	Lindsay	Kendall	Smith	Bloor	Waddington	Conroy	Busby	Scott*	Crooks	Cook
	Jackson	*Fisher*	*Roffey*	*Grealish*	*Gray*	*Roeder*	*Chiedozie*	*Bennett*	*Mayo*	*Kitchen*	*Glover**	*Clarke*
23	Jones	Dodd	Bowers	Kendall	Smith	Bloor	Waddington	Cook	Busby	Scott*	Crooks	Backos
	Wells	*Waldron*	*Peach*	*Williams**	*Nichol*	*Pickering*	*Ball*	*Holmes*	*Boyer*	*Sharpe*	*MacDougall*	*Hebberd*
24	Jones	Marsh	Bowers	Kendall	Smith	Bloor	Waddington	Cook	Busby	McGroarty	Crooks	
	Arnold	*Bird**	*Foster B*	*Sharkey*	*Foster C*	*Wood*	*Miller*	*Goodwin*	*Syrett*	*Hodgson*	*Aston*	*Cooke*
25	Jones	Marsh	Scott	Kendall	Dodd	Bloor	Waddington	Gregory	Conroy	Johnson PA	Bowers	Crooks
	Stevenson	*Scott*	*Brennan*	*Noble*	*Rodaway*	*Thompson*	*Cochrane*	*Ingham*	*Fletcher*	*Kindon*	*Morley*	
26	Jones	Marsh	Walsh	Greaves	Smith	Dodd	Waddington	Richardson	Busby	Conroy	Conroy	
	McDonagh	*Ritson*			*Jones P*	*Allardyce*	*Morgan*	*Whatmore*	*Train**	*Reid*	*Worthington*	*Nicholson*
27	Jones	Marsh	Scott	Kendall	Smith	Dodd	Waddington	Richardson	Busby	Crooks	Conroy	Walsh
	Burns	*Hinshelwood*	*Sansom*	*Holder*	*Nicholas*	*Cannon*	*Hilaire*	*Graham*	*Swindlehurst*	*Harkouk**	*Silkman*	
28	Jones	Marsh	Scott	Kendall	Smith	Dodd	Waddington	Richardson	Busby*	Crooks	Conroy	O'Callaghan
	Blackburn	*Daniel*	*De Vries*	*Bremner*	*Dobson*	*Nisbet*	*Haigh*	*Gibson*	*Warboys*	*Hawley*	*Lord**	*Sunley*
29	Jones	Marsh	Scott	Kendall	Smith	Dodd	Waddington	Richardson	Busby*	Crooks	Conroy	O'Callaghan
	Steele	*Clark*	*Williams*	*Horton*	*Rollings*	*Lawrenson*	*Potts*	*Ward**	*Maybank*	*Sayer*	*O'Sullivan*	*Poskett*
30	Jones	Marsh	Scott	Kendall	Smith	Dodd	Waddington	Richardson	Busby*	Crooks	Cook	O'Callaghan
	Brown	*Cutbush*	*Calvert*	*Flynn*	*Colquhoun**	*Franks*	*Speight*	*Stainrod*	*Campbell*	*Kenworthy*	*Edwards*	*Guy*
31	Jones	Marsh	Scott	Kendall	Smith	Dodd	Waddington	Richardson	O'Callaghan	Crooks	Gregory	
	Butcher	*Hird*	*Curtis*	*Metcalfe*	*Keeley*	*Waddington*	*Brotherston**	*Taylor*	*Radford*	*Parkes*	*Wagstaffe*	*Lewis*

Match reports

22 ORIENT — The lowest league crowd to watch a Stoke match for 27 years sees Peter Kitchen sink Stoke. In an even game Roffey crosses for the first then Kitchen beats two defenders to notch a great second. Waddington's early shot is City's only effort on target. The goals have suddenly dried up.

23 SOUTHAMPTON — Lawrie McMenemy's Saints snuff out City by playing Waldron as an extra defender. Phil Boyer flicks in Holmes' cross to clinch it. Stoke have little to offer bar Kendall's header saved by Wells. Geoff Scott cuts his eye in a penalty area melee. Smith heads over from a Bowers free-kick.

24 MANSFIELD — Rod Arnold allows Jim McGroarty's shot through his fingers for the youngster's first senior goal. The luck evens up when Dave Goodwin, ex-Stoke, sees the ball hit his thigh, loop up and land inside the far post. Mansfield, with 2 wins in 5, are happy with a point in a low key match.

25 BURNLEY — Patched up Stoke, under caretaker boss Alan A'Court after George Eastham's resignation, flounder against Burnley. Nippy Steve Kindon flicks home the deserved winner. Dave Gregory fires straight at Alan Stevenson. Harry Potts' Clarets are off the bottom for the first time this season.

26 BOLTON — Stoke land Shrewsbury boss Alan Durban after being accused of trying to poach Newcastle's Bill McGarry. Both teams struggle to make play flow in terrible conditions but City gradually gain the initiative. Their spirit is nearly rewarded by Busby's late header but McDonagh tips over.

27 CRYSTAL PALACE — Stoke shock the fancied Eagles when Viv Busby rounds Burns. Palace attack desperately but City hold firm with Smith outstanding. Crooks' volley clips the bar and Busby forces Cannon to clear his shot off the line. Graham sets up Barry Silkman but he contrives to miss an open goal.

28 HULL — Big Brendan O'Callaghan wins a place in history after scoring with his first touch on his arrival as sub. He heads home Paul Richardson's left wing corner eleven seconds after taking the field. Hard-running City finally overcome Bobby Collins' men. Peter Daniel nods just past late on.

29 BRIGHTON — Stoke's gold shorts don't exactly dazzle as they are two down before they wake up. Potts' cross curles into the far corner and then Sayer cracks past Roger Jones from 25 yards. Only after O'Callaghan's arrival on 30 mins do City threaten. Richardson fires home from 20 yards via a post.

30 SHEFFIELD UTD — Roger Jones saves John Flynn's 16th-minute penalty and Stainrod's follow up to give Stoke a platform for victory. Howard Kendall sweeps in Waddington's cross for the opener. Crooks celebrates his 20th birthday by nodding home unmarked. Blades boss Jimmy Sirrel is not amused.

31 BLACKBURN — A breathless second half as Scott cracks home from near the touchline. Crooks' first two are set up by Gregory. Then he is flattened by Hird for the penalty which completes his first hat-trick. Referee Nolan retires hurt (replaced by Mr Pearson) before Lewis scores to make a game of it.

No	Venue	Date	Opponent	Attendance	Pos	Res	Pts	Score	HT	Scorers / Opponent scorers / Referee
32	A	22/3	TOTTENHAM	30,646	14	L	31	1-3	1-0	Crooks 16 / McAllister 54, Lee 69, 90 / Ref: E Read
33	H	25/3	ORIENT	14,595	10	W	33	5-1	4-0	Kendall 3, Crooks 9, Gregory 20, Mayo 90 (Waddington 35, 73) / Ref: A Hughes
34	A	28/3	CHARLTON	7,956	10	L	33	2-3	1-3	O'Callaghan 30, Crooks 48 / Peacock 5, Robinson 6, 34 / Ref: A Gunn
35	H	1/4	CARDIFF	14,804	9	W	35	2-0	2-0	Waddington 5, O'Callaghan 32 / Ref: G Flint
36	A	4/4	SUNDERLAND	11,161	10	L	35	0-1	0-1	Kerr 22 / Ref: D Richardson
37	A	8/4	BLACKPOOL	2,261	10	D	36	1-1	1-1	O'Callaghan 15 / Wilson 18 / Ref: K McNally
38	H	12/4	MILLWALL	12,370	8	W	38	2-1	1-1	O'Callaghan 40, Crooks 66 / Seasman 10 / Ref: N Glover
39	H	15/4	LUTON	15,544	8	D	39	0-0	0-0	Ref: N Midgley
40	A	22/4	BRISTOL ROV	6,182	9	L	39	1-4	1-1	Crooks 32 / Williams 8, Randall 50, 52, White 88 / Ref: K Burns
41	H	26/4	OLDHAM	1,260	9	W	41	3-0	1-0	Kendall 44, O'Callaghan 70, Busby 80 / Ref: P Reeves
42	H	29/4	NOTTS CO	13,789	7	D	42	1-1	0-0	Crooks 84 / O'Brien 60 / Ref: A Porter

Home average: 15,114
Away average: 12,909
Average: 15,114

Line-ups (Stoke City / Opponent)

32 v Tottenham — Stoke: Jones, Marsh, Scott, Kendall, Smith, Dodd, Waddington, Richardson, O'Callaghan, Crooks*, Gregory, Thorley. Tottenham: Daines, Stead, Holmes, Hoddle, McAllister, Perryman, Pratt, McNab, Jones, Lee, Taylor.

Stoke control the first half and deservedly lead through Crooks' superb finish to O'Callaghan's flick on. Keith Burkinshaw's Spurs gradually take a grip in midfield. Hoddle sets up McAllister and Lee to beat Jones. City pile forward in numbers and Colin Lee scores on the breakaway.

33 v Orient — Stoke: Jones, Marsh, Scott, Kendall, Smith, Dodd, Waddington, Richardson, O'Callaghan, Crooks, Gregory, Busby. Orient: Jackson, Fisher, Roffey*, Payne*, Hoadley, Roeder, Godfrey, Gray, Mayo, Kitchen, Grealish, Clarke.

City overwhelm Orient with Kendall sweeping home Crooks' cross and Crooks flashing home a drive. Gregory's header and Waddington's tap in make it plain sailing. Waddington is on hand to turn the ball home after John Jackson fumbles O'Callaghan's shot to complete the nap hand.

34 v Charlton — Stoke: Jones, Marsh, Scott, Kendall*, Smith, Dodd, Waddington, Richardson, O'Callaghan, Crooks, Gregory, Busby. Charlton: Wood, Berry, Shaw, Tydeman, Shipperley, Dugdale, Powell, Robinson, Flanagan, Peacock, Brisley*, Gritt.

In a rip-roaring game Stoke have Charlton manager, Andy Nelson's nerves jangling after the Addicks seem to be in control. O'Callaghan prods home and Crooks volleys into the far corner to keep City in it. George Wood scrambles across to beat away Crooks' header in the pouring rain.

35 v Cardiff — Stoke: Jones, Marsh, Scott, Kendall, Smith, Dodd, Waddington, Richardson, O'Callaghan, Crooks, Busby. Cardiff: Healey, Thomas, Campbell*, Pethard, Larmour, Grapes, Dwyer, Williams, Went, Giles, Byrne.

Steve Waddington hammers home the rebound from Busby's shot and Big Bren volleys home a Busby cross to end the game as a contest. The referee, seemingly about to book Geoff Scott, actually takes a hanky out of his pocket and wipes mud from the astonished defender's left eye!

36 v Sunderland — Stoke: Jones, Marsh, Scott*, Kendall, Smith, Dodd, Waddington, Richardson, O'Callaghan, Crooks, Busby, Conroy. Sunderland: Siddall, Henderson, Bolton, Kerr, Clarke, Ashurst, Greenwood, Docherty, Lee, Rostron*, Rowell, Gilbert.

Steve Waddington's frustration sums up Stoke's night. He has a goal disallowed for Kendall being offside and when Henderson brings Conroy down he is booked for claiming a penalty rather too vehemently. Bobby Kerr breaks away to slot home the winner for Jimmy Adamson's side.

37 v Blackpool — Stoke: Jones, Marsh, Scott, Kendall, Smith, Dodd, Waddington, Richardson, O'Callaghan, Crooks, Busby, Conroy. Blackpool: Ward, Gardner, Milligan, Tong, McEwan, Suddaby, Chandler*, Ainscow, Wilson, Hatton, Waldron, Groves.

O'Callaghan perfectly times his leap to head in from Kendall's chip but Wilson also heads home for Pool. City are foiled by the woodwork in a hard working performance typifying Durban's new system. Crooks and O'Callaghan both hit the bar while Smith and Dodd both head wide.

38 v Millwall — Stoke: Jones, Marsh, Scott, Kendall, Smith, Dodd, Waddington, Richardson, O'Callaghan, Crooks, Busby, Conroy. Millwall: Johns, Donaldson, Moore, Allen, Kitchener, Hazell, Lee, Seasman, Pearson*, Mehmet, Chambers.

George Petchey's Millwall take a shock lead when Seasman buries at the third attempt. But they sit back and City unlock their sweeper system. Nicky Johns is booed for his timewasting tactics but Big Bren nods in Richardson's free-kick and Crooks steers home a driven cross to win it.

39 v Luton — Stoke: Jones, Marsh, Scott, Kendall, Smith, Dodd, Waddington, Richardson, O'Callaghan, Crooks*, Busby*, Cook. Luton: Aleksic, Price, Carr, Hill, McNichol, Futcher P, Stein, West, Futcher R, Fuccillo, Boersma.

City are to erect barriers at the reconstructed Stoke End after sporadic outbreaks of trouble through the season. Harry Haslam's Luton frustrate Stoke. O'Callaghan hits the post. Milija Aleksic saves from Richardson. Ron Futcher has a goal ruled out for offside. Dodd clears off the line.

40 v Bristol Rovers — Stoke: Jones, Marsh, Scott, Kendall, Smith, Dodd, Waddington, Busby, O'Callaghan, Crooks*, Conroy, Gregory. Bristol Rov: Thomas, Aitken, Bater, Williams, Harding, Prince, Barry, Pulis, Gould, White, Randall.

Rovers dampen Stoke's attacking ardour. Crooks latches on to Aitken's poor back-pass to level Williams' lob. Paul Randall's burst comes after Terry Conroy hits the bar and fires just past the far post. Steve White is supplied by Randall for the late clincher. Mid-table obscurity beckons.

41 v Oldham — Stoke: Jones, Marsh, Scott, Kendall, Smith, Dodd, Richardson*, Busby, O'Callaghan, Crooks, Waddington. Oldham: Platt, Hoolickin, Edwards S, Bell, Edwards P / Hurst, Gardner, Taylor, Young, Halom, Hilton.

Alec Lindsay, Des Backos and Alan Bloor are freed as Durban reshapes his squad for next season. City romp home against Oldham who have Paul Edwards shown the red card after the final whistle. Busby and O'Callaghan net running headers as Platt's aerial ability is cruelly exposed.

42 v Notts Co — Stoke: Jones, Marsh, Scott*, Kendall, Smith, Dodd, Richardson, O'Callaghan, Crooks, Conroy, Waddington. Notts Co: McManus, Richards, O'Brien, Chapman, Stubbs, Hunt, Carter, McVay, Bradd, Benjamin, Vinter.

Jimmy Sirrel's Magpies ensure the season's finale is far from grand with a gritty show. O'Brien's volley rocks City who are stung into action. O'Callaghan forces McManus to tip over then Crooks drives Busby's pass into the corner. Stoke claim a late penalty when Stubbs fells Busby.

LEAGUE DIVISION 2 (CUP-TIES)

Manager: Eastham ⇨ Alan Durban　　**SEASON 1977-78**

League Cup

			Att		F-A	H-T	Scorers, Times, and Referees
2	A	BRISTOL CITY	7 L		0-1	0-1	Mabbutt 8
29/8			17,877 1:18				Ref: M Sinclair

	1	2	3	4	5	6	7	8	9	10	11	12 sub used
	Shilton	Dodd	Marsh	Kendall	Smith	Bloor	Goodwin	Richardson	Gregory	Waddington	Crooks	
	Shaw	*Sweeney*	*Merrick*	*Gow**	*Collier*	*Hunter*	*Tainton*	*Ritchie*	*Mabbutt*	*Cormack*	*Whitehead*	*Gillies*

Kevin Mabbutt nods in Ritchie's cross on his debut to dump City out of the Cup. In a tame game somehow four players are booked. Whitehead is once again the main threat. He supplies Tainton and Shilton tips round at full stretch. Crooks bravely heads wide but City deserve to go out.

FA Cup

			Att		F-A	H-T	Scorers, Times, and Referees
3	H	TILBURY	15 W		4-0	3-0	Cook 5, 85, Greg'ry 25, Wadding'n 28
7/1			16,301 IS:20				Ref: J Sewell

	1	2	3	4	5	6	7	8	9	10	11	12 sub used
	Jones	Marsh	Lindsay	Kendall	Dodd	Bowers	Waddington	Gregory	Busby*	Scott	Cook	Crooks
	Armstrong	*Partner*	*Marjoram*	*Sullivan*	*Barnet*	*Linton*	*Dennis*	*Russell*	*Wallace J*	*Gray**	*Wallace C*	*Knowles*

City wrap it up inside the first half hour. Cook catches Armstrong napping for the opener. Tilbury's packed defence cannot cope with Marsh's right-wing runs. His crosses lead to Gregory and Waddington's volleys. Jeff Cook rounds it off by sliding home Dave Gregory's cross. Easy.

			Att		F-A	H-T	Scorers, Times, and Referees
4	H	BLYTH SPARTANS	15 L		2-3	0-1	Busby 56, Crooks 58
6/2			18,765 NPL:6				Johnson 11, 88, Carney S 75
							Ref: G Nolan

	1	2	3	4	5	6	7	8	9	10	11	12 sub used
	Jones	Marsh	Lindsay	Kendall	Dodd	Bloor	Waddington	Scott	Busby	Conroy*	Crooks	Cook
	Clarke	*Waterson*	*Guthrie*	*Adler**	*Scott*	*Dixon*	*Shoulder*	*Houghton*	*Johnson*	*Carney S*	*Carney R*	*Varty*

City struggle on a terrible pitch. Jones drops the ball for the first. Battling Ron Guthrie defines Blyth's spirit. Terry Johnson's shot completes a famous win. City fans applaud Spartans on a lap of honour. Brian Slane's men are the third non-league side in 50 years to reach the 5th Round.

Final League Table

	Team	P	W	D	L	F	A	W	D	L	F	A	Pts
				Home					Away				
1	Bolton	42	16	4	1	39	14	8	6	7	24	19	58
2	Southampton	42	15	4	2	44	16	7	9	5	26	23	57
3	Tottenham	42	13	7	1	50	19	7	9	5	33	30	56
4	Brighton	42	15	5	1	43	21	7	7	7	20	17	56
5	Blackburn	42	12	4	5	33	16	4	9	8	23	44	45
6	Sunderland	42	11	6	4	36	17	3	10	8	31	42	44
7	STOKE	42	13	5	3	38	16	3	5	13	15	33	42
8	Oldham	42	9	10	2	32	20	4	6	11	22	38	42
9	Crys Palace	42	9	7	5	31	20	4	8	9	19	27	41
10	Fulham	42	9	8	4	32	19	5	5	11	17	30	41
11	Burnley	42	11	6	4	35	20	4	4	13	21	44	40
12	Sheffield Utd	42	13	4	4	38	20	3	4	14	24	51	40
13	Luton	42	11	4	6	35	20	3	6	12	19	32	38
14	Orient	42	8	11	2	30	20	2	7	12	13	29	38
15	Notts Co	42	10	9	2	36	22	1	7	13	18	40	38
16	Millwall	42	8	8	5	23	22	4	6	11	26	37	38
17	Charlton	42	11	7	4	38	27	2	6	13	17	41	38
18	Bristol Rov	42	10	6	4	40	26	3	5	13	21	51	38
19	Cardiff	42	12	6	3	32	23	1	6	14	19	48	38
20	Blackpool	42	7	8	6	35	25	5	5	11	24	35	37
21	Mansfield	42	6	9	9	30	34	4	5	12	19	35	31
22	Hull	42	6	6	9	23	25	2	6	13	11	27	28
		924	235	141	86	773	462	86	141	235	462	773	924

Odds & ends

Double wins: (1) Sheffield Utd.

Double losses: (1) Tottenham.

Won from behind: (2) Bristol Rov (h), Millwall (h).

Lost from in front: (2) Blackburn (a), Tottenham (a).

High spots: Garth Crooks' 19 goals. Brendan O'Callaghan scoring after 11 seconds of his debut. Finishing in 7th spot after such a poor previous season. Stability under new manager Alan Durban.

Low spots: Knocked out of the FA Cup by minnows Blyth Spartans. Failing to beat two relegated teams, Blackpool and Mansfield. Only winning three games away from home. The continued sale of players to pay for the new stands being built. Only finishing 5 points clear of relegation.

Player of the Year: Howard Kendall (first ever!).

Ever-presents: (2) Howard Kendall, Alan Dodd.

Hat-tricks: (1) Garth Crooks.

Leading scorer: (19) Garth Crooks.

Appearances and Goals

Player	Appearances						Goals			
	Lge	Sub	LC	Sub	FAC	Sub	Lge	LC	FAC	Tot
Backos, Des	1									
Bloor, Alan	5	1	1		1					
Bowers, Ian	6	1			1					
Busby, Viv	21	1	1		2		3	1		4
Conroy, Terry	20	2			1	1	1			1
Cook, Jeff	5	3			1	1	1	2		3
Crooks, Garth	41	1	1		1		18	1		19
Dodd, Alan	42				2	1				
Goodwin, Dave	4									
Gregory, David	22	1	1		1		3	1		4
Johnson, Paul A	3	2								
Jones, Roger	39		1		2					
Kendall, Howard	42		1		2		7			7
Lindsay, Alec	20		1		2		3			3
Lumsdon, John	5									
Marsh, Jackie	34		1		2					
McGroarty, Jim	3									
O'Callaghan, Brendan	13	2	1				1			1
Richardson, Paul	32	1	1		1		6			6
Salmons, Geoff	1									
Scott, Geoff	23	1			2		2			2
Shilton, Peter	3				1					
Smith, Denis	41	1					1			1
Thorley, Dennis		1								
Waddington, Steve	36	2	1		2		4	1		5
(own-goals)							1			1
26 players used	462	20	11		22	2	53	6		59

LEAGUE DIVISION 2

Manager: Alan Durban

SEASON 1978-79

No	Date	Att	Pos	Pt	F-A	H-T	Scorers, Times, and Referees	1	2	3	4	5	6	7	8	9	10	11	12 sub used
1	A CAMBRIDGE 19/8	7,489		W 2	1-0	0-0	Richardson 87 — Ref: A Grey	Jones	Marsh	Scott	Kendall	Smith	Doyle	Waddington	Irvine	O'Callaghan*	Crooks	Richardson	Busby
	(opp)							*Webster*	*Howard*	*Smith*	*Streete*	*Fallon*	*Graham*	*Cazens*	*Buckley**	*Biley*	*Finney*	*Murray*	*Adams*
2	H CARDIFF 23/8	16,001		W 4	2-0	0-0	Smith 75, Busby 85 — Ref: G Owen	Jones	Marsh	Scott	Kendall	Smith	Doyle	Waddington*	Irvine	Busby	Crooks	Richardson	Dodd
	(opp)							*Davies*	*Thomas*	*Pethard*	*Campbell*	*Went*	*Roberts*	*Burns*	*Giles*	*Dwyer*	*Bishop*	*Byrne*	
3	H MILLWALL 26/8	15,176	1 / 13	W 6	2-0	0-0	Busby 77, Crooks 82p — Ref: R Chadwick	Jones	Marsh	Scott	Kendall	Smith	Doyle	Conroy*	Irvine	Busby	Crooks	Richardson	O'Callaghan
	(opp)							*Cuff*	*Donaldson*	*Moore*	*Allen*	*Tagg*	*Hazell*	*Hamilton*	*Walker*	*Mitchell*	*Pearson**	*Lee*	*Mehmet*
4	A OLDHAM 2/9	11,297	1 / 7	D 7	1-1	0-0	Richardson 46 / Steel 51 — Ref: C Seel	Jones	Marsh	Scott	Kendall	Smith	Doyle	Dodd	Irvine	O'Callaghan	Crooks*	Richardson	Busby
	(opp)							*McDonnell*	*Bernard**	*Blair*	*Gardner*	*Hicks*	*Hurst*	*Steel*	*Halom*	*Young*	*Chapman*	*Heaton*	*Bell*
5	A ORIENT 9/9	6,587	1 / 17	W 9	1-0	0-0	O'Callaghan 84 — Ref: A Glasson	Jones	Marsh	Scott	Kendall	Smith	Doyle	Dodd	Irvine	O'Callaghan	Crooks*	Richardson	Busby
	(opp)							*Jackson*	*Fisher*	*Roffey*	*Grealish*	*Gray*	*Went*	*Chiedozie*	*Hughton*	*Mayo*	*Kitchen*	*Bennett*	
6	A PRESTON 23/9	14,051	2 / 17	W 11	1-0	1-0	Kendall 24 — Ref: K Styles	Jones	Marsh	Scott	Kendall	Smith	Doyle	Dodd	Irvine	O'Callaghan	Crooks	Conroy*	Busby
	(opp)							*Tunks*	*McMahon**	*Wilson*	*Doyle*	*Baxter*	*Burns*	*Potts*	*Haslegrave*	*Coleman*	*Smith*	*Bruce*	*Cochrane*
7	H BRIGHTON 27/9	22,201	1 / 4	D 12	2-2	1-0	Crooks 45p, O'Callaghan 50 / Ward 50, Maybank 85 — Ref: B Martin	Jones	Marsh	Scott	Kendall	Smith	Doyle	Dodd	Irvine	O'Callaghan	Crooks	Richardson*	Busby
	(opp)							*Steele*	*Tiler*	*Williams*	*Horton*	*Rollings*	*Lawrenson*	*Ryan*	*Ward*	*Maybank*	*Clark**	*O'Sullivan*	*Sayer*
8	H CRYSTAL PALACE 30/9	19,079	1 / 2	D 13	1-1	1-0	Irvine 5 / Murphy 70 — Ref: T Mills	Jones	Marsh	Scott	Kendall	Smith	Doyle	Dodd	Irvine*	O'Callaghan	Crooks	Busby	**Johnson P**
	(opp)							*Burridge*	*Hinshelwood*	*Sansom*	*Chatterton*	*Cannon*	*Gilbert*	*Nicholas*	*Murphy*	*Swindlehurst*	*Elwiss*	*Hilaire*	
9	A FULHAM 7/10	12,534	2 / 3	L 13	0-2	0-1	Greenaway 2, Gale 70 — Ref: B Stevens	Jones	Marsh	Scott*	Kendall	Smith	Doyle	Dodd	Heath	O'Callaghan	Crooks	Richardson	Busby
	(opp)							*Peyton*	*Evans*	*Strong*	*Lock*	*Money*	*Gale**	*Bullivant*	*Davies*	*Guthrie*	*Margerrison*	*Greenaway*	*Evanson*
10	H BURNLEY 14/10	18,437	2 / 11	W 15	3-1	2-1	Richardson 14, Kendall 28, Irvine 55 / Ingham 16 — Ref: G Flint	Jones	Marsh	Johnson P	Kendall	Smith	Doyle	Dodd	Irvine	O'Callaghan	Richardson	Crooks	Busby
	(opp)							*Stevenson*	*Scott*	*Brennan*	*Noble*	*Thomson*	*Rodaway*	*Smith*	*Ingham*	*Fletcher*	*Kindon*	*James*	

Match reports

1. Mike Doyle makes a winning start after a £50,000 move from Man City. Sammy Irvine also impresses on his debut in the sweltering heat. Alan Biley misses John Docherty's sides' only chance. Paul Richardson tips home Kendall's fierce shot in front of a gate made up of 50% Stokies.

2. Stoke leave it late to beat 18-year-old keeper John Davies. Waddington is denied by his outstretched arm after 10 mins. Richardson, Doyle and Crooks pepper the goal. Finally Smith heads into the top corner and Busby's volley gives the scoreline a resemblance of Stoke's superiority.

3. City batter away at George Petchey's defence but are frustrated until Busby races onto O'Callaghan's flick to net. Crooks is fouled and buries the spot-kick himself. Busby then has a goal disallowed and O'Callaghan misses from close in as Stoke dominate. A quick return on the cards?

4. Ex-Stokie Mike Bernard tames Stoke's midfield in an explosive encounter which sees four booked and Crooks limp off. Richardson cracks one in from 18 yards but City lose their 100% record to Jim Steel's header. McDonnell saves well from Kendall. Durban is manager of the month.

5. The pressure builds on Jimmy Bloomfield's Orient as Irvine and O'Callaghan have efforts cleared off the line. Jackson saves well from Marsh. Big Bren rewards City's patience with a stooping header from Richardson's cross. Chiedozie has O's best effort cleared off the line by Irvine.

6. Howard Kendall sinks his old club with a rare headed goal from Conroy's cross. Garth Crooks should have a penalty when tripped by Steve Doyle. He then twists to blast just over. Ex-Stokie Haslegrave tests Jones from a free-kick but Stoke's composure is typified by Dodd and Doyle.

7. Alan Dodd produces a fantastic display to hold City together after the other three midfielders are injured. Rollings handles for Crooks' penalty. O'Callaghan seems to have earnt Stoke the points with his wonderful volley but Teddy Maybank nods in the rebound from O'Sullivan's effort.

8. Stoke start the better and Irvine cracks home from 25 yards. Palace press forward with Chatterton and Swindlehurst threatening but Crooks and Irvine have good chances to seal it but, as Murphy is about to be subbed, he lobs Jones from 40 yards. Durban is manager of the month again.

9. City are unsettled by the pace and verve of Bobby Campbell's men. Greenaway fires past Jones, then Gale heads home Evans' free-kick. Scott twists his ankle and will be out for a fortnight. Stoke resort to long balls to O'Callaghan which Gale laps up. The first defeat of the campaign.

10. Paul Johnson replaces the injured Scott and inspires City to a good win. He releases Irvine to cross for Richardson to head home. Then Crooks knocks back his centre for Kendall. Irvine cheekily lobs the stranded Alan Stevenson. Mike Doyle nearly adds a fourth with a 30-yard cracker.

21/10 · A WEST HAM · 0-0 1-1 · 2 D 5 16

Team: Jones, Marsh, Scott, Kendall, Smith, Doyle, Dodd, Irvine, O'Callaghan, Richardson, Crooks
Subs/Opp: Ferguson, McDowell, Brush, Holland, Taylor T, Bonds, Curtishley, Devonshire, Cross, Brooking, Robson

Richardson 8 / Brooking 85
Ref: T Buns

In a tough game four are booked and Bobby Ferguson injures his shoulder. Doyle and Smith snuff out Cross's threat until he releases Brooking to volley home on the run. City snatch a late goal through Richardson's drive in a dramatic finale. John Lyall pays tribute to Stoke's resilience.

---

12 · 28/10 · H SHEFFIELD LTD · 1 W 2-1 1-0 · 1,285 14 18

Team: Jones, Marsh, Scott, Kendall*, Smith, Doyle, Dodd, Irvine, O'Callaghan, Richardson, Crooks
Subs/Opp: Conroy, Franks, Calvert, Kenworthy, Matthews, Anderson, Keeley, Speight, Finnieson, Sabella, Hamson

O'Callaghan 7, Crooks 74p / Anderson 68
Ref: K Walmsley

Much vaunted Alex Sabella is nowhere as City outplay Harry Haslam's men. O'Callaghan bullets a header past Steve Conroy. Peter Anderson places his header out of Jones' reach. Crooks fires in a controversial penalty, given for a foul on him. United are reduced to long-range efforts.

---

13 · 4/11 · A SUNDERLAND · 1 W 1-0 0-0 · 25,170 10 20

Team: Jones, Johnson P, Scott, Kendall, Smith, Doyle, Dodd, Irvine, O'Callaghan, Crooks*, Richardson, Conroy
Subs/Opp: Siddall, Henderson, Bolton, Docherty, Clarke, Elliott, Buckley, Brown*, Entwhistle, Lee, Rowell, Greenwood

O'Callaghan 87
Ref: D Richardson

Kendall is back to his best in midfield but the home fans become restless after Jones denies Entwhistle and Docherty. In a dour battle Conroy's introduction provides the spark. He delivers a deep cross for O'Callaghan to power a header home. Richardson has a goal ruled out for offside.

---

14 · 11/11 · H CAMBRIDGE · 1 L 1-3 0-2 · 9,027 12 20

Team: Jones, Dodd, Scott, Kendall, Smith, Doyle, Conroy*, Irvine, O'Callaghan, Busby, Richardson, Crooks
Subs/Opp: Webster, Howard*, Smith, Stringer, Fallon, Leach, Garner, Spriggs, Christie, Finney, Biley, Cozens

Busby 62 / Biley 5p, Leach 17, Garner 90
Ref: D Owen

After the euphoria of cup victory in midweek City are brought back to earth by battling Cambridge. Biley heads against the bar and then slots a penalty for handball. Viv Busby gives City hope with a 15-yard drive but Garner seals it. Missiles are aimed at the linesman from the paddock.

---

15 · 18/11 · A MILLWALL · 2 L 0-3 0-1 · 6,925 22 20

Team: Jones, Marsh, Scott*, Kendall, Smith, Doyle, Dodd, Irvine, O'Callaghan, Richardson, Crooks
Subs/Opp: Cuff, Donaldson, Moore, Chatterton, Kitchener, Tagg, Towner*, Seasman, Mitchell, Walker, Mehmet, Chambers

Mitchell 2, 46, Seasman 64
Ref: L Shapter

City are mauled in the Lions' den by struggling Millwall. It's their first win since the opening day! Mitchell scores within a minute of the start of each half as Stoke go to sleep. John Seasman's close-range finish rubs it in. O'Callaghan and Richardson have headers easily saved by Cuff.

---

16 · 22/11 · H OLDHAM · 1 W 4-0 2-0 · 7,170 15 22

Team: Jones, Marsh, Johnson P, Kendall*, Smith, Doyle, Dodd, Irvine, O'Callaghan, Richardson, Crooks
Subs/Opp: McDonnell, Wood, Blair, Bell, Hicks, Hurst, Halom, Taylor, Valentine, Chapman, Sheldon, Gardner

O'Callgh'n 14, Irvine 19, Crooks 66, 78
Ref: R Toseland

Kevin Sheldon returns from his two year broken leg nightmare to lay on Crooks' first goal before going off with a twisted ankle. Stoke thrash Jimmy Frizzell's side with Irvine's drive the best effort. Crooks should have more but, as Durban says, McDonnell had adhesive on his gloves.

---

17 · 25/11 · A BLACKBURN · 2 D 2-2 0-0 · 10,841 20 23

Team: Jones, Marsh, Johnson P*, Kendall, Smith, Doyle, Dodd, Irvine, O'Callaghan, Richardson, Crooks
Subs/Opp: Butcher, Hird, Bailey, Fowler, Keeley, Fazackerley, Brotherston, Radford, Craig, Parkes, Garner

O'Callaghan 65, Crooks 76p / Hird 59, Garner 71
Ref: A Saunders

O'Callaghan and Irvine both miss easy chances before Hird cracks in from 25 yards. O'Callaghan finally buries a Crooks cross. Garner's close-range finish puts John Pickering's men ahead but a frantic second half sees Stoke grab a point through Crooks' spot-kick after Keeley handles.

---

18 · 2/12 · H LEICESTER · 2 D 0-0 0-0 · 15,590 14 24

Team: Jones, Marsh, Johnson P, Kendall, Smith, Doyle, Dodd, Irvine, O'Callaghan, Richardson, Crooks
Subs/Opp: Wallington, Whitworth, Rofe, May, Williams, Kelly, Weller, Ridley, Christie, Henderson, Hughes

Ref: J Worrall

In icy conditions both sides struggle to keep their feet. Mistakes abound and Ridley is lucky to get away with handling in the area as the referee gives him the benefit of the doubt. Crooks is closest with Irvine's drive the best effort. Mark Wallington twice keeps Jock Wallace's Foxes in the match.

---

19 · 9/12 · A NEWCASTLE · 2 L 0-2 0-0 · 23,447 9 24

Team: Jones, Marsh, Johnson P, Kendall, Smith, Doyle, Dodd*, Irvine, O'Callaghan, Richardson, Crooks
Subs/Opp: Hardwick, Brownlie, Mitchell, Cassidy, Bird, Blackley, Martin, Shoulder, Withe, Hibbitt, Connolly, Scott

Withe 68, Connolly 76
Ref: D Webb

One win in six now after Alan Shoulder inspires Bill McGarry's side to a good win. His shot is beaten out by Jones to Peter Withe for the first. In a carbon copy John Connolly nets. Stoke are forced to defend in depth to keep the score down and there is nothing to show at the other end.

---

20 · 16/12 · H WREXHAM · 2 W 3-0 1-0 · 13,358 9 26

Team: Fox, Marsh, Scott, Kendall, Smith, Doyle*, Dodd, Irvine, O'Callaghan, Richardson, Crooks
Subs/Opp: Davies, Cegielski, Jones, Davis, Roberts, Evans, Shinton, Sutton, Lyons, Dwyer*, Hill, Griffiths

Crooks 40, 72, Roberts 75 (og)
Ref: J Hunting

Stoke waltz past Wrexham with Crooks blasting home from 15 yards. He then follows up Irvine's shot. O'Callaghan pressurises John Roberts into heading past his own keeper. Richardson misses an open goal. Arfon Griffiths' men hit the bar, but City don't have to expend much effort.

---

21 · 23/12 · A BRISTOL ROV · 2 D 0-0 0-0 · 7,397 14 27

Team: Jones, Marsh, Scott, Kendall, Smith, Doyle, McGroarty, Irvine, O'Callaghan, Richardson, Crooks
Subs/Opp: Thomas, Day, Jones, Harding, Taylor, Prince, Petts*, Williams, Staniforth, Randall, Malbutt, White

Ref: C Thomas

Howard Kendall produces another fine performance but City's front men cannot beat Martin Thomas. The best chances fall to Smith and Doyle but Thomas blocks. Jones saves from the dangerous Randall. Irvine breaks though but Thomas whips the ball from his toes in the final minute.

LEAGUE DIVISION 2 — Manager: Alan Durban — SEASON 1978-79

Match summary

No	Venue	Date	Att	Pos	Opp Pos	Pt	Result	F-A	H-T	Scorers, Times, and Referees
22	H	26/12	20,841	2	11	28	D	2-2	1-0	McGroarty 30, O'Callaghan 53; Flanagan 70, 79; Ref: N Glover
23	H	30/12	21,394	2	9	30	W	2-0	1-0	Irvine 3, O'Callaghan 80; Ref: T Morris
24	A	20/1	28,071	2	3	31	D	1-1	1-1	O'Callaghan 29; Jones 17 (og); Ref: M Sinclair
25	A	6/2	16,462	1	14	32	D	0-0	0-0	Ref: A Cox
26	A	10/2	23,315	1	3	33	D	1-1	0-0	Irvine 84; Walsh 88; Ref: M Taylor
27	A	24/2	13,756	2	13	35	W	3-0	0-0	O'Callaghan 63, Randall 89, Crooks 90; Ref: G Tyson
28	H	28/2	18,177	2	13	36	D	1-1	0-1	O'Callaghan 64; Bruce 26; Ref: J Hunting
29	H	3/3	24,912	1	4	38	W	2-0	1-0	Doyle 9, Randall 85; Ref: J Bray
30	A	10/3	23,512	2	19	39	D	0-0	0-0	Ref: N Glover
31	H	14/3	13,189	2	10	41	W	3-1	2-0	Irvine 20, Crooks 30, 65; Mayo 55; Ref: R Bridges

Line-ups (Stoke row first, opponents below)

No	Team	1	2	3	4	5	6	7	8	9	10	11	12 sub used
22	Stoke	Jones	Marsh	Scott	Kendall	Smith*	Doyle	McGroarty	Irvine	O'Callaghan	Crooks	Richardson	Dodd
22	Charlton	Wood	Shaw	Campbell	Gritt	Shipperley	Berry	Brisley	Robinson	Flanagan	Madden	Powell	
23	Stoke	Jones	Marsh	Scott	Kendall	Smith	Doyle	Randall	Irvine*	O'Callaghan	Crooks	Richardson	Dodd
23	Notts Co	McManus	Richards	O'Brien	Benjamin	Stubbs	Mann	McCulloch	Masson	Hooks	Hunt	Vinter*	Blockley
24	Stoke	Jones	Dodd	Scott	Kendall	Johnson P	Doyle	Randall	Irvine	O'Callaghan	Crooks	Richardson	
24	Brighton	Moseley	Cattlin	Williams	Horton	Rollings	Lawrenson	Ryan*	Poskett	Maybank	Sayer	O'Sullivan	Ward
25	Stoke	Jones	Dodd	Scott*	Kendall	Smith	Doyle	Randall	Irvine	O'Callaghan	Crooks	Richardson	Busby
25	Luton	Lawson	Stephens	Carr	Donaghy	Turner	Price	West	Hill	Taylor	Hatton	Moss	
26	Stoke	Jones	Dodd	Scott*	Kendall	Smith	Doyle	Randall	Irvine	O'Callaghan*	Crooks	Richardson	Busby
26	Crystal Palace	Burridge	Hinshelwood	Sansom	Kember	Cannon	Gilbert	Nicholas	Murphy	Swindlehurst	Fenwick	Walsh	
27	Stoke	Jones	Dodd	Scott	Kendall	Smith	Doyle	Randall	Irvine	O'Callaghan	Crooks	Richardson	
27	Burnley	Stevenson	Scott	Brennan	Noble	Thomson	Rodaway	Robinson	Ingham	Fletcher	Kindon	James	
28	Stoke	Jones	Dodd	Scott	Kendall	Smith	Doyle	Randall	Irvine	O'Callaghan	Crooks	Richardson	
28	Preston	Tunks	Taylor	Cameron	Doyle	Baxter	O'Riordan	Coleman	Haslegrave	Robinson	Potts	Bruce	
29	Stoke	Jones	Dodd	Scott	Kendall	Smith	Doyle	Randall	Irvine	O'Callaghan	Crooks	Richardson	
29	West Ham	Parkes	McDowell	Brush	Curbishley	Martin	Bonds	Holland	Devonshire	Cross	Brooking	Robson	
30	Stoke	Jones	Marsh	Scott	Kendall	Dodd	Doyle	Randall	Irvine	O'Callaghan	Crooks	Richardson	
30	Sheffield Utd	Conroy	Speight	Garner	Kenworthy	MacPhail	Guy	Matthews	Sabella	Flood	Brown	Hamson	
31	Stoke	Jones	Marsh	Scott	Kendall	Dodd	Doyle	Randall	Irvine	O'Callaghan	Crooks	Richardson	
31	Orient	Jackson	Fisher	Roffey	Grealish	Gray	Went	Whittle	Moores	Mayo	Hughton	Coates	

Match reports

22 — CHARLTON: Stoke are cruising at 2-0 thanks to McGroarty's finish to Kendall's fine cross and O'Callaghan rounding George Wood with the referee waving aside offside appeals. Then Mike Flanagan, badly marked, sharply takes two chances and Charlton are back in it, threatening to win the match.

23 — NOTTS CO: Paul Randall starts after his £150,000 move from Bristol Rovers which means Crooks is moved out to the left. Irvine fires home left footed and O'Callaghan seals it from Crooks' cross. It should be more, but Jimmy Sirrel's team fight back. Masson probes and David Hooks tests Jones.

24 — BRIGHTON: Roger Jones fumbles Malcolm Poskett's cross into his own net to give Brighton a deserved lead. Jones atones for the error with a string of fine saves. As things begin to seem bleak, up pops O'Callaghan to head into an empty net. Alan Mullery's Seagulls deserve to win but City cling on.

25 — LUTON: After a 17-day break Stoke need time to play themselves in but show determination and grit to leave Kenilworth Road with a point. Smith and Doyle are fantastic in sub zero temperatures. Dodd keeps David Moss quiet and City nearly snatch it, but Dodd's shot is cleared by Alan West.

26 — CRYSTAL PALACE: The pacy Randall is prominent in a rugged match. Irvine heads home Kendall's near-post cross. Terry Venables' Palace, without a win in 4, are losing ground at the top but Ian Walsh snatches a draw. Alan Durban has his eye on Cardiff's Phil Dwyer as a replacement for Smith or Doyle.

27 — BURNLEY: City prevail against Harry Potts' unlucky Burnley. Kindon hits the bar from three yards and has another effort cleared off the line. O'Callaghan fires home from Randall's pass before Kendall threads the ball in to the far corner. Crooks seals it when he picks Brennan's wayward back-pass.

28 — PRESTON: Nobby Stiles' men shock City when Alex Bruce nets his 20th of the season. O'Callaghan saves Stoke's blushes with a header from Richardson's swirling corner. A series of wayward crosses all end up in Roy Tunks' grasp. He holds Paul Richardson's late effort to take a point up the M6.

29 — WEST HAM: £565,000 Phil Parkes keeps John Lyall's West Ham in the match, saving from Richardson and Kendall. Brush clears off the line from Randall and Richardson shackles England's Trevor Brooking. Doyle heads home O'Callaghan's cross then Randall skips around Parkes to seal victory.

30 — SHEFFIELD UTD: Crooks and MacPhail are involved in a dust up and four others are booked. City attack brightly but Steve Conroy superbly defies O'Callaghan, Crooks and Kendall. Randall takes the ball off Irvine's foot when he has a better shooting opportunity and Parkes hits the post from six yards.

31 — ORIENT: Stoke pummel Jimmy Bloomfield's men into submission. Irvine fires through a packed penalty area left footed and then lays on Crooks' first. Kendall flicks on for Crooks to fire home. O'Callaghan has an effort ruled out for a foul on Jackson. City are untroubled by Joe Mayo's effort.

32

---

32 — CARDIFF (A) 24/3 — W 3-1 (HT 2-0) | Att 12,869 | Pos 19 | Pts 43
Randall 16, O'Callaghan 43, Crooks 88 — *Buchanan 48p* — Ref: S Bates

Jones	Dodd	Scott	Kendall	Smith	Doyle	Randall	Irvine	O'Callaghan	Crooks	Richardson	(sub)
Jones	Dodd	Scott	Kendall	Smith	Doyle	Randall	Irvine	O'Callaghan	Crooks	Richardson	
Davies	*Roberts*	*Sullivan*	*Campbell*	*Dwyer*	*Pontin*	*Grapes*	*Bishop*	*Moore*	*Evans**	*Buchanan*	*Lewis*

Stoke turn up the heat on their promotion rivals to make it 14 without loss. Randall picks up a flick on and crashes a 22-yard drive past Davies. O'Callaghan's first-time volley flies in then Crooks turns sharply to fire home. Cardiff's penalty comes after Ronnie Moore is tripped by Scott.

---

33 — SUNDERLAND (H) 27/3 — L 0-1 (HT 0-1) | Att 24,021 | Pos 4 | Pts 43
Docherty 5 — Ref: G Flint

Jones	Dodd	Scott	Kendall	Smith	Doyle	Randall	Irvine	O'Callaghan	Crooks	Richardson	(sub)
Jones	Dodd*	Scott	Kendall	Smith	Doyle	Randall	Irvine	O'Callaghan	Crooks	Richardson	
Siddall	*Henderson*	*Bolton*	*Docherty*	*Clarke*	*Elliott*	*Buckley*	*Rostron*	*Entwhistle*	*Lee*	*Rowell*	*Busby*

Jimmy Adamson's team sneak this vital promotion battle after Docherty rounds Jones to net. Clarke and Elliott deal with O'Callaghan's aerial threat. Crooks hits the post with Stoke's best chance after 85 mins of constant pressure. Durban wants to sign Brian Kidd before the deadline.

---

34 — BLACKBURN (H) 31/3 — L 1-2 (HT 1-1) | Att 17,021 | Pos 21 | Pts 43
O'Callaghan 15 — *Craig 6, Brotherston 48* — Ref: K Styles

Jones	Dodd	Scott	Kendall	Smith	Doyle	Randall	Irvine	O'Callaghan	Crooks	Richardson	(sub)
Jones	Marsh	Scott	Kendall	Smith	Doyle	Randall	Irvine	O'Callaghan	Crooks	Richardson*	
Ramsbottom	*Rathbone*	*Bailey*	*Coughlin*	*Parkin*	*Fazackerley*	*Brotherston*	*Fowler*	*Craig*	*Parkes*	*McKenzie*	*Busby*

Noel Brotherston supplies Craig for the opener and then powers a header past Jones on the run. O'Callaghan taps in as he follows up Crooks' shot which gets stuck in the mud. Rovers sneak home after Denis Smith has a header cleared off the line and Viv Busby has his effort blocked.

---

35 — FULHAM (H) 4/4 — W 2-0 (HT 0-0) | Att 5,243 | Pos 8 | Pts 45
Smith 63, Randall 65 — Ref: R Chadwick

Jones	Dodd	Scott	Kendall	Smith	Doyle	Randall	Irvine	O'Callaghan	Crooks	Richardson	(sub)
Jones	Dodd	Scott	Kendall	Smith	Doyle	Randall	Irvine	O'Callaghan	Crooks	Richardson	
Peyton	*Evans*	*Strong*	*Lock*	*Money*	*Gale*	*Davies*	*Beck*	*Guthrie*	*Kitchen*	*Margerrison*	

The tension mounts as City fail to find a way through Fulham's well marshalled defence. Smith finally breaks the deadlock, lashing home in a frantic goalmouth scramble. Randall then notches from O'Callaghan's knockdown and the 'Magnificent' supporters are thanked by Durban.

---

36 — LEICESTER (A) 7/4 — D 1-1 (HT 1-1) | Att 7,502 | Pos 13 | Pts 46
Busby 44 — *Buchanan 33* — Ref: C Downey

Jones	Dodd	Scott	Kendall	Smith	Doyle	Randall	Irvine	O'Callaghan	Crooks	Richardson	(subs)
Jones	Dodd	Scott	Kendall	Smith	Doyle	Randall	Irvine	O'Callaghan	Crooks	Richardson	
Wallington	*Goodwin*	*Rofe*	*Williams*	*O'Neill*	*May*	*Peake*	*Kelly*	*Henderson*	*Buchanan**	*Smith*	*Heath / Christie*

Mark Wallington saves from Richardson and Irvine before Dave Buchanan races through to beat Jones. Stoke are shocked and fight back with Viv Busby's effort after Richardson's long throw. City play the ball in the air too much. Larry May and Andy Peake dominate O'Callaghan.

---

37 — CHARLTON (A) 14/4 — W 4-1 (HT 1-1) | Att 9,084 | Pos 15 | Pts 48
Richard'[son] 24, Randall 47, O'Call'han 82, [Irvine 86] — *Hales 21p* — Ref: A Gunn

Jones	Dodd	Scott	Kendall	Smith	Doyle	Randall	Irvine	O'Callaghan	Crooks	Richardson	(subs)
Jones	Dodd	Scott	Kendall	Smith	Doyle	Randall	Irvine	O'Callaghan	Crooks*	Richardson	
Wood	*Shaw*	*Warman*	*Gritt*	*Shipperley**	*Berry*	*Powell*	*Robinson*	*Hales*	*Madden*	*Peacock*	*Conroy / Brisley*

Stoke overpower Charlton, reduced to 10 for the last 25 mins after Shipperley and Warman limp off. The penalty decision baffles everyone but it sparks City into life. Richardson battles through to level, then Randall crashes one in from the edge of the box. Irvine fires home on the run.

---

38 — LUTON (H) 16/4 — D 0-0 (HT 0-0) | Att 19,214 | Pos 16 | Pts 49
Ref: A Challinor

Jones	Dodd	Scott	Kendall	Smith	Doyle	Randall	Irvine	O'Callaghan	Crooks	Richardson	(sub)
Jones	Dodd	Scott	Kendall*	Smith	Doyle	Randall	Irvine	O'Callaghan	Crooks	Richardson	
Findlay	*Stephens*	*Turner*	*Donaghy*	*Phill-Masters*	*Price*	*Hill*	*West*	*Taylor*	*Hatton*	*Birchenall*	*Conroy*

Terry Conroy's last appearance in a Stoke shirt sees City frustrated in a bruising encounter. Howard Kendall is stretchered off after 15 minutes and Smith gashes his leg after colliding with Richardson, who breaks his nose. Luton's sweeper system denies frustrated Stoke time and space.

---

39 — BRISTOL ROV (H) 17/4 — W 2-0 (HT 2-0) | Att 18,371 | Pos 14 | Pts 51
Busby 4, 27 — Ref: K Hackett

Jones	Dodd	Scott	Kendall	Smith	Doyle	Randall	Irvine	O'Callaghan	Crooks	Richardson	(subs)
Jones	Richardson	Scott	Johnson PA	Dodd	Doyle*	Randall	Irvine	O'Callaghan	Crooks	Busby	
Thomas	*Bater*	*Jones*	*Aitken*	*Taylor*	*Prince**	*Dennehy*	*Williams*	*White*	*Cook*	*Staniforth*	*McGroarty / Emmanuel / Petts*

Howard Kendall misses his first game in two seasons. Viv Busby, making a rare start, hammers home from a tight angle before half-volleying Scott's free-kick in. Doyle is injured in a challenge with Frankie Prince and Stoke lose their flow without him. Promotion is on the cards now!

---

40 — WREXHAM (A) 21/4 — W 1-0 (HT 1-0) | Att 27,215 | Pos 14 | Pts 53
O'Callaghan 44 — Ref: P Reeves

Jones	Dodd	Scott	Kendall	Smith	Doyle	Randall	Irvine	O'Callaghan	Crooks	Richardson	(sub)
Jones	Richardson	Scott	Johnson PA	Dodd	Smith	Doyle	Randall	Irvine	O'Callaghan	Crooks	Busby
Davies	*Sutton*	*Dwyer*	*Jones*	*Roberts*	*Giles*	*Shinton*	*Cartwright*	*Lyons*	*Whittle**	*Fox*	*Buxton*

Smith plays with eight stitches and a burst blood vessel to guide City to a vital win. The breakthrough comes when O'Callaghan finds space to fire Randall's pass home. Jones saves from Lyons and Jones as Wrexham pile on the pressure. Crooks nearly snatches another on the break.

---

41 — NEWCASTLE (H) 28/4 — D 0-0 (HT 0-0) | Att 23,271 | Pos 11 | Pts 54
Ref: D Sivill

Jones	Dodd	Scott	Kendall	Smith	Doyle	Randall	Irvine	O'Callaghan	Crooks	Richardson	(sub)
Jones	Dodd	Scott	Kendall	Smith	Doyle	Randall	Irvine	O'Callaghan	Crooks	Richardson	
Carr	*Nattrass*	*Mitchell**	*Barton*	*Manners*	*Bird*	*Shoulder*	*Martin*	*Withe*	*Hibbitt*	*Connolly*	*Nicholson*

Disappointment as Newcastle do neighbours Sunderland a huge favour by holding nervous Stoke to a draw. Richardson shoots wide from ten yards as does Busby. Bill McGarry's men have Peter Withe back defending at times. Doyle's late free-kick is blocked as Stoke run out of time.

---

42 — NOTTS CO (A) 5/5 — W 1-0 (HT 0-0) | Att 21,579 | Pos 6 | Pts 56
Richardson 88 — Ref: D Clarke

Jones	Dodd	Scott	Kendall	Smith	Doyle	Randall	Irvine	O'Callaghan	Crooks	Richardson	(sub)
Jones	Dodd	Scott	Kendall	Smith	Doyle	Randall	Irvine	O'Callaghan	Crooks	Richardson	
McManus	*Richards*	*O'Brien*	*Blackley*	*Stubbs*	*Mair*	*McCulloch*	*Masson*	*Hooks*	*Mann*	*Vinter*	

Sunderland's home defeat by Cardiff throws City a lifeline. A win will see them up whatever the other scores. In dramatic fashion Richardson heads home Brendan O'Callaghan's knock-back and Meadow Lane erupts. Promotion in first full season justifies Alan Durban's appointment.

Average — Home 19,108 | Away 15,451

LEAGUE DIVISION 2 (CUP-TIES) Manager: Alan Durban SEASON 1978-79

League Cup

		Att		F-A	H-T	Scorers, Times, and Referees	1	2	3	4	5	6	7	8	9	10	11	12 sub used
2	A SUNDERLAND 30/8	12,368 2:19	1 W	2-0	2-0	Irvine 3, Doyle 34 — Ref: P Richardson	Jones	Marsh	Scott	Kendall	Smith	Doyle	Dodd	Irvine	O'Callaghan	Crooks*	Richardson	Busby
							Siddall	Henderson	Bolton	Docherty	Elliott	Ashurst!	Kerr	Greenwood	Entwhistle	Gilbert	Rowell	
3	A NORTHAMPTON 3/10	11,235 4:8	1 W	3-1	1-1	Dodd 10, O'Callaghan 52, Kendall 90; Reilly 38 — Ref: R Kirkpatrick	Jones	Marsh	Scott	Kendall	Smith	Doyle	Dodd	**Heath**	O'Callaghan	Crooks	Richardson*	Busby
							Poole	Geldmintis	Mead	Woollett	Robertson	Bryant	Farrington	Williams	Cordice*	Reilly	Christie	Wassell
4	A CHARLTON 7/11	18,667 2:4	1 W	3-2	2-1	Irvine 1, Busby 20, Crooks 88p; Shipperley 37, 72 — Ref: P Reeves	Jones	Marsh	Scott	Kendall	Smith	Dodd	Conroy	Irvine	O'Callaghan	Busby*	Richardson	Crooks
							Wood	Shaw	Campbell*	Tydeman	Shipperley	Berry	Brisley	Robinson	Flanagan	Madden	Gritt	Peacock
5	H WATFORD 13/12	26,070 3:1	2 D	0-0	0-0	Ref: D Richardson	Jones	Dodd	Scott	Kendall	Smith	Doyle	Heath	Irvine	O'Callaghan	Crooks	Richardson	
							Sherwood	Stirk	Pritchett	Booth	Bolton	Garner	Pollard	Blissett	Jenkins	Joslyn	Mayes	
5R	A WATFORD 9/1	21,419 3:1	2 L	1-3 aet	0-1	Richardson 67; Jenkins 4, Blissett 93, 97 — Ref: R Kirkpatrick	Jones	Dodd	Bowers	Kendall	Smith	Doyle	McGroarty	Irvine	O'Callaghan	Crooks	Richardson*	Conroy
							Sherwood	Stirk	Pritchett	Booth	Bolton	Garner	Pollard	Blissett	Jenkins	Joslyn	Mayes	

Stoke take their chances against 10-man Sunderland who have Jack Ashurst sent off for two bookings (33 mins). Irvine heads home Kendall's cross and Doyle's screamer settles it. City silence the Roker roar. O'Callaghan draws a good save from Siddall. There is only ever one winner.

Town put the frighteners on with Reilly's near-post flick. Dodd prods in from close range before a bizarre incident when City win a penalty and as the players line up the referee gives a goal-kick saying the ball had gone out first! O'Callaghan nods home. Heath lays on Kendall's clincher.

Sammy Irvine scores from 20 yards after just 36 seconds. Bushy's near-post finish has a hint of handball about it. Stoke are in charge but Dave Shipperley's close-range finishes change things. Durban sends Crooks on. He is tripped for the penalty and lashes it home to put City through.

City quell the threat of Luther Blissett and 20-goal Ross Jenkins but have no luck at the other end. Both O'Callaghan and Heath hit the bar and Scott misses a great chance following a fine run. Kendall runs midfield but City cannot create problems for Watford's sizeable defensive wall.

Extra-time sees City slip up at Division Three Watford. After heavy Hornets pressure Ross Jenkins notches his 27th of the season. Richardson lashes home Irvine's cross. Then Luther Blissett weaves his magic to send Graham Taylor's Watford through to a semi-final date with Forest.

FA Cup

		Att		F-A	H-T	Scorers, Times, and Referees	1	2	3	4	5	6	7	8	9	10	11	12 sub used
3	H OLDHAM 17/1	16,554 2:18	2 L	0-1	0-1	Wood 19 — Ref: P Reeves	Jones	Dodd	Scott	Kendall	Smith	Doyle	McGroarty*	Irvine	O'Callaghan	Crooks	Richardson	Busby
							McDonnell	Wood	Hoult	Bell	Hicks	Hurst	Valentine	Halom	Young	Chapman	Blair	

Another slip-up in the FA Cup in a replay after the first match was abandoned due to fog with City 2-0 up. Peter McDonnell saves from Crooks and Jim McGroarty as Stoke contrive to miss chance after chance. Ian Wood's speculative 35-yard shot puts Oldham through to face Leicester.

League Table

	P	W	D	L	F	A	W	D	L	F	A	Pts
			home					Away				
1 Crys Palace	42	12	7	2	30	11	7	12	2	21	13	57
2 Brighton	42	16	3	2	44	11	7	7	7	28	28	56
3 STOKE	42	11	7	3	35	15	9	9	3	23	16	56
4 Sunderland	42	13	3	5	39	19	9	8	4	31	25	55
5 West Ham	42	12	7	2	46	15	6	7	8	24	24	50
6 Notts Co	42	8	10	3	23	15	6	6	9	25	45	44
7 Preston	42	7	11	3	36	23	5	7	9	23	34	42
8 Newcastle	42	13	3	5	35	24	4	5	12	16	31	42
9 Cardiff	42	12	5	4	34	23	4	5	12	22	47	42
10 Fulham	42	10	7	4	35	19	4	5	12	15	28	41
11 Orient	42	11	5	5	32	18	3	8	10	19	33	40
12 Cambridge	42	7	10	4	22	15	6	6	12	20	37	40
13 Burnley	42	11	6	4	31	22	3	6	12	20	40	39
14 Oldham	42	10	7	4	36	23	3	6	12	16	38	39
15 Wrexham	42	10	6	5	31	16	2	8	11	14	26	38
16 Bristol Rov	42	10	6	5	34	23	3	4	13	14	37	38
17 Leicester	42	7	8	6	28	23	3	9	9	15	29	37
18 Luton	42	11	5	5	46	24	2	5	14	14	33	36
19 Charlton	42	6	8	7	28	28	5	5	11	32	41	35
20 Sheffield Utd	42	9	6	6	34	24	2	6	13	18	45	34
21 Millwall	42	7	4	10	22	29	4	6	11	20	32	32
22 Blackburn	42	5	8	8	24	29	5	2	14	17	43	30
	924	218	142	102	725	449	102	142	218	449	725	924

Appearances / Goals

	Appearances						Goals			
	Lge	Sub	LC	Sub	FAC	Sub	Lge	LC	FAC	Tot
Bowers, Danny	8	10	1	2		1	6	1		7
Busby, Viv	3	4	1	1	1					
Conroy, Terry	3	4	1	1	1					
Cook, Jeff	1	2								
Crooks, Garth	38	2	4	1	1	1	12	1		13
Dodd, Alan	34	4	5	1	1					
Doyle, Mike	41		4		1		1		1	2
Fox, Peter	1									
Heath, Adrian	1	1	2							
Irvine, Sammy	41		4	1			7		2	9
Johnson, Paul	7	1								
Johnson Paul A	2									
Jones, Roger	41		5		1					
Kendall, Howard	40		5		1		2	1		3
Marsh, Jackie	24		3							
McGroarty, Jim	3	1	1		1		1			1
O'Callaghan, Brendan	40	1	5		1		15	1		16
Randall, Paul	20						5			5
Richardson, Paul	40		5		1		6		1	7
Scott, Geoff	37	1	4	1	1					
Sheldon, Kevin		1								
Smith, Denis	38		5		1		2			2
Waddington, Steve	2									
(own-goals)							1			1
21 players used	462	28	55	4	11	1	58	9		67

Odds & ends

Double wins: (5) Orient, Burnley, Cardiff, Wrexham, Notts Co.

Double losses: (0).

Won from behind: (1) Charlton (a).

Lost from in front: (0).

High spots: Promotion at only the second attempt.

Highest points total since 1932-33.

13-match unbeaten run in mid-season sets up promotion.

Paul Richardson's goal sparking celebrations at Meadow Lane.

Paul Randall's £150,000 purchase from Bristol Rovers.

Low spots: Losing to Division Three Watford in the League Cup, with a semi-final berth against the European Champions Forest beckoning.

Having the FA Cup Third Round match against Oldham abandoned when 2-0 up and losing the re-arranged game.

Player of the Year: Mike Doyle.

Ever-presents: (0).

Hat-tricks: (0).

Leading scorer: (16) O'Callaghan.

LEAGUE DIVISION 1   Manager: Alan Durban   SEASON 1979-80

No	Date	V	Opponent	Att	Pos	Pt	F-A	H-T	Scorers, Times, and Referees
1	18/8	H	COVENTRY	23,151	W	2	3-2	1-0	Busby 34, Crooks 50, 55 / Powell 64p, 70 — Ref: D Richardson
2	22/8	A	NOTT'M FOREST	26,147	L	2	0-1	0-0	O'Neill 82 — Ref: M Peck
3	25/8	H	TOTTENHAM	22,832	5 (22)	W 4	3-1	2-0	Crooks 35, 41p, O'Callaghan 60 / Perryman 82 — Ref: T Mills
4	1/9	A	IPSWICH	17,539	11 (12)	L 4	1-3	1-2	Butcher 20 (og) / Brazil 10, Mariner 44, Wark 89 — Ref: B Daniels
5	8/9	H	EVERTON	23,460	15 (13)	L 4	2-3	2-2	O'Callaghan 17, Smith 35 / King 12, Bailey 14, Irvine 80 (og) — Ref: A Saville
6	15/9	A	BRISTOL CITY	16,662	14 (10)	D 5	0-0	0-0	Ref: C Thomas
7	22/9	H	CRYSTAL PALACE	19,225	16 (2)	L 5	1-2	1-0	Smith 7 / Hilaire 55, Cannon 82 — Ref: J Bray
8	29/9	A	MANCHESTER U	52,357	21 (2)	L 5	0-4	0-1	Wilkins 35, McQueen 56, 85, [McIlroy 80] — Ref: D Owen
9	6/10	A	NORWICH	17,060	21 (4)	D 6	2-2	1-0	Irvine 13, Richardson 73p / Bond 58p, Reeves 76 — Ref: C Maskell
10	10/10	H	NOTT'M FOREST	28,514	19 (2)	D 7	1-1	0-0	O'Callaghan 63 / Birtles 82 — Ref: D Clarke

Line-ups (positions 1–11, 12 sub used)

1 COVENTRY (H)
Stoke: Jones, Evans, Scott, Irvine, Smith, Doyle, Busby, Heath, O'Callaghan, Crooks, Ursem* — 12: Richardson
Coventry: Blyth, Jones, McDonald, Gooding, Hutton, Collier, Hutchinson, English, Ferguson, Powell, Hunt
Busby beats Blyth with a perfectly timed header and Crooks sets City coasting with two cool left-foot finishes. Powell's penalty is for a foul on English and his lob crosses the line after hitting both posts. City return to the top flight with a win and a new stand, the 4,250 seater Stoke End.

2 NOTT'M FOREST (A)
Stoke: Fox, Evans, Anderson, Irvine, Smith, Doyle, Busby, Heath*, O'Callaghan, Crooks, Richardson — O'Neill 82
Forest: Shilton, Anderson, Gray, McGovern, Lloyd, Needham, O'Neill, Hartford*, Birtles, Woodcock, Robertson — 12: Bowyer
Brian Clough's European Champions struggle to beat late stand-in keeper Peter Fox. He defies Viv Anderson and John Robertson but cannot keep out Martin O'Neill's close-range finish.

3 TOTTENHAM (H)
Stoke: Jones, Evans, Scott, Irvine, Smith, Doyle, Busby, Heath, O'Callaghan, Crooks, Ursem* — 12: Richardson
Tottenham: Daines, Lee, Smith, Yorath, Lacy, Perryman, Pratt, Ardiles, Falco*, Hoddle, Jones — McAllister
City outplay Spurs and Heath hits the post before Crooks' brace. The penalty is for Gordon Smith's trip on Busby. Crooks bursts through to set up O'Callaghan for the third. City relax and allow Steve Perryman to fire past Jones. Busby and O'Callaghan go close as Daines is kept busy.

4 IPSWICH (A)
Stoke: Jones, Richardson, Scott, Irvine, Smith, Doyle, Randall, Heath, O'Callaghan, Crooks, Ursem* — Busby
Ipswich: Cooper, Burley, Mills, Thijssen, Butcher, Osman, Wark, Muhren, Mariner, Brazil*, Woods — Gates
Crooks, Irvine and O'Callaghan all fail to beat Cooper as Stoke are left to rue early missed opportunities. Mariner sets up Brazil to prod home unmarked then heads Ipswich 2-1 up. Butcher's headed back-pass hits the post and goes in for City's goal. Wark's diving header seals victory.

5 EVERTON (H)
Stoke: Jones, Evans, Scott, Irvine*, Smith, Doyle, Randall, Heath, O'Callaghan, Crooks, Richardson — Busby
Everton: Wood, Wright, Bailey, Lyons, Higgins, Ross, Hartford, Stanley, King, Kidd, Eastoe
City fight back after being two down against a lively Everton despite Mick Lyons containing Crooks. O'Callaghan heads home and then Smith cracks a half-cleared corner past Wood. But Sammy Irvine hasn't read the script, booting the ball into his own net when trying to clear a cross.

6 BRISTOL CITY (A)
Stoke: Jones, Evans, Scott, Irvine, Smith, Doyle, Dodd, Heath, O'Callaghan, Crooks, Richardson — Meijer
Bristol City: Shaw, Tainton, Whitehead, Gow, Sweeney, Merrick, Fitzpatrick, Ritchie, Royle*, Mann, Mabbutt
A disciplined performance brings a first away point. City have slightly the better of it as Crooks tests John Shaw. Heath slices wide when well placed and Evans heads off the line from Mabbutt. Referee Thomas pulls a muscle and has to leave a game for the first time in a 25-year career.

7 CRYSTAL PALACE (H)
Stoke: Fox, Evans, Scott, Irvine, Smith, Doyle, Busby, Richardson, O'Callaghan, Crooks*, Ursem — Kember
Palace: Burridge, Hinshelwood, Sansom, Nicholas*, Cannon, Gilbert, Murphy, Francis, Swindlehurst, Flanagan, Hilaire
Stoke grab an early lead when Smith crashes home from close in. Palace fight back. Hilaire's shot gives Fox no chance. Stoke seem to be given a penalty for a trip on Dodd but a linesman flags for offside. Jim Cannon prods home Gerry Francis' free-kick as City run out of ideas up front.

8 MANCHESTER U (A)
Stoke: Jones, Evans, Scott, Irvine, Smith, Doyle, Dodd, Heath*, O'Callaghan, Crooks, Richardson — Randall
Man U: Bailey, Nicholl, Albiston, McIlroy, McQueen, Buchan, Grimes, Wilkins, Coppell, Macari*, Thomas — Sloan
City succumb despite having the better of the opening stages. Once Wilkins whips in a cross-shot the game is up. Crooks bottles it with 50,000 United fans whistling as Bailey blocks his penalty (57 mins). The late goals arrive as Grimes cuts loose on the left, roasting Heath and Evans.

9 NORWICH (A)
Stoke: Jones, Evans, Scott, Irvine, Smith, Dodd, Johnson PA, Heath*, O'Callaghan, Crooks, Richardson* — McGuire
Norwich: Keelan, Bond, McDowell, Bennett, Hoadley, Powell, Robson*, Reeves, Fashanu, Paddon, Peters — Busby
Stoke sparkle at Carrow Road. Irvine crashes home a loose ball from 15 yards. The penalties are both for mistimed challenges in the area. Both takers have to wait for the offenders' to be booked. Kevin Reeves dives in to head the equaliser. Stoke rediscover some form after a poor spell.

10 NOTT'M FOREST (H)
Stoke: Jones, Evans, Scott, Irvine, Smith, Dodd, Johnson PA, Heath, O'Callaghan, Crooks, Richardson — Richardson
Forest: Shilton, Anderson, Gray, McGovern, Lloyd, Burns, Francis, Mills, Birtles, Woodcock, Robertson
City rock the European Champions with O'Callaghan's far-post header reward for a determined display. Only a Garry Birtles special rescues a point for Clough's men. Crooks has a goal disallowed. Both Heath and Scott bring the best out of Shilton. Stoke's best crowd since April 1977.

No	Venue	Opponent	Date	Fig1	Fig2	Fig3	Result	HT	Attendance
11	H	MIDDLESBROUGH	13/10	18	10	8	0-0	0-0	8,406
12	A	ARSENAL	20/10	18	12	9	0-0	0-0	31,501
13	H	DERBY	27/10	18	21	11	W 2-0	3-2	8,530
14	A	COVENTRY	3/11	14	15	13	W 3-1	2-1	26,719
15	H	WOLVES	10/11	16	6	13	L 0-1	0-1	23,061
16	A	ASTON VILLA	17/11	18	9	13	L 1-2	1-1	27,356
17	H	BOLTON	24/11	17	22	15	W 1-0	1-0	11,435
18	A	SOUTHAMPTON	1/12	18	12	15	L 0-1	1-3	27,295
19	H	WEST BROM	8/12	16	15	17	W 3-2	2-1	14,865
20	A	BRIGHTON	15/12	18	21	18	D 0-0	0-0	17,592
21	H	LEEDS	21/12			18	L 0-2	0-2	16,678

Player column headings (Stoke / opponent):
Jones · Evans · Scott · Doyle · Smith · Irvine* · Heath · Dodd · O'Callaghan · Crooks · Richardson · Busby

---

11 H MIDDLESBROUGH 13/10 — 0-0 (0-0) — 8,406
Stoke: Jones, Evans, Scott, Doyle, Smith, Irvine*, Heath, Dodd, O'Callaghan, Crooks, Richardson, Busby
M'boro: Platt, Craggs, Bailey, Johnston, Ashcroft*, Cochrane, Proctor, McAndrew, Hodgson, Burns, Armstrong, Ramage
Ref: G Nolan
A dog holds up play twice, proving to be the main entertainment as unadventurous Boro frustrate Stoke. Smith has powerful efforts blocked by the massed defence and Jim Platt foils Irvine and Heath. City allow the visitors too much time in midfield and the crowd's patience wears thin.

12 A ARSENAL 20/10 — 0-0 (0-0) — 31,501
Stoke: Jones, Evans, Scott, Doyle, Smith, Irvine, Heath, Johnson PA, Crooks, Richardson
Arsenal: Jennings, Rice, Nelson, Talbot, O'Leary, Young, Sunderland, Brady, Stapleton, Hollins, Rix
Ref: A Gunn
A disciplined performance sees Stoke frustrate Terry Neill's Gunners. Smith and Dodd deal well with Nelson's crosses on the overlap. Sammy Irvine fires just over when well placed. Stapleton looks dangerous but Smith, clashing heads with Talbot, embodies City's determined attitude.

13 H DERBY 27/10 — W 2-0 (3-2) — 8,530
Scorers: Richardson 11, Heath 31, Crooks 67
Stoke: Jones, Evans, Scott, Doyle, Smith, Irvine, Heath, Dodd, O'Callaghan, Crooks, Richardson
Derby: Middleton, Langan*, Buckley, Rioch, McCaffrey, Osgood, Powell S, Emery, Duncan, Davies, Hill, Greenwood
Hill 51, 55
Ref: G Owen
In an end-to-end match Heath notches his first for the club. Hill's brace are a tap-in and a brilliant lob from wide out on the left. Crooks applies the finishing touch to Heath's cross. In a pulsating finish Osgood clears off the line from Crooks and Jones pushes over Emery's 30-yard effort.

14 A COVENTRY 3/11 — W 3-1 (2-1) — 26,719
Scorers: Jones 24 (og), Heath 26, Crooks 75
Stoke: Jones, Evans, Scott, Johnson PA, Smith, Irvine, Heath, Dodd, O'Callaghan, Crooks, Richardson
Coventry: Sealey, Jones*, McDonald, Gooding, Holton, Coop, Hutchison, Wallace, English, Blair, Hunt, Whitton
McDonald 42
Ref: J Martin
Stoke take the game to Coventry and lead when Irvine crosses and David Jones deflects past Sealey. Within a minute Heath back-heads past a bewildered Les Sealey. Bobby McDonald lobs Jones splendidly. City battle gamely and Crooks' neat header from Richardson's cross seals it.

15 H WOLVES 10/11 — L 0-1 (0-1) — 23,061
Stoke: Jones, Evans, Scott, Johnson PA*, Smith, Irvine, Heath, Dodd, O'Callaghan, Crooks, Richardson, Randall
Wolves: Bradshaw, Palmer, Parkin, Daniel, McAlle, Berry, Hibbitt, Carr, Gray, Clarke, Richards
Hibbitt 33
Ref: G Courtney
Stoke give as good as they get with Irvine, O'Callaghan and Crooks going close but City lack Wolves' guile. Wolves nick the points through Hibbitt's accurate finish to Carr's pass. Jones saves superbly from Hibbitt and Gray. George Berry is a powerhouse at the back for Wanderers.

16 A ASTON VILLA 17/11 — L 1-2 (1-1) — 27,356
Scorer: Scott 10
Stoke: Jones, Swain, Scott, Johnson PA, Smith!, Irvine, Heath, Dodd, O'Callaghan, Crooks, Randall
Villa: Rimmer, Pejic, Evans, McNaught, Mortimer, Brenner, Little, Geddis, Cowans, Shaw
Mortimer 23, Evans 89p
Ref: B Newsome
In a thrilling game Denis Mortimer's screamer equalises Geoff Scott's first goal in two years when he slips Johnson's corner over the line. The dramatic finale sees a linesman give a penalty. Smith is sent off for foul and abusive language. Allan Evans slams the ball past Jones to win it.

17 H BOLTON 24/11 — W 1-0 (1-0) — 11,435
Scorer: O'Callaghan 44
Stoke: Jones, McDonagh, Scott, Johnson PA, Smith, Irvine, Heath, Dodd, O'Callaghan, Crooks, Randall*, Chapman
Bolton: Clement*, Nicholson, Greaves, Jones, Walsh, Morgan, Whatmore, Gowling, Cantello, McNab, Burke
Ref: V Callow
Mike Doyle returns to play his 500th league game. City struggle to find a way past resolute Bolton. O'Callaghan's far-post header from Evans' cross breaks the deadlock. Stoke's passing goes astray after half-time. Only Paul Randall's effort off the inside of the post troubles McDonagh.

18 A SOUTHAMPTON 1/12 — L 0-1 (1-3) — 27,295
Scorer: Irvine 67
Stoke: Jones, Wells, Scott, Johnson PA, Dodd, Irvine, Heath, Doyle, O'Callaghan, Crooks, Randall*, Chapman
Southampton: Golac, Peach, Williams S, Watson, Nicholl, Ball, Boyer, Channon, Holmes, Hebberd
Boyer 20, 89, Channon 88
Ref: M Taylor
Phil Boyer's opener is a superb shot on the run. Irvine follows up his own shot to tap in the equaliser and Stoke seem to have a point in the bag. Crooks nearly beats Peter Wells but Saints' extra class shows. Channon torments Evans down the flank and he and Boyer convert late chances.

19 H WEST BROM 8/12 — W 3-2 (2-1) — 14,865
Scorers: Crooks 11, 14, 78
Stoke: Jones, Evans, Scott, Johnson P, Richardson, Dodd, Heath, Doyle, O'Callaghan, Crooks, Randall*, Busby
WBA: Godden, Batson, Pendrey, Mills, Wile, Robertson, Trewick, Brown A, Regis, Owen*, Barnes, Deehan
Regis 35, Barnes 52p
Ref: K Walmsley
Garth Crooks bags the second hat-trick of his career. All three show his predatory instincts. He slides home Randall's cross and then intercepts Robertson's back-pass. Albion equalise when Barnes converts after Evans handles. City snatch it when Crooks latches on to Bushy's backheel.

20 A BRIGHTON 15/12 — D 0-0 (0-0) — 17,592
Stoke: Jones, Evans, Scott, Johnson PA, Dodd, Irvine, Heath, Doyle, O'Callaghan, Crooks, Randall
Brighton: Moseley, Gregory, Williams, Horton, Foster, Suddaby, Ryan, Ward, Clarke, Lawrenson, O'Sullivan*, Stevens
Ref: D Vickers
In a tough tussle Paul Johnson clears off the line from Gerry Ryan. Stoke have to rely on counter attacks using Crooks' speed. The Seagulls are more adventurous but their pressure fails to tell. They resort to long-range shots as Doyle and Johnson close down the central areas of the field.

21 H LEEDS 21/12 — L 0-2 (0-2) — 16,678
Scorers: Harris 26, Connor 32
Stoke: Jones, Evans, Scott, Johnson PA*, Dodd, Irvine, Heath, Doyle, O'Callaghan, Crooks, Randall, Busby
Leeds: Lukic, Curtis, Stevenson, Hamson, Hart, Greenhoff, Gray, Hird, Connor, Curtis, Harris*, Entwhistle
Ref: A Hamil
It's men against boys as Eddie Gray runs the game. Harris's cross-shot and Connor's strike are scant reward for Leeds' dominance. Stoke could take the lead but O'Callaghan shoots tamely at young John Lukic. Kevin Hird and Terry Connor should have more for Jimmy Adamson's men.

LEAGUE DIVISION 1

Manager: Alan Durban — SEASON 1979-80

Column headings: No | Date | (venue/opponent) | Att | Pos | Pt | F-A | H-T | 1 | 2 | 3 | 4 | 5 | 6 | 7 | 8 | 9 | 10 | 11 | 12 sub used | Scorers, Times, and Referees

Lineups (Stoke top row; opponents in italics)

No	Date	Opponent	Att	Pos	Pt	F-A	H-T	1	2	3	4	5	6	7	8	9	10	11	12 sub used
22	26/12	A MANCHESTER C	36,286	18	19	D 1-1	1-1	Fox	Evans	Johnson P	Doyle	Smith	Dodd	Heath	Irvine	O'Callaghan	Crooks	Randall	
								Corrigan	*Ranson*	*Donachie*	*Bennett*	*Caton*	*Booth*	*Henry*	*Daley*	*Robinson*	*Power*	*Shinton*	
23	29/12	A TOTTENHAM	28,810	19	19	L 0-1	0-1	Fox	Evans	Johnson P	Doyle	Smith	Dodd	Heath	Irvine	O'Callaghan	Crooks	Sheldon	
								Aleksic	*Hughton*	*Smith*	*Yorath*	*McAllister*	*Perryman*	*Ardiles*	*Jones*	*Gibson**	*Hoddle*	*Pratt*	*Galvin*
24	12/1	H IPSWICH	15,253	19	19	L 0-1	0-1	Fox	Pejic	Johnson P	Irvine	Dodd	Doyle	Heath	Richardson	O'Callaghan	Crooks	Randall*	Chapman
								Cooper	*Burley*	*Mills*	*Thijssen*	*Osman*	*Butcher*	*Wark*	*Mulhren*	*Mariner*	*Gates*	*Brazil**	*McCall*
25	2/2	H BRISTOL CITY	14,510	19	21	W 1-0	0-0	Fox	Evans	Johnson P	Irvine	Smith	Dodd	Heath	Richardson	Chapman	Crooks	Cook	
								Shaw	*Gillies*	*Whitehead*	*Tainton*	*Rodgers*	*Kenyon*	*Pritchard*	*Fitzpatrick*	*Ritchie**	*Sweeney*	*Garland*	*Doyle*
26	9/2	A CRYSTAL PALACE	21,181	18	23	W 1-0	0-0	Fox	Evans	Johnson P	Irvine	Doyle	Dodd	Heath	Richardson	Chapman	Crooks	Cook	
								Burridge	*Hinshelwood*	*Sansom*	*Nicholas*	*Cannon*	*Gilbert*	*Kember*	*Fenwick**	*Swindlehurst*	*Flanagan*	*Hilaire*	*Murphy*
27	16/2	H MANCHESTER U	28,068	17	24	D 1-1	0-0	Fox	Evans	Doyle*	Irvine	Smith	Dodd	Heath	Richardson	Chapman	Crooks	Cook	O'Callaghan
								Bailey	*Nicholl*	*Houston*	*McIlroy*	*McQueen*	*Buchan*	*Coppell*	*Wilkins*	*Jordan*	*Macari**	*Grimes*	*Ritchie*
28	23/2	A MIDDLESBROUGH	15,953	16	26	W 3-1	2-1	Fox	Evans	Johnson P	Irvine	Smith	Dodd	Heath	Richardson	Chapman	Crooks	Cook	
								Platt	*Craggs*	*Johnson*	*Hedley**	*Ashcroft*	*McAndrew*	*Cochrane*	*Proctor*	*Hodgson*	*Burns*	*Armstrong*	*Nattrass*
29	1/3	H ARSENAL	19,752	17	26	L 2-3	0-0	Fox	Evans	Johnson P	Johnson P	Smith	Dodd	Heath*	Richardson	Chapman	Crooks	Cook	O'Callaghan
								Jennings	*Devine*	*Nelson*	*Talbot*	*O'Leary*	*Young*	*Brady*	*Sunderland*	*Stapleton*	*Price*	*Rix*	
30	8/3	A DERBY	22,695	17	27	D 2-2	2-2	Fox	Evans	Doyle	Heath	Smith	Dodd	Johnson P	Richardson	Chapman	Crooks	Cook	
								McKellar	*Langan*	*Buckley*	*Powell S*	*McFarland*	*Osgood*	*Emery*	*Powell B**	*Biley*	*Swindlehurst*	*Emson*	*McCaffery*
31	15/3	H NORWICH	14,333	16	29	W 2-1	2-0	Fox	Evans	Doyle	Heath	Smith	Dodd	Johnson P	Richardson	Chapman	Crooks	Cook	
								Hansbury	*Nightingale*	*Bond*	*McGuire**	*Jones*	*Powell*	*Woods*	*Taylor*	*Robson*	*Paddon*	*Peters*	*Mendham*

Scorers, Times, and Referees — with match reports

22 — A Manchester C: Dodd 5 · Power 16 · Ref: A Challinor
Peter Fox makes the save of the season in denying Michael Robinson a certain goal with a one-handed stop. It saves a point for Stoke who lead through Dodd's shot. Unmarked Paul Power equalises when he shoots high past Fox. Heath clears off the line and Tommy Caton hits the post.

23 — A Tottenham: Pratt 43 · Ref: L Burden
Spurs test Fox through Ardiles and Pratt. Stoke threaten when O'Callaghan's cross just evades Crooks' lunge. Heath, in a new central midfield role, urges Stoke forward but Pratt's great left-footed strike makes the difference. He nearly grabs a second but Fox saves well. Slipping lower.

24 — H Ipswich: Mariner 35 · Ref: G Napthine
One of Stoke's youngest ever teams faces prodigious scorers Ipswich and nearly grab a point. Mel Pejic fills in at full-back. Gates and Wark force Fox into spectacular saves. City press Ipswich back and Osman clears off the line. Crooks hits the bar (80 mins) then Johnson fires wide.

25 — H Bristol City: Rodgers 55 (og) · Ref: M Lowe
Jeff Cook, after 5 goals in 4 games while loaned to Plymouth, starts for the first time in 10 months. John Shaw seems unbeatable until Crooks' shot deflects off Alan Rodgers and past the startled goalkeeper. Richardson misses a twice-taken penalty after Kenyon fells Chapman (61 mins).

26 — A Crystal Palace: Chapman 70 · Ref: D Hughes
Manager Alan Durban celebrates two years in charge with a vital win against relegation rivals Palace. Stoke make the early running, but Paul Hinshelwood clears Alan Dodd's header off the line. Chapman buries a loose ball in a furious scramble and Stoke survive the inevitable siege.

27 — H Manchester U: Irvine 48 · Coppell 85 · Ref: D Sivill
City nearly sneak a win against Tommy Docherty's unconvincing United. Irvine buries a 20-yarder and Crooks has a goal ruled out for offside as Stoke have the better of the match. United level through Steve Coppell's cracking shot on the run. Gary Bailey saves superbly from Crooks.

28 — A Middlesbrough: Cook 4, Crooks 28, 87 · Burns 6 · Ref: K Redfern
In a wide open game Stoke get off to a flier as Jeff Cook bags in a scramble from a corner. Crooks' brace are a fine header from Irvine's centre and an inch perfect finish to Johnson's pass. Fox saves well from Cochrane and Proctor. Crooks nearly grabs a third but Platt denies him twice.

29 — H Arsenal: Cook 54, Chapman 74 · Sunderland 48, Price 60, Brady 62 · Ref: G Flint
A car accident has jeopardised the career of Sammy Irvine. Johnson replaces him in Stoke's midfield. City struggle to keep up with Brady who runs the show, crowning his display with a coolly taken winner. Chapman's looping header gives Stoke hope, but Arsenal are worthy winners.

30 — A Derby: Cook 12, 24 · Biley 22, Osgood 33 · Ref: A Grey
Against the run of play City lead twice when Jeff Cook notches from close range. The Rams fight back with two equally scrappy goals. Stoke cause more problems after the break but Smith's header smacks the underside of the bar. There is no way past the experienced Roy McFarland.

31 — H Norwich: Heath 22, Bond 35 (og) · Bond 51p · Ref: A Porter
City get the better of a lively Canaries team featuring £120,000 signing Clive Woods. Heath puts City ahead from close in and pressures Bond into prodding past Hansbury. Richardson misses yet another penalty (25 mins) after Powell fells Crooks. Doyle fouls Robson and Bond scores.

Football League Division One — season results (matches 32–42)

32 · EVERTON (A) · 18/3 — 0-2 (HT 0-0)
- League: 16th · L · 29 pts · Att: 23,848
- Scorers: Latchford 69, Eastoe 80 · Ref: M Peck
- Stoke: Fox, Evans, Johnson P, Heath, Smith, Dodd, O'Callaghan, Richardson, Chapman, Crooks, Cook*, Lumsden
- Everton: Hodge, Gidman, Bailey, Wright, Lyons, Eastoe, Megsan, King, Latchford, Hartford, McBride, Bracewell
- Peter Fox turns in a tremendous performance in high winds, superbly denying Latchford from four yards. City's first shot comes after 52 mins when Adrian Heath hits the post. City are never in the game after Latchford shoots past Fox. John Lumsden gets his first taste of league action.

33 · WOLVES (A) · 22/3 — 0-3 (HT 0-2)
- League: 17th · L · 29 pts · Att: 27,968
- Scorers: Gray 17, Eves 30, Richards 48 · Ref: K Salmon
- Stoke: Fox, Evans, Johnson P, Heath*, Smith, Dodd, O'Callaghan, Richardson, Chapman, Crooks, Cook, Bracewell
- Wolves: Bradshaw, Palmer, Parkin, Atkinson, Hughes, Berry, Brazier, Carr, Gray, Richards, Eves
- Andy Gray gives Smith a torrid time as Stoke are put to the sword by Wolves. He sweeps home the opener, slips the ball to Mel Eves to make it two and sets up Richards for the third. Crooks goes close twice and Brazier clears off the line. Paul Bracewell makes his debut as substitute.

34 · ASTON VILLA (H) · 29/3 — 2-0 (HT 1-0)
- League: 16th · W · 31 pts · Att: 16,234
- Scorers: Evans 16p, Chapman 65 · Ref: N Midgley
- Stoke: Fox, Evans, Johnson P, Heath*, Doyle, Dodd, O'Callaghan, Richardson, Chapman, Crooks, Cook*, Bracewell
- Aston Villa: Rimmer, Linton, Gibson, Ormsly, McNaught, Heard, Brenner, Swain, Evans, Cowans, Morley*, Hopkins
- City overcome Ron Saunders' Villa. Ray Evans cracks home a penalty for his first goal after Linton trips Crooks. O'Callaghan stars in his new centre-back role and Bracewell gets 75 mins of action after Heath is injured early on. Chapman converts Cook's pass after Morley hits the bar.

35 · LIVERPOOL (A) · 1/4 — 0-1 (HT 0-1)
- League: 17th · L · 31 pts · Att: 36,475
- Scorers: Dalglish 33 · Ref: A Saunders
- Stoke: Fox, Evans, Johnson P, O'Callaghan, Doyle, Dodd, Bracewell, Richardson, Chapman*, Crooks, Cook, Randall
- Liverpool: Clemence, Neal, Kennedy A, Thompson, Hansen, Dalglish, Case, Johnson, McDermott, Souness
- City stifle the Reds, restricting them to just Dalglish's scrappy goal from Alan Kennedy's cross. Dodd clears off the line from McDermott. Fox tips round Neal's thunderbolt and saves from Dalglish point blank. Chapman forces a reflex save from Clemence but Stoke offer little up front.

36 · MANCHESTER C (H) · 5/4 — 0-0 (HT 0-0)
- League: 17th · D · 32 pts · Att: 20,451
- Ref: B Stevens
- Stoke: Fox, Evans, Johnson P, Heath*, Smith, Dodd, Johnson P, Richardson, Chapman, Crooks, Cook, O'Callaghan
- Manchester City: Corrigan, Ranson, Reid, Booth, Caton, Power, Henry, Daley, Deyna, Tueart, Reeves
- Man City, 16 games without winning, are relieved to earn a draw. City threaten constantly with Crooks and Evans both going close. Henry and Power both test Fox. Lee Chapman powers a diving header just over the bar as the stalemate cannot be broken. Two goals in five games now.

37 · LEEDS (A) · 8/4 — 0-3 (HT 0-1)
- League: 18th · L · 32 pts · Att: 15,451
- Scorers: Parlane 5, Harris 49, 84 · Ref: D Richardson
- Stoke: Fox, Evans, Johnson P, Heath*, Smith, Dodd, Johnson P, Richardson, Chapman*, Crooks, Cook, Chapman
- Leeds: Lukic, Curtis, Cherry, Flynn, Hart, Madeley, Gray, Chandler, Harris, Parlane, Dickinson
- Stoke are outclassed by Leeds' slick passing. Harris's brace are both well-worked passing movements which leave him clean through with only Fox to beat. Crooks is left out and Alan Durban says 'He will not play the way I want him to'. Evans and Dodd both fire over from close range.

38 · SOUTHAMPTON (H) · 12/4 — 1-2 (HT 1-0)
- League: 18th · L · 32 pts · Att: 5,030
- Scorers: O'Callaghan 12; Golac 62, Boyer 75 · Ref: N Glover
- Stoke: Fox, Evans, Doyle, Bracewell, Smith, Dodd, Johnson P, Richardson*, Chapman, Crooks, Cook, Randall
- Southampton: Wells, Golac, Andr'szewski/Williams S, Watson, Nicholl, Hebberd, Boyer, Channon, Holmes, Hayes
- City take the lead against the high-flying Saints through O'Callaghan's stooping header. Southampton work two fine goals to produce a second-half comeback. Stoke lose their grip after Hebberd sets up Phil Boyer for his 24th of the season. Jeff Cook has Stoke's best chance to equalise.

39 · BOLTON (A) · 19/4 — 1-2 (HT 1-0)
- League: 18th · L · 32 pts · Att: 11,304
- Scorers: Crooks 44; Carter 60, Whatmore 67 · Ref: A Bridges
- Stoke: Fox, Evans, Doyle, Bracewell, Smith, Dodd, Johnson P*, Richardson*, Chapman, Crooks, Heath, O'Callaghan
- Bolton: McDonagh, Graham, Bennett, Wilson, Allardyce, Walsh, Nowak, Whatmore, Carter, Nicholson, Reid
- Already relegated Bolton call the tune despite Stoke grabbing the lead when Crooks squeezes a header past Jim McDonagh. They hit back with a whirlwind spell prompted by Peter Reid. Neil Whatmore grabs the winner after Smith's slip. Defeat leaves City staring relegation in the face.

40 · LIVERPOOL (H) · 23/4 — 0-2 (HT 0-1)
- League: 18th · L · 32 pts · Att: 11,996
- Scorers: Johnson 32, Fairclough 62 · Ref: P Reeves
- Stoke: Fox, Evans, Doyle, Heath, Smith, Dodd, Johnson PA, Richardson*, Chapman, Crooks, Heath, Cook
- Liverpool: Clemence, Irwin*, Kennedy A, Kennedy R, Hansen, Dalglish, Johnson, Lee, Souness, Cohen
- Spirited Stoke are swept aside by Bob Paisley's Liverpool who are on the march to the title once again. Dodd's rare mistake lets in Johnson for the opener then Fairclough heads home Johnson's centre. Heath puts Crooks clear but Clemence saves bravely. Stoke are not in the same class.

41 · BRIGHTON (H) · 26/4 — 1-0 (HT 1-0)
- League: 18th · W · 34 pts · Att: 14,422
- Scorers: Heath 35 · Ref: J Hunting
- Stoke: Fox, Evans, Johnson P, Heath, Smith, Dodd, Johnson PA, Richardson, Chapman, Crooks, Ursem, Sayer
- Brighton: Moseley, Gregory, Williams, Horton, Foster, Suddaby, McNab, Ward, Clarke, Lawrenson*, Stevens
- 'Inchy' Heath nudges City towards safety after Lock Ursem blocks Williams' clearance into his path. Graham Moseley acrobatically keeps out Brendan O'Callaghan's header. Victory almost guarantees safety as Bristol City lose at home to Norwich. A point against West Brom will do.

42 · WEST BROM (A) · 3/5 — 1-0 (HT 0-0)
- League: 18th · W · 36 pts · Att: 12,270
- Scorers: Heath 57 · Ref: P Richardson
- Stoke: Fox, Evans, Johnson P, Heath, Smith, Dodd, Bracewell, Richardson, Chapman, Crooks, Ursem, Heath
- West Brom: Godden, Batson, Cowdrill, Moses, Wile, Robertson, Trewick, Monaghan, Regis, Owen, Barnes
- City complete the escape thanks to Heath's shot. He also hits the post. Albion treat the game as an end of season canter and Owen, Batson and Regis all waste easy chances. Durban runs the rule over Ron Atkinson's midfielder, John Trewick, who is available for £300,000. Safe at last!

Home 20,068 · Away 23,995 · Average

LEAGUE DIVISION 1 (CUP-TIES) Manager: Alan Durban SEASON 1979-80

League Cup

	Att		F-A	H-T	Scorers, Times, and Referees	1	2	3	4	5	6	7	8	9	10	11	12 sub used
2:1 H SWANSEA 29/8	18,004 2:6	5 D	1:1	0-0	Smith 90 / Mahoney 82 / Ref: K McNally	Jones	Evans	Scott	Irvine*	Smith	Doyle	Busby	Heath	O'Callaghan	Crooks	Ursem	Richardson
						Crudgington	*Attley*	*Marustik*	*Charles**	*Phillips*	*Rushbury*	*Craig*	*Mahoney*	*Toshack*	*Waddle*	*Callaghan*	*Baker*

The Swans snatch the lead after Roger Jones' lets Mahoney's 30-yarder slip through his fingers. Crooks misses a penalty (60 mins) when he is tripped. Geoff Crudgington punches over and seems invincible until Smith joyously crashes home in injury time. Stoke miss Kendall's passing.

	Att		F-A	H-T	Scorers, Times, and Referees	1	2	3	4	5	6	7	8	9	10	11	12 sub used
2:2 A SWANSEA 4/9	20,030 2:2	11 W	3:1 (aet)	0-1	Crooks 55, 120, Randall 93 / Craig 22p / Ref: A Cox / (Stoke win 4-2 on aggregate)	Jones	Dodd	Scott	Irvine	Smith	Doyle	Randall*	Heath	O'Callaghan	Crooks	Richardson	Busby
						Crudgington	*Attley*	*Bartley**	*Charles*	*Phillips*	*Rushbury*	*Craig*	*Mahoney*	*Toshack*	*Waddle*	*Callaghan*	*Baker*

A half-time lambasting from Durban inspires City into action. They trail to Craig's penalty after Mahoney is fouled. Crooks is a revelation and sends the tie into extra-time with a cool finish. Crooks and then Randall clinically finish off the Swans, turning Heath's passes into vital goals.

	Att		F-A	H-T	Scorers, Times, and Referees	1	2	3	4	5	6	7	8	9	10	11	12 sub used
3 H SWINDON 26/9	15,255 3:7	16 D	2:2	2-1	Crooks 6, O'Callaghan 40 / Mayes 42, Rowland 87 / Ref: R Chadwick	Fox	Evans	Dodd	Irvine	Smith	Doyle	Busby	Heath	O'Callaghan	Crooks	Richardson	
						Allan	*Lewis*	*Templeman*	*McHale*	*Tucker*	*Stroud*	*Miller*	*Carter*	*Rowland*	*Mayes*	*Williams*	

Crooks nets Heath's pass then O'Callaghan slides home with Allan stranded. Bob Smith's Swindon look dead and buried. Shameful Stoke relax and let Swindon back in. Rowland's equaliser comes as he follows up his own shot which hits a post. Even the floodlight bulbs fuse in shame!

	Att		F-A	H-T	Scorers, Times, and Referees	1	2	3	4	5	6	7	8	9	10	11	12 sub used
3R A SWINDON 2/10	15,823 3:4	21 L	1:2	0-1	Chapman 68 / McHale 32, Mayes 55 / Ref: B Hill	Jones	Evans	Dodd	Dodd	Smith*	Doyle	Irvine	Heath	Chapman	Crooks	Randall	Busby
						Allan	*Lewis*	*Templeman*	*McHale*	*Tucker*	*Stroud*	*Miller**	*Carter*	*Rowland*	*Mayes*	*Williams*	*Hamilton*

Lee Chapman scores on his debut but Swindon harass City out of their stride. Ray McHale's 25-yarder equalises and, although Andy Rowland appears to be yards offside for the winner, Swindon are worthy victors. Denis Smith is subbed after a personal nightmare. Shock of the round.

FA Cup

	Att		F-A	H-T	Scorers, Times, and Referees	1	2	3	4	5	6	7	8	9	10	11	12 sub used
3 A BURNLEY 5/1	13,478 2:20	19 L	0:1	0-0	Dobson 77p / Ref: K McNally	Fox	Evans!	Irvine	Dodd	Smith!	Doyle	Heath	Richardson	O'Callaghan	Crooks	Randall	
						Stevenson	*Scott*	*Overson*	*Burke*	*Dixon*	*Rodaway*	*Cavener*	*Dobson*	*Hamilton*	*Young*	*Smith*	

City lose to lower division opponents yet again. Denis Smith and Ray Evans are both sent off (88 mins). Smith after a tussle. Evans for arguing with the ref. Evans trips Hamilton for the penalty. Crooks goes closest as Stoke dominate and Overson clears O'Callaghan's header off the line.

League table

	P	W	D	L	F	A	W	D	L	F	A	Pts
		Home					**Away**					
1 Liverpool	42	15	6	0	46	8	10	4	7	35	22	60
2 Manchester U	42	17	3	1	43	8	7	7	7	22	27	58
3 Ipswich	42	14	4	3	43	13	8	5	8	25	26	53
4 Arsenal	42	8	10	3	24	12	10	6	5	28	24	52
5 Nott'm Forest	42	16	4	1	44	11	4	4	13	19	32	48
6 Wolves	42	9	6	6	29	20	10	3	8	29	27	47
7 Aston Villa	42	11	5	5	29	22	4	7	10	22	28	46
8 Southampton	42	14	2	5	53	24	4	7	10	12	29	45
9 Middlesbro	42	11	7	3	31	14	5	5	11	19	30	44
10 West Brom	42	9	8	4	37	23	5	5	11	17	27	41
11 Leeds	42	10	7	4	30	17	3	7	11	16	33	40
12 Norwich	42	10	8	3	38	30	3	6	12	20	36	40
13 Crys Palace	42	11	5	5	26	13	3	7	11	17	37	40
14 Tottenham	42	11	5	5	30	22	4	5	12	22	40	40
15 Coventry	42	12	2	7	34	24	4	5	12	22	42	39
16 Brighton	42	8	8	5	25	20	3	7	11	22	37	37
17 Manchester C	42	8	8	5	28	25	4	5	12	15	41	37
18 STOKE	42	9	4	8	27	26	4	6	11	17	32	36
19 Everton	42	7	7	7	28	25	2	10	9	15	26	35
20 Bristol City	42	6	6	9	22	30	3	7	11	15	36	31
21 Derby	42	9	4	8	36	29	2	4	15	11	38	30
22 Bolton	42	5	11	5	19	21	0	4	17	19	52	25
	924	228	134	100	722	437	100	134	228	437	722	924

Odds & ends

Double wins: (2) Coventry, West Brom.

Double losses: (6) Everton, Wolves, Leeds, Ipswich, Southampton, Liverpool.

Won from behind: (0).

Lost from in front: (4) Aston Villa (a), Crystal Palace (h), Bolton (a), Southampton (h).

High spots: Survival in Division One.

A winning start versus Coventry.

Blooding of the youngsters as Paul Bracewell, Adrian Heath and Lee Chapman all claim regular places.

Low spots: Garth Crooks becoming unsettled and asking to leave.

Going out of both Cups to teams from lower divisions.

Four defeats in the last six games putting the pressure on as Bristol City and Derby nearly catch up.

Sammy Irvine's career ending car accident.

Player of the Year: Alan Dodd.

Ever-presents: (0).

Hat-tricks: (0).

Leading scorer: (15) Garth Crooks.

Appearances and Goals

	Lge	Sub	LC	Sub	FAC	Sub	Goals Lge	LC	FAC	Tot
Bracewell, Paul	4	2					1			1
Busby, Viv	4	6	2	2				1		1
Chapman, Lee	14	3	1				3		1	4
Cook, Jeff	13	1					4			4
Crooks, Garth	40		4		1		12		3	15
Dodd, Alan	36	1	3		1		1			1
Doyle, Mike	28		4		1					
Evans, Ray	40		3		1		1			1
Fox, Peter	23		1		1					
Heath, Adrian	38		4		1		5			5
Irvine, Sammy	26		4		1		3			3
Jones, Roger	19		3							
Johnson, Paul	25									
Johnson, Paul A	15									
Lumsden, John		1								
O'Callaghan, Brendan	32	4	3		1		5		1	6
Pejic, Mel	1									
Randall, Paul	12	4	2		1			1		1
Richardson, Paul	34	2	2	1	1		2			2
Scott, Geoff	16		3				1			1
Sheldon, Kevin	1									
Smith, Denis	34		4		1		2		1	3
Ursem, Loek	7		1							
(own-goals)							4			4
23 players used	462	24	44	3	11		44		7	51

LEAGUE DIVISION 1 Manager: Alan Durban SEASON 1980-81

No	Date	Att	Pos	Pt	F-A	H-T	Scorers, Times, and Referees	1	2	3	4	5	6	7	8	9	10	11	12 sub used
1	A NORWICH 16/8	14,616		L 0	1-5	1-4	Heath 44 [Woods 43] Downs 7, Fashanu 32, 45, 51, Ref: R Challis	Fox	Evans	**Hampton**	Doyle	Dodd	Richardson	Ursem	Heath*	Chapman	Cook	Bracewell	Johnson PA
	Norwich							Hansbury	McDowell	Downs	Mendham	Bond	Powell	Woods	Fashanu	Royle	Paddon	Goble	
2	H WEST BROM 20/8	14,085		D 1	0-0	0-0	Ref: K Hackett	Fox	Evans	Hampton	Dodd	Thorley	Richardson	Ursem	Johnson PA	Chapman	Cook	Bracewell	
	West Brom							Godden	Trewick	Statham	Moses	Wile	Robertson	Robson	Deehan	Regis	Owen	Barnes	
3	H IPSWICH 23/8	10,722	21 / 2	D 2	2-2	1-2	Ursem 8, Chapman 80 / Brazil 15, Gates 40, Ref: A Challinor	Fox	Evans	Hampton	Dodd	Thorley	Richardson	Ursem	Johnson PA*	Chapman	Cook	Bracewell	Randall
	Ipswich							Cooper	Burley	Mills	Thijssen	Osman	Butcher	Wark	Muhren	Mariner	Brazil*	Gates	O'Callaghan
4	A NOTT'M FOREST 30/8	21,915	22 / 6	L 2	0-5	0-2	McAughtrie [Robertson 76p] Wallace 11, 79, Birtles 31, 83, Ref: P Willis	Fox	Evans	Johnson P	**McAughtrie**	Dodd	Richardson	Sheldon	Randall	Chapman	Johnson PA	Bracewell	
	Nott'm Forest							Shilton	Anderson	Gray	McGovern	Lloyd	Needham	O'Neill	Bowyer	Birtles	Wallace	Robertson	
5	H LEEDS 6/9	12,739	16 / 19	W 4	3-0	3-0	Ursem 4, Maguire 14, Heath 30, Ref: K Warmsley	Fox	Evans	Hampton	Doyle	Thorley	Dodd	**Maguire**	Heath*	Ursem	Cook	Bracewell	Johnson PA
	Leeds							Lukic	Cherry	Greenhoff	Flynn	Hart	Madeley*	Parlane	Hamson	Connor	Sabella	Graham	Harris
6	A ARSENAL 13/9	27,183	19 / 5	L 4	0-2	0-0	Hollins 57, Sansom 77, Ref: A Robinson	Fox	Evans	Hampton	Dodd	Thorley	Doyle	Maguire	Heath	Chapman	O'Callaghan	Bracewell	
	Arsenal							Jennings	Devine	Sansom	Talbot	O'Leary	Young	Hollins	Sunderland	Stapleton	Price	Rix	
7	A MANCHESTER C 20/9	29,507	16 / 21	W 6	2-1	2-1	Ursem 35, Chapman 39 / Tueart 42, Ref: R Bridges	Fox	Evans	Hampton	Dodd	O'Callaghan	Doyle	Heath*	Ursem	Chapman	Thorley	Bracewell	
	Manchester C							Corrigan	Reid	Power	Caton	Henry*	Booth	Tueart	Daley	MacKenzie	Bennett	Deyna	Palmer
8	A MIDDLESBROUGH 27/9	11,847	13 / 14	W 8	1-0	1-0	Ursem 30, Ref: A Dobson	Fox	Evans	Hampton	Dodd	O'Callaghan	Doyle	Heath	Ursem	Chapman	Thorley	Bracewell	
	Middlesbrough							Stewart	Craggs	Bailey	Johnston	Angus	McAndrew	Nattrass*	Proctor	Hodgson	Jankovic	Armstrong	Hedley
9	H TOTTENHAM 4/10	18,511	13 / 12	L 8	2-3	0-2	Hampton 50, O'Callaghan 78 / Taylor 19p, Archibald 44, Hughton 77, Ref: T Morris	Fox	Evans	Hampton	Dodd	O'Callaghan	Doyle	Heath	Ursem	Chapman	Richardson*	Bracewell	Randall
	Tottenham							Daines	Smith	Hughton	Yorath	Lacy	Perryman	Ardiles	Archibald	Villa	Taylor	Crooks*	Roberts
10	A LEICESTER 8/10	15,549	14 / 19	D 9	1-1	1-1	Chapman 8 / Wilson 5, Ref: P Richardson	Fox	Evans	Hampton	Dodd	O'Callaghan	Doyle	Heath	Ursem*	Chapman	Richardson	Bracewell	Thorley
	Leicester							Wallington	Williams	Gibson	Goodwin	May	Scott	Lineker	Buchanan*	Henderson	Wilson	Smith	Young

1 — A NORWICH. Durban has yet to spend the £650,000 from the sale of Crooks to Spurs. It shows as Norwich over-run Stoke. The first of Justin Fashanu's hat-trick, a 25-yard cracker, is the best. Heath beats two defenders to slot home a neat goal, but City have Fox to thank for not conceding any more.

2 — H WEST BROM. Denis Thorley plays his first game for over three years, Peter Fox turns in a confident display against classy West Brom. He saves from Moses and Deehan, who also hits the post.

3 — H IPSWICH. Durban reflects that 'In a month's time 50 per cent of this side may not be playing'. Loek Ursem scores his first goal for the club, slipping the ball past Cooper, before Brazil and Gates fire Ipswich ahead. Paul Randall sets up Chapman's headed equaliser with his first touch as sub. Durban is interested in Villa's Alex Cropley.

4 — A NOTT'M FOREST. City are decimated by injuries and consequently are thrashed by Forest. The floodgates open in the closing stages when Ian Wallace and Gary Birtles both notch their second goals. Anderson is fouled for the penalty by new boy Dave McAughtrie. Stoke don't trouble ex-keeper Shilton.

5 — H LEEDS. £260,000 signing Paul Maguire makes a sensational debut, turning Greenhoff inside out on the right. He crosses for Ursem to bicycle kick City into the lead and then buries a rocket of a free-kick leaving John Lukic standing. Ex-Leeds full-back Peter Hampton sets up Heath for the third.

6 — A ARSENAL. Hollins and Sansom score rare headed goals as Arsenal win convincingly despite Durban employing a 3-5-2 formation in a bid to smother their midfield. Sansom's goal is his first since moving from Palace. Willie Young kicks his boot into the stand when clearing from a rare Stoke raid.

7 — A MANCHESTER C. O'Callaghan switches to central defence in a bid to stem the flow of goals. He looks at home straight away. Ursem fires in a curling effort and Chapman dives in among the boots to clinch the points. Stoke live dangerously and winger Kazimierz Deyna finds the net but is given offside.

8 — A MIDDLESBROUGH. Boro defend deeply and it takes a fine stooping header from Loek Ursem to break the deadlock. Chapman is lively and tests Stewart. Fox saves from Armstrong and Jankovic as Boro press on looking for the equaliser. Evans goes close with a pile-driver free-kick but City hang on to win.

9 — H TOTTENHAM. Garth Crooks returns amid acrimony to win Spurs a penalty when toppling in the area. City are always just out of touch after that. Spurs clinch it when Ardiles' shot hits Hughton on the head and rebounds home. O'Callaghan's bullet header puts City back in it and Chapman blazes over.

10 — A LEICESTER. Lee Chapman wins his duel with ex-Stokie Geoff Scott to nick the ball past Wallington and finish with ease. He equalises Ian Wilson's header which squeezes past Fox and Bracewell on the line. O'Callaghan's aerial threat from defence is becoming a larger weapon in the City armoury.

Match-by-match record (fixtures 11–21)

11 — A SOUTHAMPTON — 11/10
Att 19,473 · W 2-1 · (12 / 10 · 11)
Scorers: **Munro** 50, **Hampton** 77 — *George 28p*
Ref: M Taylor
Stoke: Fox, Evans, Hampton, Dodd, O'Callaghan, Doyle, Heath, Ursem, Chapman, Richardson, **Munro**, Bracewell
Southampton: *Katalinic, Golac, McCartney*, Williams, Watson, Nichall, George, Channon, Boyer, Holmes, Baker, Hebberd*
New £165,000 arrival from St Mirren, Iain Munro, fires in after Heath allows the ball to run through his legs. George buries a penalty after Fox initially saves from McCartney but is adjudged to have moved. Hampton's well-placed cross shot wins it. A first win at the Dell for 12 seasons.

12 — H BRIGHTON — 18/10
Att 13,079 · D 0-0 · (12 / 18 · 12)
Ref: P Reeves
Stoke: Fox, Evans, Hampton, Dodd, O'Callaghan, Doyle, Heath, Ursem, Chapman, Richardson, Munro, Bracewell
Brighton: *Moseley, Gregory, Williams, Horton, Foster, Lawrenson, McHale, Robinson, Smith, Ryan*, Cohen*
Confident Stoke open brightly but Graham Moseley keeps Alan Mullery's Seagulls in it. He saves from Chapman and Evans. Munro nets but is given offside and then hits the bar with a tremendous drive. Fox has little to do but the Boothen End grow impatient as chances go begging.

13 — H MANCHESTER U — 22/10
Att 24,549 · L 1-2 · (12 / 5 · 12)
Scorers: O'Callaghan 80 — *Jordan 47, Macari 59*
Ref: R Toseland
Stoke: Fox, Evans, Hampton, Dodd, O'Callaghan, Doyle, Heath, Ursem, Chapman, Richardson, Munro, Bracewell
Manchester U: *Bailey, Nicholl, Albiston, McIlroy, Jovanovic*, Moran, Birtles, Jordan, Macari, Thomas, Duxbury*
O'Callaghan stems the threat of new million pound man Gary Birtles. Stoke's midfield is swamped by the quality of Coppell, Thomas and McIlroy. Macari's nets a fine left-foot strike. O'Callaghan's header nearly inspires a comeback as Heath hits the bar, but City are second best.

14 — A BIRMINGHAM — 25/10
Att 16,535 · D 1-1 · (13 / 14 · 13)
Scorers: Doyle 80 — *Bertschin 57*
Ref: J Hunting
Stoke: Fox, Evans, Hampton, Dodd, O'Callaghan, Doyle, Heath, Ursem, Chapman, Richardson, Munro, Bracewell
Birmingham: *Wealands, Langan, Dennis, Curbishley, Gallagher, Todd, Lynex, Bertschin, Worthington, Gemmill, Dillon*
Stoke grab a point against Jim Smith's Birmingham. Lynex and Langan cause problems for Hampton. Langan fires in a shot which Fox parries and Bertschin taps in. Fox saves superbly from Worthington and Curbishley. Mike Doyle touches home Dodd's header from a corner to level.

15 — H LIVERPOOL — 1/11
Att 22,864 · D 2-2 · (15 / 2 · 14)
Scorers: Chapman 47, Randall 90 — *Johnson 24, Dalglish 79*
Ref: K Baker
Stoke: Fox, Evans, Hampton, Dodd*, O'Callaghan, Doyle, Bracewell, Heath, Chapman, Richardson, Munro, Randall
Liverpool: *Clemence, Neal, Kennedy A, Thompson, Kennedy R, Hansen, Dalglish, Lee, Johnson, McDermott, Souness*
In a superb match Stoke are equal to everything Liverpool throw at them. The Reds' neat passing leads to Johnson's headed goal but Chapman rams home from close range. Dalglish dives to head home before Randall lashes home Chapman's header with the last kick of the game. Great!

16 — A SUNDERLAND — 8/11
Att 21,483 · D 0-0 · (15 / 12 · 15)
Ref: T Mills
Stoke: Fox, Evans*, Hampton, Dodd, O'Callaghan, Doyle, Bracewell, Heath, Chapman, Richardson, Munro, Randall
Sunderland: *Turner, Whitworth, Bolton, Allardyce, Elliott, Buckley, Arnott, Rowell, Cooke, Brown*, Cummins, Robson*
Ken Knighton's Sunderland find City a tough nut to crack. Stoke start slowly with Chapman alone up front. Fox claws away Rowell's header. Randall miskicks Stoke's best chance from 5 yards out. Fox saves point blank from Cummins and from Rowell again as City soak up pressure.

17 — H NORWICH — 15/11
Att 11,207 · W 3-1 · (12 / 20 · 17)
Scorers: Chapman 7, 51, 58 — *Royle 87*
Ref: G Nolan
Stoke: Fox, Evans, Hampton, Dodd, O'Callaghan, Doyle, Bracewell, Heath, Chapman, Richardson, Munro, Bennett
Norwich: *Hansbury, Bond, Downs, McGuire, Nightingale, Barham, Fashanu, Royle, Paddon, Woods*, Bennett*
Ken Brown's Canaries are beaten by Lee Chapman's first career hat-trick. Stoke gain revenge for the opening day humiliation when Chapman heads home Ray Evans' free-kick and slots in Richardson's cross. He rounds things off by pouncing after Hansbury drops Inchy Heath's shot.

18 — H CRYSTAL PALACE — 22/11
Att 13,422 · W 1-0 · (11 / 21 · 19)
Scorers: O'Callaghan 56
Ref: B Martin
Stoke: Fox, Evans, Hampton, Dodd, O'Callaghan, Doyle, Bracewell, Heath, Chapman*, Richardson, Munro, **Griffiths**
Crystal Palace: *Barron, Boyle, Fenwick, Nicholas, Cannon, Gilbert, Lovell, Francis, Walsh, Flanagan, Hilaire*
City have all the pressure but Paul Barron stands in their way. He saves from Heath, Chapman and Richardson. O'Callaghan, playing up front, finally finds a way past him, controlling neatly before firing home right footed. Peter Griffiths, signed from Bideford Town for £15,000, debuts.

19 — A WEST BROM — 25/11
Att 15,922 · D 0-0 · (11 / 4 · 20)
Ref: S Bates
Stoke: Fox, Evans, Hampton, Dodd, O'Callaghan, Doyle, Randall*, Heath, Chapman, Richardson, Munro, Bracewell
West Brom: *Godden, Batson, Cowdrill, Moses, Wile, Robertson, Brown, Regis, Owen, Barnes*
A committed performance sees Stoke leave the Hawthorns with a creditable draw. Ron Atkinson's men pile on the pressure but the best chance falls to O'Callaghan, Godden tipping his header on to the bar. A Ray Evans pile-driver flashes just over. Stoke are unbeaten in six away games.

20 — A WOLVES — 29/11
Att 8,786 · L 0-1 · (11 / 14 · 20)
Scorers: *Bell 55*
Ref: B Stevens
Stoke: Fox, Evans, Hampton, Thorley, O'Callaghan, Doyle, Griffiths, Heath, Chapman, Richardson, Munro, Eves
Wolves: *Bradshaw, Humphrey, Hollifield, Daniel, Brazier, Hughes, Hibbitt, Atkinson, Bell, Richards, Eves*
In slippery conditions City battle fiercely. Heath and Chapman both go close. Norman Bell nicks the only goal of the game as he beats the City offside trap. O'Callaghan goes up front for the late rally and nearly nets. Mike Doyle has a thunderous drive palmed over by Paul Bradshaw.

21 — H EVERTON — 6/12
Att 15,350 · D 2-2 · (12 / 8 · 21)
Scorers: Chapman 35, O'Callaghan 68 — *McBride 12, Varadi 60*
Ref: T Farley
Stoke: Fox, Evans, Hampton, Dodd, O'Callaghan, Doyle, Ursem*, Heath, Chapman, Bracewell, Munro, **Griffiths**
Everton: *McDonagh, Wright, Bailey, Higgins, Stanley, O'Keefe, Eastoe, McMahon, Varadi, Hartford, McBride*
England Manager Ron Greenwood sees Stoke fight back after two superb Everton strikes. Chapman buries Ursem's flick on before McDonagh saves Evans' pen (47 mins) when Higgins fouls Chapman. O'Callaghan volleys McDonagh's punched clearance back over his head to level.

LEAGUE DIVISION 1

Manager: Alan Durban

22 — A MANCHESTER U — 13/12

1	2	3	4	5	6	7	8	9	10	11	12 sub used
Fox	Evans	Hampton	Dodd	O'Callaghan	Doyle	Randall	Heath	Chapman	Bracewell	Munro	
Bailey	*Nicholl*	*Albiston*	*McIlroy*	*Jovanovic*	*Moran*	*Coppell*	*Duxbury*	*Jordan*	*Macari*	*Thomas*	

Scorers, Times, and Referees: Randall 8, Chapman 21 / *Macari 28, Jordan 68* / Ref: G Flint

Att 39,568 · Pos *4* · Pt 22 · F-A 2-2 · H-T 2-1 · (11 D)

Stoke shock Dave Sexton's United with Randall's fierce volley and Chapman's glancing header. Macari scrambles one back before Fox denies Coppell point blank as United pile on the pressure. Finally Jordan heads home McIlroy's cross. O'Callaghan fires just wide. A good point.

23 — H LEICESTER — 20/12

1	2	3	4	5	6	7	8	9	10	11	12 sub used
Fox	Evans	Hampton	Dodd	O'Callaghan	Doyle	Randall*	Heath	Chapman	Bracewell	Munro	Cook
Wallington	*Williams*	*Gibson*	*Peake*	*Scott*	*O'Neill*	*Hamill**	*Melrose*	*Young*	*Wilson*	*MacDonald*	*Goodwin*

Scorers, Times, and Referees: Chapman 18 / Ref: A Seville

Att 13,433 · Pos *21* · Pt 24 · F-A 1-0 · H-T 1-0 · (11 W)

O'Callaghan stars as City dominate the first half. His shot is turned aside by Wallington only for Chapman to score with the follow up. He also has a fierce header tipped over. The pitch churns up making passing difficult. Stoke soak up the Foxes' pressure. Wilson's drive comes closest.

24 — A ASTON VILLA — 26/12

1	2	3	4	5	6	7	8	9	10	11	12 sub used
Fox	Evans	Hampton	Dodd	O'Callaghan	Doyle	Randall*	Heath	Chapman	Bracewell	Munro	Griffiths
Rimmer	*Swain*	*Williams*	*Evans*	*McNaught*	*Mortimer*	*Bremner*	*Shaw*	*Withe*	*Cowans*	*Morley*	

Scorers, Times, and Referees: *Withe 25* / Ref: M Scott

Att 34,658 · Pos *1* · Pt 24 · F-A 0-1 · H-T 0-1 · (11 L)

Stoke huff and puff but cannot dampen confident Villa. Shaw and Withe combine well up front and produce the one decisive moment in this battling affair. Fox saves Shaw's point-blank header but Withe turns home the rebound. Doyle and O'Callaghan both direct headers just wide.

25 — H COVENTRY — 27/12

1	2	3	4	5	6	7	8	9	10	11	12 sub used
Fox	Evans	Munro	Dodd	O'Callaghan	Doyle	Ursem*	Heath	Griffiths	Bracewell	Richardson	Thorley
Sealey	*Thomas*	*Roberts*	*Blair*	*Dyson*	*Gillespie*	*Bannister*	*Daly*	*Thompson*	*Hateley*	*Hunt*	

Scorers, Times, and Referees: Doyle 52, Griffiths 69 / *Hateley 41, Thompson 82* / Ref: J Worrall

Att 17,765 · Pos *14* · Pt 25 · F-A 2-2 · H-T 0-1 · (11 D)

In a thrilling game Stoke let Gordon Milne's Sky Blues off the hook. Mark Hateley's first league goal is equalised by Doyle's header. Griffiths slides home his first goal from Richardson's ripping cross but Thompson's flying header levels it. In a pulsating finale both sides nearly win it.

26 — A CRYSTAL PALACE — 10/1

1	2	3	4	5	6	7	8	9	10	11	12 sub used
Fox	Evans	Hampton	Dodd	O'Callaghan	Doyle	Bracewell*	Griffiths	Chapman	Richardson !	Munro	
Gennoe	*Hinshelwood*	*Boyle*	*Nicholas*	*Cannon*	*Gilbert*	*Lovell*	*Francis*	*Sealy*	*Carter*	*Hilaire**	*Smillie*

Scorers, Times, and Referees: Doyle 89 / *Boyle 1* / Ref: D Letts

Att 14,154 · Pos *21* · Pt 26 · F-A 1-1 · H-T 0-1 · (11 D)

Paul Richardson becomes the last player to be shown a red card before the league bans them. He walks for two yellows. Evans is cautioned for dissent again. In a tetchy match Palace seem to have won it through Boyle's header but Mike Doyle forces the ball past Gennoe and walks it in.

27 — A IPSWICH — 31/1

1	2	3	4	5	6	7	8	9	10	11	12 sub used
Fox	Doyle	Hampton	Dodd	O'Callaghan	Munro	Bracewell	Griffiths*	Heath	Maguire	Ursem	
Cooper	*Mills*	*McCall*	*Thijssen*	*Osman*	*Butcher*	*Wark*	*Muhren*	*Mariner**	*Brazil*	*Gates*	*O'Callaghan*

Scorers, Times, and Referees: *Wark 30p, Brazil 43, 48, Gates 84* / Ref: D Vickers

Att 23,843 · Pos *1* · Pt 26 · F-A 0-4 · H-T 0-2 · (13 L)

City are soundly beaten by Bobby Robson's Ipswich. The penalty, for Munro's tackle on Gates, is dubious but the others are all classy finishes. Cooper saves Stoke's best chance, a header from Griffiths. Fox saves two more Brazil efforts and Muhren hits the bar in front of an empty net.

28 — H ARSENAL — 7/2

1	2	3	4	5	6	7	8	9	10	11	12 sub used
Fox	Johnson PA	Hampton	Dodd	O'Callaghan	Doyle	Ursem	Bracewell	Chapman	Heath	Munro	
Jennings	*Hollins*	*Sansom*	*Talbot*	*O'Leary*	*Young*	*McDermott*	*Sunderland*	*Stapleton*	*Gatting*	*Rix*	

Scorers, Times, and Referees: Ursem 12 / *Stapleton 57* / Ref: V Callow

Att 14,406 · Pos *6* · Pt 27 · F-A 1-1 · H-T 1-0 · (13 D)

Profligate City waste numerous chances. Loek Ursem is sent clear to beat Jennings early on but O'Callaghan, Heath and Munro all shoot wide. Frank Stapleton hits the bar but then goes one better, firing home via the inside of the post. O'Callaghan fires just wide again. A point dropped.

29 — A LEEDS — 14/2

1	2	3	4	5	6	7	8	9	10	11	12 sub used
Fox	Johnson PA	Hampton	Dodd	O'Callaghan	Doyle	Ursem	Heath	Chapman	Bracewell	Munro	
Lukic	*Greenhoff*	*Gray*	*Flynn*	*Hart*	*Cherry*	*Harris*	*Hird*	*Connor**	*Parlane*	*Graham*	*Sabella*

Scorers, Times, and Referees: Chapman 28, 49, 63 / *Flynn 3* / Ref: A Saunders

Att 16,530 · Pos *15* · Pt 29 · F-A 3-1 · H-T 1-1 · (13 W)

After the shock of Brian Flynn's early strike, City hit back with another Lee Chapman hat-trick. He converts Bracewell's cross, then unleashes a 25-yard effort which flies in. He beats Lukic again in a one-on-one to complete a perfect day. City's first victory at Elland Road for 21 years.

30 — H NOTT'M FOREST — 18/2

1	2	3	4	5	6	7	8	9	10	11	12 sub used
Fox	Johnson PA	Hampton	Dodd	O'Callaghan	Doyle	Bracewell	Heath	Chapman	Ursem*	Munro	Griffiths
Shilton	*Anderson*	*Gray F*	*Gray S*	*Burns*	*Gunn*	*Mills*	*Wallace*	*Francis*	*Walsh**	*Robertson*	*O'Neill*

Scorers, Times, and Referees: Heath 50 / *Doyle 9 (og), Walsh 55* / Ref: M Lowe

Att 17,305 · Pos *6* · Pt 29 · F-A 1-2 · H-T 0-1 · (14 L)

Adrian Heath's left-foot volley past a startled Shilton equalises an unlucky deflection of Mills' shot by Mike Doyle past Fox. Heath also strikes the post. The elusive Trevor Francis proves to be the difference between the sides. He accelerates past Doyle to lay on a tap-in for Colin Walsh.

31 — A MIDDLESBROUGH — 21/2

1	2	3	4	5	6	7	8	9	10	11	12 sub used
Fox	Johnson PA	Munro	Dodd	O'Callaghan	Doyle*	Ursem	Heath	Chapman	Bracewell	Maguire	Thorley
Platt	*Nattrass*	*Bailey*	*Johnston*	*Ashcroft*	*McAndrew*	*Cochrane*	*Proctor*	*Hodgson*	*Jankovic*	*Armstrong*	

Scorers, Times, and Referees: Maguire 83 / *Jankovic 44, 89p, Cochrane 69* / Ref: D Allison

Att 15,142 · Pos *10* · Pt 29 · F-A 1-3 · H-T 0-1 · (14 L)

Stoke are never in the hunt at Ayresome after Bosco Jankovic's 20-yarder sails past Fox. Despite a stomach bug Maguire starts. He pulls a goal back after latching on to Paul Johnson's free-kick. John Neal's Boro seal it when Jankovic buries a penalty after being tripped by Fox himself.

32 · A TOTTENHAM — 2-2 (15 D, 30 pts) · Att 28,742 (8)
Scorers: O'Callaghan 5, Heath 75 / Ardiles 72, Brooke 82 — Ref: D Hutchinson

Stoke	Fox	Johnson PA!	Hampton	Dodd	O'Callaghan	Doyle	Heath	Bracewell	Chapman	Munro	Maguire
Tottenham	Daines	Hughton*	Roberts	McAllister	Perryman	Ardiles	Archibald	Galvin	Haddle	Crooks	Brooke

O'Callaghan's header and Heath's cross-shot put Stoke 2-1 up. Garth Crooks is at the centre of controversy when Paul A Johnson is sent off on 76 mins for fouling him. Stoke react to Crooks' histrionics and the trouble carries on after the match finishes. City fail to hold on with 10 men.

33 · H SOUTHAMPTON — 1-2 (15 L, 30 pts) · Att 14,828 (4)
Scorers: Heath 86 / Keegan 31, 75 — Ref: D Scott

Stoke	Fox	Griffiths	Hampton	Dodd	O'Callaghan	Doyle	Heath	Bracewell	Chapman	Munro*	Maguire
Southampton	Wells	Golac	Holmes	Williams	Watson	Nicholl	Keegan	Channon	George	Moran	Ball

Kevin Keegan shows off his finishing skills by slotting two past keeper Fox. Heath's consolation effort from 18 yards doesn't unduly worry Saints as Stoke apply late pressure. Even Mike Doyle is flagged offside going forward! Maguire hits the post with a free-kick from 25 yards.

34 · H MANCHESTER C — 2-1 (11 W, 32 pts) · Att 15,802 (13)
Scorers: Doyle 45, O'Callaghan 76 / McDonald 28 — Ref: H Taylor

Stoke	Fox	Johnson PA	Hampton*	Dodd	O'Callaghan	Doyle	Munro	Heath	Chapman	Bracewell	Maguire
Man City	Corrigan	Ranson	McDonald	Reid	Power	Booth	Tueart	Buckley	MacKenzie*	Henry	Reeves · Caton

After conceding to an unmarked header from Bobby McDonald, City bounce back with ex-Blues man Mike Doyle heading home a corner. The action ebbs and fros before O'Callaghan thumps a loose ball into the roof of the net after Ray Ranson clears off the line. First home win of 1981.

35 · A BRIGHTON — 1-1 (11 D, 33 pts) · Att *3,583 (19)
Scorers: Ursem 35 / Robinson 9 — Ref: B Daniels

Stoke	Fox	Johnson PA	Munro	Dodd	O'Callaghan	Doyle	Ursem	Heath	Chapman	Williams	Maguire
Brighton	Digweed	Stevens	Williams	Horton	Foster	Ritchie	Gregory	Stille	Robinson	Smith	McNab

City equalise through Loek Ursem who touches in Brendan O'Callaghan's shot. Chapman has a goal disallowed for offside and both Heath and O'Callaghan head just over. Stoke are rarely troubled by an out-of-form Seagulls side but Durban is unsettled at the line to chances ratio.

36 · H BIRMINGHAM — 0-0 (12 D, 34 pts) · Att *4,624 (10)
Ref: A Porter

Stoke	Fox	Johnson PA	Munro	Dodd	O'Callaghan	Doyle	Ursem	Heath*	Chapman	Bertschin	Maguire
Birmingham	Wealands	Langan	Dennis	Dillon	Gallagher	Todd	Ainscow	Evans	Bertschin	Worthington · Broadhurst	Griffiths

A poor display which angers the fans with its insipidity. A high wind doesn't help. Todd clears Chapman's cross off his goal-line. Mike Doyle plays his 550th league game. Wealands saves a low Bracewell shot. Steve Parkin stars for England Schools who beat Northern Ireland 4-0.

37 · A LIVERPOOL — 0-3 (13 L, 34 pts) · Att *3,308 (5)
Scorers: — / Whelan 26, McDermott 53, 81 — Ref: P Tyldesley

Stoke	Fox	Munro		Dodd	O'Callaghan	Doyle	Whelan	Heath	Chapman		Maguire
Liverpool	Clemence	Neal	Kennedy A	Thompson	Whelan	Hansen	Dalglish	Lee	Rush	McDermott	Case

Playing on Friday night due to the Grand National Stoke are overrun by a Liverpool side resting most of its League Cup winning stars. Ronnie Whelan scores on his debut and McDermott fizzes two drives past Fox. City threaten early on as Ursem forces Clemence into a fingertip save.

38 · H SUNDERLAND — 2-0 (12 W, 36 pts) · Att 11,501 (17)
Scorers: Chapman 64, Dodd 85 — Ref: D Owen

Stoke	Fox	Evans	Munro	Dodd	O'Callaghan	Doyle	Ursem	Heath	Chapman	Rowell	Maguire
Sunderland	Siddall	Hinnigan	Bolton	Hindmarch	Allardyce	Chisholm	Arnott	Brown	Ritchie	Rowell	Cummins

Lee Chapman finally breaks stubborn Sunderland resistance when he prods home in a scramble. Alan Dodd clinches it, following up Maguire's blocked shot to fire low past Siddall. Ken Knighton's struggling Wearsiders fail to muster a single on-target effort. Only the third win of 1981.

39 · A COVENTRY — 2-2 (12 D, 37 pts) · Att 12,766 (20)
Scorers: Chapman 50, Maguire 71p / Daly 25, Thompson 45 — Ref: M Bidmead

Stoke	Fox	Evans	Hampton*	Dodd	O'Callaghan	Doyle	Hampton	Heath	Chapman	Bracewell	Maguire
Coventry	Sealey	Coop	Roberts	Blair	Dyson	Gillespie	Bannister	Daly	Thompson	English	Hunt

A fine comeback by City after two suicidal back-passes by O'Callaghan and Inchy gift Coventry a comfortable lead. Chapman heads in Evans' cross and then Maguire is brought down when clean through, converting the spot-kick himself. Desperate Coventry pressure comes to nothing.

40 · H ASTON VILLA — 1-1 (12 D, 38 pts) · Att 25,511 (1)
Scorers: O'Callaghan 25 / Withe 22 — Ref: P Willis

Stoke	Fox	Evans	Munro	Dodd	O'Callaghan	Doyle	Ursem	Hampton	Chapman	Bracewell	Maguire
Aston Villa	Rimmer	Swain	Gibson	Evans	McNaught	Mortimer	Bremner	Shaw*	Withe	Cowans	Morley · Deacy

Stoke give a very good account of themselves against the Champions elect. Brendan O'Callaghan bosses Peter Withe and still finds time to get forward to flick home a corner for the equaliser. Doyle has a header cleared off the line and Heath and Bracewell both shoot just past the post.

41 · A EVERTON — 1-0 (11 W, 40 pts) · Att *5,352 (16)
Scorers: Heath 80 — Ref: G Courtney

Stoke	Fox	Evans	Munro	Dodd	O'Callaghan	Doyle	Ursem*	Hampton	Chapman	Bracewell	Maguire
Everton	McDonagh	Barton	Bailey	Ratcliffe	Lyons	Lodge	Megson	Eastoe	Sharp	Hartford	McBride* · Varadi

Everton are urged forward by under fire boss Gordon Lee. O'Callaghan clears off the line from Lyons. Stoke's teamwork shines through. Fox returns from a cheek-bone operation. New England U-21 cap Adrian Heath scores a great 30-yarder. Lyons clears an Ursem header off the line.

42 · H WOLVES — 3-2 (11 W, 42 pts) · Att *4,929 (19)
Scorers: Bracewell 25, 68, Ursem 82 / Evans 22 (og), Hibbitt 89 — Ref: D Richardson

Stoke	Fox	Evans	Munro	Dodd	O'Callaghan	Doyle	Ursem	Hampton	Chapman	Bracewell	Maguire
Wolves	Kearns	Palmer	Hollifield	Brazier*	McAlle	Berry	Hibbitt	Carr	Gray	Richards	Teasdale · Atkinson

John Barnwell's Wolves still need a point from one of their last two games. Paul Bracewell's first league goals are both left-foot strikes. Ursem hammers home Chapman's nod down to wrap it up. Kenny Hibbitt's late goal stands despite a linesman flagging for a foul throw. Good finish.

Home · **Away 21,363** · **Average 16,253**

LEAGUE DIVISION 1 (CUP-TIES)   Manager: Alan Durban   SEASON 1980-81

League Cup

		Att		F-A	H-T	Scorers, Times, and Referees	1	2	3	4	5	6	7	8	9	10	11	12 sub used
2:1	H MANCHESTER C	21	D	1-1	1-0	Chapman 2	Fox	Evans	Hampton	Dodd	Thorley	Richardson	Ursem	Johnson PA	Chapman	Cook*	Bracewell	Randall
	27/8	13,176	18			Henry 75	Corrigan*	Ranson	Reid	Booth	Caton	Henry	Tueart	Daley	MacKenzie	Power	Reeves	Palmer
						Ref: G Napthine												

Stoke get off to a great start when Lee Chapman converts Cook's cross after 75 seconds. Corrigan and Cook collide three minutes later and the keeper is carried off leaving Tommy Booth in goal. Stoke relax and allow Henry to equalise. Fox has to make two sharp saves to avoid defeat.

		Att		F-A	H-T	Scorers, Times, and Referees	1	2	3	4	5	6	7	8	9	10	11	12 sub used
2:2	A MANCHESTER C	22	L	0-3	0-2	Henry 10, Bennett 43, 53	Fox	Evans	Hampton	Dodd	Thorley	Richardson	Johnson PA	Bracewell	Chapman	Heath*	Maguire	Randall
	3/9	21,356	18			Ref: G Owen	MacRae	Ranson	Reid	Booth	Caton	Henry	Bennett	Daley	MacKenzie	Power	Reeves	
						(Stoke lose 1-4 on aggregate)												

Dave Bennett runs Stoke ragged and is only denied a deserved hat-trick by Johnson's overhead goal-line clearance. He sets up Henry's opener and then bags two of his own. Durban has to include Maguire who is not even fully fit. Booth skies a last-minute penalty after Johnson handles.

FA Cup

		Att		F-A	H-T	Scorers, Times, and Referees	1	2	3	4	5	6	7	8	9	10	11	12 sub used
3	H WOLVES	11	D	2-2	1-2	Chapman 30, Bracewell 52	Fox	Evans	Hampton	Dodd	O'Callaghan	Doyle	Bracewell	Heath	Chapman	Richardson	Munro	
	3/1	24,737	19			Eves 26, Hibbitt 38	Bradshaw	Palmer	Hollifield	Daniel	Brazier	Barry	Hibbitt	Atkinson	Bell	Richards	Eves	
						Ref: C White												

An all-action thriller. Chapman applies the finish to Richardson's shot to equalise Eves' header. Then Hibbitt's deflected shot beats Fox before Paul Bradshaw saves wonderfully from O'Callaghan and Richardson. Bracewell turns on the edge of the box to fire home his first senior goal.

		Att		F-A	H-T	Scorers, Times, and Referees	1	2	3	4	5	6	7	8	9	10	11	12 sub used
3R	A WOLVES	11	L	1-2	1-0	Heath 34	Fox	Evans	Hampton	Dodd	Cook	Doyle	Bracewell	Heath	Chapman	Maguire*	Munro	Richardson
	6/1	22,892	19			Eves 48, Hibbitt 58	Bradshaw	Palmer	Hollifield	Daniel	McAlle	Berry	Hibbitt	Atkinson	Bell	Richards	Eves	
						Ref: C White												

Stoke surrender after Inchy Heath grabs a goal on the break, flicking the ball over Paul Bradshaw. Wolves power back as Mel Eves slots home when Richards' shot is saved. Eves also hits the bar, then Kenny Hibbitt crashes a 25-yarder past Fox. City haven't beaten Wolves in 11 games.

		P	Home					Away					Pts
			W	D	L	F	A	W	D	L	F	A	
1	Aston Villa	42	16	3	2	40	13	10	5	6	32	27	60
2	Ipswich	42	15	4	2	45	14	8	6	7	32	29	56
3	Arsenal	42	13	8	0	36	17	6	7	8	25	28	53
4	West Brom	42	15	4	2	40	15	5	8	8	20	27	52
5	Liverpool	42	13	5	3	38	15	4	12	5	24	27	51
6	Southampton	42	15	4	2	47	22	5	6	10	29	34	50
7	Nott'm Forest	42	15	3	3	44	20	4	9	8	18	24	50
8	Manchester U	42	9	11	1	30	14	6	7	8	21	22	48
9	Leeds	42	10	5	6	19	19	7	5	9	20	28	44
10	Tottenham	42	9	9	3	44	31	5	6	10	26	37	43
11	STOKE	42	8	9	4	31	23	4	9	8	20	37	42
12	Manchester C	42	10	7	4	35	25	4	4	13	21	34	39
13	Birmingham	42	11	5	5	32	23	2	7	12	18	38	38
14	Middlesbro	42	14	4	3	38	16	2	1	18	15	45	38
15	Everton	42	8	6	7	32	25	5	4	12	23	33	36
16	Coventry	42	9	6	6	31	30	4	4	13	17	38	36
17	Sunderland	42	10	4	7	32	19	4	3	14	20	34	35
18	Wolves	42	10	2	8	26	20	2	7	12	17	35	35
19	Brighton	42	10	3	8	30	26	4	4	13	24	41	35
20	Norwich	42	9	7	5	34	25	4	0	17	15	48	33
21	Leicester	42	7	5	9	20	23	6	1	14	20	44	32
22	Crys Palace	42	6	4	11	32	37	0	3	18	15	46	19
		924	243	118	101	756	472	101	118	243	472	756	924

Odds & ends

Double wins: (2) Manchester City, Leeds.

Double losses: (1) Nott'm Forest.

Won from behind: (4) Leeds (a), Manchester C (h), Southampton (a), Wolves (h).

Lost from in front: (0).

High spots: Finishing in the top half of the table.

Drawing at Old Trafford.

The first win at the Dell for 13 years.

Lee Chapman's two hat-tricks.

Brendan O'Callaghan's conversion from centre-forward to centre-half.

Low spots: The worst possible start – a thrashing at Norwich.

Heavy defeats by Forest and Ipswich.

Disappointing attendances for the top flight.

Losing manager Alan Durban at the end of the season to Sunderland.

Player of the Year: Peter Fox.

Ever-presents: (1) Peter Fox.

Hat-tricks: (2) Lee Chapman (twice).

Leading scorer: (17) Lee Chapman.

Appearances and Goals

	Appearances						Goals			
	Lge	Sub	LC	Sub	FAC	Sub	Lge	LC	FAC	Tot
Bracewell, Paul	36	4	2		2		2		1	3
Chapman, Lee	41	1	2		2		15	1	1	17
Cook, Jeff	3		1		1					
Dodd, Alan	41		2		2		4			4
Doyle, Mike	38		2		2					
Evans, Ray	32		2		2					
Fox, Peter	42		2		2					
Griffiths, Peter	5	5					1			1
Hampton, Pete	32	1	2		2		2			2
Heath, Adrian	38		1		2		6		1	7
Johnson, Paul	1									
Johnson, Paul A	11	2	2							
Maguire, Paul	15		1				3			3
McAughtrie, Dave	1									
Munro, Iain	32				2		1			1
O'Callaghan, Brendan	37				1		7			7
Randall, Paul	6	4				2	2			2
Richardson, Paul	18		2			1	1			1
Sheldon, Kevin	1									
Thorley, Dennis	8	3	2							
Ursem, Loek	24	4	1				7			7
21 players used	462	24	22	2	22	1	51	1	3	55

LEAGUE DIVISION 1

Manager: Richie Barker

SEASON 1981-82

Match results

No		Opponent	Date	Pos	Att	Res	Pos	Pt	F-A	H-T	Scorers, Times	Referee
1	A	ARSENAL	29/8		28,212	W		3	1-0	1-0	Chapman 44	Ref: T Bune
2	H	COVENTRY	2/9		13,914	W		6	4-0	2-0	Chapman 5, 77, Heath 12, 54	Ref: D Richardson
3	H	MANCHESTER C	5/9	5	25,256	L	2	6	1-3	0-1	Chapman 62 / Francis 35, 89, Boyer 65	Ref: L Robinson
4	A	WEST HAM	12/9	7	28,774	L	1	6	2-3	1-1	O'Callaghan 29, Maguire 87p / Goddard 7, 50, Stewart 68p	Ref: J Martin
5	H	NOTT'M FOREST	19/9	11	15,653	L	6	6	1-2	1-0	Heath 5 / Walsh 50, Mills 82	Ref: A Seville
6	A	ASTON VILLA	23/9	10	25,637	D	17	7	2-2	0-1	Griffiths 63, Maguire 65p / Withe 38, 46	Ref: T Morris
7	A	MIDDLESBROUGH	26/9	16	11,604	L	20	7	2-3	1-1	Griffiths 18, Chapman 80 / Cochrane 2, Woof 78, Shearer 83	Ref: C Seel
8	H	EVERTON	3/10	12	16,007	W	11	10	3-1	1-0	Chapman 2, 90, Maguire 80 / McBride 72	Ref: H Taylor
9	A	TOTTENHAM	10/10	15	30,250	L	3	10	0-2	0-0	Ardiles 65, Crooks 87	Ref: T Glasson
10	H	SWANSEA	17/10	17	14,665	L	1	10	1-2	1-0	Griffiths 35 / Stanley 67, Latchford 70	Ref: D Scott

Line-ups (1–11, 12 sub used)

Match	1	2	3	4	5	6	7	8	9	10	11	12
1 Stoke	Fox	Evans	Hampton	Dodd	O'Callaghan	Doyle	Griffiths	Heath	Chapman	Bracewell	Maguire	
1 *Arsenal*	*Jennings*	*Devine**	*Sansom*	*Talbot*	*O'Leary*	*Young*	*Davis*	*Sunderland*	*McDermott*	*Nicholas*	*Rix*	*Vaessen*
2 Stoke	Fox	Evans	Hampton	Dodd	O'Callaghan	Doyle	Griffiths	Heath	Chapman	Bracewell	Maguire	
2 *Coventry*	*Blyth*	*Thomas*	*Roberts*	*Jacobs*	*Dyson*	*Gillespie*	*Bodak**	*Daly*	*Thompson*	*Whitton*	*Hunt*	*Kaiser*
3 Stoke	Fox	Evans	Hampton	Dodd	O'Callaghan	Doyle	Griffiths	Heath	Chapman	Bracewell	Maguire*	
3 *Man C*	*Corrigan*	*Ranson*	*McDonald*	*Reid*	*Power**	*Caton*	*O'Neill*	*Gow*	*Francis*	*Hutchison*	*Reeves*	*Boyer*
4 Stoke	Fox	Evans	Hampton	Dodd	O'Callaghan	Doyle	Griffiths	Heath	Chapman	Bracewell	Maguire	
4 *West Ham*	*Parkes*	*Stewart*	*Lampard*	*Bonds*	*Martin*	*Devonshire*	*Neighbour*	*Goddard*	*Cross*	*Allen*	*Pike*	
5 Stoke	Fox	Evans	Hampton	Dodd*	O'Callaghan	Smith	Griffiths	Heath	Chapman	Bracewell	Maguire	Ursem
5 *Forest*	*Shilton*	*Anderson*	*Gray*	*McGovern*	*Burns*	*Aas*	*Proctor*	*Wallace*	*Fashanu*	*Mills*	*Walsh*	*Ursem*
6 Stoke	Fox	Evans	Hampton	Dodd	O'Callaghan	Smith	Griffiths	Heath	Chapman	Bracewell	Maguire	Ursem
6 *Aston Villa*	*Rimmer*	*Swain*	*Gibson*	*Evans*	*McNaught**	*Mortimer*	*Bremner*	*Donovan*	*Withe*	*Cowans*	*Morley*	*Blair*
7 Stoke	Fox	Evans	Hampton	Dodd	O'Callaghan	**Bould**	Griffiths	Heath*	Chapman	Bracewell	Maguire	Cook
7 *Middlesbrough*	*Platt*	*Craggs*	*Bolton*	*Ross**	*Baxter*	*McAndrew*	*Cochrane*	*Otto*	*Shearer*	*Woof*	*Askew*	*Thomson*
8 Stoke	Fox	Evans	Hampton	Dodd	O'Callaghan	Smith	Ursem	Heath	Chapman	Bracewell	Maguire	
8 *Everton*	*Arnold*	*Wright*	*Bailey**	*Walsh*	*Lyons*	*Thomas*	*McMahon*	*O'Keefe*	*Biley*	*Ross*	*McBride*	*Sharp*
9 Stoke	Fox	Evans	Hampton	Dodd	O'Callaghan	Smith	Griffiths	Heath	Chapman	Bracewell	Maguire*	Bould
9 *Tottenham*	*Clemence*	*Hughton*	*Miller*	*Roberts*	*Villa**	*Perryman*	*Ardiles*	*Archibald*	*Galvin*	*Hoddle*	*Crooks*	*Hazard*
10 Stoke	Fox	Evans	Hampton	Dodd	O'Callaghan	Smith	Griffiths	Heath	Chapman	Bracewell	Maguire	
10 *Swansea*	*Davies*	*Robinson*	*Hadziabdic*	*Rajkovic*	*Irwin*	*Mahoney*	*Curtis*	*James L**	*James R*	*Stanley*	*Latchford*	*Stanley*

Match notes

1. **Arsenal** — Lee Chapman celebrates a new contract by scoring the winner. He tackles Willie Young and fires Jennings. New manager Richie Barker's attacking philosophy is clear as City force four corners in the first 15 minutes. Dodd, Doyle and O'Callaghan swallow up Arsenal's long balls.

2. **Coventry** — Dave Sexton's Coventry are thrashed by a rampaging Stoke. Chapman's brace are both fine headers on the back post. Heath places both of his shots past Jim Blyth to perfection. He also has another tremendous goal ruled out because the referee has given him a free-kick! Fantastic stuff.

3. **Manchester C** — Trevor Francis scores twice on his debut for John Bond's men. Paul Bracewell urges Stoke back into the match after Francis' opener and feeds Chapman who shrugs off two defenders to fire home the equaliser. Blues clinch it with Phil Boyer's drive and a brilliant second from Francis.

4. **West Ham** — John Lyall's Hammers pip City in an entertaining game. O'Callaghan scores a fly-header. Maguire converts the penalty for hands by Bonds. West Ham's spot-kick comes when Fox hauls down Alan Devonshire. The lively Griffiths goes close in injury-time but Phil Parkes saves well.

5. **Nott'm Forest** — Clough sends winger John Robertson home after a pre-match argument and his replacement, Colin Walsh, equalises Heath's close-range finish to Chapman's centre. Mills' unstoppable volley wins it. Shilton touches over Evans' shot. Denis Smith returns after a year out with a cartilage.

6. **Aston Villa** — Peter Withe's brace for the Champions are both six-yard box finishes. Stoke pour forward and have Villa reeling when Griffiths converts after Heath's shot hits the upright. Ken McNaught handles and Maguire sends Rimmer the wrong way from the spot. An encouraging performance.

7. **Middlesbrough** — Another nailbiting match. Peter Griffiths' cool finish equalises Cochrane's rasping drive. Chapman notches a second equaliser, forcing the ball over the line from close range. In a frantic finale David Shearer wins it with a 25-yard shot. Steve Bould's debut – out of position at centre-half.

8. **Everton** — City overwhelm Howard Kendall's Everton. Lee Chapman's brace include a cool six-yard finish and a great left-foot finish after a Maguire short corner move involving O'Callaghan and Heath. Joe McBride's header is merely a blip. Maguire and Dodd bring good saves out of Jim Arnold.

9. **Tottenham** — Keith Burkinshaw's Spurs stop Stoke scoring for the first time this season. Spurs dominate with Archibald, Ardiles and Hoddle instrumental in pulling the strings. Ardiles turns home the rebound after Fox parries Miller's shot on to the post, then Crooks deflects Hazard's drive past Fox.

10. **Swansea** — Stoke cruise the first half and are well worth Peter Griffiths' goal from Maguire's in-swinging corner. The fightback begins when Gary Stanley replaces Leighton James. He equalises and sets up the winner as John Toshack's Swans win to top the League for the first time in their history.

11 H BIRMINGHAM 24/10 5,399 15 W 14 13 1-0 0-0
Chapman 50
Ref: R Bridges

Fox / Evans / Hampton / Dodd / O'Callaghan / Smith / Griffiths / Heath / Chapman / Bracewell / Maguire
Wealands / V d Hauwe / Hawker / Dillon / Broadhurst / Todd / Bracken / Evans / Worthington / Gemmill / Van Merlo

A dull game is won by a scrappy goal as Lee Chapman chests the ball over the line when Heath's cross is allowed to run through to him. Dodd heads a Worthington lob off the line. Griffiths misses a gilt edged chance with three mins to go. Barker is enquiring about Leeds' Brian Flynn.

---

12 A BRIGHTON 31/10 7,862 16 D 7 14 0-0 0-0
Ref: D Letts

Fox / Evans / Hampton / Dodd / O'Callaghan / Smith / Griffiths / Heath / Chapman / Bracewell / Maguire
Moseley / Shanks / Williams / Grealish* / Foster / Gatting / Case / Ritchie / Robinson / McNab / Smith / Stevens

Stoke put up a determined display to hold out against a busy Brighton side. Fox makes saves from Ritchie, Robinson and Shanks before being forced to handle outside his area. Tony Grealish fires the free-kick just wide. Heath weaves his way through but cannot beat Graham Moseley.

---

13 H SOUTHAMPTON 7/11 13,884 18 L 8 14 0-2 0-1
Armstrong 7, Keegan 67p
Ref: B Hill

Fox / Evans / Hampton / Dodd / O'Callaghan / Smith / Griffiths / Heath / Chapman / Bracewell / Maguire* / Johnson PA
Katalinic / Golac / Holmes / Williams / Nicholl / Waldron / Keegan / Channon / Moran / Armstrong / Ball

Lawrie McMenemy's Saints have too much know-how for Stoke. Maguire has a goal disallowed in the first minute for offside. Keegan's pace unsettles the tall O'Callaghan and Smith. David Armstrong's 20-yard drive and Keegan's penalty, after Fox brings him down, clinch the points.

---

14 A WEST BROM 14/11 15,787 13 W 18 17 2-1 2-1
Heath 25, Chapman 37
Smith 5 (og)
Ref: S Bates

Fox / Evans / Hampton / Dodd / O'Callaghan / Smith / Griffiths / Heath / Chapman / Bracewell / Johnson PA
Grew / Batson* / Statham / Whitehead / Wile / Robertson / Jol / Brown / Regis / Owen / MacKenzie / King

Albion set off like a steam train and force Smith to turn the ball past Fox from Whitehead's cross. Dodd gradually wins the midfield battle and Smith dominates in the air. With City on top Heath speeds clear to crack home then Chapman intercepts Statham's back-pass and rounds Grew.

---

15 H IPSWICH 21/11 13,802 12 W 3 20 2-0 0-0
Chapman 60, Maguire 90
Ref: H King

Fox / Evans / Hampton / Dodd / O'Callaghan / Smith / Griffiths / Heath* / Chapman / Bracewell / Johnson PA / Maguire
Cooper / Burley / McCall / Mills / Osman / Butcher / Wark / Mariner / Brazil / Gates

City compete well with UEFA Cup holders Ipswich. Dodd breaks up Town's passing midfield and Bracewell prompts Stoke forward. He finds Hampton whose cross is headed home in style by Chapman. Hampton hits the post and Maguire finishes off for the late clincher. A great win.

---

16 A COVENTRY 24/11 17,250 12 L 14 20 0-3 0-2
Daly 1, Thompson 4, Bradford 49
Ref: C Downey

Fox / Evans / Hampton / Dodd / O'Callaghan / Smith / Griffiths / Heath* / Chapman / Bracewell / Johnson PA / Maguire
Blyth / Thomas / Roberts / Jacobs / Dyson / Gillespie / Bradford / Daly / Thompson / Hateley / Hunt

City are caught napping by Dave Sexton's Sky Blues. Daly loops a header over Fox after 27 seconds and Garry Thompson angles a fine header in. Awful Stoke have rings run round them. Dave Bradford wraps it up with Stoke's new Swedish signing Robert Prytz watching in the stands.

---

17 A WOLVES 28/11 15,314 12 L 16 20 0-2 0-1
Palmer 25p, Matthews 89
Ref: B Stevens

McManus / Evans / Hampton / Dodd / O'Callaghan / Smith / Griffiths / Johnson PA / Ford / Chapman / Bracewell / Maguire
Bradshaw / Palmer / Parkin / Daniel / Gallagher / Berry / Matthews / Eves / Gray / Richards / Brazier

Eric McManus makes his debut in goal and gives away a penalty when he brings down John Richards. The other debutant, Steve Ford, misses Stoke's best chance. Chapman twice goes close but Mick Matthews seals it after O'Callaghan's weak clearing header falls to him 12 yards out.

---

18 H LEEDS 5/12 15,901 15 L 18 20 1-2 0-2
Heath 51
Graham 2, Hamson 34
Ref: P Tyldesley

McManus / Evans / Hampton / Dodd / O'Callaghan / Doyle / Griffiths / Heath / Chapman / Bracewell / Johnson PA / Maguire
Lukic / Cherry / Gray F / Stevenson / Hart / Burns / Harris / Graham / Butterworth / Hamson / Hird

Robert Prytz is denied a work permit and will not sign for Stoke. Allan Clarke's Leeds make a whirlwind start despite having lost nine in a row away from home. City are terrible. All three goals fly in from the edge of the area. Gary Hamson nets the decider despite being transfer listed.

---

19 A MANCHESTER C 9/1 34,491 16 D 2 21 1-1 1-0
O'Callaghan 39
Francis 62
Ref: G Owen

Fox / Evans / Kirk / Dodd / Watson / Doyle / Lumsden / Heath / Chapman / Bracewell / Johnson PA
Corrigan / Ryan / McDonald / Reid / Bond / Caton / O'Neill / Reeves / Francis / Hartford / Hutchison

Adrian Heath is sold to Everton for a club record £700,000 as Stoke are chasing Liverpool's Ray Kennedy. New £50,000 signing Dave Watson plays alongside teenager Steve Kirk. Stoke grab a good point when O'Callaghan fires across Corrigan. Trevor Francis lobs Fox from 20 yards.

---

20 H ARSENAL 20/1 8,625 18 L 10 21 0-1 0-1
Sunderland 8
Ref: D Allison

Fox / Evans / Kirk / Dodd / Watson / Doyle / Lumsden* / Griffiths / Chapman / Bracewell / Johnson PA / Griffiths
Wood / Robson / Sansom / Talbot / O'Leary / Whyte / Hollins / Sunderland / Davis / Nicholas / Rix

A woeful display as Stoke submit without a whimper. The lowest league gate for 13 years see a drab display with poor passing. Paul Bracewell gives the ball away once too often and John Hollins supplies Sunderland with a pass to crack home. Barker admits 'We are not good enough'.

---

21 H MANCHESTER U 23/1 9,662 18 L 3 21 0-3 0-1
Coppell 10, Stapleton 86p, Birtles 89
Ref: D Allison

Fox / Evans / Kirk / Dodd / Watson / Doyle / Griffiths / O'Callaghan / Chapman / Bracewell / Johnson PA* / Maguire
Bailey / Duxbury / Albiston / Wilkins / McQueen / Moran / Robson / Birtles / Stapleton / Macari / Coppell

Ron Atkinson's United put sorry Stoke to the sword. Steve Coppell's opener is a fine strike. Frank Stapleton's spot-kick is for Doyle's foul on Coppell. Gary Birtles' superb last-minute finish really sets the seal on a dismal City display. 'There is no crisis' claims manager Richie Barker.

LEAGUE DIVISION 1

Manager: Richie Barker

SEASON 1981-82

Match summary

No	Date	Venue	Opponents	F-A	H-T	Att	Pos	Pt	Scorers, Times, and Referees
22	30/1	A	NOTT'M FOREST	0-0	0-0	16,219	18 D	22	Ref: P Willis
23	6/2	H	WEST HAM	2-1	1-0	11,987	16 W	25	Chapman 10, Maguire 80 / Van der Elst 74. Ref: J Worrall
24	10/2	A	SUNDERLAND	2-0	0-0	14,317	16 W	28	O'Callaghan 65, McIlroy 70. Ref: K Hackett
25	13/2	A	EVERTON	0-0	0-0	20,656	13 D	29	Ref: A Challinor
26	20/2	H	MIDDLESBROUGH	2-0	1-0	10,473	13 W	32	O'Callaghan 29, Chapman 46. Ref: K Barrett
27	27/2	H	TOTTENHAM	0-2	0-0	20,592	15 L	32	Crooks 71, 80. Ref: T Fitzharris
28	6/3	A	SWANSEA	0-3	0-1	11,811	15 L	32	James R 34, 87, Charles 72. Ref: L Burden
29	9/3	H	LIVERPOOL	1-5	0-2	16,758	15 L	32	McIlroy 56 [Lee 83, Whelan 87] / McDermott 5, Dalglish 10, Souness 48. Ref: G Napthine
30	13/3	A	BIRMINGHAM	1-2	0-1	12,018	15 L	32	Chapman 79 / Curbishley 18, Hawker 63. Ref: K Salmon
31	20/3	H	BRIGHTON	0-0	0-0	9,120	15 D	33	Ref: N Wilson

Line-ups (Stoke City in roman; opponents in *italics*)

No	Opp	1	2	3	4	5	6	7	8	9	10	11	12 sub used
22	NOTT'M FOREST	Fox	Kirk	Hampton	Dodd	Watson	McAughtrie	Griffiths	O'Callaghan	Chapman	Bracewell	Maguire	Maguire
22	*(opp)*	*Shilton*	*Anderson*		*McGovern*	*Young*	*Bowyer*	*Robertson*	*Wallace*	*Fashanu*	*Proctor*	*Robertson*	
23	WEST HAM	Fox	Kirk	Hampton	Dodd	Watson	McAughtrie	Griffiths*	O'Callaghan	Chapman	Bracewell	Maguire	Lumsden
23	*(opp)*	*Parkes*	*Stewart*	*Brush*	*Bonds*	*Martin*	*Orr*	*Van der Elst*	*Goddard*	*Cross*	*Brooking*	*Pike*	
24	SUNDERLAND	Fox	Kirk	Hampton	Dodd	Watson	McAughtrie	McIlroy	O'Callaghan	Chapman	Bracewell	Maguire	Brown
24	*(opp)*	*Siddall*	*Nicholl*	*Hinnigan*	*Venison*	*Hindmarch*	*Elliott*	*Buckley*	*Ritchie**	*Cooke*	*Rowell*	*McGinley*	
25	EVERTON	Fox	Kirk	Hampton	Dodd	Watson	McAughtrie	McIlroy	O'Callaghan	Chapman	Bracewell	Maguire	
25	*(opp)*	*Southall*	*Borrows*	*Ratcliffe*	*Higgins*	*Wright*	*Richardson*	*Heath*	*Irvine*	*Sharp*	*Ferguson*	*Ross*	
26	MIDDLESBROUGH	Fox	Kirk	Hampton	Dodd	Watson	McAughtrie	McIlroy	O'Callaghan	Chapman	Bracewell	Maguire	
26	*(opp)*	*Platt*	*Craggs*	*Bailey*	*Angus*	*Baxter*	*Nattrass*	*Cochrane*	*Otto*	*Thomson**	*Wood*	*McAndrew*	*Woof*
27	TOTTENHAM	Fox	Kirk	Hampton	Dodd*	Watson	McAughtrie	McIlroy	O'Callaghan	Chapman	Bracewell	Maguire	
27	*(opp)*	*Clemence*	*Hughton*	*Miller*	*Price*	*Hazard*	*Perryman*	*Ardiles**	*Archibald*	*Galvin*	*Hoddle*	*Crooks*	*Roberts*
28	SWANSEA	Fox	Kirk*	Hampton	Dodd	Watson	McAughtrie	McIlroy	O'Callaghan	Chapman	Bracewell	Maguire	Griffiths
28	*(opp)*	*Davies*	*Robinson*	*Marustik*	*Irwin*	*Kennedy*	*Rajkovic*	*Curtis*	*James R*	*James L*	*Thompson*	*Charles*	
29	LIVERPOOL	Fox	Evans	Hampton	Dodd	Watson	McAughtrie	McIlroy	O'Callaghan	Chapman	Bracewell	Maguire*	Griffiths
29	*(opp)*	*Grobbelaar*	*Neal*	*Lawrenson*	*Kennedy A*	*Whelan*	*Hansen*	*Dalglish*	*Lee*	*Rush*	*McDermott*	*Souness*	
30	BIRMINGHAM	Fox	Kirk	Hampton	Dodd	Watson	McAughtrie	Griffiths	O'Callaghan	Chapman	Bracewell	Maguire*	Lumsden
30	*(opp)*	*Wealands*	*Langan*	*Broadhurst*	*Hawker*	*Scott*	*Curbishley*	*Dillon*	*Whatmore**	*Evans*	*V d Hauwe*	*Van Mierlo*	*Linney*
31	BRIGHTON	Fox	Kirk	Hampton	Dodd	Watson	McAughtrie	McIlroy	O'Callaghan	Chapman*	Bracewell	Maguire	Griffiths
31	*(opp)*	*Digweed*	*Shanks*	*Grealish*	*Nelson*	*Stevens*	*Gatting*	*Case*	*Ritchie*	*Robinson*	*McNab*	*Smith**	*Ryan*

Match reports

22 — NOTT'M FOREST (A): Peter Fox produces a brilliant display to deny Clough's men. He claws away Wallace's drive before denying Proctor with a stunning save. The profligate million pound man, Justin Fashanu, heads straight at Fox from three yards. Bryn Gunn also tests Fox low to his right. A great point.

23 — WEST HAM (H): John Lyall's Hammers succumb to a fabulous Maguire solo effort. He flashes a drive past Parkes from a tight angle. McAughtrie and Griffiths set up Chapman's opener and City look the more likely until Van der Elst's free-kick flies in. Fox saves a point-blank Trevor Brooking header.

24 — SUNDERLAND (A): Fox saves from Buckley and Ritchie as Sunderland dominate but O'Callaghan rams home Chapman's cross to snatch the lead. £350,000 record signing Sammy McIlroy marks his arrival by beating three defenders during a 50-yard run before flicking past Siddall. 'Magical' sighs Barker.

25 — EVERTON (A): Stoke frustrate Howard Kendall's Toffees. The lively Heath gives City problems, but Kirk clears off the line when he rounds Fox. Maguire hits the post, the ball rebounds off Southall and rolls agonisingly wide. Bracewell's lob almost catches Southall off his line but he recovers to save.

26 — MIDDLESBROUGH (H): Bobby Murdoch sees his Boro team well beaten as Sammy McIlroy prompts City forward. Despite facing three centre-backs O'Callaghan, with a far-post header, and Chapman, deflecting in Maguire's drive, find the net. Platt saves Chapman's header and Bracewell blasts a whisker over.

27 — TOTTENHAM (H): Garth Crooks has the last laugh to end Stoke's unbeaten run. He is put through by Hazard and then Hoddle to beat Fox. Ray Clemence's world-class save denies a fabulous Maguire volley. The Boothen End sing 'sign him up' when the transfer-listed Alan Hudson is spotted in the stand.

28 — SWANSEA (A): On a dreadful pitch Stoke are outfought. Robbie James nets two loose balls in the area and Jeremy Charles grabs a header. Fox denies Kennedy, Leighton James and Alan Curtis. Watson heads City's best chance just over while Chapman and O'Callaghan struggle to make an impression.

29 — LIVERPOOL (H): McDermott's 25-yard cracker, Souness's 20-yard rocket and Whelan's right-footed curler are all too good for Fox as Liverpool prepare well for the League Cup Final against Spurs. A shell-shocked Stoke reply through McIlroy's toe-poke, but the quality of Paisley's Reds is indisputable.

30 — BIRMINGHAM (A): Birmingham stroll to victory through Curbishley's drive and Hawker's left-foot drive. Chapman's diving header gives Stoke hope but Hawker, Dillon and Whatmore go close. Van Mierlo has a goal disallowed for a foul by McAughtrie. Denis Smith has gone on loan to York. Very poor.

31 — BRIGHTON (H): A midfield battle with few chances at either end. Lee Chapman's 17th-minute knee injury gives cause for concern. Brighton catch O'Callaghan offside continually as Stoke exert more pressure after the interval. Dodd and Maguire are both denied by Perry Digweed. City lack inspiration.

32 — A SOUTHAMPTON 27/3 — Pos 16, L, (1) 33 — Att 20,058 — **Score 3-4**

Stoke: Fox, **Parkin**, Dodd, Hampton, McAughtrie, Watson, McIlroy, O'Callaghan, **Biley**, Bracewell, Griffiths
Southampton: *Katalinic, Golac, Williams, Holmes, Waldron, Whitlock, Keegan, Channon, Puckett, Armstrong, Ball*
Scorers: Biley 49, Wat 62, McIlf 75 (Whit'k 86) / Waldron 24, Armst'g 26, Channon 33
Ref: D Axcell

A remarkable game sees City come back from the dead. On loan Alan Biley starts the recovery. Dave Watson's shot cannons in off the crossbar before McIlroy's bullet header seems to have earnt a point. Mark Whitlock's winner, a header from Channon's free-kick is his first senior goal.

---

33 — H SUNDERLAND 10/4 — Pos 17, L, 22, 33 — Att 11,399 — **Score 0-1**

Stoke: Fox, Parkin, Dodd, Hampton, McAughtrie, Watson, McIlroy, O'Callaghan, Biley*, Bracewell, Griffiths
Sunderland: *Turner, Hinnigan, Munro, Clarke, Chisholm, Buckley, Elliott, West, Rowell*, Pickering, Cummins, Ursem*
Scorers: Buckley 42
Ref: J Key

An awful display without a single clear-cut chance being created. Mick Buckley's goal seems to happen in slow motion after Fox parries Stan Cummins' shot back out. The biggest cheer of the day is for Sunderland's on-loan Stoke star substitute, Loek Ursem. City in real trouble now.

---

34 — A LIVERPOOL 13/4 — Pos 19, L, 1, 33 — Att 30,419 — **Score 0-2**

Stoke: Fox, Parkin, Dodd, Hampton, McAughtrie, Watson, McIlroy, O'Callaghan, Chapman, Bracewell, Maguire
Liverpool: *Grobbelaar, Neal, Lawrenson, Kennedy A, Whelan, Thompson, Dalglish, Lee, Rush, Johnston, Hansen*
Scorers: Kennedy A 4, Johnston 35
Ref: K Redfern

City's battling display avoids another thrashing by the Reds. Alan Kennedy's early goal means there is only ever one winner. Craig Johnston's tap-in seals it, but City's second-half grit gives hope to Barker for the run in. 'With this commitment we have no fears for the future' he says.

---

35 — A IPSWICH 17/4 — Pos 21, L, 2, 33 — Att 20,309 — **Score 0-2**

Stoke: Fox, Johnson PA, Hampton, Dodd, Biley, Watson, McIlroy, O'Callaghan, Chapman, Bracewell, Maguire
Ipswich: *Cooper, Burley, McCall, Mills, Osman, Butcher, Wark, Mariner, Brazil, Gates*
Scorers: Mariner 37, Wark 89
Ref: A Ward

City get plenty of men behind the ball. Ipswich struggle before Mariner's header finally beats Fox. He also saves from Osman and Brazil. Lee Chapman is left isolated up front. His shot hits Mills on the line and then John Wark's header is deflected past Fox by the despairing Hampton.

---

36 — H WOLVES 24/4 — Pos 18, W, 19, 36 — Att 3,797 — **Score 2-1**

Stoke: Fox, Dodd, Parkin, Johnson PA, Smith, Watson, McIlroy, Biley, Chapman, Bracewell, Maguire
Wolves: *Bradshaw, Humphrey, Hollifield, Eves, Berry, Coy, Hibbitt, Carr, Gray!, Richards*, Clarke, Matthews*
Scorers: Maguire 35p, Chapman 47 / Hibbitt 24
Ref: D Owen

Hibbitt's unstoppable drive is equalised by Maguire's penalty when Berry handles Chapman's shot. Gray receives a second caution for arguing the decision and Stoke find a way past the 10-man wall when Chapman beats Berry to fire home. Fox saves twice late on to ensure a vital win.

---

37 — A NOTTS CO 26/4 — Pos 18, L, 14, 36 — Att 8,686 — **Score 1-3**

Stoke: Fox, Parkin, Benjamin, Hampton, Smith, Watson, McIlroy, Biley*, Chapman, Bracewell, Maguire
Notts Co: *Avramovic, Benjamin, O'Brien, Goodwin*, Kilcline, Richards, Chiedozie, Harkouk*, McCulloch, Christie, Mair, Hunt*
Scorers: McCulloch 32, Harkouk 52p, Mair 60 / Chapman 27
Ref: J Bray

Dave Watson's return to Meadow Lane becomes a nightmare as he gifts Jimmy Sirrel's Magpies a penalty for a foul on Goodwin and misses a header which allows Mair to lob Fox. Chapman's cheeky finish is nearly added to by O'Callaghan but his goal is ruled out for fouling Kilcline.

---

38 — A LEEDS 1/5 — Pos 19, D, 21, 37 — Att 17,775 — **Score 0-0**

Stoke: Fox, Dodd, Parkin, Griffiths, Smith, Watson, McIlroy, O'Callaghan, Chapman, Bracewell, Maguire
Leeds: *Lukic, Hird*, Gray F, Flynn, Hart, Cherry, Gray E, Graham, Worthington, Connor, Barnes, Burns*
Ref: A Chadwick

Wind reduces an already tension packed match to a long-ball game with neither team adapting well. Fox denies Hird and Barnes while Lukic saves from Griffiths. Leeds send on Kenny Burns as an extra attacker late on but Stoke have settled for a point by then. Not enough for Leeds.

---

39 — H ASTON VILLA 5/5 — Pos 17, W, 12, 40 — Att 13,363 — **Score 1-0**

Stoke: Fox, Dodd, Parkin, Griffiths, Smith, Watson, O'Callaghan, McIlroy, Chapman, Bracewell, Maguire
Aston Villa: *Rimmer, Swain, Williams, Evans, McNaught, Mortimer, Bremner, Shaw, With, Cowans, Morley*, Blair*
Scorers: Bracewell 17
Ref: N Glover

Paul Bracewell, happier now in his central midfield role, cracks a half-cleared corner in from the edge of the area to keep Stoke above the drop zone. Tony Barton's Villa are saving themselves for the European Cup Final and rarely threaten. Maguire has a goal disallowed for handball.

---

40 — H NOTTS CO 8/5 — Pos 16, D, 15, 41 — Att 1,011 — **Score 2-2**

Stoke: McManus, Dodd, Parkin, Griffiths, Smith, Watson, McIlroy, Biley, Chapman, Bracewell, Maguire
Notts Co: *Avramovic, Benjamin, O'Brien, Goodwin*, Kilcline, Richards, Chiedozie, Hunt, McCulloch, Christie, Mair, Harkouk*
Scorers: Watson 25, Maguire 26 / Christie 38p, Richards 90
Ref: F Roberts

Stoke clutch despair from the jaws of victory. Watson's header and Maguire's interception of Richards' back-pass seem to have clinched it but O'Callaghan trips Chiedozie for the penalty. Tension mounts as City defend deeper. Richards prods in when Mair's deflected shot falls to him.

---

41 — A MANCHESTER U 15/5 — Pos 20, L, 3, 41 — Att 15,073 — **Score 0-2**

Stoke: Fox, Dodd, Parkin, Griffiths*, Smith, Watson, McIlroy, Biley, Birtles*, Bracewell, Maguire
Manchester U: *Bailey, Gidman, Albiston, Wilkins, Moran, McQueen, Robson, Whiteside, Grimes, Coppell, McGarvey*
Scorers: Robson 42, Whiteside 44
Ref: B Martin

City defend stoutly at Old Trafford and Fox saves from Wilkins and Grimes. But Bryan Robson heads a corner home and 17-year-old Norman Whiteside nods in a debut goal. City threaten little and the game peters out. Results elsewhere mean Stoke must win the final match to stay up.

---

42 — H WEST BROM 20/5 — Pos 19, W, 18, 44 — Att 9,698 — **Score 3-0**

Stoke: McManus, Dodd, Parkin, Griffiths, Smith, Watson, McIlroy, O'Callaghan, Chapman, Bracewell, Maguire*
West Brom: *Godden, Batson, Statham, Bennett, Wile, Webb*, MacKenzie, Jol, Cross, Owen, Brown, Cowdrill*
Scorers: Watson 25, Chapman 38, [O'Callaghan 73]
Ref: P Richardson

An exhausted Albion, having saved themselves from the drop two days earlier, succumb. Scenes of jubilation greet Watson's bundled opener. Chapman races in to head home and O'Callaghan rockets a header past Godden to ensure safety. Leeds boss Allan Clarke departs, head bowed.

Average — Home 14,617 — Away 22,501

LEAGUE DIVISION 1 (CUP-TIES)   Manager: Richie Barker   SEASON 1981-82

League Cup

				Att	F-A	H-T	Scorers, Times, and Referees	1	2	3	4	5	6	7	8	9	10	11	12 sub used
2:1	A	MANCHESTER C	12 L	23,146	0-2	0-1	Smith 16 (og), Hartford 83	Fox	Evans	Hampton	Dodd	O'Callaghan	Smith	Ursem	Heath	Chapman	Bracewell	Maguire	
		7/10	10				Ref: G Tyson	*Corrigan*	*Ranson*	*Wilson*	*Reid*	*Bond*	*Caton*	*Tueart*	*O'Neill*	*Hutchison*	*Hartford*	*Reeves*	
2:2	H	MANCHESTER C	15 W	17,373	2-0	0-0	Chapman 80, Evans 87	Fox	Evans	Hampton	Dodd	O'Callaghan	Smith	Johnson PA	Heath	Chapman	Bracewell	Maguire*	Griffiths
		28/10	16		aet		Ref: C Thomas	*Corrigan*	*Ranson*	*Bond*	*Reid*	*Power*	*Caton*	*Tueart*	*O'Neill**	*Hutchison*	*Hartford*	*Reeves*	*Hareide*
							(Stoke lose 8-9 on penalties)												

Denis Smith leaps to head an intended clearance past Fox. The Stoke goalkeeper then saves Dennis Tueart's 62nd-minute penalty given for an innocuous nudge by O'Callaghan. Ranson clears Dodd's shot off the line then Asa Hartford sidesteps his way past Smith before slotting home.

Man City hold out easily until Lee Chapman buries a far-post header. Ray Evans drives home to force extra-time. In a dramatic penalty shoot-out Chapman put his kick wide. Peter Griffiths has his saved by Corrigan and Stoke lose the longest penalty shoot-out ever in a British cup-tie.

FA Cup

				Att	F-A	H-T	Scorers, Times, and Referees	1	2	3	4	5	6	7	8	9	10	11	12 sub used
3	H	NORWICH	15 L	12,805	0-1	0-1	Jack 10	Fox	Evans	Hampton*	Dodd	O'Callaghan	Doyle	Griffiths	Heath	Chapman	Bracewell	Ursem	Johnson PA
		2/1	2:11				Ref: G Flint	*Woods*	*Symonds*	*Downs*	*McGuire*	*Walford*	*Watson*	*Mendham*	*Jack*	*Deehan*	*Bertschin*	*Bennett*	

Stoke put up a poor display against another lower division team. Ross Jack's scrambled goal after Deehan's corner allows the Canaries to shut up shop. The first chants of 'Barker out!' can be heard drifting down from the Boothen. Fox denies John Deehan who nearly scores a second.

League Table

#	Team	P	Home W	D	L	F	A	Away W	D	L	F	A	Pts
1	Liverpool	42	14	3	4	39	14	12	6	3	41	18	87
2	Ipswich	42	17	1	3	47	25	9	4	8	28	28	83
3	Manchester U	42	12	6	3	27	9	10	6	5	32	20	78
4	Tottenham	42	12	4	5	41	26	8	7	6	26	22	71
5	Arsenal	42	13	5	3	27	15	7	6	8	21	22	71
6	Swansea	42	13	3	5	34	16	8	3	10	24	35	69
7	Southampton	42	15	2	4	49	30	4	7	10	23	37	66
8	Everton	42	11	7	3	33	21	6	6	9	23	29	64
9	West Ham	42	9	10	2	42	29	5	6	10	24	28	58
10	Manchester C	42	9	7	5	32	23	6	6	9	17	27	58
11	Aston Villa	42	9	6	6	28	24	6	6	9	27	29	57
12	Nott'm Forest	42	7	7	7	19	20	8	5	8	23	28	57
13	Brighton	42	8	8	5	30	24	5	6	10	13	28	52
14	Coventry	42	9	4	8	31	33	4	7	10	25	38	50
15	Notts Co	42	8	5	8	32	33	5	3	13	29	36	47
16	Birmingham	42	8	8	7	29	25	2	8	11	24	36	44
17	West Brom	42	6	6	9	24	25	5	5	11	22	32	44
18	STOKE	42	9	2	10	27	28	3	6	12	17	35	44
19	Sunderland	42	6	5	10	19	26	5	6	10	19	32	44
20	Leeds	42	6	11	4	23	20	4	1	16	16	41	42
21	Wolves	42	8	5	8	19	20	2	5	14	13	43	40
22	Middlesbro	42	5	9	7	20	24	3	6	12	14	28	39
		924	214	121	127	672	501	127	121	214	501	672	1265

Odds & ends

Double wins: (1) West Brom.

Double losses: (5) Liverpool, Manchester U, Southampton, Swansea, Tottenham.

Won from behind: (2) West Brom (a), Wolves (h).

Lost from in front: (3) Nott'm Forest (h), Notts Co (a), Swansea (h).

High spots: Escape from relegation by the skin of their teeth.

A goal frenzy at the start of the season.

Thumping Coventry 4-0 to go top of the embryonic table.

Signing Sammy McIlroy and Dave Watson.

Low spots: Losing 10 home matches (worst for 22 years).

The late Notts County equaliser which plunged Stoke into trouble.

Being thrashed at home by Liverpool 1-5.

Nine games without a win from February.

Crowds reduced yet again.

Player of the Year: Peter Fox.

Ever-presents: (1) Paul Bracewell.

Hat-tricks: (0).

Leading Scorer: (17) Lee Chapman.

Appearances and Goals

Player	Appearances Lge	Sub	LC	Sub	FAC	Sub	Goals Lge	LC	FAC	Tot
Biley, Alan	8							1		1
Bould, Steve	1	1								
Bracewell, Paul	42		2		1		1			1
Chapman, Lee	40	1	2		1		16	1		17
Cook, Jeff		1								
Dodd, Alan	41		2							
Doyle, Mike	8									
Evans, Ray	22		2		1		1			1
Ford, Steve	1	1								
Fox, Peter	38		2		1					
Griffiths, Peter	27	4			1	1	3			3
Hampton, Pete	33		2		1					
Heath, Adrian	17		2		1		5			5
Johnson, Paul A	12	1	1	1						
Kirk, Steve	12									
Lumsden, John	2	3								
Maguire, Paul	32	3	2				7			7
McAughtrie, Dave	13									
McIlroy, Sammy	18						3			3
McManus, Eric	4									
O'Callaghan, Brendan	39	2	2		1		5			5
Parkin, Steve	10									
Smith, Denis	17	2	2							
Ursem, Loek	1	2	1		1					
Watson, Dave	24						3			3
25 players used	462	19	22	1	11	1	44	2		46

LEAGUE DIVISION 1   Manager: Richie Barker   SEASON 1982-83

Results summary

No	Date		Opponents	Att	Pos	Pt	Res	F-A	H-T
1	28/8	H	ARSENAL	15,504		3	W	2-1	1-0
2	1/9	A	MANCHESTER C	27,847		3	L	0-1	0-0
3	4/9	A	BIRMINGHAM	14,412	9	6	W	4-1	4-0
4	8/9	H	WEST BROM	17,447	9	6	L	0-3	0-2
5	11/9	H	SWANSEA	14,056	6	9	W	4-1	2-1
6	18/9	A	IPSWICH	19,119	4	12	W	3-2	2-2
7	25/9	H	LUTON	18,475	6	13	D	4-4	2-2
8	2/10	A	NOTT'M FOREST	17,122	8	13	L	0-1	0-0
9	9/10	A	MANCHESTER U	43,132	9	13	L	0-1	0-0
10	16/10	H	BRIGHTON	13,936	7	16	W	3-0	2-0

Match details

1 — H ARSENAL (28/8) W 2-1
Scorers: Berry 5, O'Callaghan 50 / Sunderland 54 — Ref: C Thomas

Stoke: Fox, Parkin D, Hampton, Bracewell, McAughtrie, Berry, Griffiths, McIlroy, O'Callaghan, Thomas, Ch'ber'n M.
Arsenal: Wood, Hollins, Sansom, Talbot, O'Leary, Whyte, Robson, Sunderland*, Chapman, Woodcock, Rix; sub Davis.

Mark Chamberlain destroys England left-back Sansom in a superb debut show. He crosses for fellow debutant George Berry and O'Callaghan to head home. Mickey Thomas also makes a promising start. Lee Chapman returns after his acrimonious departure and is booked after 4 mins!

2 — A MANCHESTER C (1/9) L 0-1
Scorers: Cross 46 — Ref: G Courtney

Stoke: Fox, Parkin D, Hampton, Bracewell, McAughtrie, Berry, Griffiths*, McIlroy, O'Callaghan, Thomas, Chamb'rl'n M; sub Maguire.
Man City: Corrigan, Ranson, McDonald, Baker, Bond, Caton, Hareide, Reeves, Cross, Hartford, Power.

Chamberlain's trickery forces Bond to handle, but the ref says 'not intentional'. McAughtrie's weak header falls to David Cross who fires past Fox. Stoke lack a finisher to pick up O'Callaghan's knockdowns from Chamberlain's crosses. 'You get nothing for entertainment,' says Barker.

3 — A BIRMINGHAM (4/9) W 4-1
Scorers: Hawker 20 (og), Chamberlain 33, 36, [Griffiths 43] / Curbishley 80 — Ref: D Allison

Stoke: Fox, Parkin D, Hampton, Bracewell, McAughtrie*, Berry, Griffiths, McIlroy, O'Callaghan, Thomas, Chamb'rl'n M; sub Maguire.
Birmingham: Blyth, Langan, Hawker, Scott, V'd Hauwe, Broadhurst, Van Mierlo, Dillon!, Hartford, Curbishley, Carrodus.

Chamberlain dazzles Birmingham. Kevin Dillon is sent off for taking a frustrated kick at him. Griffiths heads home after Chamberlain hits the bar. He also nets from close range.

4 — H WEST BROM (8/9) L 0-3
Scorers: Regis 23, Eastoe 28, Brown 74 — Ref: K Hackett

Stoke: Fox, Parkin D, Maguire, Bracewell, Watson, Berry, Griffiths, McIlroy, O'Callaghan, Thomas, Chamb'rl'n M.
West Brom: Grew, Batson, Whitehead, Zondervan, Bennett, Robertson, Jol, Brown, Regis, Owen, Eastoe.

Stoke pile the pressure on Albion and look certs to score. But referee Hackett overrules a linesman's flag and allows Regis' goal to stand. Peter Eastoe drives home on the break and suddenly Stoke face a 10-man wall. Maguire and O'Callaghan go close before Ally Brown fires past Fox.

5 — H SWANSEA (11/9) W 4-1
Scorers: Watson 15, Thomas 25, Davies 55 (og) / Latchford 8 [Maguire 80p] — Ref: N Wilson

Stoke: Fox, Parkin D, Hampton*, Bracewell, Watson, Berry, Griffiths, McIlroy, O'Callaghan, Thomas, Chamb'rl'n M.
Swansea: Davies, Marustik*, Habziabdic, Irwin, Kennedy, Rajkovic, Curtis, James R, James L, Stevenson, Charles; sub Latchford.

Chamberlain teases Swansea's defence into persistently fouling him, but still finds space to cross for Watson to turn and fire home. A free-kick is ripped home by Thomas before Dai Davies drops O'Callaghan's cross over the line. Chamberlain is fouled for the penalty. A very easy win.

6 — A IPSWICH (18/9) W 3-2
Scorers: Thomas 12, Maguire 18, 47p / Brazil 27, Wark 39 — Ref: M Taylor

Stoke: Fox, Parkin D, Hampton, Bracewell, Watson, Berry, Griffiths, McIlroy, O'Callaghan, Thomas, Chamb'rl'n M; sub Maguire.
Ipswich: Sivell, Burley, Mills, Thijssen, Osman*, Butcher, Wark, McCall, Mariner, Brazil, Gates; sub Parkin.

Stoke increase the pressure on new Ipswich boss Bobby Ferguson who has yet to see his side win. Thomas and Maguire coolly put City two up before Alan Brazil clips a great effort over Fox and Wark buries Mills' cross. Thijssen fouls O'Callaghan for the controversial penalty winner.

7 — H LUTON (25/9) D 4-4
Scorers: Berry 10, 22, Bracewell 50, O'Call' 84 / Walsh 20, Stein 43, 58, Donaghy 62 — Ref: G Napthine

Stoke: Fox!, Parkin D, Hampton*, Bracewell, McAughtrie, Berry, Maguire, McIlroy, O'Callaghan, Thomas*, Chamb'rl'n M.
Luton: Judge, Stephens, Money, Horton, Goodyear, Donaghy, Hill, Stein, Walsh*, Turner, Moss; sub Antic.

City lead 2-1 through Berry's headers, one from an incredible twisting cross by Chamberlain. Fox walks for handling the ball outside his box (28 mins). Walsh's superb 25-yard effort hits the bar then Moss hits the post with a last-minute spot-kick.

8 — A NOTT'M FOREST (2/10) L 0-1
Scorers: Birtles 62 — Ref: J Deakin

Stoke: Fox, Parkin D, Dodd, Bracewell, Watson, Berry, Maguire, McIlroy, O'Callaghan, Thomas, Chamb'rl'n M.
Nott'm Forest: V Breukelen, Anderson, Fairclough, Todd, Gunn, Hodge, Proctor, Robertson, Walsh, Wallace*, Birtles; sub Ward.

Bryn Gunn shackles Chamberlain and Fox saves well from Wallace and Proctor. Birtles hits the bar. In a tough game Forest sneak a win thanks to Gary Birtles who buries Hodge's pass. Mark's brother Neville goes close with an overhead kick. Stoke miss Mickey Thomas' probing runs.

9 — A MANCHESTER U (9/10) L 0-1
Scorers: Robson 80 — Ref: R Bridges

Stoke: Harrison, Parkin D, Hampton*, Bracewell, Watson, Berry, Maguire, McIlroy, O'Callaghan, Thomas, Chamb'rl'n M.
Man U: Bailey, Duxbury, Albiston, Wilkins, Moran, McQueen, Robson, Grimes, Stapleton, Whiteside, Moses.

Mark Chamberlain is picked in Robson's England squad and City nearly frustrate leaders United. Robson, Stapleton and Wilkins are all denied by debutant Mark Harrison. McIlroy's cheeky effort hits the bar then Duxbury clears off the line from Maguire. Bryan Robson finally chips in.

10 — H BRIGHTON (16/10) W 3-0
Scorers: Thomas 4, Chamberlain 41, McIlroy 50 — Ref: A Challinor

Stoke: Harrison, Parkin D, Hampton, Bracewell, Watson, McAughtrie, Maguire, McIlroy, O'Callaghan, Thomas, Chamb'rl'n M; sub Dodd.
Brighton: Moseley, Stevens, Pearce, Grealish, Foster, Gatting, Case, Ritchie, Robinson, McNab, Smith.

Stoke outplay Brighton. Mickey Thomas slots home McIlroy's centre. Chamberlain, closely marked, produces a cut inside and an angled drive for the second. Paul Maguire's near-post corner is flicked on for McIlroy to flash a header home. Moseley saves brilliantly from Chamberlain.

Match-by-match record (matches 11–21)

No	Date	V	Opponent	Att	Pos	Res	FT	HT	Pts
11	23/10	H	LIVERPOOL	29,401	8	D	1-1	1-1	17
12	30/10	A	SUNDERLAND	16,406	9	D	2-2	2-2	18
13	6/11	H	WEST HAM	17,589	7	W	5-2	4-1	21
14	13/11	A	WATFORD	18,713	9	L	0-1	0-1	21
15	20/11	A	NORWICH	13,658	10	L	2-4	1-0	21
16	27/11	H	ASTON VILLA	18,886	12	L	0-3	0-1	21
17	4/12	A	SOUTHAMPTON	17,198	13	L	0-1	0-0	21
18	11/12	H	TOTTENHAM	15,849	11	W	2-0	1-0	24
19	18/12	A	COVENTRY	10,065	14	L	0-2	0-1	24
20	27/12	H	EVERTON	25,427	12	W	1-0	0-0	27
21	28/12	A	NOTTS CO	11,600	15	L	0-4	0-2	27

---

11. LIVERPOOL 1-1 — Thomas 36 / Lawrenson 27. Ref: H Taylor
Stoke: Harrison, Parkin D, Hampton, Bracewell, Watson, McAughtrie, Maguire, McIlroy, O'Callaghan, Thomas, Chamb'rl'n M
Liverpool: Grobbelaar, Neal, Kennedy, Thompson, Whelan, Hansen, Dalglish, Lee, Rush, Lawrenson, Souness
Mickey Thomas produces a memorable strike, trapping a pass from Maguire on his thigh and belting a left-foot volley past an astonished Bruce Grobbelaar. Lawrenson's goal stems from Hampton's weak clearing header. Bracewell brings Grobbelaar to his knees with one powerful shot.

12. SUNDERLAND 2-2 — Maguire 5, Chamberlain 70 / Pickering 8, Rowell 31. Ref: M Peck
Stoke: Harrison, Parkin D, Hampton, Bracewell, Watson, McAughtrie, Maguire, McIlroy, O'Callaghan, Thomas, Chamb'rl'n M
Sunderland: Turner, Nicholl, Munro, Hindmarch, Chisholm, Pickering, Buckley, Rowell, McCoist, West, Venison
Chamberlain teases former Stokie Iain Munro and crosses for Nicholl to slam his clearance into Maguire's chest and thence past Chris Turner. Pickering and Rowell pounce from close range but Stoke stay in the hunt in an entertaining match thanks to Chambo's finish to McIlroy's pass.

13. WEST HAM 5-2 — O'Call'13, Hampton 29, Thomas 41, St'wart 41p, Pike 80 [McIl'44, 76]. Ref: F Roberts
Stoke: Harrison, Parkin D, Hampton, Bracewell, Watson, McAughtrie, Maguire, McIlroy, O'Callaghan*, Thomas, Chamb'rl'n M — sub: Berry
West Ham: Parkes, Stewart, Brush, Bonds, Martin, Devonshire, Van der Elst*, Goddard, Clark, Allen, Pike — sub: Orr
In a superb display O'Callaghan nods home the rebound after Thomas hits the bar. Hampton wallops one into the far corner and Thomas cracks a beauty past Parkes. Stewart's penalty is for McAughtrie's foul on Clark but McIlroy's pair of astute finishes are both from Chambo's passes.

14. WATFORD 0-1 — Barnes 20. Ref: D Letts
Stoke: Harrison, Parkin D, Hampton, Bracewell, Watson, McAughtrie, Maguire*, McIlroy, O'Callaghan, Thomas, Chamb'rl'n M — sub: Berry
Watford: Sherwood, Rice, Rostron, Taylor, Sims, Bolton, Callaghan, Blissett, Gilligan, Jackett, Barnes
City have two goals disallowed as O'Callaghan is harshly penalised for fouls. Barnes cracks home Taylor's cross although Jimmy Gilligan also hits the goalpost and Harrison looks edgy under a long-ball barrage. Barnes heads over from close range. Chamberlain nearly chips Sherwood.

15. NORWICH 2-4 — McIlr'y 21, O'Call' 76 [Bertschin 77] / Deehan 48p, 57p, Barham 55. Ref: M Dimblebee
Stoke: Harrison, Parkin D, Hampton, Bracewell, Watson, McAughtrie, Maguire*, McIlroy, O'Callaghan, Thomas, Chamb'rl'n M — sub: Berry
Norwich: Woods, Haylock, Hareide*, Van Wyk, Watson, Barham, Walford, O'Neill, Deehan, Bertschin, Bennett — sub: Jack
Stoke are in control thanks to McIlroy's tap-in but Ross Jack's introduction into midfield changes things and Norwich sweep forward. The pens are for handball. Barham and Bertschin nod past Harrison. Bren O'Callaghan's header is so aggressive he ends up in the back of the net with it.

16. ASTON VILLA 0-3 — Parkin 30 (og), Shaw 68, 80. Ref: D Scott
Stoke: Fox, Parkin D, Hampton, Bracewell, Watson, McAughtrie, Maguire, McIlroy, O'Callaghan, Thomas, Chamb'rl'n N
Aston Villa: Rimmer, Shaw, Williams, Evans, McNaught, Mortimer, Bremner, Shaw, Withe, Cowans, Morley
Derek Parkin deflects in Cowans' header to hand the European Champions the advantage. Shaw scores with two well-placed headers. Rimmer clings on to Maguire's shot and Neville Chamberlain has an effort disallowed for offside. Long serving defender Alan Dodd is sold to Wolves.

17. SOUTHAMPTON 0-1 — Wallace 74. Ref: D Reeves
Stoke: Fox, Parkin D, Hampton, Bracewell !, Watson, McAughtrie, Maguire*, McIlroy, O'Callaghan, Thomas, Chamb'rl'n M
Southampton: Shilton, Agboola, Mills, Williams, Nicholl, Wright, Holmes, Puckett, Moran, Armstrong, Wallace
Skipper Bracewell is sent off for fouling Steve Williams (37 mins) and City have their backs to the wall. Fox saves brilliantly from Puckett and Chamberlain is sent sprawling by Agboola but no penalty is awarded. Wallace scores from Williams' pass. City bid for Ipswich's Alan Brazil.

18. TOTTENHAM 2-0 — Watson 4, McIlroy 68. Ref: R Banks
Stoke: Fox, Parkin D, Hampton, Bracewell, Watson, Berry, Maguire, McIlroy, O'Callaghan, Thomas, Chamb'rl'n N
Tottenham: Clemence, Hughton, Price, Lacy, Villa, Roberts, Mabbutt, Archibald, Galvin, Hoddle, Crooks* — sub: Corbett
City breeze past a surprisingly lacklustre Spurs in front of England boss Bobby Robson. Dave Watson slams home unmarked from close range after a corner. McIlroy fires home on the run via a Lacy deflection. Maguire misses a sitter and Fox produces a fabulous stop to deny Hoddle.

19. COVENTRY 0-2 — Hateley 21, 50. Ref: B Stevens
Stoke: Fox, Parkin D, Hampton, Maskery, Watson, Berry, Maguire*, McIlroy, O'Callaghan, Thomas, Chamb'rl'n M — sub: Ursem
Coventry: Sealey, Thomas, Roberts, Jacobs, Dyson, Gillespie, Whitton, Francis*, Hateley, Melrose, Hunt — sub: Butterworth
George Berry's mistake allows Melrose to square for Mark Hateley to score the opener. Maguire goes close as City fight back but another error, as Parkin's back-pass falls straight to Hateley, hands Coventry the points in a disappointing performance. Thomas cracks a 20-yarder just over.

20. EVERTON 1-0 — Chamberlain 75. Ref: J Hunting
Stoke: Fox, Parkin D*, Hampton, Bracewell, Watson, Berry !, Painter, McIlroy, O'Callaghan, Thomas, Chamb'rl'n M — sub: Maskery
Everton: Arnold, Stevens*, Bailey, Ratcliffe, Higgins, McMahon, Curran, Heath, Johnson, Richardson, Sheedy — sub: Sharp
Plucky Stoke recover from Berry's 60th-minute sending-off for serious foul play as Chamberlain beats Jim Arnold from the edge of the area. On the eve of his 18th birthday Ian Painter makes a promising debut in place of Maguire (out with a bad back) against Howard Kendall's men.

21. NOTTS CO 0-4 — Mair 28, McCulloch 42, 65, [Goodwin 64]. Ref: D Axcell
Stoke: Fox, Parkin D, Hampton, Bracewell, Watson, Berry, Painter*, McIlroy, O'Callaghan, Thomas, Chamb'rl'n M — sub: Maskery
Notts Co: Avramovic, Benjamin, Worthington, Hunt, Kilcline, Richards, Chiedozie, Fashanu, McCulloch*, Goodwin, Mair — sub: Hooks
Barker risks the unfit Bracewell, Chamberlain and Thomas but in the mud City give the Magpies too much room on the flanks. Mair's shot and McCulloch's second, a shot on the run, are superb. Chiedozie supplies the other goals for Jimmy Sirrel's men. City's worst display of the year.

LEAGUE DIVISION 1 — Manager: Richie Barker — SEASON 1982-83

No	Date	1	2	3	4	5	6	7	8	9	10	11	12 sub used
22	H NORWICH 1/1	Fox	Parkin D	Hampton	Bracewell	Watson	Berry	Painter	McIlroy	O'Callaghan	Thomas*	Chamb'rl'n M	Maskery
		Woods	*Haylock*	*Deehan*	*Mendham*	*Walford*	*Watson*	*Barham*	*O'Neill*	*Channon*	*Bertschin*	*Van Wyk**	*Downs*
23	H BIRMINGHAM 3/1	Fox	Parkin D	Hampton	Bracewell	Watson	Berry	Painter	McIlroy	O'Callaghan	Thomas	Ch'b'rl'n M*	Maskery
		Coton	*Langan !*	*Dennis*	*Stevenson*	*Blake*	*Broadhurst*	*Dillon*	*Phillips*	*Harford*	*Curbishley*	*Handyside*	
24	A ARSENAL 15/1	Fox	Parkin D	Hampton	Bracewell	Watson*	Chamb'rl'n N	Painter	McIlroy	O'Callaghan	Thomas	Maskery*	Ursem
		Jennings	*Hollins*	*Sansom*	*Whyte*	*O'Leary**	*Petrovic*	*Davis*	*Sunderland* Meade*	*Woodcock*	*Rix*	*Talbot*	
25	H IPSWICH 22/1	Fox	Parkin D	Hampton	Bracewell	Watson	Berry	Painter*	McIlroy	O'Callaghan	Thomas	Maguire	Bould
		Sivell	*Steggles*	*Gernon*	*Thijssen*	*Osman*	*Butcher*	*Wark*	*McCall*	*Mariner*	*Brazil*	*Gates**	*O'Callaghan*
26	A WEST BROM 5/2	Fox	Parkin D	Hampton	Bracewell	Watson*	Berry	Painter	McIlroy	O'Callaghan	Thomas	Griffiths	Bould
		Barron	*Bennett*	*Statham*	*Zondervan*	*Wile*	*Robertson*	*Jol*	*Brown*	*Cross*	*Owen*	*Eastoe*	
27	A BRIGHTON 26/2	Fox	Parkin D	Hampton	Bracewell	Watson	Berry	Painter	McIlroy	O'Callaghan*	Thomas	Chamb'rl'n M	Lennox
		Digweed	*Ramsey*	*Gatting*	*Grealish*	*Foster*	*Stevens*	*Case*	*Ward*	*Ritchie*	*Ryan*	*Smillie*	
28	H MANCHESTER U 2/3	Fox	Parkin D	Hampton	Bracewell	Watson	Berry	Painter	McIlroy	O'Callaghan	Thomas	Chamb'rl'n M	
		Bailey	*Duxbury*	*Albiston*	*Moses*	*McGrath*	*McQueen*	*Wilkins*	*Muhren*	*Stapleton*	*Whiteside*	*Coppell*	
29	A LIVERPOOL 5/3	Fox	Grobbelaar	Hampton	Bracewell	Watson	Berry	Painter*	McIlroy	O'Callaghan	Thomas	Chamb'rl'n M	McAughtrie
			Neal	*Kennedy*	*Lawrenson*	*Whelan*	*Hansen*	*Dalglish*	*Lee*	*Rush*	*Johnston*	*Souness*	
30	H SUNDERLAND 12/3	Fox	Parkin D*	Hampton	Bracewell	Watson	Berry	Painter	McIlroy	O'Callaghan	Thomas	Chamb'rl'n M	Bould
		Turner	*Nicholl*	*Munro*	*Atkins*	*Chisholm*	*Pickering*	*Venison*	*Rowell*	*West*	*James*	*Cummins*	
31	H NOTT'M FOREST 16/3	Fox	**Parkin S**	Hampton	Bracewell	Watson	Berry	Painter	McIlroy	O'Callaghan	Thomas	Chamb'rl'n M	
		Sutton	*Anderson*	*Swain*	*Gunn*	*Young*	*Bowyer*	*Wilson*	*Wallace*	*Fairclough*	*Hodge*	*Walsh**	*Robertson*

Results, Scorers, Times and Referees

No	Team	Pos	Res	F-A	H-T	Att	Pos	Pt	Scorers / Referee
22	H NORWICH	13	W	1-0	1-0	15,669	19	30	McIlroy 32; Ref: K Walmsley
23	H BIRMINGHAM	12	D	1-1	0-1	15,428	22	31	Painter 76, Phillips 15; Ref: D Hutchinson
24	A ARSENAL	14	L	0-3	0-2	19,428	13	31	Fix 17, Petrovic 44, Hollins 62p; Ref: M James
25	H IPSWICH	12	W	1-0	0-0	14,026	11	34	Painter 58; Ref: T Mills
26	A WEST BROM	13	D	1-1	1-0	11,486	9	35	Berry 7, Cross 50; Ref: T Spencer
27	A BRIGHTON	13	W	2-1	2-1	14,937	22	38	Thomas 33, Painter 43, Ritchie 10; Ref: J Moules
28	H MANCHESTER U	11	W	1-0	0-0	20,950	3	41	O'Callaghan 75; Ref: K Barrett
29	A LIVERPOOL	12	L	1-5	0-2	30,020	1	41	Bracewell 50, Dalglish 7, 47, Neal 35, Johnston 76, [Souness 89]; Ref: J Key
30	H SUNDERLAND	13	L	0-1	0-0	12,806	15	41	Rowell 60; Ref: K Baker
31	H NOTT'M FOREST	10	W	1-0	0-0	10,880	4	44	Thomas 67; Ref: A Robinson

Match reports

22. Stoke win more convincingly than just the one goal. McIlroy bags it after John Deehan slips. Chamberlain and Bracewell force Woods to save superbly. O'Callaghan heads just over and Deehan heads another effort off the line. After Thomas limps off, City's attacking ardour dulls.

23. Chamberlain pulls up with a hamstring injury when clean through. Ron Saunders' Blues clear and Les Phillips scores before Chamberlain can receive any treatment. Ian Painter heads his first senior goal from Maskery's cross and Dave Langan walks (87 mins) for clattering into Thomas.

24. The Gunners dominate against a defence-minded City. Rix drives home when put clear. Then Vladimir Petrovic's 25-yard free-kick soars past Fox. Hollins' penalty is for Watson's debatable handball. City don't match Arsenal's desire. Watson nearly makes amends but Jennings saves.

25. Stoke hit the bar through Watson in the first minute. Ipswich are forced back as Painter, Bracewell and O'Callaghan go close, but it isn't until Painter pops up to head in Maguire's corner that City break through. Fox saves superbly from Kevin O'Callaghan but Stoke deserve their win.

26. Berry's header is adjudged to have crossed the line as Stoke dominate. The Albion fans are chanting for manager Ron Wylie's head but Cross pounces when Fox parries Eastoe's shot and the Baggies grab an undeserved draw. Fox saves acrobatically from Eastoe but City throw it away.

27. Stoke trail to Ritchie's header before Chamberlain switches to the left wing and produces a devastating display to turn the game on its head. He crosses for O'Callaghan to shoot and Thomas turns home the rebound. Then he sets up Ian Painter. Mickey Thomas is back to his tigerish best.

28. Brendan O'Callaghan finally finds a way past the superb Gary Bailey after being frustrated by two world-class saves. He flicks home Thomas' low cross as Stoke totally dominate. Bracewell and McIlroy run the show and Watson is commanding at the back. United's first defeat of 1983.

29. Another Anfield humiliation. This time Barker starts with his usual attacking line-up but Dalglish grabs two close-range finishes, then Neal and Souness spank drives in from outside the box. Rush torments Berry. Bracewell converts O'Callaghan's flick on but City are never in the hunt.

30. City do all the pressing but lose to Gary Rowell's sucker-punch goal against the run of play. Painter's overhead kick tests Turner and Berry has a header cleared off the line. Sunderland keep possession intelligently once ahead and dampen the Potters' desire to battle back into the match.

31. Ref Alan Robinson is suspended by the League after a dire display. McIlroy nets but is given a penalty for an earlier foul, which he then skies over. O'Callaghan's header is ruled out for pushing a non-existent defender. No doubt as Thomas nets when Sutton parries Bracewell's shot.

Match Summary

No	Venue	Opponent	Date	Att			Pts	Res	FT	HT	City Scorers	Opposition Scorers	Referee
32	A	WEST HAM	19/3	16,446	9	13	45		1-1	0-0	Thomas 69	Bould 52 (og)	M Bodenham
33	H	WATFORD	26/3	14,276	7	2	48	W	4-0	1-0	Thomas 10, Painter 63, Chamber'n 70, [McAughtrie 82]		R Guy
34	H	NOTTS CO	2/4	16,314	5	16	51	W	1-0	0-0	McIlroy 54p		N Midgley
35	A	EVERTON	4/4	15,360	5	11	51	L	1-3	0-0	Thomas 54	Sheedy 48, 62, Sharp 80	A Saunders
36	H	MANCHESTER C	9/4	15,372	5	17	54	W	1-0	0-0	McIlroy 61		R Milford
37	H	SWANSEA	16/4	10,100	6	20	55	D	1-1	0-1	Thomas 58	Charles 38	S Bates
38	H	SOUTHAMPTON	23/4	14,903	7	8	56	D	1-1	0-1	Berry 60	Wallace 87	N Glover
39	A	ASTON VILLA	30/4	20,944	9	4	56	L	0-4	0-1		Cowans 40, McNaught 54, Morley 75, Evans 86	C Downley
40	A	LUTON	2/5	*1,877	9	16	57	D	0-0	0-0			A Gunn
41	H	COVENTRY	7/5	12,048	11	17	57	L	0-3	0-1		Hateley 20, Hendrie 50, Thomas 81	R Chadwick
42	A	TOTTENHAM	14/5	33,391	13	4	57	L	1-4	0-2	Maguire 67p	Brazil 5, Archibald 35, 47, 82	I Borrett

Home 16,631   Average 18,741

Match Reports & Line-ups

32 — A WEST HAM
Stoke: Fox, Bould, Hampton, Bracewell, Watson, Berry, Painter, McIlroy, O'Callaghan*, Thomas, Chamb'r'n M (sub Griffiths).
West Ham: Parkes, Stewart, Lampard, Bonds, Martin, Devonshire, Van der Elst, Goddard, Morgan, Allen, Pike.
Steve Bould scores a spectacular own-goal as his back-pass loops over Fox's head. City fight back through livewire Thomas. He finishes off a thrilling Chamberlain run, beating Lampard and Bonds. Fox tips away Morgan's point-blank header. Goddard has a goal ruled out for offside.

33 — H WATFORD
Watford: Sherwood, Rice, Rostron, Taylor, Sims, Bolton, Callaghan, Blissett, Armstrong, Jackett*, Barnes (sub Lohman). Stoke sub: Ch'b'r'n M* / McAughtrie.
Stoke inflict Watford's heaviest defeat of the season with a glittering performance. Thomas' diving header sets the ball rolling. Painter fires in from 18 yards and Chamberlain, after hitting the underside of the bar, lobs Sherwood. McAughtrie, playing up front nods home Painter's cross.

34 — H NOTTS CO
Notts Co: Avramovic, Benjamin, Clarke, Hunt*, Kilcline, Richards, Harkouk, McCulloch, Lahtinen, Christie, Goodwin (sub Worthington).
City win with McIlroy's twice-taken penalty after Chamberlain is fouled off the ball. He puts the first kick wide but Avramovic is ruled to have moved so gets a second chance. Fox saves bravely when McCulloch is through and Chamberlain jinks past two defenders to force a good save.

35 — A EVERTON (Lennox* / sub Saunders)
Everton: Arnold, Richardson, Bailey, Ratcliffe, Higgins, McMahon, Ainscow, Johnson, Sharp, Heath, Sheedy.
Stoke's European ambitions are dealt a blow. Kevin Sheedy fires two left-footed shots past Fox and Graeme Sharp's close-range finish wraps it up. Thomas buries Maguire's cross but Stoke wilt under pressure. Carl Saunders, having joined the club on a work experience scheme, debuts.

36 — H MANCHESTER C
Manchester C: Williams, Ranson, McDonald, Reid, Bond, Caton, Kinsey, Reeves, Cross, Hartford, Power.
John Bonds' Man City, with 1 win in 12, play with no attacking ambitions. City find it hard to break down the resolute defence. Chamberlain's low cross sees Bracewell step over the ball to allow McIlroy a clear sight of goal. Hampton heads off the line and Power has a goal disallowed.

37 — H SWANSEA
Swansea: Sander, Marustik, Richards, Charles, Lewis, Rajkovic, Loveridge, Walsh*, James R, Robinson, Latchford (sub Stevenson).
A tight affair sees Jeremy Charles power a header past Fox from a corner. Mickey Thomas heads home O'Callaghan's back flick for a copycat goal. He also volleys just wide of Chris Sander's upright. John Toshack's Swansea press forward but the resolute Stoke back four hold up well.

38 — H SOUTHAMPTON
Southampton: Shilton, Agboola, Mills, Williams, Nicholl, Waldron, Holmes, Foyle*, Moran, Armstrong, Wallace (sub Puckett).
In a vital clash City gain the upper hand through Berry's far-post header from Chamberlain's overhead kick. Stoke look to have clinched it but Fox drops a Williams long ball and Wallace pounces. A vital point for Saints. Dave Watson's final game before joining Vancouver Whitecaps.

39 — A ASTON VILLA (subs: Chamb'r'n M / Hampton; [Evans 86]; Money 75)
Aston Villa: Spink, Williams, Gibson, Evans, McNaught, Mortimer, Curbishley*, Shaw, Walters, Cowans, Morley (sub Bremner).
City are summarily dismissed by Villa who start slowly but sparkle after the break. Tony Morley's goal is Villa's best effort. After it a group of Stoke fans run onto the pitch and the game is stopped while they are escorted away by large numbers of police. Europe looks out of reach now.

40 — A LUTON
Luton: Godden, Stephens, Money, Horton, Elliott, Donaghy, Hill, Turner, Aylott, Antic, Moss.
City frustrate Luton's desperate efforts to win with O'Callaghan dominant at the back in place of Dave Watson. Luton's fans howl with rage as Stoke catch Aylott and Moss offside continually. Painter heads against the upright as Stoke nearly snatch victory against David Pleat's Hatters.

41 — H COVENTRY (Chamb'r'n M / sub Heath)
Coventry: Sealey, Thomas, Roberts, Hrtm Inschuk, Butterworth, Gillespie, Whitton, Francis, Hateley, Hendrie, Hunt.
Stoke have an injury nightmare when O'Callaghan dislocates his shoulder then Chamberlain pulls his hamstring. Coventry's relegation fight is helped by Hateley's volley, Hendrie's cool finish and Thomas' fabulous solo goal. Gillespie miskicks against his own keeper from three yards.

42 — A TOTTENHAM (Parkin S in goal; Maskery, Maguire; sub Griffiths)
Tottenham: Clemence, Hughton, O'Reilly*, Lacy, Miller, Perryman, Mabbutt, Archibald, Galvin, Hoddle, Falco (sub Brazil).
Injury-hit Stoke are given the runaround by Keith Burkinshaw's classy Spurs. Steve Archibald's hat-trick are all close-range finishes to superb moves. He nearly snatches a fourth but his header hits the post. Maguire's spot-kick is for a foul on Maskery. City's squad needs strengthening

LEAGUE DIVISION 1 (CUP-TIES)

Manager: Richie Barker

SEASON 1982-83

Milk Cup

		Att		F-A	H-T	Scorers, Times, and Referees	1	2	3	4	5	6	7	8	9	10		12 sub used
2:1	H WEST HAM 6/10	18,709	8 D	1-1	0-0	Thomas 70 *Stewart 80p* Ref: H King	Fox	Parkin D	Hampton	Bracewell	Watson	Berry	Maguire	McIlroy	O'Callaghan	Thomas	Ch'b'rl'n M*	Griffiths
							Parkes	*Stewart*	*Lampard*	*Orr*	*Martin*	*Devonshire*	*Neighbour*	*Goddard*	*Clark*	*Allen*	*Pike*	*Neighbour*
2:2	A WEST HAM 26/10	18,349	8 L	1-2	0-0	Watson 62 *Goddard 82, Clark 84* Ref: J Martin (Stoke lose 2-3 on aggregate)	Harrison	Parkin D	Hampton	Bracewell	Watson	McAughtrie	Maguire	McIlroy	O'Callaghan	Thomas	Chamb'rl'n M	
							Parkes	*Stewart*	*Lampard*	*Bonds*	*Martin*	*Devonshire*	*Van der Elst*	*Goddard*	*Clark*	*Allen*	*Pike*	*Neighbour*

Chamberlain is injured in a clash with Devonshire and leaves the fray after just 16 mins. City take time to adjust to losing him. After relentless pressure it seems as if Thomas' left-footed piledriver has won the game, but Devonshire is tripped and Ray Stewart hammers home the penalty.

Dave Watson's far-post header seems to have done the business for City who have the better of a close game until the last 10 minutes. England U-21 international Paul Goddard hits a cracking shot from 25 yards and then provides Sandy Clark with an easy opportunity to win the match.

FA Cup

		Att		F-A	H-T	Scorers, Times, and Referees	1	2	3	4	5	6	7	8	9	10		12 sub used
3	A SHEFFIELD UTD 8/1	23,239 3:17	12 D	0-0	0-0	Ref: B Hill	Fox	Parkin D	Hampton	Bracewell	Watson	Berry	Painter	McIlroy	O'Callaghan	Thomas	Maskery	
							Waugh	*Henderson*	*Garner*	*Brazil*	*Houston*	*Kenworthy*	*Morris*	*Trusson*	*Edwards*	*Curran*	*King*	
3R	H SHEFFIELD UTD 12/1	18,315 3:17	12 W	3-2	1-2	McAug 42, Painter 48, Hender' 50 (og) *Edwards 39, Morris 44p* Ref: B Hill	Fox	Parkin D	Hampton	Bracewell	Watson	McAughtrie	Maguire	McIlroy	O'Callaghan	Thomas	Ch'b'rl'n M*	Painter
							Waugh	*Henderson*	*Garner*	*Charles*	*West**	*Houston*	*Morris*	*Trusson*	*Edwards*	*Curran*	*King*	*Brazil*
4	A LIVERPOOL 29/1	36,666 1	12 L	0-2	0-1	*Dalglish 23, Rush 88* Ref: G Courtney	Fox	Parkin D	Hampton	Bracewell	Watson	Berry	Maguire	McIlroy	O'Callaghan	Thomas	Painter	
							Grobbelaar	*Neal*	*Kennedy*	*Lawrenson*	*Johnston*	*Hansen*	*Dalglish*	*Lee*	*Rush*	*Hodgson*	*Souness*	

City are on top but never easy against a lively Blades side. Thomas puts one just over and O'Callaghan brings a great save out of Keith Waugh. Terry Curran gives Hampton problems and nearly manages to beat Fox when put through. Gary Brazil volleys over from Keith Edwards' cross.

Keith Edwards nods home in a scramble before McAughtrie flings himself full length to equalise. Fox is incensed by the penalty, for bringing down Edwards but Painter levels with a close-range header. Mike Henderson turns home Maguire's cross. Ian Porterfield's Blades are unlucky.

Richie Barker abandons his attacking principles and fields a five-man defence with just Painter up front. Ian Rush and Kenny Dalglish combine to produce two superbly crafted goals. Dalglish's beautifully angled chip is his 300th career strike. Stoke fail to trouble Bruce Grobbelaar at all.

#	Team	P		Home					Away				Pts
			W	D	L	F	A	W	D	L	F	A	
1	Liverpool	42	16	4	1	55	16	8	6	7	32	21	82
2	Watford	42	16	2	3	49	20	6	3	12	25	37	71
3	Manchester U	42	14	7	0	39	10	5	6	10	17	28	70
4	Tottenham	42	15	4	2	50	15	5	5	11	15	35	69
5	Nott'm Forest	42	12	5	4	34	18	8	4	9	28	32	69
6	Aston Villa	42	17	2	2	47	15	4	3	14	15	35	68
7	Everton	42	13	6	2	43	19	5	4	12	23	29	64
8	West Ham	42	13	3	5	41	23	7	1	13	27	39	64
9	Ipswich	42	11	3	7	39	23	4	10	7	25	27	58
10	Arsenal	42	11	6	4	36	19	5	4	12	22	37	58
11	West Brom	42	11	5	5	35	20	4	7	10	16	29	57
12	Southampton	42	11	5	5	36	22	4	7	10	18	36	57
13	STOKE	42	13	4	4	34	21	3	5	13	19	43	57
14	Norwich	42	13	6	5	30	18	4	6	11	22	40	54
15	Notts Co	42	12	4	5	37	25	3	3	15	18	46	52
16	Sunderland	42	7	10	4	30	22	5	4	12	18	39	50
17	Birmingham	42	9	7	5	29	24	3	7	11	11	31	50
18	Luton	42	7	7	7	34	33	6	6	10	31	51	49
19	Coventry	42	10	5	6	29	17	3	4	14	19	42	48
20	Manchester C	42	9	5	7	26	23	4	3	14	21	47	47
21	Swansea	42	10	4	7	32	29	0	7	14	19	40	41
22	Brighton	42	8	7	6	25	22	1	6	14	13	46	40
		924	255	111	96	810	454	96	111	255	454	810	1275

Odds & ends

Double wins: (2) Brighton, Ipswich.

Double losses: (2) Aston Villa, Coventry.

Won from behind: (2) Brighton (a), Swansea (h).

Lost from in front: (1) Norwich (a).

High spots: Fabulous attacking performances.
The emergence of Mark Chamberlain's talent.
George Berry's signing adding vigour and personality to the squad.
The midfield trio of McIlroy, Bracewell and Thomas combining brilliantly.
Beating Manchester United for the first time in seven years.

Low spots: Failing to win any of the last eight games to lose out on a place in Europe.
Only one away point between September and February.
Another thrashing by Liverpool.
League rules not allowing Dave Watson to return to the club from the USA to continue playing next season.

Player of the Year: Mickey Thomas.
Ever-presents: (0).
Hat-tricks: (0).
Leading scorer: (12) Mickey Thomas.

Appearances and Goals

Name	Appearances						Goals			
	Lge	Sub	LC	Sub	FAC	Sub	Lge	LC	FAC	Tot
Berry, George	27	4	1		2		5			5
Bould, Steve	11	3								
Bracewell, Paul	41		2		3		2			2
Chamberlain, Mark	36		2		1		6			6
Chamberlain, Neville	4									
Dodd, Alan	1	1								
Fox, Peter	35		1		3					
Griffiths, Peter	11	4		1			1			1
Hampton, Pete	38	2	2		3		1			1
Harrison, Mark	7		1							
Heath, Phil	1	1								
Lennox, Steve	1	1								
Maguire, Paul	22	2	2		2		5			5
Maskery, Chris	3	4								
McAughtrie, Dave	17	3	1		1		1		1	2
McIlroy, Sammy	41		2		3		8			8
O'Callaghan, Brendan	37		2		3		5			5
Painter, Ian	22				2	1	4	1		5
Parkin, Derek	30		2		3					
Parkin, Steve	2	1								
Saunders, Carl		1								
Thomas, Mickey	41		2		3		11		1	12
Ursem, Loek		2								
Watson, Dave	35		2		3		2	1		3
(own-goals)							2		1	3
24 players used	462	29	22	1	33	1	53	2	3	58

CANON DIVISION 1

Manager: Richie Barker ⇨ Bill Asprey   SEASON 1983-84

Match details

No	Date	Att	Pos	Pt	Res	F-A	H-T	Scorers, Times, and Referees
1	A EVERTON 27/8	22,658	—	0	L	0-1	0-1	Sharp 38. Ref: G Tyson
2	H WEST BROM 29/8	16,156	—	3	W	3-1	2-1	Painter 26, 35, Maguire 57 / Cross 25. Ref: M Peck
3	H MANCHESTER U 3/9	23,704	14 / 7	3	L	0-1	0-0	Muhren 55. Ref: M Dimblebee
4	A BIRMINGHAM 6/9	13,728	15 / 12	3	L	0-1	0-1	Blake 35p. Ref: C Downey
5	A IPSWICH 10/9	16,315	20 / 2	3	L	0-5	0-3	Burley 3, Gates 17, Wark 42, 90p [Mariner 47]. Ref: K Salmon
6	H WATFORD 17/9	12,619	20 / 12	3	L	0-4	0-1	Lohman 32, Barnes 57, 80, Jobson 65. Ref: T Mills
7	A LEICESTER 24/9	10,215	20 / 22	4	D	2-2	2-2	Painter 11, Maguire 25 / Jones 30, Lineker 45. Ref: T Spencer
8	H WEST HAM 1/10	13,825	18 / 1	7	W	3-1	1-0	McAughtrie 30, Chamberlain 70 [Thomas 80] / Stewart 60p. Ref: B Stevens
9	A SUNDERLAND 15/10	11,923	19 / 16	8	D	2-2	1-1	James 27, 70 / Thomas 26 (og), Rowell 49. Ref: D Richardson
10	A NOTTS CO 22/10	7,684	18 / 20	9	D	1-1	0-0	Bould 74 / Kilcline 60. Ref: J Moules

Line-ups (Stoke row / Opponent row)

No	1	2	3	4	5	6	7	8	9	10	11	12 sub used
1	Fox	Chamb'rl'n N	James	Savage	Dyson	Bould	Painter	Griffiths*	O'Callaghan	Thomas	Maguire	McIlroy
	Arnold	Harper	Mountfield	Bailey	Higgins	Richardson	Steven	Heath	Sharp	King	Sheedy	
2	Fox	Savage	James	Dyson	Berry	Bould	Painter	McIlroy	O'Callaghan	Thomas	Maguire	
	Barron	Robertson	Whitehead	Robson	McNaught	Bennett	Jol	Thompson	Regis	Owen	Cross	
3	Fox	Bould	Savage	James	Dyson	Berry	Painter	McIlroy	O'Callaghan	Thomas	Chamb'rl'n M	
	Bailey	Gidman	Albiston	Wilkins	Moran	McQueen	Robson	Muhren	Stapleton	Whiteside	Graham	
4	Fox	Chamb'rl'n N	James	Savage	Dyson	Bould	Painter	McIlroy	O'Callaghan*	Thomas*	Chamb'rl'n M	Maguire
	Coton	Hagan	V d Hauwe	Blake	Wright	Broadhurst	Rees*	Phillips	Harford	Halsall	McCarrick	
5	Fox	Chamb'rl'n N	Hampton	James	Dyson	Bould	Berry	McIlroy	Maguire	Thomas	Chamb'rl'n M	
	Cooper	Burley	Gernon	Parkin*	Osman	Butcher	Wark	McCall	Mariner	Gates	O'Callaghan	Putney
6	Fox	Savage	James	Dyson	Berry	Maguire	Painter	McIlroy	O'Callaghan	Thomas*	Chamb'rl'n M	Tuart
	Sherwood	Palmer	Jackett	Jobson	Sims	Franklin	Callaghan	Barnes	Reilly*	Lohman	Rostron	Gilligan
7	Fox	Bould	Hampton	James	Dyson	Berry	Painter	McIlroy	O'Callaghan	Maguire*	Chamb'rl'n M	Savage
	Wallington	Ramsey	Smith R	MacDonald	Williams	O'Neill	Lynex	Lineker	Smith A*	Jones	Wilson	Peake
8	Fox	Berry	Hampton	James	Dyson	Bould	McIlroy	McAughtrie	O'Callaghan	Thomas	Chamb'rl'n M	Savage
	Parkes	Stewart	Walford	Bonds	Martin	Devonshire	Whitton	Goddard	Swindlehurst	Brooking	Pike	
9	Fox	Bould	Hampton	James	Dyson	McAughtrie	Painter	McIlroy	O'Callaghan	Thomas	Chamb'rl'n M	
	Turner	Venison	Elliott	Atkins	Chisholm	Proctor	Bracewell	Rowell	West	Pickering	James	
10	Fox	Bould*	Hampton	James	Dyson	McAughtrie	Tuart	McIlroy	O'Callaghan	Thomas	Chamb'rl'n M	Maskery
	McDonagh	Benjamin	Worthington	Goodwin	Kilcline	Hunt	Richards	Fashanu†	Christie	Harkouk	Mair	O'Neill

Match reports

1. Richie Barker's new system of playing the early long ball means a frenzy of activity. Maguire beats the offside trap to test Arnold and Painter has a shot desperately blocked. Graeme Sharp turns to fire home the winner and despite all City's efforts in the new pin-stripe kit Everton win.

2. Painter scores two and makes a third before having a hat-trick ruled out for fouling Barron. His brace are close-range efforts. Maguire's diving header leads to wild celebrations. The long-ball policy may be paying off. Thomas makes hay down the left and Paul Dyson dominates Regis.

3. Stoke give Gary Bailey a stern test with McIlroy and Thomas twice being foiled. Thomas also nets but the referee brings it back for a free-kick to City. Arnold Muhren scores from a narrow angle and United come more into the game. The long ball is dealt with by Moran and McQueen.

4. After an aimless first half which sees Savage foul Rees and Noel Blake blast home the penalty, Stoke are more aggressive. Chamberlain thinks he has scored when Coton drags the ball back from over the line. But unsighted officials cannot give the goal and Stoke fume. A poor showing.

5. Stoke are a mess. Ipswich waltz through at will with Gates' neat finish and Mariner's fierce drive the best goals. McIlroy is glad to be subbed at 0-4. Berry fouls Wark for the spot-kick which he scores even though Fox gets his hand to it. Hampton heads off the line. Couldn't be worse.

6. 'Barker Out' shout the Boothen End after Watford win with embarrassing ease. Jan Lohman volleys past a motionless defence and John Barnes chips a beautiful free-kick past Fox. James hits Sherwood from close range when a goal seems inevitable but this is Stoke's only shot on target.

7. Two poor teams produce an exciting if low quality game. Painter's overhead kick is followed by a route one goal as Fox's kick is flicked on by O'Callaghan for Maguire to finish. Lineker turns sharply to finish. Maguire has a goal disallowed and James has a drive cleared off the line.

8. Table-topping Hammers are well beaten in a fierce match. McAughtrie produces a superb overhead kick to beat Parkes. He then fouls Goddard and Stewart crashes home the penalty before Chamberlain buries a loose ball in a scramble and Mickey Thomas does likewise. Very good win.

9. Sunderland have the edge when Thomas deflects Leighton James' cross past Fox. Stoke play more through midfield and look much better for it. Chamberlain's cross past Turner. Gary Rowell snaps up Dyson's poor clearance. Stoke play more through midfield and look much better for it.

10. Steve Bould's first goal is a scrappy affair. Chamberlain fails to control a bouncing ball and it ricochets to Bould to drive home. In a poor game Brian Kilcline sweeps home a corner which isn't cleared. James nearly buries a 30-yarder but neither side has the quality to break the deadlock.

11 H COVENTRY 29/10 — 11,836 — 19 — L — 1-3 — 1-2
Thomas 40
Bennett 12, Gibson 35, Bamber 80
Ref: D Scott / D Crone

Fox	Berry	Hampton	James	Dyson	McAughtrie	Tueart	McIlroy	O'Callaghan	Thomas	Chamb'rl'n M
Avramovic	Roberts	Singleton	Grimes	Peake	Allardyce	Bennett	Gynn	Bamber	Gibson	Platnauer

Stoke improve but their luck is out when substitute referee D Crone deflects the ball into Terry Gibson's path for the decisive second. Thomas' sharp turn and shot is all Stoke have to show for good pressure but without a cutting edge. Dave Bamber cracks home a great effort to clinch it.

---

12 H TOTTENHAM 5/11 — 14,727 — 19 — 5 — D — 1-1 — 1-1
Thomas 25
Falco 31
Ref: N Wilson

Fox	Bould	Hampton	James	O'Callaghan	McAughtrie	Maguire	McIlroy	Dyson	Thomas	Chamb'rl'n M
Clemence	Hughton	Thomas	Roberts	Stevens	Perryman	Mabbutt*	Archibald	Falco	Hoddle	Galvin	O'Reilly

In an action-packed match Mickey Thomas flies in to head home Maguire's cross. Falco stabs home after Archibald's shot hits the upright and both keepers are forced to make world-class saves. Fox from Perryman and Ray Clemence from McIlroy. The pace drops off as both teams tire.

---

13 A ASTON VILLA 12/11 — *9,272 — 18 — 8 — D — 1-1 — 1-0
Chamberlain 44
Withe 55
Ref: M Scott

Fox	Bould	Hampton	James*	O'Callaghan	McAughtrie	Maguire	McIlroy	Dyson	Withe	Chamb'rl'n M	Maskery
Day	Williams	Gibson*	Evans	Ormsby	Mortimer	Jones	Birch	Withe	McMahon	Rideout	Walters

Mark Chamberlain plays as a lone striker and scores a superb solo goal. From the halfway line he beats Evans and Ormsby before coolly firing past Mervyn Day. Peter Withe scores his customary goal against Stoke after heavy Villa pressure. City hold firm. Chamberlain nearly nicks it.

---

14 A LIVERPOOL 19/11 — *6,529 — 18 — 1 — L — 0-1 — 0-0
Rush 67
Ref: A Challinor

Fox	Bould	Hampton	James*	O'Callaghan	McAughtrie	Maguire	McIlroy	Dyson	Griffiths	Chamb'rl'n M	Savage
Grobbelaar	Neal	Kennedy	Lawrenson	Nicol	Hansen	Dalglish	Lee	Rush	Robinson	Souness

City fight for their lives. Hampton clears off the line from Rush, Robinson has a goal ruled out for offside and Fox saves Souness's raking shot as Stoke frustrate the fiery Champions. Stoke only manage to force one corner all game and finally succumb to Ian Rush's neat far-post header.

---

15 H NOTT'M FOREST 26/11 — 11,655 — 19 — 7 — D — 1-1 — 1-1
Chamberlain 7
Walsh 4p
Ref: D Allison

Fox	Bould	Hampton	McIlroy*	O'Callaghan	McAughtrie	Maguire	Maskery	Dyson	Griffiths	Chamb'rl'n M	Griffiths
Sutton	Anderson	Swain	Fairclough	Hart	Bowyer	Hodge	Thijssen	Walsh	Birtles	Davenport	Walsh

O'Callaghan fouls Davenport to hand Forest an early lead but Mark Chamberlain cuts inside and waltzes around Sutton. In an absorbing match Cloughie's Forest break well from midfield. Hodge tests Fox. Chamberlain nearly ends another long run with a superb finish but Sutton saves.

---

16 A SOUTHAMPTON 3/12 — 15,301 — 21 — 6 — L — 1-3 — 1-2
James 13
Wallace 35, Armstrong D 44, Mills 60
Ref: E Scales

Fox	Bould	Hampton	James	Dyson	McAughtrie	Heath	Maskery	Dyson	Thomas	Chamb'rl'n M
Shilton	Mills	Dennis	Williams	Armstrong K	Agboola	Holmes	Puckett	Worthington	Armstrong D	Wallace

Saints are stunned when Robbie James volleys right footed past Shilton from 18 yards. In a furious spell of attacking they reply with Wallace's shot off the underside of the bar and Armstrong's flashing header. Mills is left unmarked to drive home the third as Stoke wilt under pressure.

---

17 H LUTON 10/12 — 10,329 — 21 — 8 — L — 2-4 — 1-2
James 36p, 65
Walsh 20, 27, 90, Stein 63
Ref: C Thomas

Fox	Bould	Hampton	James	Berry	McAughtrie	Maskery	McIlroy	Painter*	Thomas	Chamb'rl'n M	Maguire
Sealey	Stephens	Thomas	Horton	Elliott	Donaghy	Hill	Stein B	Walsh	Daniel	Aylott	Daniel

Richie Barker is sacked and Bill Asprey takes charge. Stoke fall to a Paul Walsh hat-trick as the defence allow him time and space to fire three shots home from inside the box. James' penalty is for handball. He then belts a long punt by Fox in off the post to give City a glimmer of hope.

---

18 A WOLVES 17/12 — £679 — 21 — 22 — D — 0-0 — 0-0
Ref: L Shapter

Fox	Bould	Hampton	James	O'Callaghan	McAughtrie	Maskery	McIlroy	Painter	Thomas	Chamb'rl'n M
Burridge	Daniel	Palmer	Blair	Pender	Dodd	Hibbitt	Clarke	Cartwright* Mardenboro' Crainie	Eves

George Berry is stripped of the captaincy and dropped by Bill Asprey. Sammy McIlroy is the new club skipper. Chamberlain makes hay down the right but his crosses fall unkindly for Painter, James and McIlroy who all steer wide. Rock bottom Wolves are happy to settle for a point.

---

19 H NORWICH 26/12 — ~2,049 — 21 — 10 — W — 2-0 — 1-0
Maguire 23, James 82
Ref: F Roberts

Fox	Bould	Hampton	James	Dyson	McAughtrie	Maskery	McIlroy	Painter	Thomas	Chamb'rl'n M	Maguire
Woods	Haylock	Downs	Mendham	Deehan	Watson	Donowa	Channon	Devine	Bertschin	Van Wyk

Stoke end Norwich's ten-game unbeaten run when Paul Maguire turns home an O'Callaghan flick-on. Robbie James seals the win with a great 30-yard boomerang shot. Norwich barely have a sniff as Dyson dominates. Bill Asprey says 'I sense the mood is right for the coming months'.

---

20 A MANCHESTER U 31/12 — 41,164 — 21 — 2 — L — 0-1 — 0-0
Graham 75
Ref: J Key

Fox	Bould	Hampton !	James	Dyson	McAughtrie	Painter	McIlroy	O'Callaghan	Maguire	Chamb'rl'n M
Bailey	Duxbury	Albiston	Wilkins	Moran	McQueen	Moses	Muhren	Stapleton	Crooks*	Graham	Whiteside

Little New Year cheer for Peter Hampton who is dismissed following a 65th-minute fracas with Norman Whiteside. Stoke nearly hold out after Chamberlain clears off the line but Arthur Graham sneaks in to convert Stapleton's cross. United happily play keep ball to run down the clock.

---

21 H LEICESTER 2/1 — 13,728 — 21 — 18 — L — 0-1 — 0-1
Smith A 23
Ref: N Glover

Fox	Bould	Hampton	James	Dyson	McAughtrie	Painter	McIlroy	O'Callaghan	Thomas*	Chamb'rl'n M	Maguire
Wallington	Smith R	Wilson	MacDonald	Hazell	O'Neill	Lynex	Lineker	Smith A	Peake !	Banks

Alan Smith heads home Lynex's corner. Wallington saves superbly from Painter and James. Andy Peake is sent off (50 mins) for booking no 2. Maguire's arrival signals all-out attack but City cannot find a way past the massed defence. Lineker has a goal disallowed for fouling Hampton.

CANON DIVISION 1 — Manager: Richie Barker ⇨ Bill Asprey — SEASON 1983-84

Results summary (bold = attendance; italic pair = opponent position / points)

No	V	Opponent	Date	Att	Pos	italic pair	F-A	H-T	Scorers, Times, and Referees
22	H	EVERTON	14/1	**7,935**	21	*18 / 17*	D 1-1	0-0	Heath 68 / Heath 47 — Ref: B Hill
23	A	QP RANGERS	17/1	9,320	21	*6 / 17*	L 0-6	0-3	[Stewart 63, Fillery 81] Str'nrod 18, Gr'gory 35, Charles 43, 59 — Ref: A Robinson
24	A	WATFORD	21/1	14,076	21	*13 / 17*	L 0-2	0-0	Reily 82, Johnston 84 — Ref: D Axcell
25	H	ARSENAL	28/1	12,840	21	*11 / 20*	W 1-0	0-0	Maguire 75p — Ref: K Walmsley
26	A	WEST HAM	4/2	18,775	21	*3 / 20*	L 0-3	0-2	Barnes 5, Cottee 35, Stewart 70p — Ref: R Milford
27	H	IPSWICH	11/2	10,315	20	*15 / 23*	W 1-0	0-0	Painter 87 — Ref: J Worrall
28	A	COVENTRY	18/2	7,937	20	*21 / 26*	W 3-2	1-1	Hampt'n 41, Chamberlain 67, O'Call 81 / Bennett 8, Gibson 59 — Ref: J Martin
29	H	NOTTS CO	25/2	11,725	20	*21 / 29*	W 1-0	1-0	Chamberlain 8 — Ref: K Barratt
30	A	TOTTENHAM	3/3	18,271	20	*7 / 29*	L 0-1	0-1	Falco 35p — Ref: A Crickmore
31	H	ASTON VILLA	10/3	13,967	20	*12 / 32*	W 1-0	0-0	Painter 73 — Ref: G Courtney

Line-ups (top = Stoke, *italic = opponent*)

No	1	2	3	4	5	6	7	8	9	10	11	12 sub used
22	Fox / *Southall*	Bould / *Richardson*	Maskery / *Bailey*	James / *Ratcliffe*	Dyson / *Mountfield*	McAughtrie / *Reid*	Painter / *Irvine*	McIlroy / *Heath*	Heath / *Sharp*	Maguire / *Gray*	Chamb'rl'n M / *Sheedy*	/ *Micklewhite*
23	Fox / *Hucker*	Bould / *Neill*	Maskery / *Dawes*	James / *Waddock*	Dyson / *Wicks*	McAughtrie* / *Fenwick*	Painter / *Fillery*	McIlroy / *Stewart*	Heath / *Charles**	Maguire / *Stainrod*	Chamb'rl'n M / *Gregory*	/ *Micklewhite*
24	Fox / *Sherwood*	Bould / *Bardsley*	Hampton / *Rostron*	James / *Taylor*	Dyson / *Sims*	O'Callaghan* / *Franklin*	Parkin / *Callaghan*	McIlroy / *Johnston*	Maguire / *Reilly*	Maskery / *Jackett*	Chamb'rl'n M / *Barnes*	
25	Fox / *Jennings*	Bould / *Kay*	Maskery / *Sansom*	James / *Talbot*	Dyson / *O'Leary*	O'Callaghan / *Caton*	Painter / *McDermott*	McIlroy* / *Davis*	Maguire / *Woodcock*	Hudson / *Nicholas*	Chamb'rl'n M / *Rix*	/ *Heath*
26	Fox / *Parkes*	Bould / *Stewart*	Maskery / *Lampard*	James / *Walford*	Dyson / *Orr*	O'Callaghan / *Brush*	Painter / *Barnes*	McIlroy / *Cottee*	Maguire / *Swindlehurst*	Hudson / *Allen*	Chamb'rl'n M / *Dickens*	
27	Fox / *Cooper*	Bould / *Burley*	Maskery / *Gernon**	James / *Putney*	Dyson / *Osman*	O'Callaghan / *Butcher*	Maskery / *Wark*	McIlroy / *Brennan*	Maguire / *D'Avray*	Hudson / *Turner*	Ch'lr'n M* / *McCall*	/ *Dozzell*
28	Fox / *Avramovic*	Bould / *Roberts*	Hampton / *Pearce**	James* / *Gynn*	Dyson / *Peake*	O'Callaghan / *Allardyce*	Maskery / *Bennett*	McIlroy / *Hunt*	Maguire / *Thompson*	Hudson / *Gibson*	Chamb'rl'n M / *Grimes*	/ *Withey*
29	Fox / *Leonard*	Bould / *Benjamin*	Hampton / *Clarke*	James / *Richards*	Dyson / *Kilcline*	O'Callaghan* / *Hunt*	Parkin / *McP'rl'nd**	McIlroy / *McCulloch*	Maguire / *Christie*	Hudson / *Harkouk*	Chamb'rl'n M / *Chiedozie*	/ *Goodwin*
30	Fox / *Parks*	Bould / *Stevens*	Hemming / *Hughton*	James / *Roberts*	Dyson / *Miller*	O'Callaghan / *Perryman*	Maskery / *Ardiles*	McIlroy / *Brazil*	Maguire / *Falco*	Hudson* / *Hazard*	Chamb'rl'n M / *Dick**	/ *Brooke*
31	Fox / *Spink*	Bould / *Williams*	Hemming / *Gibson*	James / *Evans*	Dyson / *Ormsby*	O'Callaghan / *Mortimer*	Maskery* / *Birch*	McIlroy / *Walters*	Russell / *Withe*	Hudson* / *McMahon*	Painter / *Rideout*	Chamb'rl'n M / *Maguire*

Match reports

22 — Everton: The Heath brothers oppose each other and score! Adrian from a long Sheedy through-ball and Phil rolling the ball past Southall after being put clear by Dyson. A swirling snowstorm makes things difficult but City gain the upper hand and deserve a point. Lowest gate for nearly 15 years.

23 — QP Rangers: City fail to get to grips with Rangers' plastic pitch. Gregory, Charles and Stewart all beat Fox from over 20 yards. Stainrod scores an unmarked header. Dyson's header is ruled out for pushing. An embarrassing debacle. Last conceded six v Everton, 1969.

24 — Watford: Watford pour forward and only bad finishing delays the inevitable. Finally George Reilly finishes off Rostron's cross. He then flicks on for Mo Johnston to head in. Chamberlain produces City's only effort on target. Stoke fall deeper into the mire and something needs to be done quickly.

25 — Arsenal: Alan Hudson is the answer to the Boothen Enders' prayers. He is greeted like a long lost hero and inspires Stoke. Painter and Chamberlain both have goal-bound efforts blocked. City's pressure tells when McIlroy is tripped for the penalty. Bould quells the lively Nicholas and Woodcock.

26 — West Ham: City are easily beaten by John Lyall's Hammers. Barnes heads home unmarked. Cottee does likewise and is felled by O'Callaghan for the pen. James has Stoke's only effort of note. Dyson and Hudson clear off the line and Chamberlain is well policed by Paul Brush. Back to square one.

27 — Ipswich: Despite being on top, Town, lacking Paul Mariner sold to Arsenal, struggle to score. Irving Gernon breaks a leg. Hudson prompts City forward and eventually sub Painter provides a lifeline, latching onto Maguire's through-ball to fire past Paul Cooper for his first strike since September.

28 — Coventry: Stoke come from behind twice. Hampton's forceful shot is helped into the net by Avramovic's error. Chamberlain converts a far-post cross and O'Callaghan soars above a packed penalty area to head home the winner. Coventry are surprised by a team with so much fight. Excellent win.

29 — Notts Co: Mark Chamberlain hammers home Maguire's cross to grab the lead which City resolutely defend. Hudson probes in midfield where City's neat passing is a total contrast to the early season long-ball tactics. County have the better of the second half but fail to create any clear-cut chances.

30 — Tottenham: Spurs win an even game after O'Callaghan handles and Mark Falco sends Fox the wrong way from the spot. The lively Alan Dick causes City problems. James flashes a 30-yard drive just past the post. Hudson limps off injured and City run out of ideas as Spurs play possession football.

31 — Aston Villa: Loan signing Colin Russell makes his debut and Stoke sneak a win. He and Painter form a diminutive strikeforce which comes up trumps when Maguire's first touch as sub supplies Painter with a through pass to fire in off the far post. Withe, Walters and McMahon all go close for Villa.

Results and line-ups (matches 32–42)

#	H/A	Date	Opponent	Pos	Res	Score	HT	Att		Pts	Scorers (Stoke / Opponents)	Referee
32	H	17/3	BIRMINGHAM	19	W	2-1	1-0	13,506	15	35	Dyson 21, Bould 56 / Gayle 89	P Tyldsley
33	A	24/3	WEST BROM	19	L	0-3	0-2	13,681	17	35	— / Mackenzie 1, Hunt 38, Morley 52	N Midgley
34	H	31/3	SUNDERLAND	19	W	2-1	2-1	11,047	18	38	Painter 22, Dyson 28 / Atkins 24	R Guy
35	A	7/4	ARSENAL	19	L	1-3	0-0	21,211	7	38	Chamberlain 70 / Nicholas 55, Mariner 60, Woodcock 86	I Borrett
36	H	14/4	LIVERPOOL	19	W	2-0	1-0	24,372	7	41	Painter 21, Russell 50 / —	E Read
37	A	21/4	NORWICH	19	D	2-2	2-2	16,084	12	42	McIlroy 5, Chamberlain 70 / Rosario 54, Deehan 72	A Buksh
38	H	23/4	QP RANGERS	20	L	1-2	1-1	13,735	4	42	Russell 2 / Allen 30, Fereday 75	A Robinson
39	A	28/4	NOTT'M FOREST	20	D	0-0	0-0	13,625	5	43	— / —	R Lewis
40	H	5/5	SOUTHAMPTON	20	D	1-1	0-0	12,171	4	44	Maguire 80 / Holmes 70	D Scott
41	A	7/5	LUTON	20	W	1-0	1-0	9,867	13	47	Painter 5 / —	M James
42	H	12/5	WOLVES	18	W	4-0	2-0	13,377	22	50	Maguire 17, 41, 49p, 89p / —	C Thomas

Average: Home 13,868 — Away 15,367

Line-ups

#	Team	1	2	3	4	5	6	7	8	9	10	11	Sub
32	Stoke	Fox	Bould	Hampton	James	Dyson	O'Callaghan	Painter	McIlroy	Russell	Hudson	Chamb'rl'n M	
32	Birmingham	Coton	Roberts	Hagan	Blake	Wright	Broadhurst	Gayle	Kuhl*	Harford!	V d Hauwe	Hopkins	McCarrick
33	Stoke	Fox	Maskery	Hampton	Maguire	Dyson	O'Callaghan	Painter	McIlroy	Russell	Hudson	Chamb'rl'n M	
33	West Brom	Barron	Whitehead	Statham	Hunt	McNaught	Bennett*	Grealish	Thompson	Regis	Mackenzie	Morley	Ebanks
34	Stoke	Fox	Bould	Hampton	James	Dyson	O'Callaghan	Painter	McIlroy	Russell*	Hudson	Chamb'rl'n M	Maguire
34	Sunderland	Turner	Venison	Pickering	Atkins	Chisholm	Elliott	Bracewell	West	Chapman*	Proctor	James	Rowell
35	Stoke	Fox	Bould	Hampton	James	Dyson	O'Callaghan	Painter	McIlroy*	Russell	Hudson	Chamb'rl'n M	Maguire
35	Arsenal	Lukic	Hill	Sparrow	Talbot	O'Leary	Caton	Robson	Nicholas*	Mariner	Woodcock	Rix	Meade
36	Stoke	Fox	Bould	Hampton	James	Dyson	O'Callaghan	Painter	McIlroy	Russell	Hudson	Chamb'rl'n M	
36	Liverpool	Grobbelaar	Neal	Kennedy	Lawrenson	Whelan	Hansen	Dalglish*	Lee	Rush	Robinson	Souness	Johnston
37	Stoke	Fox	Bould	Hampton	James	Dyson	O'Callaghan	Painter	McIlroy	Russell	Hudson	Chamb'rl'n M	
37	Norwich	Woods	Devine	Downs	Mendham	Hareide*	Watson	Rosario	Channon	Deehan	Van Wyk	Donowa	Haylock
38	Stoke	Fox	Bould	Hampton	James	Dyson	O'Callaghan	Painter	McIlroy	Russell	Hudson	Chamb'rl'n M*	
38	QP Rangers	Hucker	Neill	Dawes	Fereday	Wicks	Fenwick	Micklewhite	Fillery	Allen	Stainrod	Gregory	
39	Stoke	Fox	Bould	Hampton	James	Dyson	O'Callaghan	Painter	McIlroy	Russell	Hudson	Chamb'rl'n M*	
39	Nott'm Forest	V Breukelen	Anderson	Swain	Fairclough	Hart	Bowyer	Wigley	Hodge	Davenport	Mills*	Walsh	Birtles
40	Stoke	Fox	Bould	Hampton	James	Dyson	O'Callaghan	Painter	McIlroy	Russell*	Hudson	Chamb'rl'n M	Maguire
40	Southampton	Shilton	Mills	Agboola	Golac*	Whitlock	Wright	Holmes	Moran	Baird	Armstrong	D Wallace	Puckett
41	Stoke	Fox	Bould	Hampton	James	Dyson	O'Callaghan	Painter	McIlroy	Russell*	Hudson	Chamb'rl'n M	Maskery
41	Luton	Sealey	Stephens	Thomas	Horton	Goodyear	Donaghy	Wright	Moran	Stein B	Walsh	Bum*	Antic, Nwajiobi
42	Stoke	Fox	Bould	Hampton	James	Dyson	Berry	Painter	McIlroy	Maguire	Hudson	Chamb'rl'n M	Maskery
42	Wolves	Burridge	Humphrey	Rudge	Bayly	Pender	Dodd	Crainie	Smith	McGarvey	Livingstone*	Dougherty	Buckland

Match reports

32 — Birmingham: Paul Dyson buries a great header from Painter's corner. Russell forces Coton to tip over at full stretch. Bould, returning to the pitch from being treated, steers Painter's cross in with a heavily strapped right foot. Mick Harford is dismissed for hitting Hudson. Hampton's slip lets in Gayle.

33 — West Brom: Steve Mackenzie heads home after just 75 seconds to leave Stoke's defensive policy in tatters. Hunt and Morley both bury shots from the edge of the area. Stoke are unable to find their recent form. Chamberlain's header is the only real chance. Fox saves superbly from Garry Thompson.

34 — Sunderland: In a frantic six-minute spell Painter's angled finish and Dyson's unstoppable header from a right-wing corner put Stoke in the driving seat. Ian Atkins heads home Chisholm's cross for Len Ashurst's Rokerites. Leighton James hits an upright and West hits the bar as Stoke ride their luck.

35 — Arsenal: O'Callaghan polices Mariner well and Chamberlain switches wings to good effect, then Arsenal come to life. Charlie Nicholas cracks in a great shot before Mariner turns home Woodcock's pass. Chamberlain nets from close range. Woodcock grabs a third with a return pass from Mariner.

36 — Liverpool: Painter knocks home the rebound after Grobbelaar only parries Chamberlain's shot. Russell flicks home McIlroy's driven free-kick. City tease Liverpool by playing keep ball and the Reds get frustrated. Dalglish is booked and Souness puts his hand through a window leaving the pitch.

37 — Norwich: Stoke cannot kill off a lively Norwich team. McIlroy sweeps home after Woods saves Painter's shot. Robert Rosario heads in to level. Painter's cross is tapped in by Chamberlain. Deehan replies with a sweet 15-yard half-volley. Woods touches over a Painter corner which almost flies in.

38 — QP Rangers: Stoke take an early lead through Russell's perseverance and cool finish. Then they stand off Terry Venables' QPR who put together some slick passing. A well-worked set-piece finds Allen free. Fereday zings a curling shot home. Rangers could have more. Hucker denies McIlroy twice.

39 — Nott'm Forest: In an even game City nearly snatch victory when James has his shot saved by Hans Van Breukelen. Forest have the better chances but wayward shooting means Fox is rarely extended. O'Callaghan keeps Davenport quiet and Chamberlain almost finds a way through with a 20-yard effort.

40 — Southampton: Bould has a close-range effort disallowed for a foul on Shilton. James and Chamberlain shoot just over. Stoke push forward leaving themselves open. Whitlock heads down for Holmes to finish. Stoke finally get a reward when Maguire turns in Painter's cross-shot. Bould heads just past.

41 — Luton: Ian Painter shoots first and asks questions later when he latches on to George Berry's flick on. Luton stop, looking for an offside decision. City grab a vital win with some stout defending. Maskery replaces Russell to add extra midfield bite and Stoke hold on without too many problems.

42 — Wolves: Maguire is the first Stoke player for 18 years to score four. No 1 is a far-post header. No 2; a spectacular bicycle-kick. Rumours circulate that Alan Dodd deliberately trips McIlroy to give Stoke a penalty so his beloved team would not be relegated! A fantastic second half of the season.

CANON DIVISION 1 (CUP-TIES)

Manager: Richie Barker ⇨ Bill Asprey   SEASON 1983-84

Milk Cup

2:1 H PETERBOROUGH 18 D 0-0 0-0   Att 11,085 4:5
Ref: R Banks

	1	2	3	4	5	6	7	8	9	10	11	12 sub used
Stoke	Fox	Berry	Hampton	James	Dyson	McAughtrie	Painter	McIlroy	O'Callaghan*	Thomas	Chamb'rl'n	M Maguire
Peterborough	Seaman	Chard	Imlach	Benjamin	Wile	Slack	Buchanan	Pike	Hankin	Linton*	Clarke	Firm

City are lucky not to lose against Posh whose player-manager John Wile deals with the high-ball tactics easily. Seaman touches over McIlroy's drive but with better finishing, Buchanan and Hankin could have made the visit to London Road even more difficult. City barely muster a shot.

2:2 A PETERBOROUGH 18 W 2-1 1-0   Att 9,898 4:10
Scorers: O'Callaghan 41, James 61 / Chard 62p
Ref: A Ward
(Stoke win 2-1 on aggregate)

	1	2	3	4	5	6	7	8	9	10	11	12 sub used
Stoke	Fox	Bould	Hampton	James	Dyson	McAughtrie	Tueart*	McIlroy	O'Callaghan	Thomas !	Chamb'rl'n	M Maskery
Peterborough	Seaman	Chard	Imlach	Benjamin	Wile	Slack	Buchanan*	Pike	Hankin !	Linton	Clarke	Ippolito

A dramatic game sees Ray Hankin sent off for persistent fouling after 47 mins. Thomas joins him (65 mins) for aiming a kick at Linton. James' 45-yard piledriver is an amazing shot. Dyson pushes Clarke for the penalty. City make life much more difficult for themselves than it has to be.

3 H HUDDERSFIELD 19 D 0-0 0-0   Att 14,175 2:5
Ref: D Hedges

	1	2	3	4	5	6	7	8	9	10	11	12 sub used
Stoke	Fox	Bould	Hampton	Dyson	O'Callaghan	McAughtrie	Maguire	McIlroy	James	Thomas	Chamb'rl'n M	
Huddersfield	Cox	Laws	Burke	Stanton	Sutton	Jones	Lillis	Stonehouse	Russell	Wilson	Cowling	

The Terriers' well-organised defence frustrates stale Stoke. Manager Mick Buxton is relieved to hear the whistle as City pen his team back but fail to eek out any chances in a crowded last third. Thomas and Chamberlain waste what little City create. Mark Lillis nearly snatches it late on.

3R A HUDDERSFIELD 18 W 2-0 1-0   Att 14,191 2:5
Scorers: Bould 8, Maguire 52
Ref: N Midgley

	1	2	3	4	5	6	7	8	9	10	11	12 sub used
Stoke	Fox	Bould	Hampton	James	Dyson	O'Callaghan	Maguire	Maskery	Dyson	Thomas	Chamb'rl'n M	
Huddersfield	Cox	Pugh	Burke	Stanton	Sutton*	Jones	Lillis	Doyle	Russell	Wilson	Cowling	Stonehouse

City stick to the 4-5-1 formation but break forward with more conviction after Bould's finish to the old Maguire/O'Callaghan near-post corner routine. Maguire then rockets home from 20 yards. Fox is rarely troubled. Thomas is unhappy at playing on the right, the wrong wing for him.

4 H SHEFFIELD WED 19 L 0-1 0-0   Att 18,653 2:1
Scorers: Bannister 51
Ref: K Baker

	1	2	3	4	5	6	7	8	9	10	11	12 sub used
Stoke	Fox	Bould	Hampton	James	Dyson	O'Callaghan	Maguire	Maskery	Dyson	Thomas	Ch'b'l'n M*	Griffiths
Sheffield Wed	Hodge	Sterland	Shirtliff	Smith	Lyons	Madden	Megson	Bannister	Varadi	Morris*	Heard	Pearson

A dull game has 0-0 written all over it until Gary Bannister profits from a mis-hit cross by Mel Sterland to fiercely ram home the decisive goal. The Boothen End want Barker out. He wants the ball played longer. Wednesday go through to face the mighty Liverpool in the quarter-finals.

FA Cup

3 H EVERTON 21 L 0-2 0-0   Att 16,462 16
Scorers: Gray 68, Irvine 85
Ref: M Peck

	1	2	3	4	5	6	7	8	9	10	11	12 sub used
Stoke	Fox	Bould	Hampton	James	Dyson	McAughtrie	Painter	McIlroy*	O'Callaghan	Maguire	Chamb'rl'n	M Maskery
Everton	Southall	Stevens	Bailey	Ratcliffe	Mountfield	Reid	Irvine	Heath	Sharp	Gray	Sheedy	

Neville Southall keeps Stoke at bay saving defiantly from McAughtrie, O'Callaghan and Hampton. Dyson's header hits the post. Everton score through Gray's header from Sheedy's cross and Irvine's left-footed cracker. How City could do with transfer target Bob Latchford of Swansea.

Pos	Team	P	Home					Away					Pts
			W	D	L	F	A	W	D	L	F	A	
1	Liverpool	42	14	5	2	50	12	8	9	4	23	20	80
2	Southampton	42	15	4	2	44	17	7	7	7	22	21	77
3	Nott'm Forest	42	14	4	3	47	17	8	4	9	29	28	74
4	Manchester U	42	14	3	4	43	18	6	11	4	28	23	74
5	QP Rangers	42	14	4	3	37	12	8	3	10	30	25	73
6	Arsenal	42	10	5	6	41	29	8	4	9	33	31	63
7	Everton	42	9	9	3	21	12	7	5	9	23	30	62
8	Tottenham	42	11	4	6	31	24	6	6	9	33	41	61
9	West Ham	42	10	4	7	39	24	7	5	9	21	31	60
10	Aston Villa	42	14	3	4	34	22	3	6	12	25	39	60
11	Watford	42	9	7	5	36	31	7	2	12	32	46	57
12	Ipswich	42	11	4	6	34	23	4	4	13	21	34	53
13	Sunderland	42	8	9	4	26	18	5	4	12	16	35	52
14	Norwich	42	9	8	4	34	20	3	7	11	14	29	51
15	Leicester	42	11	5	5	40	30	2	7	12	25	38	51
16	Luton	42	7	5	9	30	33	4	10	7	23	33	51
17	West Brom	42	10	4	7	30	25	4	5	12	18	37	51
18	STOKE	42	11	4	6	30	23	2	7	12	14	40	50
19	Coventry	42	8	5	8	33	33	5	6	10	24	44	50
20	Birmingham	42	7	7	7	19	18	5	5	11	20	32	48
21	Notts Co	42	6	7	8	31	36	4	4	13	19	36	41
22	Wolves	42	4	8	9	15	28	2	3	16	12	52	29
		924	226	118	118	745	505	118	118	226	505	745	1268

Odds & ends

Double wins: (0).

Double losses: (3) Manchester U, QP Rangers, Watford.

Won from behind: (2) Coventry (a), West Brom (h).

Lost from in front: (2) QP Rangers (h), Southampton (a).

High spots: Managing to stave off relegation after the club's worst start for 32 years.

Paul Maguire's four goals against Wolves to keep City in the top flight.

Barker's resignation in December, leaving Bill Asprey with enough time to turn the season around.

The return of the mercurial, if ageing, Alan Hudson.

Outplaying European Champions Liverpool at the Vic to win 2-0.

Low spots: Richie Barker's course in POMO at Lilleshall which convinced him to bypass the 'best midfield in the First Division'!

Only recording two league wins before Boxing day.

Lowest average attendance since 1961.

Player of the Year: Steve Bould.

Ever-presents: (1) Peter Fox.

Hat-tricks: (1) Paul Maguire.

Leading scorer: (10) Paul Maguire.

Appearances and Goals

Player	Appearances						Goals			
	Lge	Sub	LC	Sub	FAC	Sub	Lge	LC	FAC	Tot
Berry, George	8		1							
Bould, Steve	38		4	1			2	1		3
Chamberlain, Mark	39	1	5	1			7			7
Chamberlain, Neville	3									
Dyson, Paul	38		5				2			2
Fox, Peter	42		5							
Griffiths, Peter	3	1			1					
Hampton, Pete	31	1	5				1			1
Heath, Phil	3	1								
Hemming, Chris	3									
Hudson, Alan	16									
James, Robbie	40		5	1			6	1		7
Maguire, Paul	24	9	3		1		9	1		10
Maskery, Chris	16	3	2		1	1				
McAughtrie, Dave	17		5				1			1
McIlroy, Sammy	39		3				1			1
O'Callaghan, Brendan	37	1	5				1	1		2
Painter, Ian	30	4	1				8			8
Parkin, Steve	1									
Russell, Colin	11						2			2
Savage, Robbie	5	2								
Thomas, Mickey	16		5				3			3
Tueart, Dennis	2	1	1							
23 players used	462	26	55	3	11	1	44	4		48

CANON DIVISION 1

Manager: Bill Asprey

SEASON 1984-85

No	Date	Att	Pos	Pt	F-A	H-T	Scorers, Times, and Referees	1	2	3	4	5	6	7	8	9	10	11	12 sub used
1	A LUTON 25/8	8,626		L 0	0-2	0-1	Elliott 4, Bunn 65 — Ref: T Burns	Fox	Bould	Maskery	James	Dyson	O'Callaghan	Painter	McIlroy	Heath	Hudson	Parkin	
								Dibble	Thomas	Grimes	Breacker	North	Donaghy	Hill	Stein B	Elliott	Bunn	Moss	
2	H ASTON VILLA 27/8	12,605		L 0	1-3	1-2	Painter 44. Walters 15, 43, Withe 90 — Ref: K Walmsley	Fox	Bould	Maskery	Parkin	Dyson	O'Callaghan	Painter	McIlroy	Heath	Hudson	Hemming	
								Day	Williams	Gibson	Evans	Foster	McMahon	Bremner	Walters	Withe	Cowans	Mortimer	
3	H SHEFFIELD WED 1/9	13,032		W 3	2-1	2-0	McIlroy 35, Heath 44. Worthington 80 — Ref: K Barrett	Fox	Ebanks	Maskery	James	Dyson	O'Callaghan	Painter	McIlroy*	Heath	Chamberlain	Hemming	Parkin
								Hodge	Sterland	Shirtliff*	Smith	Madden	Worthington	Marwood	Blair	Varadi	Chapman	Shelton	Pearson
4	H LEICESTER 15/9	13,591	18 16	D 4	2-2	0-0	Hemming 65, Bould 69. Lineker 54, Lynex 75p — Ref: N Wilson	Fox	Ebanks	Maskery	James	Bould	O'Callaghan	Painter	Hudson	Heath*	Chamberlain	Hemming	Saunders
								Wallington	Wilson	Smith R	MacDonald	Hazell	O'Neill	Lynex	Lineker	Smith A	Ramsey	Peake	
5	A NORWICH 19/9	13,591	18 17	D 5	0-0	0-0	Ref: J Moules	Fox	Bould	Maskery	James	Dyson	O'Callaghan	Painter	Ebanks	Saunders	Hudson	Chamberlain	
								Woods	Haylock	Van Wyk	Mendham*	Watson	Bruce	Ordon	Farrington	Deehan	Devine	Donowa	Goss
6	A ARSENAL 22/9	26,758	18 2	L 5	0-4	0-2	Mariner 27, Sans'm 42, Wood' 82, 90p — Ref: E Read	Fox	Ebanks	Maskery	James*	Dyson	O'Callaghan	Painter	Ebanks	Heath	Hudson	Chamberlain	Saunders
								Jennings	Anderson	Sansom	Talbot	O'Leary	Caton	Robson	Rix	Mariner	Woodcock	Nicholas	
7	H SUNDERLAND 29/9	8,882	18 12	D 6	2-2	0-1	Dyson 75, Bould 87. Walker 28, Gayle 58 — Ref: F Roberts	Fox	Bould	Maskery	James	Dyson	Berry	Painter	Ebanks	Saunders	O'Callaghan	Chamberlain	
								Turner	Venison	Daniel	Bennett	Chisholm	Elliott	Berry	Gayle	Wylde	Proctor	Walker	
8	A NOTT'M FOREST 6/10	14,129	18 2	D 7	1-1	1-0	Berry 11. Davenport 87p — Ref: T Mills	Fox	Bould	Hemming	James	Dyson	Berry	Painter	Ebanks	Saunders	O'Callaghan	Chamberlain	
								Sutton	Gunn	Swain	Fairclough	Hart	Bowyer	Wigley	Metgod	Christie*	Davenport	Hodge	Walsh
9	H SOUTHAMPTON 13/10	9,643	21 12	L 7	1-3	1-2	Heath 41. Curtis 5, Dyson 16 (og), Williams 67 — Ref: J Worrall	Fox	Bould	Hemming	James	Dyson	Berry	Painter	Ebanks	Heath	O'Callaghan	Chamberlain	
								Shilton	Mills	Dennis	Williams	Wright	Bond	Holmes	Curtis	Jordan	Moran	Wallace	
10	H WEST HAM 20/10	9,945	21 7	L 7	2-4	0-1	Painter 81, Chamber'ln 90 [Allen 85]. Berry 34 (og), Cottee 56, Goddard 73 — Ref: K Cooper	Fox	Bould	Hemming	Ebanks	Dyson	Berry	Painter	McIlroy*	Heath	O'Callaghan	Chamberlain	Parkin
								McAlister	Stewart	Walford	Allen	Martin	Gale	Whitton	Goddard	Cottee	Bonds	Pike*	Orr

Match commentaries:

1. A controversial goal marks the start of things to come. Peter Fox stops expecting a foul to be given and Steve Elliott prods home. Luton swarm all over Stoke who feature five teenagers. Fox saves superbly from Hill and Stein but cannot keep out Bunn's rasping drive. Heath hits the bar

2. Mark Walters finds space in the area to turn and fire two shots past Fox. Ian Painter's reply from Maskery's cross keeps Stoke in it. The Potters put Tony Barton's men under pressure. Painter hits the bar and Heath drives just wide. Peter Withe scores again, forcing home from two yards.

3. Mark Chamberlain shows his England form providing McIlroy with an easy chance and crossing for Painter to head down for Heath to convert. Dyson walks (65 mins) for butting the provocative Chapman. Despite a midweek flu epidemic City hold out well until Worthington fires home.

4. Lineker hits the bar and then slots home Steve Lynex's centre. Carl Saunders appears on 65 mins and his first touch sets up Hemming's diving header. Bould nods in after Wallington fumbles but Maskery trips Lynex who picks himself up to score from the penalty. Two points dropped.

5. George Berry plays despite being transfer-listed after a loan spell at Doncaster. Chamberlain produces a great goal-line clearance to deny John Deehan. Wayne Ebanks links well with Hudson in midfield but Saunders is isolated on the left wing. City fail to create a single scoring chance.

6. Hudson's goal is ruled out for obstruction, then the big guns take over. Mariner beats Fox and fellow England man Kenny Sansom chips Fox expertly. Woodcock's neat finish and penalty, for Bould's trip on him, give the score-line a fair reflection of Terry Neill's team's dominance.

7. Clive Walker and Howard Gayle profit from defensive lapses. Walker torments Bould all game. An excellent fight-back against Len Ashurst's team sees Dyson power a header into the roof of the net. Chamberlain beats three men to cross for Bould to dive full length amongst the boots.

8. Berry turns the first away goal of the season past Chris Sutton. Stoke deny Forest's midfield space with a great tackling display. Then, in a mad scramble, Saunders handles and Peter Davenport cracks in the penalty for Clough's men. Cruel luck for Stoke who just cannot finish teams off!

9. Lawrie McMenemy's Saints dominate. Alan Curtis fires home and Paul Dyson nods past Fox in a mix-up. Shilton's howler allows Heath a tap-in. Shilton makes amends by saving O'Callaghan's strong header. Steve Williams curls a great free-kick past Fox to complete an easy victory.

10. Berry dives full length to head past his own keeper. Allen's excellent effort seals the win after Painter and Chamberlain grab close-range strikes against the run of play. John Lyall's men are sold to QPR for £100,000 and Asprey wants Norwich's Keith Bertschin.

Match records (Stoke City, matches 11–21):

11. A TOTTENHAM — 27/10 — Att: 23,477 — Pos 21 (3, 7) — L 0-2 (HT), 0-4 (FT)
Stoke: Fox, Bould, Hemming, Ebanks, Dyson, Berry!, Painter, Hudson, Heath, O'Callaghan, Chamberlain
Tottenham: Clemence, Stevens, Hughton, Roberts, Miller*, Perryman, Chiedozie, Falco, Allen, Hoddle, Galvin; Hazard
Scorers: Allen 5, 71, Chiedozie 10, Roberts 83p
Ref: L Burden
Glenn Hoddle celebrates his 27th birthday by running the show, providing Allen with the first for Keith Burkinshaw's in-form Spurs. Chiedozie picks up a loose pass to round Fox. Berry walks (40 mins) after a tussle with Falco who is then fouled by O'Callaghan for the spot-kick. Dismal.

12. H LIVERPOOL — 3/11 — Att: 20,567 — Pos 22 (12, 7) — L 0-0 (HT), 0-1 (FT)
Stoke: Corrigan, Bould, Maskery, Ebanks, Dyson, O'Callaghan, Painter, McIlroy, Hudson, Hudson, Chamberlain
Liverpool: Grobbelaar, Neal, Kennedy, Lawrenson, Whelan, Hansen, Dalglish, Lee, Rush, Johnston, Molby
Scorer: Whelan 86
Ref: P Tyldsley
Stoke give as good as they get in an improved display. Chamberlain causes all sorts of problems cutting in from the wing. Joe Corrigan makes his debut aged 36 and saves brilliantly to deny Ian Rush. Ronnie Whelan produces a superb angled 30-yard volley to finally defeat gallant City.

13. A WEST HAM — 10/11 — Att: 12,258 — Pos 22 (12, 7) — L 0-1 (HT), 0-2 (FT)
Stoke: Corrigan, Bould, Maskery, Saunders, Dyson, O'Callaghan, Painter, McIlroy, Hudson, Hudson, Chamberlain
West Ham: Godden, Nicholl, Statham, Hunt, Bennett, Robertson, Grealish*, Thompson, Mackenzie, Cross, Whitehead
Scorers: Hunt 23, Mackenzie 90
Ref: D Vickers
Jimmy Nicholl, a Bill Asprey target, chooses Albion instead and lines up for his debut against City. Hunt turns to fire home from 10 yards and then Steve Mackenzie flicks a cross in. Chamberlain and Painter both miss gilt-edged chances as Stoke put Johnny Giles's side under pressure.

14. A EVERTON — 17/11 — Att: 26,705 — Pos 22 (1, 7) — L 0-2 (HT), 0-4 (FT)
Stoke: Corrigan, Bould, Spearing, McIlroy, Dyson, Bould, Painter, Bertschin, Heath, Hudson*, Chamberlain; Parkin
Everton: Southall, Stevens, V d Hauwe, Ratcliffe, Mountfield, Reid, Steven, Heath, Sharp, Bracewell, Sheedy
Scorers: Heath 28, 35, Reid 70, Steven 75
Ref: M Scott
Stoke are easily beaten by Howard Kendall's Everton. Old boy Adrian Heath nips in to poach two close-range goals. Nev Southall saves when Chamberlain is through but Reid fires in Heath's pass and Trevor Steven converts a Stevens cross. City seem to give up once the third goes in.

15. H WATFORD — 24/11 — Att: 10,564 — Pos 22 (16, 7) — L 0-2 (HT), 1-3 (FT)
Stoke: Corrigan, Bould, Spearing, Maskery, Dyson, Bould, Painter, McIlroy*, Heath, Bertschin, Chamberlain; Berry*
Watford: Coton, Sinnott, Jackett, Taylor, Terry, McClelland, Sterling, Reilly*, Blissett, Rostron, Barnes; Gibbs
Scorers: Painter 58p, Reilly 37, Rostron 44, Blissett 52
Ref: D Richardson
Graham Taylor's Hornets lay siege and City fail to deal with their route one football. The goals are all scored from eight yards or less. Painter's penalty comes on a rare breakaway when Blissett hauls down Heath. Stoke are lucky to only concede three. The situation is desperate already.

16. A NEWCASTLE — 1/12 — Att: 21,135 — Pos 22 (12, 7) — L 0-1 (HT), 1-2 (FT)
Stoke: Corrigan, Bould, Spearing, Maskery, Dyson, Berry, Painter, McIlroy, Heath, Bertschin, Chamberlain
Newcastle: Carr, Brown, Saunders, Heard, Anderson, Roeder, Megson, Wharton, Waddle, Allon*, McCreery; McDonald
Scorers: McIlroy 55, Anderson 30p, Waddle 85
Ref: J Key
Stoke are competing well when John Key decides that Berry has fouled Wharton and gives a penalty. Anderson lashes in off the bar. City fight back. McIlroy diverts Heath's shot past Kevin Carr. Jack Charlton's Magpies win it when Chris Waddle's curling effort goes in off the upright.

17. A QPR — 4/12 — Att: 8,403 — Pos 22 (16, 7) — L 0-1 (HT), 0-2 (FT)
Stoke: Corrigan, Bould, Spearing!, Maskery, Dyson, Berry, Painter, Saunders, Heath, Bertschin, Chamberlain
QPR: Hucker, Neill, Dawes, Waddock, Wicks, Fenwick, Byrne*, James, Bannister, Stainrod, Gregory; Stewart
Scorers: Bannister 17, Gregory 76
Ref: D Axcell
Tony Spearing is booked twice for not retreating at a free-kick and is cheered off by the small crowd. Bannister strikes after the uneven bounce on the plastic deceives Stoke. Chamberlain misses two chances. Both sets of fans want their manager sacked. At least Rangers go home happy.

18. H IPSWICH — 8/12 — Att: 7,925 — Pos 22 (19, 7) — L 0-0 (HT), 0-2 (FT)
Stoke: Roberts, Bould, Spearing, Maskery, Dyson, Berry, Painter, McIlroy, Heath, Bertschin*, Chamberlain
Ipswich: Cooper, Burley, McCall, Zondervan, Osman, Butcher, Putney, Brennan, D'Avray, Sunderland*, Gates; Cole
Scorers: Putney 82, D'Avray 84
Ref: D Allison
17-year-old Stuart Roberts is plunged into the relegation battle, spending most of the game as a spectator. McIlroy's free-kick brings a brilliant save from Cooper. Heath also tests the keeper. Out of the blue Trevor Putney's 25-yard shot flies in and D'Avray deflects McCall's shot home.

19. A CHELSEA — 15/12 — Att: 2?,534 — Pos 22 (6, 8) — D 0-0 (HT), 1-1 (FT)
Stoke: Corrigan, Bould, Spearing, Maskery, Dyson, Berry, Painter, McIlroy*, Heath, O'Callaghan, Bertschin
Chelsea: Niedzwiecki, Wood, Rougvie, Pates, McLaughlin, Jones K, Nevin, Spackman, Dixon, Davies, Canoville*; Johnstone
Scorers: Dyson 71, Dixon 70
Ref: J Ashworth
City start with O'Callaghan in his old attacking role. Kerry Dixon gives Dyson a torrid time and finally finds room to head home after Corrigan parries Davies' header. Dyson heads an instant reply but City are penned back by John Neal's men. At least a point gives some encouragement.

20. A SHEFFIELD WED — 22/12 — Att: 9,799 — Pos 22 (7, 8) — L 1-1 (HT), 1-2 (FT)
Stoke: Corrigan, Bould, Saunders, Maskery, Dyson, Berry, Heath, McIlroy, O'Callaghan, Bertschin, Chamberlain
Sheffield Wed: Hodge, Oliver, Shirtliff, Madden, Lyons, Worthington, Marwood, Blair, Varadi, Chapman*, Shelton; Sterland
Scorers: Bould 45, Varadi 32, Chapman 60
Ref: A Saunders
Carl Saunders plays as emergency left-back. Wednesday lay siege. McIlroy clears off the line. Varadi and Marwood both go close. Varadi nods home but then Bould converts Chamberlain's cross. Finally Lee Chapman scores against his old club to clinch it for Howard Wilkinson's men.

21. H MANCHESTER U — 26/12 — Att: 2?,913 — Pos 22 (3, 11) — W 0-1 (HT), 2-1 (FT)
Stoke: Corrigan, Saunders, Spearing, Maskery, Dyson, O'Callaghan, Painter, McIlroy, Heath, Bertschin, Chamberlain
Manchester U: Bailey, Gidman, Albiston, Moses, McQueen, Duxbury, Robson, Strachan*, Hughes, Varadi, Stapleton, Muhren; Brazil
Scorers: Painter 70p, Saunders 75, Stapleton 23
Ref: K Baker
United think they can cruise it after Frank Stapleton drives home a rebound. Ron Atkinson's team get the fright of their lives when Stoke press on, forcing Albiston to handle on the line. Chamberlain's corner is flicked on for Saunders to crash into the roof of the net. A glimmer of hope?

CANON DIVISION 1

Manager: Bill Asprey

SEASON 1984-85

No	H/A	Date	Opponents	Att	Pos	Res	Pt	F-A	H-T	Scorers, Times, and Referees	1	2	3	4	5	6	7	8	9	10	11	12 sub used
22	H	29/12	QP RANGERS	10,811	15	L	11	0-2	0-2	James 20, Fillery 26 — Ref: H Taylor	Roberts	Saunders	Spearing	Maskery	O'Callaghan	Berry	Heath	McIlroy	Painter*	Bertschin	Chamberlain	Hudson
											Hucker	Chivers	Dawes	Waddock	McDonald	Fenwick	James	Fillery	Bannister	Byrne*	Gregory	Robinson
23	A	1/1	COVENTRY	9,829	19	L	11	0-4	0-3	Gibson 12, 53, Stephens 30, Hibbitt 33 — Ref: D Hedges	Roberts	Bould	Spearing	Maskery	O'Callaghan	Berry	Parkin	McIlroy	Heath	Bertschin	Chamberlain	Chamberlain
											Ogrizovic	Stephens	Pearce	Bowman	Kilcline	McGrath	Gynn	Hibbitt*	Latchford	Gibson	Adams	Bennett
24	A	12/1	LEICESTER	10,111	15	D	12	0-0	0-0	Ref: E Scales	Barron	Bould	Maskery	Hudson	Dyson	Berry	Parkin	McIlroy	Painter	Bertschin	Chamberlain	Chamberlain
											Andrews	Feeley	Wilson	Smith R	Williams	O'Neill	Lynex	Lineker	Smith A	Ramsey	Banks	
25	A	2/2	SUNDERLAND	14,762	18	L	12	0-1	0-0	Hodgson 77 — Ref: T Fitzharris	Siddall	Bould	Maskery	Hudson!	Dyson	Berry	Painter	McIlroy	O'Callaghan	Bertschin*	Dodd	Saunders
											Turner	Corner*	Pickerin	Bennett	Agboola	Elliott	Hodgson	Cooke	West	Berry	Cummins	Atkinson
26	A	23/2	LIVERPOOL	31,368	5	L	12	0-2	0-2	Nicol 14, Dalglish 28 — Ref: M Peck	Siddall	Beal	Maskery	Dodd	Dyson	Berry	Painter	McIlroy	Saunders*	Bertschin	Chamberlain	Heath
											Grobbelaar	Neal	Kennedy	Gillespie	Nicol	Hansen	Dalglish	Whelan	Rush	MacDonald	Wark	
27	H	2/3	TOTTENHAM	12,533	2	L	12	0-1	0-0	Crooks 46 — Ref: T Simpson	Siddall	Clemence	Maskery	Dodd*	Dyson	Berry	Painter	McIlroy	Saunders	Bertschin	Heath	Parkin
											Clemence	Stevens	Hughton	Roberts	Miller	Perryman	Owen	Chiedozie	Falco	Dick	Hoddle	Crooks
28	H	12/3	WEST BROM	6,885	15	D	13	0-0	0-0	Ref: N Glover	Siddall	Bould	Maskery	Dodd*	Dyson	Berry	Painter	McIlroy	Painter	Bertschin!	Chamberlain*	Parkin
											Godden	Nicholl!	Whitehead*	Hunt	Bennett!	Forsyth	Owen	Thompson	Mackenzie	Cross	Valentine	Greaish
29	A	16/3	SOUTHAMPTON	14,608	5	D	14	0-0	0-0	Ref: K Miller	Siddall	Bould	Maskery*	Dodd	Dyson	Berry	Painter	McIlroy	Painter	Bertschin	Parkin	Hemming
											Shilton	Mills	Dennis*	Curtis	Wright	Bond	Whitlock	Baker	Jordan	Armstrong	Wallace	Collins
30	H	23/3	NOTT'M FOREST	7,453	7	L	14	1-4	1-2	Parkin 10 [Davenport 78pl], Hodge 28, Hart 35, Riley 53 — Ref: G Courtney	Siddall	Bould	Hemming	Dodd*	Dyson	Berry	Parkin	McIlroy	Heath	Bertschin	Parkin	Callaghan
											Segers	McInally	Swain	Fairclough*	Hart	Bowyer	Wigley	Metgod	Riley	Davenport	Hodge	Mills
31	A	27/3	ASTON VILLA	10,874	10	L	14	0-2	0-0	Berry 71 (og), Six 85 — Ref: T Bune	Siddall	Williams	O'Callaghan	Dodd	Dyson	Berry	Painter	McIlroy	Heath	Hemming	Walters	Walker
											Spink	Williams	Dorigo	Evans*	Ormsby	McMahon	Six	Rideout	Withe	Gibson	Walters	Walker

22. Robbie James hits a fierce low drive past Rangers for his first Rangers goal against his old club. All the optimism disappears as QPR have City in turmoil at the back. Only Mike Fillery manages to score again, with Roberts performing heroics to keep out Waddock, Bannister and Byrne.

23. After Bill Asprey's sudden illness, coach Tony Lacey takes charge of demoralised City. They are thrashed by Coventry who are in trouble too. Terry Gibson's second goal is the best as he darts in to head home. Acting manager Don Mackay is not pleased with the way Coventry played!

24. In tricky conditions on-loan Paul Barron is the star, saving point-blank efforts from Alan Smith and Ramsey. Stoke's massed ranks of defenders block efforts by Banks and Ramsey. Barron saves brilliantly from Lineker. Somehow City cling on for a superb point at Jock Wallace's Foxes.

25. Alan Hudson gets himself sent off for protesting continually as the referee gives fouls against him. Backs against the wall time. Dave Hodgson glances in a running header that gives ex-Vale keeper Barry Siddall no hope. Bill Asprey, back from illness, re-signs Alan Dodd from Wolves.

26. City battle gamely but are outclassed by Joe Fagan's Reds. Nicol scores when Dalglish's shot rebounds off Siddall then Dalglish accepts a gift after McIlroy miskicks. Liverpool press forward but Stoke are resolute. Siddall saves from Nicol, Dalglish and Rush. Kennedy hits an upright.

27. Stoke are competing well until Barry Siddall's howler. He miskicks a straightforward clearance and Garth Crooks nips in to slot home. Keith Burkinshaw's team have the upper hand after that and Siddall tips Hoddle's drive on to the upright. Ray Clemence races out to deny Bertschin.

28. It's footbrawl! rather than football as Bertshin and Martyn Bennett trade blows on 28 mins and are sent off. Jimmy Nicholl follows on 65 mins for swearing at a linesman. The lowest post-war Victoria Ground crowd sees another blank score-sheet. At least this time Stoke don't concede.

29. City battle well on a pitch covered in early morning snow. Bould goes close with a 15-yard drive. Berry looks for a penalty when he is bundled over. Lawrie McMenemy's Saints don't score back but Berry leaps to clear Danny Wallace's effort off the line. A point gained rather than lost.

30. Finally a goal after 745 minutes without scoring! Parkin loops in a gentle shot after Segers and Painter tangle. It doesn't last long. Hodge is left free to rasp home and Segers saves Painter's 41st-minute penalty after Swain handles. Forest plunder three unanswered goals as City lose heart.

31. City outplay Villa but still manage to lose. Graham Turner admits his Villans could have been two down to Painter's efforts by half-time. But a youthful line-up flounder after Berry unluckily deflects Withe's shot past Siddall. Six finishes off Williams' free-kick to compound the misery.

Stoke City match-by-match results and line-ups (matches 32–42)

No.	Venue	Opponent	Date	Attendance			Res	HT	FT	Scorers	Referee
32	H	ARSENAL	30/3	7,371	22	8 17	W	0-0	2-0	Painter 55p, Dyson 62	Ref: P Willis
33	A	MANCHESTER U	6/4	42,940	22	2 17	L	0-2	0-5	Hughes 4, 65, Olsen 27, 80, [Whiteside 89]	Ref: K Redfern
34	H	LUTON	8/4	3,951	22	19 17	L	0-1	0-4	Harford 17, 47, Moss 65, Nwajiobi 70	Ref: I Hendrick
35	H	EVERTON	20/4	18,258	22	1 17	L	0-1	0-2	Sharp 23, Sheedy 46	Ref: H King
36	H	NORWICH	24/4	11,597	22	15 17	L	1-2	2-3	Bertschin 10, Saunders 90, Rosario 4, Gordon 33, Donowa 78	Ref: G Tyson
37	A	WATFORD	27/4	12,586	22	11 17	L	0-1	0-2	Blissett 33p, Jackett 52	Ref: L Burden
38	H	NEWCASTLE	4/5	7,088	22	12 17	L	0-1	0-1	Dyson 45 (og)	Ref: D Allison
39	A	IPSWICH	6/5	14,150	22	17 17	L	0-3	1-5	Bertschin 69, Wils'n 12, 26, 52, Putney 40, Gates 80	Ref: D Reeves
40	H	CHELSEA	11/5	8,905	22	6 17	L	0-1	0-1	Speedie 65	Ref: G Aplin
41	A	WEST HAM	14/5	13,362	22	17 17	L	1-5	0-3	Painter 63p, Bonds 15, 89, Pike 32, Stewart 36p, [Hilton 90]	Ref: J Martin
42	H	COVENTRY	17/5	3,330	22	20 17	L	0-1	0-0	Pearce 66p	Ref: N Midgley

Home Average 10,740 — Away 17,714

Line-ups and notes

32 – Arsenal: Siddall, Bould, Maskery, Dodd, Berry, Dyson, Painter, McIlroy, Heath, Hudson, Parkin / Lukic, Anderson, Sansom, Williams, Caton, O'Leary, Talbot, Rix, Mariner, Meade*, Nicholas, Woodcock.
At last a win, and against the most unlikely opposition. Ian Painter crashes home a penalty after O'Leary brings down Heath. Dyson dives in to head home McIlroy's cross. Hudson is influential in midfield as Stoke perform for once in front of the BBC cameras. A hard won three points.

33 – Manchester U: Siddall, Bould, Maskery, Dodd, Berry, Dyson, Painter, McIlroy, Heath, Hudson, Chamberlain* Bertschin / Bailey, Gidman, Albiston, Whiteside, McGrath, Hogg, Robson*, Strachan, Hughes, Stapleton, Olsen, Duxbury.
United overwhelm sad City who are nearly down and out. Hughes lashes home from 12 yards and powers home a header but is denied a superb hat-trick by the foot of the post. Olsen also bags a brace and sends Whiteside clear to ram home for Ron Atkinson's side. It's men against boys.

34 – Luton: Siddall, Bould, Maskery, Dodd, Berry, Dyson, Painter, McIlroy, Heath, Hudson, Chamberlain / Sealey, Breacker, Grimes, Nicholas, Turner, Donaghy, Hill*, Stein B, Harford, Nwajiobi, Preece, Moss.
Chairman Frank Edwards refuses to resign in the face of burgeoning debts and relegation but sacks Bill Asprey after a dismal display. Harford pounces when Dyson's back-pass fails to find Siddall. Nwajiobi finishes a solo run with a brilliant fourth. Awful.

35 – Everton: Siddall, Bould, Maskery, Berry, Dyson, Bertschin, Painter, McIlroy, Heath, Hudson, Heath / Southall, Stevens, V d Hauwe, Ratcliffe, Atkins, Reid, Steven, Sharp, Gray, Bracewell, Sheedy.
Classy Everton send City plummeting into Division Two. Sharp scores from a tight angle. Sheedy cracks home Berry's miscued header. Stoke create little. Everton lay siege and the crowd cheer when City make it over the halfway line! Tony Lacey is in charge after Asprey's dismissal.

36 – Norwich: Siddall, Bould, Maskery, Dodd, Berry, Dyson, Painter, McIlroy, Bertschin, Hudson*, Heath, Saunders / Woods, Haylock, Van Wyk, Rigby, Mendham, Downs, Donowa, Rosario, Deehan, Gordon, Clayton.
With their fate settled, Stoke relax. Attack-minded Norwich still need the points. Robert Rosario races through to score. Keith Bertschin scores his first goal on his 23rd appearance. Gordon and Donowa score from close range. Saunders grabs a consolation five minutes into injury-time.

37 – Watford: Siddall, Bould, Maskery, Dodd, Berry, Dyson, Painter*, McIlroy, Bertschin, Saunders, Heath / Coton, Gibbs, Rostron, Taylor, Sinnott, McClelland, Callaghan, Blissett, Johnston, Jackett, Barnes.
In a blustery wind both sides struggle to keep control of the ball. Bertschin fires a free-kick straight at Coton. Bould brings down Barnes for the penalty. Kenny Jackett nets a fierce drive. Sammy McIlroy shoots just wide. Graham Taylor's men comfortably deal with Stoke's blunt attack.

38 – Newcastle: Siddall, Bould, Maskery, Dodd, Berry, Dyson, Painter*, McIlroy, Bertschin, Saunders, Heath / Thomas, Anderson, Wharton, McCreery, Clarke, Roeder, Saunders, Reilly, Waddle, Beardsley, Heard — Chamberlain Heath.
Paul Dyson's sliced own-goal drains whatever confidence Stoke have. Reilly hits the post and Chris Waddle runs the show despite being booed by his own fans after announcing his summer transfer to Spurs. Chamberlain has Stoke's only effort saved by Thomas. Another insipid display.

39 – Ipswich: Siddall, Bould, Maskery, Dodd, Berry, Callaghan*, McIlroy, Bertschin, Saunders, Heath, Hemming / Cooper, Burley, Zondervan*, Cranson, Butcher, Putney, Brennan, D'Avray, Wilson, Gates, Dazzell.
The lowest low of the season. City give up as soon as Kevin Wilson scores the first of his unmarked hat-trick. Putney finishes a superb 40-yard run for the best goal of the game. Keith Bertschin becomes the first Stoke forward to score away from home this season netting a 20-yard drive.

40 – Chelsea: Fox, Williams, Hemming, Heath, Maskery, Heath, McIlroy, Saunders*, Painter, Saunders*, Callaghan / Niedzwiecki, Lee, Jones J, Pates, McLaughlin, Bumstead, Nevin, Spackman, Dixon, Speedie*, Thomas, Canoville.
Stoke have six teenagers in the team. Fox pulls off two superb saves to deny Dixon and Speedie, who also hits the post. He finally converts Pat Nevin's flighted free-kick. Eddie Niedzwiecki palms away Bertschin's downward header. Terry Williams makes his debut in a better showing.

41 – West Ham: Fox, Bould, Saunders, Maskery*, Dodd, Painter, McIlroy, Hemming, Williams, Heath, Callaghan / Parkes, Stewart, Brush, Gale, Martin, Pike, Orr*, Bonds, Barnes, Cottee, Goddard, Hilton.
Stoke are unlucky at Upton Park where John Martin waves aside a linesman's flag to allow Billy Bonds' opener to stand. He gives John Lyall's men a dubious penalty and they reciprocates for Stoke. West Ham are safe from the drop after a late flurry gives the score-line a lop-sided feel.

42 – Coventry: Fox, Bould, Hemming, Dyson, Heath, McIlroy, Painter, Saunders*, Beeston, Chamberlain / Ogrizovic, Butterworth, Pearce, Hibbitt*, Kilcline, Peake, Bennett, McGrath, Regis, Gibson, Adams, Gynn.
Stuart Pearce blasts home a penalty after Bould is adjudged to have handled Regis' header. Painter blasts his 83rd-minute spot-kick against the bar to leave the Sky Blues with slim hopes of survival. Stoke say goodbye to the First Division with an unenviable set of 'worst ever' records.

CANON DIVISION 1 (CUP-TIES) Manager: Bill Asprey SEASON 1984-85

Milk Cup

2:1 H ROTHERHAM 18 L 1-2 0-1 — Att 8,221 3:1 — 26/9

Saunders 65 / Birch 27, Simmons 88 / Ref: A Robinson

The Milk Cup turns sour as City produce a dismal display against George Kerr's merry Millers. Nippy Alan Birch lashes a low drive past Fox. Chamberlain shows glimpses of his old style. Painter sets up Carl Saunders for his first goal but Simmons' late lob is not undeserved. Dreadful.

	1	2	3	4	5	6	7	8	9	10	11	12 sub used
Stoke	Fox	Bould	Maskery	James	Dyson	O'Callaghan	Painter	Ebanks	Saunders	Hudson	Chamberlain	
Rotherham	Mimms	Forrest	Mitchell	Trusson	Johnson	Pickering	Birch	Gooding	Dungworth	Simmons	Kilmore	

2:2 A ROTHERHAM 18 D 1-1 1-0 — Att 6,898 3:5 — 9/10

Painter 22 / Bould 73 (og) / Ref: D Scott
(Stoke lose 2-3 on aggregate)

Stoke level the tie thanks to Painter's 12-yard finish. James hits a pile-driver which Mimms just reaches. Rotherham win a 60th-minute penalty but Fox saves Birch's kick and the gods seem to be smiling on City. They are just teasing though as Bould deflects Birch's cross-shot past Fox.

	1	2	3	4	5	6	7	8	9	10	11	12 sub used
Stoke	Fox	Parkin	Hemming	James	Dyson	Bould	Painter	Ebanks	Saunders*	O'Callaghan	Chamberlain	
Rotherham	Mimms	Forrest	Mitchell	Trusson	Johnson*	Pickering	Birch	Gooding	Dungworth	Simmons	Kilmore	Rhodes

FA Cup

3 A LUTON 22 D 1-1 0-0 — Att 7,270 21 — 5/1

Painter 78 / Foster 86 / Ref: D Reeves

Painter forces Sealey to save well before beating him in a one on one. Stoke nearly hang on but David Pleat's team equalise when Foster blasts Hill's centre high into the net. Afterwards City Manager Bill Asprey is diagnosed as having suffered complete mental and physical exhaustion.

	1	2	3	4	5	6	7	8	9	10	11	12 sub used
Stoke	Roberts	Bould	Maskery	Hudson	Dyson	O'Callaghan*	Parkin	McIlroy	Painter	Bertschin	Chamberlain	Saunders
Luton	Sealey	Breacker	Thomas	Turner	Foster	Donaghy	Hill	Stein	Harford	Daniel	Moss*	Nwajiobi

3R H LUTON 22 L 2-3 0-2 — Att 9,917 21 — 9/1

Painter 47p, Chamberlain 68 / Hill 9, Harford 12, Donaghy 63 / Ref: D Reeves

On a snow covered pitch City are knocked out by Ricky Hill's mastery of the conditions. He smashes home from 25 yards and sets up Harford. Foster fouls Parkin for the penalty then Chamberlain scores from 15 yards. Bertschin miscues when well placed. Luton will meet Huddersfield.

	1	2	3	4	5	6	7	8	9	10	11	12 sub used
Stoke	Roberts	Bould	Maskery	Hudson*	Dyson	O'Callaghan	Parkin	McIlroy	Painter	Bertschin	Chamberlain	Saunders
Luton	Sealey	Breacker	Thomas	Turner	Foster	Donaghy	Hill	Stein	Harford	Daniel	Parker	

Pos	Team	P	Home					Away					Pts
			W	D	L	F	A	W	D	L	F	A	
1	Everton	42	16	3	2	58	17	12	3	6	30	26	90
2	Liverpool	42	12	4	5	36	19	10	7	4	32	16	77
3	Tottenham	42	11	3	7	46	31	12	5	4	32	20	77
4	Manchester U	42	13	6	2	47	13	9	8	4	30	34	76
5	Southampton	42	13	4	4	29	18	6	7	8	27	29	68
6	Chelsea	42	13	3	5	38	20	5	9	7	25	28	66
7	Arsenal	42	14	5	2	37	14	5	4	12	24	35	66
8	Sheffield Wed	42	12	7	2	39	21	5	7	9	19	24	65
9	Nott'm Forest	42	13	4	4	35	18	6	3	12	21	30	64
10	Aston Villa	42	10	7	4	34	20	5	4	12	26	40	56
11	Watford	42	10	5	6	48	30	4	8	9	33	41	55
12	West Brom	42	11	4	6	36	23	5	3	13	22	39	55
13	Luton	42	12	5	4	40	22	3	4	14	17	39	54
14	Newcastle	42	11	4	6	33	26	2	9	10	22	44	52
15	Leicester	42	10	4	7	39	25	5	2	14	26	48	51
16	West Ham	42	7	8	6	27	23	6	4	11	24	45	51
17	Ipswich	42	8	7	6	27	20	5	4	12	19	37	50
18	Coventry	42	11	3	7	29	22	4	2	15	18	42	50
19	QP Rangers	42	11	6	4	41	30	2	5	14	12	42	50
20	Norwich	42	9	6	6	28	24	4	4	13	18	40	49
21	Sunderland	42	7	6	8	20	26	3	4	14	20	36	40
22	STOKE	42	3	3	15	18	41	0	5	16	6	50	17
£24		237	107	118	785	503		118	107	237	503	785	1279

Appearances / Goals

Player	Lge	Sub	LC	Sub	FAC	Sub	Lge	LC	FAC	Tot
Barron, Paul	1									
Beeston, Carl	1									
Berry, George	31	1					1			1
Bertschin, Keith	24	1	2		2		2			2
Bould, Steve	38		2		2		3			3
Callaghan, Aaron	2	3								
Chamberlain, Mark	27	1	2		2		1	1		2
Corrigan, Joe	9									
Dodd, Alan	16									
Dyson, Paul	37		2		2		3			3
Ebanks, Wayne	10		2		2					
Fox, Peter	14		2		2					
Heath, Phil	34	2		1			2			2
Hemming, Chris	14	2	1		1		1			1
Hudson, Alan	14	1	1		1					
James, Robbie	8		2		2					
Maskery, Chris	34	1	1		1					
McIlroy, Sammy	34		2		2		2			2
O'Callaghan, Brendan	20		2		2					
Painter, Ian	38		2		2		6	1	2	9
Parkin, Steve	8	5	1		1		1			1
Roberts, Stuart	3									
Saunders, Carl	17	6	2			2	2		1	3
Siddall, Barry	15									
Spearing, Tony	9									
Williams, Terry	2									
26 players used	460	22	22	1	22	2	24	2	3	29

Odds & ends

Double wins: (0).

Double losses: (11) Luton, Aston Villa, West Ham, Tottenham, Liverpool, Everton, Watford, Newcastle, QP Rangers, Ipswich, Coventry.

Won from behind: (1) Manchester U (h).

Lost from in front: (1) Nott'm Forest (h).

High spots: Beating Manchester U, Arsenal and Sheffield Wed.

Low spots: Lowest average attendances for 24 years.
Worst team ever in any division of the football league.
6 away goals scored.
Losing at home to Rotherham in the League Cup.
Record number of goals conceded/worst goal difference.
Losing last 10 games.
One goal in 10 games after Boxing Day.

Player of the Year: Sammy McIlroy.

Ever-presents: (0).

Hat-tricks: (0).

Leading scorer: (9) Ian Painter.

CANON DIVISION 2 — SEASON 1985-86

Manager: Mick Mills

Results

No	Venue	Opponent	Date	Att	Pos	Pt	Res	F-A	H-T	Scorers, Times, and Referee
1	H	SHEFFIELD UTD	17/8	11,679	–	0	L	1-3	1-1	Heath 44 / Cockerill 14, Morris 52p, 78 — Ref: N Wilson
2	A	BARNSLEY	24/8	6,598	19	1	D	0-0	0-0	Ref: M Peck
3	H	LEEDS	26/8	7,047	11	4	W	6-2	1-0	B'rry 15, Bert'n 55, 83, Ch'b'rl'n 72, 88, [Maskery 75] / Aspin 61, Snodin 70 — Ref: P Tyldesley
4	A	BRADFORD C (At Elland Road)	1/9	6,999	14	4	L	1-3	1-1	Painter 18 / Abbott 10p, 50p, Singleton 56 — Ref: G Tyson
5	H	GRIMSBY	4/9	7,362	14	5	D	1-1	0-1	Chamberlain 89 / Lund 2 — Ref: R Bridges
6	H	MILLWALL	7/9	7,187	14	6	D	0-0	0-0	Ref: J Key
7	A	MIDDLESBROUGH	10/9	4,255	12	7	D	1-1	0-0	Parkin 80 / Rowell 50 — Ref: T Mills
8	A	PORTSMOUTH	14/9	13,720	17	7	L	0-3	0-0	Morgan 53, Dillon 65p, Wood 77 — Ref: A Ward
9	A	CHARLTON	21/9	8,858	19	7	L	0-2	0-0	Stuart 78, Lee 83 — Ref: M James
10	H	CRYSTAL PALACE	28/9	7,130	19	8	D	0-0	0-0	Ref: J Worrall

Line-ups (Stoke City in bold positions 1–11, opponents in italics; 12 = sub used)

No	1	2	3	4	5	6	7	8	9	10	11	12
1	Siddall	Mills	Maskery	Hudson	Dyson	Berry	Chamberlain	Beeston*	Bertschin	Painter	Heath	Saunders
	Burridge	*Eckhardt*	*Kenworthy*	*Thompson*	*Stancliffe*	*McNaught*	*Morris*	*Cockerill*	*Withe*	*Lewington*	*Bolton*	
2	Siddall	Mills	Maskery	Hudson	Dyson	Berry	Chamberlain	Parkin	Bertschin	Painter	Heath	
	Baker	*Joyce*	*Goodison*	*Thomas*	*Burns*	*Futcher*	*Owen*	*Hirst*	*Walsh**	*Jeffels*	*Campbell*	*Plummer*
3	Siddall	Mills	Maskery	Hudson	Dyson	Berry	Chamberlain	Parkin	Bertschin	Painter	Heath	
	Day	*Irwin*	*Hamson*	*Snodin*	*Linighan*	*Aspin*	*McCluskey**	*Sheridan*	*Baird*	*Lorimer*	*Sellars*	*Wright*
4	Siddall	Bould*	Mills	Hudson	Dyson	Berry	Chamberlain	Maskery	Bertschin	Painter	Heath	Saunders
	Litchfield	*Abbott*	*Withe*	*McCall*	*Jackson*	*Evans*	*Hendrie*	*Thorpe*	*Campbell*	*Singleton*	*Graham*	
5	Siddall	Mills	Maskery	Hudson*	Dyson	Berry	Chamberlain	Parkin	Bertschin	Painter	Heath	Saunders
	Felgate	*Robinson*	*Crombie*	*Peake*	*Moore A*	*Moore K*	*Ford*	*Lund*	*Gilligan*	*Bonnyman*	*Hobson*	
6	Fox	Saunders	Mills	Hudson	Dyson	Berry	Chamberlain	Maskery	Bertschin	Painter*	Heath	Beeston
	Sansome	*Hinshelwood*	*Roffey*	*Briley*	*McLeary*	*Nutton*	*Lowndes*	*Wilson*	*Fashanu*	*Lovell*	*Kinsella*	
7	Fox	Parkin	Mills	Williams	Dyson	Berry	Chamberlain	Maskery	Bertschin	Saunders	Heath	Kernaghan
	Pears	*Laws*	*Heard*	*McAndrew*	*Mowbray*	*Beagie*	*Gill*	*O'Riordan*	*Stephens*	*Rowell*	*Currie*	
8	Fox	Parkin	Mills	Beeston	Dyson	Williams	Berry	Maskery	Bertschin	Saunders	Heath	
	Knight	*Tait*	*Swain*	*Dillon*	*Blake*	*Gilbert*	*O'Callaghan*	*Kennedy*	*Morgan*	*Channon**	*Hilaire*	*Wood*
9	Fox	Bould	Mills	Beeston	Dyson	Williams	Berry	Maskery	Bertschin	Saunders	Heath	
	Johns	*Humphrey*	*Reid*	*Loveridge*	*Thompson*	*Berry*	*Stuart*	*Shipley*	*Pearson*	*Aizlewood**	*Flanagan*	*Lee*
10	Fox	Bould	Mills	Hudson	Dyson	Berry	Adams	Maskery	Bertschin	Saunders	Heath	Parkin
	Wood	*Locke**	*Sparrow*	*Finnigan*	*Dray*	*Cannon*	*Irvine*	*Ketteridge*	*Barber*	*Gray*	*Stebbing*	

Match reports

1. City have a hangover from last season despite new player-manager Mick Mills' presence on the pitch. Hudson hits his clearance at Beeston and it falls for Glenn Cockerill to crack home. Heath buries one from 18 yards but Chamberlain trips Bolton and Morris gets his first from the spot.

2. Stoke earn their first league point since March in an entertaining game. Bertschin misses City's best chance as Baker makes a fine double save. Chamberlain is also denied. Hirst brings a fine save out of Siddall. Owen has a goal disallowed for offside. Chambo's free-kick whistles over.

3. Mark Chamberlain dazzles as City romp home. Bertschin and Berry convert his crosses to set City on their way but his second goal is the best, curled home from 15 yards. Chris Maskery loses two teeth in a challenge but still scores from Bertschin's cross. First six-goal haul since 1974.

4. City are seething after the referee awards two dubious penalties. The first seems way outside the area and the second follows Berry's attempted clearance which hits Hudson's arm. Painter deflects home Heath's shot but Stoke wilt when Martin Singleton bursts through to add a solo goal.

5. City are shocked as Tony Ford beats Mills and squares for Gary Lund to score. After that it's the Chamberlain show. He torments Mick Lyons' Mariners despite being double marked. He has two fine efforts saved before lashing the ball high past David Felgate. Steve Parkin hits the bar.

6. A physical battle. Briley flattens Saunders and is booked. Bertschin and Painter are injured. Chamberlain rises above the rough-house tactics to weave his magic down the right. Sansome is in brilliant form for George Graham's men. He denies Berry, Painter, Bertschin and Chamberlain.

7. Rowell nets from close in after O'Riordan's knockdown but City are generally well organised at the back under new skipper Berry. Carl Saunders is a live-wire all night. Mark Chamberlain bids farewell as he is sold to Sheffield Wednesday. He provides Parkin who fires a 25-yard equaliser.

8. City, down to the bare bones, keep Alan Ball's Pompey at bay until Nicky Morgan evades Dyson and Fox to finish clinically. Dyson then trips Morgan for the penalty and Paul Wood heads home Kenny Swain's cross. Steve Parkin's last-ditch tackle on Morgan stops any further damage.

9. On an emotional day Stoke lose out in the last match played at the Valley before Charlton decamp to Selhurst Park. A sit-down protest by fans dressed in black delays the second half but Charlton are unperturbed. Stuart heads home a rebound and Lee beats the offside trap to slam home.

10. Neil Adams finds space to run at Palace's mean defence but cannot produce the telling pass. Irvine has the clearest chance of the game but fires over with just Fox to beat. Heath stabs just over from close range and City run out of ideas. Alan Hudson makes his final appearance for Stoke.

#		Opponent	Date	Pos	Att			Res	Score	Scorers	Opp. scorers	Ref
11	A	HULL	5/10	17	6,890	12	11	W	2-0	Bertschin 10, Saunders 73		Ref: K Redfern
12	H	BRIGHTON	12/10	16	7,662	5	12	D	1-1	Maskery 64	Hutchings 24	Ref: T Simpson
13	A	FULHAM	19/10	18	4,007	14	12	L	0-1		Pike 38	Ref: H King
14	H	WIMBLEDON	25/10	18	6,708	5	13	D	0-0			Ref: K Cooper
15	H	HUDDERSFIELD	2/11	17	7,291	14	16	W	3-0	Heath 12, Shaw 43, Bertschin 66		Ref: K Barratt
16	A	CARLISLE	9/11	18	2,813	22	16	L	0-3		Halsall 32, Mayes 38, 69	Ref: K Walmsley
17	H	NORWICH	16/11	18	6,469	5	17	D	1-1	Bertschin 53p	Drinkell 70	Ref: G Ashby
18	A	OLDHAM	23/11	16	4,817	8	20	W	4-2	Bertschin 35, 60, Heath 44, Quinn 67p, 72 [Maskery 49]		Ref: G Aplin
19	H	SUNDERLAND	30/11	14	9,034	12	23	W	1-0	Bertschin 80		Ref: N Glover
20	H	MIDDLESBROUGH	7/12	11	7,646	21	26	W	3-2	Berry 25, Adams 33, Bertschin 55	Stephens 6, O'Riordan 56	Ref: C Trussell
21	A	SHEFFIELD UTD	14/12	10	2,370	5	29	W	2-1	Adams 7, Shaw 46	Edwards 15	Ref: C Seel

11 — HULL (A) 2-0

Stoke: Fox, Bould, Mills, Parkin, Dyson, Berry, Adams, Maskery, Bertschin, Saunders, Heath
Hull: Norman, Jobson, Pearson*, Doyle, Skipper, McEwan, Swann, Bunn, Whitehurst, Horton, Roberts, Flounders

Billy Whitehurst's height causes problems but Stoke are sharper on the deck. Bertschin slides in to finish off Maskery's effort. Fox saves from Swann and Saunders has two headers well stopped by Tony Norman. Saunders then hammers home after wrong-footing Norman. A win at last.

12 — BRIGHTON (H) 1-1

Stoke: Fox, Bould, Mills, Parkin, Dyson, Berry, Adams, Maskery, Bertschin, Saunders, Heath
Brighton: Digweed, Hutchings, Pearce, Wilson, O'Reilly, Young, Jacobs, Saunders, Ferguson, Biley*, Mortimer, Oliver

Chris Hutchings prods in the rebound when Fox tips Biley's shot onto the bar. City deservedly equalise through Maskery's 30-yard left-footed shot which sails past Perry Digweed. Saunders lobs over and Maskery fires wide. Chris Cattlin's Seagulls force a fourth successive home draw.

13 — FULHAM (A) 0-1

Stoke: Fox, Bould, Mills, Parkin, Dyson, Berry, Adams, Maskery, Bertschin, Saunders, Heath
Fulham: Peyton, Cottington, Carr, Scott, Hopkins, Parker, Marshall, Achampong, Coney, Pike, Barnett

Martin Pike has a goal disallowed before netting a legitimate effort from Dean Coney's pass. Fulham are in charge despite Neil Adams' work-rate on the wing. His crosses cause problems but Heath cannot convert. Fox saves Carr's 80th-minute spot-kick after Parkin handles on the line.

14 — WIMBLEDON (H) 0-0

Stoke: Fox, Bould, Mills*, Hemming*, Dyson, Berry, Adams, Maskery, Bertschin, Saunders, Heath, Williams
Wimbledon: Beasant, Gage, Winterburn, Galliers, Smith, Martin, Evans, Cork, Holloway, Sanchez, Thorn

Dave Bassett's Wimbledon present their usual long-ball barrage, but Berry dominates. Heath torments Gage but cannot provide the finish as 6ft 4in Dave Beasant deals comfortably with everything Stoke throw at him. Chris Hemming returns after his summer hole-in-the-heart surgery.

15 — HUDDERSFIELD (H) 3-0

Stoke: Fox, Bould, Mills*, Hemming, Dyson, Berry, Adams, Maskery, Bertschin, Shaw, Parkin
Huddersfield: Cox, Brown, Jones J, Doyle, Webster, Jones P, Curran, Cork, Tempest*, Raynor, Cowling, Stanton

City end the mini drought by comprehensively outplaying Huddersfield. Heath curls a right-foot shot in from 12 yards then Graham Shaw turns past two players before slotting a debut goal. A linesman needs attention after being flattened by Shaw and Brown slipping on the greasy pitch.

16 — CARLISLE (A) 0-3

Stoke: Fox, Bould, Hemming, Parkin, Dyson, Berry, Adams, Maskery, Bertschin, Saunders, Heath
Carlisle: Endersby, Gorman, McCartney, Ashurst, Saunders, Halsall, Mayes, Cooke, Baker, Bishop, Halpin

It looks as though the whole team have been up celebrating the birth of Peter Fox's new son as Carlisle trounce hapless City. Halsall beats Fox from 30 yards before Mayes applies the finish to two deep crosses for Bob Stokoe's men. City never get themselves together in the heavy rain.

17 — NORWICH (H) 1-1

Stoke: Fox, Bould, Williams, Parkin, Dyson, Berry, Adams, Maskery, Bertschin, Shaw, Heath
Norwich: Woods, Culverhouse, Van Wyk, Bruce, Phelan, Watson, Barham, Drinkell, Biggins, Mendham, Williams*, Gordon

Heath seems to be brought down just outside the area but Bertschin gladly rams the penalty home against his old team. Kevin Drinkell's header skids off the greasy pitch to beat Fox as Norwich fight back once Dale Gordon appears. Berry grazes the bar with a header from Heath's cross.

18 — OLDHAM (A) 4-2

Stoke: Fox, Bould, Mills, Devine, Dyson, Berry, Adams, Maskery*, Bertschin, Shaw, Heath
Oldham: Goram, Donachie, Ryan, McDonough, Hoolickin, McGuire*, Palmer, Henry, Quinn, Futcher, Atkinson, Fairclough

Debutant John Devine is the inspiration as Joe Royle's Oldham are taken apart. Bertschin fires left footed past Goram before Heath rounds off a 40-yard run with a cracking finish. Bertschin rounds it off by side-stepping Andy Goram. Micky Quinn's spot-kick is for Dyson's trip on him.

19 — SUNDERLAND (H) 1-0

Stoke: Fox, Bould, Mills, Devine, Dyson, Berry, Adams, Maskery*, Bertschin, Shaw, Heath
Sunderland: Bolder, Burley, Kennedy, Venison*, Bennett, Elliott, Gray, Pickering, Swindlehurst, Gates, Gayle, Walker

Chris Maskery, subject of interest from Man Utd, cracks a fibula in tackle with Gary Bennett. He is rushed to hospital but is out for the season. Lawrie McMenemy's men are beaten when Bertschin pounces, exchanging passes with Shaw to fire home. Devine again impresses in midfield.

20 — MIDDLESBROUGH (H) 3-2

Stoke: Fox, Bould, Mills, Devine, Dyson, Berry, Adams, Saunders, Bertschin, Shaw, Heath
Middlesbrough: Pears, Laws, McAndrew, Mowbray, O'Riordan, Pallister, Hamilton, Heard, Slaven, Stephens, Rowell*, Currie

In a superb match George Berry swoops to head home, levelling Stephens' solo opener. Neil Adams angles in a header for his first goal for the club and Bertschin stoops to head past Pears. O'Riordan's shot deflects past Fox. Heard hits a post. Bertschin has a goal disallowed for offside.

21 — SHEFFIELD UTD (A) 2-1

Stoke: Fox, Bould, Mills, Devine, Dyson, Berry, Adams, Saunders, Bertschin, Shaw*, Heath
Sheffield Utd: Burridge, Eckhardt*, Foley, Thompson, Stancliffe, McNaught, Morris, Edwards, Withe, Lewington, Arnott, Smith P

Fox saves point blank from Edwards who then slides in to equalise Neil Adams' far-post header. It takes Stoke just 18 seconds from the restart to win the game when Shaw chips over the advancing Burridge and follows up to head home. Four wins in a row for the first time in 12 years.

CANON DIVISION 2   Manager: Mick Mills   SEASON 1985-86

No	Date	Att	Pos	Pt	F-A	H-T	Scorers, Times, and Referees	1	2	3	4	5	6	7	8	9	10	11	12 sub used
22	H BARNSLEY 21/12	9,856	4	30	0-0	0-0	Ref: A Robinson. Stoke make all the running but Allan Clarke's Tykes keep them at bay. Devine has a lob held by Baker and then smashes a free-kick over. The Barnsley defence is well marshalled by Paul Futcher. Mills chases Norwich's Louie Donowa on-loan. Peter Coates is appointed vice-chairman.	Fox *Baker*	Bould *Joyce*	Hemming *Gray*	Devine *Goodison*	Dyson *May*	Berry *Futcher*	Adams *Owen*	Saunders *Thomas*	Bertschin *Walsh*	Shaw* *Hirst*	Heath *Plummer*	Williams
23	A SHREWSBURY 26/12	9,595	13	30	0-1	0-1	Dyson 45 (og). Ref: R Guy. 5,000 City fans see Ray Guy ruin the flow of the game as he stops play for petty offences. This suits the Shrews after Paul Dyson heads Daly's free-kick high past Fox in trying to clear. Shaw appears to be fouled in the box but no penalty. Shrewsbury don't extend Fox, but don't have to.	Fox *Perks*	Bould *Gunn*	Mills* *Hughes*	Devine *Cross*	Dyson *Pearson*	Berry *Griffin*	Adams *Leonard*	Saunders *Hackett*	Bertschin *Stevens*	Shaw *Robinson*	Heath *Daly*	Hemming
24	H BLACKBURN 1/1	11,875	10	31	2-2	2-1	Bertschin 33p, Adams 36; *Garner 20, Barker 48p.* Ref: K Baker. In a tale of disputed penalties Stoke have an obvious one turned down and then are surprised to get one for Gennoe and Bertschin's collision. It is Bertschin's 100th career goal. Adams dives to head in. A bobbling ball hits Berry's hand and another penalty is awarded. City are not happy.	Fox *Gennoe*	Bould *Branagan*	Hemming *Rathbone*	Devine *Barker*	Dyson *Fazackerley*	Berry *Mail*	Adams *Miller*	Saunders *Lowey*	Bertschin *Thompson*	Shaw *Garner*	Heath *Hamilton*	
25	A MILLWALL 11/1	4,611	19	34	3-2	2-1	Donowa 15, Painter 17, Bertschin 71; *Wilson 31, Lovell 65.* Ref: J Ball. A physical match flares up when Bould and Otulakowski clash. Bould is sent off (44 mins) – Mills has to go down to pitch side to calm furious players. Louie Donowa scores on his debut. City stay on the attack after going down to ten men. Bertschin nods in when Saunders hits the bar.	Fox *Sansome*	Bould ! *Roffey*	Hemming *Hinshelwood*	Devine *Briley*	Dyson *Walker*	Berry *Nutton*	Donowa *Lowndes*	Saunders *Wilson*	Bertschin *Fashanu*	Shaw *Lovell*	Painter *Otulakowski*	
26	H BRADFORD C 18/1	8,808	13	37	3-1	1-0	Shaw 41, Bertschin 48, 82; *Oliver 68.* Ref: R Groves. Shaw has a shot deflected past Peter Litchfield. Bertschin's brace see a brave diving header and a right-foot shot at the second time of asking. Gavin Oliver heads low past Fox for Trevor Cherry's Bantam's consolation goal. Hemming keeps Arthur Graham quiet.	Fox *Litchfield*	Hemming *Oliver*	Mills *Withe**	Devine *McCall*	Dyson *Jackson*	Berry *Evans*	Adams *Hendrie*	Saunders *Abbott*	Bertschin *Campbell*	Shaw *Singleton*	Donowa *Graham*	*Ellis*
27	A GRIMSBY 25/1	4,523	14	38	3-3	3-2	Shaw 10, Bertschin 22, Adams 44; *Emson 18, Bonnyman 26, Ford 67.* Ref: J Ashworth. Shaw takes advantage of Nigel Batch's miskick to slot the opener. Bertschin's brace in seven minutes is cancelled out by Mariners' player-manager Mick Lyons to crack home and Adams follows up his own header to score. Battling Town level through Tony Ford's first-time effort as the temperature drops below freezing.	Fox *Batch*	Hemming* *Robinson*	Mills *Cummings*	Devine *Peake*	Dyson *Lyons*	Berry *Crombie*	Adams *Ford*	Saunders *Lund*	Bertschin *Hobson*	Shaw *Bonnyman*	Donowa *Emson*	Painter
28	A LEEDS 1/2	10,425	14	38	0-4	0-1	*Stiles 33, Baird 52, Swan 59, 85.* Ref: K Breen. Billy Bremner's Leeds grow in stature once John Stiles' debut goal flies past Fox. Ian Baird unleashes an unstoppable shot from the edge of the area, then Peter Swan nets a pair of stooping headers. Stoke fail to move with any fluency and can't test Day. Mills is unhappy at lack of spirit.	Fox *Day*	Hemming* *Caswell*	Mills *Robinson*	Devine *Aspin*	Dyson *Snodin*	Berry *Rennie*	Adams *Ritchie*	Saunders *Swan*	Bertschin *Baird*	Shaw *Hamson*	Donowa *Stiles*	Painter
29	H FULHAM 18/2	6,449	21	41	1-0	1-0	Devine 9. Ref: J Bray. Stoke's injury list lengthens when Graham Shaw twists knee ligaments. John Devine gets his first goal for the club, firing home off a post with Shaw following in to make sure. City are in charge for the second half with Hemming and Bould using their height to good effect on the wings.	Fox *Peyton*	Bould *Cottington*	Hemming *Carr*	Devine *Gore*	Dyson *Hopkins*	Berry *Parker*	Adams *Marshall*	Saunders *Achampong*	Bertschin *Caney*	Shaw* *Donnellan*	Heath *Barnett**	Callaghan *Pike*
30	H CHARLTON 22/2	9,297	3	42	0-0	0-0	Ref: K Hackett. A tempestuous match as Bertschin is sent hurtling into the paddock wall by the force of Mark Reid's challenge. He retaliates and is cautioned. John Humphrey earns a booking for flattening Heath with a tackle from behind. Bertschin nets but is given offside. City rue missed opportunities by Saunders. No spark.	Fox *Johns*	Bould *Humphrey*	Hemming *Reid*	Devine *Curbishley*	Dyson *Thompson*	Berry *Pender*	Adams *Shipley*	Saunders *Lee*	Bertschin *Pearson*	Painter *Aizlewood*	Heath *Flanagan*	
31	H HULL 8/3	9,112	5	42	0-1	0-1	*McEwan 31.* Ref: K Barratt. Alan Curtis makes his debut on-loan from Southampton. Billy McEwan dives headlong to give Hull a hard-earned lead. Hull hound City out of their stride and only Adams, with a header against the bar, threatens in the second half. City rue missed opportunities by Saunders. No spark.	Fox *Norman*	Hemming *Swann*	Mills* *Pearson*	Devine *Doyle*	Dyson *Skipper*	Bould *McEwan*	Adams *Parker*	Saunders *Bunn*	Bertschin *Flounders*	Curtis *Askew*	Heath *Roberts*	Painter

#		Date	Opponent	Pos	Res	Score			Att
32	A	15/3	BRIGHTON	12	L	0-2	7	42	8,783
33	A	18/3	CRYSTAL PALACE	11	W	1-0	8	45	4,501
34	A	29/3	BLACKBURN	10	W	1-0	15	48	5,408
35	H	31/3	SHREWSBURY	10	D	2-2	17	49	8,988
36	A	5/4	HUDDERSFIELD	10	L	0-2	15	49	5,750
37	H	12/4	CARLISLE	11	D	0-0	21	50	7,159
38	A	19/4	NORWICH	13	D	1-1	1	51	17,757
39	H	22/4	PORTSMOUTH	11	W	2-0	3	54	3,529
40	H	26/4	OLDHAM	8	W	2-0	12	57	8,585
41	A	29/4	WIMBLEDON	9	L	0-1	3	57	4,959
42	A	3/5	SUNDERLAND	10	L	0-2	18	57	20,631
								Home	8,280
								Away	8,060
								Average	

32 — A BRIGHTON, 15/3, L 0-2
Wilson 38, Mortimer 88. Ref: D Reeves

City: Fox, Saunders, Devine*, Hemming, Bould, Berry, Adams, Painter!, Bertschin, Curtis, Heath, Callaghan
Brighton: Digweed, Jacobs, Wilson*, Hutchings, Young*, O'Reilly, Saunders, Penney, Biley, Connor, Mortimer, Gatting

City don't compete with physical Brighton. Once Wilson drives home through a crowd there is only one winner. Painter is sent off for claiming a penalty too vehemently (44 mins). Devine's broken leg in a tackle with Eric Young ends his career. Paul Dyson has been sold to West Brom.

33 — A CRYSTAL PALACE, 18/3, W 1-0
Bertschin 36. Ref: R Hamer

City: Fox, Hemming, Curtis, Hemming, Bould, Berry, Adams, Saunders, Bertschin, Painter, Heath, Heath
Crystal Palace: Hardwick, Hughton*, Brush, Taylor, Nebbeling, Cannon, Irvine, Ketteridge, Gray, Barber, Sparrow, Wright

Steve Bould keeps his place at the heart of City's defence as he prefers playing there to full-back. Bertschin darts in to loop a header over Steve Hardwick as Stoke commit daylight robbery. In a bruising game Hughton is taken to hospital with bruised ribs. For once it isn't a Stoke player.

34 — A BLACKBURN, 29/3, W 1-0
Saunders 76. Ref: R Guy

City: Fox, Callaghan, Mills, Hemming, Bould, Berry, Adams, Saunders, Bertschin, Bonnyman, Heath, Heath
Blackburn: O'Keefe, Branagan, Rathbone, Barker, Keeley, Mail, Miller, Hamilton, Quinn*, Patterson, Brotherston, Garner

Phil Bonnyman makes his debut on-loan from Grimsby. Blackburn can't find a way past Bould and Berry. A drab game sees Saunders notch a fabulous goal with a whiplash shot past O'Keefe. He then gets engaged to girlfriend Sherlyn. Mills is interested in Bury right-back Lee Dixon.

35 — H SHREWSBURY, 31/3, D 2-2
Bertschin 13p, 63 / McNally 17p, Callaghan 81 (og). Ref: V Callow

City: Fox, Callaghan, Bonnyman, Hemming, Bould, Berry, Adams, Bertschin, Bertschin, Shaw, Heath, Bates
Shrewsbury: Perks, Williams, Rees*, Johnson, Pearson, Griffin, McNally, Hackett, Stevens, Robinson, Hughes, Bates

City score another calamitous own-goal against the Shrews. This time Aaron Callaghan lobs a back-pass over Fox. It is the only way Town will get back into a game City control after the teams swap debatable penalties. Bertschin nets after a flick-on. City furiously try to win it but can't.

36 — A HUDDERSFIELD, 5/4, L 0-2
Shearer 66, 68. Ref: G Aplin

City: Fox, Callaghan, Bonnyman*, Hemming, Bould, Berry, Adams, Saunders, Bertschin, Bertschin, Heath, Beeston
Huddersfield: Cox, Brown, Doyle, Wilson Paul, Webster, Jones J, Curran, Raynor, Shearer, Wilson Phil, Cowling

Huddersfield exert pressure on City which finally pays off with two left-foot finishes by Duncan Shearer. England U-21 squad members Heath and Adams test Cox but Stoke never look like getting back level. A statue of Stan Matthews will be erected in Hanley to honour the great man.

37 — H CARLISLE, 12/4, D 0-0
Ref: T Mills

City: Fox, Mills, Bonnyman, Hemming, Bould, Berry, Adams, Saunders, Bertschin, Painter, Heath, Gorman
Carlisle: Endersby, Haigh, McCartney, Ashurst, Saunders, Halsall, Hill, Cooke, Baker, Bishop, Tolmie*

Both sides have chances. Heath hits the bar and Bertschin brings a fine save out of Endersby. Halsall and Baker test Fox. Carlisle are content to hold on as Stoke gain the initiative. Wes Saunders is rock solid. Bertschin scrapes the bar and the ball goes anywhere but in the back of the net.

38 — A NORWICH, 19/4, D 1-1
Bertschin 65 / Gordon 75. Ref: M Scott

City: Fox, Mills*, Bonnyman, Hemming, Bould, Berry, Adams, Saunders, Bertschin, Painter, Heath, Brooke
Norwich: Woods, Culverhouse, Van Wyk, Bruce, Phelan, Watson, Gordon, Drinkell, Biggins*, Deehan, Williams

Nearly promoted Norwich start at a furious pace. City cling on and Keith Bertschin heads home against his old side to give them a cheeky lead. Berry heads over but finally Ken Brown's Canaries' pressure tells when Dale Gordon fires in from Dave Watson's flick on. A very good point.

39 — H PORTSMOUTH, 22/4, W 2-0
Berry 17, Heath 45. Ref: J Worrall

City: Fox, Mills, Bonnyman*, Hemming, Bould, Berry, Painter, Quinn, Bertschin, Shaw, Shaw, McGarvey
Portsmouth: Knight, Swain, Hardyman, Dillon, Blake, Gilbert, O'Callaghan, Kennedy, Quinn, Channon*, Hilaire

Stoke outplay Pompey who look scared they may miss promotion after having a great start. Alan Ball screeches encouragement to his men but they are never in it. Berry takes time off from his duel with Mick Quinn to head home Painter's corner and Heath sweeps home Painter's cross.

40 — H OLDHAM, 26/4, W 2-0
Shaw 40, Bertschin 47. Ref: C Downey

City: Fox, Saunders, Kelly, Hemming, Bould, Berry, Painter*, McGuire, Bertschin, Shaw, Heath, Adams
Oldham: Goram, Bullock, Barlow, Jones, Linighan, Gorton, Palmer, Colville*, Futcher, Henry, Smith

City pay Wigan £80,000 for Tony Kelly who is involved in all of the best moves. He passes to Hemming who crosses for Shaw to beat Goram. Shaw provides Keith Bertschin with his 23rd of the season. Stoke test Goram from all sorts of angles. Shaw beats him but hits Jones on the line.

41 — A WIMBLEDON, 29/4, L 0-1
Cork 48. Ref: B Stevens

City: Fox, Callaghan, Mills, Hemming, Bould, Berry, Adams, Cork, Bertschin, Shaw, Heath, Painter
Wimbledon: Beasant, Gage, Winterburn, Galliers, Morris, Thorn, Hodges*, Fashanu, Sanchez, Fairweather, Downes

Dave Beasant booms long clearances as Wimbledon search frantically for the elusive goal. Shaw misses from three yards out. City provide all the finesse but the promotion-chasing Dons snatch a vital three points thanks to Alan Cork's near-post header.

42 — A SUNDERLAND, 3/5, L 0-2
Proctor 2p, Gray 68. Ref: D Hutchinson

City: Fox, Callaghan*, Mills, Hemming, Bould, Berry, Adams, Gayle*, Bertschin, Shaw, Heath, Painter
Sunderland: Dibble, Venison, Kennedy, Gray, Bennett, Elliott, Ford, Wallace, Proctor, Gates, Hodgson

Mills fouls Gates for the dubious looking spot-kick. Tempers become frayed after Gayle and Saunders come to blows. Shaw curls a free-kick wide. Sunderland's tension is eased when Gray scores from 12 yards. Mills loses to mentor McMenemy's Rokerites who just escape the drop.

CANON DIVISION 2 (CUP-TIES)　　Manager: Mick Mills　　SEASON 1985-86

Milk Cup

		Att	F-A	H-T	Scorers, Times, and Referees	1	2	3	4	5	6	7	8	9	10	11	12 sub used
2:1	A WREXHAM 19 W	5,241 4:10	1-0	0-0	Bertschin 49 Ref: I Hendrick	Fox *Hooper*	Bould *Williams*	Mills *Comstive*	Parkin *Jones*	Dyson *Keay*	Berry *Cunnington*	Adams *Muldoon*	Williams *Horne*	Bertschin *Hencher*	Saunders *Charles*	Heath *Gregory*	*Williams*
2:2	H WREXHAM 17 W	6,784 4:11	1-0	0-0	Bertschin 80 Ref: A Banks (Stoke win 2-0 on aggregate)	Fox *Hooper*	Bould *Salathiel*	Mills *Comstive*	Parkin *Williams*	Dyson *Keay*	Berry *Cunnington*	Adams *Hencher*	Maskery *Horne*	Bertschin *Edwards*	Saunders* *Charles*	Heath *Gregory*	*Williams*
3	A PORTSMOUTH 18 L	13,319 2:1	0-2	0-0	Dillon 46p, 63p Ref: A Buksh	Fox *Knight*	Bould *Stanley*	Mills* *Sandford*	Hemming *Dillon*	Dyson *Blake*	Berry *Gilbert*	Adams *O'Callaghan*	Maskery *Tait*	Bertschin *Morgan*	Parkin *Channon* *	Heath *Hilaire*	Saunders *McGarvey*

FA Cup

		Att	F-A	H-T	Scorers, Times, and Referees	1	2	3	4	5	6	7	8	9	10	11	12 sub used
3	H NOTTS CO 11 L	12,219 3:5	0-2	0-1	Waitt 41, McParland 65 Ref: G Napthine	Fox *Leonard*	Mills* *Yates*	Hemming *Clarke*	Devine *Benjamin*	Dyson *Sims*	Berry *Davis*	Adams *McParland*	Bertschin *Goodwin*	Saunders *Waitt*	Painter *Edge* *	Shaw *Hunt*	Donowa *Robinson*

Saunders is sent clear by Parkin but Hooper makes a fabulous double save. Keith Bertschin is rewarded for a great performance with a stooping header from Heath's deep cross. A large travelling support cheer Stoke's first away win in 28 attempts as Dixie McNeil's men are well beaten.

The floodlights fuse and City switch off. A dull game is enlivened only by Carl Saunders' reverse pass which wrong-foots the entire Wrexham defence to leave Bertschin clear to race through and score. Wrexham harry Stoke with Horne and Salathiel closing down doggedly in midfield.

Vince Hilaire tumbles over twice in the area to earn Pompey's penalties which Kevin Dillon dispatches past Fox with aplomb. Stoke put up a gutsy show. Heath rolls just wide of the post when through. Alan Knight produces two great saves from Parkin. Seven City players are booked.

Stoke play all the football with Fox virtually unemployed but Jimmy Sirrel's County ride their luck to win. Mick Leonard is only booked when he flattens Painter who is racing clear. Berry's clearance hits McParland's arm and rebounds for Waitt to score. McParland scores on the break.

League Table

	Team	P	Home					Away					Pts
			W	D	L	F	A	W	D	L	F	A	
1	Norwich	42	16	4	1	51	15	9	5	7	33	22	84
2	Charlton	42	14	5	2	44	15	8	6	7	34	30	77
3	Wimbledon	42	13	6	2	38	16	8	7	6	20	21	76
4	Portsmouth	42	13	4	4	43	17	9	3	9	26	24	73
5	Crys Palace	42	12	3	6	29	22	7	6	8	28	30	66
6	Hull	42	11	7	3	39	19	6	6	9	26	36	64
7	Sheffield Utd	42	10	7	4	36	24	7	4	10	28	39	62
8	Oldham	42	13	4	4	40	28	4	5	12	22	33	60
9	Millwall	42	12	3	6	39	24	5	5	11	25	41	59
10	STOKE	42	8	11	2	29	16	6	4	11	19	34	57
11	Brighton	42	10	5	6	42	30	3	8	12	22	34	56
12	Barnsley	42	9	6	6	29	26	5	8	8	18	24	56
13	Bradford C	42	14	1	6	36	22	2	5	14	15	39	54
14	Leeds	42	9	7	5	30	22	6	1	14	26	50	53
15	Grimsby	42	11	4	6	35	24	3	6	12	23	38	52
16	Huddersfield	42	10	6	5	30	23	4	4	13	21	44	52
17	Shrewsbury	42	11	5	5	29	20	3	4	14	23	44	51
18	Sunderland	42	10	6	5	33	20	6	2	12	14	32	50
19	Blackburn	42	10	4	7	30	20	2	9	10	23	42	49
20	Carlisle	42	10	2	9	30	28	3	5	13	17	43	46
21	Middlesbro	42	8	6	7	26	23	4	3	14	18	30	45
22	Fulham	42	8	3	10	29	32	2	3	16	16	37	36
		924	242	108	112	767	497	112	108	242	497	767	1278

Odds & ends

Double wins: (1) Oldham.
Double losses: (0).
Won from behind: (1) Middlesbrough (h).
Lost from in front: (0).
High spots: Good recovery from last season's debacle.
Keith Bertschin nets the highest goals total for a season for 21 years.
Thrashing Leeds 6-2.
Winning 4-2 at Boundary Park.
A solid start for Mick Mills as manager.
Low spots: Slow start to the season.
Failing to press for the play-offs after a mid-season spurt of good form.
Another disappointing FA Cup exit.
Lowest average home attendance since 1907-08.
Player of the Year: Keith Bertschin.
Ever-presents: (1) Keith Bertschin.
Hat-tricks: (0).
Leading scorer: (21) Keith Bertschin.

Appearances and Goals

Player	Appearances						Goals			
	Lge	Sub	LC	Sub	FAC	Sub	Lge	LC	FAC	Tot
Adams, Neil	31	1	3		1		4			4
Beeston, Carl	2	3								
Berry, George	41		3		1		3			3
Bertschin, Keith	42		3		1		19		2	21
Bonnyman, Phil	7									
Bould, Steve	33		3							
Callaghan, Aaron	6	2								
Chamberlain, Mark	7						3			3
Curtis, Alan	3									
Devine, John	15				1		1			1
Donowa, Louie	4					1	1			1
Dyson, Paul	31		3		1					
Fox, Peter	37		3		1					
Heath, Phil	38		3				4			4
Hemming, Chris	23	1	1		1					
Hudson, Alan	6									
Kelly, Tony	1									
Maskery, Chris	19		2				3			3
Mills, Mick	31		3		1					
Painter, Ian	15	4			1		2			2
Parkin, Steve	10	2	3				1			1
Saunders, Carl	33	4	2	1	1		2			2
Shaw, Graham	19	1			1		5			5
Siddall, Barry	5									
Williams, Terry	3	3	1		1					
25 players used	462	21	33	2	11	1	48		2	50

TODAY DIVISION 2 — Manager: Mick Mills — SEASON 1986-87

Match results

No		Opponent	Date	Att	Pos	Pt	F-A	H-T	Scorers, Times, and Referees
1	H	BIRMINGHAM	23/8	11,548		0	L 0-2	0-1	Hemming 43 (og), Whitton 69; Ref: R Groves
2	A	LEEDS	25/8	13,334		0	L 1-2	1-1	Saunders 1; Sheridan 36, Baird 72; Ref: K Redfern
3	A	CRYSTAL PALACE	30/8	6,864	22	0	L 0-1	0-0	Barber 55; Ref: M James
4	H	WEST BROM	2/9	8,668	22	1	D 1-1	1-0	Berry 29; Palmer 62; Ref: M Dimblebee
5	H	MILLWALL	6/9	7,076	16	4	W 2-0	2-0	Berry 34, Shaw 37p; Ref: T Fitzharris
6	A	OLDHAM	13/9	6,513	19	4	L 0-2	0-0	Henry 74, Futcher 75; Ref: D Allison
7	H	PORTSMOUTH	20/9	8,440	20	5	D 1-1	0-1	Kelly 58; Kennedy 31; Ref: K Baker
8	A	SUNDERLAND	27/9	14,394	21	5	L 0-2	0-2	Swindlehurst 18, Armstrong 33p; Ref: C Seel
9	A	BRIGHTON	4/10	8,341	22	5	L 0-1	0-1	Wilson 31p; Ref: J Martin
10	H	HUDDERSFIELD	11/10	7,543	22	8	W 2-0	2-0	Berry 24, Bertschin 29; Ref: D Scott

Line-ups (Stoke players in first row of each pair, opponents in italics)

No	Team	1	2	3	4	5	6	7	8	9	10	11	12 sub used
1	Stoke	Fox	Dixon	Hemming	Kelly	Bould	Berry	Ford*	Maskery	Bertschin	Shaw	Heath	Saunders
1	*Birmingham*	*Hansbury*	*Jones*	*Dicks*	*Hagan*	*Overson*	*Kuhl*	*Bremner*	*Rees*	*Whitton*	*Mortimer*	*Hopkins*	
2	Stoke	Fox	Dixon	Mills*	Kelly	Bould	Berry!	Ford	Maskery	Bertschin	Saunders	Heath	Shaw
2	*Leeds*	*Sinclair*	*Aspin*	*Thompson*	*Snodin*	*Ashurst*	*Rennie*	*Stiles*	*Sheridan*	*Baird*	*Edwards*	*Ritchie*	
3	Stoke	Fox	Dixon	Hemming	Saunders	Bould	Berry	Ford	Maskery	Bertschin	Shaw	Heath*	Kelly
3	*Crystal Palace*	*Wood*	*Finnigan*	*Brush*	*Taylor*	*Droy*	*Cannon*	*Irvine*	*Ketteridge*	*Barber*	*Wright*	*Otulakowski*	
4	Stoke	Fox	Naylor	Hemming	Mills*	Bould	Berry	Ford	Maskery	Saunders	Shaw	Heath	Parkin
4	*West Brom*		*Whitehead*	*Burrows*	*Bennett*	*Dyson*	*Dickinson*	*Palmer*	*Evans*	*MacKenzie*	*Williamson*	*Thompson*	
5	Stoke	Fox	Dixon	Hemming	Parkin	Bould	Berry	Ford	Maskery	Saunders	Shaw	Heath	
5	*Millwall*	*Horne*	*Stevens*	*Coleman N*	*Briley*	*Walker*	*Salman*	*Byrne*	*McLeary*	*Sheringham*	*Marks*	*Mehmet*	
6	Stoke	Fox	Dixon	Hemming	Parkin	Bould	Callaghan	Saunders*	Maskery	Bertschin	Shaw	Heath	Williams
6	*Oldham*	*Goram*	*Irwin*	*Donachie*	*Jones*	*Linighan*	*Barlow*	*Palmer*	*Henry*	*Ellis**	*Futcher*	*Milligan*	*McGuire*
7	Stoke	Fox	Dixon	Hemming	Kelly	Bould	Berry	Ford	Parkin	Bertschin	Shaw	Heath	Williams
7	*Portsmouth*	*Knight*	*Swain*	*Hardyman !*	*Dillon*	*Blake*	*Gilbert*	*Tait*	*Kennedy*	*Mariner*	*Quinn**	*Hilaire*	*O'Callaghan*
8	Stoke	Fox	Dixon	Hemming	Kelly	Bould	Berry	Ford	Maskery	Bertschin	Parkin	Heath	Williams
8	*Sunderland*	*Hesford*	*Burley*	*Kennedy*	*Armstrong*	*Corner*	*Bennett*	*Lemon*	*Doyle*	*Swindlehurst*	*Gray*	*Buchanan*	
9	Stoke	Fox	Dixon	Hemming	Kelly	Bould	Callaghan*	Ford	Parkin	Bertschin	Williams	Heath	Crooks
9	*Brighton*	*Digweed*	*Berry*	*Hutchings*	*Wilson*	*Gatting*	*O'Regan*	*Penney*	*Saunders*	*Armstrong*	*Hughes*	*Jasper*	
10	Stoke	Fox	Dixon	Parkin	Talbot	Bould	Berry	Ford	Kelly	Shaw	Bertschin	Heath*	Maskery
10	*Huddersfield*	*Cox*	*Trevitt*	*Wilson Paul*	*Banks*	*Webster*	*Jones*	*Raynor**	*Winter*	*Shearer*	*Wilson Phil*	*Cowling*	*Cork*

Match reports

1. Stoke parade new signings Tony Ford and Lee Dixon. A tetchy affair erupts when Hagan seems to foul Shaw but no penalty is given. Five are booked as City lose their young heads. Chris Hemming slices Dicks' cross into his own goal and a mix-up in defence gifts Whitton the second.

2. City score from their first corner. Saunders nets after Maskery's shot hits a post. John Sheridan then takes over and curls in a fine equaliser. He crosses for Edwards to head against the bar. Bould slips in the rain leaving Ian Baird clean through. Berry is sent off (87 mins) for two bookings.

3. Palace put City under intense pressure and from their 12th corner Phil Barber wallops home from close range. Wright's over-head kick is tipped onto the bar by Fox. Alan Irvine torments Hemming. Micky Droy overshadows Shaw. 'We should have lost by five' says Mills, disconsolately.

4. Ford impresses on the right as Stoke produce some stylish football for the first time this season. George Berry characteristically heads home his corner. Fox tips Stuart Evans' header on to the bar. Gangling Carlton Palmer fires home to grab Ron Saunders' Baggies a draw. A point at last.

5. Saunders moves into a striker's role and looks good as John Docherty's Millwall are totally outplayed. Berry sweeps in his cross. Shaw scores one penalty for a foul on Bould but misses another (46 mins) for a trip on Saunders. Berry vows to wear his new red trousers until Stoke lose.

6. City are caught offside continually as they struggle to cope with the 250 tons of sand which have been spread on Boundary Park's plastic pitch. Shaw misses from an acute angle after rounding Goram. Henry and Futcher score for Joe Royle's Oldham who have yet to concede this season.

7. Tony Kelly returns after losing a stone in an intensive training programme to score a picture-book free-kick. Knight saves Bertschin's 44th-min penalty. Peter Fox breaks the City goalkeepers appearance record in his 239th game. Paul Hardyman is sent off as he is stretchered off the field.

8. Mills lashes out at City's undisciplined defence after Berry tries to dribble out of a crowded area only to hand possession to Swindlehurst who scores. Dixon's handball is punished by Armstrong. Lawrie McMenemy's team have it won by the break. Tony Ford wastes two good chances.

9. City produce a lamentable performance. Callaghan, Kelly and Bertschin all miss free headers and Williams misses from five yards. Callaghan commits a stupid foul to gift Brighton a penalty and is substituted. Fox makes a wonder save from Hughes. Where are George's trousers now?

10. Brian Talbot signs from Watford for £25,000. The PFA Chairman gives Stoke stability in midfield allowing Kelly to rove forward. Berry nets a flicked on corner and Bertschin hooks another home. Shaw nets a third but Berry is given offside despite lying prone after running into a post.

Match-by-match results grid (matches 11–21). Columns across the top list the Stoke City line-up; the name beneath each is the opposing player. Figures after the attendance are the two running totals printed in the grid (the second is cumulative points).

---

11 · H BLACKBURN · 18/10 — Pos 18 · W 1-0 (0-0) · Att 7,715 · 19 · 11
Scorer: Shaw 49. Ref: L Hamer.
Stoke: Fox, Dixon*, Parkin, Talbot, Bould, Berry, Kelly, Ford, Shaw, Bertschin, Heath, Saunders
Blackburn: O'Keefe, Price, Branagan, Barker, Fazakerley, Mail, Brotherston, Patterson, Quinn, Garner, Rathbone
Kelly and Talbot run midfield. City waste a host of chances. Bertschin hits the bar and Bould turns the rebound against the post. Don Mackay's men hold out until Shaw cracks home after Vince O'Keefe parries Heath's drive. Kelly hasn't had a beer in six weeks and is down to 13 stone.

---

12 · A IPSWICH · 25/10 — Pos 20 · L 0-2 (0-1) · Att 1,054 · 6 · 11
Scorers: Wilson 42, 50. Ref: M Reed.
Stoke: Fox, Dixon*, Parkin, Talbot, Bould, Berry, Kelly, Ford, Shaw, Bertschin, Heath, Saunders
Ipswich: Cooper, Yallop, Zondervan, Atkins, Dazzell, Cranston, Gleghorn, Brennan, Cole, Deehan*, Wilson, Atkinson
Kevin Wilson plays on Steve Parkin's defensive weaknesses to pinch two goals. City hit the post through Heath and the ball rolls tantalisingly along the goal-line before being cleared. Cooper tips a Berry header over and a Saunders header round. City just cannot score at Mills' old club.

---

13 · H DERBY · 1/11 — Pos 22 · L 0-2 (0-1) · Att 2,358 · 7 · 11
Scorers: Williams 42, Gee 78. Ref: J Worrall.
Stoke: Fox, Dixon*, Parkin, Talbot, Bould, Berry, Kelly*, Ford, Shaw, Bertschin, Heath, Saunders
Derby: Wallington, Sage, Forsyth, Williams, Hindmarch, MacLaren, Micklewhite, Gee, Davison, Gregory, Harbey
Stoke slip back to the bottom after Derby survive a furious onslaught. Berry's header is cleared off the line. Wallington touches Shaw's shot on to the bar. Williams and Gee notch breakaway goals for Arthur Cox's disciplined Rams. Mills takes off Kelly (65 mins) who is not best pleased.

---

14 · A HULL · 8/11 — Pos 19 · W 4-0 (3-0) · Att 5,252 · 14 · 14
Scorers: Ford 16, McEwan 37 (og), Morgan 41, Bertschin 64. Ref: K Lupton.
Stoke: Fox, Dixon*, Parkin, Talbot, Bould, Berry, Kelly, Ford, **Morgan**, Bertschin, Heath, Saunders
Hull: Norman, Jobson, Heard, Parker, Skipper*, McEwan, Williams, Bunn, Saville, Roberts, Flounders
At last City find the right formula with on-loan Nicky Morgan providing the perfect foil for Bertschin. Ford crashes in from six yards and then McEwan lobs over his own keeper under pressure. Morgan scores a debut tap-in. Bertschin rounds off a great show heading in Morgan's flick.

---

15 · A SHEFFIELD U'D · 15/11 — Pos 20 · L 1-3 (1-2) · Att 11,177 · 5 · 14
Scorers: Bertschin 19; Dixon 4 (og), Withe 38, Beagrie 75. Ref: W Flood.
Stoke: Fox, Dixon, Parkin, Talbot, Saunders, Berry, Kelly, Ford, Morgan, Bertschin, Heath*, Shaw
Sheffield U'd: Tomlinson, Barnsley, Pike, Arnott, Stancliffe, Glover, Daws, Wigley, Withe, Foley, Beagrie
City miss Bould (knee) and Talbot is moved into the back four. But the midfield malfunctions without him. Dixon nets trying to keep out Paul Stancliffe's header. Bertschin buries a free header. Peter Withe scores against City yet again. Beagrie heads home after Fox misjudges a cross.

---

16 · H READING · 22/11 — Pos 18 · W 3-0 (1-0) · Att 7,465 · 14 · 17
Scorers: Bertschin 12, 58, 79. Ref: T Mills.
Stoke: Fox, Dixon, Parkin, Talbot, Bould, Berry, Kelly, Ford, Morgan, Bertschin, Heath, Saunders
Reading: Westwood, Williams, Richardson, Beavon, Bailie, Crombie, Rogers, Hurlock, Senior, Bremner, Gilkes*, Horrix
Keith Bertschin's hat-trick of headers is the first treble by a Stoke player for three years. He scores from a flicked-on corner, Heath's cross and after Westwood parries Morgan's effort. Ian Branfoot's third choice central defensive pair struggle. Mills offers to buy Morgan from Pompey.

---

17 · A BRADFORD C · 29/11 (at Odsal Stadium) — Pos 16 · W 4-1 (2-0) · Att 5,191 · 19 · 20
Scorers: Saunders 17, 65, Ford 35, Berry 60p; Hendrie 58. Ref: C Trussell.
Stoke: Fox, Dixon, Parkin, Talbot, Bould, Berry, Kelly, Ford, Morgan, Bertschin, Heath, Saunders
Bradford C: Nixon, Abbott, Withe, McCall, Oliver, Evans, Hendrie, Goodman, Leonard, Singleton, Ellis*, Ormondroyd
Stoke outshine the Bantams with stand-in striker Saunders the brightest star. He buries Kelly's cross and then leaps over Ford's shot to deceive Nixon. Saunders is tripped by Hendrie for the penalty and Berry, the new taker, crashes home. Saunders buries Morgan's cross to round it off.

---

18 · H PLYMOUTH · 6/12 — Pos 12 · W 1-0 (0-0) · Att 11,043 · 3 · 23
Scorer: Berry 64p. Ref: R Wiseman / K Hoare.
Stoke: Fox, Dixon, Parkin, Talbot, Bould, Berry, Kelly, Ford, Morgan, Bertschin, Heath, Saunders
Plymouth: Cherry, Nisbet, Cooper L*, Goodyear, Burrows, Uzzell, Hodges, Rowbotham, Tynan, Clayton, Summerfield, Nelson
Substitute ref Mr K Hoare spots Cherry's foul on Morgan, allowing Berry to score from the spot again. Says Mills 'Some of the lads fell about when I handed George the job, but he loves it'. Fox changes direction in mid-air to save Tynan's shot. Parkin is more comfortable at left-back.

---

19 · A GRIMSBY · 13/12 — Pos 12 · D 1-1 (0-0) · Att 4,642 · 9 · 24
Scorers: Saunders 88; Rawcliffe 71. Ref: J Watson.
Stoke: Fox, Dixon, Parkin, Talbot, Bould, Berry, Kelly, Ford, Morgan, Bertschin, Heath, Saunders
Grimsby: Felgate, Moore D, Agnew, Robinson, Lyons, Moore K, Walsh, Turner, Henshaw, O'Riordan, Grocock*, Rawcliffe
City have to wear Town's damp change kit as Grimsby object to Stoke wearing striped shirts. Saunders' shooting fails to match good approach work as Mick Lyons' men defend in depth. Saunders finally scores after Felgate saves from Morgan. Morgan looks great value for £40,000 fee.

---

20 · H LEEDS · 21/12 — Pos 11 · W 7-2 (5-0) · Att 12,358 · 8 · 27
Scorers: Mrg'n 5, 35, 72, S'nders 11, Dix'n 21, B'rd 51, Sher 73p [Klly 44, F'rd 62]. Ref: I Hemley.
Stoke: Fox, Dixon, Parkin, Talbot, Bould, Berry, Kelly, Ford, Morgan, Bertschin, Heath, Saunders
Leeds: Day, Aspin, Robinson*, Thompson, Ashurst, Swan, Doig, Sheridan, Baird, Edwards, Rennie, Ritchie
A magnificent seven for Stoke. Morgan blasts a trio of shots home from inside the box. Lee Dixon's superb overhead kick and Kelly's cheeky free-kick beat Day all ends up. John Sheridan's penalty is for Dixon's handball. 'We've threatened goals for some time.' Says Mills. Fantastic.

---

21 · A BARNSLEY · 26/12 — Pos 10 · W 2-0 (1-0) · Att 6,436 · 21 · 30
Scorers: Saunders 30, Kelly 87. Ref: N Midgley.
Stoke: Fox, Dixon, Parkin, Talbot, Bould, Berry, Kelly, Ford, Morgan, Bertschin, Heath, Saunders
Barnsley: Baker, Ogley, Cross, Thomas, May, Futcher, Agnew, Foreman, Ferry*, MacDonald, Gray, Hedworth
Tony Kelly makes Saunders' goal and rounds off a classy Stoke performance by powering a shot past Baker. Saunders also has a goal ruled out for a foul. Allan Clarke's Barnsley put in a lot of hard work but Fox is equal to Gwyn Thomas' headers. Bould is City's most improved player.

TODAY DIVISION 2

Manager: Mick Mills

SEASON 1986-87

Position →	1	2	3	4	5	6	7	8	9	10	11	12 sub used

22 — H SHEFFIELD UTD — 27/12
Att 17,320 / 9 · Pos 7 · W · Pt 33 · F-A 5-2 · H-T 2-0
Scorers, Times, and Referees: Bould 5, Saunders 17, 55, 82, Morris 70p, 87 [Morgan 77] — Ref: K Breen

1	2	3	4	5	6	7	8	9	10	11	12 sub used
Fox	Dixon	Parkin	Talbot	Bould	Berry	Ford	Kelly	Morgan	Saunders	Heath	
Burridge	Barnsley	Pike	Dempsey	Stancliffe	Smith	Morris	Wigley	Withe *	Foley	Frain	Daws

United regret playing the offside trap against a rampaging City attack. Berry and Bould combine for the opener from Tony 'Zico' Kelly's free-kick. Saunders' trio of excellent finishes is completed by an exultant header. The penalty is for Berry's foul on Morris. 28 goals in nine games.

23 — H SHREWSBURY — 1/1
Att 19,382 / 15 · Pos 5 · W · Pt 36 · F-A 1-0 · H-T 1-0
Scorers: Saunders 1 — Ref: D Hedges

1	2	3	4	5	6	7	8	9	10	11	12 sub used
Fox	Dixon	Parkin	Talbot	Bould	Berry	Ford	Kelly	Morgan*	Saunders	Heath	
Perks	Williams	Johnson	Leonard*	Pearson	Linighan	McNally	Hackett	Brown	Robinson	Daly	Green

Carl Saunders pounces after 52 seconds, slipping the ball to Heath and running on to finish a well-worked move involving Morgan and Talbot. Shrews' good midfield play is spoilt by their woeful crossing. City find it a hard slog on a rain-soaked pitch. Ford blazes wide of an open goal.

24 — A MILLWALL — 3/1
Att 6,134 / 9 · Pos 6 · D · Pt 37 · F-A 1-1 · H-T 1-1
Scorers: Heath 32, Leslie 10 — Ref: G Napthine

1	2	3	4	5	6	7	8	9	10	11	12 sub used
Fox	Dixon	Parkin	Talbot	Bould	Berry	Ford	Kelly	Morgan	Saunders	Heath	
Horne	Coleman N	Coleman P	Briley	Walker	McLeary	Byrne	Morgan	Sheringham	Leslie	Salman	

City recover from a bout of flu to earn a creditable draw as John Docherty's Millwall. Heath stabs home after Bould flicks on Berry's free-kick to equalise John Leslie's tap-in. Stoke have slightly the better of the second half but tire. Mills is made Manager of the Month on his birthday.

25 — A BIRMINGHAM — 24/1
Att 10,641 / 11 · Pos 6 · D · Pt 38 · F-A 0-0 · H-T 0-0
Ref: H King

1	2	3	4	5	6	7	8	9	10	11	12 sub used
Fox	Dixon	Parkin	Talbot	Bould	Berry	Ford	Kelly	Morgan	Saunders	Heath	
Hansbury	Ranson	Roberts	Williams	Dicks	Mortimer	Bremner	Handysides	Whitton	Rees	Kuhl	

Blues boss John Bond reflects that handing Lee Dixon a free transfer while manager at Burnley may not have been a great move. He is superb, both overlapping and defending as Stoke end Birmingham's record of scoring in each home game. Saunders flashes wide as City nearly win it.

26 — H CRYSTAL PALACE — 7/2
Att 13,154 / 8 · Pos 4 · W · Pt 41 · F-A 3-1 · H-T 1-0
Scorers: Ford 2, Dixon 64, Berry 73p, Ketteridge 65 — Ref: F Roberts

1	2	3	4	5	6	7	8	9	10	11	12 sub used
Fox	Dixon	Parkin	Talbot	Bould	Berry	Ford	Kelly	Morgan*	Saunders*	Heath	
Wood	Stebbing	Brush	Taylor*	O'Reilly	Cannon	Gray	Ketteridge	Bright	Wright	Barber	Finnigan

City start like a whirlwind. Ford takes Morgan's pass in his stride and fires into the far corner, Heath hits a post and Wood makes a great save. Dixon volleys a corner home. O'Reilly fells Bertschin and Berry tucks in the penalty. Berry subdues the famous Wright and Bright strikeforce.

27 — A WEST BROM — 14/2
Att 12,366 / 11 · Pos 6 · L · Pt 41 · F-A 1-4 · H-T 0-3
Scorers: Bertschin 80, Crooks 13, 73, Reilly 14, 20p — Ref: R Groves

1	2	3	4	5	6	7	8	9	10	11	12 sub used
Segers	Dixon	Parkin	Talbot	Bould	Berry	Ford	Kelly	Morgan	Bertschin	Heath !	
Naylor	Palmer	Statham	Whitehead	Dyson	Bradley	Hopkins	Anderson	Reilly	MacKenzie	Crooks	

The wheels come off as ex-Stokie Garth Crooks finishes coolly twice and is tripped by Berry for the pen. Heath walks (42 mins) for a second booking after flattening Hopkins who keeps fouling him. The ten men force seven corners but only Bertschin's close-range finish beats Naylor.

28 — A PORTSMOUTH — 28/2
Att 14,607 / 1 · Pos 6 · L · Pt 41 · F-A 0-3 · H-T 0-2
Scorers: Quinn 12, 67, Dillon 31p — Ref: A Seville

1	2	3	4	5	6	7	8	9	10	11	12 sub used
Fox	Dixon	Parkin	Talbot*	Bould	Berry	Ford	Maskery	Morgan	Bertschin	Saunders	
Knight	Swain	Hardyman	Dillon	Blake	Gilbert	O'Callaghan* Tait	Mariner	Quinn	Hilaire	Collins	

Suspensions tell as Stoke lose Kelly and Heath for this vital clash. Mick Quinn scorches a drive past Fox. Mariner is upended by Berry for the penalty. Quinn rises to head home Kevin Dillon's free-kick. 'An extra day training next week to make up for the day off here.' grumbles Mills.

29 — A BLACKBURN — 14/3
Att 10,075 / 17 · Pos 9 · L · Pt 41 · F-A 1-2 · H-T 0-0
Scorers: Morgan 83, Price 74, Berry 80 (og) — Ref: G Tyson

1	2	3	4	5	6	7	8	9	10	11	12 sub used
Fox	Dixon	Hemming*	Maskery	Bould	Berry	Ford	Parkin	Morgan	Saunders	Heath	
O'Keefe	Price	Sulley	Barker	Keeley	Mail	Miller	Ainscow	Hendry	Patterson	Branagan* Sellars	

A poor display. George Berry has a nightmare deflecting Chris Price's shot inside the far post and turning a cross past Fox. Nicky Morgan heads home a consolation but Stoke are not worth a point. Mills describes the performance as 'Relegation form'. Where has all the form gone?

30 — H SUNDERLAND — 17/3
Att 9,420 / 15 · Pos 7 · W · Pt 44 · F-A 3-0 · H-T 1-0
Scorers: Berry 21p, Dixon 60, Morgan 89 — Ref: P Harrison

1	2	3	4	5	6	7	8	9	10	11	12 sub used
Fox	Dixon	Parkin	Talbot	Hemming	Berry	Ford	Kelly	Morgan	Shaw	Heath	
Hesford	Agboola *	Gray	Armstrong	Hetzke	Bennett	Lemon	Doyle	Swindlehurst Proctor	Buchanan	Atkinson	

City splash their way to a comfortable win against struggling Sunderland. Morgan is fouled by Hetzke and after a long delay for protests Berry cracks in. Dixon finishes off Hemming's incisive pass. It is revealed that Chris Hemming will become the first pro player to wear a pacemaker.

31 — A HUDDERSFIELD — 21/3
Att 7,222 / 18 · Pos 7 · D · Pt 45 · F-A 2-2 · H-T 0-1
Scorers: Ford 67, Bertschin 87, Shearer 25, Cork 61 — Ref: D Allison

1	2	3	4	5	6	7	8	9	10	11	12 sub used
Fox	Dixon	Parkin	Talbot	Hemming	Berry	Ford	Kelly	Morgan	Saunders	Heath*	
Cox	Brown	Burke	Banks	Webster	Jones	Winter	Cork	Shearer	Wilson Phil	Cowling	Bertschin

City do well to fight back after Shearer's quality strike and Cork's bobbling finish. Ford beats the offside trap to score. Bertschin scores a well-taken equaliser. He is set to join Sunderland to bring in cash for deadline day signings. Banks hits the post and Webster hits Parkin on the line.

32 | H IPSWICH | 25/3 | 7 D 0-0 46 | Att: 11,805

Stoke: Fox, Dixon, Parkin, Talbot, Hemming, Berry, Kelly, Ford, Morgan, Saunders*, Heath, Maskery
Ipswich: Cooper, Yallop, McCall, Atkins, Dozzell, Cranson, Brennan, D'Avray, Deehan, Wilson, Zondervan, Shaw

Stoke, disrupted by injuries, battle all the way to earn a deserved point against Bobby Ferguson's Ipswich. Late City pressure sees Cooper save from Morgan and Ford. D'Avray commits a bad challenge on Lee Dixon, injuring his knee. Parkin clears off the line. Fox saves his knee.

Ref: K Hackett

---

33 | H BRIGHTON | 28/3 | 8 D 1-1 47 | Att: 10,216 (22)

Goals: Morgan 47 / Wilson 1

Stoke: Fox, Dixon, Parkin, Talbot, Hemming, Berry, Kelly, Ford, Morgan, Daly*, Heath, Shaw
Brighton: Digweed, Hutchings, Wilson, Hughes, Isaac, Young, Crumplin, Gatting, Tiltman, Connor, Jasper

Bottom club Brighton are a goal up after 28 seconds when 'constructive' play from the back allows Wilson to seize the ball from Berry and fire past Fox. City never flow and their only chance is Morgan's diving header from Tony Kelly's free-kick. Newcomer Gerry Daly strains a thigh.

Ref: M Bailey

---

34 | H HULL | 4/4 | 8 D 1-0 48 | Att: 8,146 (20)

Goals: Talbot 15 / Bunn 84

Stoke: Fox!, Dixon, Parkin, Talbot, Hemming, Berry, Kelly, Ford, Morgan, Shaw*, Heath, Gayle
Hull: Norman, Palmer, Heard, Jobson, Skipper, Parker*, Dyer, Bunn, Saville, Askew, Roberts, Payton

Talbot's 15-yard finish puts Stoke ahead but Brian Horton's Hull equalise. Fox is sent off (86 mins) for the second time in his career. His foul on Andy Saville is deemed 'professional' by the referee. Stand-in keeper Tony Kelly makes a superb save from Garreth Roberts in injury-time.

Ref: A Buksh

---

35 | A DERBY | 11/4 | 9 D 0-0 49 | Att: 9,038 (1)

Stoke: Fox, Dixon, Parkin, Talbot, Hemming, Berry, Kelly, Ford, Morgan, Shaw, Heath
Derby: Steele, Blades, Forsyth, Williams, Hindmarch, MacLaren, Micklewhite, Gee, Davison, Gregory, Callaghan

City expose Derby's weak defence and only Eric Steele stands between them and victory. Steele thwarts Shaw, making two saves with his legs. Heath and Talbot head against the woodwork. Arthur Cox's Rams, on course for promotion, will have to play better than this in the top flight.

Ref: D Hedges

---

36 | A SHREWSBURY | 18/4 | 9 L 1-4 49 | Att: 6,777 (18)

Goals: Saunders 88 (Dixon 85 og) / Robinson 4, Geddis 7, Tester 24, Tester 24

Stoke: Reece, Dixon, Parkin, Talbot, Hemming, Berry, Kelly, Ford, Morgan, Shaw, Heath*, Saunders
Shrewsbury: Perks, Williams, Johnson, Steele, Pearson, Linighan, McNally, Hackett, Geddis, Robinson, Tester

Kick-off is delayed by 10 minutes but Stoke never get started. Poor defending allows Robinson, Geddis and Tester all to find their way through easily. Dixon turns Reece's save past the prone keeper and it just isn't City's day. Saunders taps in but Chic Bates' Shrews are worthy winners.

Ref: H King

---

37 | H BARNSLEY | 20/4 | 10 L 1-2 49 | Att: 7,263 (13)

Goals: Morgan 52 / Thomas 29, Clarke 58

Stoke: Reece, Dixon, Parkin, Talbot, Hemming, Berry, Maskery, Ford, Morgan, Saunders*, Gayle*, Heath
Barnsley: Baker, Joyce, Hedworth, Thomas, Gray, Futcher, Agnew, Wylde, Dobbin, MacDonald, Clarke

Stoke miss Steve Bould's influence. Paul Reece saves Stuart Gray's 12th-minute penalty after Hemming fouls Hedworth. Thomas to supply Clarke in the City defence, waltzing through to fire past Reece. Morgan heads in but City's defence parts again to allow MacDonald to supply Clarke.

Ref: B Hill

---

38 | A READING | 25/4 | 9 W 1-0 52 | Att: 5,927 (13)

Goals: Morgan 12

Stoke: Fox, Dixon, Parkin, Talbot, Hemming, Berry, Saunders, Ford, Morgan, Shaw, Heath*, Maskery
Reading: Francis, Bailie, Richardson, Beavon, Hicks, Peters, Williams*, Taylor, Senior, Bremner, Smillie, Wood

Saunders reverts to midfield as Stoke put an end to their poor run. Morgan heads in Talbot's free-kick at the far post. Fox saves Reading's only chance, denying Trevor Senior from six yards. Peters clears off the line and Morgan shoots just wide. City's first visit to Elm Park since 1931.

Ref: M Bodenham

---

39 | H OLDHAM | 28/4 | 9 L 0-2 52 | Att: 7,228 (3)

Goals: — / Henry 39, Williams 75

Stoke: Fox, Dixon, Parkin, Talbot, Hemming, Berry, Kelly, Ford, Morgan, Saunders, Gayle
Oldham: Goram, Irwin, Barlow, McGuire, Hoolickin, Moore, Ormondroyd, Henry, Palmer, Milligan, Williams

Stoke's play-off dreams are in tatters after another poor home performance. Oldham's five-man midfield takes control and Tony Henry drives a 30-yarder high past Fox. Goram saves well from Saunders' leaping header. Williams heads home after Henry hits the bar. Joe Royle is ecstatic.

Ref: R Milford

---

40 | H BRADFORD C | 2/5 | 9 L 2-3 52 | Att: 5,229 (12)

Goals: Gayle 81, 86 / Abbott 44p, 71, Hendrie 79

Stoke: Fox, Dixon, Mills*, Talbot, Hemming, Berry, Parkin, Ford, Morgan, Saunders, Gayle
Bradford C: Litchfield, Graham, Goddard, McCall, Oliver, Evans, Hendrie, Abbott, Futcher, Palin, Ellis

Ford fouls Hendrie for the penalty which tips the balance. Stoke go to pieces. At 0-3 angry season-ticket holders throw their books on the track as City lose their third home game in a row. Howard Gayle's late goals are both close-range finishes. Mills makes plans for wholesale changes.

Ref: P Tyldesley

---

41 | A PLYMOUTH | 4/5 | 8 W 3-1 55 | Att: 13,774 (6)

Goals: Saunders 35, 38, Talbot 46 / Coughlin 55p

Stoke: Fox, Dixon, Mills, Talbot, Hemming, Berry, Parkin*, Ford, Morgan, Saunders, Gayle
Plymouth: Cherry, Nisbet, Cooper L, Law, McElhinney, Matthews*, Hodges, Coughlin, Tynan, Evans, Nelson, Summerfield

A comprehensive win on the south coast. Saunders finishes off two great moves and nearly bags a hat-trick but Steve Cherry saves well. Mills makes light of his 38 years to turn in a superb performance. Reading's twice-taken penalty is for Gayle's trip. Fox saves but moves too early.

Ref: J Deakin

---

42 | H GRIMSBY | 9/5 | 8 W 5-1 58 | Att: 6,406 (21)

Goals: K'ly 6, Talb't 14, B'rry 40p, S'nders 57, [Ford 76] / McGarvey 19p

Stoke: Fox, Dixon*, Mills, Talbot, Hemming, Berry, Kelly, Ford, Morgan, Saunders, Heath, Gayle [Ford 76]
Grimsby: Pratt, Burgess, Agnew, Turner, Moore A, Crombie, McDermott, Halsall*, Coughlin, O'Riordan, Bonnyman, Henshaw

An end of season romp as City overwhelm the Mariners. Kelly sidesteps two defenders before beating Pratt. Talbot bravely dives in to head in. McGarvey 19p. Saunders neatly controls Morgan's pass to slip home. Ford's cross-shot nestles in the corner. Too little too late. The penalties are both for fouls.

Ref: M Peck

Home 9,991 | Away .604 | Average 9,604

TODAY DIVISION 2 (CUP-TIES) Manager: Mick Mills SEASON 1986-87

Littlewoods Cup

		Att	F-A	H-T	Scorers, Times, and Referees	1	2	3	4	5	6	7	8	9	10	11	12 sub used
2:1	A SHREWSBURY 23/9	5,343 17	20 L 1-2	1-0	Maskery 17 / Robinson 60, Waller 78 / Ref: R Nixon	Fox / Perks	Dixon / Williams*	Hemming* / Johnson	Kelly / Hughes	Bould / Pearson	Berry / Green	Ford / McNally	Parkin / Hackett	Maskery^ / Waller	Shaw / Robinson	Heath / Daly	Call'/Crooks / Tester

City run the first half and should have more than just Maskery's shot from 18 yards. They regret sitting back on the lead. Gerry Daly takes over after the break and prompts the Shrews to score through two headers. Ford brings a superb save out of Perks. At least Stoke have an away goal.

		Att	F-A	H-T	Scorers, Times, and Referees	1	2	3	4	5	6	7	8	9	10	11	12 sub used
2:2	H SHREWSBURY 8/10	6,468 17	22 D 0-0	0-0	Ref: K Hackett (Stoke lose 1-2 on aggregate)	Fox / Perks	Dixon / Williams	Parkin / Johnson	Kelly / Daly	Bould / Pearson	Hemming / Green	Ford / McNally	Maskery / Hackett*	Shaw / Waller	Bertschin / Robinson	Heath* / Tester	Williams / Leonard

Stoke hit rock bottom as they fail to find a way past Chic Bates' Shrews. Phil Heath blasts over from 12 yards and Dixon completely misses his kick. Frustration is voiced from the Boothen End at which City have yet to score this season. Kelly is transfer listed after a bust up with Mills.

FA Cup

		Att	F-A	H-T	Scorers, Times, and Referees	1	2	3	4	5	6	7	8	9	10	11	12 sub used
3	A GRIMSBY 10/1	7,367 13	6 D 1-1	1-0	Saunders 38 / Walsh 60 / Ref: T Mills	Fox / Felgate	Dixon / Burgess	Parkin / Agnew	Talbot / Turner	Bould / Lyons	Berry / Moore K	Ford / Robinson	Kelly / Walsh	Morgan / Bonnyman	Saunders / O'Riordan	Heath / Cumming	Bertschin / Rawcliffe

The game goes ahead in a blizzard and Saunders manages to pick the white ball out clearly enough to head home Ford's corner. Walsh snaffles a half chance from Cumming's cross to snatch a draw. Kelly's free-kick is saved by Felgate. Stoke are the better side and Berry curls one wide.

		Att	F-A	H-T	Scorers, Times, and Referees	1	2	3	4	5	6	7	8	9	10	11	12 sub used
3R	H GRIMSBY 26/1	14,340 12	6 D 1-1 aet	0-0	Saunders 71 / Moore 82 / Ref: T Mills	Fox / Batch	Dixon / Burgess	Parkin / Agnew	Talbot / Turner	Bould / Lyons	Berry / Moore K	Ford / Robinson	Kelly / Walsh	Morgan* / Bonnyman*	Saunders / O'Riordan	Heath / Henshaw	Bertschin / Rawcliffe

Stoke have so much possession there seems to be only one possible result. After a night of frustration City seem to have won it when Saunders slams home Heath's square pass but the Mariners hit back through Kevin Moore's 20-yard snapshot which beats Fox. Fifth draw in two years.

		Att	F-A	H-T	Scorers, Times, and Referees	1	2	3	4	5	6	7	8	9	10	11	12 sub used
3 RR	H GRIMSBY 28/1	12,087 12	6 W 6-0	4-0	Morgan 10, 48, Talbot 17, Heath 22, [Saunders 41, 81] / Ref: R Bridges	Fox / Batch	Dixon / Burgess	Parkin / Agnew	Talbot / Turner	Bould / Lyons	Berry / Moore K	Ford / Robinson	Kelly / Walsh	Morgan / Bonnyman	Saunders* / O'Riordan	Heath / Henshaw	Bertschin

City finally tame Mick Lyons' men. They overwhelm the Mariners in a superb first-half display. Morgan and Talbot both finish Kelly's passes. Berry sets up Heath and Kelly crosses for Saunders and Morgan. Saunders buries Heath's cutback and now has 13 goals in 12 games. Brilliant.

		Att	F-A	H-T	Scorers, Times, and Referees	1	2	3	4	5	6	7	8	9	10	11	12 sub used
4	H CARDIFF 31/1	20,423 4:17	6 W 2-1	1-1	Saunders 33, Heath 70 / Wimbleton 15 / Ref: K Hackett	Fox / Moseley	Dixon / Kerr	Parkin / Ford	Talbot / Wimbleton	Bould / Brignull	Berry / Boyle	Ford / Platnauer	Kelly / Bartlett	Morgan / Pike*	Saunders* / Curtis	Heath / Marustik	Bertschin / Davies

Frank Burrows' Cardiff battle hard and take a shock lead through Paul Wimbleton's left-foot shot. After a spate of corners City's pressure tells when Saunders races on to Kelly's pass. Heath strikes Dixon's cross inside the far post to put Stoke in the fifth round for first time in 11 years.

		Att	F-A	H-T	Scorers, Times, and Referees	1	2	3	4	5	6	7	8	9	10	11	12 sub used
5	H COVENTRY 21/2	31,255 1:8	6 L 0-1	0-0	Gynn 71 / Ref: R Nixon	Fox / Ogrizovic	Dixon / Barrows	Parkin / Downs	Talbot / Gynn	Bould / Kilcline	Berry / Peake	Ford / Bennett*	Kelly / Phillips	Morgan* / Regis	Saunders / Houchen	Heath / Pickering	Bertschin / Sedgley

In front of the biggest gate for seven years John Sillett and George Curtis' Coventry break swiftly out of defence and Micky Gynn produces an angled finish. Referee Nixon amazingly fails to give Stoke a penalty when Phillips fells Dixon. Bertschin forces Ogrizovic into a brilliant save.

Appearances and Goals

Player	Appearances						Goals			
	Lge	Sub	LC	Sub	FAC	Sub	Lge	LC	FAC	Tot
Berry, George	40		1		5		8			8
Bertschin, Keith	16	5	1			4	8			8
Bould, Steve	28		2		5		1			1
Callaghan, Aaron	2			1						
Crooks, Paul						1				
Daly, Gerry	1									
Dixon, Lee	42		2		5		6			6
Ford, Tony	41		2		5					
Fox, Peter	39		2		5					
Gayle, Howard	4	2					2			2
Heath, Phil	37	1	2			5	1		2	3
Hemming, Chris	21	1	2		5		3			3
Kelly, Tony	32	3	2			5	4			4
Maskery, Chris	10	3	2					1		1
Mills, Mick	6									
Morgan, Nicky	29					5	10		2	12
Parkin, Steve	37	1	2			5				
Reece, Paul	2									
Saunders, Carl	26	5				5	14		5	19
Segers, Hans	1									
Shaw, Graham	15	3	2				2			2
Talbot, Brian	32					5	3		1	4
Williams, Terry	1	2				1				
20 players used	**462**	**27**	**22**	**3**	**55**	**4**	**62**	**1**	**10**	**73**

League Table

		P	Home					Away					Pts
			W	D	L	F	A	W	D	L	F	A	
1	Derby	42	14	6	1	42	18	11	3	7	22	20	84
2	Portsmouth	42	17	2	2	37	11	6	7	8	16	17	78
3	Oldham	42	13	6	2	36	16	9	3	9	29	28	75
4	Leeds	42	15	4	2	43	16	4	7	10	15	28	68
5	Ipswich	42	12	6	3	29	10	5	7	9	30	33	64
6	Crys Palace	42	12	4	5	35	20	7	1	13	16	33	62
7	Plymouth	42	12	6	3	40	23	4	7	10	22	34	61
8	STOKE	42	11	5	5	40	21	5	5	11	23	32	58
9	Sheffield Utd	42	10	8	3	31	19	5	5	11	19	30	58
10	Bradford C	42	10	5	6	36	27	5	5	11	26	35	55
11	Barnsley	42	8	7	6	26	23	6	6	9	23	29	55
12	Blackburn	42	11	4	6	30	22	4	6	11	15	33	55
13	Reading	42	11	4	6	33	23	3	7	11	19	36	53
14	Hull	42	10	6	5	25	22	3	8	10	16	33	53
15	West Brom	42	8	6	7	29	22	5	6	10	22	27	51
16	Millwall	42	10	5	6	27	16	4	4	13	12	29	51
17	Huddersfield	42	9	6	6	38	30	4	6	11	16	31	51
18	Shrewsbury	42	11	3	7	24	14	4	3	14	17	39	51
19	Birmingham	42	8	9	4	27	21	3	8	10	20	38	50
20	Sunderland *	42	8	6	7	25	23	4	6	11	24	36	48
21	Grimsby	42	5	8	8	18	21	5	6	10	21	38	44
22	Brighton	42	7	6	8	22	20	2	6	13	15	34	39
		924	232	122	108	693	438	108	122	232	438	693	1264

* relegated after play-offs

Odds & ends

Double wins: (2) Plymouth, Reading.
Double losses: (1) Oldham.

Won from behind: (0).
Lost from in front: (1) Leeds (a).

High spots: Scoring seven against Leeds.
28 goals in 9 games leading up to the turn of the year.
Tony Kelly's form after his battle for fitness.
Hat-tricks from three separate players for the first time since 1958.

Low spots: Missing the play-offs by just six points.
Terrible form from February to May.
Being beaten 1-4 at the Hawthorns.
The departure of Tony Kelly.

Player of the Year: Lee Dixon.
Ever-presents: (1) Lee Dixon.
Hat-tricks: (3) Bertschin, Morgan, Saunders.
Leading scorer: (19) Carl Saunders.

BARCLAYS DIVISION 2 — Manager: Mick Mills — SEASON 1987-88

Match details

No	Match	Date	Att	Pos	Pt	F-A	H-T	Scorers, Times, and Referees
1	A BIRMINGHAM	15/8	13,137	–	L 0	0-2	0-1	Rees 1, 50 — Ref: A Buksh
2	H HULL	18/8	9,139	–	D 1	1-1	0-1	Ford 68 / Parker 37 — Ref: M Reed
3	H MIDDLESBROUGH	22/8	9,345	11	W 4	1-0	0-0	Berry 60p — Ref: D Elleray
4	A IPSWICH	29/8	11,149	15	L 4	0-2	0-1	Hemming 18 (og), Lowe 82 — Ref: C Downey
5	H LEICESTER	31/8	9,948	8	W 7	2-1	2-1	Saunders 4, Heath 45 / McAllister 31 — Ref: K Cooper
6	A SHEFFIELD UTD	5/9	10,086	10	D 8	0-0	0-0	— Ref: V Callow
7	H BRADFORD C	12/9	9,571	13	L 8	1-2	0-1	Berry 50 / Futcher 7, Ellis 80 — Ref: L Shapter
8	A READING	16/9	5,349	12	W 11	1-0	0-0	Parkin 50 — Ref: B Stevens
9	A MANCHESTER C	19/9	19,322	14	L 11	0-3	0-2	Varadi 2, 27, 48 — Ref: G Tyson
10	H HUDDERSFIELD	26/9	8,665	15	D 12	1-1	0-1	Ford 74 / Cooper 22 — Ref: J Deakin
11	A LEEDS	30/9	17,208	15	D 13	0-0	0-0	— Ref: P Vanes

Line-ups (Stoke City in roman, opponents in *italic*; opponent league position shown in brackets)

No	1	2	3	4	5	6	7	8	9	10	11	subs used
1	Fox	Dixon	Parkin	Talbot	Hemming	Berry	Ford	Daly	Morgan	Saunders	Allinson*	Heath
1	*Godden*	*Ranson*	*Dicks*	*Overson*	*Williams*	*Handysides*	*Bremner*	*Kennedy*	*Whitton*	*Rees*	*Wigley*	
2	Fox	Dixon	Parkin	Talbot^	Hemming	Berry	Ford	Daly*	Morgan	Saunders	Allinson	Carr / Heath
2	*Norman*	*Palmer*	*Heard*	*Jobson*	*Skipper*	*Parker*	*Roberts*	*Bunn*	*Saville*	*Askew*	*Daniel*	
3	Fox	Dixon	Carr	Talbot	Hemming	Berry	Ford	Daly*	Morgan	Saunders	Allinson	Parkin
3	*Pears (18)*	*Glover*	*Cooper*	*Mowbray*	*Parkinson*	*Pallister*	*Slaven*	*Stephens*	*Hamilton**	*Kerr*	*Ripley*	*Kernaghan*
4	Fox	Dixon	Carr	Talbot	Hemming	Berry	Ford	Parkin	Morgan	Saunders	Allinson*	Heath
4	*Hamilton (6)*	*Stockwell*	*Harbey*	*Yallop*	*Dozzell*	*Cranson*	*Lowe*	*Brennan*	*D'Array*	*Zondervan*	*Gleghorn*	
5	Fox	Dixon	Carr	Talbot	Hemming	Berry	Ford	Parkin	Morgan	Saunders	Heath	
5	*Andrews (20)*	*James*	*Venus*	*Osman*	*Horner*	*Ramsey^*	*Ford*	*Moran*	*Reid**	*McAllister*	*Wilson*	*Russell / Morgan*
6	**Barrett**	Dixon	Carr	Talbot	Hemming	Berry	Ford	Parkin	Morgan	Saunders	Heath	
6	*Leaning (19)*	*Barnsley^*	*Pike*	*Kuhl*	*Stancliffe*	*Eckhardt*	*Marsden**	*Withe*	*Cadette*	*Dempsey*	*Beagrie*	*Philliskirk / Wilder*
7	Barrett	Dixon	Carr	Talbot	Hemming	Berry	Ford	Parkin	Morgan	Saunders*	Heath	Daly
7	*Tomlinson (3)*	*Mitchell*	*Goddard*	*McCall*	*Oliver*	*Evans*	*Hendrie*	*Sinnott*	*Futcher*	*Palin**	*Ellis*	*Abbott*
8	Barrett	Dixon	Carr	Talbot	Bould	Berry	Ford	Parkin	Morgan	Daly	Heath	
8	*Francis (17)*	*Jones*	*Richardson*	*Tait*	*Hicks*	*Peters*	*Smillie*	*Taylor*	*Gordon*	*Joseph**	*Canoville*	*Gilkes*
9	Fox	Dixon	Carr	Talbot	Bould	Berry	Ford	Parkin	Morgan	Daly*	Allinson	Shaw
9	*Nixon (9)*	*Gidman*	*Hinchcliffe^*	*Lake*	*Simpson*	*Redmond*	*White*	*Stewart*	*Varadi*	*Scott*	*McNab*	
10	Fox	Dixon	Carr	Daly*	Bould	Berry	Ford	Parkin	Morgan	Shaw	Heath	Allinson
10	*Cox (23)*	*Bray*	*Burke*	*Banks*	*Webster*	*Tucker*	*Barham**	*May*	*Cooper*	*Ward*	*Cork*	*Trevitt*
11	Fox	Dixon	Carr	Parkin	Bould	Berry	Ford	Saunders	Morgan	Shaw	Heath	Pearson
11	*Day (11)*	*Aspin*	*Adams*	*Haddock*	*Ashurst*	*Rennie*	*De Mange*	*Sheridan*	*Melrose**	*Taylor*	*Snodin*	

Match reports

1. Birmingham (A): City concede the first goal of the season when Mark Rees turns Bremner's cross past Fox. Rees' second arrives after Dixon's back-pass falls to Whitton. Heath has his shot cleared off the line but Stoke lack conviction at either end. A great start for new Birmingham boss Garry Pendrey.

2. Hull (H): Mills is enraged by City's lack of passion. Garry Parker rounds Fox to put Hull ahead but it takes the introduction of two subs to change things. New signing Ian Allinson crosses for Ford to pick his spot. Berry heads against the bar, but Stoke don't deserve to beat Brian Horton's Tigers.

3. Middlesbrough (H): It's George Berry's day. He blasts home a penalty for Pallister's foul on Saunders and is then fouled for Pallister's foul on Saunders; Berry loops into the net and City escape with a free-kick. Cliff Carr is a hit on his full debut after moving from Fulham. Dixon is watched by Liverpool manager Dalglish.

4. Ipswich (A): New Ipswich boss John Duncan sees City take a stranglehold on the game. That is until Chris Hemming over-hits a lobbed back-pass to Fox. His face is as red as his hair. City never recover. David Lowe curls a beauty past Fox. Hemming nearly makes amends but puts a free header wide.

5. Leicester (H): Stoke are lively but profligate. Ford's superb cross finds Saunders unmarked to head home. McAllister rams home the rebound after Fox saves from Moran. Osman nullifies Morgan but Heath races clear to beat Andrews to Hemming's long ball. Mills isn't happy even though Stoke win.

6. Sheffield Utd (A): Mills is happier as the defence seem more of a unit after three days of intense training. On-loan Scott Barrett, from Wolves, replaces Fox, out with a swollen hand. Parkin stars in midfield as City have slightly the better of a very dour game. Billy McEwan is unhappy.

7. Bradford C (H): The back four malfunctions again and City are lucky to only concede two. Futcher picks his spot from 10 yards before Barrett saves well twice. Bradford hit bar and post. Berry powers a header home but Terry Dolan's men win through the speedy Mark Ellis who buries Hendrie's cross.

8. Reading (A): Steve Bould returns early from a back operation to add solidity to City's defence. Steve Parkin glances a header past Steve Francis for his first goal in two years. Barrett makes two superb close-range saves. A much more confident performance. Morgan still needs more support up front.

9. Manchester C (A): Mills admits he got the tactics wrong as Imre Varadi takes advantage of three defensive errors. Lee Dixon is pulled out of position for the first. Berry kicks the air to allow the ball to run to Varadi for the second. The defence marks each other rather than Varadi who nods home his third.

10. Huddersfield (H): Dixon inexplicably tries to back head to Fox from the halfway line and Graham Cooper races in to score. Dixon atones by curling a cross in for Ford to power a header home, but Stoke's performance is a complete shambles. Mills accuses the team of 'Failing to wear the shirt with pride'.

11. Leeds (A): Stoke match Leeds' work-rate and nearly snatch a win when Morgan blasts over from close range. Fox saves Snodin's late drive. Steve Parkin marks the dangerous John Sheridan out of the game. He loses his temper and is booked for kicking out at Parkin. A rare point at Elland Road.

Season results grid (matches 12–23)

No	Venue	Opponent	Date	Pos	Res	FT	HT	Att	Opp Pos	Pts
12	H	BOURNEMOUTH	3/10	10	W	1-0	0-0	8,104	21	16
13	H	PLYMOUTH	10/10	9	W	1-0	1-0	8,275	19	19
14	A	BLACKBURN	17/10	10	L	0-2	0-1	7,280	12	19
15	A	SWINDON	20/10	10	L	0-3	0-1	9,160	4	19
16	H	ASTON VILLA	24/10	10	D	0-0	0-0	13,494	4	20
17	A	BARNSLEY	31/10	15	L	2-5	0-2	5,908	11	20
18	H	WEST BROM	7/11	14	W	3-0	2-0	9,992	18	23
19	A	CRYSTAL PALACE	14/11	14	L	0-2	0-0	8,309	5	23
20	H	MILLWALL	21/11	14	L	1-2	1-0	7,998	7	23
21	A	SHREWSBURY	28/11	14	W	3-0	3-0	5,158	20	26
22	H	OLDHAM	8/12	14	D	2-2	1-1	6,470	20	27
23	A	MIDDLESBROUGH	12/12	15	L	0-2	0-0	7,289	1	27

---

12 · H BOURNEMOUTH · 3/10 — W 1-0
Scorer: Ford 77. Ref: K Barratt
City: Fox, Dixon, Carr^, Parkin, Bould, Berry, Ford, Saunders, Morgan*, Shaw, Heath; subs Daly/Allinson
Bournemouth: Peyton, Newson, Morrell, Brooks, Williams, Whitlock, O'Driscoll, Richards, Aylott, Pulis*, Cooke; sub O'Connor
Fox saves from Richards, Aylott and Williams. Richards hits the woodwork and Saunders clears off the line from Newson. Tony Ford, City's best player, pops up to clip home Gerry Peyton's punch out. Harry Redknapp cannot believe his Bournemouth team don't have at least a point.

13 · H PLYMOUTH · 10/10 — W 1-0
Scorer: Heath 10. Ref: N Midgley
City: Fox, Dixon, Carr, Parkin, Bould, Berry, Ford, Daly*, Saunders^, Shaw, Heath; subs Allinson/Hemming
Plymouth: Crudgington, Brimacombe, Cooper L, Tynan, Law, Smith, Hodges, Summerfield, Clayton, Evans, Anderson*; sub Rowbotham J
Plymouth play an offside game but Heath breaks through bravely heading past Crudgington from Daly's cross. Daly is still troubled by injury and departs after thirty mins but has done enough. Ian Allinson says he is ready to leave. A much better show stretches the unbeaten run to six

14 · A BLACKBURN · 17/10 — L 0-2
Scorers: Sellars 28, Garner 52. Ref: G Courtney
City: Fox, Dixon, Carr, Parkin, Bould, Berry, Ford, Parkin, Hemming, Shaw*, Heath; sub Heath
Blackburn: Gennoe, Price, Sulley, Barker*, Hendry, Mail, Miller, Reid, Patterson, Garner, Sellars; sub Ainscow
Another shoddy performance. Mills is down to just 11 fit pros and introduces a sweeper system but Scott Sellars is allowed to angle a left-foot shot home. Garner rifles in via an upright. With no threat at the other end Mills' patience snaps and he vows to put players on the transfer list.

15 · A SWINDON · 20/10 — L 0-3
Scorers: Quinn 1, White 60, 71. Ref: A Ward
City: Fox, Dixon, Mills^, Talbot!, Parkin^, Berry, Ford, Parkin, Shaw, Daly, Heath; sub Shaw
Swindon: Digby, Hockaday, King^, Kamara, Calderwood, Bamber, White, Quinn, Foley, Barnard; sub Henry
Brian Talbot is sent off for retaliation on 34 mins. Stoke are already one down to Jimmy Quinn's free-kick. Steve White swoops to convert two crosses as City fall apart. Fox makes a great save to deny him a hat-trick. Steve Foley also manages to miss two open goals. A miserable night

16 · H ASTON VILLA · 24/10 — D 0-0
Ref: I Hemley
City: Fox, Dixon, Carr, Talbot, Hemming, Berry, Ford, Daly, Morgan, Shaw, Heath
Aston Villa: Spink, Gage, Gallacher, Lillis, Sims, Keown, Birch, Aspinall*, McInally, Hunt D, Walters; sub Shaw
Stoke show some pride and passion to hold Villa to a draw. Shaw hits the post, obviously missing his partner Nicky Morgan. Villa's only clear opening comes when Hemming miskicks and McNally fires wide. The match peters out as Villa fail to find the key to City's resolute defence.

17 · A BARNSLEY · 31/10 — L 2-5
Scorers: Shaw 62, Ford 75 [Lowndes 77] / MacD'ld 30, Wylde 40, 48, Dobbin 70. Ref: T Holbrook
City: Fox, Dixon, Parkin, Talbot, Hemming, Berry, Ford, Daly, Morgan, Shaw, Heath; sub Saunders
Barnsley: Baker, Joyce, Cross, Thomas, Futcher, Wylde, Dobbin, Lowndes, MacDonald*, Gray; sub Foreman
In an enthralling encounter Shaw's close-range finish and Ford's smart turn and shot keep City in the hunt. MacDonald's cracker is the best of Allan Clarke's men's goals. Dobbin heads in unmarked. Barnsley win it as Lowndes and Wylde net from close in. 'Unprofessional' says Mills.

18 · H WEST BROM · 7/11 — W 3-0
Scorers: Berry 16p, Heath 45, Parkin 77. Ref: L Dilkes
City: Fox, Dixon, Carr, Talbot, Hemming, Berry, Ford, Daly, Morgan, Shaw, Heath*; sub Saunders
West Brom: Naylor, Palmer, Burrows, Hogg, Reilly, Kelly, Lynex, Williamson*, Gray, Bradley^, Morley; subs Robson/Anderson
Parkin stars as City finally find some form. Berry converts a penalty after Hogg handles Shaw's cross. Heath races clear to round Naylor. Steve Lynex wastes a penalty for Ron Atkinson's team after Berry's push (58 mins). Parkin blasts home right footed to send the Boothen End wild.

19 · A CRYSTAL PALACE · 14/11 — L 0-2
Scorers: Bright 63, Wright 84. Ref: J Martin
City: Fox, Dixon, Carr, Daly*, Hemming, Berry, Ford, Daly*, Morgan, Shaw, Heath; sub Talbot
Crystal Palace: Wood, Stebbing, Burke, Pardew, Nebbeling, O'Doherty, Redfearn, Thomas, Bright, Wright, Barber; sub Talbot
City are beaten by the 27 goal Wright/Bright partnership. Bright admits to nudging Berry before beating him to a header for the opener. Wright arches backwards to angle a header inside the post. Steve Coppell's men easily cope with what little City have to offer. Mills wants new blood.

20 · H MILLWALL · 21/11 — L 1-2
Scorers: Heath 36 / Cascarino 57, 83. Ref: C Trussell
City: Barrett, Dixon, Parkin, Talbot, Hemming, Berry, Ford, Saunders, Morgan, Shaw, Heath; sub Carr
Millwall: Horne, Salman, Coleman, Stevens, Walker, McLeary, Byrne, Sheringham, Cascarino, Carter; sub Carr
City start well and Heath races on to Gerry Daly's through-ball to lift over Horne. Tony Ford's inexperience as a stand-in centre-half shows and Cascarino nods in after picking up his weak header. Battling Millwall score a second simple headed goal to continue their charge up the table.

21 · A SHREWSBURY · 28/11 — W 3-0
Scorers: Dixon 22, Ford 25, Saunders 32. Ref: M Reeves
City: Barrett, Dixon, Carr, Talbot, Hemming*, Berry, Ford, Daly, Saunders, Shaw, Heath; sub Holmes
Shrewsbury: Perks, Green, Williams B, Priest*, Moyes, Linighan, Milligan, Steele, Brown, Robinson, Tester; sub Leonard
1,500 away fans see Dixon glance Ford's corner home. Ford then crashes home a classic volley. Saunders hits his goal so hard it flies back out off the stanchion. McNally hits the bar for managerless Shrews. Andy Holmes is impressive on his debut coming on for the injured Hemming.

22 · H OLDHAM · 8/12 — D 2-2
Scorers: Shaw 14, Heath 77 / Bunn 29, Henry 46p. Ref: V Callow
City: Fox, Dixon, Carr, Talbot*, Holmes, Berry, Ford, Daly, Morgan, Shaw, Heath; sub Heath
Oldham: Gorton, Irwin, Barrett, Flynn, Linighan, Milligan, Kelly J, Henry A, Bunn*, Wright, Ritchie; sub Barlow
Stoke are second best but salvage a point. Shaw opens the scoring with a running header but Joe Royle's men doggedly fight back with Bunn's fierce cross-shot and Henry's penalty after Parkin fouls Kelly. Morgan hits the bar before Heath heads Daly's probing cross past Gorton.

23 · A MIDDLESBROUGH · 12/12 — L 0-2
Scorers: Hamilton 46, Slaven 72. Ref: J Penrose
City: Barrett, Dixon, Carr, Talbot*, Bould, Berry, Ford, Henry, Morgan, Shaw, Heath; sub Heath
Middlesbrough: Pears, Glover, Cooper, Mowbray, Laws, Pallister, Slaven, Kernaghan, Hamilton, Kerr, Ripley*; sub Parkinson
The referee is the only person not to see Kernaghan knock the ball out of Barrett's hands. Hamilton prods in and a goal is given. Pandemonium as even mild mannered Sammy Chung flies out of the dugout. When it dies down Slaven makes sure with a lucky bounce off the bumpy pitch.

BARCLAYS DIVISION 2 — SEASON 1987-88

Manager: Mick Mills

Each playing position lists the Stoke player; the opponent in that position is shown in *italics*.

No	Date	Att / Pos / Pt	F-A	H-T	Scorers, Times, and Referees	1	2	3	4	5	6	7	8	9	10	11	subs used
24	H READING 19/12	6,968 / 14 W / 23 30	4-2	0-0	Morgan 52, Talbot 72, Henry 82, Moran 59, Gilkes 80 [Ford 85]. Ref: S Lodge	Barratt *Francis*	Dixon *Bailie*	Carr *Gilkes*	Parkin *Beavan*	Bould *Hicks*	Berry *Curle*	Ford *Williams*	Henry *Madden**	Morgan *Tait*	Shaw* *Moran*	Heath *White*	Talbot / Horrix
25	A HUDDERSFIELD 26/12	9,510 / 14 W / 21 33	3-0	0-0	Morgan 55, Parkin 75, Shaw 84. Ref: E Parker	Barratt *Martin*	Dixon *Trevitt*	Carr *Bray*	Parkin *Banks*	Bould *Mitchell*	Berry *Walford^*	Ford *Ward*	Henry *Hutchings*	Morgan *Cooper*	Shaw *May*	Heath *Cork*	Shearer/Brown
26	H MANCHESTER C 28/12	18,020 / 15 L / 7 33	1-3	0-2	Berry 82p. Stewart 24, 44, Brightwell 55. Ref: J Ashworth	Barratt *Nixon*	Dixon *Brightwell*	Carr *Hinchcliffe*	Parkin *Clements*	Bould *Lake*	Berry *Redmond*	Ford *White*	Henry *Stewart*	Morgan *Varadi*	Shaw *McNab*	Heath* *Simpson*	Saunders / Scott
27	H IPSWICH 1/1	9,976 / 15 L / 6 33	1-2	1-1	Morgan 8. Lowe 40, D'Avray 52. Ref: D Scott	Barratt *Hamilton*	Dixon *Yallop*	Carr *Harbey*	Parkin *Atkins*	Bould *Humes*	Berry *Cranson*	Ford *Lowe*	Henry* *Brennan*	Morgan *D'Avray*	**Stainrod*** *Dozzell*	Shaw *Stockwell*	Talbot/Daly
28	A BRADFORD C 2/1	12,223 / 14 W / 6 36	**4-1**	3-0	Morgan 10, Ford 14, Dixon 39, Ormondroyd 69 [Henry 64]. Ref: K Breen	Barratt *Tomlinson*	Dixon *Mitchell*	Carr *Ormondroyd*	Talbot *McCall*	Bould *Oliver*	Berry *Evans*	Ford *Hendrie^*	Henry *Sinnott*	Morgan *Leonard*	Stainrod *Palin*	Parkin *Ellis*	Staunton
29	H BIRMINGHAM 16/1	10,076 / 14 W / 15 39	3-1	1-1	Talbot 7, Henry 82, 87. Kennedy 10. Ref: R Milford	Barratt *Hansbury*	Dixon *Ranson*	Carr *Dicks*	Talbot *Roberts*	Bould *Overson*	Berry *Williams*	Ford *Bremner*	Henry *Childs*	Morgan* *Kennedy**	Stainrod *Trewick*	Heath^ *Handysides*	Shaw/Daly … Rees
30	H SHEFFIELD UTD 6/2	9,344 / 12 W / 18 42	1-0	0-0	Saunders 63. Ref: T Fitzharris	Barratt *Segers*	Parkin *Barnsley*	Carr *Pike*	Saunders *Todd*	Bould *Stancliffe*	**Beeston** *Smith*	Ford *Duffield*	Henry *Phillskirk^*	Shaw *Cadette**	Stainrod *Frain*	Heath *Beagrie*	Morris/Downes
31	A HULL 13/2	6,424 / 12 D / 8 43	0-0	0-0	Ref: M Peck	Barratt *Norman*	Parkin *Palmer*	Carr *Heard*	Saunders *Jobson*	Bould *Skipper*	Beeston *Parker*	Ford *Roberts*	Henry *Payton*	Shaw *Dyer*	Stainrod *Askew*	Heath *Williams**	Saville
32	H LEEDS 23/2	10,129 / 10 W / 7 46	2-1	1-0	Heath 35, Berry 90. Pearson 55. Ref: A Seville	Barratt *Day*	Beeston *Williams*	Carr *Adams*	Parkin *Aizlewood*	Bould *Ashurst*	Berry *Haddock*	Ford *Batty*	Henry *Sheridan*	Shaw *Pearson*	Stainrod* *Davison*	Heath *Snodin*	Morgan
33	A BOURNEMOUTH 27/2	6,871 / 10 D / 19 47	0-0	0-0	Ref: D Elleray	Barratt *Peyton*	Beeston *Langan*	Carr *Morrell*	Parkin *Brooks**	Bould *Williams*	Berry *Whitlock*	Ford *O'Driscoll*	Henry *Newson*	Morgan* *Aylott*	Stainrod *Cooke*	Heath *Close*	Shaw … Armstrong
34	H BLACKBURN 5/3	14,098 / 9 W / 2 50	2-1	1-0	Morgan 14, Shaw 76. Price 50. Ref: K Cooper	Barratt *Gennoe*	Beeston *Price*	Carr *Sulley*	Parkin *Barker*	Bould *Hendry*	Berry *Mackay*	Ford *Dawson*	Henry *Reid*	Morgan *Archibald*	Shaw *Garner*	Heath *Sellars*	Shaw

Match reports

24 — Reading: In a bruising game Shaw is kicked while on the ground and Dixon is caught badly by Tait. City keep their heads. Morgan heads in and Talbot, influential, sweeps home from 10 yards. Reading peg City back, but Henry buries a spectacular left-foot volley. Ford's fierce drive clinches it.

25 — Huddersfield: City weather the early storm. Cork miskicks with the goal gaping. Dixon pulls off a last-ditch tackle on Hutchings. Once Morgan heads home Henry's free-kick there is only one winner. Parkin scores with a rasping low drive before Shaw taps in Ford's cross. An excellent performance.

26 — Manchester C: Stoke are never at the races against Mel Machin's talented, young Man City side. The Blues plunder three classy goals. Paul Stewart rounds off two great moves. Ian Brightwell heads home. Berry's penalty, as Shaw is fouled, is academic. Heath breaks his jaw and is out for three weeks.

27 — Ipswich: City sit back after Morgan's left-footed finish to Berry's flick-on. Bobby Ferguson's Ipswich play accurate flowing football. Stoke just cannot match them. David Lowe turns in Humes' header. Mich D'Avray hammers home from five yards. Lowe also has a goal disallowed for offside.

28 — Bradford C: What a difference a day makes! Stoke profit from dreadful Bantams defending. Morgan nips in as the defence stands static then Tomlinson lets Ford's effort slip between his legs. Dixon, inspirational down the right, cuts in to crack home and Tony Henry scores a splendid goal. Brilliant.

29 — Birmingham: In a tight game Talbot curls home Heath's cross before Kennedy latches on to Overson's knockdown. Berry has an overhead kick saved. Stoke take their time to break down Birmingham's five-man defence. Tony Henry follows up Stainrod's shot and then heads in Talbot's free-kick.

30 — Sheffield Utd: Carl Beeston wins a two-year battle with glandular fever to play an important role filling in at centre-half. In a tight match Stoke pip the Blades under new boss Dave Bassett. Saunders accepts a return pass from Ford to crack home the decider. Lee Dixon is sold to Arsenal for £300,000.

31 — Hull: A dour game with Hull keeping things tight under orders from Brian Horton having just been thrashed at Bournemouth. Tony Norman's goal is never under threat Stoke's midfield struggles for fluidity. Stainrod has an overhead kick saved on the line. Shaw's free-kick whizzes just over.

32 — Leeds: Heath heads home unmarked at the far post before Pearson beats Barrett to a cross to equalise. Berry, on his return from suspension, stoops to force in Bould's flick-on in added time. 'What a beauty' he grins! Sheridan hits the woodwork. Snodin fires just wide for Billy Bremner's men.

33 — Bournemouth: City dominate but waste the best chances. Stainrod's goalless spell drags on as he freezes when put clean through. Gerry Peyton touches over a great Ford effort. Bournemouth field new record signing £90,000 Shaun Close but he is anonymous. Berry and Bould snuff out Aylott's threat.

34 — Blackburn: City deservedly beat promotion-chasing Rovers. Don Mackay's men have a large following who see Bould foul Price but it is given outside the box. Morgan fires home. Price whips a low shot past Barratt. Parkin's 40-yard run sets up Shaw who curls home brilliantly. 17 points from 21.

Stoke City season results (matches 35–44)

No.	Venue	Opponent	Date	Att.	Pos.	Res	Pts	Opp pos	Score (FT)	(HT)	Scorers / Opp scorers	Referee
35	A	PLYMOUTH	12/3	8,749	10	L	50	14	0-3	0-2	Tynan 30, 32, Uzzell 85	Ref: J Carter
36	A	LEICESTER	16/3	10,502	10	D	51	16	1-1	0-1	Shaw 72 / Mauchlen 43	Ref: K Morton
37	H	BARNSLEY	19/3	8,029	9	W	54	15	3-1	3-1	Daly 53, Henry 60, Hemming 78 / Rees 69	Ref: P Harrison
38	A	ASTON VILLA	26/3	20,392	8	W	57	1	1-0	0-0	Heath 71	Ref: A Buksh
39	A	WEST BROM	2/4	12,144	8	L	57	18	0-2	0-1	Gray 25, Talbot 90p	Ref: P Foakes
40	H	CRYSTAL PALACE	4/4	9,613	9	D	58	6	1-1	1-0	Shaw 43 / Bright 58	Ref: F Roberts
41	A	OLDHAM	9/4	6,505	9	L	58	10	1-5	1-2	Heath 23 [Callaghan 90] / Palmer 3, 71, 83, Ritchie 33.	Ref: K Lupton
42	H	SWINDON	23/4	6,293	8	W	61	12	1-0	1-0	Stainrod 16	Ref: J Deakin
43	A	MILLWALL	30/4	12,636	10	L	61	1	0-2	0-0	Sheringham 52, O'Callaghan 63p	Ref: R Gifford
44	H	SHREWSBURY	2/5	7,452	11	D	62	19	1-1	0-1	Stainrod 59 / Brown 28	Ref: K Hackett

Average: Home 10,469 Away 8,591

35 — A PLYMOUTH 12/3
Stoke: Barrett, Beeston, Carr, Parkin, Bould, Berry, Ford, Henry, Morgan*, Shaw, Hackett^ Heath/Hemming
Plymouth: Cherry, Brimacombe, Uzzell, Burrows, Marker, Smith, Hodges^, Matthews, Tynan, Evans*, Summerfield Clayton/Anderson
A disaster from start to end. New signing Gary Hackett plays despite a pain-killing injection and breaks down. Morgan limps off to leave Stoke without a recognised striker. Tommy Tynan pounces twice from close range to reach 200 career league goals for Dave Smith's Plymouth side.

36 — A LEICESTER 16/3
Stoke: Barrett, Hemming, Carr, Parkin, Bould, Berry, Ford, Henry, Shaw, Beeston, Heath
Leicester: Cooper, Mauchlen, Morgan, Osman, Walsh, Ramsey, McAllister, Cross, Newell, Reid, Weir
With only one fit striker Stoke play a defensive system and in a physical game Berry and Bould deal well with Leicester's direct approach. The Foxes go ahead when Ally Mauchlen's 25-yarder beats Barrett. Beeston, playing in midfield, sparks the move for Shaw's close-range equaliser.

37 — H BARNSLEY 19/3
Stoke: Barrett, Hemming, Carr, Parkin, Bould, Berry*, Ford, Henry, Shaw, Beeston, Heath Daly
Barnsley: Baker, Joyce, Cross, Thomas, McGugan, Futcher, Currie, Blair, Lowndes, Beresford, Rees
Berry's injury brings the introduction of Gerry Daly who sparks City into life. He picks up Henry's flick to fire low past Clive Baker and then sets up Henry. Hemming coolly finishes after Shaw's shot is blocked. Even with new signing Andy Blair, Allan Clarke's Tykes are never in it.

38 — A ASTON VILLA 26/3
Stoke: Barrett, Parkin, Carr, Daly*, Bould, Beeston, Ford, Henry, Shaw, Puckett, Heath Stainrod
Villa: Spink, Gage, Gallacher, Gray A^, Evans, Keown, Birch, McInally, Thompson* Gray S, Platt Daley/Lillis
City are down to the last 11 fit pros after Gerry Daly is carried off on 15 mins. Beeston is superb as a gritty defensive display frustrates leaders Villa. David Puckett hooks off the line from Alan McInally. Heath slides the ball under Nigel Spink to complete a perfect smash and grab raid.

39 — A WEST BROM 2/4
Stoke: Barrett, Parkin, Carr, Puckett, Bould, Beeston, Henry, Stainrod*, Shaw, Heath, Hemming
West Brom: Naylor, Hodson, Cowdrill, Talbot, North, Dyson, Hopkins, Phillips, Gray*, Palmer, Anderson Robson
City are always second best against Ron Atkinson's relegation escapees. In the dazzling sunshine Andy Gray, who Carr has lost after bombing forward, sweeps home a Robert Hopkins cross. Ex-Stokie Brian Talbot is delighted to bang home a penalty after Beeston fouls Carlton Palmer.

40 — H CRYSTAL PALACE 4/4
Stoke: Barrett, Parkin, Carr, Beeston, Bould, Berry*, Ford, Henry, Shaw*, Puckett, Heath Gibbons
Palace: Suckling, Finnigan, Burke, Pennyfather Nebbeling, Cannon, Redfearn* Thomas^, Bright, Wright, Berber Salako/Pardew
Graham Shaw's 30-yard volley rockets past a bemused Perry Suckling. Stoke relax after the break and play-off chasing Palace look dangerous. Mark Bright applies the finishing touch to Thomas' left-wing centre. City drop two more home points. No chance of making the play-offs now.

41 — A OLDHAM 9/4
Stoke: Barrett, Parkin, Carr, Beeston*, Bould, Berry, Ford, Henry, Shaw, Puckett, Heath Fowler
Oldham: Rhodes, Irwin, Barrett, Flynn, Callaghan, Barlow, Donachie* Bunn, Palmer, Wright, Ritchie Kelly N
City capitulate to Roger Palmer's hat-trick of superb left-footed finishes. Ex-Stoke player Aaron Callaghan rubs it in with the last goal. Heath's header after Berry hits the bar is irrelevant. YTS lad Lee Fowler makes his debut replacing the injured Carl Beeston. Stoke hate plastic pitches.

42 — H SWINDON 23/4
Stoke: Barrett, Parkin, Carr, Bould, Berry, Ford, Henry, Shaw, Stainrod*, Puckett, Heath Hemming
Swindon: Digby, Hockaday, King, McLoughlin Parkin, Gittens, Bamber, Quinn, Barnes, Foley, Wegerle* White
Swindon's shooting is unbelievably bad. Quinn hits the bar. Barrett saves from White, McLaughlin and Quinn. Barrett is even left stranded but the shot still goes wide. Stainrod grabs a long overdue first strike. Lou Macari is furious. Mills says he has never been defeated by a win before.

43 — A MILLWALL 30/4
Stoke: Barrett, Parkin, Carr*, Puckett, Bould, Hemming, Ford, Henry, Shaw, Stainrod, Heath Lewis
Millwall: Horne, Stevens, Coleman, Hurlock, Wood, McLeary, Carter, Briley, Cascarino, Sheringham, O'Callaghan
Millwall brush City aside with a dominant display. Sheringham bundles the ball, Carr and himself into the net. Kevin Lewis handles nine mins after coming on for disjointed City. George Graham's Lions roar on to automatic promotion. A summer rebuilding programme is on the cards.

44 — H SHREWSBURY 2/5
Stoke: Barrett, Parkin, Carr*, Ware, Bould, Hemming, Ford, Henry, Shaw, Puckett, Heath
Shrewsbury: Perks, Green, Williams B, Priest*, Pratley, Linighan, Kasule, McNally, Geddis, Brown, Bell Melrose
City, with only ten fit pros, include Paul Ware (aged 16). Michael Brown atones for an earlier miss by heading home Kasule's cross. Stainrod heads home after Perks fumbles Shaw's centre. Ian McNeill's Shrews avoid relegation. A muted finale to a season that never really got going.

BARCLAYS DIVISION 2 (CUP-TIES)   Manager: Mick Mills   SEASON 1987-88

Littlewoods Cup

	Att	F-A	H-T	Scorers, Times, and Referees	1	2	3	4	5	6	7	8	9	10	11	subs used
2:1 H GILLINGHAM 22/9 14 W	7,198 3:2	2-0	1-0	Shaw 18, 65 — Ref: D Hedges	Fox	Dixon	Carr	Daly	Bould	Berry	Allinson	Ford	Morgan	Shaw	Heath	Eves
					Kite	*Haylock*	*Pearce*	*Quow*	*West*	*Greenall*	*Pritchard*	*Shearer**	*Lovell*	*Elsey*	*Smith**	
2:2 A GILLINGHAM 6/10 10 W	5,039 3:12	1-0	1-0	Morgan 12 — Ref: R Lewis (Stoke win 3-0 on aggregate)	Fox	Dixon	Carr	Parkin	Bould	Berry	Ford	Daly	Morgan*	Shaw	Heath	Eves/Lillis
					Kite	*Haylock*	*Pearce*	*Quow*	*West*	*Berry*	*Pritchard*	*Shearer^*	*Lovell*	*Elsey*	*Smith**	
3 H NORWICH 27/10 10 W	8,603 1:18	2-1	2-0	Daly 14, Talbot 17 — Bruce 76 — Ref: J Moules	Fox	Dixon	Carr	Talbot	Hemming	Berry	Ford	Parkin	Shaw	Daly	Heath	Crook/Butterworth
					Gunn	*Culverhouse*	*Elliott*	*Bruce*	*Phelan*	*Ratcliffe*	*Fox*	*Drinkell*	*Biggins*	*Williams**	*Bowen^*	
4 A ARSENAL 17/11 14 L	30,058 1:1	0-3	0-1	O'Leary 18, Rocastle 48, Richards'n 84 — Ref: K Hackett	Barrett	Dixon	Parkin	Daly	Hemming	Berry	Ford	Saunders	Morgan	Shaw	Heath	
					Lukic	*Thomas*	*Sansom*	*Williams*	*O'Leary*	*Adams*	*Rocastle*	*Davis*	*Smith*	*Groves**	*Richardson*	*Hayes*

FA Cup

	Att	F-A	H-T	Scorers, Times, and Referees	1	2	3	4	5	6	7	8	9	10	11	subs used
3 H LIVERPOOL 9/1 14 D	31,979 1:1	0-0	0-0	Ref: T Mills	Barrett	Dixon	Carr	Talbot	Bould	Berry	Ford	Henry	Morgan	Stainrod*	Parkin	Shaw
					Hooper	*Gillespie*	*Lawrenson*	*Nicol*	*Whelan*	*Hansen*	*Beardsley*	*Aldridge*	*Houghton*	*Barnes*	*McMahon*	
3R A LIVERPOOL 12/1 14 L	39,147 1:1	0-1	0-1	Beardsley 9 — Ref: T Mills	Barrett	Dixon	Carr	Talbot	Bould	Berry	Ford	Henry	Morgan	Stainrod*	Parkin	Shaw
					Hooper	*Gillespie*	*Lawrenson*	*Nicol*	*Whelan*	*Hansen*	*Beardsley*	*Aldridge*	*Houghton**	*Barnes*	*McMahon*	*Johnston*

2:1 GILLINGHAM: Graham Shaw poaches two close-range goals as his partnership with Morgan develops. Stoke are in third gear after the second goal and cannot press home their advantage. Keith Peacock's Gills fail to test Fox. The boo-boys target new signing Ian Allinson, who looks very disinterested.

2:2 GILLINGHAM: A Sunday morning meeting has cleared the air and Steve Bould's dominance inspires the team to keep Gillingham at bay. City kill off the Gills through Nicky Morgan's far-post header. On Stoke's first ever visit to Priestfield, Morgan is injured and an x-ray reveals a dislocated shoulder.

3 NORWICH: Stoke threaten to overrun the Canaries as Daly's 25-yard shot zips along the wet turf and in off the post. Talbot perfectly times his run to meet Shaw's centre. Bruce heads home and Daly clears off the line but it is Ken Brown who wants to sell his team rather than Mills after the match.

4 ARSENAL: Stoke look comfortable until Barrett drops a corner for O'Leary to score. He makes up for it by saving Thomas' 25th-minute penalty, which is retaken but the shaken Thomas skies it. City battle hard but create little. Richardson rounds off a good Thomas and Hayes move for the third.

3 LIVERPOOL: City throttle the Anfield goal machine. Carr closes down Liverpool's right flank. Barnes and Beardsley both test Barrett. Graham Shaw nearly steals it, but he hesitates when put clean through as he thinks he is offside allowing Hooper to close him down. Best performance of the season.

3R LIVERPOOL: It's the Scott Barrett show as his wonderful display denies Liverpool time and again. Barnes, Whelan and Aldridge are all denied by wonderful saves. It takes a mis-hit from Peter Beardsley to sink brave Stoke. He drives his shot straight into the ground and it bounces over Barrett

Pos	Team	P	Home					Away					Pts
			W	D	L	F	A	W	D	L	F	A	
1	Millwall	44	15	3	4	45	23	10	4	8	27	29	82
2	Aston Villa	44	9	7	6	31	21	13	5	4	37	20	78
3	Middlesbro *	44	15	4	3	44	16	7	8	7	19	20	78
4	Bradford C	44	14	3	5	49	26	8	8	6	25	28	77
5	Blackburn	44	12	8	2	38	22	9	6	7	30	30	77
6	Crys Palace	44	16	3	3	50	21	6	6	10	36	38	75
7	Leeds	44	14	4	4	37	18	5	8	9	24	33	69
8	Ipswich	44	14	3	5	38	17	5	6	11	23	35	66
9	Manchester C	44	11	4	7	50	28	8	4	10	30	32	65
10	Oldham	44	13	4	5	43	27	5	7	10	29	37	65
11	STOKE	44	12	6	4	34	22	5	5	12	16	35	62
12	Swindon	44	10	7	5	43	25	6	4	12	30	35	59
13	Leicester	44	12	5	5	35	25	4	6	12	19	41	59
14	Barnsley	44	11	4	7	42	32	4	8	10	19	30	57
15	Hull	44	10	8	4	32	22	4	7	11	22	38	57
16	Plymouth	44	12	4	6	44	26	4	4	14	21	41	56
17	Bournemouth	44	7	7	8	36	30	6	3	13	20	38	49
18	Shrewsbury	44	7	8	7	23	22	4	8	10	19	32	49
19	Birmingham	44	7	9	6	20	24	4	6	12	21	42	48
20	West Brom	44	8	7	7	29	26	4	4	14	21	43	47
21	Sheffield U **	44	8	6	8	27	28	5	1	16	18	46	46
22	Reading	44	5	7	10	20	25	5	5	12	24	45	42
23	Huddersfield	44	4	6	12	20	38	2	4	16	21	62	28
		1012	246	127	133	830	559	133	127	246	559	830	1391

* promoted after play-offs
** relegated after play-offs

Appearances / Goals

Player	Lge	Sub	LC	Sub	FAC	Sub	Lge	LC	FAC	Tot
							Goals			
Allinson, Ian	6	3	1	1						
Barrett, Scott	27		1		2					
Beeston, Carl	12									
Berry, George	35	1	4		2		5			5
Bould, Steve	30		2		2					
Carr, Cliff	39	2	3		2					
Daly, Gerry	16	5	4				1		1	2
Dixon, Lee	29		4		2		2			2
Ford, Tony	44		4		2		7			7
Fowler, Lee		1								
Fox, Peter	17		3							
Gibbons, Ian		1								
Hackett, Gary	1									
Heath, Phil	32	7	4				8			8
Hemming, Chris	20	4	2				1			1
Henry, Tony	22				2		5			5
Holmes, Andy	1	1								
Lewis, Kevin		1								
Mills, Mick	1									
Morgan, Nicky	27		3		2		5		1	6
Parkin, Steve	42	1	3		2		3			3
Puckett, David	7									
Saunders, Carl	15	2	1				3			3
Shaw, Graham	30	3	4			2	6		2	8
Stainrod, Simon	11	1			2		2			2
Talbot, Brian	19	3	1		2		2		1	3
Ware, Paul	1									
28 Players used	484	37	44	1	22	2	50		5	55

Odds & ends

Double wins: (1) Reading.
Double losses: (3) Ipswich, Manchester C, Millwall.

Won from behind: (0).
Lost from in front: (2) Ipswich (h), Millwall (h).

High spots: 7 games without defeat up to February.
Winning at Villa Park for the first time since 1965.
Beating high-flying Norwich in the Littlewoods Cup.
Having the best chance of the game in the first Liverpool match.

Low spots: A tame end of season.
Losing in all three cups to the defeated finalists.
The continuing plastic pitch nightmare.
The lack of a goal-scoring forward after an early injury to Nicky Morgan.

Player of the Year: Steve Parkin.
Ever-presents: (1) Tony Ford.
Hat-tricks: (0).
Leading scorer: (8) Phil Heath, Graham Shaw.

BARCLAYS DIVISION 2

SEASON 1988-89

Manager: Mick Mills

No	Date	Att	Pos	Pt	F-A	H-T	Scorers, Times, and Referees	1	2	3	4	5	6	7	8	9	10	11	subs used
1 H IPSWICH	27/8	8,639		D 1	1-1	1-0	Kamara 43 / Humes 80 / Ref: A Seville	Fox / *Forrest*	Gidman / *Yallop*	Parkin / *Hill*	**Kamara** / *Zondervan*	Beeston / *Humes*	Henry / *Linighan*	Hackett* / *Lowe*	Ford / *Dazzell*	Shaw / *D'Avray**	Saunders / *Atkinson*	**Beagrie** / *Wark*	Morgan / *Milton*
2 A BRADFORD C	29/8	11,918		D 2	0-0	0-0	Ref: K Lupton	Fox / *Tomlinson*	Gidman / *Mitchell*	Parkin / *Goddard !*	Kamara* / *Banks*	Beeston^ / *Oliver*	Henry / *Evans*	Hackett / *Thomas*	Ware / *Sinnott*	Morgan / *Ormondroyd*	Saunders / *Kennedy*	Beagrie / *Jewell**	Carr/Shaw / *Leonard*
3 A BARNSLEY	3/9	5,682	15	L 2	0-1	0-0	Agnew 86 / Ref: E Parker	Fox / *Baker*	Carr / *Beresford^*	Parkin / *Joyce*	Kamara / *Thomas*	Gidman / *Dobbin*	Henry / *Futcher*	Hackett / *Lowndes*	Ford / *Agnew*	Morgan / *Cooper*	Saunders / *Currie !*	Beagrie / *Clarke**	Broddle/MacDonald
4 H BLACKBURN	10/9	8,624	17	L 2	0-1	0-1	Hendry 5 / Ref: H Taylor	Fox / *Gennoe*	Gidman / *Atkins*	Carr / *Millar*	Kamara / *Finnigan*	Beeston / *Hendry*	Henry / *Mail*	Hackett / *Miller*	Ford / *Hildersley**	Shaw / *Gayle*	Saunders / *Garner*	Beagrie / *Sellars^*	Ainscow/Dawson S
5 A PLYMOUTH	17/9	7,823	23	L 2	0-4	0-2	Tynan 35, 45, 64, Marker 54 / Ref: W Burge	Fox / *Cherry*	Carr / *Brown*	Parkin / *Cooper*	Kamara / *Burrows*	Beeston / *Marker*	Henry / *Smith*	Hackett / *Plummer*	Ford / *Matthews*	Stainrod^ / *Tynan*	Saunders / *McCarthy*	Beagrie / *Brimacombe*	Morgan/Shaw
6 H PORTSMOUTH	20/9	7,025	23	D 3	2-2	1-1	Stainrod 28, Hackett 90 / Horne 17, Aspinall 85 / Ref: W Flood	Fox / *Knight*	Carr / *Sandford*	Parkin / *Hardyman*	Kamara / *Dillon*	Hemming / *Hogg*	Henry / *Whitehead*	Hackett / *Chamberlain*	Saunders / *Horne*	Stainrod / *Aspinall*	Stainrod / *Connor*	Beagrie / *Kelly*	
7 A WALSALL	24/9	7,795	19	W 6	2-1	1-1	Morgan 4, Stainrod 75 / Callaghan 23 / Ref: P Don	Fox / *Barber*	Carr / *Dornan*	Carr / *Taylor M*	Kamara / *Shakespeare^ Forbes*	Hemming /	Henry / *Hart*	Hackett / *Mower*	Saunders / *Goodwin**	Morgan / *Taylor A*	Stainrod / *Callaghan*	Beagrie / *Naughton*	Pritchard/Rees
8 H BOURNEMOUTH	1/10	7,485	16	W 9	2-1	1-0	Shaw 33, Beagrie 69 / Brooks 81 / Ref: R Gifford	Fox / *Peyton*	Hemming / *Newson*	Hemming / *Morrell*	Kamara / *Bond*	Higgins / *Williams*	Henry / *Whitlock^*	Hackett / *Richards*	Saunders / *Brooks*	Morgan* / *Aylott*	Stainrod / *Bishop*	Beagrie / *O'Connor*	Shaw / *Close*
9 H SHREWSBURY	4/10	8,075	16	D 10	0-0	0-0	Ref: R Bridges	Fox / *Green Ron*	Ford / *Williams W*	Beeston / *Green Rich'd*	Kamara / *Moyes*	Higgins / *Rougvie*	Henry / *Finley*	Hackett / *Bell*	Saunders / *McNally*	Shaw / *Geddis*	Stainrod / *Griffiths**	Beagrie / *Thomas*	Brown
10 A OLDHAM	8/10	6,600	19	D 11	2-2	0-2	Kamara 57, Stainrod 85 / Kelly 10, Bunn 44 / Ref: F Nixon	Fox / *Litchfield*	Ford / *Donachie*	Beeston / *Blundell*	Kamara / *Barrett*	Higgins / *Marshall*	Henry / *Williams**	Hackett / *Palmer*	Saunders / *Kelly*	Shaw* / *Bunn*	Stainrod / *Ritchie*	Beagrie / *Wright*	Gidman / *Cecere*
11 A LEICESTER	15/10	10,312	20	L 11	0-2	0-1	Newell 7, 51 / Ref: D Phillips	Barrett / *Cooper*	Ford / *Parris*	Carr / *Morgan*	Henry / *Groves*	Higgins / *Walsh*	Berry / *Brown*	Hackett / *Reid*	Ware* / *Cross*	Saunders / *Newell*	Stainrod / *McAllister*	Beagrie / *Weir^*	Shaw / *Williams*

Match commentaries

1. Stoke use up a whole season's worth of luck but still only draw. After Kamara's debut glancing header, Parkin clears off the line and Fox saves Zondervan's penalty after Saunders fouls Atkinson. D'Avray has a goal disallowed. Finally Tony Humes heads home unmarked from a corner.

2. Stoke again line up without a recognised centre-half and the giraffe-like Ormondroyd causes mayhem in the box. Stand-in skipper Henry flings himself to block Ian Banks' effort on the line. Karl Goddard is sent off (41 mins) for scything down Hackett. Kamara fractures his cheekbone.

3. Baker saves Morgan's overhead free-kick and half-volley as City start on top. Julian Broddle's arrival (50 mins) gives Allan Clarke's Barnsley impetus. Parkin and Carr both make last-ditch tackles. Agnew beats Fox from 18 yards. David Currie walks for foul and abusive. 'Mills out!'

4. Kamara and Fox leave the ball to each other and Hendry nips in to head in unchallenged. John Millar bicycle-kicks Hackett's cross off the line and also blocks Shaw's shot. Saunders hits the bar. Plenty of high crosses in but no-one to finish them off. Mills needs to spend the money fast.

5. Tommy Tynan's hat-trick is assisted by woeful defending. Four players fail to clear before he prods in a corner. Unmarked close-range tap-ins complete his first treble in four years for Ken Brown's team. Nicky Marker is allowed to run 50 yards for the killer third. Mills under pressure.

6. Bury centre-half Mark Higgins is seen watching from the stands. Mark Chamberlain returns to the Vic and sets up Barry Horne before his own effort is ruled out for Alan Ball's men. Stainrod powers in after Morgan flattens the keeper. Hackett cashes in when a blunder leaves him clear.

7. City just make it in time due to M6 traffic. Tommy Coakley's men have just hammered Birmingham 5-0. Alex Taylor beats the offside trap to set up Callaghan. Beagrie crosses for Morgan. Stainrod overhead-kicks Morgan's cross in from 12 yards. 3,500 Stokies revel in the first win.

8. Shaw gives City good mobility up front and whistles a fierce shot past Peyton from the angle. Beagrie scores an unbelievable goal, beating five players after picking the ball up in his own box and celebrating with a somersault. Kamara and Hackett dominate midfield. Mills is happy now.

9. Ian McNeil's five-man defence comfortably nullify Stoke's wing play. Saunders blasts a good chance over. Richard Green clears his own back-pass off the line. Fox foils David Geddis. More bookings, five, than shots on target. Nicky Morgan has knee surgery and is out for four months.

10. Kelly and Bunn score easily and Fox's foot denies Roger Palmer. City's remarkable comeback is sparked by Gidman's arrival (55 mins). Ford moves forward to prompt Kamara to fire home and Stainrod to lash in exultantly in the pouring rain. First point secured on an artificial surface.

11. David Pleat's Foxes snatch the lead against the run of play when Mike Newell cracks in a bobbling loose ball in the box. Beagrie has a dipping 30-yarder tipped over by Cooper. Newell heads in McAllister's centre and Stoke give up. Without Kamara the midfield is clueless. A bad loss.

This page presents a season's match-by-match results grid (Stoke City). Each match block lists: match number, venue (H/A), opponent, date, three figures, attendance, result (W/D/L), final score, half-time score, scorers, referee, the line-ups (Stoke player / opponent player per position), and a match report.

Player-position column headers (Stoke): **Fox · Ford · Carr · Kamara · Higgins · Berry · Hackett · Henry · Saunders · Stainrod · Beagie · (Roberts)**

---

12 · H · WATFORD · 22/10 — 17 / 2 / 14 — Att 7,878 — W 2-0 (1-0)
Scorers: Coton 29 (og), Beagie 84 · Ref: I Hendrick

Pos	Stoke	Opponent
Fox	Fox	Coton
Ford	Ford	Gibbs
Carr	Carr	Rostron
Kamara	Kamara	Jackett
Higgins	Higgins	H'worth^ / D'vid McClelland
Berry	Berry	McClelland
Hackett	Hackett	Sterling*
Henry	Henry	Wilkinson
Saunders	Saunders	Blissett
Stainrod	Stainrod	Porter
Beagie	Beagie	Holden
Roberts	Roberts	Roberts

Tony Coton's bizarre own-goal sees three of Steve Harrison's Hornets touch the ball after the last Stoke player. Long-ball Watford cannot deal with Kamara and Hackett's bite. Berry polices Luther Blissett. Beagie's neat sidestep and rapier-like finish round off a splendid team display.

---

13 · A · BIRMINGHAM · 25/10 — 14 / 24 / 17 — Att 6,262 — W 1-0 (0-0)
Scorers: Stainrod 73 · Ref: A Buksh

Opponents: Thomas, Roberts, Frain^, Atkins, Overson, Peer, Bremner, Childs, Richards, Robinson*, Wigley, Sturridge/Bird

An easy three points against inept Blues. Stainrod dives to head home the impressive Ford's cross. He also misses two other easy chances. Fox superbly saves Robinson's shot. Shaw is the target of the boo-boys and misses badly. Roberts flattens Beagie and is lucky to stay on the pitch.

---

14 · H · CRYSTAL PALACE · 29/10 — 11 / 8 / 20 — Att 9,118 — W 2-1 (1-0)
Scorers: Shaw 1, Henry 62 (Bright 46) · Ref: D Hedges

Opponents: Parkin, Pemberton, Burke*, Pardew, Hopkins, O'Reilly, Redfearn, Thomas, Bright, Salako, Berber, Shaw

Shaw nips in to score when Burke heads against his own bar after only 30 secs. Kamara and Pemberton have a running feud. In a vibrant game Palace level when Berry misjudges a long ball. Ford goes close twice. Henry turns in the winner when Parkin can only smother Stainrod's shot.

---

15 · A · SUNDERLAND · 5/11 — 10 / 8 / 21 — Att 17,923 — D 1-1 (1-0)
Scorers: Shaw 7 (Doyle 52) · Ref: P Tyldesley

Opponents: Hesford, Gray, Agboola*, Ord, MacPhail, Doyle, Owers, Armstrong, Gabbiadini, Whitehurst, Pascoe, Bennett

Shaw heads home Hackett's deep cross and Denis Smith's Sunderland lay siege. Berry twice heads off the line. Gabbiadini hits the post. Doyle finally cracks in off the bar. Hackett brings a brilliant save from Hesford. Lack of depth in the squad will soon show when suspensions kick in.

---

16 · H · HULL · 13/11 — 8 / 14 / 24 — Att 10,505 — W 4-0 (1-0)
Scorers: Henry 20, Beagie 48, Hackett 65, [Carr 74] · Ref: K Hackett

Opponents: Norman, Palmer, Jacobs, Warren, Jobson, Terry, Roberts^, De Mange, Moore, Edwards, Jenkinson, Payton

Another good performance as Eddie Gray's Hull are torn apart. Henry crashes into the roof of the net and Beagie dances through to score from 12 yards. Saunders takes a quick free-kick to set up Hackett. Cliff Carr notches his first goal, beating three players and firing home. Great stuff.

---

17 · H · SWINDON · 19/11 — 7 / 19 / 27 — Att 9,339 — W 2-1 (0-0)
Scorers: Berry 50p, Shaw 85 (Jones 55) · Ref: T West

Opponents: Digby, Hockaday, King, Jones, Parkin, Gittens, Foley, Calderwood, Henry, White, Barnes*, Shearer

Henry, Stainrod and Hackett all see chances go begging, but Stoke get a penalty when Gittens fouls Stainrod. Berry nets on his birthday! Jones takes time off man-marking Beagie to fire a superb 20-yard leveller. Carr strikes a post. Shaw heads the winner from Beagie's perfect centre.

---

18 · A · LEEDS · 26/11 — 8 / 14 / 27 — Att 19,933 — L 0-4 (0-2)
Scorers: Baird 20, 75, Davison 30, Sheridan 48p · Ref: M Reed

Opponents: Day, Aspin, Snodin, Aizlewood, Blake, Rennie, Whitlow, Sheridan*, Baird, Davison, Hilaire, Batty

An atrocious display. Carr and Berry tackle each other to allow Snodin to set up Baird. Higgins stops, expecting offside and Davison nets. Carr palms away a shot but the officials miss his indiscretion. Stoke fans sing 'Oh Maradona'! Fox fouls Davison for the penalty. Baird heads home.

---

19 · H · CHELSEA · 3/12 — 10 / 2 / 27 — Att 12,288 — L 0-3 (0-1)
Scorers: Roberts 6p, Wilson C 52, McAllister 72 · Ref: R Hart

Opponents: Freestone, Hall, Dorigo, Roberts, Lee, Wood, Nicholas !, Wilson K, Dixon, McAllister, Wilson C, Saunders/Beeston

Despite Nicholas's dismissal on five mins for butting Stainrod, Chelsea take the lead when Carr trips Kevin Wilson, although it seems outside the box. Clive Wilson nets after hapless Berry miscues. The frustrated Stainrod is sent off for hacking at McAllister. Stoke totally demoralised.

---

20 · A · BRIGHTON · 10/12 — 12 / 22 / 28 — Att 7,443 — D 1-1 (1-0)
Scorers: Beagie 26 (Gatting 79) · Ref: D Reeves

Opponents: Keeley, Chivers, Dublin, Wilkins, Beeston, Gatting, Bissett, Nelson, Curbishley, Bremner, Crumplin, Codner

City survive the Seagulls' onslaught as the ball pings around the area, hits the bar and even goes in, to be given offside. From nowhere Beagie latches onto a weak clearance to ram in. The defence holds out until Berry and Beeston combine to help on a corner for Steve Gatting to score.

---

21 · A · WEST BROM · 18/12 — 13 / 4 / 28 — Att 17,634 — L 0-6 (0-2)
Scorers: Robson 2, 86, Goodman 32, 84, [Paskin 70, 76] · Ref: G Aplin

Opponents: Naylor, Hodson, Albiston, Talbot, Whyte, North, Dobbins, Goodman, Robson, Paskin, Anderson (Stoke: Ford !, Gidman, Shaw)

Stoke are thrashed by Brian Talbot's Baggies. Gary Robson heads in unmarked to start proceedings. Paskin's double includes an acrobatic leap to make it four. Ford is sent off for kicking out after Anderson's vicious foul. Don Goodman also bags a brace. Mills' future is under a cloud.

---

22 · H · MANCHESTER C · 26/12 — 10 / 5 / 31 — Att 24,056 — W 3-1 (0-1)
Scorers: Kamara 48, Bamber 54, Berry 59p (Gleghorn 9) · Ref: K Barratt

Opponents: Dibble, Seagraves, Hinchcliffe, Gayle, Brightwell, Redmond, White^, Marley, Gleghorn, Biggins*, Beckford/Moulden (Stoke: Butler, Ware*, Bamber)

New signings John Butler and Dave Bamber inspire Stoke. High-flying Blues, cheered on by several thousand fans carrying inflatable bananas, see Gleghorn score. Bamber heads down for Kamara to blast in and then deflects his shot past Dibble. He is also upended for Berry's penalty.

---

23 · H · OXFORD · 31/12 — 10 / 18 / 34 — Att 10,562 — W 1-0 (1-0)
Scorers: Henry 24 · Ref: P Harrison

Opponents: Judge, Bardsley, Phillips J, Phillips L*, Lewis, Greenall, Smart, Foyle, Hill, Shelton, Simpson^, Heath/Leworthy (Stoke: Butler, Bamber, Ford)

An entertaining match sees both teams miss a host of chances. Beagie's jinking runs torment Mark Lawrenson's Oxford. Phil Heath replaces Les Phillips who dislocates a shoulder and is roundly booed. Henry heads the only goal from Ford's centre. The play-offs are still in reach?

BARCLAYS DIVISION 2 — Manager: Mick Mills — SEASON 1988-89

Match summary

(Pos = Stoke's league position; Res = result; figure in brackets after the opponent = opponent's league position, shown in italic in the original.)

No	Date	Opponents	Pos	Res	Att	Pt	F-A	H-T	Scorers, Times, and Referees
24	2/1	A BLACKBURN (3)	13	L	11,654	34	3-4	3-2	S'ders 20, 22, B'grie 44 (Hidersl'y 52) Atkins 17, Gayle 35p, Kennedy 50. Ref: W Flood
25	14/1	H BRADFORD C (18)	11	W	9,919	37	2-1	2-1	Hackett 14, Henry 34 Banks 38 Ref: G Ashby
26	21/1	A IPSWICH	13	L	14,692	37	1-5	0-0	Bamber 74 [Yallop 78] Baltacha 46, Dozzell 50, 79, Kiwomya 63, Ref: A Ward
27	4/2	A SHREWSBURY (22)	12	W	6,646	40	2-1	0-1	Moyes 46 (og), Shaw 82 Priest 1 Ref: G Pooley
28	11/2	H OLDHAM (21)	10	D	10,992	41	0-0	0-0	Ref: A Buksh
29	25/2	H LEICESTER (16)	12	D	9,666	42	2-2	2-2	Beagrie 35, Bamber 37 Reid 4, Walsh 32 Ref: S Lodge
30	28/2	A BIRMINGHAM (24)	9	W	7,904	45	1-0	1-0	Berry 33 Ref: D Allison
31	4/3	A HULL (17)	7	W	5,915	48	4-1	4-0	Hackett 13, Morgan 20, Beeston 37, 40 Whitehurst 70 Ref: G Tyson
32	11/3	H SUNDERLAND (14)	7	W	12,489	51	2-0	1-0	Hackett 30, Beagrie 86 Ref: P Wright
33	18/3	A PORTSMOUTH (13)	9	D	7,624	52	0-0	0-0	Ref: H King
34	25/3	H BARNSLEY (12)	10	D	10,209	53	1-1	1-0	Berry 32p Currie 85p Ref: V Callow

Line-ups

(For each match the first row is Stoke City; the second, italic row in the original is the opposition.)

No	Team	1	2	3	4	5	6	7	8	9	10	11	subs used
24	Stoke	Fox	Butler	Carr	Kamara	Higgins	Berry	Hackett	Henry	Bamber	Saunders	Beagrie	
24	Blackburn	Gennoe	Atkins	Sulley	Finnigan	Hendry	Mail*	Gayle	Hildersley	Kennedy	Garner	Sellars	Ainscow
25	Stoke	Fox	Butler	Carr	Kamara	Higgins	Berry	Hackett	Henry	Bamber	Saunders	Beagrie	
25	Bradford C	Tomlinson	Mitchell	Abbott^	Banks*	Jackson	Evans	Palin	Sinnott	Ormondroyd	Kennedy	Leonard	Jewell/Oliver
26	Stoke	Fox	Butler	Parkin	Kamara	Higgins	Berry	Ford	Henry	Bamber	Saunders*	Beagrie	Hackett
26	Ipswich	Fearon	Yallop	Harbey	Zondervan	Redford	Linighan	Kiwomya	Dozzell	Wark*	Hill	Baltacha	D'Avray
27	Stoke	Barrett	Butler	Carr	Kamara	Higgins	Berry	Hackett	Henry*	Ford	Shaw	Beagrie	Saunders
27	Shrewsbury	Hughes	Green Richd't*	Williams B	Priest*	Moyes	Pratley	Brown	Kasule !	Griffiths	Irvine	Bell	Kelly/Steele
28	Stoke	Barrett	Butler	Carr	Kamara	Higgins	Berry	Hackett	Ford^	Bamber	Shaw^	Beagrie	Henry/Saunders
28	Oldham	Hallworth	Irwin	Barrett	Kelly J	Marshall	Skipper	Palmer	Wright	Milligan	Ritchie	Adams	
29	Stoke	Barrett	Butler	Carr	Ford	Higgins	Berry	Hackett	Saunders	Bamber	Shaw^	Beagrie	Morgan
29	Leicester	Hodge	Mauchlen	Spearing	Ramsey*	Walsh	Paris	Reid	Cross	Newell	McAllister	Turner*	Quinn/Groves
30	Stoke	Barrett	Butler	Carr	Henry	Higgins	Berry	Hackett	Ford	Bamber	Shaw	Beagrie	Morgan
30	Birmingham	Thomas	Ashley	Frain	Atkins	Overson	Clarkson	Bremner	Peer*	Whitton	Robinson^	Wigley	Langley/Sturridge
31	Stoke	Barrett	Butler	Carr	Beeston	Higgins	Berry	Hackett	Saunders	Shaw	Morgan	Beagrie	
31	Hull	Hesford	Brown	Jacobs	De Mange	Jobson	Buckley	Askew	Roberts	Whitehurst	Edwards	Daniel	
32	Stoke	Barrett	Butler	Carr	Kamara	Higgins	Berry	Hackett	Beeston	Bamber	Shaw	Beagrie	
32	Sunderland	Norman	Bennett	Gray	Agboola	MacPhail	Doyle	Cullen^	Armstrong	Gates*	Gabbiadini	Pascoe	Hauser/Owers
33	Stoke	Barrett	Butler	Carr	Kamara	Higgins	Berry	Hackett	Beeston	Bamber	Shaw*	Beagrie	Saunders
33	Portsmouth	Gosney	Neill	Whitehead	Dillon*	Hogg	Maguire	Chamberlain	Horne	Quinn	Aspinall	Fillery^	Kuhl/Kelly
34	Stoke	Barrett	Butler	Carr	Beeston	Higgins	Berry	Hackett	Saunders	Bamber*	Shaw	Beagrie	Morgan
34	Barnsley	Baker	Joyce	Broddle	Dobbin	Tiler	Futcher	Robinson*	Agnew	Lowndes	Currie	MacDonald	Cooper

Match notes

24 — Blackburn: City's attacking intentions are signalled by Saunders' first goals for 11 months. The first after Hildersley's back-pass hits his own bar. Beagrie's shot is helped in by Atkins. Gayle's penalty is for Higgins' challenge on Kennedy. The winner is a Hildersley diving header. A pulsating game.

25 — Bradford C: Gary Hackett runs riot. He scores after Bamber's shot is blocked by Abbott and hits the post after beating three defenders. Tomlinson saves his firm header before a neat return pass sets up Henry's goal. Banks heads home unmarked to liven things up but Stoke are well worth the points.

26 — Ipswich: A travelling army of inflatable Pink Panthers greets Sergei Baltacha, the first Russian to play in England. He responds by opening the scoring. Ipswich walk it. Bamber notches after a prolonged scramble. 'Delilah' bursts forth from dispirited Stokies to applause from Ipswich supporters.

27 — Shrewsbury: City are a goal down within a minute as Priest taps in unmarked. David Moyes nets his third own-goal in six matches for unlucky Shrews who have won one home game all season. Kasule is sent off for flooring Beagrie who refuses to be subbed. Shaw fires in Beagrie's centre to win it.

28 — Oldham: An absolutely dreadful match with no attempts at goal to seriously trouble either keeper. Mills is worried that the players have lost the spirit of Christmas time. No new signings are on the horizon due to lack of funds and the Boothen End is restless. 'Coates out!' is the new shout heard.

29 — Leicester: On a snow-covered pitch Stoke gift Leicester two goals with charitable marking. Beagrie cuts loose and buries one looping effort in the far top corner. Hackett's twice-taken free-kick finds Bamber's head. Butler's rampaging runs are not matched by poor finishing and the Foxes hold on.

30 — Birmingham: Stoke fans expect the floodgates to open after the referee rules that Berry's looping header has crossed the line. They don't. Rock-bottom Blues deal easily with the ineffective Bamber. Beagrie and Carr are reduced to firing long-range efforts into the Boothen End. 'Mills out' once again.

31 — Hull: Stoke run riot on Humberside again with Carl Beeston the star of the show. He powers two shots past Hesford to firmly put his glandular fever nightmare behind him. Hackett cracks in from 20 yards and Morgan heads home Hackett's centre. Barrett saves Edwards' 53rd-minute penalty.

32 — Sunderland: City outbattle Denis Smith's Rokerites. New England U-21 cap Gabbiadini misses glaringly before Shaw chips for Hackett to head in at the far post. Shaw has a header disallowed and is booked by the fussy ref for protesting. Beagrie waltzes in when Norman and Bennett get tangled up.

33 — Portsmouth: In the face of a gale neither side create much. The match is reduced to a series of offside decisions and the linesman's flag collapses with over-use! Fratton Park is slowly being dismantled for rebuilding and the backdrop reflects the game. Awful. Tony Ford is sold to West Brom (£50k).

34 — Barnsley: Play-off dreams are ended by George Berry's handball, which gifts Barnsley a penalty. Jim Dobbin also handles for City's spot-kick. Kamara is suspended and Stoke miss his drive from midfield. Beagrie has a tremendous shot blocked by Futcher while Barrett tips over Agnew's header.

No	V	Date	Opponent	HT	FT	Pos	Opp Pos	Pts	Att
35	A	27/3	MANCHESTER CITY	0-1	1-2	11	2	53	28,303
36	H	1/4	PLYMOUTH	2-0	2-2	11	17	54	8,363
37	H	4/4	WEST BROM	0-0	0-0	11	3	55	11,151
38	A	8/4	OXFORD	1-2	2-3	12	15	55	5,297
39	A	11/4	WATFORD	1-2	2-3	12	6	55	9,086
40	A	15/4	BOURNEMOUTH	0-0	1-0	11	12	58	6,834
41	H	22/4	WALSALL	0-2	0-3	11	23	58	3,132
42	H	29/4	LEEDS	2-1	2-3	13	10	58	3,051
43	A	1/5	CHELSEA	1-1	1-2	13	1	58	14,946
44	A	6/5	SWINDON	0-0	0-3	13	6	58	9,543
45	A	9/5	CRYSTAL PALACE	0-1	0-1	13	4	58	12,159
46	H	13/5	BRIGHTON	1-1	2-2	13	19	59	5,841

Home 9,887   Away 10,258

---

35 — MANCHESTER CITY (A), 27/3 — 1-2
Stoke: Barrett, Butler, Carr, Kamara, Higgins, Berry, Hackett, Beeston*, Bamber, Shaw^, Beagie, Henry/Saunders
Man City: Cooper, Lake, Hinchcliffe, Gayle, Megson, Redmond, White, Maulden, Oldfield*, McNab, Morley, Gleghorn
Scorers: Butler 65 / Oldfield 22, Hinchcliffe 48p
Ref: T Holbrook
Stoke battle hard but after Bamber misses a gilt-edged chance Oldfield nips in to score for Man City. Beeston limps off before Carr trips White and Hinchcliffe buries the penalty. Beagie also limps off after the second sub is made but Stoke's ten men grab a life-line through John Butler.

36 — PLYMOUTH (H), 1/4 — 2-2
Stoke: Barrett, Butler, Carr, Kamara, Higgins*, Berry, Hackett, Beeston, Bamber, Saunders, Beagie, Shaw/Morgan
Plymouth: Wilmot, Brown, Uzzell, Burrows, Marker, Smith, Ford, Byrne*, McCarthy, Matthews, Stuart, Hodges
Scorers: Bamber 25, Henry 44 / Tynan 52p, McCarthy 56
Ref: R Pawley
Plymouth make April Fools of Stoke. Bamber and Henry both prod in rebounds after Wilmot fails to hold rasping shots. Hackett runs midfield but Stuart is fouled by Barrett and Tynan scores. McCarthy strikes a superb equaliser. Tynan has a second spot-kick saved by Barrett (58 mins).

37 — WEST BROM (H), 4/4 — 0-0
Stoke: Barrett, Butler, Carr, Kamara, Higgins, Berry, Hackett, Henry, Bamber, Shaw, Beagie, Saunders
West Brom: Naylor, Bradley, Albiston, Talbot, Whyte^, North, Bartlett, West, Robson^, Anderson, Paskin/Banks
Ref: J Key
Kamara welcomes back Chris Whyte from suspension with a sliding tackle, which leaves him needing 10 stitches. In a ferocious match Albion seek reprisals led by player-manager Talbot. Barrett turns over Banks' drive and Stoke fail to trouble Naylor. Tony Ford plays for West Brom.

38 — OXFORD (A), 8/4 — 2-3
Stoke: Barrett, Butler, Carr, Kamara, Higgins, Hemming!, Hackett, Henry, Bamber, Saunders*, Beagie, Shaw
Oxford: Hucker, Smart, Phillips J, Shelton, Lewis, Greenall, Briggs, Foyle*, Mustoe, Durnin, Hill, Leworthy
Scorers: Bamber 37, Henry 73 / Hill 9, 55, Durnin 15
Ref: K Morton
Referee Morton sends off Chris Hemming for an innocuous foul on Shelton. Stoke are already 0-2 behind to Hill's free header and Durnin's 20-yard effort. The ten men battle. Bamber drives high past Hucker. Henry heads in Hackett's free-kick. Barrett lets Hill's shot through his hands.

39 — WATFORD (A), 11/4 — 2-3
Stoke: Barrett, Butler, Carr, Kamara, Higgins, Berry, Hackett, Henry, Bamber, Morgan, Beagie, Beeston
Watford: Coton, Gibbs, Jackett, Falconer, Miller, McClelland, Thomas*, Wilkinson^, Thompson, Porter, Hodges, H'wrth D'd
Scorers: Morgan 30, 87 / Porter 8, Falconer 18, Hodges 82
Ref: D Vickers
Stoke are always off the pace in an entertaining game. Gary Porter's wind-assisted shot goes in off the post. Barrett then watches as Falconer's chip sails over him. Morgan heads home Bamber's cross. Glyn Hodges punishes more defensive hesitancy before Morgan bundles in a corner.

40 — BOURNEMOUTH (A), 15/4 — 1-0 (W)
Stoke: Barrett, Butler, Carr, Kamara, Higgins, Beeston, Hackett, Morgan, Bamber, Morgan, Beagie, Ware
Bournemouth: Peyton, Newson, Morrell, Teale, Pulis, O'Driscoll, Barnes^, Shearer*, Aylott, Bishop, Blissett, Brooks/O'Connor
Scorers: Ware 67
Ref: K Cooper
Gerry Peyton gifts Stoke the win after City are outplayed. He drops a mis-hit through-ball over the line to the amusement of City fans who sing 'Gerry is a Stokie'. Harry Redknapp's men hit the post five times. Bamber heads straight at Peyton. This is the day of the Hillsborough tragedy.

41 — WALSALL (H), 22/4 — 0-3
Stoke: Barrett, Butler, Carr, Kamara!, Beeston, Berry, Hackett, Morgan, Bamber*, Saunders, Beagie, Ware
Walsall: Barber, Rees, Mower, Shakespeare, Forbes, Smith, Pritchard, Rimmer*, Saville, Naughton, Hawker, Bertschin
Scorers: Rimmer 12, Saville 17, 85
Ref: K Lupton
Stoke are outplayed by already relegated Saddlers. Rimmer nets off a post. Saville scores from 20 yards. Ex-Stokie Bertschin sets up Saville's second. Kamara is dismissed for striking Craig Shakespeare. The game kicks off at 3.06pm in remembrance of those who died at Hillsborough.

42 — LEEDS (H), 29/4 — 2-3
Stoke: Barrett, Butler, Carr, Kamara, Higgins, Berry, Hackett, Morgan, Bamber, Beeston, Beagie, Ware
Leeds: Williams A, Whitlow, Aizlewood*, Blake, Fairclough, Strachan, Sheridan, Davison, Hilaire, Haddock/Batty, Baird
Scorers: Bamber 22, 33 / Sheridan 25p, Davison 54, Strachan 74
Ref: J Martin
Bamber puts City 2-1 up with two close-range finishes. Sheridan's penalty is for Carr's foul. He then threads a superb pass through to Bobby Davison to equalise. Gordon Strachan scores his first goal since his £300,000 move from Man Utd, chipping over Higgins on the line to win it.

43 — CHELSEA (A), 1/5 — 1-2
Stoke: Fox, Butler, Carr, Kamara, Higgins, Beeston, Hackett, Henry*, Bamber, Ware^, Beagie, Morgan/Saunders
Chelsea: Beasant, Clarke, Dorigo, Roberts, McLaughlin*, Bumstead, McAllister, Dixon, Wilson C, Wilson K, Monkou
Scorers: Higgins 12 / Dixon 43, Roberts 86p
Ref: R Gifford
Stoke snatch a surprise lead against Bobby Campbell's champions elect. Mark Higgins heads home his first Stoke goal from Ware's flag-kick. Bamber misses a great opportunity just before Kerry Dixon equalises. Higgins turns villain, bringing down Clarke for Roberts' penalty winner.

44 — SWINDON (A), 6/5 — 0-3
Stoke: Fox, Butler, Carr^, Ware, Higgins!, Beeston*, Hackett, Henry*, Bamber, Ware, Beagie, Berry/Morgan
Swindon: Digby, Hockaday, King, Jones, Calderwood, Parkin, Foley, Shearer, MacLaren, White
Scorers: Shearer 62, 87, Jones 86
Ref: P Danson
Stoke hold their own against play-off bound Swindon. Fox makes a string of saves until Shearer beats him at his left-hand post. Higgins is sent off for a bad foul, leaving Stoke with the second worst disciplinary record in the league. Late goals reflect the ten men's desire to chase a point.

45 — CRYSTAL PALACE (A), 9/5 — 0-1
Stoke: Fox, Butler, Carr, Ware, Higgins, Berry, Hackett, Henry, Bamber, Ware, Beagie, Beagie
Crystal Palace: Suckling, Hedman, Burke, Madden, Hopkins, Nebbeling, McGoldrick, Pardew, Bright, Wright, Berber
Scorers: Madden 40p
Ref: D Elleray
Higgins is again the villain as he climbs all over Bright and Madden converts the penalty. City's best chance comes when Jeff Hopkins almost slices the ball into his own goal. Fox makes three brilliant saves. His best is from Ian Wright's overhead kick. Where does Mills go from here?

46 — BRIGHTON (H), 13/5 — 2-2
Stoke: Keeley, Butler, Carr, Ware, Higgins, Berry, Hackett, Beeston, Bamber, Morgan, Beagie
Brighton: Chivers, Dublin, Wilkins, Gatting, Chapman, Nelson, Bremner, Cadner, Curbishley, Trusson
Scorers: Morgan 30, Beagie 53 / Nelson 5, Wilkins 85
Ref: L Dilkes
In the glorious sunshine City contrive to draw with a poor Brighton side. Nelson volleys in before Morgan's flying header and Beagrie's cross-shot lead to the customary acrobatics. Wilkins hits Fox from two yards but the ball rebounds onto him and into the net. Why Why Why Mills?

BARCLAYS DIVISION 2 (CUP-TIES) Manager: Mick Mills SEASON 1988-89

Littlewoods Cup

				Att	F-A	H-T	Scorers, Times, and Referees	1	2	3	4	5	6	7	8	9	10	11	subs used
2:1	A	LEYTON ORIENT 27/9	19 W	3,154 4:21	2-1	0-1	Morgan 48, Kamara 73 / Juryeff 36 / Ref: M Bodenham	Fox / *Wells*	Ford / *Howard*	Beeston* / *Dickenson*	Kamara / *Hales*	Henry / *Day*	Hemming / *Ward*	Hackett / *Baker*	Saunders / *Harvey**	Morgan / *Shiners*	Stainrod / *Juryeff*	Beagrie / *Comfort*	Gidman / *Ketteridge*
2:2	H	LEYTON ORIENT 11/10	19 L	5,756 4:19	1-2	0-1	Stainrod 86p / Hales 41p, Comfort 90 / Ref: T Fitzharris / (Stoke lose 2-3 on penalties)	Barrett / *Wells*	Gidman^ / *Howard*	Beeston / *Dickenson*	Kamara / *Hales*	Hemming / *Day*	Henry / *Sitton*	Hackett* / *Baker**	Ford / *Ward*	Shaw / *Hull*	Stainrod / *Juryeff*	Beagrie / *Comfort*	Ware/Carr / *Harvey*

Match 2:1 — Ian Juryeff cracks a 30-yard shot into the far corner for Frank Clark's lowly Orient. Morgan heads in Stainrod's cross and Kamara prods home when Wells drops the ball from a corner. Orient's pressure dwindles once behind. Stainrod produces some party tricks once victory is assured.

Match 2:2 — Stoke contrive to lose even when Stainrod converts from the spot after Beagrie skies an earlier penalty. Hales scores Orient's pen for Barrett's foul on Ian Juryeff. Alan Comfort sends the tie into extra-time. Stainrod then misses the final spot-kick to send Orient through to meet Ipswich.

FA Cup

				Att	F-A	H-T	Scorers, Times, and Referees	1	2	3	4	5	6	7	8	9	10	11	subs used
3	H	CRYSTAL PALACE 27/1	13 W	12,294 2:8	1-0	0-0	Shaw 74 / Ref: J Key	Fox / *Suckling*	Ware / *Pemberton*	Carr / *Burke*	Kamara / *Pennyfather*	Higgins / *Hopkins*	Berry / *Nebbeling*	Hackett / *Salako*	Henry / *Thomas*	Bamber / *Bright*	Saunders* / *Wright*	Beagrie / *Barber*	Shaw
4	H	BARNSLEY 28/1	13 D	18,592 2:8	3-3	1-3	Bamber 29, Berry 77, Beagrie 83 / Currie 6, 30, MacDonald 24 / Ref: P Tyldesley	Fox / *Baker*	Ford / *Joyce*	Carr / *Beresford*	Kamara / *Dobbin*	Higgins / *McGugan*	Berry / *Futcher*	Hackett / *Lowndes*	Henry / *Agnew*	Bamber / *Cooper*	Saunders* / *Currie*	Beagrie / *MacDonald*	Shaw
4R	A	BARNSLEY 31/1	13 L	21,086 2:8	1-2	0-1	Bamber 64 / MacDonald 4, Cooper 70 / Ref: G Aplin	Barrett / *Baker*	Ford / *Joyce*	Carr / *Beresford*	Kamara / *Dobbin*	Higgins / *McGugan*	Berry / *Futcher*	Hackett / *Lowndes*	Henry / *Agnew*	Bamber / *Cooper*	Shaw* / *Currie*	Beagrie / *MacDonald*	Saunders / *Rees^/Shotton*

Match 3 — A potteries mist shrouds the Vic as an end-to-end game culminates with Shaw's flick over the onrushing Perry Suckling. Steve Coppell's team lay siege but Stoke cling on with Paul Ware filling in for the cup-tied Butler. Bright and Wright hit the bar. Fox tips over a thunderous header.

Match 4 — Taking the field to Henry Mancini's Pink Panther theme seems appropriate as City gift Barnsley three simple goals and only manage Bamber's right-foot shot after having 80% of the play. Berry bullets a header in off the bar. Beagrie salvages a draw with a wonderful sidestep and drive.

Match 4R — A cracking game seen by 6,000 Stokies, mostly let in free when the coaches arrive late. Barrett saves well from Joyce but MacDonald slots the rebound. Bamber hits the bar before heading in Beagrie's cross. Cooper slots in and out-somersaults Beagrie as Barnsley go on to face Everton.

League Table

Pos	Team	P	Home W	Home D	Home L	Home F	Home A	Away W	Away D	Away L	Away F	Away A	Pts
1	Chelsea	46	15	6	2	50	25	14	6	3	46	25	99
2	Manchester C	46	12	8	3	48	28	11	5	7	29	25	82
3	Crys Palace *	46	15	6	2	42	17	8	6	9	29	32	81
4	Watford	46	14	5	4	41	18	8	7	8	33	30	78
5	Blackburn	46	16	4	3	50	22	6	7	10	24	37	77
6	Swindon	46	13	8	2	35	15	7	8	8	33	38	76
7	Barnsley	46	12	8	3	37	21	8	6	9	29	37	74
8	Ipswich	46	13	3	7	42	23	9	4	10	29	38	73
9	West Brom	46	13	7	3	43	18	5	11	7	22	23	72
10	Leeds	46	12	6	5	34	20	5	10	8	25	30	67
11	Sunderland	46	12	8	3	40	23	4	7	12	20	37	63
12	Bournemouth	46	13	3	7	32	20	5	5	13	21	42	62
13	STOKE	46	9	4	9	33	22	5	5	13	23	47	59
14	Bradford C	46	8	11	4	29	22	6	6	12	23	37	56
15	Leicester	46	11	6	6	31	20	2	10	11	25	43	55
16	Oldham	46	9	10	4	49	32	2	11	10	26	40	54
17	Oxford	46	11	6	6	40	34	3	6	14	22	36	54
18	Plymouth	46	11	4	8	35	22	3	8	12	20	44	54
19	Brighton	46	11	5	7	36	24	3	4	16	21	42	51
20	Portsmouth	46	10	6	7	33	21	3	6	14	20	41	51
21	Hull	46	7	9	7	31	25	4	5	14	21	43	47
22	Shrewsbury	45	4	11	8	25	31	4	7	12	15	36	42
23	Birmingham	45	6	4	13	21	33	2	7	14	10	43	35
24	Walsall	45	3	10	10	27	42	2	6	15	14	38	31
		1104	261	163	128	884	581	128	163	261	581	884	1493

* promoted after play-offs

Odds & ends

Double wins: (3) Birmingham, Bournemouth, Hull.

Double losses: (3) Blackburn, Chelsea, Leeds.

Won from behind: (3) Manchester C (h), Shrewsbury (a), Walsall (a).

Lost from in front: (3) Blackburn (a), Leeds (h), Chelsea (a).

High spots: Pushing for a play-off spot until March.

Putting eight goals past Hull.

Beating Man City 3-1.

Peter Beagrie's stunning goal against Bournemouth.

Low spots: Losing to Orient in the Littlewoods Cup.

Being thrashed at the Hawthorns.

Not winning a home game after 11 March.

Only scoring one goal in the first five games.

George Berry's early-season injury.

Unrest about the future of manager Mills.

Player of the Year: Chris Kamara.

Ever-presents: (0).

Hat-tricks: (0).

Leading scorer: (9) Dave Bamber, Peter Beagrie.

Appearances and Goals

Player	Appearances Lge	Sub	LC	Sub	FAC	Sub	Goals Lge	LC	FAC	Tot
Bamber, Dave	23						7		2	9
Barrett, Scott	17		1		1	3				
Beagrie, Peter	41		2		2	3	8		1	9
Beeston, Carl	22	1	2		2		2			2
Berry, George	32	1			3		4		1	5
Butler, John	25						1			1
Carr, Cliff	40	1	1	1	3		1			1
Ford, Tony	27		2		2					
Fox, Peter	29		1		2					
Gidman, John	7	3	1	1	1					
Hackett, Gary	45	1	2		3		5			5
Henning, Chris	4		2							
Henry, Tony	37	3	2	3	3		6			6
Higgins, Mark	33				3		1			1
Kamara, Chris	38		2	2	3		3		1	4
Morgan, Nicky	11	7	1				5	1		6
Parkin, Steve	4									
Saunders, Carl	27	6	1	1	2	1	2			2
Shaw, Graham	19	9	1		1	2	5	1		6
Stainrod, Simon	16	2	2		1		4	1		5
Ware, Paul	9	2		1	1	1	1			1
(own-goals)							2			2
21 players used	506	34	22	3	33	3	57	3	5	65

BARCLAYS DIVISION 2

Manager: Mick Mills ⇨ Alan Ball

SEASON 1989-90

Match results

No		Opponent	Date	Att	Pos	Pt	F-A	H-T	Scorers, Times, and Referees
1	H	WEST HAM	19/8	16,058		1	D 1-1	0-1	Biggins 81 / Keen 28 / Ref: J Apln
2	A	PORTSMOUTH	26/8	7,433	15/20	2	D 0-0	0-0	Ref: I Hemley
3	H	LEEDS	2/9	14,570	14/11	3	D 1-1	1-0	Cranson 29 / Strachan 60 / Ref: R Milford
4	A	BARNSLEY	5/9	8,564	16/10	3	L 2-3	1-2	Berry 19p, Morgan 58 / Agnew 2, Cooper 40, Lowndes 62 / Ref: R Hart
5	A	WOLVES	9/9	15,659	19/23	4	D 0-0	0-0	Ref: P Don
6	H	OLDHAM	16/9	10,673	22/13	4	L 1-2	0-2	Bamber 65 / Palmer 15, Ritchie 37 / Ref: A Ward
7	H	PORT VALE	23/9	27,032	23/18	5	D 1-1	0-0	Palin 66 / Earle 50 / Ref: T Simpson
8	H	BRADFORD C	26/9	9,346	22/19	6	D 1-1	0-1	Cranson 55 / Tinnion 2 / Ref: A Seville
9	A	IPSWICH	30/9	10,389	21/16	7	D 2-2	0-2	Palin 47p, Saunders 50 / D'Avray 11, Dozzell 23 / Ref: D Elleray
10	A	PLYMOUTH	7/10	6,940	21/7	7	L 0-3	0-1	Hodges 44, Tynan 52p, Thomas 74 / Ref: R Lewis
11	H	HULL	14/10	9,955	21/23	8	D 1-1	1-0	Biggins 3 / McParland 59p / Ref: D Vickers

Line-ups (top line = Stoke, bottom line = opponents)

No	1	2	3	4	5	6	7	8	9	10	11	subs used
1	Fox	Butler	Statham	Kamara	Cranson	Beeston	Hackett	Scott*	Bamber	Biggins	Beagie	Saunders
	Parkes	Potts	Paris	Gale	Martin	Keen	Ward	McAvennie*	Slater	Brady	Ince	Kelly D
2	Fox	Butler	Statham	Kamara	Cranson	Beeston	Hackett	Scott	Bamber	Biggins*	Beagie	Morgan
	Knight	Neill	Maguire	Fillery	Sandford	Ball	Wigley	Chamberlain Kelly*	Connor	Black	Whittingham	
3	Fox	Butler	Statham	Kamara	Cranson	Beeston	Hackett	Scott	Bamber	Saunders*	Beagie	Morgan
	Day	Sterland	Whitlow	Jones	Fairclough	Haddock	Strachan	Batty	Baird	Davison*	Hendrie	Speed
4	Fox	Butler	Statham	Kamara	Beeston	Berry	Hackett	Scott	Bamber	Morgan*	Beagie	Saunders
	Baker	Shotton	Broddle	Dobbin	Banks	Futcher*	Lowndes	Agnew	Cooper	Currie	Robinson	Tiler
5	Fox	Butler	Statham	Kamara	Cranson	Beeston	Hackett	Scott*	Bamber	Biggins	Beagie	Ware
	Lange	Chard*	Venus	Robertson	Westley	Vaughan	Thompson	Gooding	Bull	Mutch	Dennison	Paskin
6	Fox	Butler	Statham	Kamara	Cranson	Beeston	Hackett	Saunders*	Bamber	Morgan^	Beagie	Ware/Boughey
	Rhodes	Irwin	Barlow	Henry	Marshall	Barrett	Palmer	Ritchie	Bunn	Milligan	Holden R	
7	Fox	Butler	Statham	Kamara	Cranson	Beeston	Ware*	Palin^	Bamber	Beagie		Saunders/Hackett
	Grew	Webb	Hughes	Mills	Aspin	Glover	Porter	Earle*	Futcher	Beckford^	Jefers	Walker/Jepson
8	Fox	Butler	Statham	Kamara	Cranson	Beeston	Hackett	Palin	Bamber	Morgan*	Beagie	Saunders
	Tomlinson	Abbott	Tinnion	Aizlewood	Sinnott	Evans D^	Megson	Duxbury	Leonard	Quinn	Wharton*	Ellis/Jackson
9	Fox	Butler	Statham	Kamara	Cranson	Beeston	Hackett	Palin	Bamber	Saunders	Beagie	Saunders
	Forrest	Humes	Palmer	Zondervan	Redford*	Linighan	Lowe	Dozzell	Wark*	D'Avray	Stockwell	Donowa/Thompson
10	Barrett	Butler	Statham	Kamara	Cranson	Beeston	Hackett*	Palin	Bamber	Biggins	Beagie	Thomas
	Wilmot	Brown	Brimacombe	Marker	Burrows	Morrison	Byrne	Hodges*	Tynan	Campbell	Stuart	
11	Barrett	Butler	Statham	Ware	Cranson*	Beeston	Palin*	Saunders	Bamber	Biggins	Beagie	Boughey/Higgins
	Hesford	Warren	Jacobs	Swan	Terry	Jobson	Askew	Roberts	McParland	Whitehurst	Doyle*	Jenkinson

Match reports

1. West Ham. Over £1 million worth of new talent, including record £450,000 Ian Cranson, snatch a deserved late draw. Phil Parkes arches to palm over from Biggins. Keen pokes past Fox in a scramble. Martin shackles Bamber. Kamara breaks McAvennie's ankle. Biggins nips in to poke past Parkes.

2. Portsmouth. An entertaining game sees Beagrie sting Knight's fingers with a free-kick. John Gregory's Pompey have a string of corners but City hold firm. Ian Scott knits the midfield together and Derek Statham roams down the left flank. Fox's one save of note is from Kenny Black's 30-yard shot.

3. Leeds. Vinnie Jones is booed by the Boothen but proceeds to prompt Leeds on to the attack. Cranson powers home a free-kick against the run of play. Bamber hits the post. Gordon Strachan chips Fox with a quickly taken free-kick. Butler clears off the line from Hendrie's effort. Another draw.

4. Barnsley. Stoke come unstuck after just 70 secs when Agnew threads in. Berry's penalty is for Agnew's handball. Cooper loops in a header and Morgan replies with a volley. Dobbin nearly heads into his own net. Steve Lowndes wins it and Allan Clarke's men still have the Indian sign over City.

5. Wolves. 3,500 Stokies witness a half-hearted affair at dilapidated Molineux. Scott is carried off after a tackle by Chard. Cranson hits the bar. Bamber is tripped but Statham hits a poor penalty straight at Tony Lange. Andy Mutch heads wide from four yards. Lange saves from Biggins. Dour fare.

6. Oldham. The Boothen End make their feelings plain. 'Mills out!' they chant as Joe Royle's Latics snap up two gifts from City's generous defence. Dave Bamber contrives to lob into Andy Rhodes' hands when clean through but then thumps in Beagrie's curling pass as the heavens open. Terrible.

7. Port Vale. John Rudge's Valiants take the lead in the first local derby since 1957. A sell-out crowd see Robbie Earle rifle past Fox. Mark Grew saves well from Bamber. Leigh Palin, on-loan from Bradford, volleys home from nine yards. Vale hit the bar and Cranson heads just wide. Honours even.

8. Bradford C. Beeston misjudges the soggy turf and his under-hit back-pass leads to Tinnion converting Leonard's cross. Saunders appears at half-time and is lively. Cranson heads home a free-kick. Bamber misses chance after chance. The team is jeered off for failing to beat Terry Yorath's Bantams.

9. Ipswich. Stoke fall apart at the back. Kamara's wayward pass allows D'Avray to head in off the post. Fox fails to prevent Jason Dozzell's powerful shot crossing the line. The break sees a turnaround. Bamber is fouled for the penalty. Saunders finishes calmly. Bamber misses again from close in.

10. Plymouth. Ken Brown's Pilgrims romp home as sorry Stoke register their worst start for years. Beagrie, watched by Chelsea manager Bobby Campbell, forages well. The profligate Bamber wastes three excellent chances. Hackett limps off injured, Statham trips Greg Campbell for the spot-kick.

11. Hull. Wayne Biggins heads home a brilliant Beagrie cross to give Stoke a great start. Cranson, captain for the day, is troubled by the lively Askew. Ian McParland nets after Roberts' shot is handled on the line. 'Will we ever win a game' drifts down from the Boothen End. Post-match demos.

12 — 17/10 H WEST BROM — Att 11,991 (13 · 11) — pos 19 — W 2-1
Hackett 8, Biggins 32 / Bartlett 49 — Ref: G Tyson

Stoke: Barrett, Butler, Statham, Scott, Beeston, Hackett*, Palin, Bamber, Biggins, Beagrie, Ware^/Higgins
West Brom: Naylor, Parkin, Burgess, Robson*, North, Ford, Goodman, Thomas, McNally, Barham^, Talbot/Bartlett

Stoke start with two wingers and one scores when Scott pulls back for Hackett. Biggins turns in the six-yard box to finish Beagrie's cross. Only the second win in 26 league games. Ware has a goal ruled out for offside. Kevin Bartlett scores four minutes after coming on, but City hold out.

13 — 21/10 A SHEFFIELD UTD — Att 16,873 (1 · 11) — pos 21 — L 1-2
Palin 67p / Bradshaw 14, Booker 25 — Ref: J Lloyd

Stoke: Barrett, Butler, Statham, Scott, Beeston, Ware*, Palin, Bamber, Biggins, Beagrie, Boughey
Sheffield Utd: Tracey, Hill, Rostron, Booker, Morris, Bradshaw, Gannon, Agana, Deane, Bryson*, Francis

League leaders United show City how to finish. Carl Bradshaw turns to fire home. The statuesque defence allows Booker to net from 18 yards. Bamber misses from close in but is fouled for the penalty. New team coach Alan Ball urges City forward but Dave Bassett's Blades win easily.

14 — 28/10 H SUNDERLAND — Att 12,480 (5 · 11) — pos 21 — L 0-2
Bracewell 77, Gabbiadini 79 — Ref: P Tyldesley

Stoke: Barrett, Butler, Statham, Scott^, Beeston, Hackett*, Palin, Bamber, Saunders, Hackett, Morgan
Sunderland: Carter, Kay, Hardyman*, MacPhail, Owers, Bracewell, Armstrong, Gates, Gabbiadini, Pascoe, Cullen

Beagrie is sold to Everton for £750,000. Denis Smith's Rokerites take over. Bracewell hits the bar. Gates misses from two yards. Finally Bracewell scores via the underside of the bar. Gabbiadini curls home a beauty. No pride. Mills is clinging on.

15 — 1/11 A OXFORD — Att 4,375 (16 · 11) — pos 22 — L 0-3
Durnin 6, Foster 65, Mustoe 70 — Ref: R Wiseman

Stoke: Barrett, Butler, Statham, Cranson, Beeston, Palin, Scott^, Bamber, Saunders, Hackett*, Ware/Morgan
Oxford: Judge, Smart, Phillips J*, Lewis, Foster, Mustoe^, Ford, Durnin, Stein, Heath, McClaren/Simpson

Cranson allows the ball to squeeze under his foot for John Durnin to finish clinically. Judge saves Bamber's header superbly. Foster nudges in from close range and Robbie Mustoe heads in Mark Stein's centre. Foster clears off the line from Bamber. Post-match demos demand changes.

16 — 4/11 A SWINDON — Att 7,825 (7 · 11) — pos 23 — **L 0-6**
McL'ghlin 7, Sh'rer 23, 78, B'mber 47 (og), [White 68, 86] — Ref: P Alcock

Stoke: Barrett, Butler, Statham, Cranson, Beeston, Higgins*, Bamber, Biggins*, Saunders, Hackett/Ware
Swindon: Digby, Hockaday, Bodin, McLoughlin, Calderwood, Shearer, White, MacLaren, Simpson

Mick Mills is finally sacked after the most atrocious performance in living memory. The defence is carved to pieces time and again. Bamber's own-goal is the first time he has found the net for seven weeks! Duncan Shearer's 25-yard pile-driver is the best goal for Ossie Ardiles' Robins.

17 — 11/11 H BRIGHTON — Att 10,346 (12 · 14) — pos 23 — W 3-1
Beeston 1, Bamber 25, Kamara 30 / Codner 13, Bremner 72 — Ref: A Wilkie

Stoke: Barrett, Butler, Statham, Kamara, Berry, Hilaire^, Beeston, Bamber, Biggins*, Hackett, Ware/Saunders
Brighton: Keeley, Chivers, Chapman, Cuthshley, Bissett, Jones, Nelson, Bremner, Codner, Wilkins, Crumplin

Caretaker boss Ball reinstates Berry and plays on-loan Vince Hilaire. Beeston, in midfield, waltzes through to score on 35 secs. Bamber nets a header. Kamara flicks in Beeston's cross. Berry puts a 60th-minute penalty wide to set up a nail-biting finish after Kevin Bremner cracks home.

18 — 18/11 A BOURNEMOUTH — Att 6,412 (13 · 14) — pos 24 — L 1-2
Hilaire 30 / Brooks 31, Moulden 53 — Ref: A Gunn

Stoke: Barrett, Butler, Statham, Kamara, Beeston, Hilaire, Berry, Bamber, Biggins, Brooks, Ware^/Hackett
Bournemouth: Peyton, Bond, Coleman, Teale, Peacock, Lawrence*, Moulden*, Williams^, O'Driscoll, Blissett, O'Connor/Miller

Cranson's injury forces Beeston into the back four and weakens the midfield. Fox drops a cross and Shaun Brooks nets. Peyton drops Hilaire's cross over the line. Paul Ware injures himself kicking air rather than ball. Good news. Sir Stanley Matthews is made Life President of the club.

19 — 25/11 H LEICESTER — Att 12,264 (22 · 14) — pos 24 — L 0-1
Mills 65 — Ref: G Ashby

Stoke: Fox, Butler, Carr, Kamara, Higgins, Hackett, Beeston, Bamber, Biggins*, Saunders, Ware^/Hackett
Leicester: Hodge, Mauchlen*, Morgan, Ramsey, Walsh, Reid, Moran, Campbell, Mills, Wright, James

A vital relegation battle and Stoke are unable to score despite Hilaire and Hackett providing numerous chances. Martin Hodge saves well from Biggins and Dave Bamber. Gary Mills cracks home a free-kick from 18 yards. David Pleat's Foxes win their first away match for a year.

20 — 2/12 A WEST HAM — Att 7,704 (7 · 15) — pos 23 — D 0-0
Ref: B Hill

Stoke: Fox, Butler, Carr, Kamara, Higgins, Hackett, Beeston, Bamber, Saunders, Ward, Kelly Di/Foster
West Ham: Parkes, Potts, Dicks, Martin, Strodder, Devonshire*, Brady, Slater, Keen, Fasanu^, Kelly Di/Foster

Fox saves superbly from Kevin Keen after just 15 seconds. Lou Macari's West Ham are below par. Julian Dicks wastes a 55th-minute penalty, saved brilliantly by Fox. Kamara harasses Liam Brady into a rare booking. Saunders has a good strike well saved by Phil Parkes. A good draw.

21 — 9/12 A BARNSLEY — Att 13,163 (20 · 15) — pos 24 — L 0-1
Cooper 72 — Ref: K Morton

Stoke: Fox, Butler, Carr, Kamara, Higgins, Hackett*, Beeston, Bamber, Saunders, Currie, Hilaire
Barnsley: Baker, Dobbin, Cross, Lowndes, Shotton, Brady, McCord, Agnew, Cooper, Archdeacon, Archdeacon

A four-day break in Jersey to 'get to know each other' doesn't work. Hackett misses pathetically and Saunders miscues a header. Steve Cooper blasts in after Berry passes straight to Agnew. Stoke are booed off the pitch. Ball is after Luton's Steve Williams and Plymouth's Mark Smith.

22 — 26/12 H NEWCASTLE — Att 14,878 (6 · 18) — pos 24 — W 2-1
Biggins 78, Beeston 90 / Scott 5 — Ref: J Worrall

Stoke: Fox, Saunders, Carr, Kamara, Beeston, Hackett*, Palin, Ellis, Biggins, Ellis, Holmes
Newcastle: Burridge, Ranson, Sweeney, Dillon, Scott, Gallacher*, Kristensen, Brock, Cooper, Quinn, Brazil^/Stimson

New coach Graham Paddon sees City fight back after conceding to Kevin Scott's header from a corner. New men Tony Ellis and Lee Sandford add steel. Biggins slides the ball under Burridge. Cliff Carr's superb knock-on sees sub Beeston to crack home an unstoppable shot.

23 — 30/12 H WATFORD — Att 13,228 (9 · 19) — pos 24 — D 2-2
Biggins 23, 26p, Hodges 21, Penrice 66 — Ref: K Redfern

Stoke: Fox, Butler, Carr, Kamara, Holmes, Saunders*, Fowler, Beeston, Biggins, Ellis, Hackett
Watford: Coton, Gibbs*, Ashby, Richardson, Hw'rth/D'vid/Roeder, Henry, Wilkinson, Penrice, Porter, Quinn, Thomas

In a cracking game Biggins nets a fantastic goal from Ellis' knockdown to equalise Glyn Hodges' close-range finish. Biggins then slots home a penalty after Ellis is tripped. Steve Harrison's Hornets subject City to a long-ball barrage and Gary Penrice finishes off a flick on. Much better.

BARCLAYS DIVISION 2

Manager: Mick Mills ⇨ Alan Ball

SEASON 1989-90

No	Date	Match	Att	Pos	Pt	F-A	H-T	Scorers, Times, and Referees	1	2	3	4	5	6	7	8	9	10	11	subs used
24	A 1/1	MIDDLESBROUGH W	16,238	20	22	1-0	0-0	Ellis 61 / Ref: T West	Fox	Butler	Carr	Kamara!	Holmes	Fowler*	Pain	Beeston	Ellis	Biggins	Sandford	Saunders
		(opp.)							*Pears*	*Parkinson*	*Cooper*	*Mowbray*	*Coleman*	*Ripley*	*Slaven*	*Proctor*	*Kernaghan**	*Brennan*	*Davenport*	*Burke*
25	H 13/1	PORTSMOUTH L	12,051	19	22	1-2	0-2	Sandford 70; Whittingham 14, Hazard 40 / Ref: J Watson	Fox	Butler	Carr	Kamara	Holmes*	Fowler	Bamber	Beeston	Ellis	Biggins	Sandford	Saunders/Hackett
		(opp.)							*Knight*	*Neill*	*Stevens*	*Fillery*	*Hogg^*	*Ball*	*Wigley^*	*Black*	*Whittingham*	*Hazard*	*Chamberlain*	*Fillery/Gilligan*
26	A 20/1	LEEDS L	29,318	1	22	0-2	0-0	Strachan 68p, Hendrie 74 / Ref: G Tyson	Fox	Butler	Carr*	Saunders	Holmes	Fowler	Ware^	Beeston	Palin	Biggins	Sandford	Hackett/Palin
		(opp.)							*Day*	*Beglin*	*Whitlow*	*Jones*	*Fairclough*	*Haddock*	*Strachan*	*Batty*	*Chapman*	*Davison**	*Hendrie*	*Pearson*
27	A 27/1	BLACKBURN L	9,132	9	22	0-3	0-2	Kennedy 4, Gayle 37p, Sellars 77 / Ref: C Trussell	Fox	Butler	Statham	Beeston	Holmes	Fowler*	Ware	Ellis	Palin	Biggins	Sandford	Saunders
		(opp.)							*Gennoe*	*Atkins*	*Sulley*	*Reid*	*Moran*	*Mail*	*Kennedy*	*Millar*	*Stapleton*	*Gayle*	*Sellars*	
28	A 3/2	PORT VALE D	22,075	10	23	0-0	0-0	Ref: P Tyldesley	Fox	Butler	Carr	Beeston	Sandford	Berry	Kelly*	Ellis	Palin	Biggins	Kevan	Hackett
		(opp.)							*Grew*	*Mills*	*Walker*	*Aspin*	*Glover*	*Porter*	*Earle*	*Cross^*	*Beckford*	*Jeters*	*Millar*	
29	A 10/2	OLDHAM L	10,028	4	23	0-2	0-0	Palmer 54, Ritchie 64 / Ref: M Peck	Fox	Butler	Carr	Beeston	Blake	Sandford	Kevan	Ellis	Palin	Biggins	Kelly*	Scott
		(opp.)							*Hallworth*	*Irwin*	*Barlow*	*Henry*	*Marshall*	*Holden A*	*Adams*	*Ritchie*	*McGarvey**	*Milligan*	*Holden R*	*Palmer*
30	H 17/2	WOLVES W	17,870	6	26	2-0	0-0	Biggins 34, Hackett 75 / Ref: T Lunt	Fox	Butler	Sandford	Beeston	Blake	Berry	Smith*	Ellis	Kevan	Biggins	Carr	Hackett
		(opp.)							*Kendall*	*Bennett*	*Venus*	*Westley*	*Downing*	*Streete*	*Jones^*	*Cook*	*Bull*	*Mutch*	*Dennison*	*McLoughlin*
31	A 24/2	LEICESTER L	12,245	13	26	1-2	1-0	Biggins 41; Oldfield 66, Reid 79 / Ref: L Shapter	Fox	Butler	Sandford	Beeston	Blake	Berry	Hackett	Ellis	Kevan	Biggins	Carr*	Kelly
		(opp.)							*Hodge*	*Mauchlen*	*Spearing*	*Mills*	*Walsh*	*James*	*Reid*	*Oldfield*	*Kitson^*	*McAllister*	*Wright**	*Ramsey/North*
32	H 3/3	BOURNEMOUTH D	10,988	13	27	0-0	0-0	Ref: J Key	Fox	Butler	Sandford	Beeston	Blake	Berry	Brooke	Ellis	Kevan	Biggins	Carr	Morgan
		(opp.)							*Peyton*	*Bond*	*Morrell*	*Teale*	*Miller*	*Peacock*	*Lawrence**	*Mouldin^*	*Shearer*	*O'Driscoll*	*Blissett*	*Brooks/Aylott*
33	H 6/3	IPSWICH D	10,815	12	28	0-0	0-0	Ref: I Hemley	Fox	Butler	Sandford	Beeston	Blake	Berry	Brooke	Ellis	Kevan	Biggins	Palin	Fowler
		(opp.)							*Forrest*	*Stockwell*	*Thompson*	*Zondervan*	*Gayle*	*Linighan*	*Lowe*	*Dozzell*	*Wark*	*Milton*	*Pennyfather*	
34	A 10/3	BRADFORD C L	9,269	22	28	0-1	0-0	Woods 87 / Ref: G Singh	Fox	Butler	Sandford	Beeston	Blake	Berry	Brooke	Ellis	Kevan	Biggins	Carr*	Morgan
		(opp.)							*Tomlinson*	*Mitchell*	*Tinnion*	*Abbott*	*Sinnott*	*Jackson*	*Aizlewood*	*Davies*	*Leonard*	*Adcock*	*Woods*	

24 — Middlesbrough (A): Chris Kamara is sent off in the middle of the first half for a bad retaliatory foul. City resolutely cling on against Bruce Rioch's Middlesbrough. Tony Ellis cracks home to round off the best performance of the season. Ball is confirmed as the new manager with Paddon as his number two.

25 — Portsmouth (H): Stoke are outplayed by Alan Ball's old team in a vital relegation game. Guy Whittingham nods in a Mickey Hazard cross. On his debut Hazard slams home from close in. Black hits the post with a 38th-minute pen after Chamberlain is felled by Fox but nets the rebound himself. No goal!

26 — Leeds (A): Profligate City waste two fine opportunities to kill the game. Biggins sees his penalty saved by Day (48 mins) after Beeston is fouled. Saunders miscues when bearing down on goal. Strachan nets his penalty after ex-Stokie Lee Chapman is fouled. Hendrie forces home from close range.

27 — Blackburn (A): Howard Gayle scores from the spot, after Fox saves Atkins' 1st-minute penalty. The other goals are from close in. 'Men against boys' says Ball.

28 — Port Vale (A): Saunders is sold to Bristol Rovers for £70,000 and replaced by Tony Kelly, signed from St Albans for £20,000. Dave Kevan signs on-loan from Notts County. Lacklustre Stoke cling on to a point at Vale Park. Vale have two goals disallowed for fouls. Ellis blasts over from five yards out.

29 — Oldham (A): City lose again on plastic where the Latics are unbeaten in their last 30 matches. Noel Blake makes his debut after signing from Leeds. Ex-Stokie Neil Adams crosses for Palmer to guide home. Blake allows the ball to run to Ritchie for the clincher. Beeston drives just past the post.

30 — Wolves (H): In an exuberant game Gary Hackett replaces the on-loan Mark Smith from Dunfermline to produce a superb show. He sets up Biggins to shoot home from 15 yards and then nets after Ellis robs Streete in the box. Graham Turner's Wolves pile forward. The five-man back-line hold firm.

31 — Leicester (A): Biggins' drive hits post and bar before bouncing out but he scores with a cracking free-kick low into the far corner. The ball bobbles in front of Fox and Oldfield profits. Reid pounces when Berry dallies on the ball. Beeston's overhead kick goes wide. Why, why, why are Stoke so poor?

32 — Bournemouth (H): On-loan Gary Brooke becomes City's 30th player this season, a record. In a strong wind City miss Biggins (out with tonsillitis). Morgan hits the upright from three yards. Fox saves well from Lawrence. Noel Blake's header hits a defender on the line as Stoke launch a late cavalry charge.

33 — Ipswich (H): John Duncan's Ipswich are as bad as City. Both sides create just one chance each. Gary Brooke contrives to fire over from three yards out after Craig Forrest parries Palin's effort. The whistles from the Boothen End start well before the referee blows his.

34 — Bradford C (A): Managerless Bradford steal the points thanks to a dubious Neil Woods goal. He later admits to handling the ball before firing past Fox. A huge following see Stoke battle hard but Brooke blasts over and Morgan delays too long. Heads drop when the goal goes in. Relegation a certainty.

35 A PLYMOUTH 17/3 — Att 9,452 | P24 D | Pos 20 | Pts 29 | HT 0-0 | FT 0-0

Fox, Butler, Carr, Beeston, Blake, Smith, Sandford, Ellis*, Kevan, Biggins, Brooke, Morgan
Wilmot, Brown, Braddle, Blacwell, Burrows, Morrison, Hodges, McCarthy, Tynan, Byrne, Fiore, Scott

Ref: V Callow

City fail to overcome a dire Pilgrims side in an atrocious game. In bright sunshine Mark Smith sets up several chances but Rhys Wilmot is not tested. Tynan scuffs an open goal. McCarthy lobs wide. Ellis sees his goalbound shot hit a defender on the line. Ball is exasperated by ill luck.

---

36 A HULL 20/3 — Att 6,456 | P24 D | Pos 19 | Pts 30 | HT 0-0 | FT 0-0

Fox, Butler, Carr, Beeston, Blake, Berry, Palin, Morgan, Kevan, Biggins, Fowler, Scott
Hesford, Brown, Jacobs, Jobson, Shotton, De Mange, Roberts*, Payton, Bamber, Askew^, Atkinson, McParland/Hunter

Ref: T Mills

Lee Fowler plays as sweeper in a five-man back-line. Stoke start well but Andy Payton is fouled and then hits the bar with the penalty. Brooke needs eight stitches after a collision with Jacobs. De Mange clears off the line from Biggins. Stoke are unbeaten at Boothferry Park since 1960.

---

37 A WEST BROM 24/3 — Att 12,771 | P24 D | Pos 16 | Pts 31 | HT 0-1 | FT 1-1

Fox, Butler, Carr*, Thomas, Blake, Barnes, Sandford, Ellis, Kevan, Biggins^, Fowler, Scott/Kelly
Naylor, Burgess, Harbey, Shakespeare North, Whyte, Ford, Goodman, Bannister, Bradley, Hackett

Ellis 78, Ford 22. Ref: D Phillips

Paul Barnes from Notts Co and the returning Mickey Thomas start against Brian Talbot's Albion featuring ex-Stokies Hackett and Ford. They combine for the Baggies' goal. Thomas' cross allows Ellis to head past the startled Naylor. Fox produces four great saves to earn a point.

---

38 H SHEFFIELD UTD 31/3 — Att 14,898 | P24 L | Pos 2 | Pts 31 | HT 0-0 | FT 0-1

Fox, Butler, Carr, Beeston, Blake, Berry^, Sandford, Ellis, Kevan, Biggins, Brooke*, Barnes/Fowler
Tracey, Hill, Hardyman, Todd, Stancliffe, Morris, Barnes, Gannon, Whitehurst*, Deane, Wood^, Agana/Booker

Deane 81. Ref: M James

Stoke weather the Blades' long-ball storm. Fox tips over Brian Deane's header. City improve after Barnes arrives. He fires into the side netting from a well-worked opening. Agana's pace proves to be the difference. His cross is headed home by Deane. Fox tips over Ian Bryson's volley.

---

39 A SUNDERLAND 7/4 — Att 17,119 | P24 L | Pos 5 | Pts 31 | HT 1-2 | FT 1-2

Fox, Butler, Carr, Scott, Blake, Kelly^, Sandford, Ellis, Barnes, Thomas, Kevan, Brooke
Norman, Kay, Heathcote, MacPhail, Owers, Bracewell, Armstrong, Pascoe, Gabbiadini, Brady*, Gates

Gabbiadini 46, Armstrong 57; Ellis 63. Ref: S Lodge

The ageless Thomas is everywhere as City create chances for Ellis and Barnes but both fire wide. Marco Gabbiadini scores after 13 seconds of the second half from 12 yards. Armstrong's header is adjudged to have gone over the line. Ellis turns on a sixpence to half-volley past Norman.

---

40 H OXFORD 10/4 — Att 8,139 | P24 L | Pos 11 | Pts 31 | HT 1-0 | FT 1-2

Fox, Butler, Carr, Scott, Blake, Barnes*, Sandford, Ellis, Thomas, Biggins, Kevan, Brooke
Judge, Smart, Ford, Lewis, Foster, Penney, Evans, Mustoe, Durrin, Stein, Simpson

Sandford 42; Simpson 65p, 89. Ref: D Allison

At last Stoke have some luck. Sandford scores a soft goal from 10 yards. Ellis is tripped for a 48th-minute penalty and a win seems on the cards, but Biggins hits Judge's trailing legs and collapses to the turf in disbelief. Stein is fouled for Oxford's pen. Simpson shows Biggins what to do.

---

41 H MIDDLESBROUGH 14/4 — Att 8,636 | P24 D | Pos 22 | Pts 32 | HT 0-0 | FT 0-0

Fox, Butler, Carr, Fowler, Blake, Kevan^, Sandford, Ellis, Thomas, Biggins, Carr, Berry/Kelly
Pears, Parkinson, Phillips, Kernaghan, Coleman, Slaven, McBee*, Proctor, Baird, Brennan, Davenport, Ripley

Ref: J Deakin

Another lame performance as Stoke seem to freeze whenever goal is sighted. Thomas attempts to drive Stoke forward and Coleman misjudges his pass to leave Ellis clear but his effort is parried by Steve Pears. Berry comes on for a cameo role as a centre-forward as things get desperate.

---

42 A NEWCASTLE 16/4 — Att 26,190 | P24 L | Pos 2 | Pts 32 | HT 0-3 | FT 0-2

Fox, Butler, Carr, Sandford, Blake, Berry, Thomas, Ellis*, Kevan, Biggins, Kevan, Scott/Barnes
Burridge, Scott, Stimson, Aitken, Anderson, Ranson*, Brock, Dillon^, Quinn, McGhee, Kristensen, Bradshaw/O'Brien

Kristensen 3, 70, Quinn 32. Ref: N Midgely

Relegation is finally confirmed after weeks of waiting. Jim Smith's 'Toon never get out of second gear. Bjorn Kristensen scores a classy brace. Mick Quinn notches his 35th of the season – more then the entire Potters squad! 'We're not bothered anymore!' opine the small away gathering.

---

43 H BLACKBURN 21/4 — Att 9,305 | P24 L | Pos 4 | Pts 32 | HT 0-1 | FT 0-0

Fox, Ware, Scott, Sandford, Blake, Berry, Sandford!, Ellis, Kevan, Biggins, Thomas*, Gallimore
Gennoe, Atkins, Dawson, Reid, Moran, Mail, Kennedy, Millar, Stapleton^, Garner, Sellars, Gayle

Mail 65p. Ref: J Martin

Tony Ellis flings himself dramatically when fouled in the box and nothing is given. A second crude challenge earns him a red card. Ball bloods another youngster, Tony Gallimore.

---

44 A WATFORD 24/4 — Att 8,073 | P24 D | Pos 15 | Pts 33 | HT 1-1 | FT 1-1

Fox, Butler, Ware, Fowler, Blake, Berry, Sandford*, Ellis, Kevan, Biggins, Thomas*, Kelly/Farrell
Coton, Gibbs, Williams, Richardson^, H'worth D'vid Roeder, Allison*, Penrice, Wilkinson, Falconer, Thomas, Drysdale/Harrison

Biggins 30; Thomas 36. Ref: R Gifford

Peter Fox apologises to his team-mates after criticising them for 'not being 100% behind Stoke City' on live TV. Perhaps his words sting Stoke into action. Biggins opens the scoring, but 19-year-old Rod Thomas nets his 6th of the year for Colin Lee's Hornets. Some hope for next year?

---

45 A BRIGHTON 28/4 — Att 8,614 | P24 W | Pos 17 | Pts 36 | HT 4-1 | FT 0-0

Fox, Butler, Carr, Beeston, Blake, Berry, Sandford, Boughey^, Ellis, Biggins, Ware, Scott/Sale
Digweed, Crumplin, Chapman, Curdishley, McCarthy, Robinson, Dublin, Gatsmanov, Bremner, Codner, Wilkins

Ellis 51, 76, Biggins 70, Scott 80; Bremner 47. Ref: P Jones

In a party atmosphere, with many Stokies sporting fancy dress, City produce the best ten-minute spell of the season. Biggins hammers low into the corner. Ellis chips Digweed and turns to fire home. Ian Scott loops a header in. Fox makes a wonder stop from Gotsmanov. Wonderful day.

---

46 H SWINDON 5/5 — Att 11,386 | P24 D | Pos 4 | Pts 37 | HT 1-1 | FT 1-1

Noble, Butler, Fowler*, Beeston, Blake, Wright*, Boughey, Ellis, Kevan, Biggins, Ware, Scott/Farrell
Digby, Kerslake, Bodin, McLoughlin, Calderwood Gittens, Shearer^, Jones^, Shearer, White, MacLaren, Foley, Simpson/Cornwall, Sale

Ellis 12; Shearer 12. Ref: T Holbrook

Ball fields a young team. Danny Noble's handling is sound and Darren Boughey's 40-yard run leads to Ellis sweeping home. Shearer glances a header in before the celebrations have finished. City play three at the back after the break and hold their own against play-off contenders Town.

Home 12,458
Away 2,640
Average 12,458

BARCLAYS DIVISION 2 (CUP-TIES)

Manager: Mick Mills ⇒ Alan Ball

Littlewoods Cup

	Att	F-A	H-T	Scorers, Times, and Referees	1	2	3	4	5	6	7	8	9	10	11	subs used
2:1 H MILLWALL 19/9	22 8,030	W 1:5	1-0	Morgan 32 Ref: J Deakin	Fox *Horne*	Butler *Stevens*	Statham *Dawes*	Kamara *Hurlock*	Cranson *Wood !*	Higgins *McLeary*	Palin* *Carter*	Ware *Briley*	Bamber *Sheringham*	Morgan *Cascarino*	Beagrie *Anthrobus**	Hackett *Waddock*

A win against higher division opposition for once. City cope with the loss of the injured Beeston and Biggins. Morgan exultantly volleys home Bamber's knock-down. Steve Wood is dismissed (66 mins) for stamping on the prone Beagrie. Hurlock hits the post. A brilliant performance.

	Att	F-A	H-T	Scorers, Times, and Referees	1	2	3	4	5	6	7	8	9	10	11	subs used
2:2 A MILLWALL 3/10	21 8,637	L 1:5	0-2 aet 0-1	Sheringham 42, Cascarino 119 Ref: B Stevens (Stoke lose 1-2 on aggregate)	Fox *Horne*	Butler *Stevens*	Statham *Dawes*	Kamara *Hurlock*	Cranson *Sparham*	Higgins* *Thompson*	Hackett *Carter*	Beeston *Waddock*	Bamber *Sheringham*	Palin *Cascarino*	Beagrie *Anthrobus*	Saunders

Stoke's five-man defence battle admirably in a bruising match. Carter crosses for Teddy Sheringham to nod in. Stoke have the better chances in extra-time but lose to a clearly offside Tony Cascarino who is allowed to race through and beat Fox. Mills has to be restrained on the touchline.

FA Cup

	Att	F-A	H-T	Scorers, Times, and Referees	1	2	3	4	5	6	7	8	9	10	11	subs used
3 H ARSENAL 6/1	24 23,827	L 1:3	0-1 0-0	Quinn 74 Ref: N Midgley	Fox *Lukic*	Butler *Dixon*	Carr *Davis*	Kamara *Thomas**	Holmes *O'Leary*	Fowler *Adams*	Ware* *Quinn*	Beeston *Richardson*	Saunders *Groves*	Biggins *Bould*	Sandford *Merson^*	Hackett *Jonsson/Rocastle*

Stoke are never in the hunt against George Graham's Gunners. Niall Quinn heads the only goal from a corner. Carr rugby tackles Perry Groves but escapes with a booking. Saunders wastes a glorious chance with two minutes left, failing to make Lukic save. Respectable but out of depth.

League Table

#	Team	P	Home W	Home D	Home L	Home F	Home A	Away W	Away D	Away L	Away F	Away A	Pts
1	Leeds	46	16	6	1	46	18	8	7	8	33	34	85
2	Sheffield Utd	46	14	5	4	43	27	10	8	5	35	31	85
3	Newcastle	46	17	4	2	51	26	5	10	8	29	29	80
4	Swindon	46	12	6	5	49	29	8	8	7	30	30	74
5	Blackburn	46	10	9	4	43	30	9	8	6	31	29	74
6	Sunderland *	46	10	8	5	41	32	6	6	7	29	32	74
7	West Ham	46	14	5	4	50	22	6	7	10	30	35	72
8	Oldham	46	15	7	1	50	23	4	7	12	20	34	71
9	Ipswich	46	13	7	3	38	22	6	5	12	29	44	69
10	Wolves	46	12	5	6	37	20	6	8	9	30	40	67
11	Port Vale	46	11	9	3	37	20	4	7	12	25	37	61
12	Portsmouth	46	9	8	6	40	34	6	8	9	22	31	61
13	Leicester	46	7	8	8	34	29	6	6	12	33	50	59
14	Hull	46	6	7	8	27	31	7	8	8	31	34	58
15	Watford	46	11	6	6	41	28	3	9	11	17	32	57
16	Plymouth	46	9	8	6	30	23	5	5	13	28	40	55
17	Oxford	46	9	6	8	35	31	7	2	14	31	35	54
18	Brighton	46	10	6	7	28	27	5	3	15	28	45	54
19	Barnsley	46	7	9	7	22	23	6	6	11	27	48	54
20	West Brom	46	6	8	9	35	37	6	7	10	32	34	51
21	Middlesbro	46	10	3	10	33	29	3	8	12	19	34	50
22	Bournemouth	45	8	6	9	30	31	4	6	13	27	45	48
23	Bradford C	43	9	6	8	26	24	0	8	15	18	44	41
24	STOKE	43	4	11	8	20	24	2	8	13	15	39	37
		1·04	252	165	135	886	640	135	165	252	640	886	1491

* promoted after play-offs

Appearances and Goals

Player	App Lge	App Sub	App LC	App Sub	App FAC	App Sub	Goals Lge	Goals LC	Goals FAC	Goals Tot
Bamber, Dave	20			2			2			2
Barnes, Paul	4	1								
Barrett, Scott	7									
Beagrie, Peter	13		2							
Beeston, Carl	38		1		1					
Berry, George	15	1			1					
Biggins, Wayne	35						10			10
Blake, Noel	18									
Boughey, Darren	4	3								
Brooke, Gary	6	2								
Butler, John	44		2		2					
Carr, Cliff	22				1					
Cranson, Ian	17		2				2			2
Ellis, Tony	24						6			6
Farrell, Steve		2								
Fowler, Lee	13	2	2							
Fox, Peter	38				2					
Gallimore, Tony		1								
Hackett, Gary	18	8	1	1	1		2			2
Higgins, Mark	4	2	2							
Hilaire, Vince	5						1			1
Holmes, Andy	5	1			1					
Kamara, Chris	22			2	1		1			1
Kelly, Tony	5	4								
Kevan, David	17									
Morgan, Nicky	6	7	1				1	1		2
Noble, Danny	1									
Palin, Leigh	17	2	2				3			3
Sale, Mark		2								
Sandford, Lee	23				1		2			2
Saunders, Carl	12	10		1	1		1			1
Scott, Ian	14	5					1			1
Smith, Mark	2									
Statham, Derek	19		2							
Thomas, Mickey	8									
Ware, Paul	9	7	1		1					
Wright, Ian	1				1					
37 players used	506	60	22	2	11	1	35	1		36

Odds & ends

Double wins: (1) Brighton.

Double losses: (7) Barnsley, Blackburn, Leicester, Oldham, Oxford, Sheffield Utd, Sunderland.

Won from behind: (2) Brighton (a), Newcastle (h).

Lost from in front: (2) Leicester (a), Oxford (h).

High spots: Holding Arsenal to only one goal in the FA Cup.
Improved attendances.
The departure of the floundering Mills.
Beating Millwall at home in the League Cup.
Party time at Brighton.

Low spots: Relegation 13 points adrift in bottom position.
Another dreadful start.
Only 6 wins and 35 goals scored.
The 0-6 thrashing at Swindon.
The arrival of the floundering Ball.
Ian Cranson's bad injury.
Just 3 goals in the last 8 home matches.

Player of the Year: Peter Fox.

Ever-presents: (0).

Hat-tricks: (0).

Leading scorer: (10) Wayne Biggins.

BARCLAYS DIVISION 3

Manager: Alan Ball ⇒ Graham Paddon — SEASON 1990-91

In each line-up table the top row is City, the italic row is the opponents. Positions 1–11 plus substitutes used.

---

1. ROTHERHAM (H) — 25/8
W 3 · F-A 3-1 · H-T 2-0 · Att 13,048 · Ref: R Lewis
Scorers: Blake 15, Kennedy 44p, Thomas 49 — *Williamson 60*

	1	2	3	4	5	6	7	8	9	10	11	subs used
City	Fox	Butler	Statham	Beeston	Blake	Fowler	**Kennedy**	Ellis	Thomas	Biggins	Kelly*	Ware
Opp	*O'Hanlon*	*Forrest*	*Scott*	*Goodwin*	*Law*	*Robinson*	*Buckley**	*Spooner*	*Williamson*	*Mendonca*	*Hazel*	*Dempsey*

Mick Kennedy, from Luton, is cash-strapped City's only new signing. He slots the penalty when Biggins is fouled. Noel Blake dives to head in a flicked on corner. 'Mad' Mickey Thomas belts in to the far corner to send the crowd, higher than most of the Division two gates, into ecstasy.

---

2. TRANMERE (A) — 31/8
W 6 · F-A 2-1 · H-T 2-1 · Att 10,327 · Ref: E Parker
Scorers: Ellis 36, Kennedy 43p — *Muir 21p*

	1	2	3	4	5	6	7	8	9	10	11	subs used
City	Fox	Butler	Statham	Beeston	Blake	Sandford	Kennedy	Ellis	Thomas*	Biggins	Ware	Kelly
Opp	*Nixon*	*Mungall*	*McCarrick**	*McNab*	*Hughes^*	*Vickers*	*Morrissey*	*Harvey*	*Steel*	*Muir*	*Thomas*	*Martindale/Irons*

Paul Ware handles and Ian Muir sends Fox the wrong way from the spot. Ellis' back header creeps into the far corner. Kennedy's spot-kick is courtesy of Vickers' foul. A new yellow and black away kit is christened with six bookings. 'We're going to win the league' chant the Stokies.

---

3. BIRMINGHAM (H) — 8/9
L 6 · F-A 0-1 · H-T 0-0 · Att **16,009** · Pos 7/2 · Ref: J Deakin
Scorers: — *Gleghorn 57*

	1	2	3	4	5	6	7	8	9	10	11	subs used
City	Fox	Butler	Statham	Beeston*	Blake	Sandford	Kennedy	Ellis	Thomas	Biggins	Kelly	Ware
Opp	*Thomas*	*Ashley*	*Downs*	*Frain*	*Fox*	*Matthewson*	*Peer*	*Bailey*	*Moran**	*Gleghorn*	*Tait*	*Sturridge*

A midfield battle. Stoke hold the upper hand but Moran and Tait threaten on the break. Dean Peer's deep cross falls to Nigel Gleghorn who nets from three yards. Stoke's long-ball game fails to trouble Dave Mackay's Blues. Fox saves Tait's shot well. More creativity needed in midfield.

---

4. BOURNEMOUTH (A) — 15/9
D 7 · F-A 1-1 · H-T 0-0 · Att 6,374 · Pos 6/20 · Ref: P Alcock
Scorers: Statham 84 — *Bissett 47p*

	1	2	3	4	5	6	7	8	9	10	11	subs used
City	Fox	Butler	Statham	Beeston	Blake	Sandford	Kennedy	Ellis*	Kelly*	Biggins	Ware	Thomas /Fowler
Opp	*Guthrie*	*O'Driscoll*	*Morrell*	*Teale*	*Shearer*	*Bond*	*Lawrence**	*Peacock*	*Aylott*	*Holmes*	*Blissett*	*Ekoku*

Blissett scores from the spot after Butler barges Holmes. Kelly has a goal disallowed for offside even though the referee appears to have played advantage. Stoke push forward in numbers and Statham ghosts into the box to bag his first goal for the club. City are over £1.5 million in debt.

---

5. CHESTER (A) — 18/9
D 8 · F-A 1-1 · H-T 1-0 · Att 3,579 · Pos 8/9 · Ref: P Harrison
Scorers: Thomas 7 — *Ellis 87*

	1	2	3	4	5	6	7	8	9	10	11	subs used
City	Fox	Butler	Statham	Beeston	Blake	Sandford	Kennedy	Ellis	Ware	Biggins	Thomas	
Opp	*Stewart*	*Preece*	*Pugh*	*Butler*	*Abel*	*Lane*	*Bennett*	*Barrow*	*Painter**	*Dale*	*Ellis*	*Lightfoot*

Over 500 Stokies are locked out. They are the lucky ones as City stumble against Harry McNally's Chester. Thomas nets from a narrow angle. Chester's wind-assisted onslaught sees Fox save well from Dale and Barrow. The midfield disintegrates and Ellis loops a header in. Booed off.

---

6. SOUTHEND (H) — 22/9
W 11 · F-A 4-0 · H-T 2-0 · Att 11,901 · Pos 7/2 · Ref: K Cooper
Scorers: Ware 38, Biggins 41, 49, Cornwell 68 (og)

	1	2	3	4	5	6	7	8	9	10	11	subs used
City	Fox	Butler	Statham	Beeston	Blake	Sandford	Kennedy	Ellis	Thomas^	Biggins	Ware^	Kelly
Opp	*Sansome*	*Austin*	*Powell*	*Martin*	*Cornwell*	*Clark*	*Butler*	*Ansah*	*Benjamin*	*Angell**	*Kelly*	*Cook*

Southend have won all their games so far but buckle under intense City pressure. Ware cracks home from 15 yards. Biggins rams in exultantly. His second slips through Paul Sansome's grasp. Cornwell heads Ware's centre into his own net. Blake has a header palmed over. More like it.

---

7. SHREWSBURY (H) — 29/9
L 11 · F-A 1-3 · H-T 1-2 · Att 12,672 · Pos 10/19 · Ref: P Vanes
Scorers: Sandford 26 — *Spink 34, Sandford 40 (og), Worsley 63*

	1	2	3	4	5	6	7	8	9	10	11	subs used
City	Fox	Butler	Statham	Beeston*	Blake	Sandford	Kennedy	Ellis	**Evans**	Biggins	Ware	Thomas/Cranson
Opp	*Perks*	*Worsley*	*Gorman*	*Kelly*	*Heathcote*	*Blake*	*Moore*	*Coughlin*	*Spink*	*Brown**	*Griffiths*	*Wimbledon*

Sandford chests down a Kennedy cross to crash in from 15 yards. City sit back and allow ex-Stokie Tony Kelly to run midfield. He crosses for Spink and forces Sandford to turn past Fox. Worsley converts Moore's centre and it is all over bar the booing. Shrews' first win of the season.

---

8. CREWE (A) — 2/10
W 14 · F-A 2-1 · H-T 1-0 · Att 7,200 · Pos 6/22 · Ref: T Fitzharris
Scorers: Biggins 42, Ware 77 — *Foreman 60*

	1	2	3	4	5	6	7	8	9	10	11	subs used
City	Fox	Butler	Statham	Ware	Blake	Sandford	Kennedy	Ellis	Evans	Biggins	Thomas	
Opp	*Greygoose*	*Lennon*	*Carr*	*Smart !*	*Swain*	*Rose*	*Jasper*	*Foreman**	*Hignett*	*Gardiner^*	*Sussex*	*Callaghan/Jones*

Wayne Biggins scores a superb solo goal, beating two Alex defenders before firing home from outside the box. Foreman prods in after the ball rebounds off the post. Colin Smart is sent off for felling a clean through Ellis. Ware lunges to head in Cliff Carr's resulting left-wing free-kick.

---

9. BOLTON (A) — 6/10
W 17 · F-A 1-0 · H-T 0-0 · Att 8,521 · Pos 4/23 · Ref: P Wright
Scorers: Evans 61

	1	2	3	4	5	6	7	8	9	10	11	subs used
City	Fox	Butler	Statham	Ware	Blake	Sandford	Kennedy	Ellis	Evans	Biggins	Thomas*	Kelly* /Fowler
Opp	*Felgate*	*Brown*	*Burke**	*Green*	*Seagraves*	*Winstanley*	*Lee*	*Thompson*	*Reeves^*	*Phillskirk*	*Darby*	*Cowdrill/Stevens*

City dominate but Biggins and Ellis waste golden opportunities. Finally a cushioned Evans header from Kennedy's left-wing cross beats David Felgate. Bolton wobble and City should have more. A late panic sees Fox scrambling when a deflected free-kick loops onto the roof of the net.

---

10. FULHAM (H) — 13/10
W 20 · F-A 2-1 · H-T 1-0 · Att 12,394 · Pos 3/23 · Ref: T West
Scorers: Ellis 26, 68 — *Rosenior 32*

	1	2	3	4	5	6	7	8	9	10	11	subs used
City	Fox	Butler	Statham	Beeston	Blake	Sandford	Kennedy	Ellis	Evans	Biggins	Ware	
Opp	*Stannard*	*Newson*	*Pike*	*Ferney**	*North*	*Morgan*	*Kelly*	*Davies**	*Rosenior*	*Brazil*	*Marshall*	*Cobb/Milton*

Alan Dicks' Fulham, fresh from their first victory of the season, begin brightly. Leroy Rosenior's overhead kick just misses. Ellis cracks home Biggins' flick on. He then drags the ball back to wrong-foot three defenders before slotting past Jim Stannard. Fox makes a superb double save.

---

11. CAMBRIDGE (H) — 20/10
D 21 · F-A 1-1 · H-T 0-1 · Att 12,673 · Pos 3/8 · Ref: H King
Scorers: Biggins 54 — *Dublin 14*

	1	2	3	4	5	6	7	8	9	10	11	subs used
City	Fox	Butler	Statham	Beeston	Blake	Sandford	Kennedy	Ellis	Evans	Biggins	Ware*	Thomas
Opp	*Vaughan*	*O'Shea*	*Kimble*	*Wilkins*	*Chapple*	*Daish*	*Cheetham**	*Leadbitter**	*Dublin*	*Taylor*	*Philpott*	*Claridge/Bailie*

Dion Dublin finishes brilliantly to stun Stoke. He then hits the foot of the post as City fumble for form. Possession means nothing against John Beck's well-organised defence. Biggins heads in Evans' corner to grab a point but puts an easier header wide. U's 20 away matches unbeaten.

12 A BRADFORD C 24/10 — 8,086 — pos 3, 16 — **W 2-1** (HT 0-1) — 24

Kelly 58, Thomas 88 / McCarthy 48 — Ref: A Flood

Fox, Butler, Statham, Beeston, Blake, Sandford, Kennedy^, Ellis, Thomas, Biggins*, Ware, Kelly/Carr
Tomlinson, Mitchell, Babb, James, Oliver, Simnott, Duxbury, Jewell, McCarthy, Leonard, Stuart, Carr/Kevan

Despite a dreadful showing Stoke snatch the win against John Docherty's Bantams. McCarthy nods in after heavy Bradford pressure. Fox pulls off two fantastic saves. The game turns when Mitchell miscues against his own post and Kelly prods in, then Thomas cashes in on Babb's error.

---

13 A GRIMSBY 27/10 — 10,799 — pos 3, 2 — **L 0-2** (HT 0-0) — 24

Watson 55, Childs 70 — Ref: P Tyldesley

Fox, Butler, Statham, Beeston, Blake, Sandford, Kennedy^, Ellis, Thomas, Biggins*, Ware, Kelly*
Sherwood, McDermott, Jobling, Tilson, Lever, Cunnington, Childs, Gilbert, Rees, Watson, Woods, Carr/Kevan

A bad day as Kelly is crocked by a tackle from behind and City lose to two poor goals emanating from defensive blunders. A post-match pitch invasion is the cue for fights between rival supporters. Director Geoff Manning resigns under the pressure of running the club on a shoestring.

---

14 H READING 3/11 — 12,245 — pos 3, 9 — **L 0-1** (HT 0-1) — 24

Moran 2 — Ref: T Simpson

Fox, Butler, Statham, Beeston, Blake, Sandford, Scott, Ellis, Thomas, Barnes*, Ware, **Bright**
Burns, Jones, Gilkes, McPherson, Hicks, Williams, Gooding, Taylor, Senior, Conroy, Moran*, Maskell

Ball's squad is down to the bare bones. Paul Barnes starts and is replaced by youth starlet David Bright. Ellis blasts a great chance over the bar before Steve Moran prods home. Stoke cannot find the net despite the one-way traffic. Sandford, Ellis, Ware and Statham waste good chances.

---

15 H WIGAN 10/11 — 12,756 — pos 3, 11 — **W 2-0** (HT 1-0) — 27

Biggins 20, Kennedy 68 — Ref: P Jones

Fox, Butler, Statham, Beeston, Blake, Sandford, Kennedy^, Ellis, **Whitehurst**, Biggins, Ware^, Ellis
Atkins, Parkinson, Tankard, Atherton, Johnson, Langley, Woods, Daley*, Rimmer, Page, Griffiths B, Patterson

Mickey Thomas is at the centre of everything as Stoke outplay woeful Wigan. Biggins neatly loops a header in. Billy Whitehurst makes a quiet debut but offers another option up front. Thomas is tripped for a penalty after scampering clear. Atkins saves. Kennedy rams home the rebound.

---

16 A BURY 14/11 — 5,118 — pos 3, 8 — **D 1-1** (HT 0-0) — 28

Thomas 47, McGinlay 77 — Ref: R Shepherd

Fox, **Rennie**, Statham, Beeston, Blake*, Sandford, Kennedy, Ellis, Thomas^, Biggins, Ware*, Fowler/Kelly
Kelly, Hill, Stanislaus^, Mauge, Valentine, Knill, Lee*, Parkinson, Robinson, McGinlay, Patterson, Cunningham/Feeley

In pouring rain 3,000 Stokies witness an ill-tempered affair. Biggins and Thomas take punishment but Blake and Kennedy redress the balance. Ellis crosses for Thomas to head home superbly. John McGinlay pounces when Rennie and Cranson get in a mix up. A game City should win.

---

17 A EXETER 1/12 — 5,377 — pos 3, 18 — **L 0-2** (HT 0-0) — 28

Neville 72, Eshelby 79 — Ref: R Wiseman

Fox, Rennie, Statham, Beeston, Blake, Cranson, Kennedy, Ellis, Whitehurst*, Biggins, Sandford, Thomas
Miller, Hiley, Dryden, Cawley, Taylor, Cooper, Marshall, Bailey, Morgan, Neville, Eshelby, Thomas

Stoke's first ever visit to the other St James' Park ends in disaster when Steve Neville and Paul Eshelby wrap up the game for Terry Cooper's Grecians. Stoke wilt, the fans boo and the referee books the Exeter trainer who enters the pitch to treat a player without permission! Outplayed.

---

18 H BRENTFORD 16/12 — 10,995 — pos 5, 6 — **D 2-2** (HT 1-1) — 29

Hilaire 10, Sandford 65 / Cadette 44, Smillie 46 — Ref: G Aplin

Fox, Ware, Statham, Beeston, Blake, Sandford, Thomas, Ellis, Whitehurst*, Biggins, Hilaire*, Ellis
Benstead, Ratcliffe, Fleming, Millen, Cousins, Buckle, Jones, Godfrey*, Cadette, Blissett, Smillie, Gayle

Vince Hilaire celebrates his permanent transfer from Leeds by riding a tackle and firing past Graham Benstead. Transfer-listed Richard Cadette fires the Bees level and Neil Smillie's deflected shot beats Fox. Ellis' arrival sparks the fightback. Sandford rises to head home from six yards.

---

19 A PRESTON 22/12 — 7,532 — pos 7, 17 — **L 0-2** (HT 0-1) — 29

Swann 17, 64 — Ref: S Lodge

Fox, Kelly, Statham, Beeston, Blake, Sandford, Kennedy, Thomas, Ware*, Biggins, Hilaire, Kelly/Gallimore
Kelly, Senior, Williams, Flynn, Hughes, Wrightson, Mooney, Bogie, Joyce, Shaw, Swann, Swann

Ex-Stokie Shaw sets up Gary Swann to fire low past Fox and then sees his own effort disallowed for offside. Stoke's dislike of the plastic pitch is clear. Ball kicks an advertising hoarding when City foul up a set-piece. The second comes from Blake's mis-hit back-pass. It's 'Ball out' now.

---

20 H SWANSEA 26/12 — 12,534 — pos 8, 16 — **D 2-2** (HT 1-1) — 30

Biggins 44, Thomas 70 / Gilligan 17, 89p — Ref: T Lunt

Fox, Butler, Statham, Beeston, Cranson, Fowler, Ellis*, Thomas, Biggins, Ware, Hilaire, Kelly
Bracey, Hough, Coleman, Walker, Harris, Davies, Raynor^, Coughlin, Gilligan, Connor, Legg*, Hutchison/D'Auria

Stoke are awful and concede to Jimmy Gilligan's header. Out of the blue Biggins skips a tackle and drives home. Stoke are galvanised. Hilaire torments the Swans' defence. Thomas heads in Kelly's centre. After dropping a high cross at his feet, Fox brings down Gilligan for the penalty.

---

21 H HUDDERSFIELD 29/12 — 1,869 — pos 8, 14 — **W 2-0** (HT 1-0) — 33

Ellis 15, 48 — Ref: G Aplin

Fox, Butler, Fowler, Beeston, Cranson, Sandford, Kennedy, Ellis, Thomas, Biggins, Hilaire, Smith
Martin, Trevitt, Parsley*, O'Doherty, Mitchell, Jackson, O'Regan, Donovan, Roberts, Barnett, Onuora, Smith

Tony Ellis scores two great goals as Stoke end a terrible year on a bright note. He shrugs off Simon Trevitt to fire beat Lee Martin then cleverly clips a first-time shot past the advancing Jackson and Martin. Carl Beeston runs midfield and fires wide after a superb flowing four-man move.

---

22 A LEYTON ORIENT 1/1 — 6,371 — pos 6, 7 — **W 2-0** (HT 1-0) — 36

Ellis 9, Thomas 59 — Ref: M Pierce

Fox, Butler, Fowler, Beeston, Blake, Sandford, Ware, Ellis, Thomas, Biggins, Hilaire, Harvey
Heald, Baker, Howard, Sitton, Whitbread, Pike, Carter, Castle, Nugent, Achampong, Berry*, Harvey

Tony Ellis latches onto a long Fox punt to ram home from 15 yards. Frank Clark's O's cause problems with Kenny Achampong prominent on the right. Sandford contains him well. Thomas nips in to notch another brave header as City counter attack. Is form returning at the right time?

---

23 H TRANMERE 12/1 — 13,461 — pos 7, 6 — **D 1-1** (HT 0-1) — 37

Butler 77 / Brannan 31 — Ref: P Taylor

Fox, Butler, Statham, Beeston, Blake, Sandford, Kennedy, Ellis, Thomas*, Biggins, Hilaire, Kelly
Nixon, Higgins, Brannan, Irons, Hughes, Vickers, Morrissey*, Harvey, Steel, Muir, Mungall, Cooper

Tempers fray as neither side can get a hold on the match. Hilaire and Hughes have a running battle. Biggins and Vickers lock foreheads. Butler deflects Brannan's shot over Fox before firing a long-range shot past Eric Nixon. Thomas is lucky to stay on after a set-to with Steve Mungall.

BARCLAYS DIVISION 3 Manager: Alan Ball ⇨ Graham Paddon SEASON 1990-91

Column headers (per match): 1, 2, 3, 4, 5, 6, 7, 8, 9, 10, 11, subs used — each cell lists the Stoke player first, the opposition player in *italics*.

No	Date	Att	Pos	Pt	F-A	H-T	Scorers, Times, and Referee
24	A ROTHERHAM 19/1	6,236	24	38	0-0	0-0	Ref: I Hendrick
25	H CHESTER 2/2	11,037	10	38	2-3	0-1	Kelly 60, Hilaire 68; Dale 29, Bishop 52, 54. Ref: A Bennett
26	A SOUTHEND 5/2	5,164	11	38	0-1	0-1	Angell 41. Ref: M James
27	H BURY 16/2	9,885	13	39	2-2	1-0	Biggins 45, 65; Hulme 73, 30. Ref: R Bigger
28	A WIGAN 23/2	3,728	15	39	0-4	0-1	Daley 36, 52, Patterson 64, Page 88. Ref: V Callow
29	H BOURNEMOUTH 27/2	7,797	16	39	1-3	0-0	Biggins 50; Jones 61, Lawrence 76, Blissett 84. Ref: J Lloyd
30	H EXETER 2/3	8,536	15	42	2-1	1-1	Biggins 27, 85; Cooper 29p. Ref: M Peck
31	A MANSFIELD 5/3	2,941	15	43	0-0	0-0	Ref: J Moules
32	A BRENTFORD 9/3	7,249	13	46	4-0	0-0	Thomas 64, Blake 69, Beeston 86, [Clarke 90]. Ref: G Willard
33	H CREWE 13/3	15,455	11	49	1-0	0-0	Devlin 90. Ref: R Hamer
34	A SHREWSBURY 16/3	6,210	12	49	0-2	0-2	Lyne 31, 44. Ref: K Barratt

Line-ups (Stoke / *opponent*):

No	1	2	3	4	5	6	7	8	9	10	11	subs used
24	Fox / *O'Hanlon*	Fowler / *Forrest*	Statham / *Russell*	Ware / *Thompson*	Blake / *Law*	Sandford / *Robinson*	Kennedy / *Goodwin**	Ellis / *Dempsey*	Thomas / *Goater*	Biggins* / *Mendonca*	Hilaire / *Hazel*	Kelly / *Spooner*
25	Fox / *Stewart*	Butler / *Butler*	Cranson / *Painter*	Ware / *Lightfoot*	Blake / *Abel*	Sandford / *Pugh*	Kevan* / *Bishop*	Ellis / *Barrow*	Thomas* / *Morton**	Kelly / *Dale*	Hilaire / *Croft*	Carr/Devlin / *Bennett*
26	Fox / *Sansome*	Butler / *Austin*	Carr / *Powell*	Ware* / *Martin*	Blake / *Scully*	Sandford / *Tilson*	Devlin / *Clark*	Ellis / *Butler*	Kelly / *Ansah*	Rice / *Benjamin*	Hilaire^ / *Angell*	Scott/Cranson
27	Fox / *Kelly*	Butler / *Feeley*	Carr / *Stanislaus*	Beeston / *Kearney*	Blake / *Valentine*	Cranson / *Greenall*	Devlin* / *Lee*	Ellis / *Robinson*	Ware / *Cunningham*	Biggins / *Parkinson*	Rice / *Hulme*	Thomas
28	Fox / *Hughes*	Butler / *Patterson*	Carr / *Tankard*	Beeston / *Atherton*	Blake / *Johnson*	Fowler / *Langley*	Kennedy / *Jones*	Ellis / *Rimmer*	Ware / *Daley*	Biggins* / *Page*	Rice / *Griffiths B*	Devlin
29	Fox / *Peyton*	Butler* / *Mundee*	Statham / *Morrell*	Beeston / *Teale*	Blake / *Watson*	Sandford / *O'Driscoll*	Kennedy! / *Wood*	Ellis^ / *Holmes**	Rice / *Jones*	Biggins / *Pulis*	Devlin / *Blissett*	Thomas/Barnes / *Lawrence*
30	Fox / *Miller*	Beeston / *Hiley*	Statham / *Brown*	Devlin* / *McNichol*	Blake / *Taylor*	Sandford / *Cooper*	Kennedy / *Dryden*	Ellis* / *Batty^*	Kennedy / *Morgan*	Biggins / *Neville*	Barnes / *Marshall*	Ware / *Rowbottham*
31	Fox / *Beasley*	Ware / *Chambers**	Statham* / *Murray*	Devlin / *Withe*	Blake / *Foster*	Cranson / *Gray*	Kennedy / *Kent*	Thomas / *Charles*	Rice / *Hathaway*	Biggins / *Wilkinson*	Barnes^ / *Fairclough*	Carr/Kelly / *Christie*
32	Fox / *Benstead*	Beeston / *Ratcliffe*	Carr / *Carstairs*	Devlin / *Fleming*	Blake / *Evans*	Fowler / *Buckle^*	Kennedy / *Jones*	Thomas / *Cockram*	Thomas / *Holdsworth*	Biggins / *Cadette**	Rice / *Godfrey*	Gayle/Rostron
33	Fox / *Beresford*	Rennie^ / *Swain*	Statham* / *Callaghan*	Devlin / *Smart*	Blake / *Carr*	Fowler / *Lennon*	Kennedy / *Murphy^*	Thomas / *Hignett^*	Clarke / *Gardiner*	Biggins / *Edwards R*	Rice* / *Doyle/McKearney*	Kelly/Ware
34	Fox / *Hughes*	Beeston / *Blake*	Carr / *Lynch*	Devlin / *Kelly*	Blake / *Heathcote*	Sandford / *Clements*	Kennedy / *Brown*	Thomas / *Spink*	Thomas / *Summerfield*	Biggins* / *Taylor*	Rice^ / *Lyne*	Ellis/Kelly

Match reports

24 — 3,000 Stokies bask in the South Yorkshire sun but see little to believe that City will go up. Ellis twice shoots straight at Kelham O'Hanlon and Hilaire does likewise when clean through. Fox's brilliant flying save denies Des Hazel. Billy McEwan's rock-bottom Millers deserve the point.

25 — An abysmal performance. Chester are applauded by the Boothen after their third goal. City lack discipline, imagination and heart. Mark Devlin is the honourable exception on his debut as substitute. Kelly and Hilaire convert easy chances but the Potters' lack of commitment is worrying.

26 — City play without direction and fail to muster a shot in the first half. Brett Angell bundles the ball in for his 22nd of the season as Dave Webb's uncultured Shrimpers stay top. Brian Rice, on-loan from Forest, looks out of place in Div 3. Fox keeps the score down. Blake is booked again.

27 — Biggins flicks in against the run of play. Roger Stanislaus incredibly fires over from two yards with Fox beaten. Biggins heads the second from Rice's perfect cross but Hulme is left unmarked for two headers and Bury nearly snatch it in added time. Totally inept. Ball's job is on the line.

28 — Alan Ball resigns, leaving Stoke in their worst ever position in the league after taking a fearful hammering from Bryan Hamilton's Latics. Fox has a brilliant game, keeping the score respectable. Carr and Biggins both miss good chances. The team has no confidence left. Truly appalling.

29 — Graham Paddon is in charge of the demoralised troops who manage to take the lead through Biggins' header from Rice's centre. The Cherries' rough-house tactics see Butler stretchered off and Mick Kennedy snaps. He is sent off for kicking Matt Holmes. Bournemouth take advantage.

30 — Relief as City finally win. Kevin Miller allows a long ball to slip past him and Biggins pounces. Blake handles for the penalty but City manage to put their troubles behind them and dominate the second period. Biggins' deserved second is a superb run and shot. His fifth in four matches.

31 — City revert to type against George Foster's relegation-haunted Stags. Kennedy has a shot cleared off the line and Kelly and Biggins both fail to beat Andy Beasley one-on-one. Ian Cranson is carried off at the end. Forgive us Delilah but Stoke cannot take any more.

32 — Stoke run riot in the second half and for once everything that they hit goes in. Thomas glances a header home and Blake lobs Graham Benstead from 10 yards. Beeston twists past two defenders to drive in and Wayne Clarke, on-loan from Man City, taps home from two yards. Fabulous.

33 — A totally forgettable night. Crewe battle tigerishly in their battle to avoid the drop. City rarely threaten. They somehow contrive to score when Devlin nets from Thomas's good approach work. Over 15,000 witness Stoke's undeserved win, almost as many as watch Man Utd at the Dell.

34 — Neil Lyne, on-loan from Forest, scores twice after Stoke defenders fail to clear. He also hits the post. Shrewsbury's first home league win since 9 Nov. Clarke has an overhead kick cleared off the line. Ellis head-butts Lynch but escapes a red card when he is carried off with concussion.

Stoke City match-by-match results

---

35 — A — 19/3 — FULHAM | 3,131 | 9 | 22 | 52 | W 1-0
Biggins 61
Ref: B Hill
Lineup: Fox, Ware, Carr, Beeston, Blake, Sandford, Devlin, Thomas, Clarke, Biggins, Rice
(opp: Stannard, Morgan, Thomas, Eckhart, North, Talbot, Milton*, Scott, Stant, Brazil, Pike^, Davies/Cobb)
A paltry crowd witness a dour match with Stoke just having the edge. Neither side has brought its shooting boots. Blake produces a moment of rare inspiration, breaking free to cross for Biggins to fire in. The Fulham faithful want boss Alan Dicks out. No new manager until the summer.

36 — H — 23/3 — BOLTON | 13,889 | 10 | 3 | 53 | D 2-2
Devlin 47, Kelly 55; Darby 80, Storer 81
Ref: D Frampton
Lineup: Fox, Ware, Carr, Beeston, Blake, Sandford, Devlin, Thomas, Clarke, Kelly, Rice
(opp: Felgate, Brown, Burke, Patterson*, Seagraves, Stubbs, Storer, Thompson, Reeves, Philliskirk, Darby, Green)
Yet again Stoke fail to win a match after scoring the first goal. Thomas buzzes around in midfield and sets up Devlin's tap-in and Kelly's close-range header. Stoke self-destruct. Blake loses Darby who fires home and Storer rifles in unchallenged from the edge of the area. Thrown away.

37 — H — 26/3 — MANSFIELD | 9,113 | 9 | 20 | 56 | W 3-1
Clarke 30, 60, Blake 53; Smalley 46
Ref: N Midgley
Lineup: Fox, Beeston, Carr, Devlin, Blake, Sandford, Kennedy, Thomas, Clarke, Biggins, Rice
(opp: Beasley, Chambers, Smalley, Spooner, Kearney, Gray, Ford, Smith, Christie*, Wilkinson, Fairclough, Stringfellow)
The City back four look jittery against Gary Ford's direct running but in attack Stoke move freely. Clarke heads home Kelly's cross to finish a move he begins. Blake heads in Rice's free-kick and Clarke rounds off the scoring from another Rice centre. One defeat in eight since Ball left.

38 — A — 30/3 — SWANSEA | 4,418 | 10 | 19 | 56 | L 1-2
Ellis 88; Legg 8, Harris 81
Ref: A Buksh
Lineup: Fox, Fowler, Carr, Blake, Blake, Sandford*, Kennedy, Thomas, Clarke, Kelly, Rice
(opp: Bracey, Williams, Coleman, Hough, Harris, Legg, Raynor, Davies, Gilligan, Coughlin, Penney, Ware/Ellis)
Newly installed Swans boss Frank Burrows sees his men ride their luck. Legg's shot takes a deflection to beat Fox. Devlin has a header cleared off the line and Kelly hits the bar. Harris picks up a wayward Stoke throw in to shoot past Fox. Ellis buries a snapshot but City run out of time.

39 — H — 1/4 — PRESTON | 11,524 | 10 | 17 | 56 | L 0-1
Shaw 85
Ref: W Flood
Lineup: Fox, Ware, Carr, Beeston^, Blake, Fowler, Kennedy, Hilaire*, Clarke, Biggins, Rice
(opp: Kelly, Senior, James, Joyce, Flynn, Wrightson, Thompson*, Bogie, Shaw, Harper, Ashcroft, Kelly/Devlin)
Vince Hilaire is brought back into the team despite going AWOL for three days in midweek. He is subbed after 39 mins and never plays again. Predictably ex-Stokie Graham Shaw notches the only goal from Steve Senior's cross. No manager, no play-offs, no hope for Stoke. Dark days.

40 — A — 6/4 — HUDDERSFIELD | 6,520 | 13 | 6 | 56 | L 0-3
O'Regan 34p, Quinlan 49, Wright 55
Ref: W Burns
Lineup: Fox, Ware!, Carr, Beeston, Blake, Kelly*, Kennedy, Thomas, Clarke, Biggins, Rice
(opp: Hardwick, Trevitt, Wright, Marsden, Mitchell, Jackson, O'Regan, Onoura*, Donovan, Quinlan, Barnett, Edwards)
A comprehensive defeat against promotion-seeking Town. O'Regan's penalty is for Carr's trip on Donovan. Quinlan beats Fox at his near post. As the rain pours down, Fox drops Mark Wright's cross over the line and Paul Ware is sent off for two yellows. Beeston is lucky not to follow.

41 — H — 13/4 — LEYTON ORIENT | 7,957 | 13 | 14 | 56 | L 1-2
Beeston 27; Cooper 65, 71
Ref: A Wilkie
Lineup: Fox, Butler, Carr, Beeston, Blake, Fowler^, Devlin, Thomas, Clarke, Biggins*, Rice
(opp: Heald, Baker, Howard, Day, Whitbread, Bart-Williams, Carter*, Castle, Nugent, Cooper, Berry^, Harvey/Hales)
Stoke play some football for half an hour. Kelly springs the offside trap and Biggins side-foots home. Kelly fires wide after a post. Then Orient's physical forwards batter Fowler. Cooper beats him to head in and threads a shot in off a post. The stunned fans depart in total silence.

42 — A — 16/4 — BIRMINGHAM | 6,729 | 13 | 11 | 56 | L 1-2
Ellis 45; Matthewson 7, Hopkins 21
Ref: J Key
Lineup: Noble, Butler, Carr*, Beeston, Blake, Fowler, Devlin, Ellis, Kelly, Biggins, Rice^
(opp: Thomas, Clarkson, Frain, Yates, Overson, Matthewson, Rodgerson, Aylott*, Robinson, Glephorn, Hopkins, Gallimore/Baines, Gordon)
Stoke take the game to Lou Macari's Blues after Matthewson nets a free header. Kelly's speed troubles the big Birmingham back four. Noble palms Frain's penalty (26 mins) round the post. Hopkins sweeps home a corner. Ellis powers past two defenders to blast past Martin Thomas.

43 — A — 20/4 — CAMBRIDGE | 5,743 | 15 | 4 | 56 | L 0-3
Claridge 51, Cheetham 63, Dublin 71
Ref: G Pooley
Lineup: Noble, Butler, Gallimore, Devlin*, Blake, Wright, Kennedy, Ellis, Kelly, Biggins, Baines^
(opp: Vaughan, Fensome, Leadbitter, Bailie, Chapple, O'Shea, Cheetham, Wilkins^, Claridge, Taylor*, Philpott, Carr/Barnes, Dublin/Dennis)
City's smallest away following of the season witness another debacle. Claridge fires high past Noble. Cheetham shins the ball in from six yards and Dublin scores from close in. Biggins is booked for throwing the ball at an opponent. Kennedy heads off the line twice. Six straight defeats.

44 — H — 27/4 — BRADFORD C | 5,946 | 13 | 12 | 59 | W 2-1
Ellis 17, Butler 45; Babb 18
Ref: P Danson
Lineup: Fox, Kevan, Butler, Devlin, Blake, Gallimore, Ware, Thomas, Kelly, Biggins, Rice
(opp: Tomlinson, James, Timmon, Duxbury, Oliver, Sinnott, McCarthy, Jewell, Babb, Torpey*, Reid!, Abbott)
Paul Ware's lunging 8th-minute challenge brings swift retribution from Paul Reid who is promptly sent off. Thomas twists to centre for Ellis to score but no deluge follows. Instead Babb heads a hopeful long punt over Fox. Butler saves Stoke's blushes, firing in after a rare foray upfield.

45 — H — 4/5 — GRIMSBY | 11,832 | 14 | 2 | 60 | D 0-0
Ref: K Cooper
Lineup: Fox, Kevan, Butler, Devlin, Blake, Ware, Devlin, Ellis*, Thomas, Kelly, Biggins
(opp: Sherwood, McDermott, Jobling, Futcher, Lever, Cunnington, Watson, Gilbert, Birtles*, Cockerill, Woods, Smith, Gallimore)
Angry City fans invade the pitch with 15 minutes left of a sterile match. The game is held up for 18 mins while the police herd supporters back to the terraces. Mr Cooper blows early as the teams play out time. Demonstrations. Talk of the fences going up again despite the Taylor report.

46 — A — 11/5 — READING | 4,101 | 14 | 15 | 60 | L 0-1
Senior 15
Ref: R Gifford
Lineup: Fox, Kevan, Butler, Devlin*, Blake, Ware, Devlin, Ellis*, Thomas, Kelly, Biggins
(opp: Francis, Richardson, Conroy, McPherson, Hicks, Bailey, Gooding*, Lovell, Senior, Maskell, Taylor, Seymour)
Stoke lose to new manager Mark McGhee's Royals, who are on a worse run than City (five defeats in five). City's new boss will have his work cut out to turn a poor side, with no passion, into any kind of team. Senior heads a free-kick in unchallenged. Blake clears off the line. Pathetic.

Home Average 11,587
Away 6,150

BARCLAYS DIVISION 3 (CUP-TIES)

Manager: Alan Ball ⇨ Graham Paddon — SEASON 1990-91

Rumbelows Cup

1:1 H SWANSEA — 29/8 — D 0-0 (H-T 0-0) — Att 7,806
Ref: C Trusson

	1	2	3	4	5	6	7	8	9	10	11	subs used
Stoke	Fox	Butler	Statham	Beeston	Blake	Fowler	Kennedy	Ellis*	Thomas	Biggins	Kelly	Boughey
Swansea	*Bracey*	*Raynor*	*Coleman*	*Hough*	*Harris*	*Walker*	*Thornber*	*Davies*	*Gilligan*	*Connor*	*Legg*	

In torrential rain Stoke hold the upper hand. Tony Kelly heads straight at Lee Bracey. Kennedy's shot appears to hit the bar and bounce over the line, but no goal is awarded. 36-year-old Thomas runs himself into the ground but Terry Connor fluffs Terry Yorath's Swans' best opportunity.

1:2 A SWANSEA — 4/9 — W 1-0 (H-T 0-0) — Att 4,464
Kelly 86
Ref: K Cooper
(Stoke win 1-0 on aggregate)

	1	2	3	4	5	6	7	8	9	10	11	subs used
Stoke	Fox	Butler	Statham	Beeston	Blake	Sandford	Kennedy	Ellis	Thomas*	Biggins	Ware	Kelly
Swansea	*Bracey*	*Raynor*	*Coleman*	*Trick*	*Harris*	*Walker**	*Thornber*	*Davies*	*Gilligan*	*Connor*^	*Legg*	*D'Auria/Watson*

Stoke escape after Fox brilliantly tips Mark Harris' header over and parries Keith Walker's point-blank effort. Tony Kelly latches on to Trick's back-pass and beats Bracey to spare Alan Ball's blushes. An unimaginative midfield struggle all night and hard-working Swansea are unlucky.

2:1 A WEST HAM — 26/9 — 7 — L 0-3 (H-T 0-1) — Att 15,870 — 2:3
Dicks 43p, Keen 64, Quinn 86
Ref: B Hill

	1	2	3	4	5	6	7	8	9	10	11	subs used
Stoke	Fox	Butler	Statham^	Beeston	Blake	Sandford	Kennedy	Evans	Kelly^	Biggins	Ware	Thomas/Fowler
West Ham	*Miklosko*	*Potts*	*Dicks*	*Foster*	*Martin*	*Keen*	*Bishop*	*Quinn*	*Slater*	*Allen**	*Morley*	*Parris*

Despite thrashing Southend, Ball makes changes and introduces on-loan Gareth Evans from Hibs. Stoke are never at the races after Morley falls in the box to win a spot-kick. Billy Bonds' Hammers put the tie out of reach through Keen's 30-yarder and Quinn latching onto Fowler's error.

2:2 H WEST HAM — 10/10 — 4 — L 1-2 (H-T 1-0) — Att 8,411 — 2:3
Evans 37 / Allen 64, 73
Ref: N Midgley
(Stoke lose 1-5 on aggregate)

	1	2	3	4	5	6	7	8	9	10	11	subs used
Stoke	Fox	Butler	Carr	Ware	Blake	Sandford	Scott	Evans	Ellis	Biggins	Kevan*	Boughey
West Ham	*Miklosko*	*Potts*	*Dicks*	*Foster*	*Martin*	*Keen**	*Bishop*	*Parris*	*Quinn*^	*Allen*	*Morley*	*Gale/McAvennie*

Evans nips in between Ludo Miklosko and Julian Dicks to lob home. All hope is set aside when Clive Allen clinically plants a pin-point header past Fox and flicks home with the outside of his boot. Hammers run Stoke ragged as the gulf in class between the divisions is clearly visible.

FA Cup

1 A TELFORD — 17/11 — 3 — D 0-0 (H-T 0-0) — Att 3,709
Ref: J Lloyd

	1	2	3	4	5	6	7	8	9	10	11	subs used
Stoke	Fox	Butler*	Statham	Beeston	Blake	Cranson	Kennedy	Ellis	Thomas	Biggins	Sandford	Fowler
Telford	*McDonagh*	*Salathiel*	*Dyson*	*Myers*	*Brindley*	*Humphreys*	*McGinty*	*Grainger*	*Crawley*	*Buxton**	*Nelson*^	*Brown/Bailey*

Stoke face non-league opposition for the first time since Blyth Spartans – and ex-Stokie Paul Dyson. The TV cameras see Stoke out-intimidate Telford. Butler is carried off with a twisted knee. City deal with the Telford threat comfortably. Ian Cranson makes his first start for 12 months.

1R H TELFORD — 21/11 — 3 — W 1-0 (H-T 1-0) — Att 11,880
Sandford 14
Ref: J Lloyd

	1	2	3	4	5	6	7	8	9	10	11	subs used
Stoke	Fox	Rennie^	Statham	Beeston	Blake	Cranson	Kennedy	Whitehurst*	Thomas	Biggins	Sandford	Ellis/Fowler
Telford	*McDonagh*	*Salathiel*	*Dyson*	*Myers*	*Brindley*	*Humphreys*	*McGinty*	*Grainger*	*Crawley*	*Benbow**	*Nelson*^	*Brown/Daly*

Fox makes good saves from Crawley and Brindley. Biggins has a goal ruled out for offside. Sandford outjumps Dyson to bury Kennedy's cross as City edge past battling Telford. Statham and Myers exchange punches but referee Lloyd only books them. Paul Rennie makes a good debut.

2 A BURNLEY — 12/12 — 3 — L 0-2 (H-T 0-0) — Att 12,949 — 4:3
Francis 72, White 84
Ref: K Hackett

	1	2	3	4	5	6	7	8	9	10	11	subs used
Stoke	Fox	Ware	Statham	Sandford	Blake	Cranson*	Kennedy	Thomas	Whitehurst	Biggins	Hilaire*	Beeston/Ellis
Burnley	*Pearce*	*Measham*^	*Deakin*	*Deary*	*Pender*^	*Davis*	*White*	*Futcher**	*Francis*	*Jakub*	*Grewcock*	*Mumby/Farrell*

Frank Casper's Burnley are caused problems by Biggins and Hilaire but lead through a freak goal when Francis' shot hits the post but rebounds into the net off Ware. City lose their heads. Kennedy is intent on kicking anything that moves. White taps in after Fox tips onto the bar. Awful.

Appearances / Goals

Player	Lge	Sub	LC	Sub	FAC	Sub	Lge	LC	FAC	Tot
Baines, Paul	1	1								
Barnes, Paul	3	3					2			2
Beeston, Carl	37		3		2	1				
Biggins, Wayne	36	2	4		3		12			12
Blake, Noel	44		4		3		3			3
Boughey, Darren						2				
Bright, Dave		1								
Butler, John	31		4		1		2			2
Carr, Cliff	15	5	1							
Clarke, Wayne	9									
Cranson, Ian	7	2			3					
Devlin, Mark	18	3								
Ellis, Tony	33	5	3		1	2	2			2
Evans, Gareth	5	2	2				9			9
Fowler, Lee	14	3	1	1	1	2	1		1	2
Fox, Peter	44		4		3					
Gallimore, Tony	4	3								
Hilaire, Vince	10		1				2			2
Kelly, Tony	16	13	2	1			3	1		4
Kennedy, Mick	32		3		3		3			3
Kevan, David	4	1	1							
Noble, Danny	2									
Rennie, Paul	3					1				
Rice, Brian	18									
Sandford, Lee	32		3		3		2	1		3
Scott, Ian	1	1	1							
Statham, Derek	22		3		3		1			1
Thomas, Mickey	32	6	2	1	3		7			7
Ware, Paul	29	5	3		1		2			2
Whitehurst, Billy	3				2					
Wright, Ian	1									
(own-goals)							1			1
31 players used	506	54	44	5	33	5	55	2	1	58

League Table

	Team	P	W	D	L	F	A	W	D	L	F	A	Pts
1	Cambridge	46	14	5	4	42	22	11	6	6	33	23	86
2	Southend	46	13	6	4	34	23	13	1	9	33	28	85
3	Grimsby	46	16	3	4	42	13	8	8	7	24	21	83
4	Bolton	46	14	5	4	33	18	10	6	7	31	32	83
5	Tranmere *	46	13	5	5	38	21	10	4	9	26	25	78
6	Brentford	46	12	4	7	30	22	9	9	5	29	25	76
7	Bury	46	13	6	4	39	26	7	7	9	28	30	73
8	Bradford C	46	13	3	7	36	22	7	7	9	26	32	70
9	Bournemouth	46	14	6	3	37	20	5	7	11	21	38	70
10	Wigan	46	14	6	3	40	20	6	6	11	21	34	69
11	Huddersfield	46	13	3	7	37	23	6	10	8	20	28	67
12	Birmingham	46	8	9	6	21	21	8	8	7	24	28	65
13	Leyton Orient	46	15	2	6	35	19	3	8	12	20	39	64
14	STOKE	46	7	7	9	36	29	7	5	11	19	30	60
15	Reading	46	11	5	7	34	28	5	3	14	19	38	59
16	Exeter	46	12	6	5	35	16	4	3	16	23	36	57
17	Preston	46	11	5	7	33	29	4	6	13	21	38	56
18	Shrewsbury	46	8	7	8	29	22	6	3	14	32	46	52
19	Chester	46	10	3	10	27	27	4	6	13	19	31	51
20	Swansea	46	8	6	9	31	33	5	3	15	18	39	48
21	Fulham	46	8	8	7	27	22	2	8	13	14	34	46
22	Crewe	46	6	9	8	35	35	5	2	16	27	45	44
23	Rotherham	46	5	10	8	31	38	5	2	16	19	49	42
24	Mansfield	46	5	8	10	23	27	3	6	14	19	36	38
		1134	265	134	153	805	576	153	134	265	576	805	1522

* promoted after play-offs

Odds & ends

Double wins: (3) Bradford C, Crewe, Fulham.
Double losses: (4) Birmingham, Preston, Reading, Shrewsbury.

Won from behind: (2) Bradford C (a), Tranmere (a).
Lost from in front: (3) Bournemouth (h), Orient (h), Shrewsbury (h).

High spots: A good start, hitting third spot in November.
The good form of Wayne Biggins.
Beating early season leaders Southend 4-0.
Winning on the opening day for the first time since 1982.
7 away victories, most since 78-79.

Low spots: Lowest ever finish in the Football League.
Alan Ball's failure to turn things around.
An abysmal 0-4 defeat at Wigan.
The appalling behaviour of fans towards the departing Alan Ball.
Losing at Burnley in the FA Cup.
Six defeats towards the end of the season.

Player of the Year: Mickey Thomas.
Ever-presents: (0).
Hat-tricks: (0).
Leading scorer: (12) Wayne Biggins.

BARCLAYS DIVISION 3   Manager: Lou Macari   SEASON 1991-92

No	Date		Att	Pos	Pt		F-A	H-T	Scorers, Times, and Referees	1	2	3	4	5	6	7	8	9	10	11	subs used
1	A	BRADFORD C	7,556	–	0	L	0-1	0-1	Timion 17 / Ref: C Trussell	Kearton / *Tomlinson*	Butler / *Mitchell*	Cranson / *Dowson*	Blake / *James*	Fowler* / *Oliver*	Kevan / *Gardner*	Gallimore / *Babb*	Beeston / *Duxbury L*	Kelly / *Torpey*	Biggins / *Timmion*	Sandford / *Stuart*	Ellis
2	H	BOURNEMOUTH	10,011	18	1	D	1-1	1-1	Biggins 17p, Quinn 42 / Ref: S Bell	Kearton / *Bartram*	Butler / *Baker*	Scott* / *Morrell*	Kevan / *Morris*	Blake / *Watson*	Sandford / *O'Driscoll*	Ellis / *Bond*	Beeston / *Jones^*	Kelly / *Quinn*	Biggins / *Case*	Fowler / *Holmes**	Gallimore / Cooke/Mundee
3	A	PETERBOROUGH	7,174	6	2	D	1-1	1-1	Biggins 1, Kimble 16 / Ref: J Moules	Kearton / *Barber*	Overson / *White*	Scott / *Butterworth Halsall*	Kevan / *Halsall*	Blake / *Robinson*	Kennedy / *Welsh*	Cranson / *Sterling*	Beeston / *Ebdon*	Kelly* / *Gavin*	Biggins / *Riley^*	Fowler / *Kimble^*	Ellis, McInerney/Sterling
4	H	SHREWSBURY	10,182	6	5	W	1-0	0-0	Biggins 53 / Ref: K Breen	Kearton / *Hughes*	Overson / *Gorman*	Scott / *Lynch*	Kevan / *Henry*	Blake / *Heathcote*	Kennedy / *Blake*	Cranson / *Smith*	Beeston / *Summerfield Spink**	Kelly* /	Biggins / *Hopkins*	Fowler / *Lyne*	Ellis, O'Toole
5	A	DARLINGTON	4,230	17	8	W	1-0	0-0	Ellis 57 / Ref: M Peck	Kearton / *Prudhoe*	Butler / *Coatsworth Gray**	Sandford / *Willis*	Kevan / *Smith*	Blake / *Tait*	Kennedy / *Trotter*	Cranson / *Cook*	Beeston / *Toman*	Ellis / *Barthwick**	Biggins* / *Mardenboro' Tait*	Fowler /	Fowler /Scott, Cork/Ellison
6	H	FULHAM	10,567	11	9	D	2-2	1-0	Biggins 25, Cranson 53 / Cole 56, Newson 75 / Ref: R Shepherd	Kearton / *Stannard*	Sandford / *Marshall*	Sandford / *Pike*	Kevan / *Newson*	Blake* / *Eckhardt*	Kennedy / *Thomas*	Cranson / *Kelly**	Beeston / *Onwere*	Ellis / *Cole*	Biggins* / *Brazil*	Fowler^ / *Scott*	Kelly/Overson, Georgiou
7	H	HARTLEPOOL	9,394	14	12	W	3-2	2-0	Biggins 37, 39, Butler 75 / Baker 50, Olsson 65 / Ref: I Hendrick	Kearton / *Hodge*	Butler / *Nobbs*	Sandford / *McKinnon*	Kevan / *Tinkler*	Blake* / *MacPhail*	Kennedy / *Bennyworth Rush**	Cranson /	Overson / *Olsson*	Overson / *Baker*	Biggins / *Honour**	Scott / *Dalton*	Fowler, McCreery/Tupling
8	A	PRESTON	6,345	19	13	D	2-2	1-1	Biggins 41, 59 / Jepson 7, Swann 60 / Ref: I Cruikshanks	Kearton / *Kelly*	Overson / *Senior*	Sandford / *Wrightson*	Kevan / *Swann*	Blake* / *Flynn*	Kennedy / *James J*	Cranson / *Greenwood* Joyce*	Beeston / *Jepson*	Ellis / *Jepson*	Biggins / *Shaw*	Fowler / *James M*	Thompson
9	H	STOCKPORT	12,954	4	14	D	2-2	2-0	Biggins 14p, 28 / Lillis 55, Francis 87 / Ref: R Poulain	Kearton / *Edwards*	Butler / *Knowles*	Sandford / *Williams P*	Scott / *Thorpe*	Overson / *Barras*	Kennedy / *Williams B*	Cranson / *Gannon*	Beeston / *Paskin*	Stein / *Francis*	Biggins / *Ward*	Fowler^ / *Lillis**	Kilner
10	A	CHESTER (at Moss Rose)	4,212	21	15	D	0-0	0-0	Ref: A Dawson	Kearton / *Stewart*	Butler / *McGuinness Albiston*	Sandford / *Pugh*	Scott / *Abel**	Overson / *Whelan*	Kennedy / *Bishop*	Cranson / *Barrow*	Beeston / *Morton*	Stein / *Bennett*	Biggins / *Croft*	Blake / *Butler*	
11	H	BOLTON	12,420	9	18	W	2-0	1-0	Biggins 16, Scott 80 / Ref: R Gifford	Kearton / *Dibble*	Butler / *Brown P*	Sandford / *Burke^*	Kevan* / *Kelly*	Overson / *Came*	Kennedy / *Stubbs*	Cranson / *Brown M*	Beeston / *Patterson*	Stein / *Reeves*	Biggins / *Green**	Fowler / *Darby*	Scott, Stone/Seagraves

Match reports

1. After an on-off saga, Lou Macari is the new manager. He sees a makeshift side beaten by Brian Timmion's strike from 16 yards, which flies past on-loan Jason Kearton. Despite neat approach play, shot-shy Stoke don't look promotion material. Macari knows the squad needs improving.

2. Bournemouth look the better side before Kelly is brought down by Vince Bartram. Stoke hold the upper hand until Jimmy Quinn nips in to fire past Kearton. City lack midfield bite and the forwards look uninterested without service. Ellis' near-post header is the only other on-goal effort.

3. 'Bertie' Biggins turns on the edge of the area to crash home right footed at Chris Turner's newly-promoted Borough. He then has another effort mysteriously disallowed for offside. Gary Kimble pounces when Blake miskicks in the box and Stoke leave with one point not three. Typical.

4. City beat ex-Stokie Tony Henry's unbeaten Shrews thanks to Biggins' flying header from Kevan's cross. Hughes fingertips his earlier volley over. Biggins, Beeston and Kennedy are booked as City cling on. Solid defending indicates the tactical thinking of Macari. A first win at last.

5. City maul Darlington but the referee fails to spot a blatant handball and doesn't award a penalty. Kevan's free-kick rattles the crossbar. It looks like being another one of those days but Tony Ellis pops up at the far post to drill home. Cranson marshals the defence superbly. Much better.

6. Stoke sweep into the lead thanks to Biggins' tap in after Blake beats Stannard and Cranson's header from Kevan's corner; then surrender after Biggins is subbed. Scott hits the bar. Cole and Newson finish well-worked moves. Stoke lose their shape and are lucky to cling on for a point.

7. Biggins pounces when Hodge fumbles. He then heads Butler's centre in. But another two-goal cushion is let slip. Blake's error gifts Paul Baker his opportunity. Paul Olsson outpaces the back four to smash home a long ball. Grafting City snatch victory thanks to Butler's far post header.

8. For once Stoke look comfortable on plastic despite Jepson scoring with Les Chapman's Preston's only first-half shot. On-loan Mark Stein links well with Biggins who rounds Alan Kelly. Beeston's cushion header sets up Bertie's second. Sandford's clearance hits Swann and rebounds in.

9. Bertie cracks home a penalty after Stein is felled by Edwards. City look settled and Biggins' second arrives when the County defence stop and leave him free to score. Danny Bergara's County steal a point thanks to debutant Mark Lillis's scrambled shot and giant Kevin Francis' header.

10. Chester, playing at Macclesfield's ground as they wait for a new stadium, reduce Stoke to kick and rush football. Six are booked and the game deteriorates into a series of long balls. Biggins and Stein miss open nets. Vince Overson's tribunal fee is £50k. Cranson signs for another year.

11. City's five-man defensive system begins to bear fruit as they shut out Phil Neal's Bolton. Biggins nabs a lucky 13th with a low shot. Scott chips home with his first touch as sub. Stein is superb but hits the bar and is denied by Dibble's fantastic save. Macari is set to sign him from Oxford.

12 A SWANSEA 19/10 — 9 L 1-2 0-2 22 18 — Att 3,363

Kearton Butler Sandford Kevan Overson Kennedy Cranson Beeston Ellis Biggins Fowler*
Freestone Jenkins Ford Coughlin Harris Brazil Bowen Davies Gilligan Raynor Legg — Scott

Ellis 88 / Harris 9, Davies 14
Ref: D Frampton

Stoke lose their way in the swirling wind. Frank Burrows' Swans fly into a two-goal lead as Mark Harris soars above the supposedly strong-in-the-air defence to nod home and then Alan Davies rams home Jimmy Gilligan's neat cross. Ellis fires in Kevan's corner but too late to matter.

---

13 H LEYTON ORIENT 26/10 — 6 W 2-0 1-0 10 21 — Att 9,555

Kearton Butler Sandford Kevan Overson Kennedy Cranson Beeston Ellis Biggins Fowler
Turner Howard Hackett Achampong Day Hales* Bart-Williams Jones Nugent Castle Otto — Harvey

Biggins 36, Cranson 71
Ref: A Wilkie

Kearton keeps City in it with a brilliant one-handed save from Nugent. Biggins scores from close in after Tony 'Elvis' Ellis's shot is deflected to him. Cranson bullets home a Kevan corner. Turner palms Biggins' shot round the post. The long-ball tactics seem lost without a target man.

---

14 H HUDDERSFIELD 2/11 — 8 L 0-2 0-2 4 21 — Att 10,116

Kearton Butler Sandford Kevan Overson Kennedy Cranson Beeston Ellis* Biggins Fowler
Clarke Trevitt Charlton Marsden Mitchell Jackson! O'Regan Stapleton Roberts Starbuck Bennett

Roberts 12, 14
Ref: W Burge

Kearton's howlers allow Iwan Roberts to grab two close-range goals. First he lets a shot through his legs, then he fails to collect a cross to give Roberts a free header. Jackson's second caution is for hauling back Biggins (74 mins). Stoke make no more chances against 10 than 11 men.

---

15 A BURY 5/11 — 6 W 3-1 1-1 19 24 — Att 3,245

Kearton Butler Sandford Kevan Overson Kennedy Cranson Beeston Ellis Biggins Fowler*
Kelly Wilson D Robertson Kearney Valentine Greenall Smith Robinson Stevens Cullen Wilson I* — Ware Parkinson

Ellis 3, 78, Overson 53 / Stevens 7
Ref: K Redfearn

Stoke murder a poor Shakers team. Ellis heads home a corner. Remarkably Bury level when Stevens turns sharply to fire in. Overson converts another corner and Ellis cuts past two defenders to score. Two shots are cleared off the line. A blatant penalty is turned down. Should be more.

---

16 A EXETER 19/11 — 5 D 0-0 0-0 6 25 — Att 5,309

Sinclair Butler Sandford Kevan Overson Kennedy Cranson Beeston Stein Biggins Fowler
Howells Hiley Brown Williams Daniels Whiston Hilaire* Wimbleton Moran Chapman^ Kelly — Hodge/Dolan

Ref: M Pierce

Exeter manager Alan Ball is the target of a Stoke hate mob. His team carry out vengeful tackles and are lucky to keep 11 men on. Jon Brown's challenge on Butler is the worst but he escapes with a yellow card. After the whistle, mindless idiots invade the pitch and the police are needed.

---

17 H TORQUAY 23/11 — 5 W 3-0 2-0 23 28 — Att 9,124

Sinclair Ware Sandford Kevan Overson Kennedy Cranson Beeston Stein^ Biggins* Fowler
Holmes P Uzzell* Compton* Elliott Holmes M Rowbotham Hall Joyce Chapman^ Loram Edwards — Ellis/Barnes Hodges/Myers

Biggins 2, Stein 34, 60
Ref: P Alcock

Torquay have lost eight in a row away from home. Biggins pounces on a loose ball to sweep home. The Gulls concede Stein's first Stoke goals after his move from Oxford. Howells fails to stop his shot crossing the line and a harmless looking shot deflects wickedly, stranding the keeper.

---

18 A WEST BROM 30/11 — 5 D 2-2 1-1 3 29 — Att 17,207

Sinclair Ware Sandford Kevan Overson Kennedy Cranson Beeston Stein^ Biggins* Fowler
Naylor Parkin Harbey Bradley Strodder^ Burgess McNally Goodman Robson White* Kelly* — Barnes Williams/Rogers

Overson 40, 52 / Shakespeare 17, Goodman 83
Ref: K Cooper

Stoke are shocked by Craig Shakespeare's cool finish after they have all the early play against Bobby Gould's men. Vince Overson notches his first goals for Stoke. He cracks home Beeston's pass and nods in Ware's corner. Don Goodman turns a cross shot home to save Albion a point.

---

19 H WIGAN 14/12 — 5 W 3-0 2-0 20 32 — Att 4,419

Sinclair Butler Sandford Kevan Overson Kennedy Cranson Beeston Stein Biggins Kelly
Adkins Parkinson Tankard Jones Patterson Langley Powell* Connelly Pilling Worthington* Griffiths — Johnson/Daley

Stein 17, Kelly 43, Biggins 81
Ref: M Reed

City romp home against Bryan Hamilton's hapless Latics. Stein fires home his third in three games. Kelly and Biggins both race clear to score coolly. The thick fog prevents many fans arriving or seeing much when they do finally get there. On-loan Ronnie Sinclair looks good in goal.

---

20 A BOURNEMOUTH 21/12 — 4 W 2-1 1-1 12 35 — Att 5,436

Sinclair Ware Bartram Kevan Overson Kennedy Cranson Beeston Stein Biggins Kelly
Bartram Bond Rowland Morris Mundee O'Driscoll Cooke Wood^ Quinn Case Holmes* — Lawrence/Mitchell

Biggins 10, Kelly 76 / Wood 5
Ref: G Poll

Paul Wood loops a header in off the far post but Stoke storm back. Bertie turns to drive past Bartram and with the wind at their backs City win thanks to Kelly's header from Stein's clever cut-back. Overson dominates dangerman Quinn. Sinclair saves brilliantly from George Lawrence.

---

21 H PETERBOROUGH 26/12 — 5 D 3-3 2-2 12 36 — Att 14,732

Sinclair Barber Luke Johnson^ Halsall Robinson D Welsh Sterling Cooper Riley Charlery Kimble* — Sandford Culpin/Robinson R

Kevan 7, Stein 30, Biggins 70 / Robinson D 17, Halsall 35, Sterling 81
Ref: T Lunt

Stoke let Posh off the hook as they present Chris Turner's side with three equalisers. Kevan deflects home Biggins' piledriver. Robinson is left unmarked to head in. Halsall's rocket follows Stein's superb run and shot. Barber lets Biggins' effort wriggle in but Sterling's tap-in squares it.

---

22 H BRADFORD C 28/12 — 5 D 0-0 0-0 19 37 — Att 14,208

Sinclair Ware Butler Kevan Overson Sandford Cranson Beeston Stein Biggins Kelly*
Tomlinson Mitchell Williams Stapleton Leonard Babb McCarthy Duxbury L Torpey McHugh Jewell — Barnes

Ref: K Barratt

Hampered by a heavy pitch, Stoke struggle against Frank Stapleton's Bantams. Butler and Kelly have poor games — Kelly fouling Torpey for a penalty (55 mins) which Lee Duxbury thankfully blasts over. Tomlinson saves Barnes' deflected effort. Neither keeper is unduly troubled.

---

23 A SHREWSBURY 1/1 — 5 L 0-1 0-1 11 37 — Att 6,557

Sinclair Ware Butler Kevan Overson Cranson Beeston Stein Biggins Kelly
Perks Worsley Lynch* Henry Spink Blake Donaldson Gallimore Summerfield Griffiths^ MacKenzie Lyne — Clark/Hopkins

Summerfield 8
Ref: P Taylor

Tony Gallimore, on his return from loan at Carlisle, proves ineffective as Macari searches for width. Tony Henry sets up Kevin Summerfield's early goal. Stoke attack all out. Biggins, Ware, Butler and Beeston all go close but Steve Perks stands firm. Kelly misses a glorious open goal.

BARCLAYS DIVISION 3   Manager: Lou Macari   SEASON 1991-92

No	Date	Team	Att	Pos	Pt	F-A	H-T	Scorers, Times, and Referees	1	2	3	4	5	6	7	8	9	10	11	subs used
24	H 4/1	BIRMINGHAM	18,914	5	40	W 2-1	0-0	Ware 52, Biggins 77 / Beckford 49 / Ref: R Milford	Sinclair	Ware	Butler	Kevan	Overson	Sandford	Cranson	Beeston	Stein	Biggins	**Russell**	**Russell**
									Miller	Frain	Matthewson	Cooper	Hicks	Mardon^	Rodgerson	Rowbotham	Paskin	Glephorn	Beckford	Okenla
25	A 11/1	BRENTFORD	9,004	6	40	L 0-2	0-1	Luscombe 4, Holdsworth 60 / Ref: P Scobie	Sinclair	Ware	Butler	Kevan*	Overson	Sandford	Cranson	Beeston	Stein	Biggins !	Russell	Ellis
									Benstead	Bates	Manuel	Millen	Evans	Ratcliffe	Luscombe	Booker	Holdsworth	Blissett^	Smillie	Godfrey/Gayle
26	H 18/1	READING	10,835	6	43	W 3-0	1-0	Jones 24 (og), Butler 64, Stein 71 / Ref: B Coddington	Sinclair	Foley	Butler*	Kevan	Overson	Sandford	Cranson	Beeston	Stein	Biggins	Russell	**Grimes**
									Leighton	Jones	Dillon !	Taylor	Williams	Streete !	Gooding	Bailey	Senior	Lovell^	Gilkes^	Cockram/Gray
27	A 25/1	HULL	4,996	4	46	W 1-0	1-0	Russell 20 / Ref: P Harrison	Sinclair	Foley	Butler	Kevan*	Blake	Sandford	Cranson	Beeston	Stein	Ellis	Russell	Grimes
									Fettis	Norton	Jacobs*	Mail	Wilcox	Shotton	Palin	Stoker	Pearson	Windass	Jenkinson	France
28	H 1/2	SWANSEA	11,299	3	49	W 2-1	1-0	Ware 41, Beeston 90 / Gilligan 61 / Ref: T Fitzharris	Sinclair	Ware	Butler	Kevan	Blake^	Sandford	Cranson	Beeston	Stein	Ellis^	Russell	Kennedy/Grimes
									Freestone	Agboola	Ford	Walker	Harris	Chapple^	Williams	Coughlin	Gilligan	Raynor	Legg	Thornber
29	A 8/2	LEYTON ORIENT	9,153	2	52	W 1-0	1-0	Beeston 4 / Ref: G Willard	Sinclair	Foley	Butler	Kevan	Overson	Sandford	Cranson	Beeston	Stein*	Biggins	Ware	Barnes
									Turner	Howard^	Hackett	Burnett	Day	Whitbread	Carter	Achampong	Jones*	Nugent	Berry	Cooper/Castle
30	H 12/2	WEST BROM	23,645	1	55	W 1-0	1-0	Stein 28 / Ref: I Hendrick	Sinclair	Foley	Butler	Kevan*	Overson	Sandford	Cranson	Beeston	Stein	Biggins	Ware	Ware
									Naylor	Hodson*	Harbey	Bradley	Shakespeare	Burgess	Fereday	Taylor	Robson	Roberts	Hackett	Bannister
31	A 15/2	WIGAN	5,695	2	55	L 0-1	0-1	Griffiths 15p / Ref: C Wilkes	Sinclair	Foley	Butler	Kevan	Overson	Sandford	Cranson	Beeston	Stein	Biggins	Ware	Rennie*
									Adkins	Parkinson	Tankard	Johnson	Patterson^	Langley	Jones	Collins	Daley	Taylor	Griffiths*	Worthington/Skipper
32	H 22/2	BRENTFORD	16,417	1	58	W 2-1	1-0	Butler 10, Stein 65 / Blissett 47 / Ref: G Ashby	Sinclair	Foley	Butler	Kevan	Overson	Sandford	Cranson	Beeston	Stein*	Biggins	Ware	Steele
									Benstead	Bates	Manuel	Millen	Evans	Ratcliffe	Finnigan^	Booker	Holdsworth	Blissett*	Smillie	Gayle/Sealy
33	H 29/2	BIRMINGHAM	22,162	1	59	D 1-1	0-1	Barnes 89 / Frain 20p / Ref: R Wiseman	Sinclair	Foley	Butler	Kevan	Overson	Sandford	Cranson	Beeston	Stein	Biggins	Steele*	Barnes
									Miller	Clarkson	Frain	Rennie	Hicks	Mardon	Rodgerson	Tait	Rowbotham	Glephorn	Sturridge*	Donowa^/O'Neill
34	A 4/3	READING	4,362	1	62	W 4-3	2-2	Stein 28, F'ley 30, Ware 60, McP'n 66 (og) / Lovell 8, Williams 36, Gooding 58 / Ref: D Frampton	Sinclair	Foley	Butler	Kevan	Ware	Sandford	Cranson	Beeston	Stein*	Biggins	Steele*	Barnes
									Keeley	Jones	Richardson	McPherson	Gooding	Streete	Dillon	Tait	Williams	Maskell	Lovell*	McGhee

24. Kevin Russell gives Stoke the width Macari wants. The game comes to life when on-loan Jason Beckford fires past Sinclair from Frain's pass. Ware replies with a fine 30-yard effort. Biggins wriggles through to crack a rising shot past Kevin Miller. Steino is felled but no pen is awarded.

25. A vital promotion clash. City look lively but Lee Luscombe sets the Bees buzzing with a header from their first chance. Biggins walks (46 mins) for a clash with Billy Manuel. Div 3 leading marksman Dean Holdsworth taps in to seal it. Sinclair's lack of height is giving cause for concern.

26. A brilliant performance helped by strict refereeing. Mr Coddington sends off Floyd Streete (44 mins) for handball and Kevin Dillon (50 mins) for dissent. Jones helps Biggins' shot over the line after it hits the bar. Butler heads in and Stein rounds Jim Leighton to score easily. Classy.

27. Kevin Russell volleys home a beauty to send sorry Hull into the relegation zone. Their fans chant 'sack the board' after failing to score in 480 mins. Biggins and Overson are both suspended but Stoke easily contain Terry Dolan's team. Pearson fires the Tigers' best chances at Sinclair.

28. Stoke swarm all over Swansea. Stein is sent sprawling but no penalty is given. Finally Ware latches on to Ellis' pass to fire home. Stoke relax. Jimmy Gilligan exposes Sinclair's lack of height by heading over him. Beeston volleys in a splendid late winner from Kennedy's long throw.

29. A dreadful game. The action begins and ends in the fourth minute when Beeston slots home after Adrian Whitbread blocks Steve Foley's shot on the line. Paul Ware's overhead kick sails over. The game deteriorates into a long ball/offside battle. Competent but hardly very entertaining.

30. Kick-off is delayed for 15 mins to allow the huge crowd in. Stein pounces to head home a left-wing corner, flicked on by Overson. Stein taunts the Baggies defence, sending the whole back four the wrong way once. He also hits the side netting. Biggins has an effort ruled out for offside.

31. City's best run of victories since 1946-7 comes to an end when Steve Foley handles on the line. Brian Griffiths converts. Stoke pump long balls forward but the strong wind spoils the tactic. The suspended Ware is missed in midfield. Macari still wants to improve the squad for the run in.

32. On-loan Tim Steele, from Wolves, sets up Butler's header. Blissett taps in Bees' only chance. A niggly game turns sour when Beeston is felled and retaliates by dragging his assailant along the ground. Stein atones for earlier misses by mopping up when Benstead parries Overson's shot.

33. All hell breaks loose when Barnes nets after Biggins pressurises Miller into dropping the ball. Fans run onto the pitch and a full-scale invasion follows Sinclair's save which Blues claim crosses the line. The sides leave the pitch but return to end the game behind closed doors. A sad day.

34. A superb see-saw game. Biggins sets up Stein with a great cross to level Lovell's header. Foley plays a one-two with Biggins to fire in. Ware's fantastic 25-yard effort equalises Gooding's volley. Keith McPherson finds his own net in trying to clear Biggins' goal-bound header. Brilliant.

Match log (games 35–46)

No	V	Opponent	Date	Att	Opp pos	Pts	Stoke pos	Res	FT	HT	Scorers (Stoke / opponent)	Referee
35	H	HULL	7/3	13,563	19	62	1	L	2-3	0-1	Barnes 52, Stein 73 / Jenkinson 5, 55, Atkinson 48	Ref: J Worrall
36	H	BURY	11/3	12,385	19	62	1	L	1-2	0-0	Barnes 85 / Stevens 55, 73	Ref: M Peck
37	A	HUDDERSFIELD	14/3	10,156	7	65	1	W	2-1	2-0	Biggins 27, Stein 27 / Starbuck 55p	Ref: E Parker
38	H	EXETER	21/3	13,634	14	68	1	W	5-2	3-1	Biggins 16, St'n 33, B'ston 42, Grimes 61, [St'le 90] / Whiston 45, Th'pstone 72	Ref: V Callow
39	A	TORQUAY	28/3	3,260	23	68	1	L	0-1	0-1	Dobie 17	Ref: H King
40	A	FULHAM	31/3	5,779	11	69	1	D	1-1	0-1	Stein 72 / Haag 20	Ref: G Singh
41	H	DARLINGTON	3/4	13,579	24	72	1	W	3-0	2-0	Biggins 10p, 20, Stein 69	Ref: P Don
42	A	HARTLEPOOL	11/4	4,360	11	73	1	D	1-1	1-1	Stein 44 / Olsson 39	Ref: S Lodge
43	H	PRESTON	18/4	16,151	18	76	2	W	2-1	1-1	Stein 44, Biggins 50p / Thompson 20	Ref: B Hill
44	A	STOCKPORT	20/4	3,129	4	77	2	D	0-0	0-0		Ref: J Watson
45	H	CHESTER	25/4	18,474	18	77	2	L	0-1	0-0	Bennett 59	Ref: R Pawley
46	A	BOLTON	2/5	5,997	13	77	4	L	1-3	1-0	Stein 7 / Patterson 49, Seagraves 69, Walker 90	Ref: K Lupton

Home 12,982 | Away 7,378 | Average

Line-ups (Stoke player / opponent player, by position)

Position columns: 1 Sinclair · 2 Foley · 3 Butler* · 4 Kevan · 5 Overson · 6 Sandford · 7 Cranson · 8 Ware · 9 Stein · 10 Barnes · 11 Steele · 12 Beeston

No	1	2	3	4	5	6	7	8	9	10	11	12
35	Sinclair / Fettis	Foley / Hockaday	Butler* / Brown	Kevan / Mail	Overson / Wilcox	Sandford / Warren	Cranson / Norton	Ware / Atkinson	Stein / Pearson	Barnes / Windass	Steele / Jenkinson	Beeston / Ellis
36	Pressman / Kelly	Foley / Greenall	Butler / Hughes	Kevan / Flitcroft	Overson / Valentine	Sandford / Knill	Beeston / Hulme	Ware / Smith	Stein / Stevens	Barnes / Kearney	Steele* / Stanislaus	Biggins / Ellis
37	Pressman / Clarke	Foley / Trevitt	Butler / Charlton	Kevan / McNab	Overson / Mitchell	Beeston / Jackson	Cranson / O'Regan	Ware / Kelly*	Stein / Roberts	Barnes / Starbuck	Steele / Onuora	Biggins / Booth
38	Pressman / Miller	Foley / Brown	Butler / Cook	Ware* / Williams^	Overson / Daniels	Cranson / Whiston	Kevan / Thompstone	Biggins / Morris*	Stein / Kelly	Beeston / Hilaire	Steele / Marshall	Grimes / Cooper
39	Pressman / Howells	Foley / Holmes P	Butler / Herrera*	Ware / Saunders	Overson / Curran	Sandford / Compton^	Cranson / Hall	Bent^ / Joyce	Stein / Dobie	Barnes / Myers	? / Trollope	Grimes / Davis/Colcombe
40	Sinclair / Stannard	Foley / Morgan	Butler / Pike	Kevan / Marshall	Overson / Nebbeling	Sandford / Thomas	Cranson / Eckhardt	Beeston / Kelly	Stein / Byrne	Barnes / Brazil	Heath / Haag	Biggins / ?
41	Sinclair / Prudhoe	Foley / Hinchley	Butler / Pickering	Beeston / Sunley	Overson / Gregan	Kevan / Tait*	Cranson / Gaughan	Grimes / Toman^	Stein / Cusack	Biggins / Borthwick	Heath / Cork	? / Reed/Isaacs
42	Sinclair / Jones	Grimes / McCreery	Butler / Cross	Foley / MacPhail	Kevan / McGuckin	Sandford / Nobbs	Cranson / Southall*	Beeston / Olsson	Stein / Johnrose	Barnes* / Fletcher	Heath / Dalton	? / Thomas
43	Sinclair / Farnworth	Ware / Williams	Butler / James M	Kevan / Cartwright	Overson* / Flynn	Sandford / Greenall	Grimes / Ashcroft	Beeston / Joyce	Stein / Jepson*	Biggins / Shaw	Heath^ / Thompson	? / Blake/Barnes
44	Sinclair / Edwards	Foley / Thorpe	Butler / Carstairs^	Kevan / Frain	Blake / Barras	Sandford / Williams B	Wright / Gannon	Beeston / Ward	Stein / Francis	Biggins / Beaumont	? / Loram*	? / Preece/Miller
45	Sinclair / Stewart	Foley / Preece	Butler / Albiston	Kevan / Comstive	Blake / Abel	Sandford / Lightfoot	Wright* / Bennett	Beeston / Barrow	Stein / Butler	Biggins / Rimmer	Heath / Pugh	Grimes / Heath/Grimes
46	Sinclair / Felgate	Foley / Spooner	Brown P / Darby	Kevan / Seagraves	Cranson / ?	Sandford / Lydiate	Heath / Green	Beeston / Stubbs	Stein / Walker	Biggins / Phillskirk	Grimes / Patterson	? / ?

Match reports

35 – Hull: Lowly Hull surprise Stoke. Leigh Jenkinson floats the ball into an empty net with Sinclair grounded. Barnes taps in. Alan Fettis saves Beeston's effort. Jenkinson scores the goal of the game, drifting into the area and cracking in. Stein's finish sparks the Alamo but Barnes' header is saved.

36 – Bury: Kevin Pressman is signed on-loan from Sheff Wed. Barnes hits the bar but Ian Stevens snaffles two chances from 12 yards out. Bury shut up shop. City's long ball fails to find the diminutive Stein and Barnes. The pressure tells when Barnes volleys in off the post. Three points wasted.

37 – Huddersfield: Eoin Hand's Terriers are stunned when Biggins latches onto a wind-assisted goal-kick to score. Direct from the restart Stein pounces to crack home. The referee gives a penalty after Starbuck's cross hits Overson's arm from two yards. Ten mins of injury-time keeps the nerves jangling.

38 – Exeter: Stoke sweep aside Alan Ball's hapless Exeter. Tim Steele's cross allows Biggins to blast home. Beeston taps in. Stein nets a fine angled drive. Ashley Grimes nets his first from Biggins' cut-back and Steele grabs his first to hand City their biggest win since December 1986. Going up!?

39 – Torquay: Macari is livid after City lose to Ivan Golac's men. He bans Wayne Biggins from attending the PFA dinner, even though he has been named in the 3rd Division Team of the Season, along with Vince Overson. Macari wants Biggins to concentrate on the crunch midweek game at Fulham.

40 – Fulham: Stein grabs a vital equaliser after the tall Kelly Haag puts Don Mackay's Fulham ahead. City face stubborn resistance from Jim Stannard, who denies Stein and Biggins. Adrian Heath returns to the club after 10 years away, signing from Manchester City for £50,000. Nerves are jangling.

41 – Darlington: Biggins, out of contract in June, sends out a 'Come and get me!' message to the big clubs with a fantastic performance capped by two quality finishes. Played on a Friday night to alleviate fixture congestion due to Monday's televised Autoglass Trophy semi-final against Peterborough.

42 – Hartlepool: Stoke visit the other Victoria Ground for the first time since 1926. Paul Olsson rams home a weak clearance. Stein's screaming 20-yard volley flies into the back of the net. Lenny Johnrose threatens for Hartlepool. Barnes, Kevan and Ware all test debutant teenage keeper Steven Jones.

43 – Preston: David Thompson stuns Stoke with a neat finish from ex-Stokie Graham Shaw's pass. Ashcroft torments Grimes and only a clinical strike from Stein keeps Stoke in the hunt. Simon Farnworth saves three efforts before Flynn fells Biggins who converts the spot-kick himself. Nearly there.

44 – Stockport: City stave off the challenge of Danny Bergara's County to ensure it will be either they or Birmingham who go up in the second automatic spot. Stoke keep County quiet with Noel Blake subduing the 6ft 7in Kevin Francis. Biggins goes closest for City. It's all down to the last two games.

45 – Chester: Relegation-threatened Chester steal the points to leave Stoke short of automatic promotion. Gary Bennett is sent clear to beat Sinclair. Heath's arrival sparks Stoke into life. Despite Sandford playing as centre-forward and three shots cleared off the line, it's the play-offs for the first time.

46 – Bolton: Stein's clinical finish seems to give Stoke the upper hand but Bolton fight back to land their first win in ten. Patterson volleys in at the far post. The impressive Walker drives home. A disappointing end to a fabulous first season for Macari. Now for Stockport.

BARCLAYS DIVISION 3 (CUP-TIES)

Manager: Lou Macari

SEASON 1991-92

Play-offs

			Att	F-A	H-T	Scorers, Times, and Referees	1	2	3	4	5	6	7	8	9	10	11	subs used
SF 1	A	STOCKPORT 10/5	7,537	L 0-1	0-1	Ward 40 Ref: A Buksh	Sinclair *Edwards*	Fowler *Knowles**	Butler *Todd*	Kevan *Frain*	Blake *Barras*	Sandford *Williams B*	Cranson *Gannon*	Beeston ! *Ward*	Stein *Francis*	Biggins *Beaumont*	Grimes *Preece*	Wheeler
SF 2	H	STOCKPORT 13/5	16,170	D 1-1	0-1	Stein 81 Beaumont 1 Ref: K Hackett (Stoke lose 1-2 on aggregate)	Sinclair *Edwards*	Foley *Knowles*	Butler *Todd*	Kevan^ *Frain*	Blake* *Barras*	Sandford *Williams B*	Cranson *Gannon*	Fowler *Ward*	Stein *Francis*	Biggins *Beaumont*	Grimes *Preece**	Kelly/Heath Wheeler

Carl Beeston lives up to his nickname 'The Beast' and flattens Lee Todd after a bad challenge on Biggins. He is sent off and immediately Peter Ward scores from a free-kick just outside the box. City battle hard to restrict County's chances. A one-goal lead should be assailable at the Vic.

Disaster as a long ball allows Chris Beaumont to loop a header past Sinclair. Stoke lose their cool and it takes an hour to regain it. Cranson hits the bar. Paul Edwards saves from Butler. Stein lobs Edwards to set up a grandstand finish but County hold on despite exuberant penalty claims.

Rumbelows Cup

			Att	F-A	H-T	Scorers, Times, and Referees	1	2	3	4	5	6	7	8	9	10	11	subs used
1:1	H	CHESTERFIELD 21/8	7,815	W 1-0	1-0	Ellis 20 Ref: H King	Fox *Leonard*	Butler *Dyche*	Cranson *Williams*	Kevan *Rogers*	Blake *Brien*	Sandford *McGugan*	Ellis *Gunn*	Beeston *Hewitt**	Kelly *Morris*	Biggins* *Benjamin^*	Fowler *Grayson*	Barnes Cooke/Evans
1:2	A	CHESTERFIELD 27/8	5,391 *4:11*	W 2-1	1-0	Kelly 22, Beeston 68 Lancaster 58 Ref: T Fitzharris (Stoke win 3-1 on aggregate)	Fox	Barnes *Leonard !*	Cranson *Dyche*	Kevan *Rogers*	Blake *Brien*	Fowler *McGugan*	Kevan *Gunn*	Beeston *Cooke**	Kelly* *Lancaster*	Biggins *Grayson*	Scott* *Morris^*	Ellis/Kennedy Turnbull/Evans
2:1	A	LIVERPOOL 25/9	18,389 *1:9*	D 2-2	1-1	Cranson 28, Kelly 88 Rush 16, 71 Ref: K Lupton	Fox *Grobbelaar*	Butler *Ablett*	Sandford *Burrows*	Scott *Nicol*	Overson *Marsh*	Kennedy *Tanner*	Cranson *Saunders**	Beeston *McManaman Rush*	Ellis*	Biggins *Walters*	Kelly *McMahon*	Kelly Rosenthal
2:2	H	LIVERPOOL 9/10	22,335 *1:9*	L 2-3	0-1	Biggins 75p, 88 McManaman 9, Saunders 56, Walters 84 Ref: A Smith (Stoke lose 4-5 on aggregate)	Fox *Hooper*	Butler *Harkness*	Sandford *Burrows*	Scott *Nicol*	Overson *McManaman*	Kennedy *Tanner*	Cranson^ *Saunders*	Beeston *Houghton*	Kelly* *Rush*	Biggins *Walters*	Fowler *McMahon*	Wright/Kevan

Fox plays as Everton do not want Kearton cup-tied. Stoke fail to impose themselves on Chris McMenemy's awful Spireites team. Ellis glances in from Butler's centre but City lose their way. Biggins looks awkward up front and is subbed. Mick Leonard saves well from Kelly and Ellis.

Stoke are comfortable on their first visit to Saltergate since 1965. Kelly and Beeston pounce after Leonard only parries Biggins effort and then Kennedy's header. Leonard is sent off (69 mins) for bringing down the charging Biggins. Kelly scores but the ref awards a free-kick to Stoke.

A magical night. 6,000 Stokies go wild when Cranson heads Scott's corner past Bruce Grobbelaar. Rush's brace are classic poachers finishes. Record transfer man Dean Saunders is kept quiet by Vince Overson. The hordes are sent silly by Tony Kelly nut-megging Grobbelaar. Superb!

The biggest crowd for three years sees Tony Kelly's back-pass fall to Ian Rush who squares to Dean Saunders to effectively end the game as a contest. Biggins converts a penalty after Tanner handles Overson's header on the line. He then grabs a consolation header after Walters taps in.

FA Cup

			Att	F-A	H-T	Scorers, Times, and Referees	1	2	3	4	5	6	7	8	9	10	11	subs used
1	H	TELFORD 15/11	9,974 *C:6*	D 0-0	0-0	Ref: I Borrett	Fox *Acton*	Butler* *Humphreys*	Sandford *Brindley*	Kevan *Dyson*	Overson *Nelson*	Kennedy *Whittington*	Cranson *Myers*	Beeston *Grainger*	Stein *Benbow*	Biggins *Langford*	Fowler *Parrish*	Ellis
1R	A	TELFORD 26/11	4,032 *C:8*	L 1-2	0-1	Beeston 81 Benbow 29, 83 Ref: I Borrett	Fox *Acton*	Ware *Humphreys*	Sandford^ *Brindley*	Kevan *Dyson*	Overson *Nelson*	Kennedy *Whittington*	Cranson *Myers*	Beeston *Grainger*	Stein *Benbow*	Biggins *Langford*	Scott* *Parrish*	Ellis/Blake

Stoke's new double strength floodlights are the only bright spot of a dour game. City lack a flank player to unlock a Telford defence headed by ex-Stokie Paul Dyson. Acton saves well from Cranson. Ellis hits the bar with a drive. Gerry Daly's plucky Conference side deserve to cling on.

City plumb further depths at Bucks Head. Ian Benbow's intelligently finished opener seems enough as former YTS trainee Darren Acton saves well from Ware and Biggins. Finally Beeston crashes a 30-yarder into the top corner. Relief is short-lived as Benbow finishes Langford's cross.

Football League Table

Pos	Team	P	Home					Away					Pts
			W	D	L	F	A	W	D	L	F	A	
1	Brentford	46	17	2	4	55	29	8	5	10	26	26	82
2	Birmingham	46	15	6	2	42	22	8	6	9	27	30	81
3	Huddersfield	46	15	4	4	36	15	7	8	8	23	23	78
4	STOKE	46	14	5	4	45	24	7	9	7	24	25	77
5	Stockport	46	15	5	3	47	19	7	5	11	28	32	76
6	Peterborough*	46	13	7	3	38	20	7	7	9	27	38	74
7	West Brom	46	12	6	5	45	25	8	8	8	19	24	71
8	Bournemouth	46	13	4	6	33	18	7	7	9	19	30	71
9	Fulham	46	11	7	5	29	16	8	6	9	28	37	70
10	Leyton Orient	46	12	7	4	36	18	6	4	13	26	34	65
11	Hartlepool	46	12	5	6	30	21	6	11	6	27	36	65
12	Reading	46	9	8	6	33	27	6	8	9	26	35	61
13	Bolton	46	10	9	4	26	19	5	5	13	26	37	59
14	Hull	46	9	4	10	28	23	8	4	11	31	43	59
15	Wigan	46	9	6	6	33	21	6	8	9	25	31	59
16	Bradford C	46	8	10	5	36	30	6	6	11	26	31	58
17	Preston	46	12	7	4	42	32	3	5	15	19	40	57
18	Chester	46	10	6	7	34	29	4	8	11	22	30	56
19	Swansea	46	10	9	4	35	24	4	5	14	20	41	56
20	Exeter	46	11	7	5	34	25	3	4	16	23	55	53
21	Bury	46	8	7	8	31	31	5	5	13	24	43	51
22	Shrewsbury	46	7	7	9	30	31	5	4	14	23	37	47
23	Torquay	46	13	3	7	29	19	0	5	18	13	49	47
24	Darlington	46	5	5	13	31	39	2	2	16	25	51	37
		1104	272	146	134	858	577	134	146	272	577	858	1510

* promoted after play-offs

Odds & ends

Double wins: (3) Darlington, Leyton Orient, Reading.

Double losses: (0).

Won from behind: (4) Birmingham (h), Bournemouth (a), Preston (h), Reading (a).

Lost from in front: (1) Bolton (a).

High spots: The remarkable resurgence under Lou Macari. Going top of the Division in February. Winning the Autoglass Trophy at Wembley. The arrival of Mark Stein and his formidable partnership with Biggins. Ian Cranson finally having an injury-free season.

Low spots: Only making the play-offs having been top with four games to go. Conceding in the first minute at home to Stockport in the play-offs. Losing at home to relegation candidates Chester to miss out on automatic promotion.

Player of the Year: Wayne Biggins.

Ever-presents: (0).

Hat-tricks: (0).

Leading scorer: (24) Wayne Biggins.

Appearances and Goals

Player	Appearances						Goals			
	Lge	Sub	LC	Sub	FAC	Sub	Lge	LC	FAC	Tot
Barnes, Paul	3	10	1	1			3			3
Beeston, Carl	42	1	4		2		3	1	1	5
Bent, Junior	1									
Blake, Noel	12	1	2			1				
Biggins, Wayne	41		4		2		22	2		24
Butler, John	42		4		1		3			3
Cranson, Ian	41		4		2		2		1	3
Ellis, Tony	9	6	2	1	2	2	4	1		5
Foley, Steve	20		2				1			1
Fowler, Lee	15	1	4		1					
Fox, Peter			4		2					
Gallimore, Tony	2	1								
Grimes, Ashley	4	6					1			1
Heath, Adrian	5	1								
Kearton, Jason	16									
Kelly, Tony	10	3	3	1			2	2		4
Kennedy, Mick	19	1	2	1	2		2			2
Kevan, David	43		2		2		1			1
Overson, Vince	34	1	2		2		3			3
Pressman, Kevin	4									
Rennie, Paul	1									
Russell, Kevin	5									
Sandford, Lee	37	1	3		2		1			1
Scott, Ian	6	3	3		1					
Sinclair, Ronnie	26									
Steele, Tim	7									
Stein, Mark	36				2		16			16
Ware, Paul	22	2			1		3			3
Wright, Ian	3	1				1				
(own-goals)							2			2
29 players used	506	38	44	6	22	3	69	7	1	77

BARCLAYS DIVISION 2 Manager: Lou Macari SEASON 1992-93

No	Date	Att	Pos	Pt	F-A	H-T	Scorers, Times, and Referees	1	2	3	4	5	6	7	8	9	10	11	subs used
1	A HULL 15/8	9,088		L 0	0-1	0-0	Hunter 82 Ref: I Cruikshank	Sinclair	Butler	**Harbey**	Cranson	Overson	Sandford	Foley	Ware	Stein	Kelly*	**Russell**	**Shaw**
								Fettis	Hockaday	Hobson	Mail	Lund	Warren	Stoker*	Atkinson	Hunter	Windass	Jenkinson	France
2	H WIGAN 22/8	12,902	15 / 22	W 3	2-1	1-0	Biggins 7, Foley 70 Griffiths 55 Ref: R Pawley	Sinclair	Butler	Harbey	Cranson	Overson	Sandford	Foley	Devlin	Stein	Biggins	Russell	Russell
								Adkins	Parkinson	Tankard	Robertson	Doolan	Langley^	Jones	Powell	Daley	Worthington^	Griffiths	Sharratt/Appleton
3	A EXETER 29/8	4,106	13 / 21	D 4	2-2	2-1	Stein 23, 25 Jepson 5, Harris 90 Ref: P Scobie	Sinclair	Butler	Harbey	Cranson	Overson	Sandford!	Foley	Devlin	Stein	Biggins	Russell*	Kevan
								Miller	Hiley	Cooper	Kelly	Brown	Whiston	Collins*	Harris	Jepson	Chapman	Hodge	Williams
4	A BRADFORD C 2/9	5,959	15 / 8	L 4	1-3	1-1	Stein 18 Jewell 29, 64, Duxbury L 77 Ref: T West	Sinclair	Butler	Harbey	Cranson	Overson	Kelly*	Foley	Devlin	Stein	Biggins	Russell	Shaw
								Pearce	McDonald	Heseltine	Duxbury L	Blake	Hoyle	Jewell	Duxbury M	McCarthy	Tinnion	Reid	
5	H BOLTON 5/9	14,252	15 / 7	D 5	0-0	0-0	Ref: A Smith	Sinclair	Butler	Harbey	Cranson	Overson	Sandford	Foley*	Ware	Stein	Biggins	Russell*	Kevan / Brown M
								Branagan	Brown P	Butler	Darby	Seagraves	Winstanley	Green	Stubbs	Walker	Phillskirk*	Kelly	Brown M
6	A PLYMOUTH 12/9	8,208	16 / 13	D 6	1-1	1-0	Stein 34 Walker 83 Ref: K Cooper	Sinclair	Butler	Harbey	Cranson	Overson	Wright	Foley	Ware	Stein	Biggins*	Russell	Kelly
								Kite	Poole	Morgan	Morrison	Walker	Marker	Skinner	McCall	Nugent	Marshall	Evans*	Adcock
7	H BRIGHTON 16/9	10,867	17	D 7	1-1	1-0	Sandford 1 Wilkins 83 Ref: P Wright	Sinclair	Butler	Harbey	Cranson	Overson	Sandford	Foley*	Ware	Stein	Biggins	Russell	Kelly
								Beeney	Chivers	Chapman	Wilkinson*	Crumplin	Foster	Edwards	Moulden	Cotterill	Codner	Wilkins	Macciochi
8	A WEST BROM 19/9	18,674	14 / 1	W 10	4-3	1-1	Foley 45, Russell 46, 76, Cranson 83 Taylor 27, 71, Garner 74 Ref: E Parker	Parks	Butler	Harbey	Cranson	Overson	Sandford	Foley	Ware	Stein	Biggins	Russell	Kelly
								Naylor	Coldicott^	Lilwall^	Bradley	Raven	Shakespeare	Garner	Hamilton	Taylor	McNally	Robson	Hackett/Fereday
9	A MANSFIELD 26/9	6,826	11 / 20	W 13	4-0	3-0	Stein 33, 45, Ware 41, Biggins 61 Ref: I Hemley	Parks	Butler	Harbey	Cranson	Overson^	Sandford	Foley	Ware	Stein	Biggins	Russell*	Beeston/Kelly
								Pearcey	Parkin	Charles	Holland	Fee	Walker	Spooner	McCord	Stant	McLoughlin^	Noteman*	Wilhe/Wilkinson
10	A CHESTER 3/10	5,237	11 / 23	D 14	1-1	0-0	Beeston 61 Bishop 69 Ref: P Harrison	Horne	Butler	Harbey	Cranson	Overson	Sandford	Foley	Ware	Stein	Biggins	Russell	Beeston
								Stewart	Preece	Goodwin^	Butler^	Abel	Garnett	Thompson	Barrow	Rimmer	Bishop	Kelly	Ryan/Whelan
11	H LEYTON ORIENT 10/10	12,640	10 / 3	W 17	2-1	0-0	Stein 87, 89 Otto 53 Ref: E Wolstenholme	Fox	Butler	Harbey*	Cranson	Overson	Sandford	Foley	Ware	Stein	Shaw	Beeston	Kelly
								Turner	Bellamy	Howard	Hales	Kitchen	Whitbread	Otto	Achampong	Jones^	Taylor	Okai*	Zoricich/Cooper

Match reports

1 — HULL: 4,000 Stokies see another poor start to a season. Paul Hunter's first goal for two years arrives after £95,000 signing Kevin Russell hits the post. City use a 5-3-2 formation but miss the suspended Biggins. Galling news: recent departures Scott, Barnes and Ellis all net for their new clubs.

2 — WIGAN: Biggins heads home a Russell corner after an early flurry. Foley, Stein and Russell all miss good chances. From nowhere Bryan Griffiths waltzes past three tackles to fire home. Livewire Russell crosses for Foley to stoop and head home. Langley clears Biggins' header off the line.

3 — EXETER: In the new purple away kit City start badly. Renowned Potters fan Ronnie Jepson fires Exeter ahead. Stein's brace puts Stoke in a comfortable position. Sandford is sent off (70 mins) for a bad tackle and Alan Ball's men storm forward. Stoke hold firm until the 10th minute of injury-time.

4 — BRADFORD C: Stoke swarm all over Frank Stapleton's Bradford. Cranson heads inches wide before Stein volleys a sweet left-foot shot home. On a rare attack Paul Jewell hammers his first and then as the balance tips beats Sinclair in a one-on-one. Lee Duxbury pounces after Tony Kelly loses the ball.

5 — BOLTON: Free transfer Keith Branagan stonewalls a dominant City. He stops a fierce Stein shot with his legs and palms away Biggins' shot. Alan Stubbs heads Bolton's only chance over the bar. Branagan saves from Biggins, Russell hits the post and Ware's late shot is tipped away spectacularly.

6 — PLYMOUTH: Ex-Stokie Peter Shilton is suspended for Argyle, but his Plymouth team grab a point thanks to Alan Walker's header. A stop-start match is not helped by both sides' offside tactics. Stein profits when Marker and the on-loan Phil Kite get mixed up. Another strong position thrown away.

7 — BRIGHTON: Lee Sandford returns from suspension to net a header after just 45 secs. Stoke press hard but Stein heads over and Biggins, considering a move to Barnsley, heads wide. Graham Wilkins curls a free-kick past the despairing Sinclair. Kelly stubs a golden chance into Mark Beeney's hands.

8 — WEST BROM: Loan keeper Tony Parks fluffs a clearance and Bob Taylor nets. Foley nips in to fire home. Russell swoops after Naylor tips away Stein's cross and then neatly sidesteps the keeper. Taylor and Garner finish well for Ossie Ardiles' men. Cranson soars high to bullet a header in off the bar.

9 — MANSFIELD: Stoke beat George Foster's Stags at a canter. Stein rounds Pearcey to score and Ware follows suit. Stein side-foots 'Rooster' Russell's cross in. Russell is injured and replaced by Beeston who sets up Wayne Biggins to turn and fire his last goal in a Stoke shirt before moving to Barnsley.

10 — CHESTER: City visit Chester's new Deva Stadium for the first time. Beeston runs the game and hits the post before volleying home sweetly from 12 yards. On-loan Brian Horne misses a corner and Bishop gratefully accepts Harry McNally's men's only chance. A tribunal sets Biggins' fee at £200k.

11 — LEYTON ORIENT: Peter Fox appears to have his 400th appearance ruined after Chris Turner saves Stein's 46th-minute penalty following a trip by Bellamy. Ricky Otto scores with a good drive. Stein makes amends, turning home after Beeston hits the bar and then nonchalantly side-footing in Shaw's cross.

Stoke City — match-by-match results (games 12–23)

12 · A · PRESTON · 17/10
Att 8,138 · Opp pos 17 · Pos 7 · W 2-1 (HT 2-0) · Pts 20
Butler 13, Sandford 40 — Callaghan 48 · Ref: W Flood
Stoke: Sinclair, Butler, Harbey, Cranson, Overson, Sandford, Foley, Ware, Stein, Shaw*, Beeston, Kelly
Opp: Farnworth, Davidson, Fowler, Tinkler, Flynn, Callaghan, Ashcroft!, Cartwright, Leonard, Ellis, James*, Kidd
Stoke produce an impressive display to secure a first ever win on a plastic pitch. Butler nods home Harbey's cross. His free-kick is headed in by Sandford. Ex-Stokie Aaron Callaghan nets from Ellis' pass. Lee Ashcroft is sent off for swearing (64 mins). Farnworth saves from Harbey.

13 · H · PORT VALE · 24/10
Att 24,459 · Opp pos 9 · Pos 4 · W 2-1 (HT 0-0) · Pts 23
Cranson 69, Stein 86p — Kerr 68 · Ref: J Watson
Stoke: Sinclair, Butler, Gleghorn, Cranson, Overson, Sandford, Foley, Ware*, Stein, Shaw, Beeston, Russell
Opp: Musselwhite, Sandeman, Sulley, Walker, Swan, Glover, Aspin, Taylor, Cross, Houchen, Van der Laan*, Kerr
A capacity crowd see a dour first half. Vale lead through Kerr's strike after Ian Taylor's run, but Ian Cranson rises to head home Russell's free-kick. A clean-though Stein collides with Musselwhite whose lengthy protests earn a caution but don't put off Stein who nets the penalty. Great.

14 · A · BURNLEY · 31/10
Att 16,667 · Opp pos 14 · Pos 2 · W 2-0 (HT 2-0) · Pts 26
Shaw 21, 37 · Ref: M Reed
Stoke: Sinclair, Butler, Gleghorn, Cranson, Overson, Sandford, Harbey, Ware, Stein*, Shaw, Beeston, Russell
Opp: Beresford, Measham, Jakub, Davis, Monnington, Farrell, Penney*, Deary, Heath, Conroy, Harper, Eli
4,500 Stokies witness Burnley' first home defeat of the season. Nigel Gleghorn, £100k Birmingham, leads an inspired midfield who are first to every ball. Jimmy Mullen's much vaunted defence are ripped apart. Shaw beats Beresford at the third attempt and then lashes high into the net.

15 · A · FULHAM · 3/11
Att 5,903 · Opp pos 10 · Pos 3 · D 0-0 (HT 0-0) · Pts 27
Ref: R Gifford
Stoke: Sinclair, Butler, Harbey, Cranson, Overson, Sandford, Foley, Ware*, Stein, Shaw, Beeston, Russell
Opp: Stannard, Morgan*, Pike, Eckhardt, Nebbeling, Thomas, Hails, Marshall, Farrell, Brazil, Lewis, Onwere
Stoke look lively up front but Shaw fluffs from six yards. Paul Ware has a nightmare and is replaced by Russell who sets up Stein for the best chance of the night but his shot is saved by Jim Stannard. Overson is dominant in a flat back four which snuffs out Don Mackay's men's threat.

16 · H · BOURNEMOUTH · 7/11
Att 5,146 · Opp pos 17 · Pos 2 · W 2-0 (HT 0-0) · Pts 30
Stein 47p, 52 · Ref: I Hendrick
Stoke: Sinclair, Butler, Sandford, Cranson, Overson, Gleghorn, Foley, Russell, Stein*, Shaw, Beeston, Regis
Opp: Bartram, Mundee, Morrell^, Morris, Watson, Shearer, O'Driscoll, McGorry*, Lovell, Scott, Rowland, Murray/Masters
Tony Pulis' Cherries string eight men across the back but can't contain Stein. He cracks home when Russell is floored in the box and slots past Vince Bartram from a tight angle. Dave Regis, £100,000 from Plymouth, finally makes his debut after being non-playing sub for three games.

17 · A · BLACKPOOL · 21/11
Att 8,028 · Opp pos 24 · Pos 1 · W 3-1 (HT 2-1) · Pts 33
Russell 19, 46, Stein 26 — Ward 15 · Ref: K Redfern
Stoke: Sinclair, Butler, Sandford, Cranson, Overson, Gleghorn, Foley, Russell, Stein*, Shaw, Beeston, Regis
Opp: Martin, Burgess, Harvey, Horner, Briggs, Ward, Rodwell, Sinclair*, Mitchel^, Gouck, Eyres, Bonner/Murphy
City hit the top of the League after easing past Billy Ayre's Tangerines. Ashley Ward, on-loan from Leicester, gives Pool the lead but Russell scores twice as the fans rejoice at rain-swept Bloomfield Road. Aussie Ernie Tapei, £60k from Adelaide City, has been granted a work permit.

18 · H · SWANSEA · 28/11
Att *3,867 · Opp pos 12 · Pos 1 · W 2-1 (HT 0-0) · Pts 36
Shaw 47, Stein 80p — Cullen 53 · Ref: T Lunt
Stoke: Sinclair, Butler, Sandford, Cranson, Overson, Gleghorn, Foley*, Russell, Stein, Shaw, Beeston, Ware
Opp: Freestone, Lyttle, Jenkins!, Agboola, Harris, Connor, Cullen, Cornforth, Legg, West*, Bowen, McFarlane
City roar on at the top despite the midweek Cup exit. Shaw crashes in off the post from Russell's chip. Tony Cullen blasts a 30-yard rocket past Sinclair but Shaw is upended by Reuben Agboola and Stein cracks home another penalty. Steve Jenkins gets himself sent off for two bookings.

19 · H · HUDDERSFIELD · 12/12
Att 13,377 · Opp pos 23 · Pos 1 · W 3-0 (HT 0-0) · Pts 39
Ware 75, 83, Cranson 87 · Ref: P Taylor
Stoke: Sinclair, Butler, Sandford, Cranson, Overson, Gleghorn, Foley, Russell, Stein, Shaw*, Beeston*, Harbey/Ware
Opp: Clarke, Parsley, Charlton, Mooney, Mitchell, Jackson, Barnett, O'Regan, Roberts, Dunn, Stuart^, Starbuck
Sub Paul Ware finds a way past Neil Warnock's gritty Terriers after a frustrating afternoon. He latches on to Russell's looping cross to nod over the advancing Tim Clarke. Gleghorn then flicks on a corner for him to head home. Cranson blasts a 20-yard piledriver into the top corner.

20 · A · HARTLEPOOL · 19/12
Att 4,021 · Opp pos 9 · Pos 1 · W 2-1 (HT 1-0) · Pts 42
Regis 7, Gleghorn 90 — Honour 71 · Ref: J Kirkby
Stoke: Sinclair, Butler, Sandford, Cranson, Overson, Gleghorn, Foley, Russell, Stein, Shaw, Beeston, Ware
Opp: Hodge*, Cross R, Cross P, Gilchrist, MacPhail, Emerson, Johnrose, Olsson, Saville, Honour, Johnson^, Southall/Peverell
Regis and Gleghorn both open first goalscoring accounts as City steal the points at the other Victoria Ground. Manager Alan Murray, who has led Hartlepool to their highest ever position in the League, cannot believe it when Nigel Gleghorn's shot beats stand-in keeper John MacPhail.

21 · A · READING · 26/12
Att 7,269 · Opp pos 16 · Pos 1 · W 1-0 (HT 1-0) · Pts 45
Regis 37 · Ref: K Cooper
Stoke: Sinclair, Butler, Sandford, Cranson, Overson, Gleghorn, Foley, Russell, Stein, Shaw, Beeston, Regis
Opp: Francis, Richardson*, Hopkins, McPherson, Williams, Parkinson, Gilkes, Dillon, Moody, Lambert, Jones^, Gooding/Lovell
Stoke extend their unbeaten run to 17 league games thanks to Dave Regis' poachers goal. Stein brings a fantastic save out of Steve Francis but Regis prods in. Francis is outstanding, pushing a Russell drive round the post and clutching Overson's header. Stoke are moving into top gear.

22 · H · ROTHERHAM · 28/12
Att 21,714 · Opp pos 5 · Pos 1 · W 2-0 (HT 1-0) · Pts 48
Beeston 40, Foley 81 · Ref: P Vanes
Stoke: Sinclair, Butler, Sandford*, Cranson, Overson, Gleghorn, Foley, Russell, Stein, Shaw, Beeston, Regis
Opp: Mercer, Pickering, Hutchings, Banks, Johnson, Law, Hazel, Goodwin, Cunningham, Howard, Barrick*, Goater
City knock the stuffing out of Phil Henson's Millers. Kevin Russell hits the bar. He then crosses for Beeston to nod home. Regis tees up Foley for a thunderous 20-yard drive. An eighth straight league win ends the year on a high. Lou Macari has taken on a god-like status with the fans.

23 · A · BRIGHTON · 9/1
Att 2,622 · Opp pos 8 · Pos 1 · D 2-2 (HT 0-0) · Pts 49
Stein 48, Foley 89 — Nogan 61, Overson 63 (og) · Ref: D Axcell
Stoke: Sinclair, Butler, Sandford*, Cranson, Overson, Gleghorn, Foley, Russell, Stein, Shaw, Beeston, Regis
Opp: Beeney, Chivers, Gallacher, Wilkins, Foster, Bissett, Crumplin, Kennedy, Nogan, Codner, Walker, Shaw
Sandford's injury means Gleghorn fills in at left-back. His roving runs set up the darting Stein. Brighton, facing a winding-up order, fight back. Nogan beats three men to level. Overson volleys Crumplin's cross past Sinclair. Foley's late strike ensures a club record of 19 games unbeaten.

BARCLAYS DIVISION 2   Manager: Lou Macari   SEASON 1992-93

No	Date	Att	Pos	Pt	F-A	H-T	Scorers, Times, and Referees	1	2	3	4	5	6	7	8	9	10	11	subs used
24	H 16/1	14,643	21	52	W 4-0	2-0	Russell 14, Gray 40 (og), Regis 64, [Overson 70] Ref: D Gallagher	Sinclair	Butler	Harbey	Cranson	Overson	Gleghorn	Foley	Russell	Stein	Regis	Ware	
MANSFIELD								*Pearcey*	*Peer*	*Gray*	*Foster*	*Walker*	*With*	*Holland*	*Charles*	*Ford*	*Rowbotham* Noteman*	*Wilkinson*	

Stoke profit from Stags errors. Player-boss Foster lets in Russell to score. Russell's shot is saved by Pearcey but cannons off Gray into the net. Regis holds off Walker to crack in on the turn. Overson swoops to power a short corner home. City steam on. Macari is manager of the month.

No	Date	Att	Pos	Pt	F-A	H-T	Scorers, Times, and Referees	1	2	3	4	5	6	7	8	9	10	11	subs used
25	A 23/1	29,341	3	55	W 2-1	1-1	Gleghorn 11, Stein 69 Taylor 22 Ref: M Bodenham	Sinclair	Butler	Sandford	Cranson	Overson	Gleghorn	Foley	Russell	Stein	Regis*	Beeston	Shaw
WEST BROM								*Naylor*	*Fereday*	*Lilwall*	*Bradley*	*Raven*	*Strodder*	*Speedie*	*Hamilton^*	*Taylor*	*McNally*	*Donovan**	*Hackett/Heggs*

Gleghorn heads in a corner but Albion have City on the ropes after Bob Taylor races clear to finish calmly. Foley and Beeston sit back to deny classy Albion space. David Speedie has a quiet debut policed well by Overson. Stein deflects Russell's shot past Naylor. 7,500 Stokies go mad.

No	Date	Att	Pos	Pt	F-A	H-T	Scorers, Times, and Referees	1	2	3	4	5	6	7	8	9	10	11	subs used
26	H 27/1	14,181	15	56	D 1-1	1-1	Regis 38 Cook 24 Ref: S Bell	Sinclair	Butler	Sandford	Cranson	Overson*	Gleghorn	Foley	Russell	Stein	Regis	Beeston	Shaw
EXETER								*Miller*	*Hiley*	*Cook*	*Bailey*	*Daniels !*	*Whiston*	*Harris*	*Brown*	*Jepson*	*Tonge*	*Hodge*	

Having lost 0-5 to Orient on Saturday Alan Ball's men take a shock lead. Regis nets his fifth goal in a month. Scott Daniels sees red (52 mins) for fouling Regis when he is through on goal. Stoke lack the ideas to break down Exeter's ten men. First home points dropped since 6 Sept.

No	Date	Att	Pos	Pt	F-A	H-T	Scorers, Times, and Referees	1	2	3	4	5	6	7	8	9	10	11	subs used
27	A 30/1	4,775	20	57	D 1-1	1-1	Beeston 36 Pilling 41 Ref: K Hackett	Sinclair	Butler	Sandford	Cranson	Overson	Gleghorn	Foley	Russell	Stein	Regis	Beeston	
WIGAN								*Adkins*	*Appleton*	*Tankard*	*Johnson*	*Pilling*	*Langley*	*Skipper*	*Powell**	*Jones*	*Woods*	*Griffiths*	*Robertson*

Carl Beeston chips Nigel Adkins exquisitely from 40 yards to put Stoke ahead. City sit back and Bryan Griffiths tricks his way down the wing to cross for Andy Pilling to head in unmarked. Griffiths is a nuisance throughout a poor second half. One of Stoke's worst performances so far.

No	Date	Att	Pos	Pt	F-A	H-T	Scorers, Times, and Referees	1	2	3	4	5	6	7	8	9	10	11	subs used
28	H 6/2	15,341	18	60	W 3-0	2-0	Ware 5, Foley 43, Stein 86 Ref: R Lewis	Sinclair	Butler	Harbey	Cranson	Sandford	Gleghorn	Foley	Russell	Stein	Ware	Beeston	
HULL								*Wilson*	*Hockaday*	*Brown**	*Mail*	*Wilcox*	*Abbott*	*Norton*	*Atkinson*	*Lund*	*Windass*	*Jenkinson*	*Millar*

Against Terry Dolan's men Ware belts Stein's cross home from the box. Foley drives home from Stein's pass and Stein curls a 20-yarder past Steve Wilson. Stein has another goal ruled out and a free-kick awarded on the edge of the box. Foley drives home from Stein's pass and Stein curls a 20-yarder past Wilson for what he describes as his best goal of the season so far.

No	Date	Att	Pos	Pt	F-A	H-T	Scorers, Times, and Referees	1	2	3	4	5	6	7	8	9	10	11	subs used
29	H 20/2	16,494	9	63	W 1-0	0-0	Kevan 89 Ref: R Groves	Sinclair	Butler	Sandford	Cranson	Overson	Gleghorn	Ware	Russell*	Stein	Shaw	Kevan	Regis
BRADFORD C								*Tomlinson*	*Williams*	*Heseltine*	*Duxbury L*	*Oliver*	*Hoyle*	*Jewell*	*Duxbury M*	*McCarthy*	*Timmion*	*Reid*	

Suspension rules out Foley and Beeston but Overson returns. Stoke find Paul Tomlinson in impressive form. He saves from Sandford, Russell and Stein. Dogged Bradford resist a barrage until Ware sends Stein clear to curl a shot over the keeper and off the bar. Kevan follows up to net.

No	Date	Att	Pos	Pt	F-A	H-T	Scorers, Times, and Referees	1	2	3	4	5	6	7	8	9	10	11	subs used
30	A 27/2	10,798	3	63	L 0-1	0-1	Cooper 43 Ref: D Frampton	Sinclair	Butler	Sandford	Cranson	Overson	Gleghorn	Ware	Russell	Stein	Shaw*	Kevan	Taylor
LEYTON ORIENT								*Heald*	*Bellamy*	*Howard*	*Carter*	*Whitbread*	*Ludden*	*Ryan*	*Benstock*	*Hackett*	*Otto**	*Cooper*	

A snowstorm swirls as the players pay their respects to the late Bobby Moore with a minute's silence. A hard pitch allows little good football. The glorious 25-match unbeaten run is ended by Mark Cooper's firm header. Heald tips over Russell's shot. Stein squanders two good chances.

No	Date	Att	Pos	Pt	F-A	H-T	Scorers, Times, and Referees	1	2	3	4	5	6	7	8	9	10	11	subs used
31	H 6/3	14,534	24	66	W 4-0	2-0	Stein 23, 63, Shaw 41, Foley 66 Ref: M Peck	Sinclair*	Kevan*	Sandford*	Cranson	Overson	Gleghorn	Foley	Russell	Stein	Shaw*	Beeston	Regis
CHESTER								*Stewart*	*Whelan**	*Albiston*	*Comstive*	*Abel*	*Lightfoot*	*Kelly*	*Wheeler*	*Rimmer*	*Butler*	*Pugh*	*Thompson*

Stoke outplay caretaker-boss Graham Barrow's Chester. Stein volleys his first for a month. Shaw heads past Stewart. Stein taps in Gleghorn's cross. Foley bundles in after Stein's lob hits the bar. Gleghorn misses from six yards. Stoke secure their first win over Chester in six attempts.

No	Date	Att	Pos	Pt	F-A	H-T	Scorers, Times, and Referees	1	2	3	4	5	6	7	8	9	10	11	subs used
32	A 9/3	17,484	4	69	W 2-1	0-0	Stein 47, Gleghorn 77 Francis 48 Ref: A Dawson	Sinclair	Hockaday	Sandford	Cranson	Overson	Gleghorn	Foley	Russell	Stein	Shaw	Beeston	Williams PA
STOCKPORT								*Edwards*	*Todd*	*Williams PR*	*Frain*	*Miller*	*Barras*	*Gannon*	*Ward*	*Francis*	*Beaumount*	*Preece**	

Stein nets when Sandford's header is blocked on the line. Francis sticks out a long leg to level. Gleghorn's shot crosses the line despite County defenders' best efforts. After the final whistle Stein reacts to Gannon's racist abuse by clouting him. Mayhem ensues. The case ends in court.

No	Date	Att	Pos	Pt	F-A	H-T	Scorers, Times, and Referees	1	2	3	4	5	6	7	8	9	10	11	subs used
33	A 13/3	7,129	15	70	D 1-1	0-0	Stein 68p Ekoku 89 Ref: R Eamer	Sinclair^	Butler	Hockaday	Cranson	Sandford	Gleghorn	Foley	Russell	Stein	Shaw^	Beeston	Ware/Regis
BOURNEMOUTH								*Bartram*	*Mundee*	*Masters*	*Morris*	*Watson*	*McGorry*	*Wood^*	*Shearer*	*Fletcher**	*Ekoku*	*Rowland*	*Murray/O'Driscoll*

Overson starts another suspension but Butler returns. Ronnie Sinclair is injured in a scramble. Gleghorn takes over in goal. Stein is tripped for the penalty. Gleghorn performs well but cannot stop the speedy Efan Ekoku who races clear to shoot home. Ware volleys into the side netting.

No	Date	Att	Pos	Pt	F-A	H-T	Scorers, Times, and Referees	1	2	3	4	5	6	7	8	9	10	11	subs used
34	H 20/3	17,935	14	73	W 1-0	0-0	Stein 72p Ref: T Lunt	Grobbelaar	Butler	Hockaday	Cranson*	Sandford	Gleghorn	Foley	Russell	Stein	Shaw^	Beeston	Ware/Regis
FULHAM								*Stannard*	*Tucker*	*Pike**	*Onwere*	*Newson*	*Thomas*	*Hails*	*Marshall*	*Farrell*	*Brazil*	*Kelly*	*Ferney*

Bruce Grobbelaar pulls out of a Zimbabwe international to rescue Stoke's goalkeeping crisis. His debut is largely untroubled by a poor Fulham side. Mark Stein cracks home another penalty for his 50th goal in a Stoke shirt. 'This is the best run of form we've had in my time' Macari says.

Football season results record — matches 35–46.

No	V	Opponent	Date	Att	Pos			W/L/D	Score	HT	Scorers / Ref
35	A	SWANSEA	23/3	£366	1	10	76	W	2-1	0-1	Gleghorn 51, Foley 74; Legg 17; Ref: J Carter
36	H	BLACKPOOL	27/3	1,918	1	20	76	L	0-1	0-0	Sinclair 89; Ref: P Alcock
37	A	PORT VALE	31/3	2,373	1	2	79	W	2-0	1-0	Stein 4, Gleghorn 64; Ref: R Milford
38	A	STOCKPORT	3/4	£402	1	3	80	D	1-1	1-0	Regis 40; Ward 70; Ref: T Fitzharris
39	A	HUDDERSFIELD	7/4	7,089	1	16	80	L	0-1	0-1	Dunn 17; Ref: R Hart
40	H	READING	10/4	£919	1	8	83	W	2-0	1-0	Shaw 35, Gleghorn 69; Ref: K Redfern
41	A	ROTHERHAM	12/4	£021	1	10	86	W	2-0	1-0	Stein 2, 54; Ref: R Pawley
42	H	HARTLEPOOL	17/4	1,363	1	18	86	L	0-1	0-1	Johnrose 10; Ref: R Dilkes
43	H	PRESTON	24/4	1,334	1	21	89	W	1-0	0-0	Stein 55; Ref: S Dunn
44	H	PLYMOUTH	28/4	1,718	1	14	92	W	1-0	1-0	Gleghorn 4; Ref: D Elleray
45	A	BOLTON	4/5	1,238	1	2	92	L	0-1	0-1	Darby 7; Ref: K Lupton
46	H	BURNLEY	8/5	2,840	1	13	93	D	1-1	0-1	Stein 64; Randall 40; Ref: D Gallagher

Home / Away / Average 15,831

35 SWANSEA — Grobbelaar, Butler, Sandford, Hockaday*, Overson, Gleghorn, Foley, Kevan*, Stein, Regis, Beeston, Russell. Subs: Freestone, Lyttle, Jenkins, Walker, Harris, Ford^, Bowen, Coughlin*^, McFarlane, Conforth, Legg, Wimbleton/Chapple.
Stoke produce some great football but Andy Legg's superb left-foot volley snatches the lead for Frank Burrows' Swans. Stoke hit back through Gleghorn who heads Dave Hockaday's free-kick home. Beeston supplies Foley with a perfect pass for the winner. Stein has two efforts saved.

36 BLACKPOOL — Grobbelaar, Butler, Sandford, Cranson, Overson, Gleghorn, Foley, Russell, Stein, Regis*, Beeston, Shaw. Subs: Dickins, Bailey, Thornber*, Horner, Briggs, Gare, Leitch, Sinclair, Bamber, Murphy, Eyres, Stoneman.
Promotion jitters as Stoke fail to take advantage of heavy pressure against relegation-threatened Blackpool. Lilleshall graduate Trevor Sinclair scores his first league goal for Billy Ayre's men. Macari has failed to sign Birmingham striker John Gayle after the clubs could not agree a fee.

37 PORT VALE — Grobbelaar, Butler, Sandford, Cranson, Overson, Gleghorn, Foley, Kevan, Stein, Regis*, Ware*, Shaw/Russell. Subs: Musselwhite Kent, Sulley*, Walker, Swan, Glover, Slaven, Van der Laan Houchen, Billing^, Kerr, Jeffers/Cross.
Paul Ware produces a magnificent performance as City overpower Vale. Stein lashes home after a scramble to settle early nerves. Macari keeps Vale waiting at the break and Stoke run out to a cacophony of sound. Vale are stunned. Gleghorn bundles a corner past Musselwhite. Delirium.

38 STOCKPORT — Fox, Butler, Sandford, Cranson, Overson, Gleghorn, Foley, Kevan, Stein, Regis, Beeston, Russell. Subs: Kite, Connolly, Williams PR, Frain*, Miller, Flynn, Gannon, Ward, Francis, Beaumont, Duffield^, James/Williams PA.
A poor match sees on-loan Phil Kite parry Gleghorn's effort but Regis follows up to fire home the rebound. Amid a succession of niggly fouls Peter Ward curls a free-kick home left footed. Stein and Beeston miss good opportunities. Nearly there as Stockport cannot now catch Stoke.

39 HUDDERSFIELD — Fox, Butler, Sandford, Cranson, Overson, Gleghorn, Foley, Kevan*, Stein, Regis, Beeston, Russell. Subs: Clarke, Parsley, Charlton, Robinson, Cooper, Jackson, Barnett, O'Regan, Roberts, Onuora, Dunn.
Iain Dunn's superb volley gives Fox no chance as it lodges in between the angle of bar and post. Onuora and Roberts prove a handful. Foley wastes the best opportunity, blazing wide when clean through. Russell's cross is turned just past the post by a defender. Seven points clear still.

40 READING — Fox, Butler, Sandford, Cranson, Overson, Gleghorn, Foley, Kevan, Stein, Shaw*, Beeston*, Russell/Ware. Subs: Francis, McDonald*, Holzman, McPherson, Hopkins, Parkinson, Bass^, Dillon, Quinn, Lovell, Taylor, Lambert/Gray.
Stoke are wasteful against the play-off chasing Royals. Cranson rounds Francis but fluffs the chance. Foley heads over from seven yards. Stein miskicks in front of goal. The breakthrough arrives when Francis clears against Shaw and the ball rolls in. Gleghorn rockets a free-kick home.

41 ROTHERHAM — Fox, Butler, Sandford, Cranson, Overson, Gleghorn, Foley*, Kevan*, Stein, Regis, Hockaday, Ware. Subs: Mercer, Pickering, Taylor, Wilder, Law, Richardson, Hazel, Goodwin, Cunningham* Varadi, Barrick, Page.
Stein swivels brilliantly to wrong-foot the entire Rotherham defence before beating Billy Mercer. He then scores an even better goal, cracking a dipping drive home from 25 yards. A late effort is cleared off the line to deny him his first Stoke hat-trick. 4,500 Stokies party on in the rain.

42 HARTLEPOOL — Fox, Butler, Sandford, Cranson, Overson, Gleghorn, Ware, Kevan*, Stein, Regis*, Foley*, Russell/Shaw. Subs: Hodge, Cross R, Gilchrist, MacPhail, Nobbs, Southall*, Olsson, Johnrose, Honour, Tait, Peverell.
Hartlepool haven't won in four months but Lenny Johnrose pounces after Fox parries his shot. Pool shut up shop and lethargic Stoke struggle. Stein volleys over and Hodge saves two flying headers. He also saves Stein's penalty (44 mins) with his legs after Stein is nudged in the box.

43 PRESTON — Fox, Butler, Sandford, Cranson, Overson, Gleghorn, Foley, Kevan, Stein, Regis, Shaw, Ware. Subs: Farnworth, Callaghan, Lucas, Ainsworth, Kidd, Greenall, Cartwright* Leonard, Watson, Burton, Ashcroft, Tinkler.
John Beck's Preston side offer stern resistance. The Boothen End is becoming restless before Stein grabs another opportunist strike to put City three points away from automatic promotion and the championship. Another powerful team performance. Stoke's long wait is close to ending.

44 PLYMOUTH — Fox, Butler, Sandford, Cranson, Overson, Gleghorn, Foley, Kevan, Stein, Regis*, Shaw*, Russell/Regis. Subs: Shitton, Poole, McCall, Adcock, Regis, Garner, Castle, Morgan, Marshall, Spearing, Barlow.
The early goal, after Gleghorn chests down Ware's cross and side-foots home, makes City nervous as they fight to cling on. Fox saves superbly from Castle. Marshall threatens up front. City cling on and the celebrations begin. Several rousing Delilah's later Overson collects the trophy.

45 BOLTON — Fox, Butler, Sandford, Cranson, Overson, Gleghorn, Foley, Kevan, Stein, Regis*, Hockaday, Russell. Subs: Branagan, Brown, Burke, Lee, Seagraves, Stubbs, Kelly, McAteer, Darby*, McGinlay, Patterson, Green.
Stoke are greeted by a flurry of red and white ticker tape. Gleghorn's error lets in Julian Darby to score. John Butler revels in his new free role in front of the back four. Hockaday, Stein and Cranson all go close. Bolton go above Vale into second place and everybody goes home happy!

46 BURNLEY — Fox, Butler*, Sandford, Cranson, Overson, Gleghorn, Foley, Kevan, Stein, Russell, Hockaday*, Regis/Shaw. Subs: Beresford*, Farrell, Wilson, Monington, Pender, Deary, Francis, Randall, Heath, Conroy, Harper, Painter.
A champions' welcome greets the team who take the field down a tunnel of Burnley players. Adrian Randall beats Fox to give Jimmy Mullen's Clarets the lead. Stein notches his 33rd goal of the season in all competitions. Peter Fox makes his farewell Stoke appearance. A wonderful day!

BARCLAYS DIVISION 2 (CUP-TIES)

Manager: Lou Macari

SEASON 1992-93

Coca-Cola Cup

Match	No.	Att	Res	F-A	H-T	Scorers, Times, and Referees	1	2	3	4	5	6	7	8	9	10	11	subs used
1:1 A PRESTON 8/8		5,581	L	1-2	1-1	Stein 8 / *Tinkler 41, Ellis 51* / Ref: A Wilkie	Sinclair / *Farnworth*	Butler / *Davidson*	Harbey / *Fowler*	Cranson / *Tinkler*	Overson / *Flynn*	Sandford / *Callaghan*	Foley / *Ashcroft*	Ware* / *Cartwright*	Stein / *Leonard*	Shaw / *Ellis*	Russell / *James*	Kelly / *James*
1:2 H PRESTON 26/8	15	9,745	W	4-0	0-0	Stein 90, Overson 95, Biggins 102, 105 / Ref: B Coddington / (Stoke win 5-2 on aggregate) *aet*	Sinclair / *Farnworth*	Butler / *Davidson^*	Harbey / *Fowler*	Cranson / *Tinkler*	Overson / *Flynn*	Sandford* / *Callaghan*	Foley / *Ashcroft*	Devlin / *Cartwright*	Stein^ / *Leonard*	Biggins / *Ellis**	Russell / *James*	Kelly/Shaw / *Eaves/Fitcroft*
2:1 A CAMBRIDGE 22/9	14	3,426 1:19	D	2-2	1-1	Stein 34, 63 / *Philpott 37, Chapple 89* / Ref: P Alcock	Parks / *Sheffield*	Butler / *Fensome*	Harbey / *Kimble*	Cranson / *Dennis**	Overson / *Chapple*	Sandford / *Daish*	Foley / *Rowett*	Ware / *Leadbitter*	Stein / *Raynor*	Biggins / *Cheetham^*	Russell / *Philpott*	*Fowler/Francis*
2:2 H CAMBRIDGE 7/10	11	10,732 1:20	L	1-2	0-1	Shaw 68 / *Fowler 36, Francis 80* / Ref: T Fitzharris / (Stoke lose 3-4 on aggregate)	Horne / *Sheffield*	Butler / *Clayton*	Harbey / *Kimble*	Cranson / *Rowett*	Wright* / *Chapple**	Sandford / *Daish*	Foley / *Raynor*	Ware / *Leadbitter*	Stein / *White*	Shaw / *Cheetham^*	Beeston / *Philpott*	Devlin / *Fowler/Francis*

FA Cup

Match	No.	Att	Res	F-A	H-T	Scorers, Times, and Referees	1	2	3	4	5	6	7	8	9	10	11	subs used
1 H PORT VALE 16/11	2	24,490	D	0-0	0-0	Ref: V Callow	Sinclair / *Musselwhite Sandeman*	Butler / *Sulley*	Sandford / *Walker*	Cranson / *Swan*	Overson / *Glover*	Gleghorn / *Aspin*	Foley / *Kerr^*	Russell / *Cross**	Stein / *Houchen*	Shaw / *Taylor*	Beeston	Foyle/Jeffers
1R A PORT VALE 24/11	1	19,810	L	1-3	1-2	Sandford 24 / *Foyle 24, 90, Porter 45* / Ref: V Callow	Sinclair / *Musselwhite Sandeman*	Butler / *Sulley*	Sandford / *Walker*	Cranson / *Swan*	Overson / *Glover*	Gleghorn / *Aspin**	Foley / *Porter*	Russell / *Cross*	Stein / *Foyle*	Shaw* / *Taylor*	Beeston / *Jeffers*	Regis / *Jeffers*

Stein latches on to Shaw's flick to finish into the far corner. City are coasting. A first ever win on plastic seems a foregone conclusion. Ashcroft suddenly has the beating of Graham Harbey. His crosses cause panic and Tinkler prods home. Confidence drains, Ellis scores and Stoke slump.

Stein, Sandford and Biggins all waste good chances in front of the largest first round crowd. City fall foul of the new back-pass law but Sinclair saves the free-kick. Finally Stein lashes in a great shot. The floodgates open. Overson and Biggins head home corners. Biggins neatly chips in.

In heavy rain City match John Beck's physical Cambridge. Stein pounces from long passes to shoot past Jon Sheffield as Stoke create several good chances. Parks struggles to deal with Cambridge's deep crosses. Philpott scores and Phil Chapple heads a free-kick home at the far post.

Injury-hit Stoke fail to deal with Cambridge's long-ball tactics. Phil Chapple is carried off injured and his replacement scores after hesitancy in the City box. Stein's overhead kick is blocked on the line. Shaw nets when clean through but Francis heads Philpott's cross past a static Horne.

In torrential rain a capacity crowd, and several million on TV, see Stoke swarm all over Vale. John Rudge's team hold firm and Shaw springs to nod Houchen's looping header off the line. A midfield stalemate ensues. Musselwhite tips Gleghorn's late shot round the post as nerves fray.

Sandford nets from close in but Vale's quick reply comes courtesy of Martin Foyle. Andy Porter nets a beauty. In dreadful conditions the ball stops on Vale's line after Regis beats Musselwhite to a through-ball. Foyle then nicks the ball past Sinclair after the ball sticks in the mud again.

League Table

		P	Home					Away					Pts
			W	D	L	F	A	W	D	L	F	A	
1	STOKE	46	17	4	2	41	13	10	8	5	32	21	93
2	Bolton	46	18	2	3	48	14	9	7	7	32	27	90
3	Port Vale	46	14	7	2	44	17	12	4	7	35	27	89
4	West Brom *	46	17	3	3	56	22	8	7	8	32	32	85
5	Swansea	46	12	4	7	38	17	8	6	9	27	30	73
6	Stockport	46	11	11	1	47	18	8	4	11	34	39	72
7	Leyton Orient	46	16	4	3	49	20	5	5	13	20	33	72
8	Reading	46	14	4	5	44	20	4	11	8	22	31	69
9	Brighton	46	13	4	6	36	24	7	5	11	27	35	69
10	Bradford C	46	12	5	6	36	24	6	9	8	33	43	68
11	Rotherham	46	9	7	7	30	27	8	7	8	30	33	65
12	Fulham	46	9	9	5	28	22	7	8	8	29	33	65
13	Burnley	46	11	8	4	38	21	4	8	11	19	38	61
14	Plymouth	46	11	6	6	38	28	5	6	12	21	36	60
15	Huddersfield	46	10	6	7	30	22	7	3	13	24	39	60
16	Hartlepool	46	8	6	9	19	23	6	6	11	23	37	54
17	Bournemouth	46	7	10	6	28	24	5	7	11	17	28	53
18	Blackpool	46	9	9	5	40	30	3	6	14	23	45	51
19	Exeter	46	5	8	10	26	30	6	9	8	28	39	50
20	Hull	46	9	5	9	28	26	4	6	13	18	43	50
21	Preston	46	8	5	10	41	47	5	3	15	24	47	47
22	Mansfield	46	7	8	8	34	34	4	3	16	18	46	44
23	Wigan	46	6	6	11	26	34	6	5	14	17	38	41
24	Chester	46	6	2	15	30	47	2	3	18	19	55	29
		1104	259	146	147	875	604	147	146	259	604	875	1510

* promoted after play-offs

Appearances and Goals

	Appearances						Goals			
	Lge	Sub	LC	Sub	FAC	Sub	Lge	LC	FAC	Tot
Beeston, Carl	25	2	1		2		3			3
Biggins, Wayne	8		2				2	2		4
Butler, John	44		4		2		1			1
Cranson, Ian	45		4		2		3			3
Devlin, Mark	3		1	1						
Foley, Steve	44		4		2		7			7
Fox, Peter	10									
Gleghorn, Nigel	34						7			7
Grobbelaar, Bruce	4									
Harbey, Graham	16	1	4							
Hockaday, Dave	7									
Horne, Brian	1		1							
Kelly, Tony	2	5			2					
Kevan, Dave	13	2					1			1
Overson, Vince	43		3		2		1		1	2
Parks, Tony	2		1							
Regis, Dave	16	9	3			1	5			5
Russell, Kevin	30	10	3		2		5			5
Sandford, Lee	42		4		2		2		1	3
Shaw, Graham	20	9	2	1	2		5		1	6
Sinclair, Ronnie	29		2		2					
Stein, Mark	46		4		2		26	4		30
Ware, Paul	21	7	3				4			4
Wright, Ian	1				1					
24 players used	506	45	44	4	22	1	72	8	1	81

Odds & ends

Double wins: (7) Mansfield, Port Vale, Preston, Reading, Rotherham, Swansea, West Brom.

Double losses: (0).

Won from behind: (5) West Brom (h), Leyton Orient (h), Port Vale (h), Blackpool (a), Swansea (a).

Lost from in front: (1) Bradford C (a).

High spots: Promotion as Champions.

The 25-match club record unbeaten run.

Mark Stein becoming the first City player to score 30 goals in a season since John Ritchie in 1963-64.

Peter Fox finally making his 400th league appearance in goal for the club.

Low spots: Losing at Leyton Orient to end the unbeaten run.

A nervous blip at Huddersfield and against Hartlepool to delay winning promotion.

Player of the Year: Mark Stein.

Ever-presents: (1) Mark Stein.

Hat-tricks: (0).

Leading scorer: (30) Mark Stein.

ENDSLEIGH DIVISION 1 — Manager: Lou Macari ⇨ Joe Jordan — SEASON 1993-94

No	Date	H/A	Opponent	Att	Pos	Pt	F-A	H-T	Scorers, Times, and Referees
1	14/8	H	MILLWALL	18,766	–	0	L 1-2	1-1	McCarthy 28 (og) / Bogie 14, Murray 55 / Ref: J Kirkby
2	21/8	A	BOLTON	11,328	20	1	D 1-1	0-0	Stein 69 / Coyle 48 / Ref: J Watson
3	28/8	H	WEST BROM	17,948	16	4	W 1-0	0-0	Stein 68 / Ref: J Lloyd
4	4/9	A	PORTSMOUTH	12,552	16	5	D 3-3	1-3	Stein 17, 65, Regis 84 / Durnin 3, Walsh 12, Gittens 39 / Ref: A Groves
5	11/9	H	TRANMERE	17,296	21	5	L 1-2	1-0	Martindale 25 (og) / Thomas 70, Muir 72 / Ref: P Jones
6	14/9	A	MIDDLESBROUGH	13,189	14	8	W 2-1	1-0	Carruthers 42, Foley 84 / Hignett 86 / Ref: R Poulain
7	19/9	A	NOTT'M FOREST	20,843	7	11	W 3-2	2-0	Regis 16, Stein 25p, 49 / Phillips 50, Pearce 66 / Ref: K Lupton
8	25/9	H	SOUTHEND	16,145	9	11	L 0-1	0-0	Mooney 34 / Ref: K Leach
9	2/10	A	CRYSTAL PALACE	12,880	12	11	L 1-4	0-3	Stein 75 / Southgate 24, Salako 31, 44, 88 / Ref: R Bigger
10	10/10	A	OXFORD	6,489	15	11	L 0-1	0-1	Penney 41 / Ref: D Elleray
11	16/10	H	GRIMSBY	14,696	14	14	W 1-0	0-0	Orlygsson 69 / Ref: E Wolstenholme

Line-ups (positions 1–11, subs used) and match reports

1. MILLWALL — Prudhoe, Butler, Sandford, Harbey, Overson, Lowe, Orlygsson*, Foley, Stein, Bannister^, Gleghorn. Subs: Gynn/Carruthers.
Opponents: Keller, Cunningham, Dawes, Maguire, McCarthy, Stevens, Roberts, Bogie, Murray*, Kerr, Dolby, Byrne.
A new-look Stoke line-up fail to settle against Mick McCarthy's Millwall. Lowe and Orlygsson tire after a good start in midfield. Bogie's shot finds it way past Prudhoe. The Lions' player-manager lobs the ball over his own keeper. Bruce Murray taps on his debut. A struggle ahead?

2. BOLTON — Prudhoe, Butler, Sandford, Cranson, Overson, Lowe*, Williams, Foley, Stein, Regis^, Gleghorn. Subs: Orlygsson/Carruthers.
Opponents: Branagan, Brown, Phillips, Kelly, Burke, Stubbs, Lee, McAteer, Coyle*, McGinlay, Thompson, Patterson.
Ian Cranson, back from injury, and on-loan Brett Williams bolster the shaky-looking defence. Ex-Stokie Tony Kelly and Jason McAteer have a grip on midfield. Owen Coyle volleys home. Thompson blazes over the bar when clean through. Regis crosses for Stein to nod in the equaliser.

3. WEST BROM — Prudhoe, Butler, Sandford, Cranson, Overson, Lowe^, Gynn, Foley*, Stein, Regis, Gleghorn. Subs: Orlygsson/Carruthers.
Opponents: Lange, Fereday, Lilwall, Bradley, Raven, Burgess, Hunt, Hamilton, Taylor, O'Regan, Donovan.
Baggies threaten through Bob Taylor and new signing Kieran O'Regan. Micky Gynn tests Tony Lange from 20 yards. His free-kick is floated to Cranson whose header is cracked in by Stein. Prudhoe fingertips Paul Raven's volley on to the bar. Darren Bradley also hits the woodwork.

4. PORTSMOUTH — Prudhoe, Butler, Sandford, Cranson, Overson, Orlygsson^, Gynn, Foley, Stein, Regis, Gleghorn. Subs: Carruthers/Lowe.
Opponents: Horne, Awford*, Burns, McLoughlin, Gittens, Daniel, Neill, Blake, Durnin, Walsh*, Butters, Price/Powell.
Walsh is lively for Jim Smith's Pompey. He sets up Durnin and fires in from 20 yards. Stein belts home a free-kick but Gittens' header restores the lead. All change after Brett Williams is subbed at half-time. Stein lashes in after Home picks up a back-pass. Regis smashes home to level.

5. TRANMERE — Prudhoe, Butler*, Sandford, Cranson, Overson, Kevan, Gynn, Foley, Stein, Regis^, Gleghorn. Subs: Bannister/Carruthers.
Opponents: Nixon, Higgins, Mungall, Irons, Martindale, Nevin, Aldridge, Muir, Brannan, Thomas.
City outclass John King's Tranmere but only manage one goal when Stein's header is brilliantly saved by Eric Nixon but rebounds into the net off Martindale. The ref misses a blatant handball and gives a dodgy free-kick for a back-pass. Rovers score and nick it when Muir lobs Prudhoe.

6. MIDDLESBROUGH — Prudhoe, Clarkson, Sandford, Cranson, Harbey, Orlygsson, Carruthers, Foley, Stein^, Regis, Gleghorn. Subs: Lowe/Wright.
Opponents: Pears, Morris, Liburd, Pollock, Kernaghan, Whyte, Hendrie, Hignett, Wilkinson, Mustoe*, Moore.
Promotion favourites Boro are well beaten at Ayresome. Stein wastes a great chance having rounded Stephen Pears. Carruthers buries a similar shot. Foley rounds off a superb move by steering past Pears. Craig Hignett's free-kick flies in but City hang on for a great win. Settling in now.

7. NOTT'M FOREST — Prudhoe, Clarkson, Sandford, Cranson, Overson, Orlygsson, Gynn*, Foley, Stein, Regis, Gleghorn. Subs: Lowe/Gemmill.
Opponents: Crossley, Lyttle, Pearce, Blatherwick, Chettle, Stone, Phillips, Glover, Roasio^, Collymore, Woan.
3,000+ Stokies are present despite this being City's first live league match. Regis rolls the ball past Crossley and inside the post. Stein converts the penalty when Gynn is floored. Stein volleys a beautiful goal. Delilah sounds out. Phillips and Pearce put on the pressure but Stoke cling on.

8. SOUTHEND — Prudhoe, Clarkson, Sandford*, Cranson, Overson, Orlygsson, Gynn^, Foley, Stein, Carruthers, Gleghorn. Subs: Sturridge/Lowe.
Opponents: Sansome, Poole, Powell, Jones !, Howell, Bressington, Ansah, Payne, Lee, Otto, Allan*, Mooney.
Both teams have early goals disallowed. Simon Sturridge is City's tenth debutant this season. Stoke press forward once captain Keith Jones is sent off for swearing (52 mins). Barry Fry's Southend nick the points thanks to Tommy Mooney's strike from a long punt by Paul Sansome.

9. CRYSTAL PALACE — Prudhoe, Clarkson, Cowan, Cranson, Overson, Orlygsson, Gynn*, Foley^, Stein, Carruthers, Gleghorn. Subs: Shaw/Sturridge.
Opponents: Martyn, Humphrey, Coleman, Southgate, Young, Thorn, Shaw, Bowry, Whyte, Salako*, Rodger, Williams.
City attack in the pouring rain but pay for their cavalier approach when Gareth Southgate poaches a rare goal. John Salako notches two tap-ins on his return from a two-year injury lay-off. Stein glances in on-loan Tom Cowan's cross but Salako completes his hat-trick with a neat header.

10. OXFORD — Muggleton, Clarkson, Cowan, Cranson, Overson, Orlygsson, Gynn, Foley*, Stein, Sturridge, Gleghorn. Subs: Carruthers.
Opponents: Whitehead, Collins, Ford M, Lewis, Robinson, Rogan, Magilton, Beauchamp, Druce*, Penney, Allen^, Wanless/Ford R.
Stoke waste chance after chance as Denis Smith's men lead a charmed life. Phil Whitehead saves from Stein and Sturridge. Muggleton saves a Magilton penalty but cannot stop Penney's header. Foley's awful miss sums up a preoccupied Stoke, wondering if Macari and Stein will leave.

11. GRIMSBY — Muggleton, Clarkson, Cowan*, Cranson, Overson, Orlygsson, Gynn^, Carruthers, Stein, Sturridge, Gleghorn. Subs: Lowe/Foley.
Opponents: Crichton, McDermott, Agnew, Futcher, Lever, Dobbin, Childs, Gilbert*, Daws, Mendonca, Groves, Shakespeare/Jobling.
City end their worst sequence since Macari became manager in his last home game. A quiet game is won by a deflected Toddy Orlygsson shot. Crichton saves from Stein and Cranson. Cranson heads off the line with Muggleton beaten. Fans stage 'Macari must stay' demos at the whistle.

Stoke City — Match Log (matches 12–23)

#	Venue	Opponent	Date	HT	FT	Result	Pos	No.	Pts	Att.
12	A	WOLVES	23/10	1-1	1-1	D	14	17	15	20,421
13	H	BARNSLEY	30/10	2-3	5-4	W	11	22	18	14,679
14	H	SUNDERLAND	3/11	0-0	1-0	W	9	14	21	13,551
15	A	WATFORD	6/11	1-1	3-1	W	8	14	24	7,767
16	H	LEICESTER	14/11	1-0	1-0	W	9	3	27	15,984
17	A	NOTTS CO	20/11	0-0	0-2	L	8	15	27	9,815
18	A	LUTON	27/11	2-3	2-6	L	10	15	27	7,384
19	H	WATFORD	4/12	0-0	2-0	W	6	22	30	13,465
20	H	MIDDLESBROUGH	11/12	2-0	3-1	W	7	15	33	13,777
21	A	MILLWALL	19/12	0-0	0-2	L	9	3	33	8,930
22	H	BIRMINGHAM	26/12	1-0	2-1	W	8	17	36	16,584
23	A	CHARLTON	29/12	0-1	0-2	L	10	3	36	8,416

Match details

12 — A WOLVES, 23/10 (1-1)
Scorers: Stein 33 / Kelly D 23. Ref: P Harrison
Stoke: Mugleton, Clarkson, Cowan, Cranson, Overson, Orlygsson*, Foley, Carruthers, Stein, Sturridge^, Sandford/Butler; Regis
Wolves: Stowell, Simkin, Venus, Thompson, Mountfield, Shirtliff, Cook, Kelly J*, Kelly D, Dennison, Keen
Rebuilt Molineux has three complete sides ready to see Graham Turner's Wolves. Regis sets up Kelly who scores at the second attempt. Andy Thompson puts a 32nd-minute penalty wide after Sturridge fouls Cook. Stein poaches a simple goal. City shut up shop. Job done.

13 — H BARNSLEY, 30/10 (5-4)
Scorers: Flem'g 23 (og), Bish'p 25 (og), Glegh'n 50, [Overson 55, Carruthers 64] / Redf'rn 6, O'C'nl 7, Brys'n 42, Arch'n 86. Ref: R Gifford
Stoke: Mugleton, Butler, Cowan, Cranson, Overson, Orlygsson, Foley, Carruthers, Shaw, Sturridge^, Gleghorn
Barnsley: Butler, Fleming, Boden, Wilson, Bishop, Anderson^, O'Connell, Rammell*, Bryson, Redfearn, Eaden; Lowe, Archdeacon/Liddell
A crazy week ends with a crazy game. Stoke lack Macari (to Celtic) and Stein (to Chelsea) but score five for the first time in seven years. Two copycat own-goals keep Stoke in the hunt. Gleghorn curls a shot in from 25 yards. Overson flicks a header in. Carruthers strolls around Butler.

14 — H SUNDERLAND, 3/11 (1-0)
Scorers: Orlygsson 86. Ref: T Lunt
Stoke: Mugleton, Sandford, Cowan, Cranson, Overson, Orlygsson, Foley, Carruthers, Shaw, Gray Martin*, Gleghorn
Sunderland: Chamberlain, Ball, Bennett, Owers, Melville, Atkinson, Goodman, Gray P, Smith, Armstrong, Gray Michael
A poor crowd reflects the feeling after Macari's departure. No replacement is on the horizon. Caretaker boss Chic Bates keeps to Macari's tried and tested formation. Orlygsson produces a sublime moment to win the game, beating four men to crash the ball into Chamberlain's far corner.

15 — A WATFORD, 6/11 (3-1)
Scorers: Orlygsson 10, Carruthers 53, Regis 84 / Dyer 30. Ref: G Willard
Stoke: Mugleton, Butler, Sheppard, Cranson, Overson, Orlygsson, Foley, Carruthers, Regis, Cowan, Gleghorn
Watford: Sheppard, Lavin, Drysdale^, Hessenthaler, Holdsworth, Dublin, Dyer, Soloman, Charley^, Porter, Nogan; Ashby/Harding
Orlygsson volleys a beauty past Simon Sheppard. Overson polices Ken Charley well but Bruce Dyer poaches an equaliser. Carruthers heads in and Regis shrugs off two players to power home and seal a first ever win at Glenn Roeder's Hornets. Still no sign of a replacement for Macari.

16 — H LEICESTER, 14/11 (1-0)
Scorers: Gleghorn 43. Ref: J Parker
Stoke: Prudhoe, Butler, Ward, Sandford, Overson, Orlygsson, Foley, Carruthers, Regis, Cowan, Gleghorn
Leicester: Ward, Grayson, Mills^, Whitlow, Carey, Hill, Joachim, Thompson, Speedie, Oldfield, Gibson*; Philpott/Smith
New manager Joe Jordan presides over an excellent performance as Stoke defeat Brian Little's high-flying Foxes. Sandford and Overson have Speedie and Joachim in their pockets allowing City to attack at will. Gleghorn's swirling 35-yard drive beats Ward. Overson heads off the line.

17 — A NOTTS CO, 20/11 (0-2)
Scorers: Robinson 50, Turner 82. Ref: K Lynch
Stoke: Prudhoe, Butler, Cherry, Sandford, Overson, Orlygsson*, Foley, Carruthers, Regis, Cowan, Gleghorn
Notts Co: Cherry, Gallagher, King, Robinson, Johnson, Turner, Devlin, Draper, Lund, Wilson, Agana
Stoke dominate and miss three good chances. Carruthers hits Cherry from eight yards. Regis heads over and shoots tamely when clean through. County capitalise when Phil Robinson's overhead kick goes in off the bar. Turner prods home after Prudhoe makes a mess of a long-range shot.

18 — A LUTON, 27/11 (2-6)
Scorers: Regis 3, Linton 19 (og) [Hartson 89] / Dixon 22, 71, 79, Hughes 32, Oakes 37. Ref: B Hill
Stoke: Marshall, Summer, Linton, Sandford, Overson, Orlygsson, Foley, Carruthers*, Regis, Cowan, Gleghorn
Luton: Sommer, Linton, Thomas, Harper, Peake, Campbell, Hughes, Oakes, Dixon, Rees*; Dickov^, Hartson/Thorpe
An appalling display after being 2-0 to the good sees ex-England striker Kerry Dixon bag a hat-trick and on-loan keeper Gordon Marshall have a nightmare debut. Hughes fires in a free-kick. An ill-tempered game is not helped by ineffectual refereeing. City miss the influential Cranson.

19 — H WATFORD, 4/12 (2-0)
Scorers: Bannister 53, Regis 63. Ref: J Lloyd
Stoke: Marshall, Sheppard, Lavin, Cranson, Overson, Orlygsson, Foley, Bannister, Regis, Cowan, Gleghorn
Watford: Sheppard, Lavin, Dublin, Johnson, Watson, Dyer, Holdsworth, Soloman, Charley*, Nogan, McCarthy; Willis
City put the Luton humiliation behind them. Regis cuts in from the touchline, eludes two defenders and fires in a 20-yard shot. Fantastic stuff. Marshall doesn't have to make a save. An easy victory.

20 — H MIDDLESBROUGH, 11/12 (3-1)
Scorers: Bannister 18, Orlygsson 32, 69 / Peake 70. Ref: T Holbrook
Stoke: Marshall, Pears, Fleming*, Cranson, Overson, Orlygsson, Foley, Bannister, Regis, Cowan, Gleghorn
Middlesbrough: Pears, Fleming*, Liburd, Vickers^, Mohan, Whyte, Peake, Hignett, Wilkinson, Mustoe, Moore; Hendrie/Gannon
Stoke profit when Stephen Pears' clearance hits Regis and Bannister pounces. Orlygsson cracks home a beauty on the run and then thrashes the ball in after Regis' shot is saved. Clarkson looks good down the right. Pears saves Regis' drive. Marshall fails to stop Peake's deflected shot.

21 — A MILLWALL, 19/12 (0-2)
Scorers: Rae 87, Kennedy 90. Ref: K Martin
Stoke: Marshall, Keller, Dolby, Cranson, Overson, Orlygsson, Foley, Bannister, Regis, Cowan, Gleghorn
Millwall: Keller, Dolby, Barber*, Roberts, Carter, Stevens, Rae, Verveer, Mitchell, Goodman^, Huxford; Beard/Kennedy
Gordon Marshall continues his atrocious form by gifting Mick McCarthy's men both late goals. City test USA international Keller three times before Marshall starts the Panto season early. New Birmingham boss, Barry Fry, wants to swap his keeper Kevin Miller for striker Dave Regis.

22 — H BIRMINGHAM, 26/12 (2-1)
Scorers: Orlygsson 12, Sandford 69 / Peschisolido 60. Ref: K Cooper
Stoke: Marshall, Miller, Fenwick^, Cranson, Overson, Orlygsson*, Foley, Bannister, Regis, Cowan, Gleghorn
Birmingham: Miller, Fenwick^, Cooper, Lowe, Dryden, Whyte, McMinn, Wallace*, Peschisolido, Saville, Harding; Shutt/Barnett
Orlygsson runs half the length of the pitch to crack past Kevin Miller. Blues counter attack well, but the final pass is lacking until Peschisolido beats three players to slot home. Stoke, urged on by a small Xmas crowd, pour forward and Sandford lashes home after Miller drops a corner.

23 — A CHARLTON, 29/12 (0-2)
Scorers: Leaburn 23, McLeary 80. Ref: R Bigger
Stoke: Marshall, Salmon, Brown, Cranson, Overson, Orlygsson*, Foley, Bannister!, Regis, Cowan, Gleghorn
Charlton: Salmon, Brown, Minto, Pardew, McLeary, Chapple, Robson, Leaburn, Pitcher, Grant*, Nelson; Gynn/Carruthers, Walsh
A stormy game sees Jordan and Asa Hartford ordered from the bench and Bannister sent off for hitting Pitcher (36 mins). City's ten men chase shadows as the Addicks build on Carl Leaburn's header. McLeary heads a second. Cranson risks a red for fouling Pitcher who is clean through.

ENDSLEIGH DIVISION 1 — Manager: Lou Macari ⇨ Joe Jordan — SEASON 1993-94

No	H/A	Date	Team	Att	Pos	Pt	F-A	H-T	Scorers, Times, and Referees	1	2	3	4	5	6	7	8	9	10	11	subs used
24	H	1/1	DERBY	20,307	7	W 39	2-1	1-1	Foley 35, Orlygsson 49 / Gabbiadini 15 / Ref: G Singh	Marshall	Clarkson	Sandford	Cranson	Overson	Orlygsson	Foley	Bannister*	Regis	Butler	Gleghorn	Sturridge
										Taylor	*Charles*	*Forsyth*	*Kuhl**	*Short*	*Wassall*	*Harkes*	*Ramage^*	*Johnson*	*Gabbiadini*	*Williams*	*Simpson/Kavanagh*
25	A	3/1	BRISTOL CITY	11,132	12	D 40	0-0	0-0	Ref: P Durkin	Marshall	Clarkson	Sandford	Cranson	Overson	Orlygsson	Foley	Bannister	Regis	Butler*	Gynn	Gynn
										Welch	*Munro*	*Scott*	*Shail*	*Bryant*	*Edwards*	*Martin*	*Robinson*	*Baird**	*Allison*	*Tinnion*	*Brown*
26	A	15/1	GRIMSBY	8,577	19	D 41	0-0	0-0	Ref: T Heilbron	Marshall	Butler	Sandford	Cranson	Overson	Orlygsson	Foley	Carruthers*	Regis	Potter	Gleghorn	Sturridge
										Crichton	*Ford*	*Croft*	*Futcher*	*Handyside*	*Dobbin*	*Watson**	*Gilbert^*	*Groves*	*Mendonca*	*Shakespeare*	*Agnew/Rees*
27	H	22/1	OXFORD	14,689	22	D 42	1-1	1-0	Regis 12 / Beauchamp 85 / Ref: T Lunt	Marshall	Butler	Sandford	Cranson	Overson	Orlygsson	Foley	Carruthers*	Regis	Sturridge^	Gleghorn	Shaw/Gynn
										Whitehead	*Elliott*	*Ford M*	*Lewis*	*Robinson*	*Rogan*	*Magilton*	*Beauchamp*	*Cusack^*	*Byrne*	*Dyer^*	*Allen/Saunders*
28	H	5/2	WOLVES	22,579	9	D 43	1-1	0-1	Overson 53 / Blades 37 / Ref: N Barry	Prudhoe	Butler	Sandford	Cranson	Overson	Orlygsson	Foley	Carruthers*	Regis	Potter	Gleghorn	Sturridge
										Stowell	*Rankine*	*Thompson*	*Venus*	*Blades*	*Shirtliff*	*Marsden*	*Ferguson*	*Regis*	*Kelly D*	*Keen*	
29	A	12/2	BARNSLEY	7,561	10	L 43	0-3	0-1	Rammell 20, Redfearn 58, Taggart 74 / Ref: M Bailey	Prudhoe	Butler	Sandford	Cranson*	Overson	Orlygsson	Foley^	Bannister	Regis	Clark	Gleghorn	Carruthers/Potter
										Butler	*Eaden*	*Fleming*	*Wilson*	*Taggart*	*Bishop*	*O'Connell*	*Redfearn*	*Rammell*	*Payton*	*Archdeacon*	
30	A	19/2	PETERBOROUGH	7,428	8	D 44	1-1	1-1	Gleghorn 45 / Bradshaw 6 / Ref: W Flood	Prudhoe	Butler	Sandford	Cranson	Overson	Orlygsson	Foley	Carruthers	Regis	Clark	Gleghorn	Sturridge
										Barber	*Bradshaw*	*Carter*	*Greenman*	*Howarth*	*Welsh*	*Williams*	*McGorry*	*Adcock*	*Charlery*	*Brissett*	
31	H	23/2	BOLTON	14,257	6	W 47	2-0	1-0	Orlygsson 45, Regis 85 / Ref: J Worrall	Prudhoe	Butler	Sandford	Cranson	Overson	Orlygsson	Foley^	Carruthers*	Regis	Clark	Gleghorn	Walker/Lee
										Davison	*Lydiate*	*Kelly*	*Phillips*	*McAteer*	*Seagraves*	*Thompson^*	*Burke*	*Coyle**	*McGinlay*	*Patterson*	
32	H	26/2	PORTSMOUTH	14,506	5	W 50	2-0	1-0	Orlygsson 45p, Carruthers 84 / Ref: J Parker	Prudhoe	Butler	Sandford	Cranson	Overson	Orlygsson	Foley*	Carruthers	Regis	Clark	Gleghorn	Powell/Wood
										Knight	*Stimson^*	*Butters*	*Burns*	*Symons**	*Awford*	*Neill*	*Durnin*	*Creaney*	*Walsh*	*Kristensen*	
33	A	5/3	WEST BROM	16,060	19	D 51	0-0	0-0	Ref: G Pooley	Prudhoe	Butler	Sandford	Cranson	Overson	Orlygsson	Foley	Carruthers	Regis	Clark	Gleghorn	Hamilton
										Naylor	*Burgess*	*Edwards*	*Bradley*	*Mardon*	*Raven*	*Hunt*	*McNally**	*Naylor*	*Donovan*	*Smith*	
34	H	12/3	NOTT'M FOREST	20,550	8	L 51	0-1	0-1	Webb 40 / Ref: J Kirkby	Prudhoe	Butler	Sandford	Cranson	Overson	Orlygsson	Foley	Bannister*	Regis	Clark	Gleghorn	Sturridge
										Crossley	*Lyttle*	*Pearce*	*Cooper*	*Chettle*	*Stone*	*Phillips*	*Bohinen*	*Lee*	*Webb*	*Black*	

24 DERBY — A mediocre first half is only enlivened by Gabbiadini's close-range finish. Foley scores after Regis beats the offside trap. Roy McFarland's £13 million Rams are ripped apart after the break Orlygsson rounds off a good move by charging down Craig Short's clearance which rebounds in.

25 BRISTOL CITY — Bristol City fail to make much impression on Stoke's well-drilled defence. Marshall has his best match so far. Even knocking out Ian Baird in an aerial challenge. Welch saves well from Foley and Gleghorn. Baird rounds Marshall but fires wide. Idle mutterings about the play-offs start!

26 GRIMSBY — A dreadful match with little incident. Jordan reshuffles the defence after the cup debacle v Bath. Youngster Graham Potter makes his debut at left-back. Butler reverts to his favoured right side. Neither Cowan nor Muggleton can be signed up due to lack of funds. No ambition shown.

27 OXFORD — Not for the first time Stoke fade badly after a whirlwind start. Regis runs onto Sturridge's through-ball to beat Whitehead. Denis Smith's Oxford battle back. Only Marshall's superb save denies Magilton. Sandford clears off the line. Finally Beauchamp sees his effort creep past Marshall.

28 WOLVES — A minute's silence is observed for ex-Stoke manager Tony Waddington. Wolves start the brighter and Paul Blades latches onto Marsden's pass to beat Prudhoe. Big Cyrille wins the battle of the Regis brothers after a crunching early tackle. Overson hooks in after Carruthers hits the bar.

29 BARNSLEY — Stoke are ripped apart by Viv Anderson's confident Tykes. Andy Rammell races through to beat Prudhoe. Cranson is injured and debutant Jon Clark moves to defence from up front as cover. Barnsley take advantage as Redfearn chips Prudhoe. Taggart ferociously heads a corner home.

30 PETERBOROUGH — Lowly Posh score when Prudhoe drops a corner and Darren Bradshaw nets. Stoke struggle and are lucky to equalise when Gleghorn beats Fred Barber at his near post for City's first away goal in six games. Disquiet is voiced about not investing in players with the play-offs still in reach.

31 BOLTON — The arctic conditions mean an orange ball has to replace the original white one. Orlygsson's left-footed piledriver beats Aidan Davison. Owen Coyle chips just over the bar. Butler and Cranson combine to provide for Regis to slot the clincher, killing off Bruce Rioch's battling Trotters.

32 PORTSMOUTH — Alan Knight is lucky to stay on the pitch after felling Carruthers in the act of scoring. Carruthers is then tripped for the penalty. Orlygsson slots the kick to become joint top scorer. Carruthers races on to a Regis flick on to score at the second attempt. Pompey are tumbling down the table.

33 WEST BROM — A truly awful game in which neither side can string more than three passes together. The away end is being rebuilt so 2,000 Stokies get soaked to boot. Stoke are reluctant to commit to all-out attack. A point may not be enough when the play-off spots are being decided in May. Dreadful.

34 NOTT'M FOREST — Forest are without Collymore and Gemmill but still stroll past subdued City. Steve Stone robs Cranson and squares for the portly Neil Webb to net. Stoke attack but Frank Clark's Forest defend well. Prudhoe saves from Bohinen. Pearce and Orlygsson square up after a crunching tackle.

No	H/A	Date	Opponent	Attendance	Pos	—	Res	Score	Pts
35	A	15/3	TRANMERE	2,346	9	8	L	0-2	51
36	A	19/3	SOUTHEND	4,542	9	12	D	0-0	52
37	H	26/3	CRYSTAL PALACE	18,071	10	1	L	0-2	52
38	H	30/3	BRISTOL CITY	13,208	9	16	W	3-0	55
39	A	2/4	BIRMINGHAM	15,568	11	23	L	1-3	55
40	H	4/4	CHARLTON	15,569	9	8	W	1-0	58
41	A	9/4	DERBY	17,593	9	6	L	2-4	58
42	H	13/4	PETERBOROUGH	10,181	8	24	W	2-0	61
43	A	16/4	SUNDERLAND	17,406	7	13	W	1-0	64
44	H	23/4	NOTTS CO	13,470	9	7	D	0-0	65
45	A	30/4	LEICESTER	15,291	9	4	D	1-1	66
46	H	8/5	LUTON	5,911	10	20	D	2-2	67

Average: Home 15,965 Away 11,658

Match 35 — TRANMERE (A)
Stoke: Prudhoe, Butler, Sandford, Cranson, Overson, Orlygsson, Foley, Carruthers, Regis, Clark, Gleghorn
Tranmere: Nixon, Higgins, Nolan, Brannan, Garnett, O'Brien, Morrissey, Aldridge, Jones, Nevin, Thomas
Aldridge 47, 85 — Ref: G Singh
Another inept away performance. Two corners in the first two mins flatters to deceive. Tranmere take over and Pat Nevin back-heels to set up Aldridge to score easily. Jon Clark hits the post. Aldridge seals it with a looping header from ten yards. 'Jordan out!' is heard for the first time.

Match 36 — SOUTHEND (A)
Stoke: Prudhoe, Butler, Sandford, Cranson, Gynn*, Orlygsson, Foley, Carruthers, Regis, Clark, Gleghorn
Southend: Sansome, Poole, Powell, Sussex, Scully, Edwards, Ansah^, Payne*, Beadle, Otto, Nogan — subs: Gridelet/Hunt
Ref: P Vanes
Another dull and uninspiring display. The supporters are restless despite a solid defensive display, which snuffs out the threat of Peter Taylor's Southend. Stoke fail to create a worthwhile chance. The frontline has lost all confidence. Is Jordan the man to restore it? Play-offs out of reach.

Match 37 — CRYSTAL PALACE (H)
Stoke: Prudhoe, Butler, Sandford, Cranson, Adams, Orlygsson, Foley, Carruthers*, Biggins, Clark, Walters
Palace: Martyn, Humphrey, Gordon, Southgate, Young*, Coleman, Rodger, Shaw, Armstrong^, Stewart, Dyer — subs: Salako/Williams
Gordon 55p, Williams 69 — Ref: T Holbrook
A much improved display against the runaway leaders. Three deadline day signings bolster the attack. Biggins apparently sings 'Delilah' all down the M6 from Celtic to sign for City! The penalty is for a dubious foul on the lumbering Paul Stewart. Martyn dominates. Stoke are better.

Match 38 — BRISTOL CITY (H)
Stoke: Prudhoe, Butler, Sandford, Cranson, Adams, Orlygsson^, Foley, Carruthers, Biggins*, Clark, Walters
Bristol: Welch, Harriott, Munro, Shail, Bryant, Scott, Hoyland^, Hewlett*, Martin, Allison, Tinnion — subs: Robinson/Milsom !
Adams 8, 78, Biggins 59p — Ref: M Reed
Micky Adams scores Stoke's first goal in March with a diving header. Biggins converts a penalty after Mark Walters is floored. Allison brings a great save out of Prudhoe. Welch saves from Walters. Adams crashes in an unstoppable shot. Paul Milsom is sent off (90) for two bookings.

Match 39 — BIRMINGHAM (A)
Stoke: Prudhoe, Butler, Sandford, Cranson, Adams, Gleghorn, Foley, Carruthers, Biggins*, Clark, Walters
Birmingham: Bennett, Hiley, Frain, Harding, Barnett, Daish, Ward, Claridge, Saville, Willis, Doherty — subs: Regis
Carruthers 33 — Claridge 35, Ward 57, Willis 59 — Ref: C Wilkes
Carruthers heads home a Walters cross for Stoke's first away goal for seven weeks. But the defence stand and watch as the ball bobbles around the area. Claridge pounces to level. Walters is lucky to stay on after a bad tackle and Ward blasts the free-kick home. Willis heads in the third.

Match 40 — CHARLTON (H)
Stoke: Prudhoe, Butler, Sandford, Cranson, Overson, Orlygsson^, Foley, Carruthers, Biggins*, Adams, Walters
Charlton: Salmon, Balmer, Minto, Garland*, McLeary, Chapple, Bennett, Sturgess^, Gorman, Nelson, Pardew — subs: Regis/Gynn, Grant/Walsh
Orlygsson 31 — Ref: E Wolstenholme
Easter Monday sees a dreadful game won by Toddy Orlygsson's shot from the edge of the box. The Addicks, under managerial duo Steve Gritt and Alan Curbishley fail to create a chance of note. Hardly a game between two play-off chasing sides dreaming of a place in the Premiership!

Match 41 — DERBY (A)
Stoke: Prudhoe, Butler, Sandford, Cranson, Overson, Orlygsson*, Foley, Carruthers, Biggins, Adams, Walters
Derby: Taylor, Charles, Nicholson, Harkes, Short, Williams, Cowans, Johnson, Kitson, Pembridge, Simpson — subs: Regis
Biggins 77p, Adams 81 — [Kitson 66] Simps'n 20, Pmbridge 22, Cranson 62(og) — Ref: G Poll
City is simply awful for an hour in the mud. Simpson's came curls straight in. Pembridge and Kitson both score well-worked goals. Cranson tops a poor display by heading a corner past Prudhoe. Somehow Stoke fight back. Regis is fouled for the penalty. Adams scores at the far post.

Match 42 — PETERBOROUGH (H)
Stoke: Prudhoe, Butler^, Sandford, Cranson, Overson, Orlygsson*, Foley, Gynn, Regis, Adams, Walters
Peterborough: Barber, Bradshaw, Carter, Williams, Peters, Welsh, Iorfa^, McGlashan, Funnell, Charlery, McGee* — subs: Carruthers/Gynn, McGarry/Hackett
Regis 14, Biggins 36, Walters 79 — Ref: K Leach
A deathly atmosphere surrounds the ground as City have nothing to play for. They are still too good for rock-bottom Posh. Barber's howler lets in Regis to score. Gynn crosses for Biggins to head in. Barber saves a brilliant Orlygsson effort. Mark Walters follows up his own shot to net.

Match 43 — SUNDERLAND (A)
Stoke: Prudhoe, Clark, Sandford, Cranson, Overson, Orlygsson, Foley, Biggins*, Regis, Adams, Walters^
Sunderland: Chamberlain, Kubicki, Gray Michael, Bennett, Ferguson, Melville, Ball, Goodman, Gray P, Smith, Russell — subs: Carruthers/Gleghorn
Walters 28 — Ref: D Allison
Walters' determination and style allow him time to crack a short free-kick into the far corner of the net. He also hits the post with a thunderous effort. In a swirling wind the defence copes well with Mick Buxton's team's desperate long-ball game. Stoke's first away league win of 1994.

Match 44 — NOTTS CO (H)
Stoke: Prudhoe, Butler*, Sandford, Cranson, Overson, Orlygsson, Gynn, Biggins*, Regis, Adams, Walters^
Notts Co: Cherry, Wilson, Yates, Turner!, Dijkstra^, Devlin!, Palmer, Draper, Lund, Agana, McSwegan — subs: Foley, Bannister, McSwegan Johnson
Ref: R Poulain
Another sterile match enlivened by County's bizarre turquoise and purple kit! Cherry changes direction to palm a deflected Biggins shot away. McSwegan hits the bar. Paul Devlin elbows Sandford and sees red. Turner follows (85 mins) for yet another foul on Regis. City still can't win.

Match 45 — LEICESTER (A)
Stoke: Prudhoe, Butler, Sandford, Cranson, Overson, Orlygsson, Gynn, Biggins*, Regis, Adams, Walters
Leicester: Poole, Grayson, Lewis, Willis, Carey*, Gibson^, Joachim, Blake, Coatsworth, Gee, Johnson — subs: Ormondroyd Philpott/Kerr
Regis 48, Willis 61 — Ref: K Cooper
A more encouraging performance albeit against an under-strength Foxes side. Regis takes advantage of poor defending to bobble the ball past Kevin Poole. Leicester's goal is just as soft. Prudhoe misjudges a cross and Jimmy Willis beats Cranson to nod past him.

Match 46 — LUTON (H)
Stoke: Prudhoe, Butler, Sandford, Cranson!, Overson, Gleghorn, Gynn*, Biggins, Regis, Adams, Walters
Luton: Davis, Linton, James, Harper^, Peake, Greene, Telfer, Oakes*, Hartson, Hughes, Thorpe — subs: Orlygsson, Campbell/McLaren
Biggins 16, Regis 32 — Oakes 47, Telfer 80p — Ref: J Key
'Bertie' Biggins strokes the ball home after a scramble. Adams is upended in the area but the referee plays advantage for Regis to slot in to an empty net. Oakes' classy volley screams in. Cranson produces a superb one-handed save on the line. He is sent off. Telfer levels from the spot.

ENDSLEIGH DIVISION 1 (CUP-TIES)

Manager: Lou Macari ⇒ Joe Jordan

SEASON 1993-94

Coca-Cola Cup

		Att		F-A	H-T	Scorers, Times, and Referees	1	2	3	4	5	6	7	8	9	10	11	subs used
1:1 H MANSFIELD 18/8	D	8,976		2-2	1-2	Gleghorn 2, Carruthers 80 / Noteman 18 McLoughlin 28 / Ref: D Allison	Prudhoe	Butler	Sandford	Kevan	Overson !	Lowe	Orlygsson	Foley*	Stein	Regis^	Gleghorn	Gynn/Carruthers
							Pearcey	*Foster S**	*Platnauer*	*Fairclough*	*Gray*	*Clarke*	*Noteman*	*Holland*	*McLoughlin*	*Wilkinson*	*Wilson*	*Stringfellow*
1:2 A MANSFIELD 24/8	W	4,214	aet	3-1	1-1	Stein 17, 93, Regis 117 / Stant 8 / Ref: T Holbrook (Stoke win 5-3 on aggregate)	Prudhoe	Butler	Sandford	Cranson	Lowe*	Overson	Gleghorn	Foley	Stein	Wilkinson^	Regis	Gynn
							Pearcey	*Foster S*	*Platnauer*	*Fairclough*	*Gray*	*Clarke*	*Noteman*	*Holland*	*Stant**	*Wilkinson*	*McLoughlin*	*Stringfellow/Wilson*
2:1 H MANCHESTER U 22/9 8 P:1	W	23,327		2-1	1-0	Stein 32, 74 / Dublin 66 / Ref: J Key	Prudhoe	Clarkson	Sandford	Cranson	Overson	Orlygsson	Gynn	Foley	Stein	Carruthers	Gleghorn	Bruce/Sharpe
							Schmeichel	*Martin*	*Irwin*	*Phelan**	*Kanchelskis*	*Pallister*	*Robson^*	*Ferguson*	*McClair*	*Hughes*	*Dublin*	
2:2 A MANCHESTER U 6/10 12 P:1	L	41,387		0-2	0-0	Sharpe 47, McClair 85 / Ref: K Cooper (Stoke lose 2-3 on aggregate)	Muggleton	Clarkson	Cowan	Cranson	Overson	Orlygsson	Gynn	Foley	Stein	Sturridge*	Gleghorn	Carruthers
							Schmeichel	*Irwin*	*Martin**	*Bruce*	*Sharpe*	*Pallister*	*Robson*	*Kanchelskis*	*McClair*	*Hughes*	*Keane*	*Giggs*

Commentary:

1:1 — Gleghorn rams the ball home from six yards. The Stags attack fiercely. Noteman waltzes through a very ill-at-ease defence. McLoughlin cracks a poor clearance home. Overson is sent off (48 mins) for elbowing Lee Wilson in the eye. Carruthers drives in from 20 yards to sighs of relief.

1:2 — Phil Stant diverts the ball past Prudhoe to give Andy King's Stags a shock lead. Pearcey misses a corner and Stein heads into an empty net. No clear-cut openings are created until extra-time when Stein taps in at the far post. Regis finishes the job, shrugging off three defenders to score.

2:1 — City shine against the Champions. Stein turns Mike Phelan inside out before unleashing a raking shot past Schmeichel. Against the run of play United level when Dion Dublin heads in a Sharpe centre. Stein bags another spectacular turn and shot that sends the Boothen berserk.

2:2 — City put up stern resistance against a side packed with internationals. Hughes' acrobatic volley is well saved by Carl Muggleton. 9,000 Stokies roar on their heroes but Sharpe volleys in at the far post. Brain McClair wraps it up from 10 yards as United turn on the style. Good team spirit

FA Cup

		Att		F-A	H-T	Scorers, Times, and Referees	1	2	3	4	5	6	7	8	9	10	11	subs used
3 H BATH 8/1 7 C:4	D	14,159		0-0	0-0	Ref: P Wright	Marshall	Clarkson	Sandford	Cranson	Overson	Orlygsson*	Foley	Bannister	Regis	Butler	Gleghorn	Sturridge
							Mogg	*Gill*	*Dicks*	*Batty*	*Hedges*	*Cousins*	*Banks*	*Chenoweth* Adcock*		*Mings*	*Brooks*	*Smart/Vernon*
3R A BATH 18/1 8 C:6	W	6,213		4-1	2-0	Regis 5, 57, Cranson 38, Orlygsson 83 / Chenoweth 90 / Ref: P Wright	Marshall	Clarkson	Sandford	Cranson	Overson	Orlygsson	Foley	Carruthers*	Regis	Sturridge	Gleghorn	Shaw
							Mogg	*Gill*	*Dicks*	*Batty*	*Hedges*	*Cousins**	*Banks*	*Chenoweth Adcock^*		*Mings*	*Brooks*	*Smart/Vernon*
4 A OLDHAM 29/1 8 P:21	D	14,465		0-0	0-0	Ref: P Jones	Prudhoe	Butler	Sandford	Cranson	Overson	Orlygsson	Foley	Carruthers	Regis	Potter	Gleghorn	Palmer
							Hallworth	*Fleming*	*Makin*	*Pointon*	*Jobson*	*Redmond**	*Adams*	*Bernard*	*Sharp*	*Milligan*	*Holden*	
4R H OLDHAM 9/2 9 P:20	L	19,871		0-1	0-1	Beckford 3 / Ref: P Jones	Prudhoe	Butler	Sandford	Cranson	Overson	Orlygsson	Foley	Bannister	Regis	Potter*	Gleghorn	Sturridge
							Hallworth	*Fleming*	*Makin*	*Pointon*	*Jobson*	*McDonald*	*Bernard*	*Beckford*	*Sharp*	*Milligan*	*Holden*	

Commentary:

3 — Stoke lack any semblance of confidence against non-league Bath. Jordan fields a five-man defence which restricts Bath to one shot at goal, but City struggle for ideas against Tony Ricketts' men. To fail to either score or win is embarrassing. Jordan wants to buy Sheff Weds' Phil King.

3R — Regis and Cranson head home corners to settle the tie. City score a fourth in the pouring rain as Orlygsson races through onto Gleghorn's pass. Marshall's howler from a late free-kick allows Bath some comfort. Lou Macari is present to see City's first away FA Cup victory for 23 years.

4 — Joe Royle's Latics look far from Premier League class. On an awful pitch Stoke dominate. Foley wins the midfield battle and Orlygsson sets up Carruthers to nod wide from close in. Ex-Stokie Adams causes problems on the right but City, backed by massive vocal support, earn a replay.

4R — An atrocious game decided by a ridiculous goal as Darren Beckford gets in the way of a clearance and the ball loops over Prudhoe's head into the net. City fail to make a decent chance all night. Oldham are as bad. They go on to reach the semi-finals. City's FA Cup curse strikes again.

League Table

Pos	Team	Home					Away					Pts
		W	D	L	F	A	W	D	L	F	A	
1	Crys Palace	16	4	3	39	18	11	5	7	34	28	90
2	Nott'm Forest	12	9	2	38	22	11	5	7	36	27	83
3	Millwall	14	8	1	36	17	5	9	9	22	32	74
4	Leicester *	11	9	3	45	30	8	7	8	27	29	73
5	Tranmere	15	3	5	48	23	6	6	11	21	30	72
6	Derby	15	3	5	44	25	5	8	10	29	43	71
7	Notts Co	16	3	4	43	26	4	5	14	22	43	68
8	Wolves	12	10	1	34	19	7	7	9	26	28	68
9	Middlesbro	12	6	3	40	19	6	7	10	26	35	67
10	STOKE	14	4	5	35	19	4	9	10	22	40	67
11	Charlton	14	3	6	39	22	5	5	13	22	36	65
12	Sunderland	14	2	7	35	22	5	6	12	19	35	65
13	Bristol City	11	7	5	27	18	5	9	9	23	32	64
14	Bolton	10	8	5	40	31	5	6	12	23	33	59
15	Southend	10	5	8	34	28	7	3	13	29	39	59
16	Grimsby	7	14	2	26	16	6	6	11	26	31	59
17	Portsmouth	10	6	7	29	22	5	7	11	23	36	58
18	Barnsley	9	3	11	25	26	7	4	12	30	41	55
19	Watford	10	5	8	39	35	5	4	14	27	45	54
20	Luton	12	4	7	38	25	2	7	14	18	35	53
21	West Brom	9	7	7	38	31	4	5	14	22	38	51
22	Birmingham	9	7	7	28	29	4	5	14	24	40	51
23	Oxford	10	5	8	33	33	3	5	15	21	42	49
24	Peterborough	6	9	8	31	30	2	4	17	17	46	37
		276	144	132	864	586	132	144	276	586	864	1512

* promoted after play-offs

Appearances and Goals

Player	Appearances						Goals			
	Lge	Sub	LC	Sub	FAC	Sub	Lge	LC	FAC	Tot
Adams, Micky	10									3
Bannister, Gary	10	5				2	2			2
Biggins, Wayne	10						4			4
Butler, John	34	1	2		4					
Carruthers, Martin	24	10	1	2	2		5	1		6
Clark, Jon	12									
Clarkson, Ian	14	2	2		1					
Cowan, Tom	14	1	1							
Cranson, Ian	44	3			4					
Foley, Steve	43	1	4		4		2			2
Gleghorn, Nigel	38	2	4	2	4		3	1		4
Gynn, Micky	14	7	2	2						
Harbey, Graham	2									
Kevan, David	1	1								
Lowe, Kenny	3	6			2					
Marshall, Gordon	10				2					
Mugleton, Carl	6	1								
Orlygsson, Toddy	42	3	4		4		10		1	11
Overson, Vince	39		4		4		2			2
Potter, Graham	2	1			2					
Prudhoe, Mark	30		3		2					
Regis, Dave	33	5	2		4		10	1	2	13
Sandford, Lee	40	1	3		4		1			1
Shaw, Graham	2	2				1				
Stein, Mark	12		4				8		4	12
Sturridge, Simon	5	8	1		1	2				
Walters, Mark	9						2			2
Ware, Paul	1									
Williams, Brett	2									
29 players used	506	52	44	4	44	3	52	7	4	63

Odds & ends

Double wins: (3) Middlesbrough, Sunderland, Watford.
Double losses: (3) Crystal Palace, Millwall, Tranmere.

Won from behind: (2) Barnsley (h), Derby (h).
Lost from in front: (3) Birmingham (a), Luton (a), Tranmere (h).

High spots: Mid-table stability in Division Two.
Beating Manchester United in the home leg of the Coca-Cola Cup.
Winning an away FA Cup-tie for the first time since 1971.
Eight home wins in a row from late October.

Low spots: Mark Stein's record £2.5m transfer to Chelsea.
The departure of Lou Macari.
Falling from 5th in March to 11th by early April to drop out of the play-off picture.
Over-reliance on loan players to bolster the squad.
Crowds dropping by a third once the play-offs are out of reach.

Player of the Year: Ian Cranson.
Ever-presents: (0).
Hat-tricks: (0).
Leading scorer: (13) Dave Regis.

ENDSLEIGH DIVISION 1

Manager: Joe Jordan ⇨ Lou Macari — SEASON 1994-95

No	Venue	Opponent	Date	Att	Pos	Pt	Res	F-A	H-T
1	H	TRANMERE	13/8	15,915	–	3	W	1-0	0-0
2	A	BURNLEY	20/8	15,331	6	4	D	1-1	0-1
3	H	SUNDERLAND	27/8	13,159	14	4	L	0-1	0-1
4	A	READING	30/8	7,103	18	4	L	0-4	0-0
5	A	BOLTON	3/9	11,515	22	4	L	0-4	0-1
6	H	SOUTHEND	10/9	11,808	16	7	W	4-1	2-0
7	H	CHARLTON	14/9	10,643	10	10	W	3-2	2-0
8	A	NOTTS CO	17/9	8,281	6	13	W	2-0	1-0
9	A	DERBY	25/9	11,782	8	13	L	0-3	0-2
10	H	WEST BROM	2/10	14,203	7	16	W	4-1	2-1
11	H	LUTON	9/10	11,712	7	16	L	1-2	0-1

Line-ups

No	Team	1	2	3	4	5	6	7	8	9	10	11	subs used
1	Stoke	Muggleton	Clark	Sandford	Dreyer	Overson	Orlygsson	Carruthers*	Wallace	Biggins	Peschisolido	Gleghorn	Beckford
1	Tranmere	Coyne	Higgins	Mungall	Braman	Garnett*	O'Brien	Morrissey	Aldridge	Irons	Nevin	Thomas	Muir
2	Stoke	Muggleton	Clark	Sandford	Dreyer	Overson	Orlygsson*	Carruthers^	Wallace	Biggins	Sturridge	Gleghorn	Butler/Shaw
2	Burnley	Beresford	Parkinson	Vinnicombe	Davis	Winstanley	Joyce	Harper*	Gayle	Heath	Robinson	McMinn	Deary
3	Stoke	Muggleton	Clark	Sandford	Dreyer	Cranson	Downing	Peschisolido	Wallace	Biggins	Sturridge*	Gleghorn	Carruthers
3	Sunderland	Norman	Owers	Kubicki	Bennett	Ferguson	Melville	Atkinson	Goodman	Gray P	Gray M*	Ball	Cunnington
4	Stoke	Muggleton	Clark	Sandford	Dreyer	Overson!	Downing	Peschisolido*	Wallace	Biggins!	Butler	Gleghorn	Carruthers
4	Reading	Hislop	Hopkins*	Kerr	Wdowczyk	Williams	Parkinson	Gilkes	Gooding	Quinn	Lovell	Osborn	Taylor/Holsgrove
5	Stoke	Muggleton	Clark*	Sandford	Dreyer	Overson	Downing	Peschisolido	Wallace	Biggins	Beckford	Gleghorn	Butler
5	Bolton	Branagan	Lydiate	Phillips	McAteer	Kernaghan	Stubbs	Fisher	Sneekes	McGinlay	Paatelainen	Kelly	
6	Stoke	Muggleton	Butler	Sandford	Dreyer	Overson	Orlygsson	Beckford	Downing	Biggins*	Peschisolido	Gleghorn	Carruthers/Wallace
6	Southend	Sansome	Hone	Powell	Jones	Edwards	Bressington	Hunt	Whelan	Thomson	Otto	Forrester	Kelly
7	Stoke	Muggleton	Butler	Sandford	Dreyer	Cranson	Orlygsson	Wallace	Downing	Carruthers	Peschisolido	Gleghorn	
7	Charlton	Ammann	Brown	Sturgess	Walsh	Chapple	McCleary	Newton*	Nelson	Garland^	Whyte	Robson	Grant/Pardew
8	Stoke	Muggleton	Butler	Sandford	Dreyer	Cranson	Orlygsson	Wallace	Downing	Carruthers	Peschisolido	Gleghorn	
8	Notts Co	Cherry	Gallagher	Emenalo	Turner	Johnson	Yates	Jemson*	Legg	Devlin	McSwegan	Simpson	Lund
9	Stoke	Muggleton	Butler	Sandford	Dreyer	Cranson	Orlygsson	Wallace	Downing	Carruthers	Peschisolido	Gleghorn	
9	Derby	Taylor	Charles	Forsyth	Hodge	Short	Williams	Cowans	Gabbiadini	Johnson*	Pembridge	Carsley^	Simpson/Harkes
10	Stoke	Muggleton	Wallace	Sandford	Dreyer	Cranson	Orlygsson	Butler*	Downing	Carruthers	Peschisolido*	Gleghorn	Biggins/Overson
10	West Brom	Naylor	Parsley	Lilwall	Phelan	Stradder	Herbert	Hunt	Ashcroft	Taylor	McNally*	Smith	Coldicott
11	Stoke	Muggleton	Wallace^	Sandford	Dreyer!	Cranson	Orlygsson	Butler	Downing	Carruthers	Peschisolido*	Gleghorn	Overson/Beckford
11	Luton	Sommer	James	Johnson	Waddock	Thomas	Peake	Telfer	Hughes	Hartson	Preece	Marshall	Oakes

Scorers, Times, and Referees

1. Tranmere (H): Gleghorn 49. Ref: J Kirkby.
The summer boardroom wranglings have released cash for Dreyer and record £600,000 signing Peschisolido. Rumours spread of the imminent return of Macari who has been sacked by Celtic. Jordan's team win thanks to Nigel Gleghorn's right-footed effort through a crowd of players.

2. Burnley (A): Dreyer 90; Davis 42. Ref: W Flood.
Steve Davis takes advantage of City's unconvincing defence. His diving header flashes home. Gary Parkinson has his 40th-minute spot-kick for Sandford's handball saved by Muggleton. City get out of jail via John Dreyer's volley from Shaw's cross in the 93rd minute. Worryingly poor.

3. Sunderland (H): Gray P 23. Ref: G Lurt.
Stoke look sluggish despite dominating possession. The excitement generated by winning in Cosenza in midweek is dampened by the brilliant form of 37-year-old Tony Norman. He denies Pesch, Sturridge and Biggins. Phil Gray's great solo goal wins it for Mick Buxton's Wearsiders.

4. Reading (A): Lovell 61, Kerr 71, Gilkes 85, Taylor 90. Ref: G Pooley.
Nightmare at Elm Park! Biggins and Overson are sent off (55 mins) following a dust up near the corner flag as City are enjoying the best spell of the game. Lovell's first-time volley opens the floodgates as the nine men capitulate. Kerr's brilliant 25-yard strike fizzes into the top corner.

5. Bolton (A): [Paatelainen 79] McGinlay 41p, McAteer 59, 66. Ref: A Dawson.
One of the worst performances in years. Bolton outplay the poor Potters in every department. Jason McAteer's second is a great 30-yard drive. Clark trips McGinlay for the pen. Things are no better in the boardroom as Bob Kenyon and Paul Wright have sold their shares amid acrimony.

6. Southend (H): Orlygsson 10, Edwards 13 (og), Dreyer 47, Butler 67 (og) [Biggins 62]. Ref: I Cruikshanks.
Joe Jordan has left the club. Reportedly pushed rather than of his own doing. City respond with an upbeat display against Peter Taylor's woeful team. Orlygsson beats three players to lash in. Andy Edwards diverts a centre past Sansome. Dreyer heads in. Biggins latches on to a back-pass.

7. Charlton (H): Glegh' 17, Orlygsson 22, Peschisolido 55; Nelson 72, Whyte 77. Ref: K Lynch.
Caretaker manager Asa Hartford selects Cranson and Wallace for suspended Overson and Biggins. Gleghorn dives to head in Wallace's cross. Orlygsson cracks in a low free-kick. Pesch touches home Dreyer's header. Nelson and Whyte finish off far-post crosses as Stoke get the jitters.

8. Notts Co (A): Peschisolido 31, 70. Ref: E Wolstenholme.
Pesch wins over some of his critics with two strikers' goals. He nods in after Cherry saves his initial shot, then sidefoots a Carruthers pass into the corner. Dreyer marshals the defence impressively as County retaliate. Asa Hartford rules himself out of the running for the manager's role.

9. Derby (A): Hodge 22, Gabbiadini 38, Charles 89. Ref: N Barry.
Stoke start brightly but Pesch's shot is cleared off the line and Roy McFarland's Rams score when Steve Hodge turns in a rebound off the post. Gabbiadini finishes with aplomb. Downing and Orlygsson toil but City lack a playmaker. Muggers is beaten by an unkind bounce for the third.

10. West Brom (H): Carr 24, 87, Wallace 35, Peschisolido 68; Taylor 32. Ref: I Cruikshanks.
Lou Macari is hailed as the saviour after superb Stoke put Alan Buckley's Baggies to the sword. Carruthers pounces on a weak clearance. Bob Taylor taps in. Ray Wallace's first goal for City is a rasping shot after a one-two. Pesch touches home. Carruthers finishes from a tight angle.

11. Luton (H): Carruthers 80; Marshall 22, Preece 81. Ref: P Alcock.
Stoke start well but Dreyer fluffs a clearance and Dwight Marshall fires home. Dreyer gives away a penalty but Muggleton saves yet again. A horrendous personal afternoon sees Dreyer sent off for hauling down Marshall. Carruthers taps in but Hatters score a neat goal from the restart.

Stoke City match-by-match record (matches 12–23)

#		Opponent	Date	Att				HT	FT	City scorers	Opponents' scorers	Referee
12	A	MILLWALL	15/10	7,856	7	0	17	1-1	0-1	Peschisolido 55	Goodman 15	Ref: T West
13	A	OLDHAM	22/10	8,954	9	13	18	0-0	0-0			Ref: R Hart
14	H	WOLVES	30/10	5,928	11	1	19	1-1	1-1	Keen 17	Bull 40	Ref: J Holbrook
15	H	SHEFFIELD UTD	2/11	11,556	11	19	20	0-1	1-1	Gleghorn 77	Gage 15	Ref: K Lynch
16	A	BARNSLEY	5/11	5,117	16	7	20	0-2	0-1		O'Connell 42, Sheridan 77	Ref: P Wright
17	H	GRIMSBY	19/11	12,055	13	6	23	3-0	2-0	Peschisolido 23, 44, Carruthers 60		Ref: J Lloyd
18	A	WATFORD	26/11	7,126	14	9	24	0-0	0-0			Ref: P Foakes
19	A	PORTSMOUTH	30/11	7,272	11	21	27	1-0	0-0	Beeston 74		Ref: I Hemley
20	H	OLDHAM	4/12	12,558	12	14	27	0-1	0-0		McCarthy 90	Ref: K Leach
21	H	BURNLEY	10/12	13040	11	18	30	2-0	0-0	Orlygsson 68p, 83		Ref: C Wilkes
22	A	TRANMERE	17/12	7,501	9	4	33	1-0	0-0	Carruthers 81		Ref: R Poulain
23	H	SWINDON	26/12	17,462	8	19	34	0-0	0-0			Ref: D Allison

12 — A MILLWALL 15/10
City: Muggleton, Overson, Sandford, Dreyer, Cranson, Orlygsson, Butler, Downing, Carruthers, Peschisolido*, Gleghorn, Wallace
Millwall: Keller, Cunningham, Thatcher, Connor, Witter^, Roberts, Savage, Rae, Cadette, Goodman*, Kennedy, Mitchell/Dawes
City's defence is all over the shop as Cadette and Goodman threaten. John Goodman steals in to bury Thatcher's centre. The Lions should have more. Pesch wins the ball 40 yards out, beats two men, beats Keller and nets via the post. Carruthers and Pesch hit the woodwork. Good draw.

13 — A OLDHAM 22/10
City: Muggleton, Overson, Sandford, Dreyer, Cranson, Orlygsson, **Keen**, Potter^, Carruthers, Peschisolido*, Gleghorn, Biggins/Beeston
Oldham: Gerrard, Halle, Pointon, Henry, Jobson, Redmond, Rickers, Banger, Graham, McCarthy, Holden
A capable performance as the five-man defence is more organised. Beeston returns from his injury worries to provide midfield bite for the last 30 mins. Muggleton saves Neil Pointon's stinging drive. Oldham force 20 corners but only Sandford comes close, heading against his own bar.

14 — H WOLVES 30/10
City: Muggleton, Overson, Sandford, Dreyer, Cranson, Orlygsson, Keen, Beeston, Carruthers, Peschisolido*, Gleghorn, Biggins
Wolves: Stowell, Smith^, Thompson, Emblen*, Blades, Venus, Walters, Thomas, Bull, Kelly, Froggatt, Ferguson/Stewart
£300,000 signing Kevin Keen stuns his former team-mates by finishing a superb move involving nine City players. Pesch and Carruthers waste chances as City dominate. Steve Bull cracks home for an undeserved draw. The club may build a new ground in response to the Taylor report.

15 — H SHEFFIELD UTD 2/11
City: Muggleton, Overson, Sandford, Dreyer, Cranson, Orlygsson, Keen*, Beeston, Carruthers, Peschisolido*, Gleghorn, **Wade**, Sturridge
Sheffield Utd: Kelly, Gage, Nilsen, Harfield, Beesley, Marshall, Rogers, Veart*, Starbuck, Blake, Whitehouse, Scott
Dave Bassett's Blades dominate from the off. Dane Whitehouse hits the post before Kevin Gage whacks home a well-worked free-kick. Stoke improve in the second half when Keen crosses for Gleghorn to ram home. The pony-tailed Shaun Wade debuts. Beeston is booked once again.

16 — A BARNSLEY 5/11
City: Muggleton, Clarkson, Sandford, Cranson, Orlygsson, Keen, Beeston, Carruthers, Peschisolido*, Gleghorn, Sturridge
Barnsley: Watson, Eaden, Fleming, Wilson, Taggart, Davis, O'Connell, Redfearn, Jackson, Liddell, Sheridan
Dave Watson recovers to save after Orlygsson rounds him. Brendan O'Connell heads in Eaden's cross. Darren Sheridan trips Orylgsson when clear but the ref only books him. He rubs it in by lobbing the advancing Muggleton from 30 yards. Macari tries three at the back but to no avail.

17 — H GRIMSBY 19/11
City: Muggleton, Butler, Sandford, Cranson, Orlygsson, Keen, Beeston, Carruthers, Peschisolido*, Gleghorn, Gilbert
Grimsby: Crichton, Croft, Jobling, Handyside, Lever, Groves, Watson*, Dobbin, Livingstone^, Woods, Gilbert, Childs/McDermott
Stoke take control against the Mariners who have won their last three under caretaker boss John Cockerill. Pesch steers home from close range. Overson has a header cleared off the line. Pesch taps in Carruthers' cross-shot. Crichton denies Orylgsson but from a corner Carruthers scores.

18 — A WATFORD 26/11
City: Muggleton, Butler, Sandford, Cranson, Orlygsson, Keen, Beeston, Carruthers, Peschisolido*, Gleghorn, Biggins
Watford: Miller, Lavin, Johnson, Foster*, Holdsworth, Ramage, Hessenthaler/Nugan, Millen, Porter, Mooney, Moralee
A tight game sees Gleghorn crack a right-footed volley just over. Cranson and Clarkson impress as Ramage and Hessenthaler drive the Hornets on. Watford spurn four good chances. Moralee and Mooney both hit the woodwork. The squad needs improving to avoid a season of struggle.

19 — A PORTSMOUTH 30/11
City: Muggleton, Butler, Sandford, Cranson, Orlygsson, **Sigurdsson**, Beeston, Carruthers, Peschisolido*, Gleghorn, Hall*
Portsmouth: Knight, Gittens, Daniel, McLoughlin, Symons, Dobson, Pethick, Kristensen, Powell, Creaney, Hall*, Radosavljevic
Stoke survive the woodwork being hit twice. Larus Sigurdsson, Orlygsson's cousin, makes his debut and proceeds to join in battle with Gerry Creaney. Beeston cracks through a crowd of players from the edge of the box for the winner. Chairman Coates wants to move to a new ground.

20 — H OLDHAM 4/12
City: Muggleton, Clarkson, Sandford, Cranson, Orlygsson, Keen*, Beeston, Carruthers, Peschisolido*, Gleghorn, Biggins
Oldham: Gerrard, Makin, Pointon, Henry, Jobson, Redmond, Richardson, Ritchie*, McCarthy, Graham, Holden*, Banger/Brennan
Defeat is snatched from the jaws of a bore draw when Muggleton blasts a clearance straight at Sean McCarthy. The ball bobbles back to him but he tries to kick rather than pick up the ball and falls over. McCarthy manages to stop his sides splitting to tap the ball in. Hilarious but unfunny.

21 — H BURNLEY 10/12
City: Muggleton, Clarkson, Sandford, Cranson, Orlygsson, Shaw*, Beeston, Carruthers, Peschisolido*, Gleghorn, Biggins/Sigurdsson
Burnley: Beresford, Parkinson, Hoyland, Davis, Winstanley/Randall*, Shaw*, Harper*, Gayle, Robinson, Eyres, Phillskirk/Mullin
Jimmy Mullen's Clarets have Mark Winstanley sent off for a professional foul and Orlygsson blasts home the penalty. His second is a 25-yard screamer following a one-two with Pesch. Muggers redeems himself after last week's howler to save brilliantly twice from the big John Gayle.

22 — A TRANMERE 17/12
City: Muggleton", Butler, Sandford, Cranson, Orlygsson, Clarkson, Beeston*, Carruthers*, Peschisolido*, Gleghorn, Dreyer/Biggins/Sinclair
Tranmere: Nixon, Stevens, Brannan*, McGreal, Higgins, Irons, Clarkson, Morrissey, Aldridge, O'Brien, Thomas, Branch
City inflict a first home defeat of the season on John King's Rovers. Pesch, Cranson, Orlygsson and Gleghorn all miss decent chances. Sinclair replaces the injured Muggleton at the break and is brilliant. Carruthers heads over from five yards but swoops to slide home Pesch's low cross.

23 — H SWINDON 26/12
City: Muggleton, Butler, Sandford, Cranson, Orlygsson, Clarkson, Keen, Carruthers, Peschisolido*, Gleghorn, **Williams**
Swindon: Digby, Robinson, Bodin, Culverhouse/Nijholt, Dreyer, Taylor, Horlock, Beauchamp, Fjortoft, Ling, Scott
Stoke edge a dull first half. Carruthers hits the post and finds Fraser Digby in fine form. Culverhouse is lucky to stay on after a heavy challenge on Pesch. Muggers tips Taylor's header onto the bar. Cranson clears. Stoke are only the second team in 1994 not to score at home to Swindon.

ENDSLEIGH DIVISION 1   Manager: Joe Jordan ⇨ Lou Macari   SEASON 1994-95

No	Date		Att	Pos	Pt	F-A	H-T	Scorers, Times, and Referees	1	2	3	4	5	6	7	8	9	10	11	subs used
24	27/12	A BRISTOL CITY	8,500	23	34	1-3	0-0	Cranson 83 / Bryant 66, Allison 78, 80; Ref: P Vanes	Sinclair / Welch	Butler / Hansen	Sandford / Munro	Cranson / Shair*	Dreyer^ / Bryant	Orlygsson / Tinnion	Sigurdsson / Parris	Clarkson / Bent	Biggins* / Baird^	Williams / Allison	Gleghorn / Owers	Peschisolido/Shaw; Partridge/Dryden
25	31/12	H MIDDLESBROUGH	15,914	7	35	1-1	1-1	Gleghorn 20 / Vickers 9; Ref: U Rennie	Muggleton* / Miller	Butler / Morris	Sandford / Fleming	Cranson / Vickers	Overson / Pearson	Orlygsson / Mustoe	Clarkson / Robson	Scott / Pollock	Carruthers* / Wilkinson	Downing / Hendrie	Gleghorn / Hignett	Williams/Sinclair
26	14/1	A WOLVES	28,298	2	35	0-2	0-1	Kelly 17, Dennison 87; Ref: J Winter	Sinclair / Jones	Clarkson / Blades	Sandford / Venus	Cranson / Emblen	Overson / De Wolf	Orlygsson / Law	Butler / Birch	Dreyer^ / Kelly	Scott* / Mills	Peschisolido / Cowans	Gleghorn / Dennison	Biggins/Williams
27	4/2	H PORTSMOUTH	9,704	18	35	0-2	0-0	Preki 54, Creaney 90; Ref: W Burns	Sinclair / Knight	Clarkson^ / Gittens	Dreyer* / Daniel	Cranson / McLoughlin	Sigurdsson / Symons	Allen / Butters	Orlygsson / Pethick	Peschisolido / Preki*	Scott^ / Powell	Downing / Creaney	Gleghorn / Rees	Butler/Leslie; Hall
28	11/2	A SHEFFIELD UTD	13,900	7	36	1-1	0-1	Peschisolido 26 / Starbuck 6; Ref: P Richards	Sinclair / Kelly	Clarkson / Ward	Butler / Nilsen^	Cranson / Gannon	Sigurdsson / Gayle	Allen / Beesley	Orlygsson / Rogers	Peschisolido / Veart*	Scott^ / Starbuck	Downing* / Flo	Gleghorn / Whitehouse	Dreyer/Gayle; Littlejohn/Scott
29	21/2	A GRIMSBY	6,384	7	37	0-0	0-0	Ref: E Parker	Sinclair / Crichton	Sigurdsson / Croft	Sandford / Jobling	Cranson / Handyside	Overson / Rodger	Orlygsson / Groves	Allen / Watson	Peschisolido / Dobbin^	Scott* / Woods	Butler / Mendonca	Gleghorn / Gilbert	Wallace; Laws
30	25/2	A WEST BROM	16,591	19	40	3-1	1-1	Scott 34, Peschisolido 65, 80 / Hamilton 21; Ref: E Wolstenholme	Sinclair / Lange	Sigurdsson / Parsley*	Sandford / Agnew	Cranson / Bradley	Overson / Burgess	Orlygsson / Raven	Butler / Donovan^	Allen / Ashcroft	Peschisolido* / Taylor	Gleghorn^ / Hunt	Scott / Hamilton	Keen/Sturridge; O'Regan/Rees
31	4/3	H DERBY	13,462	13	41	0-0	0-0	Ref: E Lomas	Sinclair / Hoult	Sigurdsson / Kavanagh*	Sandford / Nicholson	Cranson / Trollope	Overson / Short	Orlygsson* / Yates	Butler / Harkes	Peschisolido* / Pembridge	Allen / Mills	Beeston / Gabbiadini	Gleghorn / Simpson	Gleghorn/Keen; Wassall
32	11/3	A SUNDERLAND	12,282	17	41	0-1	0-0	Melville 87; Ref: J Lloyd	Sinclair / Norman	Sigurdsson / Kubicki*	Sandford / Scott	Cranson / Ball	Overson / Ferguson	Beeston / Melville	Allen / Agnew	Carruthers / Russell	Peschisolido* / Howey	Carruthers* / Smith	Gleghorn* / Armstrong	Keen/Sturridge; Brodie
33	14/3	A PORT VALE	19,510	15	42	1-1	1-1	Sandford 33 / Naylor 2; Ref: A Dawson	Sinclair / Musselwhite	Butler / Sandeman	Sandford / Tankard	Cranson / Porter	Overson / Aspin	Orlygsson* / Billing	Sigurdsson / Guppy	Beeston / Van der Laan Glover L^	Peschisolido^ / Naylor	Allen / Walker*	Gleghorn / Naylor	Keen/Allen; Kent/Allon
34	18/3	H READING	10,006	6	42	0-1	0-1	Taylor 8; Ref: A Flood	Sinclair / Hislop	Butler* / Bernal	Sandford / Kerr	Cranson / Widowczyk	Overson / McPherson	Orlygsson / Holsgrove	Sigurdsson / Gilkes	Beeston / Quinn	Carruthers / Gooding	Allen / Parkinson	Scott* / Taylor*	Gleghorn/Sturridge; Nogan

24 — John Williams, on loan from Coventry, makes his first start. A poor surface contributes to a dismal game. It is brought to life by Matt Bryant's 30-yard thunderbolt. Allison nets twice from close in as Stoke capitulate against old boss Joe Jordan's Robins who have lost six on the bounce.

25 — Stoke's shaky start sees Steve Vickers powerfully head home Craig Hignett's cross for Bryan Robson's Boro. City recover thanks to Overson's and Orlygsson's solid performances. Gleghorn slides home Carruthers' cross at the far post. Quiet debut for £300k Keith Scott from Swindon.

26 — City are never in the running after David Kelly puts Graham Taylor's Wolves ahead when Rob De Wolf flicks on a corner. Robbie Dennison's late clincher is his fourth strike in six matches. Stoke have appointed their first ever Chief Executive, Jez Moxey, previously at Partick Thistle.

27 — City lack any kind of confidence against managerless Pompey. Preki cracks home left footed from the edge of the area. Gerry Creaney waltzes past Sinclair to net. Scott scoops over from two yards. Most of City's lowest league gate for five years leave early. Stoke are plummeting fast.

28 — A slightly improved performance despite conceding to Phil Starbuck's early effort. The Blades have most of the play but Pesch's header levels matters. Stoke create good chances after half-time but Pesch and Scott are wasteful. Blades fans leave en masse disgusted at their performance.

29 — Another non-event counts as a moral victory for Stoke over high-flying Grimsby. The Mariners' attack is reduced to long-range pot shots. The best chance falls to Pesch but Crichton saves his flick. Lack of confidence means the Potters settle for an away point. 11 games without a win.

30 — City run into a side who are even worse than they are. Albion are outplayed. Pesch hits the post. Hamilton's speculative shot flies past Sinclair. Paul Allen runs midfield. Sandford crosses for Scott to slide in his first goal. Pesch heads in from five yards and pokes a long ball past Lange.

31 — Another goalless game. Pesch scores but is controversially given offside. He and Orlygsson are both carried off after fierce clashes. Sigurdsson restricts Marco Gabbiadini to one mis-hit shot. Roy McFarland's Rams best chance falls to Mills but his shot is saved. Four matches unbeaten.

32 — The proverbial relegation six-pointer goes the way of Peter Reid's Sunderland. The two lowest scoring sides in the division struggle in front of goal. Scott hits the bar. Sinclair saves Howey's header. Andy Melville heads home a free-kick for Sunderland's first home win in three months.

33 — A nearly full Vale Park sees a pulsating encounter. Orlygsson nearly scores but Vale break out and Tony Naylor pounces on a weak clearance. A free-kick for obstruction inside the box is chipped for Sandford to head home. Delilah resounds around the stadium as Stoke glimpse safety.

34 — Jimmy Quinn and Mick Gooding's promotion-hunting Royals snatch a win when City's offside trap fails, leaving Scott Taylor free to fire past Sinclair. The profligate Scott, Carruthers and Sturridge all miss clear chances. Shaka Hislop makes two great saves. Just one win in 16 games.

Matches 35–46 (Stoke City)

No	V	Opponent	Date	Pos	Opp Pos	Pts	Att	Res	FT	HT	Scorers (Stoke / Opponents)	Ref
35	A	SOUTHEND	21/3	20	16	42	4,240	L	2–4	0–2	Allen 48, Biggins 59p / Jones 17, Tilson 26, Edwards 57 [Sussex 78p]	Ref: P Alcock
36	H	NOTTS CO	25/3	19	24	45	10,204	W	2–1	1–0	Gleghorn 13, Sturridge 77 / White 89	Ref: N Barry
37	A	CHARLTON	1/4	18	13	46	10,208	D	0–0	0–0		Ref: G Barber
38	H	WATFORD	4/4	16	10	49	9,576	W	1–0	1–0	Sigurdsson 43	Ref: I Cruikshanks
39	A	MIDDLESBROGH	8/4	18	1	49	20,867	L	1–2	1–1	Peschisolido 30 / Pearson 13, Moore 69	Ref: M Riley
40	H	BARNSLEY	12/4	18	6	50	10,752	D	0–0	0–0		Ref: K Cooper
41	H	BRISTOL CITY	15/4	16	23	53	10,172	W	2–1	1–1	Andrade 27, Peschisolido 89 / Shail 17	Ref: D Allison
42	A	SWINDON	17/4	14	21	56	10,549	W	1–0	1–0	Orlygsson 35	Ref: G Singh
43	H	PORT VALE	22/4	17	14	56	20,429	L	0–1	0–0	Foyle 67	Ref: S Dunn
44	H	MILLWALL	29/4	15	11	59	9,111	W	4–3	2–2	Scott 15, Gleghorn 39, 65, Keen 90 / Dixon 22, Webber 42, Oldfield 50	Ref: J Kirkby / F Stretton
45	H	BOLTON	3/5	15	3	60	5,557	D	1–1	1–1	Orlygsson 12p / McGinlay 22	Ref: P Wright
46	A	LUTON	7/5	11	16	63	8,252	W	3–2	0–1	Orlygsson 52, Peschisolido 79, Scott 87 / Harvey 43, Waddock 83	Ref: G Pooley

Home Average 12,832 Away 11,188

Line-ups (Stoke / Opposition)

35 v Southend — Stoke: Sinclair, Butler, Cranson, Sandford*, Overson, Orlygsson, Allen, Sigurdsson, Biggins!, Beeston^, Gleghorn, Sturridge/Gayle. Southend: Royce, Hone, Whelan, Powell, Badley, Edwards!, Hails, Sussex, Jones!, Tilson, Dublin, Gridelet.

36 v Notts Co — Stoke: Sinclair, Butler, Cranson, Sandford, Overson, Orlygsson, Allen^, Beeston, Peschisolido*, Scott, Gleghorn, Sturridge/Keen. Notts Co: Cherry, Short, Forsyth, Murphy, Turner, Hogg*, Devlin, White, Emenalo, Nicol, Legg^, Mills/Russell.

37 v Charlton — Stoke: Sinclair, Butler, Cranson, Sigurdsson, Overson, Keen, Allen, Beeston^, Scott, Peschisolido*, Gleghorn, Carruthers/Clarkson. Charlton: Salmon, Brown, Jones, Mortimer, Rufus, Balmer, Robson^, Leaburn, Pardew, Grant, Robinson*, Whyte/Newton.

38 v Watford — Stoke: Sinclair, Butler, Cranson, Sigurdsson, Overson, Keen, Allen, Downing, Peschisolido*, Scott, Gleghorn, Clarkson/Johnson. Watford: Miller, Lavin, Foster, Holdsworth, Millen, Ramage*, Payne, Hessenthaler, Beadle, Gibbs, Phillips, Johnson.

39 v Middlesbrogh — Stoke: Sinclair, Butler, Clarkson, Sigurdsson, Overson, Downing, Allen, Carruthers, Peschisolido, Gayle*, Gleghorn, Andrade/Moore^. Middlesbrough: Miller, Cox*, Whyte, Vickers, Pearson, Kavanagh, Hignett, Pollack, Fjortoft, Hendrie, Moore, Blackmore/Moreno.

40 v Barnsley — Stoke: Sinclair, Butler, Clarkson, Sigurdsson, Overson, Orlygsson, Downing, Allen, Peschisolido*, Scott, Gleghorn, Andrade/Rammell. Barnsley: Watson, Eaden, Fleming, Wilson, Taggart, Shotton, O'Connell, Bullock, Payton, Liddell*, Sheridan, Rammell.

41 v Bristol City — Stoke: Sinclair, Butler, Clarkson, Sigurdsson, Overson, Orlygsson, Allen^, Downing*, Peschisolido, Andrade, Gleghorn, Carruthers/Keen. Bristol City: Welch, Hansen, Munro^, Shail, Dryden, Tinnion, Martin^, Bent, Flatts, Allison, Owers, Baird/Edwards.

42 v Swindon — Stoke: Sinclair, Butler, Clarkson, Sigurdsson, Overson, Orlygsson, Allen^, Carruthers, Peschisolido, Andrade*, Gleghorn, Wallace/Scott. Swindon: Digby, Todd, Viveash, Nijholt, Taylor, Ling^, Beauchamp, Gooden, Thorne, McMahon, Thomson/O'Sullivan.

43 v Port Vale — Stoke: Sinclair, Butler, Cranson!, Sigurdsson, Overson, Orlygsson, Allen, Carruthers, Peschisolido, Andrade*, Gleghorn, Gayle. Port Vale: Musselwhite, Sandeman, Tankard, Porter, Aspin, Glover D, Bogie, Van der Laan, Foyle, Naylor, Guppy, Gayle.

44 v Millwall — Stoke: Sinclair, Butler, Cranson, Sigurdsson, Overson, Wallace, Allen, Keen, Peschisolido, Scott^, Gleghorn, Van Blerk. Millwall: Keller, Beard, Thatcher, Roberts, Webber, Stevens^, Savage*, Rae, Dixon, Oldfield, Van Blerk, Taylor/Forbes.

45 v Bolton — Stoke: Sinclair, Butler, Cranson, Sigurdsson, Overson, Orlygsson, Allen, Keen, Peschisolido, Scott^, Gleghorn, Sandford/Carruthers. Bolton: Davison!, Bergsson, McAteer, Stubbs, Seagraves*, Lee^, Patterson, Paatelainen, McGinlay, Thompson, Green/Shilton.

46 v Luton — Stoke: Sinclair, Butler, Sandford, Sigurdsson, Overson, Orlygsson, Wallace, Keen, Peschisolido*, Scott, Gleghorn, Clarkson. Luton: Davis, Johnson, Waddock, Thomas, Peake, Telfer, Oakes, Taylor, Preece, Woodsford*, Marshall, Harvey.

Match notes

35: Southend pummel Stoke. Jones heads in. Tilson turns to drive past Sinclair. Allen scores with a low shot but Edwards' header restores the lead. He is then sent off for handball and Biggins nets the spot-kick. He also departs after protesting the penalty is given for Overson's handball.

36: Nigel Gleghorn scores Stoke's first home goal of 1995, sweeping in an Orlygsson corner. Cherry tips over Toddy's thunderous free-kick. Scott fires over from two yards. Sturridge has a shot kicked off the line but rounds Cherry to net Stoke's first goal at the Boothen End since October.

37: A poor game ends goalless as Stoke shut up shop. Allen is industrious in midfield. Steve Gritt and Alan Curbishley's Addicks have most of the play. Sinclair tips John Robinson's shot onto the post and recovers brilliantly to deny Grant. Pesch looks sharper after his recent injury lay-off.

38: The relief is tangible when Larus Sigurdsson floats a header between Kevin Miller and the far post. With confidence boosted City dominate the second half. Miller saves superbly from Pesch twice. Allen heads Foster's header off the line but Keen's 20-yard cracker tests Miller to the full.

39: John Gayle makes his first start in a side lacking nine first teamers. Bryan Robson's leaders storm forward. Vickers flicks on for Nigel Pearson to head in. Pesch slams a deserved goal after Carruthers' run and cross. City battle hard but Boro's class tells. Alan Moore cracks in on the run.

40: 2,000 travelling fans out-sing a dismal home crowd. Barnsley play neat football but lack penetration. Allen tests Watson from 25 yards. Pesch finishes well but is ruled to have fouled a defender. Jose Andrade (aka Zay Angola) makes his home debut and nearly scores from a loose ball.

41: Bristol City skipper Mark Shail forces a Gary Owers corner over the line as the Robins look for the win they need to avoid relegation. Andrade nets his first for Stoke against the run of play. Both sides have chances but Pesch's late winner virtually condemns Joe Jordan's team to Div 2.

42: A smash and grab raid at Lou Macari's old club. City are quicker to the ball and grab a scrappy goal thanks to Toddy Orlygsson in a goalmouth melee. Trialist Jose Andrade has his leg broken in a fierce challenge. Steve McMahon's Robins are now in deep trouble at the foot of the table.

43: A poor game. Martin Foyle glances home Steve Guppy's inswinging corner at the near post. Pesch hits the foot of Musselwhite's post. Cranson becomes the first player to be dismissed in a derby match, for two bookings. City's first home league defeat by Vale for 67 years. Humiliating!

44: A pulsating game. Gleghorn cracks in two outstanding strikes. Scott scores at the near post and fluffs an easier chance. Mick McCarthy's Lions lead as Oldfield taps in with Sinclair stranded. Linesman Stretton replaces the ref and denies Stoke a penalty but Keen nets the resulting corner.

45: A frantic game sees Aidan Davison dismissed for fouling Pesch. Orlygsson nets the penalty against Peter Shilton making his 998th appearance. Ten-man Trotters fight hard. John McGinlay scores at the second attempt after Sinclair makes a great reaction stop. Pesch misses an open goal.

46: Fancy dress again. Richard Harvey fires in from 20 yards for Terry Westley's Town. Gleghorn heads against the bar. Wallace hits the post but Wallace punishes a defensive error. The woeful Scott hits the bar from two yards but heads home from Gleghorn's cross. Keen sets up Pesch. Waddock punishes a defensive error.

ENDSLEIGH DIVISION 1 (CUP-TIES) Manager: Joe Jordan ⇨ Lou Macari SEASON 1994-95

Coca-Cola Cup

	Att	F-A	H-T	Scorers, Times, and Referees	1	2	3	4	5	6	7	8	9	10	11	subs used
2:1 A FULHAM 20/9	6 L 3,721 3:17	2-3	0-0	Orlygsson 69p, Gleghorn 70 / Moore 60, Haworth 76, Blake 85 / Ref: M Bailey	Muggleton	Butler	Sandford	Cranson	Dreyer	Orlygsson	Wallace	Downing	Carruthers	Peschisolido	Gleghorn	
(Fulham)					*Stanmard*	*Morgan*	*Herrera*	*Hurlock*	*Moore*	*Blake*	*Marshall*	*Jupp*	*Cork*	*Brazil*	*Haworth*	

Lou Macari watches from the stand as Pesch is upended for the penalty. Gleghorn's cool finish puts Stoke 2-1 up. The linesman awards a spot-kick, but as Muggers saves wants a retake. Muggers keeps that out too but the rebound is lashed in. Mark Blake heads the winner on his debut.

	Att	F-A	H-T	Scorers, Times, and Referees	1	2	3	4	5	6	7	8	9	10	11	subs used
2:2 H FULHAM 28/9	8 W 7,440 3:15	1-0	1-0	Peschisolido 2 / Ref: J Watson / (Stoke win on away goals)	Muggleton	Butler	Sandford	Dreyer	Cranson	Orlygsson	Carruthers	Downing	Biggins	Peschisolido	Gleghorn	Bedrossian/Haworth
(Fulham)					*Stanmard*	*Morgan*	*Adams*	*Mison*	*Moore**	*Blake*	*Marshall*	*Jupp*	*Bartley^*	*Brazil*	*Thomas*	

Pesch's early goal allows City to progress thanks to the away goals rule. Ian Branfoot and Mickey Adams' team of journeymen pros fight hard but Stoke are generally in control. Macari is confirmed as next manager. For the first time in a long while everything is rosy. Better days ahead.

	Att	F-A	H-T	Scorers, Times, and Referees	1	2	3	4	5	6	7	8	9	10	11	subs used
3 A LIVERPOOL 25/10	7 L 32,060 P:5	1-2	1-1	Peschisolido 41 / Rush 4, 55 / Ref: J Holbrook	Muggleton	Butler	Sandford	Cranson	Overson	Orlygsson	Beeston	Clarkson	Carruthers*	Peschisolido	Gleghorn^	Biggins/Potter
(Liverpool)					*James*	*Jones*	*Bjornebye*	*Scales*	*Babb*	*Ruddock*	*McManaman Redknapp*	*Clarkson*	*Rush*	*Barnes*	*Fowler*	

Ian Rush nets and City fans reach for their calculators. To their astonishment Stoke fight back. Babb is lucky not to see red after felling Pesch. Gleghorn hits the post. Pesch fires Carruthers' cross home to spark scenes of delirium. Rush's winner is his 100th cup goal for the Reds. Great!

FA Cup

	Att	F-A	H-T	Scorers, Times, and Referees	1	2	3	4	5	6	7	8	9	10	11	subs used
3 A BRISTOL CITY 7/1	12 D 9,683 23	0-0	0-0	Ref: K Cooper	Sinclair	Butler	Sandford	Cranson	Overson	Orlygsson	Clarkson	Downing*	Scott	Peschisolido^	Gleghorn	Sturridge/Sigurdsson
(Bristol City)					*Welch*	*Hansen*	*Munro*	*Shail*	*Bryant*	*Tinnion*	*Kuhl*	*Bent*	*Baird**	*Allison*	*Owers*	*Partridge*

A terrible game on a heavily sanded pitch. Pesch is one of eight booked as he flicks the ball past Welch with his hand before netting. Sandford clears Partridge's shot off the line. Ex-Stoke loanee Junior Bent fires just past the upright. Keith Welch smothers Keith Scott's last-minute shot.

	Att	F-A	H-T	Scorers, Times, and Referees	1	2	3	4	5	6	7	8	9	10	11	subs used
3R H BRISTOL CITY 18/1	14 L 11,579 23 aet	1-3	1-0	Scott 17 / Bent 70, Baird 93, Tinnion 119 / Ref: K Cooper	Sinclair	Clarkson*	Sandford	Cranson	Overson	Orlygsson	Butler	Wallace	Scott	Peschisolido	Gleghorn	Edwards/Partridge
(Bristol City)					*Welch*	*Hansen*	*Munro*	*Shail*	*Bryant*	*Tinnion*	*Kuhl**	*Bent*	*Baird*	*Allison**	*Owers*	

Keith Scott glances a header in from a corner. Welch fumbles and the ball trickles along the line to safety. Bent scores with Bristol's first effort on target. Baird profits after Overson miskicks. Brian Tinnion fires in from 20 yards. Joe Jordan has the last laugh as Bristol will meet Everton.

League Table

Pos	Team	P	Home W	D	L	F	A	Away W	D	L	F	A	Pts
1	Middlesbro	46	15	4	4	41	19	8	9	6	26	21	82
2	Reading	46	12	7	4	34	21	11	3	9	24	32	79
3	Bolton *	46	16	6	1	43	13	5	8	10	24	43	77
4	Wolves	46	14	6	3	39	18	6	8	9	38	43	76
5	Tranmere	46	17	4	2	51	23	5	6	12	16	35	76
6	Barnsley	46	15	6	2	42	19	5	6	12	21	33	72
7	Watford	46	14	6	3	33	17	5	7	11	19	29	70
8	Sheffield Utd	46	12	9	2	41	21	5	8	10	33	34	68
9	Derby	46	11	7	5	44	23	6	6	11	22	28	66
10	Grimsby	46	12	7	4	36	19	5	7	11	19	32	65
11	STOKE	46	10	7	6	31	21	6	8	9	19	32	63
12	Millwall	46	11	8	4	36	21	5	6	12	24	38	62
13	Southend	46	13	2	8	33	25	5	6	12	21	48	62
14	Oldham	46	12	7	4	34	21	4	6	13	26	39	61
15	Charlton	46	11	6	6	33	25	5	5	13	25	41	59
16	Luton	46	11	5	7	35	30	5	5	13	26	40	58
17	Port Vale	46	12	5	6	30	24	4	8	11	28	40	58
18	Portsmouth	46	9	8	6	31	28	6	5	12	22	35	58
19	West Brom	46	13	3	7	33	24	3	7	13	18	33	58
20	Sunderland	46	5	12	6	22	22	7	6	10	19	23	54
21	Swindon	46	9	6	8	28	27	3	6	14	26	46	48
22	Burnley	46	8	7	8	36	33	3	6	14	13	41	46
23	Bristol City	46	8	8	7	26	28	4	4	16	16	35	45
24	Notts Co	46	7	8	8	26	28	2	5	16	19	38	40
		1104	275	153	124	838	551	124	153	275	551	838	1503

* promoted
after play-offs

Odds & ends

Double wins: (3) Notts County, Tranmere, West Brom.

Double losses: (2) Reading, Sunderland.

Won from behind: (4) Bristol City (h), Luton (a), Millwall (h), West Brom (a).

Lost from in front: (0).

High spots: The return of Lou Macari. Toddy Orlygsson's form in midfield. Playing so well at Anfield. Beating Cosenza, Udinese and Piacenza in the Anglo-Italian Cup. Winning at fellow strugglers Swindon to ensure survival.

Low spots: Losing at home to Bristol City in the FA Cup. The sacking of Joe Jordan after an awful start. Poor performances after Christmas leading to a scramble to avoid relegation. Losing another Potteries derby.

Player of the Year: Larus Sigurdsson.

Ever-presents: (0).

Hat-tricks: (0).

Leading scorer: (13) Paul Peschisolido.

Appearances and Goals

Player	Appearances Lge	Sub	LC	Sub	FAC	Sub	Goals Lge	LC	FAC	Tot
Allen, Paul	17						1			1
Andrade, Jose	2	2								
Beckford, Jason	2	2								
Beeston, Carl	15		1		1		1			1
Biggins, Wayne	8	9	1	1	1		2			2
Butler, John	38	3	3		3					
Carruthers, Martin	26	6	3			1	5			5
Clark, Jon	5									
Clarkson, Ian	15	3	1							
Cranson, Ian	37		3		2		1			1
Downing, Keith	16		2		1					
Dreyer, John	16	2	2		2		2			2
Gayle, John	1	3								
Gleghorn, Nigel	44	2	3		2		6	1		7
Keen, Kevin	15	6	6				2			2
Leslie, Steve		1	1							
Muggleton, Carl	24		3							
Orlygsson, Toddy	38	3	3		2	1	7	1		8
Overson, Vince	33	2	1		2					
Peschisolido, Paul	39	1	3		2	2	13	2		15
Potter, Graham	1			1						
Sandford, Lee	34	1	3		2		1			1
Scott, Keith	16	2	2		2		3		1	4
Shaw, Graham	1	2								
Sigurdsson, Larus	22	1	1				1			1
Sinclair, Ronnie	22	2	2		2					
Sturridge, Simon	2	6				1	1			1
Wade, Shaun		1								
Wallace, Ray	16	4	1		1		2			2
Williams, John	1	3					1			1
(own-goals)										
30 players used	506	65	33	2	22	2	50	4	1	55

ENDSLEIGH DIVISION 1

Manager: Lou Macari — SEASON 1995-96

Results

No	Date	Venue	Opponent	Att	Pos	Pt	Result	F-A	H-T	Scorers, Times, and Referees
1	12/8	H	READING	11,932	—	1	D	1-1	1-0	Wallace 12 / Williams A 83. Ref: J Kirkby
2	19/8	A	LEICESTER	17,719	4	4	W	3-2	3-0	Peschisolido 9, 23, Gleghorn 33 / Walsh 71, Parker 74p. Ref: R Gifford
3	27/8	H	PORT VALE	14,283	14	4	L	0-1	0-0	Bogie 48. Ref: G Singh
4	30/8	A	IPSWICH	10,848	18	4	L	1-4	0-1	Peschisolido 83 / Slater 38, 62, Mathie 82, 86. Ref: M Bailey
5	2/9	H	OLDHAM	8,663	23	4	L	0-1	0-0	Overson 69 (og). Ref: K Lynch
6	9/9	A	WATFORD	7,130	23	4	L	0-3	0-2	Ramage 27, 54, Mooney 44. Ref: P Rejer
7	12/9	A	BIRMINGHAM	19,005	23	5	D	1-1	0-1	Carruthers 52 / Hunt 30. Ref: I Cruickshanks
8	16/9	H	TRANMERE	8,618	22	6	D	0-0	0-0	Ref: S Mathieson
9	24/9	H	WEST BROM	9,612	22	9	W	2-1	1-0	Peschisolido 14, Keen 51 / Hunt 62p. Ref: T Lunt
10	20/9	A	CRYSTAL PALACE	14,613	21	10	D	1-1	1-1	Carruthers 36 / Freedman 31. Ref: A D'Urso
11	7/10	H	NORWICH	12,016	21	11	D	1-1	1-1	Wallace 67 / Akinbiyi 32. Ref: G Cain

Line-ups (Stoke in roman, opponents in italic)

No	1	2	3	4	5	6	7	8	9	10	11	subs used
1	Muggleton	Clarkson	Sandford	Sigurdsson	Overson	Orlygsson	Keen	Wallace	Peschisolido*	Scott	Gleghorn	Sturridge
1	*Sheppard*	*Bernal^*	*Gooding*	*Parkinson*	*Williams A*	*McPherson*	*Gilkes*	*Jones*	*Nogan**	*Lovell*	*Williams M*	*Morley/Wdowczyk*
2	Muggleton	Clarkson	Sandford	Sigurdsson	Overson	Orlygsson	Keen	Wallace	Peschisolido*	Scott	Gleghorn	Sturridge/Gayle
2	*Poole*	*Grayson^*	*Whitlow*	*Willis**	*Walsh*	*Parker*	*Joachim*	*Taylor*	*Robins*	*Corica*	*Lawrence"*	*Roberts/Hill/Lewis*
3	Muggleton	Clarkson	Sandford	Sigurdsson	Overson	Orlygsson*	Keen	Wallace	Peschisolido*	Scott	Gleghorn	Sturridge/Potter
3	*Musselwhite*	*Hill*	*Tankard*	*Bogie*	*Griffiths*	*Glover*	*McCarthy*	*Porter*	*Mills*	*Glover**	*Guppy*	*Naylor*
4	Muggleton	Clarkson	Sandford	Sigurdsson	Overson	Orlygsson	Keen*	Wallace	Peschisolido	Scott	Gleghorn	Sturridge
4	*Forrest*	*Stockwell*	*Vaughan*	*Sedgley*	*Palmer*	*Williams**	*Uhlenbeek*	*Milton^*	*Mathie*	*Chapman*	*Slater*	*Taricco/Tanner*
5	Muggleton	Clarkson	Sandford	Sigurdsson	Overson	Orlygsson	Keen^	Wallace	Peschisolido	Scott	Gleghorn	Sturridge
5	*Hallworth*	*Makin*	*Pointon*	*Henry*	*Jobson*	*Redmond*	*Halle*	*Bernard*	*McCarthy*	*Banger**	*Brennan*	*Pemberton*
6	Sinclair	Clarkson	Sandford*	Sigurdsson	Overson	Orlygsson^	Keen*	Wallace	Peschisolido	Carruthers	Gleghorn	Scott/Dreyer/Devlin
6	*Miller*	*Gibbs*	*Johnson*	*Foster*	*Holdsworth*	*Ramage*	*Bazeley^*	*Payne*	*Mooney**	*Porter*	*Phillips*	*Moralee/Pitcher*
7	Muggleton	Clarkson	Sandford	Sigurdsson	Overson	Potter	Keen*	Wallace	Peschisolido	Scott^	Gleghorn"	Sturridge/Carruthers/Br'well
7	*Bennett*	*Poole*	*Johnson*	*Ward*	*Edwards*	*Daish*	*Hunt*	*Claridge*	*Bowen*	*Charlery**	*Cooper^*	*Tait/Otto*
8	Prudhoe	Clarkson	Sandford	Sigurdsson	Overson	Potter	Keen*	Wallace	Peschisolido	Carruthers	Gleghorn	Orlygsson
8	*Coyne*	*Stevens^*	*Thomas*	*McGreal*	*Teale*	*O'Brien**	*Brennan*	*Aldridge*	*Bennett*	*Irons*	*Nevin*	*Moore/Jones*
9	Prudhoe	Clarkson	Sandford	Sigurdsson	Overson	Potter	Keen*	Wallace	Peschisolido	Carruthers*	Gleghorn	Sturridge
9	*Naylor*	*Burgess*	*Edwards**	*Coldicott*	*Mardon*	*Raven*	*Donovan*	*Gilbert*	*Taylor^*	*Hamilton*	*Hunt*	*Ashcroft/Rees*
10	Prudhoe	Clarkson	Sandford	Sigurdsson	Overson	Potter	Sturridge	Wallace	Peschisolido*	Carruthers	Gleghorn	
10	*Martyn*	*Edworthy*	*Vincent**	*Hopkin*	*Coleman*	*Shaw*	*Houghton*	*Pitcher**	*Freedman*	*Taylor*	*Gordon*	*Roberts/Launders*
11	Prudhoe	Clarkson	Sandford	Sigurdsson	Overson	Potter	Sturridge	Wallace	Peschisolido	Carruthers	Gleghorn	
11	*Gunn*	*Ullathorne*	*Bowen*	*Crook*	*Newsome*	*Prior*	*Adams**	*Fleck^*	*Akinbiyi*	*Johnson*	*O'Neill**	*Milligan/Polston/Sheran*

Match notes

1. **Reading (H)** — Work will begin on Stoke's stadium at Sideway next year. The lack of new signings suggests the move is eating deep into the club's resources. Wallace's effort is reward for a bright opening. Adrian Williams nets a soft equaliser to earn an undeserved point for Quinn/Gooding's Royals.

2. **Leicester (A)** — Stoke soak up heavy pressure and play on the break. Pesch's shot dribbles in. Willis is lucky not to go after felling the diminutive Canadian. A great move allows Pesch to head in. Gleghorn puts City in control. Sandford's foul on Walsh for the pen is as good as Mark McGhee's men get.

3. **Port Vale (H)** — Stoke sport new Broxap sponsored shirts after finally clinching a deal. The lowest ever gate at a Potteries derby sees Vale outplay City for long periods. Ian Bogie turns on a one-man show and beats Muggleton at his near post. Sturridge lobs the keeper but also past the post. Depressing.

4. **Ipswich (A)** — City perform well with some slick passing moves but George Burley's Ipswich finish brilliantly. Slater's second is a brilliant turn and shot. Ex-Stokie Lee Chapman misses an open goal. Pesch's rounds Forrest. City's passion elicits a standing ovation from the visiting fans at the whistle.

5. **Oldham (H)** — An atrocious game is won by Graeme Sharp's Oldham when Vince Overson, Stoke's best player, miskicks the ball past the shocked Mugglers. New coach Mike Pejic conducts a 45-min post-match inquest. Amid rumours of a move upstairs Macari is looking at Willie Falconer of Celtic.

6. **Watford (A)** — Goalkeeper Ronnie Sinclair has a nightmare of a game. Glenn Roeder's Hornets have two first-half efforts. Both go in. Kevin Phillips balloons a spot-kick over the bar after Overson's foul. Ramage's second is a great free-kick. Macari is close to signing Oldham's winger Rick Holden.

7. **Birmingham (A)** — The Holden deal has fallen through due to lack of funds. Macari demands action. Contract rebel Orlygsson is omitted after speaking out in the press. Blues boss Barry Fry offers six players in exchange for the in-form Paul Peschisolido. David Brightwell is taken on loan from Man City.

8. **Tranmere (H)** — The lowest gate for five years see the best performance of the season. Stoke are out of luck when Keen and Overson hit the woodwork. Danny Coyne saves Ian Clarkson's volley brilliantly. Boardroom turmoil as Chairman Peter Coates says he will sell for the right price. £10m anyone?

9. **West Brom (H)** — Pesch shrugs off two players to beat Naylor. Carruthers thumps a header against the bar from two yards. Keen is booked for taking his shirt off to celebrate his goal. Andy Hunt goes down dramatically in the area for the penalty. 13 matches unbeaten against the Baggies. First home win!

10. **Crystal Palace (A)** — Palace's £2.5m investment pays off when Dougie Freedman lashes home Gareth Taylor's flick on. Carruthers is put through by Pesch to waltz round Nigel Martyn and score in front of Selhurst's impressive new stand. Prudhoe saves Taylor's header. Another solid away performance.

11. **Norwich (H)** — Stoke are down to the bare bones against Martin O'Neill's strong Canaries. Ade Akinbiyi taps in after Prudhoe superbly saves Andy Johnson's effort. 'Razor' Wallace finishes a fine left-wing move by slotting in past Bryan Gunn. More support up front required to win matches like this.

Season Match Record (matches 12–23)

12 · A · WOLVES · 14/10
Gleghorn 36, Potter 41, Wallace 85, Carruthers 90
Thompson 65p [Carruthers 90]
16 · W · 4-1 · 2-0 · 19/14 · 26,4??
Ref: D Allison

Prudhoe	Clarkson	Sandford	Sigurdsson	Overson	Potter	Keen	Wallace	Peschisolido	Carruthers*	Gleghorn*	Sturridge
Stowell"	*Emblem*	*Thompson*	*Atkins*	*Young*	*Richards*	*Wright*	*Goodman*	*Venus**	*Ferguson**	*Williams*	*Bull/Cowans/Smith*

City put Graham Taylor's Wolves to the sword after Gleghorn hammers home. Potter stabs in his first for the club. Mike Stowell is injured in a clash with Young. Dean Richards goes in goal. Wallace's shot squirms past him. Pesch has a goal ruled out. First win at Molineux since 1967.

---

13 · H · DERBY · 22/10
Keen 66
Van der Laan 89
16 · D · 1-1 · 0-0 · 17/15 · 9,4??
Ref: G Furnandiz

Prudhoe	Clarkson	Sandford*	Sigurdsson	Overson	Potter	Keen	Wallace	Peschisolido	Carruthers	Gleghorn	Dreyer
Hoult	*Carsley*	*Nicholson*	*Preece^*	*Yates*	*Rowett*	*Van der Laan*	*Wrack**	*Willems*	*Gabbiadini*	*Trollope*	*Simpson/Flynn*

Kevin Keen volleys a wonderful goal from Gleghorn's chip but is again booked for taking his shirt off in celebration. Robin Van der Laan runs clear to give Jim Smith's Rams an undeserved draw. Nine without defeat. Stoke report Birmingham to the FA over illegal approaches to Pesch.

---

14 · A · GRIMSBY · 28/10
Groves 51
19 · L · 0-1 · 0-0 · 10/15 · 5,4??
Ref: T West

Prudhoe	Clarkson	Sandford	Sigurdsson	Overson	Potter	Keen*	Wallace	Peschisolido	Carruthers	Gleghorn	Gayle
Crichton	*Laws*	*Croft*	*Handyside*	*Lever*	*Groves*	*Childs**	*Dobbin*	*Woods*	*Bonetti*	*Southall^*	*Livingstone/Forrester*

Paul Groves slips in to fire past Prudhoe. Gleghorn has a shot blocked on the line. Carruthers slices a great chance wide. Brian Laws' men look dangerous on the break. No win at Blundell Park since 1947. Keith Scott is wanted by old team Wycombe. Bradford are chasing John Dreyer.

---

15 · H · LUTON · 4/11
Peschisolido 14, Sturridge 73, 87, [Gayle 75, Gleghorn 90]
15 · W · 5-0 · 1-0 · 24/18 · 9,8??
Ref: J Lloyd

Prudhoe	Clarkson"	Sandford	Sigurdsson	Overson	Potter	Keen	Wallace	Peschisolido^	Carruthers^	Gleghorn	Sturridge/Gayle/Gleghorn
Feuer	*Peake*	*Johnson*	*Davis*	*Hughes*	*Vilstrup**	*Alexander*	*Oakes*	*Riseth*	*Marshall*	*Harvey*	*Oldfield*

6ft 7in Ian Feuer is beaten by Pesch. Sturridge comes on for the injured Carruthers at half-time and his direct running sparks the avalanche. He cracks in from 22 yards for his first. Gayle scores the goal of the game from our on the left. The superb Gleghorn robs a defender to fire home.

---

16 · A · SOUTHEND · 11/11
Sturridge 32, 63, 75, Gleghorn 65
Belsvik 25, Hails 54
13 · W · 4-2 · 1-1 · 16/21 · 5,3??
Ref: M Pierce

Prudhoe	Cranson	Sandford	Sigurdsson	Overson	Potter	Keen	Wallace^	Gayle*	Sturridge	Gleghorn"	Carruthers/**Devlin/Whittle**
Royce	*Dublin*	*Powell*	*Lapper*	*Bodley*	*Gridelet*	*Marsh*	*Byrne*	*Regis*	*Belsvik**	*Hails^*	*Thomson/Read*

Debutant Peter Belsvik glances a header home. Potter is fouled in the area but an indirect free-kick is given. Sturridge turns in Keen's pass. He completes his hat-trick with two superb individual efforts. Gleghorn neatly shoots through Simon Royce's legs. A first ever win at Roots Hall.

---

17 · A · PORTSMOUTH · 18/11
Gayle 29, 61, Sturridge 63
McLoughlin 16p, 56, Walsh 44
14 · D · 3-3 · 1-2 · 22/22 · 8,7??
Ref: C Wilkes

Prudhoe	Cranson*	Sandford	Sigurdsson	Overson	Potter^	Keen	Wallace	Gayle	Sturridge	Gleghorn	Devlin/**Sheron**
Knight	*Pethick*	*Russell*	*McLoughlin*	*Whitbread*	*Butters*	*Walsh*	*Allen*	*Durnin*	*Hall*	*Carter**	*Burton*

Paul Walsh runs the show. He is tripped for penalty and scores himself after Prudhoe fails to hold his shot. McLoughlin's header puts Pompey in the driving seat. Gayle's brace are from close in. Sturridge turns well to fire home. Ex-Canary Mike Sheron misses a sitter in the last minute.

---

18 · H · SUNDERLAND · 22/11
Wallace 21
12 · W · 1-0 · 1-0 · 4/25 · 11,7??
Ref: R Harris

Prudhoe	Clarkson	Sandford	Sigurdsson	Overson*	Potter^	Keen^	Wallace	Gayle	Sturridge*	Gleghorn	Carruthers/**Dreyer/Sheron**
Chamberlain	*Kubicki*	*Scott*	*Bracewell**	*Ball*	*Melville*	*Gray M*	*Ord*	*Kelly^*	*Gray P*	*Russell**	*Howey/Smith/Aiston*

Phil Gray and Kevin Russell waste good chances for Peter Reid's Sunderland. Wallace latches on to Keen's header to put Stoke undeservedly in the lead. Prudhoe makes two brilliant saves as the Rokerites pour forward. Gleghorn has a good effort saved. Sunderland's first defeat in 11.

---

19 · H · MILLWALL · 25/11
Gleghorn 62
9 · W · 1-0 · 0-0 · 1/28 · 12,5??
Ref: P Taylor

Prudhoe	Clarkson	Sandford	Sigurdsson	Overson	Potter	Keen^	Wallace	Gayle*	Sturridge*	Gleghorn	Carruthers/**Dreyer/Sheron**
Keller	*Lavin*	*Thatcher*	*Bowry*	*Webber*	*Stevens*	*Fuchs*	*Rae*	*Dixon**	*Makin*	*Van Blerk*	*Savage*

Ian Cranson, finally fully fit after his long injury lay-off, is superb as Stoke contain league leaders Millwall. Gleghorn's 20-yard effort deflects off Ben Thatcher leaving Kasey Keller stranded. Mick McCarthy's men's first away loss of the season. Five are booked in a competitive game.

---

20 · A · NORWICH · 2/12
Gleghorn 53
7 · W · 1-0 · 0-0 · 4/31 · 15,7??
Ref: I Hemley

Prudhoe	Clarkson	Sandford	Sigurdsson	Cranson	Potter*	Keen	Wallace	Peschisolido*	Sturridge^	Gleghorn	Sheron/**Beeston**
Gunn	*Sutch^*	*Ullathorne*	*Adams*	*Newsome*	*Prior*	*Bowen*	*Fleck*	*Ward*	*Scott*	*Eadie*	*Akinbiyi*

An inspired Stoke display against a Canaries team which would be top with a win. Pesch sets up Gleghorn to win it. Prudhoe stops everything Norwich throw at him. Cranson is brilliant in defence. Macari is censured by the League for remarks about the referee in the Newcastle cup-tie.

---

21 · A · WEST BROM · 9/12
Peschisolido 35
5 · W · 1-0 · 1-0 · 16/34 · 14,8??
Ref: T Helibron

Prudhoe	Clarkson	Sandford	Sigurdsson	Cranson	Potter^	Dreyer	Wallace^	Peschisolido*	Sturridge*	Gleghorn	Keen/**Carruthers/Sheron**
Naylor	*Burgess*	*Smith*	*Darby*	*Edwards*	*Raven*	*Hamilton*	*Gilbert**	*Taylor*	*Hunt*	*Ashcroft^*	*Donovan/Coldicott*

3,000 Stokies see Naylor deny Wallace in almighty goalmouth scramble. Daryl Burgess heads against the bar. Pesch turns to blast past Naylor. Sigurdsson impresses at the back. Kevin Donovan fires wide when clean through. Albion have lost eight in a row. Stoke into the play-off zone.

---

22 · H · CRYSTAL PALACE · 16/12
Sheron 87
Freedman 24, Taylor 71
8 · L · 1-2 · 0-1 · 16/34 · 12,0??
Ref: K Breen

Prudhoe	Clarkson	Sandford	Sigurdsson	Cranson	Potter*	Dreyer	Wallace	Sheron	Sturridge	Gleghorn	Peschisolido
Martyn	*Edworthy*	*Gordon*	*Roberts*	*Cundy*	*Vincent*	*Bowen*	*Houghton*	*Freedman*	*Taylor^*	*McKenzie^*	*Dyer/Boere*

A wonder goal from Sheron can't save City after a poor display. Freedman takes advantage of sloppy defending to ram home. Sturridge rounds Martyn but can't convert. Prudhoe fluffs a cross and Taylor nods in his first goal for Palace. Five without a win against Steve Coppell's Eagles.

---

23 · H · SHEFFIELD UTD · 23/12
Gleghorn 27, Sheron 46
Patterson 7, White 74
8 · D · 2-2 · 1-1 · 23/35 · 1?,3??
Ref: E Wolstenholme

Prudhoe	Clarkson	Sandford	Sigurdsson	Cranson!	Potter	Sheron^	Wallace	Peschisolido	Sturridge	Gleghorn	Dreyer
Kelly	*Rogers*	*Fitzgerald*	*Gannon^*	*Vonk**	*Tuttle*	*White*	*Patterson*	*Battersby*	*Holland*	*Ward*	*Hodges/Heath*

Howard Kendall's Blades score when new signing Mark Patterson volleys in. Gleghorn deflects Cranson's shot in. Potter has a goal disallowed for Pesch's offside. Sheron flicks in Potter's centre. David White levels with a far-post header. Cranson walks (76 mins) for a second booking.

ENDSLEIGH DIVISION 1 — Manager: Lou Macari — SEASON 1995-96

No	H/A	Opponent	Date	Att	Pos	Pt	F-A	H-T	Scorers, Times, and Referees	1	2	3	4	5	6	7	8	9	10	11	subs used
24	A	BARNSLEY	26/12	9,229	13	L 35	1-3	0-2	Gleghorn 68 / Redfearn 30, Rammell 43, Liddell 62 / Ref: N Berry	Prudhoe	Clarkson*	Sandford	Sigurdsson	Cranson	Potter	Dreyer	Wallace	Peschisolido	Sheron	Gleghorn	Devlin
										Watson	Eaden	Shirtliff	Sheridan	Davis	Moses	Liddell	Redfearn	O'Connell	Rammell	Archdeacon	
25	A	HUDDERSFIELD	30/12	15,071	6	D 36	1-1	0-0	Sheron 47 / Prudhoe 73 (og) / Ref: I Cruickshanks	Prudhoe	Clarkson	Sandford	Sigurdsson	Cranson	Potter	Keen	Wallace	Peschisolido*	Sheron	Gleghorn	Sturridge/Carruthers
										Francis	Dyson^	Cowan	Collins	Sinnott	Gray	Dalton*	Makel	Booth	Jepson		Rowe/Turner
26	H	LEICESTER	13/1	13,669	5	W 39	1-0	1-0	Sturridge 27 / Ref: J Kirkby	Prudhoe	Clarkson	Sandford	Sigurdsson	Cranson	Potter^	Keen^	Wallace	Sturridge	Carruthers*	Gleghorn	Gayle/Beeston
										Poole	Grayson	Whitlow	Hill	Walsh	Parker	Carica	Taylor^	Robins^	Smith^		Joachim/Philpott/Lowe
27	A	READING	20/1	8,082	18	L 39	0-1	0-0	Gooding 67 / Ref: G Pooley	Prudhoe	Clarkson	Sandford	Sigurdsson	Cranson	Potter	Keen	Wallace	Gayle*	Sturridge	Gleghorn	Peschisolido
										Sutton	Bernal		Williams A	Wdowczyk^	Booty	Quinn	Parkinson	Morley^	Nogan	Holsgrove	Gilkes/Lambert
28	H	IPSWICH	10/2	12,239	9	W 42	3-1	1-0	Sheron 37, 75, Gleghorn 65 / Scowcroft 54 / Ref: G Cain	Prudhoe	Clarkson	Sandford	Sigurdsson	Cranson	Potter^	Beeston	Wallace	Sheron	Sturridge*	Gleghorn	Peschisolido/Dreyer
										Wright	Uhlenbeek	Taricco	Mowbray	Thomsen	Williams	Mason^	Sedgley	Scowcroft	Marshall	Milton^	Stockwell/Slater
29	H	BIRMINGHAM	17/2	15,716	13	W 45	1-0	1-0	Sturridge 25 / Ref: T Helibron	Prudhoe	Clarkson	Sandford	Sigurdsson	Cranson	Potter^	Beeston*	Wallace	Sheron	Sturridge	Gleghorn	Keen/Dreyer
										Griemink	Bass	Frain	Samways	Edwards	Johnson	Hunt^	Bowen^	Francis	Sheridan	Donowa*	Otto/Bull/Breen
30	A	TRANMERE	24/2	8,312	17	D 46	0-0	0-0	Ref: D Allison	Prudhoe	Clarkson	Sandford	Sigurdsson	Cranson	Potter	Beeston	Wallace	Sheron*	Sturridge*	Gleghorn	
										Coyne	Stevens	Rogers	Teale	Garnett*	O'Brien	Brannan	Aldridge	Bennett^	Irons	Branch	Mungall/Morrissey/Jones
31	H	WATFORD	28/2	10,114	24	W 49	2-0	0-0	Cranson 48, Wallace 62 / Ref: T West	Prudhoe	Clarkson	Sandford	Sigurdsson	Cranson	Potter	Beeston	Wallace*	Sheron*	Sturridge	Gleghorn	Keen/Peschisolido
										Miller	Gibbs	Barnes	Hessenthaler	Holdsworth	Millen	Penrice^	Palmer	White	Mooney^	Phillips	Bazeley/Ludden
32	H	BARNSLEY	2/3	12,663	6	W 52	2-0	1-0	Keen 39, Sheron 70 / Ref: R Gifford	Prudhoe	Clarkson	Sandford	Sigurdsson	Cranson	Potter*	Beeston	Wallace	Sheron	Sturridge	Gleghorn	Dreyer
										Watson	Eaden	Shirtliff	Bullock	Archdeacon	De Zeeuw	Liddell	Redfearn	O'Connell	Payton	Sheridan	Hurst
33	A	SHEFFIELD UTD	9/3	14,468	17	D 53	0-0	0-0	Ref: R Furnandiz	Prudhoe	Clarkson	Sandford	Sigurdsson	Cranson	Potter^	Keen	Wallace	Sheron*	Sturridge	Gleghorn	Peschisolido/Dreyer
										Kelly	Short	Nilsen	Cowans	Hodgson	Ablett	White	Ward	Taylor	Hutchison^	Whitehouse	Walker
34	A	PORT VALE	12/3	16,737	22	L 53	0-1	0-1	Bogie 1 / Ref: E Lomas	Prudhoe	Clarkson	Sandford	Sigurdsson	Cranson	Wallace	Beeston^	Keen*	Sheron	Sturridge	Gleghorn	Potter/Gayle
										Musselwhite	Stokes	Bogie*	Griffiths	Aspin	Hill	McCarthy	Porter	Foyle	Glover^	Guppy	Walker/Naylor

Match reports

24 — The noon kick-off doesn't suit Stoke, neither does the rock-hard surface. Atrocious. City only have studded boots and slide all over the place. Barnsley are astonished to only score three after dominating. Stoke look for £500,000 from the tribunal after Ortygsson finally moves to Oldham.

25 — A moment of total embarrassment as Prudhoe slices a routine clearance into his own net from a seemingly impossible angle. It wrecks hopes of leaving Town's new McAlpine Stadium with a win thanks to Sheron's volley. Keen hits the bar. Jepson clears off the line. Quite unbelievable!

26 — Sturridge runs onto Wallace's pass to fire in. Martin O'Neill's Foxes change shape with a triple substitution and look ominous. Prudhoe denies Joachim who also puts a free header just over. Cranson dominates Iwan Roberts and goes close himself. The Ortygsson fee is set at just £180k.

27 — The poor pitch and high winds make for a forgettable match. Sturridge hits the woodwork twice. Gayle rounds the portly Steve Sutton but also hits the post. The midfield, on a rare off day, allows Mick Gooding to run 40 yards, waltz past three players and fire past the helpless Prudhoe.

28 — Carl Beeston returns from his self-imposed contractual exile and sets up Sheron to curl round Richard Wright. Negative Town level when Jamie Scowcroft heads a free-kick in unmarked. Gleghorn bags a rare header. Sheron controls Sturridge's flick on and lashes into the roof of the net.

29 — The biggest league gate thus far sees Stoke pinch the points in a tight affair. Sturridge smashes wide of Bart Griemink after cutting inside. Barry Fry's team force Prudhoe into a great double save. Potter skins Frain at will but Stoke cannot find a finish. Highest league position since 1985.

30 — A bright start tails off into a midfield slog in the Birkenhead mud. John King's Rovers are denied by Sigurdsson's last-ditch tackle on Aldridge. Sheron's goalbound header is palmed away by Danny Coyne. Pesch heads narrowly over. City settle for a draw rather than looking for the win.

31 — After a woeful first half Cranson buries a loose ball after Kevin Miller saves twice in a scramble. The first goal by a Stoke defender for a year! Watford wilt visibly. A great move ends with Gleghorn stepping over the ball for the onrushing Wallace to blast home. Play-offs here we come.

32 — Keen, returning from injury, nips in to poach a vital goal in a tight game. Danny Wilson's Tykes waste good chances. Liddell and Payton both at fault. Prudhoe palms O'Connell's shot over. Sturridge's cross is converted easily by Sheron. Level on points with third-placed Charlton now.

33 — An end-to-end game amazingly ends goalless. The tension shows as chances go begging at both ends. Sturridge is tripped when breaking clear. Keen works tirelessly. Whitehouse and Taylor waste great openings for Howard Kendall's United. Only two goals conceded in eight matches.

34 — Ian Bogie scores with a ferocious cross-shot after just 12 secs without a City player touching the ball. Shell-shocked Stoke battle back. Sheron hits both posts, the ball rebounds into Musselwhite's hands. Potter gees things up when he arrives but Vale withstand the onslaught to cling on.

35 — H HUDDERSFIELD 16/3 · Att 3,157 · 5/6 · D · 54 · HT 0-0 · FT 1-1
Prudhoe; Clarkson (*Jenkins*); Sandford (*Cowan*); Cranson (*Bullock*); Sigurdsson (*Sinnott*); Potter (*Gray*); Beeston (*Edwards*); Wallace (*Makel*); Sheron (*Booth*); Sturridge (*Dunn**); Gleghorn (*Thornley*); *Baldry*
Sturridge 66 / *Edwards 88* · Ref: K Lynch
Brian Horton's Terriers play neat football as the game starts at a furious pace. Stoke gain superiority. Wallace and Sturridge hit the post. Potter heads back a cross for Sturridge to bury and his corner hits the woodwork again. New signing Rob Edwards levels via the underside of the bar.

36 — A CHARLTON 23/3 · Att 2,770 · 5/4 · L · 54 · HT 1-0 · FT 1-2
Ammann; Clarkson (*Brown**); Sandford (*Sturges*); Cranson (*Mortimer*); Sigurdsson (*Rufus*); Potter* (*Whyte C*); Beeston (*Newton*); Wallace (*Leaburn*); Sheron^ (*Robinson*); Sturridge (*Grant**); Gleghorn (*Bowyer*); Keen/*Carruthers*
Sheron 41 / *Mortimer 83p, Whyte D 89* · Ref: A Butler
Stoke are in control after Sheron bravely heads Clarkson's chip past the onrushing Ammann. It is City's first goal away from the Vic in 1996. Gleghorn fires straight at the keeper. Charlton finish strongly. The penalty is for Clarkson's handball. Whyte heads in after Keen fails to clear.

37 — A DERBY 30/3 · Att 7,245 · 6/2 · L · 54 · HT 1-0 · FT 1-3
Hoult; Clarkson (*Wassall*); Sandford (*Powell C*); Cranson (*Powell D*); Keen (*Yates*); Sigurdsson (*Stimac^*); Potter* (*——*); Beeston (*Flynn*); Wallace (*Ward**); Sheron (*Willems*); Sturridge (*Gabbiadini*); Gleghorn (*Carsley*); Carruthers; Simpson/*Sturridge*
Sheron 22 / *Sturridge 53, 79, Powell D 58* · Ref: S Mathieson
Pesch is sold to Birmingham for £475,000 without Macari's knowledge on deadline day. A sell-out crowd see Sheron dive to head City ahead. Once again Stoke fail to hold on. Dean wins the battle of the Sturridge brothers scoring two after appearing as a half-time sub. Rams almost up.

38 — H WOLVES 1/4 · Att 6,361 · 6/11 · W · 57 · HT 2-0 · FT 2-0
Stowell; Clarkson (*Smith"*); Sandford (*Thompson*); Cranson (*Young*); Sigurdsson (*Venus^*); Potter* (*Richards*); Beeston* (*Corica*); Wallace (*Goodman*); Sheron (*Bull*); Sturridge (*Froggatt*); Gleghorn (*Osborn**); Keen/Dreyer/*Carruthers*; Rankine/Ferguson/*Atkins*
Sheron 3, Sturridge 58 · Ref: M Pierce
The biggest league gate so far sees Sheron delicately flick Gleghorn's drive past the keeper. Wallace fires wide before hitting the post. Sheron blazes the follow up over. Sturridge whips Potter's centre into the corner of the net after the ever-improving Sigurdsson weaves out of defence.

39 — H GRIMSBY 6/4 · Att 2,524 · 8/15 · L · 57 · HT 1-2 · FT 1-2
Crichton; Clarkson (*McDermott^*); Sandford (*Gallimore*); Cranson (*Smith*); Sigurdsson (*Handyside*); Potter (*Groves*); Beeston (*Flatts**); Wallace (*Shakespeare Woods*); Sheron; Sturridge* (*Mendonca^*); Gleghorn^ (*Childs*); Carruthers/*Beeston*; Southall/Fickling/*Forrester*
Sheron 35 / *Groves 47, Gallimore 55* · Ref: E Wolstenholme
City lead when Sheron's backheel dumbfounds Paul Crichton. Just 194 Grimsby fans witness a smash and grab win. Paul Groves sweeps home after a good move. Ex-Stokie Tony Gallimore fires in from 20 yards. City are well below par. The new ground is granted planning permission.

40 — A LUTON 9/4 · Att 7,589 · 7/23 · W · 60 · HT 2-1 · FT 2-1
Feuer; Clarkson (*Alexander*); Sandford (*Thomas*); Cranson (*Waddock*); Sigurdsson (*Johnson*); Potter (*Patterson*); Dreyer^; Beeston* (*Guenthchew*); Wallace (*Thorpe^*); Sheron* (*Oldfield^*); Sturridge (*Grant*); Gleghorn^ (*Oakes*); Keen/Potter/*Carruthers*; Taylor/*Tomlinson*
Sturridge 86, Sheron 90 / *Grant 45* · Ref: U Rennie
Justin Whittle makes a nervous start to his full debut. Kim Grant gives Lennie Lawrence's Hatters hope of beating the drop. Prudhoe produces three excellent saves as City hang on. Then Sturridge weaves into the box and pokes past Feuer and Sheron heads in a deep free-kick. Bedlam.

41 — H PORTSMOUTH 13/4 · Att 11,471 · 5/21 · W · 63 · HT 1-0 · FT 1-0
Knight; Clarkson (*Pethick !*); Sandford (*Awford*); Sigurdsson (*McLoughlin Thomson*); Potter (*Butters*); Beeston* (*Allen*); Wallace (*Durnin*); Sheron (*Burton*); Sturridge (*Hall*); Gleghorn (*Carter**); Devlin/*Igoe*
Wallace 7, Sheron 90 / *Butters 61* · Ref: M Bailey
Wallace follows up to score after Sheron causes havoc. Pethick is dismissed for swearing (20 mins) but Pompey fight hard. With Sigurdsson off for treatment Butters heads in unmarked. Sheron nicks it with a cross-shot. Cranson misses the rest of the season after having knee surgery.

42 — A CHARLTON 17/4 · Att 12,369 · 5/4 · W · 66 · HT 1-0 · FT 1-0
Petterson; Clarkson (*Jackson*); Sandford (*Stuart**); Sigurdsson (*Jones^*); Potter* (*Whyte C*); Devlin (*Balmer*); Wallace (*Newton*); Sheron (*Robinson*); Sturridge (*Allen*); Gleghorn (*Brown^*); Dreyer/Robson/Whyte D/*Nelson*
Sheron 29 · Ref: M Riley
Mike Sheron sets a club record of scoring in seven consecutive matches. He dispatches Sturridge's chip into the far corner of the net in front of an ecstatic Boothen End. Play-off certs Charlton are dreadful. 12 cautions in the last seven games means City will not win the fair play award.

43 — A SUNDERLAND 21/4 · Att 21,276 · 4/1 · D · 67 · HT 0-0 · FT 0-0
Prudhoe (*Chamberlain*); Clarkson (*Kubicki*); Sandford (*Scott**); Sigurdsson (*Bracewell Ball*); Potter* (*Melville*); Devlin (*Gray M*); Wallace (*Ord*); Sheron* (*Russell"*); Sturridge (*Howey*); Gleghorn (*Agnew^*); Carruthers/*Dreyer*; Hall/Alston/*Bridges*
Ref: G Singh
Stoke are party poopers as Peter Reid's team celebrate winning the Championship. Sigurdsson and Whittle are superb. Michael Bridges hits the post. Potter's dipping drive is tipped onto the bar by Alec Chamberlain. Devlin slices wide when well placed. Ex-Stokie Bracewell impresses.

44 — A MILLWALL 27/4 · Att 17,105 · 4/19 · W · 70 · HT 2-0 · FT 3-2
Keller; Clarkson (*Connor*); Sandford (*Thatcher*); Sigurdsson (*Newman*); Potter^ (*Van Blerk*); Devlin (*Stevens*); Wallace (*Weir*); Sheron* (*Makin*); Sturridge (*Rae*); Gleghorn (*Bowry^*); Carruthers/*Dreyer*; Savage/*Neill*
Sheron 28, Sturridge 32, 70p / *Rae 80p, 89* · Ref: R Harris
City sport a natty duo-tone blue kit. Sheron cracks in a fierce shot on the run. Sturridge latches onto a long punt to blast home. His penalty, for Thatcher's foul, is City's first of the season. Millwall look doomed to the drop despite Alex Rae's late brace. The pen is for Sigurdsson's foul.

45 — A OLDHAM 30/4 · Att 17,271 · 4/19 · L · 70 · HT 0-2 · FT 0-1
Hallworth; Clarkson (*Makin*); Sandford (*Serrant*); Sigurdsson (*Fleming*); Potter (*Graham*); Devlin (*Rickers*); Wallace (*Richardson Beckford*); Sheron (*Orlygsson*); Sturridge (*Creaney*); Gleghorn (*Redmond*); Carruthers
Richardson 27p, Creaney 72 · Ref: K Leach
A win ensures a play-off berth but a huge support leaves disappointed as City fail to perform. The inexperienced Whittle trips Beckford for the penalty. Ex-Stokie Orlygsson runs midfield. Creaney flicks in Richardson's cross. Gleghorn hits the bar. Seven without a goal against Oldham.

46 — H SOUTHEND 5/5 · Att 14,897 · 4/14 · W · 73 · HT 1-0 · FT 1-0
Royce; Clarkson (*Hails*); Sandford (*Stinson*); Sigurdsson (*McNally*); Potter* (*Badley*); Devlin (*Marsh*); Wallace (*Byrne"*); Sheron (*Dublin*); Sturridge (*Rammell**); Gleghorn (*Tilson*); Dreyer/Lapper/*Roge*
Sheron 12 · Ref: M Barry
Tentative City are relieved to get the early clinching goal. Sheron's unstoppable shot finds the roof of the net. Cue 'Delilah'. Prudhoe saves in a one-on-one as he sees the end of season pitch invasion is about to start early. Phew!

Average — Home 12,279 · Away 12,515

ENDSLEIGH DIVISION 1 (CUP-TIES) Manager: Lou Macari SEASON 1995-96

Play-offs

	Att	F-A	H-T	Scorers, Times, and Referees	1	2	3	4	5	6	7	8	9	10	11	subs used
SF A LEICESTER 12/5	20,325	D 0-0	0-0	Ref: W Burns	Prudhoe *Poole*	Clarkson *Grayson*	Sandford *Whitlow*	Sigurdsson *Watts*	Whittle *Walsh*	Potter *Izzet*	Devlin *Lennon*	Wallace *Taylor*	Sheron *Claridge*	Sturridge *Robins**	Gleghorn *Heskey*	*Parker*

Stoke pummel Martin O'Neill's team but can't find the back of the net. Sturridge picks up Steve Claridge's back-pass but Poole saves with his legs. Poole's brilliant flying save denies Potter point blank. Clarkson heads off the line from Walsh but the Foxes are poor. Roll on Wembley!

	Att	F-A	H-T	Scorers, Times, and Referees	1	2	3	4	5	6	7	8	9	10	11	subs used
SF H LEICESTER 15/5	21,037	L 0-1	0-0	Parker 46 / Ref: J Singh / (Stoke lose 0-1 on aggregate)	Prudhoe *Poole*	Clarkson *Grayson*	Sandford *Whitlow*	Sigurdsson *Watts*	Whittle *Walsh*	Potter* *Izzet*	Devlin *Lennon*	Wallace *Taylor*	Sheron *Claridge*	Sturridge *Parker*	Gleghorn *Heskey*	Carruthers *Heskey*

Leicester gradually get the better of an out-of-sorts Stoke who fail to deal with the fans' expectations. Emile Heskey is superb up front, holding off Whittle as Leicester build moves around him. One moment of magic wins it: Parker's superb left-foot volley at the far post. Totally gutting.

Coca-Cola Cup

	Att	F-A	H-T	P	Scorers, Times, and Referees	1	2	3	4	5	6	7	8	9	10	11	subs used
2:1 H CHELSEA 20/9	15,574	D 0-0	0-0	P:9	Ref: T West	Prudhoe *Kharine*	Clarkson *Clarke*	Sandford *Minto*	Sigurdsson *Gullit*	Overson *Johnsen*	Potter *Sinclair*	Keen *Newton*	Wallace *Hughes*	Peschisolido *Spencer**	Carruthers *Burley*	Gleghorn *Wise*	*Furlong*

A stunning performance to hold Glenn Hoddle's all-star team. Ruud Gullit's assured sweeping keeps Chelsea in it. Carruthers wastes two great chances. Overson heads against the post. The start of something good? After the match Macari asks to have out-of-favour Mark Stein on loan.

	Att	F-A	H-T	P	Scorers, Times, and Referees	1	2	3	4	5	6	7	8	9	10	11	subs used
2:2 A CHELSEA 4/10	16,272	W 1-0	0-0	P:10	Peschisolido 75 / Ref: K Cooper / (Stoke win 1-0 on aggregate)	Prudhoe *Kharine*	Clarkson *Burley*	Sandford *Barness*	Sigurdsson *Gullit*	Overson *Johnsen*	Potter *Sinclair*	Keen *Spackman**	Wallace *Hughes*	Peschisolido *Furlong*	Carruthers *Peacock**	Gleghorn *Wise*	*Stein/Lee*

A stupendous night is crowned by Pesch's opportunist strike. Delilah resounds around Stamford Bridge as City use up a season's worth of luck against profligate Blues. Sandford heads off the line. Gullit, Furlong and Stein all miss sitters: Stein in the last minute from six yards. Brilliant.

	Att	F-A	H-T	P	Scorers, Times, and Referees	1	2	3	4	5	6	7	8	9	10	11	subs used
3 H NEWCASTLE 25/10	23,000	L 0-4	0-2	P:1	Beardsley 29, 39, Ferdinand 52, [Peacock 73] / Ref: G Ashby	Prudhoe *Hislop*	Clarkson! *Barton*	Sandford *Elliott*	Sigurdsson *Clark*	Overson *Peacock*	Potter* *Howey*^	Keen *Lee**	Wallace *Beardsley*	Peschisolido *Ferdinand*	Carruthers *Ginola*	Gleghorn *Gillespie*	Cranson *Watson/Albert*

A sell-out crowd see a superb performance by Kevin Keegan's Toon. Beardsley's brace puts the game out of reach. Pesch and Carruthers have good chances saved by £1.5m Hislop. Clarkson is sent off (45) for two fouls on the theatrical Ginola. Ferdinand and Peacock net from close in.

FA Cup

	Att	F-A	H-T	P	Scorers, Times, and Referees	1	2	3	4	5	6	7	8	9	10	11	subs used
3 H NOTT'M FOREST 6/1	17,947	D 1-1	1-0	P:7	Sturridge 27 / Pearce 82 / Ref: D Gallagher	Prudhoe *Crossley*	Clarkson *Lyttle*	Sandford *Pearce*	Sigurdsson *Cooper*	Dreyer *Chettle*	Potter *Stone*	Keen *Bart-Williams*	Wallace *Gemmill*	Sturridge *Campbell*	Carruthers *Roy**	Gleghorn *Woan*	*Lee*

A reshuffled City play Forest off the park. Sturridge finishes well but Gleghorn has a header cleared off the line. Potter hits the upright and the ball rebounds to Crossley. Sturridge's shot hits Dreyer with the keeper beaten. Jason Lee miskicks and Pearce buries at the far post. Travesty.

	Att	F-A	H-T	P	Scorers, Times, and Referees	1	2	3	4	5	6	7	8	9	10	11	subs used
3R A NOTT'M FOREST 17/1	17,372	L 0-2	0-1	P:6	Campbell 16, Pearce 55p / Ref: D Gallagher	Prudhoe *Crossley*	Clarkson *Lyttle*	Sandford *Pearce*	Sigurdsson *Cooper*	Cranson *Chettle*	Potter *Stone*	Keen *Bart-Williams*	Wallace *Gemmill*	Sturridge *Campbell**	Peschisolido* *Roy*^	Gleghorn *Woan*	Gayle *Lee/Phillips*

Forest are in control from the start against the strangely subdued Potters. Campbell turns adroitly to blast past Prudhoe. Potter gives Des Lyttle the runaround but Pesch fails to convert any of his crosses. Sandford fells Stone for the penalty. Lee misses an open goal. Forest meet Oxford.

League Table 1996–97

	P	W	D	L	F	A	W	D	L	F	A	Pts
		Home					**Away**					
1 Sunderland	46	13	8	2	32	10	9	9	5	27	23	83
2 Derby	46	14	8	1	48	22	9	8	8	23	29	79
3 Crys Palace	46	9	9	5	34	22	9	6	8	33	26	75
4 STOKE	46	13	6	4	32	15	7	7	9	28	34	73
5 Leicester *	46	9	7	7	32	29	10	7	6	34	31	71
6 Charlton	46	8	11	4	28	23	9	5	9	29	22	71
7 Ipswich	46	13	5	5	45	30	6	7	10	34	39	69
8 Huddersfield	46	14	4	5	42	23	3	8	12	19	35	63
9 Sheffield Utd	46	9	7	7	29	25	7	7	9	28	29	62
10 Barnsley	46	9	10	4	34	28	5	8	10	26	38	60
11 West Brom	46	11	5	7	34	28	5	7	11	26	39	60
12 Port Vale	46	10	5	8	30	29	5	10	8	29	37	60
13 Tranmere	46	9	9	5	42	29	4	6	13	22	31	59
14 Southend	46	11	8	4	30	22	4	6	13	22	39	59
15 Birmingham	46	11	7	5	37	23	4	6	13	24	41	58
16 Norwich	46	11	7	9	26	24	7	6	10	33	31	57
17 Grimsby	46	8	10	5	27	25	6	4	13	28	44	56
18 Oldham	46	10	7	6	33	20	4	7	12	21	30	56
19 Reading	46	8	7	8	28	30	5	10	8	26	33	56
20 Wolves	46	8	9	6	34	28	5	7	11	22	34	55
21 Portsmouth	46	8	6	9	34	32	5	7	11	27	37	52
22 Millwall	46	7	6	10	23	28	6	7	10	20	35	52
23 Watford	46	7	8	8	40	33	3	10	10	22	37	48
24 Luton	46	7	6	10	30	34	4	6	13	10	30	45
	1104	233	177	142	804	613	142	177	233	613	804	1479

* promoted after play-offs

Odds & ends

- **Double wins:** (6) Leicester, Luton, Millwall, Southend, West Brom, Wolves.
- **Double losses:** (3) Grimsby, Oldham, Port Vale.
- **Won from behind:** (2) Luton (a), Southend (a).
- **Lost from in front:** (3) Charlton (a), Derby (a), Grimsby (h).
- **High spots:** Making the play-offs.
- The Sheron/Sturridge partnership.
- Simon Sturridge's hat-trick at Roots Hall.
- Beating Ruud Gullit's Chelsea at Stamford Bridge in the Coca-Cola Cup.
- Outplaying Nottingham Forest at home in the FA Cup.
- The doubling of attendances over the course of the season.
- **Low spots:** Losing to Leicester after having the best of the first leg of the play-offs.
- Not winning the home FA Cup-tie with Forest.
- Losing both Potteries derbies.
- Saying goodbye to Paul Peschisolido.
- Being thrashed by Newcastle in the Coca-Cola Cup.
- **Player of the Year:** Ray Wallace and Mark Prudhoe.
- **Ever-presents:** (3) Gleghorn, Sandford, Sigurdsson.
- **Hat-tricks:** (1) Simon Sturridge.
- **Leading scorer:** (15) Mike Sheron.

Appearances & Goals

Player	Lge	Sub	LC	Sub	FAC	Sub	Lge	LC	FAC	Tot
	Appearances						**Goals**			
Beeston, Carl	13	3								
Brightwell, David		1								
Carruthers, Martin	10	14	3		1		3			3
Clarkson, Ian	43		3		2					
Cranson, Ian	23	1		1	1		1			1
Devlin, Mark	5	5								
Dreyer, John	4	15				1				
Gayle, John	5	5					3			3
Gleghorn, Nigel	46		3		2		3			3
Keen, Kevin	27	6	2		2		3			3
Muggleton, Carl	6		3							
Orlygsson, Toddy	6	1			1					
Overson, Vince	18		3		2					
Peschisolido, Paul	20	6	3		1		6	1		7
Potter, Graham	38	3	3		2		1			1
Prudhoe, Mark	39		3		2					
Sandford, Lee	46		3		2					
Scott, Keith	6	1								
Sheron, Mike	23	5	3				15			15
Sigurdsson, Larus	46		3		2					
Sinclair, Ronnie	1									
Sturridge, Simon	30	11	1		2		13		1	14
Wallace, Ray	44		3		2		6			6
Whittle, Justin	7	1								
24 Players used	506	78	33	1	22	1	60	1	1	62

NATIONWIDE DIVISION 1

Manager: Lou Macari

SEASON 1996-97

Column headings: No | Date | Att | Pos | Pt | F-A | H-T | Scorers, Times, and Referees | 1 | 2 | 3 | 4 | 5 | 6 | 7 | 8 | 9 | 10 | 11 | subs used

---

1 — A OLDHAM (17/8)
Att 8,021 · W 2-1 · Pt 3 · H-T 2-0
Scorers: Sheron 27, 43; Redmond 76. Ref: U Rennie

	1	2	3	4	5	6	7	8	9	10	11	subs used
Stoke	Prudhoe*	Pickering	Dreyer	Sigurdsson	Cranson	Forsyth	Worthing'n	Wallace	Gayle	Sheron	Beeston	Devlin^/Keen
Oldham	Hallworth	Halle	Serrant	Fleming	Graham	Redmond	Ohlgsson*	Richardson	McCarthy	Barlow^	Rickers	Beresford/Morrow

Sheron pokes in a long punt and nets when Gayle's shot is parried. Latics have goals ruled out for two fouls on Prudhoe. He is injured – Cranson takes over (31 mins). In the sweltering heat Cranson makes two good saves. Redmond buries a short free-kick. First win at Oldham for 9 years.

---

2 — H MANCHESTER C (24/8)
Att 21,116 · Pos 5 (opp 15) · W 2-1 · Pt 6 · H-T 2-0
Scorers: Forsyth 27, Sheron 32; Rosler 58. Ref: I Cruikshanks

	1	2	3	4	5	6	7	8	9	10	11	subs used
Stoke	Mugleton	Pickering	Dreyer	Sigurdsson	Cranson	Forsyth	Worthington	Wallace	Sturridge*	Sheron*	Beeston	Gayle/Macari
Man C	Immel	Brightwell	Kernaghan	Lomas	Symons	Brown*	Summerbee	Clough	Kawalashvili^	Kinkladze	Rosler	Phillips/Dickov

Stoke open the last ever season at the Vic with a good win over the promotion favourites. Sturridge's effort is only parried and Forsyth taps in. Sheron outpaces Kit Symons to score. Rosler picks up a loose ball to pull one back, but Man C are awful. Alan Ball resigns as their manager.

---

3 — H BRADFORD C (28/8)
Att 11,918 · Pos 2 (opp 12) · W 1-0 · Pt 9 · H-T 0-0
Scorer: Sheron 90p. Ref: E Lomas

	1	2	3	4	5	6	7	8	9	10	11	subs used
Stoke	Mugleton	Pickering	Dreyer	Sigurdsson	Cranson	Forsyth	Sturridge*	Wallace	Gayle	Sheron	Beeston	Keen
Bradford	Roberts	Liburd	Mitchell	Cowans	Mohan	Sas	Hamilton	Duxbury	Shutt	Stalard	Kiwomya	

City attack from the off. Sheron fires just wide. The much-improved Gayle holds the ball up well. He loops a header just over. Chris Kamara's Bantams threaten via the dangerous Andy Kiwomya. Sheron is tripped by Richard Liburd in the 3rd minute of injury-time and bangs in the pen.

---

4 — A READING (31/8)
Att 8,414 · Pos 1 (opp 15) · D 2-2 · Pt 10 · H-T 1-1
Scorers: Sheron 25, Forsyth 76; Morley 7p, Holsgrove 79. Ref: A Butler

	1	2	3	4	5	6	7	8	9	10	11	subs used
Stoke	Mugleton	Pickering	Dreyer	Sigurdsson	Cranson	Forsyth	Gayle^	Wallace	Sturridge	Sheron	Beeston*	Keen/Da Costa
Reading	Bibbo	Booty	Bodin	Holsgrove	Hopkins	Wdowczyk	Parkinson*	Williams	Morley	Nogan^	Gooding	Lovell/Gilkes

Morley's penalty goes in via a post after Cranson trips Booty. Sheron curls in a superb free-kick. On-loan Hugo Da Costa (Benfica) appears as Macari opts for five at the back. Forsyth cracks in from 20 yards. Paul Holsgrove blazes a volley home. City are top as Bolton have yet to play.

---

5 — H CRYSTAL PALACE (7/9)
Att 13,540 · Pos 3 (opp 12) · D 2-2 · Pt 11 · H-T 2-2
Scorers: Sheron 20, Dreyer 32; Hopkin 13, Freedman 22. Ref: K Lynch

	1	2	3	4	5	6	7	8	9	10	11	subs used
Stoke	Mugleton	Pickering	Dreyer	Sigurdsson	Cranson	Forsyth	Worthington	Wallace	Sturridge*	Sheron	Beeston	Gayle
Palace	Day	Edworthy	Muscat	Roberts	Tuttle	Hopkin	Boxall	Houghton	Freedman*	Dyer	Veart	Ndah/Andersen

Dave Bassett's Eagles take the game to Stoke. Hopkin scores from 20 yards. Sheron beats Day when clean through. Freedman turns to fire past Muggers. Sturridge is fouled, but Sheron's penalty hits the post (26 mins). Dreyer nods in Pickering's centre. Macari is Manager of the Month.

---

6 — A BARNSLEY (10/9)
Att 11,696 · Pos 5 (opp 1) · L 0-3 · Pt 11 · H-T 0-1
Scorers: Davis 17, Thompson 88, Liddell 90. Ref: R Pearson

	1	2	3	4	5	6	7	8	9	10	11	subs used
Stoke	Mugleton	Pickering	Dreyer	Sigurdsson	Cranson	Forsyth	Worthing'n^	Wallace	Sturridge*	Sheron	Beeston	Gayle/Macari
Barnsley	Watson	Eaden	Appleby	Sheridan*	Davis	De Zeeuw	Marcelle	Redfearn	Wilkinson^	Liddell	Thompson	Bosancic/Regis

Danny Wilson's Tykes pull Stoke all over the park. Steve Davis heads in one of numerous corners. The remorseless pressure tells as City snap. Neil Thompson thumps home a great 30-yarder and Andy Liddell finishes with a flourish. Barnsley retain the only 100% record in the division.

---

7 — A BIRMINGHAM (14/9)
Att 18,612 · Pos 7 (opp 15) · L 1-3 · Pt 11 · H-T 0-2
Scorer: Forsyth 66; Furlong 2, 65, Legg 32. Ref: E Wolstenholme

	1	2	3	4	5	6	7	8	9	10	11	subs used
Stoke	Mugleton	Pickering	Dreyer	Sigurdsson	Da Costa	Forsyth	Worthing'n*	Wallace	Sturridge	Sheron	Beeston^	Keen/Kavanagh
Birmingham	Bennett	Poole	Ablett	Bruce	Breen	Holland	Bowen^	Newell*	Furlong	Legg	Horne	Devlin/Castle/Donowa

Lack of depth in the squad is exposed. Da Costa starts but will return to Portugal. Muggers' clearance is blocked and Furlong mops up. Players are left unmarked for the other goals. Forsyth scores against his old club. Graham Kavanagh, loaned by Middlesbro', replaces the hurt Beeston.

---

8 — H HUDDERSFIELD (22/9)
Att 9,147 · Pos 4 (opp 14) · W 3-2 · Pt 14 · H-T 1-2
Scorers: Gayle 41, Sheron 77, 85; Worthington 7 (og), Stewart 36. Ref: C Wilkes

	1	2	3	4	5	6	7	8	9	10	11	subs used
Stoke	Mugleton	Pickering	Worthington	Sigurdsson	Dreyer	Devlin*	McMahon	Wallace	Gayle	Sheron	Beeston^	Keen
Huddersfield	Francis	Jenkins	Cowan	Bullock	Sinnott*	Gray	Makel	Burnett	Stewart	Payton	Lawson^	Collins/Edwards/Reid

An amazing comeback tells when Gayle turns to fire in. Worthington nets a dreadful own-goal before Stewart scores with Town's first shot on goal. Incessant pressure tells when Gayle turns to fire in. Sheron scores two superb goals to snatch victory. Gerry McMahon (Spurs) signs for £250k.

---

9 — A BOLTON (28/9)
Att 16,195 · Pos 6 (opp 1) · D 1-1 · Pt 15 · H-T 0-1
Scorers: Kavanagh 90; Blake 42. Ref: F Stretton

	1	2	3	4	5	6	7	8	9	10	11	subs used
Stoke	Mugleton	Pickering	Worthington	Sigurdsson	Dreyer	Devlin^	Wallace	Gayle"	Sheron	Kavanagh		Keen/McMahon
Bolton	Branagan	Bergsson	Phillips	Frandsen	Taggart	Fairclough	Johansen^	Sellars*	Blake	McGinlay	Thompson	Lee/Todd/Taylor

Leaders Bolton dominate. Muggers saves a Frandsen free-kick. Fairclough blasts wide. Sigurdsson's weak back-pass to score. Colin Todd's Trotters pile on the pressure but Kavanagh grabs a point, put in by Forsyth. Macari is linked with the vacancy at Man City.

---

10 — A PORT VALE (13/10)
Att 14,396 · Pos 8 (opp 17) · D 1-1 · Pt 16 · H-T 0-0
Scorer: Keen 65; Mills 90. Ref: K Leach

	1	2	3	4	5	6	7	8	9	10	11	subs used
Stoke	Mugleton	Pickering	Worthington	Sigurdsson	Dreyer	Forsyth	Devlin^	Wallace	McMahon^	Sheron*	Kavanagh	Keen/Macari/Whittle
Port Vale	V Heusden	Hill*	Tankard	Porter	Griffiths	Aspin^	McCarthy	Bogie^	Talbot	Naylor	Guppy	Foyle/Mills/Glover

Kavanagh's £250,000 fee is confirmed by Boro. Sheron signs for a further two years. He wants premiership football but won't find it with City if they concede more late strikes. Lee Mills heads home a cross in the fifth minute of injury-time after Keen loops a great over Van Heusden.

---

11 — A WEST BROM (16/10)
Att 16,501 · Pos 7 (opp 14) · W 2-0 · Pt 19 · H-T 1-0
Scorer: Wallace 33, Forsyth 72. Ref: D Allison

	1	2	3	4	5	6	7	8	9	10	11	subs used
Stoke	Mugleton	Pickering	Worthington	Sigurdsson	Dreyer	Forsyth	Devlin^	Wallace	Gayle"	Sheron^	Kavanagh	Keen/Macari/Whittle
West Brom	Crichton	Holmes*	Nicholson	Sneekes	Mardon	Burgess	Hamilton	Gilbert^	Ashcroft	Hunt	Groves	Taylor/Peschisolido

Albion's methodical play is easily snuffed out by Sigurdsson and Dreyer. Wallace is superb in midfield. He starts and ends a move, converting Gayle's cross. Forsyth relieves the mounting pressure with a great strike off the bar. Ten wins and a draw in the last eleven against the Baggies.

No.		Opponent	Date	Pos	Res		Pts	Att	HT	FT
12	H	SHEFFIELD UTD	19/10	10	L	6	19	15,531	0-3	**0-4**
13	H	PORTSMOUTH	26/10	7	W	20	22	16,259	0-1	**3-1**
14	A	OXFORD	29/10	9	L	13	22	8,301	0-2	**1-4**
15	A	QP RANGERS	2/11	9	D	11	23	13,354	1-1	**1-0**
16	A	GRIMSBY	16/11	10	D	24	24	5,601	1-1	**1-1**
17	A	SOUTHEND	23/11	12	L	17	24	12,221	0-1	**1-2**
18	A	PORTSMOUTH	30/11	18	L	11	24	7,249	0-1	**0-1**
19	H	CHARLTON	4/12	15	W	12	27	7,556	0-0	**1-0**
20	H	TRANMERE	7/12	10	W	6	30	8,931	1-0	**2-0**
21	H	SWINDON	14/12	7	W	13	33	13,002	1-0	**2-0**
22	A	IPSWICH	21/12	8	D	14	34	12,159	1-1	**1-1**
23	H	BARNSLEY	26/12	7	W	3	37	18,125	0-0	**1-0**

---

12 — SHEFFIELD UTD (H), 19/10
City: Muggleton, Pickering, Whittle, Sigurdsson, Dreyer^, Forsyth, Holdsworth, Devlin^, Gayle*, Wallace, Sheron*, Kavanagh, Keen/McMahon
Opp: Kelly, Ward, Sandford, Hutchison^, Vonk, White, Patterson, Katchuro*, Whitehouse, Taylor/Hawes
Scorers: Vonk 8, 19, Walker 16, Taylor 77
Ref: P Rejer
Three defensive changes allow United to score unmarked headers from their first three corners. City's discipline is in tatters. Muggers fumbles the ball for the third. Sheron has a goal ruled out for offside but Taylor scores on the turn. Macari is linked to Anderlecht full-back Isaac Asare.

13 — PORTSMOUTH (H), 26/10
City: Muggleton, Devlin, Worthington, Sigurdsson, Whittle, Forsyth, McMahon, Wallace^, Keen*, Sheron*, Kavanagh, Macari/Griffin/Mackenzie
Opp: Flahavan, Russell", McLoughlin, Perrett, Awford, Carter*, Simpson!, Durnin, Hall/Igoe/Thomson
Scorers: McMahon 59, 75, Sheron 71, Bradbury 37
Ref: W Burns
Stoke play well, but Pompey net from a corner. The tables are turned when Fitzroy Simpson is deservedly sent off (53 mins). City take charge. McMahon's second is a gem. Sheron scores via a deflection. Mackenzie and Griffin come on despite playing for the A-team four hours earlier.

14 — OXFORD (A), 29/10
City: Muggleton, Devlin, Worthington^r'n, Sigurdsson, Whittle, Forsyth, McMahon, Wallace, Keen^, Sheron, Kavanagh, Macari/Griffin
Opp: Whitehead, Robinson, Ford M, Smith, Elliott, Purse, Angel", Gray, Aldridge^, Jemson, Beauchamp, Rush/Moody
Scorers: Gray 5, Angel 27, Jemson 78, Aldridge 80
Ref: M Bailey
City's pedestrian full-backs are exposed by Denis Smith's use of nippy wingers. Oxford score their first goals in 592 minutes. Joey Beauchamp crosses for Gray and Angel to finish. Sheron turns in a flash to notch a beauty but City capitulate. The unhappy Dreyer is to move to Bradford.

15 — QP RANGERS (A), 2/11
City: Muggleton, Pickering, Worthington^r'n, Sigurdsson, Whittle, Forsyth, McMahon, Wallace, Keen^, Sheron, Kavanagh, Devlin/Griffin
Opp: Sommer, Graham, Brevett, Barker, McDonald, Ready, Brazier*, Murray, Dichio, Slade, Sinclair, Impey
Scorers: Kavanagh 4, Sinclair 65
Ref: A D'Urso
City are poor but Kavanagh waltzes through a stunned Rangers' back four to score joyously. Backs to the wall as Stewart Houston's men pour forward. Finally Trevor Sinclair's overhead kick beats Muggers. A battling point. Sturridge's knee operation will keep him out for five months.

16 — GRIMSBY (A), 16/11
City: Muggleton, Pickering, Devlin, Sigurdsson, Whittle, Forsyth, McMahon^, Wallace, Keen*, Sheron, Kavanagh, Macari/Griffin/Carruthers
Opp: Pearcey, Jobling*, Gallimore, Smith, Rodger, Widdrington, Childs^, Livingstone, Mendonca, Black, Shakespeare, Fickling/Forrester
Scorers: Forsyth 30, Mendonca 20p
Ref: G Pooley
Forsyth makes amends for tripping Childs for the penalty by firing a fine low shot past Jason Pearcey. Kenny Swain is Town's second manager in as many games. Muggers pulls off a great double save. Loanee Mirko Taccola returns to Napoli after the Italians refuse to clear him to play.

17 — SOUTHEND (A), 23/11
City: Prudhoe, Pickering*, Devlin", Sigurdsson, Whittle, Forsyth, McMahon^, Wallace, Keen^, Stein, Sheron, Kavanagh, Macari/McMahon/Griffin
Opp: Royce, Harris, Dublin, McNally, Lapper*, Nielsen, Gridelet, Rammell, Hails*, Williams, Tilson, Stimson/Byrne"/Boere
Scorers: Forsyth 52, Williams 37, Sigurdsson 51 (og)
Ref: A Leake
Ian Cranson announces his retirement through injury and is given a standing ovation before kick-off. How Stoke miss him as Ronnie Whelan's Southend grab a goal on the break. Then Sigurdsson slices past Prudhoe. On-loan Mark Stein wastes a one-on-one. Forsyth nets from 12 yards.

18 — PORTSMOUTH (A), 30/11
City: Prudhoe, Pickering", Devlin", Sigurdsson, Whittle, Forsyth, Griffin, Wallace, Stein*, McMahon*, Kavanagh, Gayle/Macari/Stokoe
Opp: Flahavan, Whitbread, McLoughlin, Perrett, Igoe, Carter*, Simpson, Durnin, Turner, Hall
Scorers: Turner 4
Ref: C Wilkes
Stoke are even worse than dreadful Pompey. Without Sheron, whose wife has given birth, Stoke fail to score away from home for the first time in 10 games. Andy Turner heads in Carter's corner. Dreyer's fee is set at a measly £25k. Carruthers joins Posh. A tribunal to decide the fee too.

19 — CHARLTON (H), 4/12
City: Prudhoe, Pickering, Griffin, Sigurdsson, Whittle, Forsyth, McMahon, Wallace, Stein*, Sheron, Kavanagh^, Macari/Mackenzie
Opp: Salmon, Poole, Barness, O'Connell, Rufus, Chapple, Newton*, Leaburn, Robinson*, Whyte, Kinsella, Lisbie/Robson
Scorers: Sheron 49
Ref: R Poulain
Both sides revert to route one football. The loudest cheer arrives when Prudhoe bowls the ball out instead of kicking. Sheron celebrates his first child by burying the rebound when Stein's effort is parried. Stein then blazes over. A lucky win in front of the lowest league crowd since 1991.

20 — TRANMERE (H), 7/12
City: Prudhoe, Pickering, Griffin, Sigurdsson, Whittle, Forsyth^, McMahon, Wallace, Stein, Sheron, Kavanagh^, Mackenzie/Keen
Opp: Nixon, Stevens, Irons", Higgins, Teale, O'Brien, Brannan, Aldridge, Thomas, Nevin^, Cook, Morrissey/Jones
Scorers: Sheron 27, Higgins 82 (og)
Ref: R Harris
Sheron outshines the prolific John Aldridge. He stabs home to finish a good right-wing move. Young Andy Griffin impresses at left-back. Stein and Sheron begin to combine well up front. Sheron squares after rounding Eric Nixon and Dave Higgins runs the ball into his own net. Bizarre.

21 — SWINDON (H), 14/12
City: Prudhoe, Pickering, Griffin, Sigurdsson, Whittle, Forsyth, McMahon, Wallace, Devlin*, Stein*, Sheron, Kavanagh, Mackenzie
Opp: Digby, Kerslake, Elkins, O'Sullivan", Robinson, Darras*, Culverhouse, Watson, Cowe, Allison, Collins/Smith/McMahon
Scorers: Stein 44, 64
Ref: A Kaye
Steve McMahon's under-strength Swindon struggle. Fraser Digby's clearance hits Stein but he recovers to save. Sigurdsson's overhead kick is touched over. Stein nets two classic goals as he rediscovers his sharpness in front of goal. Prudhoe pulls off a superb stop from Wayne Allison.

22 — IPSWICH (A), 21/12
City: Prudhoe, Pickering, Griffin, Sigurdsson, Whittle, Forsyth, McMahon, Wallace, Stein*, Sheron, Kavanagh^, Macari/Mackenzie
Opp: Wright, Stockwell*, Taricco, Cundy, Sedgley, Williams, Uhlenbeek, Sonner, Naylor", Scowcroft, Mason, Tanner/Jean
Scorers: Sheron 23, Mason 45
Ref: P Taylor
City start on top. Sheron volleys a brilliant goal from the angle of the penalty box into the far top corner. George Burley's men swarm forward and after a scramble Paul Mason nets. Stein blazes over from two yards after McMahon's mazy run. Wright pulls off a great save from Sheron.

23 — BARNSLEY (H), 26/12
City: Prudhoe, Pickering, Griffin, Sigurdsson, Whittle, Forsyth^, McMahon, Wallace, Devlin^, Stein, Sheron, Kavanagh, Devlin
Opp: Watson, Eaden, Appleby, Bosancic", Davis, De Zeeuw, Hendrie, Jones", Marcelle*, Wilkinson, Sheridan!, Liddell/Bullock/Moses
Scorers: Sheron 72
Ref: T Heilbron
A frenetic game sees Prudhoe tip over Marcelle's effort. Wallace rampages forward at will. Sheridan loses it and walks for elbowing Kavanagh in front of the referee (52 mins). Sheron belts an angled drive past Watson. Kav hits the bar. Pickering clears off the line with Prudhoe beaten.

NATIONWIDE DIVISION 1 — Manager: Lou Macari — SEASON 1996-97

No	Date	Opponent	Att	Pos	Pt	Res	F-A	H-T	Scorers, Times, and Referees	1	2	3	4	5	6	7	8	9	10	11	subs used
24	A 1/1	HUDDERSFIELD	12,019	9 12	37	L	1-2	1-1	Stein 18 / Makel 6, Edwards 63 / Ref: N Barry	Prudhoe / Norman	Pickering* / Jenkins	Griffin / Cowan	Sigurdsson / Bullock	Whittle / Sinnott*	Forsyth / Heary	McMahon / Makel	Wallace / Crosby	Stein / Lawson	Sheron" / Payton	Kavanagh^ / Edwards	Devlin/Macari/Stokoe / Dyson
25	H 10/1	BIRMINGHAM	10,049	7 15	40	W	1-0	1-0	Wallace 18 / Ref: R Furnandiz	Prudhoe / Bennett	Pickering* / Brown	Griffin / Grainger	Sigurdsson / Bruce	Whittle / Johnson	Forsyth / O'Connor	McMahon / Devlin	Wallace / Tait	Stein / Legg*	Sheron / Horne	Kavanagh / Bowen^	Furlong/Bass
26	A 18/1	CHARLTON	9,901	5 16	43	W	2-1	2-0	Sheron 42, 43 / Barness 49 / Ref: D Orr	Prudhoe / Petterson	Pickering / Brown^	Griffin / Barness	Sigurdsson / O'Connell	Whittle / Rufus	Forsyth / Chapple	McMahon / Newton"	Wallace / Leaburn	Stein / Robson	Sheron / Whyte^	Kavanagh / Kinsella	Macari / Jones/Robinson/Lisbie
27	H 22/1	NORWICH	10,179	7 5	43	L	1-2	1-2	Stein 14 / O'Neill 4, Eadie 11 / Ref: M Bailey	Prudhoe / Gunn	Pickering^ / Newman	Griffin / Jackson	Sigurdsson / Eadie	Whittle / Scott	Forsyth* / Kevin Sutch	McMahon / Adams	Wallace / Crook^	Stein / Rocastle	Sheron / Carey	Kavanagh / O'Neill*	Macari/Mackenzie / Scott Keith/Ottosson
28	H 29/1	BOLTON	15,645	7 1	43	L	1-2	0-1	Macari 84 / Pollock 28, McGinlay 54 / Ref: I Cruikshanks	Muggleton / Ward	Pickering* / Bergsson	Griffin / Small	Sigurdsson / Pollock	Whittle / Taggart	Forsyth / Fairclough	McMahon / Frandsen	Wallace / Sellars	Mackenzie / Blake !	Sheron / McGinlay	Kavanagh / Thompson	Macari
29	A 1/4	WOLVES	27,408	9 2	43	L	0-2	0-1	Bull 16, 55 / Ref: R Poulain	Muggleton / Stowell	Pickering* / Thompson	Griffin / Froggatt	Sigurdsson / Atkins	Whittle / Williams	Forsyth / Curle	McMahon / Corica	Wallace / Emblem	Macari / Bull	Sheron / Goodman*	Kavanagh / Osborn	Devlin / Roberts
30	H 7/2	OXFORD	8,609	7 13	46	W	2-1	2-0	Mackenzie 9, Macari 37 / Moody 88 / Ref: S Mathieson	Muggleton / Whitehead	Mackenzie / Robinson	Griffin M / Ford M	Sigurdsson / Smith	Whittle / Purse*	Forsyth / Gilchrist	McMahon / Angel	Wallace / Gray	Macari / Gabbiadini"	Sheron / Jenson"	Kavanagh / Beauchamp	Nyamah / Ford B/Aldridge/Moody
31	A 15/2	SOUTHEND	4,625	7 21	46	L	1-2	0-1	Harris 70 (og) / Thomson 34, Rammell 89 / Ref: M Pierce	Muggleton / Royce	Mackenzie / Harris	Griffin / Dublin	Sigurdsson / McNally	Whittle / Roget	Rodger* / Poric	McMahon / Gridelet	Wallace* / Byrne	Macari / Boere"	Sheron / Thomson*	Kavanagh / Hails^	Devlin / Williams/Nielsen/Rammell
32	H 22/2	QP RANGERS	13,121	10 12	47	D	0-0	0-0	Ref: R Pearson	Muggleton / Sommer	Mackenzie / Yates	Griffin / Brevett	Sigurdsson / Barker	Whittle / McDonald	Pickering / Ready	McMahon / Murray	Rodger^ / Peacock	Macari / Hateley	Wallace / Dichio*	Kavanagh / Sinclair	Nyamah / Charles
33	A 28/2	TRANMERE	9,127	10 11	48	D	0-0	0-0	Ref: P Rejer	Muggleton / Nixon	Mackenzie / Thomas	Griffin / Rogers	Sigurdsson / Challinor	Whittle / Higgins	Rodger* / O'Brien	McMahon / Brannan	Wallace / Moore	Macari^ / Branch*	Sheron / Irons*	Kavanagh / Nevin	Mackenzie/Nyamah / Aldridge/Mahon
34	H 5/3	GRIMSBY	8,621	8 23	51	W	3-1	0-1	Southall 48 (og), Kavanagh 50, Griffin 78 / Livingstone 25 / Ref: E Lomas	Muggleton / Love	Pickering / Fickling	Griffin / Shakespeare	Sigurdsson / Rodger	Whittle / Southall	Rodger^ / Widdrington	McMahon^ / Appleton	Wallace / Livingstone^	Macari / Woods	Sheron / Mendonca	Kavanagh / Oster*	Mackenzie/Nyamah / Childs/Lester

Match notes:

24 — Huddersfield: Macari is Manager of the Month again. Prudhoe is cheered by both sets of fans after last year's comic performance and he is soon at it again, allowing Lee Makel to fire the orange ball past him from 35 yards and spilling Edwards' effort which trickles in. Stein cracks home left footed.

25 — Birmingham: Forsyth's cross-shot finds Wallace who forces the ball home from close in. A tight match becomes trickier as the conditions take an Arctic turn. £4m is needed to finish constructing the new ground. Millionaire Uttoxeter racecourse owner Stan Clarke is reportedly interested in investing.

26 — Charlton: Prudhoe allows a Kinsella shot to squirm out of his hands but the ball spins past the post. Mike Sheron grabs two brilliant predatorial goals. He flicks in Stein's low cross and fires home with the inside of his foot from Kav's slide rule pass. Barness' swerving shot flies in at the near post.

27 — Norwich: O'Neill and Eadie crack home balls over the top and Norwich defend in depth. Stein bids farewell in depth. The new ground will be called the Britannia Stadium as the Building Society will be its sponsor for 10 years. Sheron is runner-up in Sky TV's Nationwide Player of the Year.

28 — Bolton: Leaders Bolton give City a footballing lesson. Pollock strokes in to finish a fine move. Blake is sent off (40 mins) for poleaxing Sigurdsson, but TV replays suggest a dive. Ten-man Trotters remain in charge. McGinlay shrugs off Whittle to calmly beat Muggers. Macari swivels to fire in.

29 — Wolves: Steve Bull is the difference, exposing City's weak defence. He powers in a floated Froggatt free-kick and stoops to head home Emblem's cross. Macari heads just over the bar. West Ham offer £2.7m for Sheron. Mike Moors resigns from the board after his offer to inject funds is refused.

30 — Oxford: A young Stoke side make it three out of three on Sky TV. Sheron's shot is blocked but Neil Mackenzie finishes coolly. His confidence boosted, Mackenzie runs midfield and forces Whitehead into a sharp save. Macari cracks in after U's twice hit the bar. Moody nets with his first touch.

31 — Southend: Sheron's header hits the bar. McMahon wastes two good chances. Andy Thomson cracks a great shot home. Stoke keep pressing and a Sheron shot rebounds off the keeper and Harris into the net. Andy Rammell fires into the top corner seconds after coming on. Sigurdsson's 100th game.

32 — QP Rangers: Sheron is out with a neck strain. Simon Rodger, on loan from Palace, makes his home debut. Gavin Peacock's volley skims the bar. Stoke have 17 shots but Jurgen Sommer saves well from Mackenzie and Kav. An absorbing game peters out. John Gayle is sold to Northampton for £25k.

33 — Tranmere: Debutant Dave Challinor introduces City to his incredible long throw which causes panic in the defence. Nevin takes on Griffin but the 17-year-old emerges on top. Muggers saves when Ian Moore is clean through. Sheron muffs an easy chance. Sixth clean sheet in a row against Rovers.

34 — Grimsby: The first half is littered with errors. Steve Livingstone steals beyond Whittle to steer a long ball past Nicky Southall turns Sheron's cross into his own net. Kav rockets a free-kick in and suddenly it's party time. Griffin plays a one-two with Mackenzie to score.

Match-by-match results log (games 35–46):

35. H IPSWICH — 8/3 — Result 0-1 (HT 0-1) — Pos 9 L — 6 — 51 — Att 11,933
Stoke: Muggleton, Pickering, Griffin, Sigurdsson, Whittle, Rodger*, McMahon^, Wallace, Macari, Sheron, Kavanagh, subs Mackenzie/Nyamah
Opp: Wright, Mowbray, Taricco, Vaughan, Swailes, Williams, Dyer, Sonner, Naylor*, Scowcroft, Mason*, Milton/Gregory
Scorers: Taricco 7 — Ref: E Wolstenholme
A sterile display. Mauricio Taricco pounces on a loose ball after a free-kick. Town are quicker to the ball. Even Ally Pickering's new red boots cannot inspire Stoke. Muggers saves brilliantly from Jamie Scowcroft's flying header. Macari blasts Nyamah's cross over. Poor.

36. A SWINDON — 15/3 — Result 0-1 (HT 0-1) — Pos 12 L — 10 — 51 — Att 8,57?
Stoke: Muggleton, Pickering, Griffin, Sigurdsson, Whittle, Forsyth, McMahon^, Beeston, Macari, Sheron, Kavanagh^, subs Keen/Mackenzie
Opp: Digby, Robinson, Drysdale^, Bullock, Watson, Broomes, Culverhouse Cowe", Thorne", Allison !, Smith, Finney/Elkins/Pattimore
Scorers: Thorne 26 — Ref: B Knight
The Robins react to a 0-7 thrashing at Bolton by stifling jaded City. Justin Whittle misses a clearing header and Peter Thorne slips the ball past Muggleton. Wayne Allison is dismissed for elbowing Whittle (27 mins) but Stoke fail to take advantage despite having 25 shots to Town's six.

37. H WOLVES — 18/3 — Result 1-0 (HT 0-0) — Pos 9 W — 2 — 54 — Att 15,68?
Stoke: Muggleton, Pickering, Griffin, Sigurdsson, Whittle, Forsyth, McMahon^, Wallace, Macari, Sheron, Beeston, subs Kavanagh
Opp: Stowell, Thompson, Venus, Atkins, Emblen, Curle, Corica", Thomas", Bull, Roberts, Osborn^, Ferguson/Goodman/Dennison
Scorers: Forsyth 47 — Ref: J Kirkby
Corica and Bull miss good chances straight from the kick-off for Mark McGhee's Wolves. A dour game is lit up by Forsyth's left-footed curler beyond the despairing Mike Stowell. Steve Bull hits the post and forces Muggleton into two brilliant saves. The play-offs are still a possibility.

38. A MANCHESTER C — 22/3 — Result 0-2 (HT 0-2) — Pos 9 L — 15 — 54 — Att 28,49?
Stoke: Muggleton, Pickering^, Griffin, Sigurdsson, Whittle, Forsyth, McMahon^, Wallace, Macari, Sheron, Kavanagh, subs Devlin/Mackenzie
Opp: Wright, Brightwell, McGoldrick, Lomas, Symons, Braman, Summerbee Atkinson*, Horlock, Kinkladze, Rosler, Kavelashvili
Scorers: Atkinson 65, Lomas 68 — Ref: T Lunt
The kick-off is delayed due to a small fire. Wallace goes man-to-man on Kinkladze. He is quiet but Stoke rarely threaten. Griffin slices against his own bar. Debutant Dalian Atkinson nods in McGoldrick's cross. Steve Lomas repeats the feat. QPR offer £2.5m for Sheron.

39. H OLDHAM — 29/3 — Result 2-1 (HT 2-0) — Pos 10 W — 23 — 57 — Att 11,?55
Stoke: Muggleton, Pickering, Griffin, Sigurdsson, Whittle, Forsyth, Beeston*, Macari, Sheron, Kavanagh
Opp: Kelly, Duxbury, Serrant, Snodin, Hodgson, Fleming, Rush^, Rickers*, McCarthy", Barlow, Reid, Graham/Richardson/Ritchie
Scorers: Sheron 17, Macari 40 / Barlow 87 — Ref: P Richards
Oldham are awful. City lack confidence. Sheron sees his penalty, for a foul on Wallace, saved but he nicks in the rebound. Macari scores when put clear by Forsyth. Kav whacks an 89th-min pen against the post. Stan Clarke takes a third share in Stoke, installing Paul Doona on the board.

40. A BRADFORD C — 31/3 — Result 0-1 (HT 0-1) — Pos 11 L — 21 — 57 — Att 13,579
Stoke: Muggleton, Wallace, Griffin, Sigurdsson !, Whittle, Forsyth, McNally, Beeston, Macari, Sheron, Flynn^, subs Mackenzie
Opp: Davison, Liburd", Jacobs, Dreyer, Mohan, O'Brien, Murray, Kulcsar, Newell, Edinho, Pepper, Wilder
Scorers: Pepper 49 — Ref: G Frankland
Nigel Pepper cracks in a 20-yarder. Controversy as the referee awards a penalty after Sigurdsson and Edinho clash. Siggy is sent off. Muggers saves the feeble kick. Newell stays on the pitch after a terrible foul on new boy McNally. Angry Macari is banished to the stand for protesting.

41. H READING — 5/4 — Result 1-1 (HT 1-1) — Pos 11 D — 17 — 58 — Att 6,931
Stoke: Muggleton, Devlin^, Griffin, Sigurdsson, Whittle, Forsyth, Flynn*, Wallace, Macari, Sheron, Beeston, subs Kavanagh/Mackenzie
Opp: Mautone, Bernal, Bodin, Parkinson, Blatherwick McPherson, Lambert, Williams*, Quinn^, Newell, Nogan*, Gooding, Meaker/Holsgrove/Lovell
Scorers: Forsyth 65 / Lambert 1 — Ref: W Burns
A cataclysmic start as Whittle and Muggleton mess up a clearance and James Lambert lobs home. Boos all around the ground. Stoke take time to regroup. More inept defending sets up Jimmy Quinn but he blazes wide. McMahon's shot is charged down and Forsyth fires in the rebound.

42. A NORWICH — 12/4 — Result 0-2 (HT 0-2) — Pos 13 L — 7 — 58 — Att 17,605
Stoke: Muggleton, McNally, Griffin", Sigurdsson, Whittle^, Forsyth, Kavanagh^, Wallace, Macari, Sheron, Mackenzie, subs Pickering/Beeston/Devlin
Opp: Marshall, Newman, Jackson, Crook, Bradshaw, Sutch, Adams, Fleck^, Milligan*, Eadie, O'Neill", Mills/Polston/Broughton
Scorers: O'Neill 1, Eadie 53 — Ref: M Bailey
Mike Walker's Canaries stroll to victory when Keith O'Neill rams in Kav's poor back-pass after 12 seconds. Despite having 89 minutes to level, Stoke only trouble Andy Marshall when Forsyth's shot is saved. Norwich pile on the pressure. Eadie runs onto O'Neill's through-ball to score.

43. A CRYSTAL PALACE — 15/4 — Result 0-2 (HT 0-2) — Pos 13 L — 7 — 58 — Att 17,?82
Stoke: Muggleton, Flynn, Griffin, Sigurdsson, Whittle^, Forsyth, Beeston^, Wallace, Macari, Sheron, McMahon*, subs Kavanagh/Devlin/Nyamah
Opp: Nash, Edworthy, Gordon, Roberts, Davies, Linighan, Hopkin*, Houghton, Shipperley" Dyer*, Rodger, Muscat/Freedman/McKenzie
Scorers: Dyer 6, 21 — Ref: U Rennie
The season limps to a conclusion. City fans cheer when the Potters get through the first 60 seconds unscathed. It doesn't last long. Bruce Dyer curls in after skipping past Pickering and nods Shipperley's cross home. Macari has a good shot saved by Carlo Nash. Palace into the play-offs.

44. H PORT VALE — 20/4 — Result 1-0 (HT 2-0) — Pos 13 W — 6 — 61 — Att 16,246
Stoke: Muggleton, Mussellwhite Hill, Griffin, Sigurdsson, Whittle, Forsyth, Flynn*, Wallace, Macari, Sheron, McMahon^, subs Mackenzie
Opp: Tankard, Bogie, Aspin, Glover, McCarthy", Porter, Mills, Naylor, Koordes^, Beeston^, Talbot/Corden
Scorers: Sheron 44, 85 — Ref: D Allison
Macari announces he will be stepping down to fight his court case against Celtic at the end of the season. Rumours abound that he was pushed. Beeston's aggression wins the midfield fight. Sheron belts in two corkers, one via an outrageous deflection off Glover, to defeat the arch rivals.

45. A SHEFFIELD UTD — 25/4 — Result 0-1 (HT 0-0) — Pos 13 L — 4 — 61 — Att 25,596
Stoke: Muggleton, Pickering, Griffin, Sigurdsson, Whittle, Forsyth, McNally^, Wallace, Macari, Sheron, Beeston^, subs Kavanagh/Mackenzie
Opp: Kelly, Ward, Sandford, Hutchison, Tiler, Holdsworth White, Henry, Fjortoft, Katchuro", Naylor, Whitehouse Scott
Scorers: Tiler 66 — Ref: 1 Cruickshanks
Chic Bates and Mike Pejic are in charge. Papers link Dave Webb to the manager's job. United drop admission to £5 and gain their biggest gate all season. Sheron is fouled when clean through but Kelly escapes with a yellow. In a desperate scramble the ball hits Carl Tiler and trickles in.

46. H WEST BROM — 4/5 — Result 2-1 (HT 1-0) — Pos 12 W — 16 — 64 — Att 22,500
Stoke: Muggleton, Pickering, Griffin, Sigurdsson, Whittle, Forsyth, McMahon, Wallace, Macari, Sheron^, Beeston, subs Kavanagh
Opp: Miller, McDermott Smith, Sneekes, Murphy, Raven, Coldicott Butler*, Peschisolido Hunt, Groves^, Nicholson/Donovan, Mackenzie
Scorers: McMahon 33, Kavanagh 69 / Hunt 85p — Ref: R Poulain
In a carnival atmosphere Stoke bid farewell to the oldest league ground in the world. Ex-players including Sir Stan, Jimmy Greenhoff and John Ritchie parade before kick-off. McMahon's flying header and Kav's cheeky lob set the seal on a great day. Whittle trips Hunt, who slots the pen.

Average: Home 12,748 — Away 12,865

NATIONWIDE DIVISION 1 (CUP-TIES)

Manager: Lou Macari

SEASON 1996-97

Coca-Cola Cup

2:1 H NORTHAMPTON 7 W 1-0 0-0   Att 6,093 3:20

Worthington 60
Ref: N Barry

1	2	3	4	5	6	7	8	9	10	11	subs used
Muggleton	Pickering	Dreyer	Sigurdsson	Devlin	Forsyth*	Worthington	Wallace	Gayle^	Sheron	McMahon*	Keen/Macari/Da Costa
Woodman	Clarkson	Maddison	Sampson	Rennie	O'Shea	Grayson	Peer*	White^	Parris	Hunter	Gibb/Colkin

Stoke are second best for most of the match. John Gayle has a nightmare. Andy Woodman denies him well on three occasions. Muggers clears desperately with Jason White bearing down on him and twice denies Grayson. Sheron's shot is saved but falls to Worthington who fires home.

2:2 A NORTHAMPTON 4 W 2-1 aet 0-0   Att 5,088 3:20

Sheron 100, 108
Gayle 89 (og)
Ref: G Cain
(Stoke win 3-1 on aggregate)

1	2	3	4	5	6	7	8	9	10	11	subs used
Muggleton*	Pickering	Dreyer	Sigurdsson	Devlin	Da Costa^	Worthington	Wallace	Gayle	Sheron	McMahon*	Prudhoe/Macari/Keen
Woodman	Clarkson	Maddison	Sampson	Rennie	O'Shea	Gibb*	Parrish^	Cooper	Hunter	Colkin*	White/Peer/Grayson

City seem to have survived Ian Atkins' Cobbler's onslaught until Pickering's clearance hits Gayle and rebounds past an astonished Muggleton. Stoke abandon the negative tactics and look good. Sheron flicks the ball over a defender to net before placing Gayle's cross beyond Woodman.

3 H ARSENAL 10 D 1-1 1-0   Att 20,804 P:2

Sheron 26
Wright 78
Ref: K Burge

1	2	3	4	5	6	7	8	9	10	11	subs used
Muggleton	Pickering*	Worthington	Sigurdsson	Dreyer	Forsyth	Whittle	Wallace	Keen	Sheron	Kavanagh	McMahon
Seaman	Dixon	Winterburn	Keown	Bould	Adams	Platt	Wright	Merson	Bergkamp*	Vieira	Hartson

Arsene Wenger's Gunners are given a stern test by a vibrant Stoke side. Lone striker Sheron is a nuisance to the famed back four. He nips in to turn the ball past David Seaman. Stoke cling on as Arsenal get narked and have five booked. Wright turns well to level with a hint of handball.

3R A ARSENAL 9 L 2-5 1-1   Att 33,962 P:2

Sheron 35, 88 [Merson 73]
Wright 41p, 63, Platt 46, Bergkamp 68
Ref: G Willard

1	2	3	4	5	6	7	8	9	10	11	subs used
Muggleton*	Pickering*	Devlin	Sigurdsson	Whittle	Forsyth	McMahon^	Wallace	Keen*	Sheron	Kavanagh	Griffin/Macari/Carruthers
Seaman	Dixon	Winterburn	Keown	Bould	Adams	Platt	Wright	Merson	Bergkamp*	Vieira*	Hartson/Morrow

Sheron subtly clips the ball past Seaman as Stoke start on top. Bergkamp tumbles theatrically for the pen. Arsenal run riot after half-time. Platt chests in from a yard out. Wright nets from a corner. Bergkamp scores from 20 yards and Merson in a scramble. Sheron flicks in a consolation.

FA Cup

3 H STOCKPORT 7 L 0-2 0-1   Att 9,961 2:5

Durkan 25, Armstrong 90
Ref: A D'Urso

1	2	3	4	5	6	7	8	9	10	11	subs used
Prudhoe	Pickering	Griffin	Sigurdsson	Whittle	Forsyth	McMahon	Wallace	Devlin*	Sheron	Kavanagh	Macari/Mackenzie
Jones	Connelly	Todd	Bennett	Flynn	Gannon	Durkan*	Marsden	Angel^	Armstrong	Cavaco	Dinning/Mutch

Another atrocious Cup performance sees City lose to lower league opponents yet again. Kieron Durkan turns neatly to fire past Prudhoe. A direct second half sees Stoke fail to put sufficient pressure on David Jones' huge defence. Armstrong's strike ensures this is the last cup-tie at the Vic.

			Home					Away						Odds & ends
		P	W	D	L	F	A	W	D	L	F	A	Pts	
1	Bolton	46	18	4	1	60	20	10	10	3	40	33	98	Double wins: (3) Charlton, Oldham, West Brom.
2	Barnsley	46	14	4	5	43	19	8	10	5	33	36	80	Double losses: (1) Norwich, Sheffield Utd, Southend.
3	Wolves	46	10	5	8	31	24	9	6	5	37	27	76	
4	Ipswich	46	12	7	3	44	23	7	9	8	24	27	74	Won from behind: (3) Grimsby (h), Huddersfield (h), Portsmouth (h).
5	Sheffield Utd	46	13	5	5	46	23	7	8	8	24	29	73	Lost from in front: (0).
6	Crys Palace *	46	13	7	6	39	22	9	7	7	39	26	71	
7	Portsmouth	46	12	4	7	32	24	8	4	11	27	29	68	High spots: The electric form of Mike Sheron.
8	Port Vale	46	9	9	5	36	28	8	7	8	22	27	67	A carnival day for the last match at the Vic.
9	QP Rangers	46	10	5	8	33	25	8	7	8	31	35	66	Leading Arsenal 1-0 at Highbury.
10	Birmingham	46	11	7	5	30	18	6	8	9	22	30	66	The emergence of the talented Andy Griffin.
11	Tranmere	46	10	9	4	42	27	7	5	11	21	29	65	Having the second best home record in the division.
12	STOKE	46	9	3	5	28	22	7	7	13	17	35	64	Keeping up the hoodoo on the Baggies.
13	Norwich	46	9	10	4	34	18	8	2	13	35	50	63	
14	Manchester C	46	9	4	7	34	25	5	6	12	25	35	61	Low spots: Falling away from the play-off zone with a poor run in March.
15	Charlton	46	7	8	4	36	28	8	6	15	16	38	59	
16	West Brom	46	7	7	9	37	33	7	8	8	31	39	57	Being thrashed at home by Sheffield United.
17	Oxford	46	14	3	6	44	26	2	6	15	20	42	57	Losing at home to Stockport in the FA Cup.
18	Reading	46	13	7	3	37	24	2	5	16	21	43	57	The sale of Sheron to Queen's Park Rangers.
19	Swindon	46	11	6	6	36	27	4	3	16	16	44	54	Failure to sign a forward once Sturridge is injured.
20	Huddersfield	46	10	7	6	28	20	3	8	12	20	41	54	Saying an emotional goodbye to the Victoria Ground.
21	Bradford C	46	10	5	8	29	32	2	7	14	18	40	48	Only winning three away games.
22	Grimsby	46	7	7	9	31	34	4	6	13	29	47	46	Losing home and away against bottom club Southend.
23	Oldham	46	6	8	9	30	30	4	5	14	21	36	43	
24	Southend	46	7	9	7	32	32	1	6	16	10	54	39	
		1104	262	150	140	872	604	140	150	262	604	872	1506	

* promoted after play-offs

	Appearances						Goals			
	Lge	Sub	LC	Sub	FAC	Sub	Lge	LC	FAC	Tot
Beeston, Carl	17	1								
Carruthers, Martin		1			1					
Cranson, Ian	6									
Da Costa, Hugo	1	1	1		1					
Devlin, Mark	13	8	3		1					
Dreyer, John	12		3				1			1
Flynn, Sean	5									
Forsyth, Richard	40	3	3		1		8			8
Gayle, John	8	4	2				1			1
Griffin, Andy	29	5		1	1		1			1
Kavanagh, Graham	32	6	2		1		4			4
Keen, Kevin	5	11	2		2		1			1
Macari, Mike	15	15	3			1	3			3
Mackenzie, Neil	5	17				1	1			1
McMahon, Gerry	31	4	3	1	1		3			3
McNally, Mark	3									
Muggleton, Carl	33		4							
Nyamah, Kofi		7								
Pickering, Ally	39	1	4							
Prudhoe, Mark	13				1	1				
Rodger, Simon	5									
Sheron, Mike	41	4	4		1		19	5		24
Sigurdsson, Larus	45	4	4		1					
Stein, Mark	11						4			4
Stokoe, Graham		2								
Sturridge, Simon	5									
Wallace, Ray	45	4		1			2			2
Whittle, Justin	35	2	2	1						
Worthington, Nigel	12		3						1	1
(own-goals)							3			3
29 Players used	506	85	44	10	11	2	51	6		57

Player of the Year: Andy Griffin.
Ever-presents: (0).
Hat-tricks: (0).
Leading scorer: (24) Mike Sheron.

NATIONWIDE DIVISION 1

Manager: Chic Bates ⇨ Chris Kamara — SEASON 1997-98

No	V	Opponent	Date	Att	Pos	Opp Pos	Pt	Res	F-A	H-T	Scorers / Times	Referee
1	A	BIRMINGHAM	9/8	20,608			0	L	0-2	0-1	Devlin 33, Ndlovu 87	E Wolstenholme
2	H	BRADFORD C	15/8	13,823			1	D	0-0	0-0		T Heilbron
3	A	MIDDLESBROUGH	23/8	30,122	12	17	4	W	1-0	0-0	Stewart 60	P Barnes
4	H	SWINDON	30/8	23,000	13	4	4	L	1-2	1-0	Forsyth 34 / Allison 78, Hay 80	G Frankland
5	H	WEST BROM	3/9	17,500	13	3	5	D	0-0	0-0		E Lomas
6	H	STOCKPORT	13/9	11,743	13	23	8	W	2-1	1-0	Wallace 28, Thorne 50 / Mutch 48	B Coddington
7	A	IPSWICH	20/9	10,665	14	22	11	W	3-2	2-0	Thorne 13, 30, Stewart 55 / Scowcroft 48, Holland 67	B Knight
8	A	NOTT'M FOREST	27/9	19,018	15	1	11	L	0-1	0-0	Campbell 67	M Fletcher
9	A	BURY	4/10	11,760	11	17	14	W	3-2	0-0	Angola 63, Forsyth 69, Thorne 73 / Swan 70, Gray 85p	C Foy
10	H	PORT VALE	12/10	20,125	7	11	17	W	2-1	2-1	Forsyth 5, Keen 34 / Naylor 21	C Wilkes
11	A	CHARLTON	19/10	12,345	7	4	18	D	1-1	0-0	Wallace 51 / Kinsella 79	R Furnandiz

Line-ups (Stoke City top row / opponents below)

No	Team	1	2	3	4	5	6	7	8	9	10	11	subs used
1	Stoke	Muggleton	Pickering	Nyamah	Sigurdsson	Whittle	Keen^	Forsyth	Wallace	Thorne	Stewart	Kavanagh	Sturridge
	Birmingham	Bennett	Wassall	Grainger	Bruce	Ablett	O'Connor*	Devlin^	Hey^	Hughes	Robinson	Ndlovu	Holland/Francis/Johnson
2	Stoke	Muggleton	Pickering	Nyamah	Sigurdsson	Tweed	Keen	Forsyth	Wallace	Thorne	Stewart	Kavanagh	
	Bradford	Prudhoe	Wilder	Jacobs	Beagrie	Youds	Dreyer	Lawrence"	Pepper	Steiner"	Edinho"	Murray"	Blake/Sundqvist/Ramage
3	Stoke	Muggleton	Pickering	Griffin	Sigurdsson	Tweed	Keen	Forsyth	Wallace	Thorne^	Stewart*	Kavanagh	McMahon/Angola
	Middlesbrough	Roberts	Liddle	Fleming	Vickers	Festa	Stamp	Hignett^	Mustoe	Moore^	Merson	Ravanelli	Beck/Freestone
4	Stoke	Muggleton	Pickering	Griffin	Sigurdsson	Tweed	Keen	Forsyth	Wallace	Thorne	Stewart*	Kavanagh	Angola
	Swindon	Digby	Darras	Drysdale*	Leitch^	Seagraves	McDonald	Walters	Cuervo	Hay	Allison	Gooden	Bullock/Smith
5	Stoke	Muggleton	Pickering	Griffin	Whittle	Tweed	Keen	Forsyth	Wallace	Thorne^	Stewart	Kavanagh	Angola
	West Brom	Miller	Holmes	Nicholson	Sneekes	Burgess	Raven	Flynn	Butter	Taylor^	Hunt^	Smith	Hamilton/Thomas
6	Stoke	Muggleton	Pickering	Griffin	Sigurdsson	Tweed	Keen	Forsyth	Wallace	Thorne	Stewart*	Kavanagh^	McMahon/Angola
	Stockport	Nixon	Connelly	Woodthorpe	Bennett	McIntosh	Gannon	Durkan*	Marsden	Angell^	Mutch	Cooper	Richardson/Grant
7	Stoke	Muggleton	Pickering	Griffin	Sigurdsson	Tweed	Keen	Forsyth	Wallace	Thorne	Stewart	Kavanagh	Cundy
	Ipswich	Wright	Stockwell	Tanico	Williams	Venus	Swailes	Dyer	Holland	Stein	Scowcroft	Sonner^	
8	Stoke	Muggleton	Pickering	Griffin	Sigurdsson	Tweed	Keen	Forsyth^	Wallace	Thorne	McMahon^	Kavanagh	Crowe/MacKenzie
	Nott'm Forest	Beasant	Lyttle	Rogers	Cooper*	Chettle	Armstrong	Saunders	Gemmill	V Hooijdonk	Campbell	Bart-Williams	Bart-Williams/Johnson
9	Stoke	Muggleton	Pickering	Griffin	Sigurdsson	Tweed	Keen	Forsyth	Wallace	Thorne	Angola^	Kavanagh	McMahon
	Bury	Kiely	Hughes^	Morgan	Daws	Lucketti	Butler	Gray	Johnson	Swan	Johnrose		Randall/Woodward
10	Stoke	Muggleton	Pickering	Griffin	Sigurdsson	Tweed	Keen	Forsyth	Wallace	Thorne	Angola*	Kavanagh	Crowe
	Port Vale	Musselwhite	Hill^	Tankard	Talbot	Aspin	Snijders	Ainsworth	Porter	Mills*	Naylor	Koordes"	Foyle/Bogie/Corden
11	Stoke	Muggleton	Pickering	Griffin	Sigurdsson	Tweed	Keen	Forsyth	Wallace	McMahon^	Angola^	Kavanagh	Whittle/Macari
	Charlton	Petterson	Bowen	Barnss	Jones	Rufus	Chapple	Newton^	Kinsella	Robinson	Mendonca	Jones^	Holmes/Allen

Match reports

1 — Birmingham (A): The new era at the Britannia Stadium will start late as building work is not quite ready. Coach Chic Bates is the new manager. At sun-kissed St Andrews, Whittle misses a long ball and Paul Devlin nods over the stranded Muggleton. Thorne rounds Bennett but fires wide of a gaping goal.

2 — Bradford C (H): Chris Kamara has his Bradford side, with three ex-Stokies in it, fired up. They have the better of it. Steiner, Edinho and Beagrie. Mark Prudhoe tips Steven Tweed's header over. Eddie Youds trips Thorne in the area but the ref waves play on.

3 — Middlesbrough (A): Tweed snuffs out the threat of Ravanelli. Moore and Stamp blaze wide as Boro fail to register a shot on target. A superb move ends with Paul Stewart sweeping into the net. Victory on Stoke's first ever visit to the Cellnet Stadium. Alan Durban has returned to the club to assist Bates.

4 — Swindon (H): City run out of steam in the blazing sun as Steve McMahon's Robins finish strongly. Richard Forsyth nets the first league goal at the Brit, after Stan Matthews sets a hideous precedent by failing to find the net from 12 yards in the opening ceremony. Allison and Hay crack in on the turn.

5 — West Brom (H): City lose Sigurdsson but Albion miss Peschisolido on international duty. In atrocious conditions both teams attack but neither can find a finish. Sneekes' volley flies narrowly wide. City fail to hit the target. Sturridge will be out until January with a recurrence of his knee ligament injury.

6 — Stockport (H): Wallace pokes home in a scramble. County are poor, but still push City all the way after Andy Mutch heads in a free-kick. Thorne slides home Stewart's cross. Gannon clears off the line. The whole ground rises to protest about Coates' refusal to back Chic Bates with funds for transfers.

7 — Ipswich (A): Indecision allows Thorne to loop a header over Richard Wright. Keen's corner is not cleared and Thorne nets in the scramble. Town change to 4-4-2. Scowcroft dives to head in. Stewart races clear to score. Stein puts Holland through to beat Muggleton. First win at Ipswich for 15 years.

8 — Nott'm Forest (A): Keen hits the bar. Tweed allows Van Hooijdonk to cross and Kevin Campbell heads in. Stoke launch a wave of attacks against Dave Bassett's unconvincing Forest. In injury-time Sigurdsson heads against the bar only for Muggleton to mis-hit the rebound against a defender on the line.

9 — Bury (A): Stan Tement's Shakers fight all the way after Jose Angola scores on his debut. Wallace misses a sitter. Forsyth nips in to finish in a scramble. Swan collects Griffin's poor back-pass to score. Thorne smashes Keen's centre home. Gray's penalty is for Pickering's foul on David Johnson.

10 — Port Vale (H): Keen's cross finds Forsyth who rises to head in unmarked. Tony Naylor glances a header past Muggers despite being only 5ft 7in. Keen accepts Kav's killer pass to fire precisely into the corner. Six wins in seven.

11 — Charlton (A): Siggy tackles Jones brilliantly as he races clear. Wallace races on to Kav's square pass to rocket home from 20 yards. Charlton pour forward as Stoke sit deep. Kinsella fires in via Wallace's knee. Another lead lost. City cannot afford £300k for ex-Stokie Graham Potter from West Brom.

No		Date	Pos	W/D/L	Score	HT	Attendance
12	A MANCHESTER C	22/10	6	W	1-0	0-0	25,355 / 21 21
13	H SUNDERLAND	25/10	9	L	1-2	0-1	14,381 / 10 21
14	A HUDDERSFIELD	1/11	12	L	1-3	0-0	10,213 / 24 21
15	H OXFORD	4/11	12	D	0-0	0-0	8,423 / 18 22
16	H WOLVES	8/11	9	W	3-0	2-0	18,350 / 8 25
17	A QP RANGERS	15/11	10	D	1-1	1-0	11,923 / 13 26
18	A TRANMERE	22/11	12	L	1-3	1-1	8,079 / 16 26
19	H READING	29/11	13	L	1-2	0-1	11,103 / 18 26
20	A SHEFFIELD UTD	2/12	13	L	2-3	1-0	14,547 / 4 26
21	A PORTSMOUTH	6/12	14	L	0-2	0-2	7,272 / 24 26
22	H CREWE	13/12	15	L	0-2	0-1	14,323 / 20 26
23	A NORWICH	20/12	15	D	0-0	0-0	2,265 / 13 27

12 — A MANCHESTER C, 22/10

Stoke: Muggleton, Pickering, Griffin, Sigurdsson, Tweed, Keen, Forsyth, Wallace, McMahon, Stewart*, Kavanagh, Nyamah

Man City: Margetson, Brightwell, Van Blerk, McGoldrick, Symons, Edghill, Brannan*, Horlock, Heaney^, Kinkladze, Dickov, Summerbee/Conlon

Wallace 63

Ref: A Leake

Frank Clark's Blues have Stoke under the cosh. Heaney fires just over. Muggers brilliantly saves Horlock's effort. Dickov gives Tweed a torrid time. Brannan has a header tipped away. Stoke gradually get a grip. Wallace belts in a half-cleared corner. Muggers denies Eddie McGoldrick.

13 — H SUNDERLAND, 25/10

Stoke: Muggleton, Pickering^, Nyamah, Sigurdsson, Tweed, Keen, Forsyth, Wallace, McMahon, Stewart, Kavanagh^, Whittle/Angola

Sunderland: Perez, Holloway, Gray, Clark, Ball, Craddock, Johnston, Williams, Bridges*, Phillips, Smith^, Russell/Mullin

Stewart 81; Clark 40, 70

Ref: S Baines

£2.3m Lee Clark, who cost Peter Reid more than the entire City team, peppers Muggleton with shots. His first two fly wide, but he cracks in as Wallace slips in the box. McMahon fires at Lionel Perez. Clark's ferocious 25-yard shot from flies in. Stewart hammers in Angola's flick-on.

14 — A HUDDERSFIELD, 1/11

Stoke: Muggleton, Pickering, Griffin, Sigurdsson, Tweed, Keen, Forsyth, Wallace*, McMahon, Stewart, Kavanagh, Angola/McMahon

Huddersfield: Bartam, Jenkins, Edmundson, Dyson, Morrison, Gray, Dalton, Horne, Stewart, Richardson, Edwards^, Lawson

Griffin 79; Richardson 46, Stewart 80, Dalton 90

Ref: K Lynch

The Terriers register their first win of the season against out of sorts Stoke. Kav shaves the post. Richardson hammers in from 25 yards. Griffin weaves through to net from a tight angle. Marcus Stewart nips in. Muggers goes up for a corner but it is cleared and Paul Dalton slots past Kav.

15 — H OXFORD, 4/11

Stoke: Muggleton, Pickering, Griffin, Sigurdsson, Tweed, Keen, Forsyth, Wallace, McMahon, Stewart*, Kavanagh, Angola/McMahon

Oxford: V Heusden, Gilchrist, Ford M, Robinson, Purse^, Wilsterman, Ford B, Smith, Banger, Jemson*, Beauchamp, Aldridge/Murphy

Ref: R Pearson

Griffin's 30-yarder startles on-loan Van Heusden but he recovers to scoop up his parry. Total lack of invention enrages the fans who single out Ally Pickering as a scapegoat. He responds with a gesture which wins him no friends. 'Where has all the money gone?' sing the North Stand.

16 — H WOLVES, 8/11

Stoke: Muggleton, Pickering, Griffin, Sigurdsson, Tweed, Keen, Forsyth, Wallace, McMahon, Stewart, Kavanagh, Angola

Wolves: Stowell, Muscat, Froggatt, Robinson^, Willems, Curle, Keane, Ferguson, Bull, Freedman, Simpson, Naylor

Kavanagh 8, 23p, Forsyth 60

Ref: E Wolstenholme

Bull's rocket pings against the bar with Muggers stranded. Immediately Kavanagh sweetly fires home from the edge of the box. Kevin Muscat handles in a scramble and Kav slots the penalty. Forsyth hits an absolute pearler from 35 yards past the astonished Mike Stowell. Triumphant!

17 — A QP RANGERS, 15/11

Stoke: Muggleton, Pickering, Nyamah, Sigurdsson, Tweed, Keen, Forsyth, Wallace, McMahon, Stewart, Kavanagh

QPR: Roberts, Perry, Brazier, Barker, Ready, Yates, Spencer, Peacock, Murray*, Sheron, Sinclair, Quashie

Forsyth 7; Barker 61p

Ref: M Bailey

Ex-Stokie Sheron is roundly booed. Forsyth leaps to head Kav's far-post cross past Roberts. City absorb heavy pressure. Spencer fires over but referee Bailey spots shirt pulling by Sigurdsson and Simon Barker nets the spot-kick. Muggers produces a great point-blank save from Sinclair.

18 — A TRANMERE, 22/11

Stoke: Muggleton, Pickering, Griffin, Sigurdsson, Tweed, Keen, Forsyth, Wallace*, McMahon, Stewart, Kavanagh, McMahon

Tranmere: Simonsen, Stevens, Thompson, McGreal*, Thorn, Irons, Mellon, Aldridge*, Kelly, O'Brien, Jones L*, Jones G/Morrissey/Mahon

Kavanagh 35p; Jones L 9, Aldridge 66, O'Brien 87

Ref: G Laws

Over 2,200 Stokies see Rovers' ageing side outfight City's lightweight midfield. Lee Jones heads in at the far post. Kav's penalty arrives when Andy Thompson pushes Stewart. Player-manager Aldridge guides a header in. O'Brien lashes in a third. Stoke in tatters. It does not bode well.

19 — H READING, 29/11

Stoke: Muggleton, Pickering, Griffin, Sigurdsson, Tweed, Keen, Forsyth, Angola^, McMahon, Stewart*, Kavanagh, Mackenzie/Tiatto

Reading: Hammond, Booty, Swales, Lambert*, McPherson, Primus, Parkinson, Houghton, Asaba^, Morley, Williams^, Hodges/Caskey/Thorp

Thorne 81; Morley 32p, 59

Ref: T Jones

The miserable weather is matched by Stoke's performance. 36-year-old Trevor Morley torments the central defenders. He misses a sitter from six yards before slotting a penalty after Sigurdsson fouls Williams and then side-foots home unmarked. Thorne hammers in Mackenzie's cross.

20 — A SHEFFIELD UTD, 2/12

Stoke: Muggleton, Pickering, Griffin, Sigurdsson, Tweed, Keen, Forsyth, Mackenzie, Thorne, Tiatto*, Kavanagh

Sheffield Utd: Tracey, Bartokis, Nilsen^, Hutchison*, Dallas, Holdsworth, Patterson", Marker, Fjortoft, Deane, Stuart, Taylor/Woodhouse/Ford

Thorne 8, 63; Taylor 46, Fjortoft 64, Deane 80

Ref: G Frankland

On a bitter night City play excellent football. Thorne guides the ball under Simon Tracey. New boy Danny Tiatto looks lively. Nigel Spackman makes three changes at the break. Taylor scores from close in. Fjortoft taps in after Muggers can only parry. Deane turns the ball past Muggers.

21 — A PORTSMOUTH, 6/12

Stoke: Muggleton, Pickering, Griffin, Sigurdsson, Tweed, Keen, Forsyth, Mackenzie^, Thorne, Tiatto*, Kavanagh, McMahon

Portsmouth: Knight, Pethick, Thomson, McLoughlin, Whitbread, Awford, Hall, Foster^, Aloisi*, Aloisi^, Hillier, Igoe/Durnin

Aloisi 31, Svensson 43

Ref: P Rejer

Sigurdsson's shot is superbly saved by veteran Alan Knight. Hall finds John Aloisi who spins to fire into the roof of the net. Sigurdsson misses a tackle and Paul Hall sets up Matthias Svensson for a simple tap-in. Stoke are abject. Under-fire Terry Fenwick's first home win since August.

22 — H CREWE, 13/12

Stoke: Muggleton, Pickering, Griffin*, Sigurdsson, Tweed, Keen, Forsyth, Mackenzie, Thorne, Tiatto, Kavanagh

Crewe: Kearton, Bignot, Smith, Unsworth, Foran, Lunt*, Rivers, Holsgrove, Adebola^, Johnson, Street, Garvey/Little

Smith 11, Little 75

Ref: A Wiley

Stoke lose for the third time this season against the bottom side. Dario Gradi's youthful side revel in the open spaces at the Brit. Captain Shaun Smith fires a free-kick past a static Muggers. Boos ring out. City lack the imagination to carve a chance. Colin Little finishes from close range.

23 — A NORWICH, 20/12

Stoke: Muggleton, Pickering, Griffin, Sigurdsson, Tweed, Keen, Forsyth, Mackenzie, Thorne, Stewart, Kavanagh

Norwich: Marshall, Segura, Mills, Grant, Scott, Jackson, Forbes, Carey^, Roberts, Bellamy, Fugelstad, O'Neill

Ref: R Harris

Mike Walker's Canaries are as bad as Stoke. At least their future is ensured as millionaire cook Delia Smith has taken control. 364 Stokies see a sterile game. Marshall claws Mackenzie's weak shot away. Forsyth nods straight at the keeper. Griffin heads off the line from Victor Segura.

NATIONWIDE DIVISION 1

Manager: Chic Bates ⇨ Chris Kamara

SEASON 1997-98

No	Date	Att	Pos	Pt	F-A	H-T	Scorers, Times, and Referees	1	2	3	4	5	6	7	8	9	10	11	subs used
24	H SHEFFIELD UTD 26/12	19,723	4	28	2-2	0-0	Forsyth 66, Thorne 86 / Taylor 59, Deane 90 / Ref: S Mathieson	Muggleton	Pickering	Griffin	Sigurdsson	Tweed	Forsyth	Keen	Mackenzie	Thorne*	Stewart*	Kavanagh	Tiatto/Gabbiadini
								Kelly	Borbokis^	Woodhouse^ Ford		Lee	Nilsen		Marker	Taylor	Deane	Stuart	Katchoura/Hutchison

Reserve keeper Alan Kelly produces a fine display to keep the Blades in it. He denies Stewart, Griffin and Keen. Kav hits the post. Taylor nods in. Forsyth finally beats Kelly from six yards. Thorne seems to have won it but Deane loops a header home. Eight without a win.

No	Date	Att	Pos	Pt	F-A	H-T	Scorers, Times, and Referees	1	2	3	4	5	6	7	8	9	10	11	subs used
25	A WEST BROM 28/12	17,690	7	29	1-1	0-0	Thorne 47 / Hunt 62 / Ref: P Danson	Muggleton	Griffin	Nyamah*	Sigurdsson	Tweed	Keen	Forsyth	Mackenzie*	Thorne	Stewart*	Kavanagh	Whittle/Wallace/Gabbiadini
								Miller	McDermott Smith		Sneekes	Burgess	Murphy	Butler	Hamilton^	Hughes	Hunt	Kilbane	Codicott*/Evans

Denis Smith's first home game in charge of Albion sees Stewart loop a header against the post. Thorne slots from close range after Mackenzie miscues his shot. Muggers is injured. Stewart, in goal, fails to hold Sneekes' free-kick. Andy Hunt profits. 18 without loss against the Baggies.

No	Date	Att	Pos	Pt	F-A	H-T	Scorers, Times, and Referees	1	2	3	4	5	6	7	8	9	10	11	subs used
26	H BIRMINGHAM 10/1	14,940	8	29	0-7	0-3	Hghes 4, 9, F'ster 26, Furlong 50, 69, 87 [McCarthy 65] / Ref: T Helibron	Muggleton	Griffin	Nyamah*	Sigurdsson	Tweed	Keen	Forsyth	Mackenzie	Thorne	Stewart*	Kavanagh	Wallace/Gabbiadini
								Bennett	Bass	Charlton	Bruce^	Ablett	Marsden	McCarthy	O'Connor	Furlong	Hughes	Forster*	Ndlovu/Johnson

The most appalling defeat in the club's history. It comes soon after nine players discover via the press they are surplus to requirements. Hughes and Forster waltz through. Paul Furlong's hat-trick completes a biggest ever home defeat. Protesters climb into the stand to confront the board.

No	Date	Att	Pos	Pt	F-A	H-T	Scorers, Times, and Referees	1	2	3	4	5	6	7	8	9	10	11	subs used
27	H BRADFORD C 16/1	10,459	11	32	2-1	2-1	Forsyth 35p, Thorne 42 / McGinlay 21 / Ref: R Pearson	Muggleton	Pickering	Griffin	Sigurdsson	Tweed	Keen	Forsyth	Wallace	Thorne	Gabbiadini*	Whittle	McMahon
								Walsh	Wilder	Small^	Murray	Youds	O'Brien	Lawrence*	McGinlay	Jacobs	Blake	Beagrie	Edinho/Bolland

Peter Coates announces his resignation as Chairman but retains a controlling interest in the club. Keith Humphreys is the new Chair. 2,000 fans register their disgust by arriving 15 mins late only to see McGinlay's header. Forsyth's pen is for handball. Thorne cracks in Keen's fine pass.

No	Date	Att	Pos	Pt	F-A	H-T	Scorers, Times, and Referees	1	2	3	4	5	6	7	8	9	10	11	subs used
28	A SWINDON 28/1	6,683	10	32	0-1	0-0	Robinson 71 / Ref: A Hall	Muggleton	Pickering	Nyamah	Whittle	Tweed	Keen	Holsgrove	Wallace	Thorne	Scully*	Kavanagh*	McMahon/Gabbiadini
								Mildenhall	Borrows	Robinson	Thompson	Taylor	Collins	Cuervo	Howe	Hay	Finney	Drysdale*	Leitch

Chris Kamara replaces Chic Bates. Andy Griffin is sold to Newcastle for £2.3m. Loan signings Paul Holsgrove and Tony Scully cannot inspire Stoke to find a way past youth keeper Steve Mildenhall. Mark Robinson cracks home. Former Stokie Ian Moores dies of throat cancer aged 44.

No	Date	Att	Pos	Pt	F-A	H-T	Scorers, Times, and Referees	1	2	3	4	5	6	7	8	9	10	11	subs used
29	H MIDDLESBROUGH 1/2	13,242	2	32	1-2	1-1	Kavanagh 36p / Pearson 17, Moreno 81 / Ref: P Richards	Muggleton	Pickering	McKinlay1	Whittle	Tweed*	Keen	Holsgrove	Wallace	McMahon	Scully	Kavanagh	Gabbiadini
								Schwarzer	Baker	Kinder	Vickers	Pearson	Mustoe	Hignett	Townsend	Campbell^	Merson	Summerbell*	Beck/Moreno

Bryan Robson's Boro are a class above City. Tosh McKinlay, on loan from Celtic, helps Pearson's header past Muggers. Mark Schwarzer tips Kav's shot over. McKinlay is tripped by Baker for the pen, but is sent off for slapping Hignett (84 mins). Jaime Moreno scores from 20 yards.

No	Date	Att	Pos	Pt	F-A	H-T	Scorers, Times, and Referees	1	2	3	4	5	6	7	8	9	10	11	subs used
30	H IPSWICH 7/2	11,416	13	33	1-1	1-0	Holsgrove 15 / Holland 78 / Ref: M Pike	Muggleton	Pickering	McKinlay	Sigurdsson	Whittle	Keen	Holsgrove	Wallace	McMahon	Scully*	Kavanagh*	Macari/Gabbiadini
								Wright	Stockwell	Taricco!	Williams^	Clapham	Cundy	Uhlenbeek*	Holland	Mathie	Scowcroft	Dyer	Sonner/Johnson

The Victoria Ground has finally been demolished. Much like City's season. Holsgrove slides in to convert McKinlay's cross. Muggers makes a fine save from Clapham as George Burley's men fight back. Matt Holland nods in a corner. Taricco walks (86 mins) for a third foul on Scully.

No	Date	Att	Pos	Pt	F-A	H-T	Scorers, Times, and Referees	1	2	3	4	5	6	7	8	9	10	11	subs used
31	A STOCKPORT 14/2	8,701	8	33	0-1	0-0	Grant 82 / Ref: G Laws	Muggleton	Pickering	McKinlay*	Sigurdsson	Whittle	Gabbiadini*	Holsgrove	Wallace	McMahon*	Scully	Kavanagh	Tweed/Macari/Mackenzie
								Nixon	Connelly	Woodthorpe Byrne^	Flynn		Dinning	Gannon	Cook^	Angell	Mutch^	Cooper	Grant/Travis/Phillips

Holsgrove skims the bar from 25 yards. Andy Mutch heads just wide. Sean Connelly misses a sitter after Wallace gives possession away. Steve Grant's aimless cross sails over Muggleton and nestles in the bottom corner. The death of long-serving club secretary Mike Potts is announced.

No	Date	Att	Pos	Pt	F-A	H-T	Scorers, Times, and Referees	1	2	3	4	5	6	7	8	9	10	11	subs used
32	A BURY 17/2	5,802	23	34	0-0	0-0	Ref: J Robinson	Muggleton	Pickering	Tiatto	Sigurdsson	Whittle	Crowe	Holsgrove	Wallace	Xausa	Scully	Kavanagh	Swan/Rigby/Matthews
								Kiely	Woodward	Small	Daws	Lucketti	Butler	Jenson^	Patterson	Armstrong	Johnrose^	Battersby^	

Kamara's selection smacks of panic. Davide Xausa, on loan from St Johnstone, is awful. Kav hits the keeper when put clear. Crowe strikes the upright. Pickering nods off the line. Sheffield United turn down £750k for striker Gareth Taylor. Lou Macari loses his court case against Celtic.

No	Date	Att	Pos	Pt	F-A	H-T	Scorers, Times, and Referees	1	2	3	4	5	6	7	8	9	10	11	subs used
33	H NOTT'M FOREST 21/2	16,899	2	35	1-1	1-0	Crowe 32 / Moore 87 / Ref: D Pugh	Muggleton	Pickering	Tiatto	Sigurdsson	Whittle	Scully*	Holsgrove	Wallace	Crowe	Lightbourne	Kavanagh^	Keen/Mackenzie
								Beasant	Lyttle	Rogers	Cooper	Chettle*	Johnson A^	Johnson D^	Gemmill	Moore	Campbell	Bonnalair	Armstrng/Thomas/Brt-Wilms

£500k man Kyle Lightbourne, from Coventry, starts despite not fully recovering from flu. Dean Crowe nets his first goal from Tiatto's corner. Ian Moore's effort eludes everyone and trickles into the net. Former player Robbie James collapses and dies while playing for Llanelli aged 40.

No	Date	Att	Pos	Pt	F-A	H-T	Scorers, Times, and Referees	1	2	3	4	5	6	7	8	9	10	11	subs used
34	H CHARLTON 25/2	10,027	4	35	1-2	1-1	Kavanagh 42 / Robinson 17, Barness 73 / Ref: R Furnandiz	Muggleton	Pickering*	Tiatto	Sigurdsson	Whittle	Scully	Keen^	Wallace	Crowe	Lightbourne	Kavanagh	Tweed/Thorne
								Ilic	Brown	Bowen	Jones	Chapple	Balmer	Barness	Kinsella	Robinson	Mendonca	Lishie*	Newton

John Robinson is tackled in the act of shooting but the ball spoons up and over the stranded Muggers. Kavanagh fires a brilliant short free-kick past Sasa Ilic and celebrates wildly with club mascot Pottermuss! Anthony Barness nets at the second attempt after Robinson carves City open.

35 · A · 1/3 · PORT VALE · 13,85? · D 0-0 · 23 24 36

Southall · Pickering Hill · Tiatto Tankard^ · Sigurdsson Bogie · Whittle Glover · Tweed^ Carragher · Forsyth Ainsworth · Wallace Porter · Thorne Mills* · Lightbourne Kavanagh Foyle Jansson · Crowe Naylor/Snijders
V Heusden

Ref: P Rejer

Neville Southall, on loan from Everton, becomes the third oldest player in Stoke's history. A grim derby sees the teams occupy the bottom two places in the division after the awful pitch makes good football impossible. Coach Mike Pejic has been sacked and replaced by Martin Hunter.

36 · A · 4/3 · WOLVES · 21,05? · D 1-1 · 23 9 37

Crowe 89
Freedman 22

Ref: E Wolstenholme

Southall · Pickering^ Hill · Tiatto Atkins · Sigurdsson Naylor · Whittle Richards · Holsgrove^ Curle · Forsyth Keane^ · Wallace Robinson · Thorne Bull · Lightbourne Kavanagh Freedman* Osborn · Crowe/McNally Paatelainen/Muscat
Segers

Whittle allows Freedman's speculative shot under his foot and the ball speeds into the bottom corner. In pouring rain Dean Crowe profits from lackadaisical defending to shoot through a mass of players as Wolves' minds turn to their forthcoming FA Cup quarter-final tie at Elland Road.

37 · H · 7/3 · HUDDERSFIELD · 12,55? · L 1-2 · 24 21 37

Tiatto 90
Barnes 15, Stewart 18

Ref: E Lomas

Southall · Pickering" Phillips · Tiatto Jenkins · Sigurdsson Browning · Whittle Watts · Holsgrove Gray · Forsyth Richardson* Barnes^ · Wallace Stewart · Thorne Allison · Lightbourne* Kavanagh^ Keen/Crowe/Woods Johnson · Edwards/Baldry
Harper

Stoke go to pieces after Peter Jackson's Terriers score two early goals. Ex-Stokie Paul Barnes profits from awful defending. Stewart powers in from 15 yards. 'Bring on the Hippo!' chorus the North Stand.

38 · A · 14/3 · OXFORD · 7,3?0 · L 1-5 · 24 13 37

Crowe 69 [Beauchamp 87]
Murphy 45, 61, Francis 65, 68.

Ref: B Knight

Southall · Pickering Robinson · Tiatto^ Marsh · Sigurdsson Tweed · Whittle ! Davis · Keen* Gilchrist · Forsyth Murphy* · Wallace Smith · Donaldson Kavanagh Cook^ Beauchamp · Crowe/Heath Banger/Powell
Whitehead

Stoke surrender abjectly. Wallace heads straight to Murphy who nets. Kevin Francis turns in from close range twice. Kamara slams his players. Relegation is edging ever closer. On-loan O'Neill Donaldson (Sheffield Wed) replaces Lightbourne, having blood tests as his illness continues.

39 · H · 21/3 · QP RANGERS · 11,0?1 · W 2-1 · 23 18 40

Dowie 21 (og), Crowe 51
Barker 90p

Ref: A Leake

Southall · McNally Yates" · Tiatto Morrow · Sigurdsson Kulcsar^ · Whittle ! Ready · Holsgrove Maddix · Forsyth Barker · Wallace Baraclough · Thorne Dowie* · Donaldson* Stewart^ Kavanagh Sheron Scully · Crowe Gallen/Slade/Heinola
Harper

The players appeal for fans to be more positive during games. City pour forward. Dowie slices the ball into his own net. Jorg Sobiech, on loan from NEC Nijmegen, sets up Crowe for the second. Whittle is sent off for fouling Mike Sheron in the box. Only the second win in 23 months.

40 · H · 28/3 · TRANMERE · 16,?9? · L 0-3 · 23 16 40

Jones G 26, Mellon 39, Kelly 60

Ref: M Fletcher

Southall · McNally" Kubicki* · Tiatto Thompson · Sigurdsson McGreal · Whittle Challinor · Holsgrove* Irons · Forsyth Morrissey · Crowe Jones G · Thorne Kelly · Stewart^ Kavanagh O'Brien Jones L · Tiatto/Lightbourne/Taaffe Mellon
Simonsen

The club slash prices to £10 for adults and kids £4. A bumper crowd assembles to witness another abject performance. Challinor's long throw lands at Gary Jones' feet. Micky Mellon profits when Whittle fails to clear twice. Diminutive David Kelly rises above two defenders to nod in.

41 · A · 4/4 · READING · 10,3?8 · L 0-2 · 24 23 40

O'Neill 32, Meaker 48

Ref: F Stretton

Southall · Pickering Bernal · Tiatto^ Gray · Sigurdsson Parkinson · Whittle Primus · Holsgrove* McNally Crawford · Forsyth Meaker* · Wallace* Caskey · Thorne McIntyre^ · Crowe O'Neill · Kavanagh^ Lambert · Keen/Lightbourne/Tweed Asaba/Fleck
Howie

Tommy Burns fields four deadline day signings as Reading halt a run of seven straight defeats. O'Neill outjumps six players to loop his header past Southall. Meaker nets without a defender in sight. Stokies don't know whether to shout 'Kamara out!' or 'Sack the board!' Utterly abject.

42 · H · 11/4 · PORTSMOUTH · 15,5?9 · W 2-1 · 23 22 43

Pickering 78, Lightbourne 90
Durnin 69

Ref: R Furmandiz

Southall · Pickering Pethick · Tiatto Robinson · Sigurdsson McLoughlin* Whitbread · Holsgrove^ Awford · Keen Hillier · Forsyth" Simpson · Wallace Aloisi" · Thorne^ Durnin · Crowe* Thomson · Kavanagh Hall/Svensson/Allen · Whittle/Lightbourne/Heath
Flahavan

Chris Kamara has resigned after just 14 games as manager leaving Alan Durban to see the season out. John Durnin puts Alan Ball's relegation-haunted Pompey ahead. Ally Pickering's rocket almost tears the net off the stanchion. Lightbourne finally scores his first goal when he lobs in.

43 · A · 13/4 · CREWE · £759 · L 0-2 · 23 13 43

Westwood 16, Lightfoot 48

Ref: R Harris

Southall · Pickering Bignot · Tiatto Smith · Sigurdsson Westwood* Walton · Holsgrove^ Lightfoot · Keen Street" · Wallace Whalley · Thorne Anthrobus" Johnson · Heath Kavanagh^ Crowe Little · Mackenzie/Taaffe Unsworth/Rivers/Tierney
Kearton

Ashley Westwood prods in after Little flicks on Seth Johnson's rehearsed set-piece. Stoke rock visibly. Little makes a hash of an easy chance. Chris Lightfoot lunges in to poke home Gareth Whalley's flighted free-kick. A thumb injury will keep Muggleton out for the rest of the season.

44 · H · 18/4 · NORWICH · 13,?08 · W 2-0 · 21 17 46

Sigurdsson 19, Lightbourne 50

Ref: G Cain

Southall · Pickering Sutch · Tiatto Fudelstad" Segura^ · Sigurdsson Segura" · Keen Jackson · Forsyth" Adams · Wallace Bellamy · Heath Roberts Fenn^ · Crowe* Kavanagh Llewellyn · Thorne Grant/Coote/Polston
Marshall

Stoke pour forward. Kav crosses into a crowded box and Sigurdsson heads inside the near post. Tiatto releases Heath whose inch-perfect centre finds Lightbourne unmarked. Southall pulls off a miracle save from Ex-Stokie Neil Adams. Stoke out of the bottom three – a glimmer of hope?

45 · A · 25/4 · SUNDERLAND · 4?,?14 · L 0-3 · 22 2 46

Williams 6, Phillips 54, 88

Ref: T Jones

Southall · Pickering Holloway · Tiatto^ Gray · Sigurdsson Clark · Heath Craddock · Forsyth^ Williams · Wallace Summerbee Ball · Lightbourne* Crowe Dunn* · Keen Phillips · Heath Whittle/Thorne/Holsgrove Johnston Dichio
Perez

Stoke's first visit to the magnificent Stadium of Light sees them taken apart by Peter Reid's Champions. Darren Williams scores after Ball hits the bar from a corner. Southall is kept busy. Kevin Phillips races clear twice to rack up thirty goals for the season. It all rests on the last match.

46 · H · 3/5 · MANCHESTER C · ?6,664 · L 2-5 · 23 22 46

Thorne 62, 87 [Horlock 90]
Goater 32, 71, Dickov 49, Bradbury 64,

Ref: M Bailey

Southall · Pickering Edghill · Tiatto Horlock · Sigurdsson Wiekens · Heath Symons · Forsyth Vaughan · Wallace Whitley Jim* Pollock · Thorne Whitley"/Kavanagh · Lightbourne* Taaffe · Goater^ Dickov" Bradbury · Br'man/Kink'dze/Whit'y Jeff
Margetson

Stoke fall apart after Shaun Goater chips Southall to put Joe Royle's Blues ahead. The sell-out crowd see dreadful defending punished by close-range finishes by Dickov and Bradbury. Thorne nets twice from six yards. Fighting erupts out as both clubs learn their joint fate. An awful day.

Home 14,945
Away -4,563
Average -

NATIONWIDE DIVISION 1 (CUP-TIES)

Manager: Chic Bates ⇒ Chris Kamara   SEASON 1997-98

Coca-Cola Cup	Att	F-A	H-T	Scorers, Times, and Referees	1	2	3	4	5	6	7	8	9	10	11	subs used
1:1 A ROCHDALE 12/8	2,509	W 3-1	1-1	Kavanagh 26, Thorne 67, Forsyth 70 / Painter 32 / Ref: D Pugh	Muggleton	Pickering	Nyamah	Sigurdsson	Tweed	Keen	Forsyth	Wallace	Thorne	Stewart*	Kavanagh	Sturridge^/McMahon
					Key	*Fensome*	*Barlow*	*Hill*	*Farrell*	*Gouck*	*Bailey*	*Painter*	*Leonard*	*Carter*	*Stuart*	
1:2 H ROCHDALE 27/8	12 12,768 3:18	D 1-1	0-0	Kavanagh 85 / Russell 90 / Ref: S Mathieson (Stoke win 4-2 on aggregate)	Muggleton	Pickering	Griffin	Sigurdsson	Tweed*	Keen	Forsyth	Wallace*	Thorne	Stewart	Kavanagh	Whittle/Schreuder
					Key	*Fensome*	*Bayliss*	*Hill*	*Farrell*	*Gouck*	*Russell*	*Painter*	*Leonard**	*Bailey^*	*Stuart*	*Carter/Smith*
2:1 A BURNLEY 16/9	13 4,175 2:24	W 4-0	1-0	Thorne 37, 62, Kavanagh 68, 80 / Ref: J Kirkby	Muggleton	Pickering	Griffin	Sigurdsson	Tweed	Keen	Forsyth	Wallace^	Thorne	Angola*	Kavanagh	Whittle/MacKenzie
					Beresford	*Weller*	*Brass*	*Williams*	*Blatherwick*	*Moore*	*Matthew**	*Ford*	*Howey^*	*Barnes*	*Eyres*	*Waddle/Little*
2:2 H BURNLEY 24/9	14 6,041 2:24	W 2-0	1-0	Keen 36, Thorne 71 / Ref: A D'Urso (Stoke win 6-0 on aggregate)	Muggleton	Pickering	Griffin	Sigurdsson	Tweed*	Keen^	Forsyth	Wallace*	Thorne	Crowe	MacKenzie	Whittle/Kavnagh/Schreuder
					Beresford	*Brass*	*Vinnicombe*	*Matthew**	*Gentile*	*Moore*	*Waddle^*	*Creaney*	*Cooke"*	*Cowans*	*Eyres*	*Huxford/Weller/Little*
3 H LEEDS 15/10	7 16,203 P:8	L 1-3 aet	0-0	Kavanagh 66p / Kewell 69, Wallace 93, 105 / Ref: P Jones	Muggleton	Pickering	Griffin	Sigurdsson	Tweed	Keen	Forsyth	Wallace	McMahon*	Angola^	Kavanagh^	Crowe/Nyamah/Whittle
					Martyn	*Kelly*	*Robertson*	*Haaland*	*Radebe*	*Wetherall*	*Wallace*	*Ribiero**	*Hopkin^*	*Halle*	*Kewell*	*Lilley/Bowyer*

Kavanagh has his shooting boots on. His 30-yard free-kick whistles into the corner. Robbie Painter is sent clear by a long ball over the top and duly levels. Thorne finishes Keen's whipped cross and City score from a corner for the first time since 1995-6 when Forsyth nods in a flick-on.

A rather quiet first-ever competitive match at the Brit is enlivened by Graham Kavanagh's 25-yard belter which rockets into the top corner for a superb first goal at the new ground. City go to sleep. Alex Russell pounces to net from 12 yards. Dutchman Dick Schreuder makes his debut.

City put Chris Waddle's Clarets to the sword. A superb move out of defence allows Thorne to crash the ball home on the run. Pickering's cross falls to Thorne to volley in. Kav slams home from 20 yards and then hits a belter from slightly further out after Thorne's dummy outwits Brass.

A professional performance. Keen beats keeper Marlon Beresford to a dropped ball in the box to score. Stoke saunter through the motions. An increasingly angry Waddle is the only booking. Thorne swivels adroitly to finish across Beresford. Dean Crowe, on fire in the reserves, debuts.

Stoke's best cup run for 14 years ends at the hands of George Graham's Leeds. Wetherall hits the post before Griffin's run is ended by a pincer tackle and Kav wallops in the pen. Delirium is cut short by Harry Kewell's first Leeds goal from 25 yards. City run out of steam in extra-time.

FA Cup

FA Cup	Att	F-A	H-T	Scorers, Times, and Referees	1	2	3	4	5	6	7	8	9	10	11	subs used
3 A WEST BROM 13/1	16 17,598 7	L 1-3	0-2	Gabbiadini 61 / Sneekes 28, 32, Kilbane 78 / Ref: P Jones	Muggleton	Pickering	Griffin	Sigurdsson	Tweed*	Keen	Forsyth	Wallace	Gabbiadini	Stewart	Whittle	Thorne
					Miller	*Holmes*	*Nicholson*	*Sneekes*	*Murphy*	*Dobson*	*Evans**	*Hamilton*	*Hughes*	*Hunt*	*Kilbane*	*Butler*

City's FA Cup hoodoo outweighs the unbeaten run against West Brom. Richard Sneekes cracks a free-kick under the unguarded far post. Then a shot is deflected past the helpless Muggers. Stewart has a strike ruled out for offside. Gabbiadini pokes home. £1m Kilbane heads the clincher

	Team	P	Home					Away					Pts
			W	D	L	F	A	W	D	L	F	A	
1	Nott'm Forest	46	18	7	3	52	20	10	8	5	30	22	94
2	Middlesbro *	46	17	4	2	51	12	10	6	7	26	29	91
3	Sunderland	46	14	7	2	49	22	12	5	6	37	28	90
4	Charlton *	46	17	5	1	48	17	9	9	9	32	32	88
5	Ipswich	46	14	5	4	47	20	9	5	9	30	23	83
6	Sheffield Utd	46	13	5	2	44	20	3	12	8	25	34	74
7	Birmingham	46	13	8	5	27	15	9	9	5	33	20	74
8	Stockport	46	14	6	3	46	21	5	2	16	25	48	65
9	Wolves	46	13	6	4	42	25	5	5	13	15	28	65
10	West Brom	46	9	8	6	27	26	7	5	11	23	30	61
11	Crewe	46	10	2	11	30	34	8	3	12	28	31	59
12	Oxford	46	2	6	5	36	20	4	4	15	24	44	58
13	Bradford C	46	10	9	4	26	23	4	6	13	20	36	57
14	Tranmere	46	9	8	6	34	26	5	6	12	20	31	56
15	Norwich	46	9	8	6	32	27	5	5	13	20	42	55
16	Huddersfield	46	9	5	9	28	28	5	6	12	22	44	53
17	Bury	46	7	10	6	22	22	4	9	10	20	36	52
18	Swindon	46	9	6	8	28	25	5	4	14	14	48	52
19	Port Vale	46	7	6	10	25	24	6	4	13	31	42	49
20	Portsmouth	46	8	6	9	28	30	5	4	14	23	33	49
21	QP Rangers	46	8	9	6	28	21	2	10	11	23	42	49
22	Manchester C	46	6	6	11	28	26	6	6	11	28	31	48
23	STOKE	46	8	5	10	30	40	3	8	12	14	34	46
24	Reading	46	8	4	11	27	31	3	5	15	12	47	42
		1104	262	146	144	835	575	144	146	262	575	835	1510

* promoted after play-offs

Odds & ends

Double wins: (0).

Double losses: (7) Birmingham, Crewe, Huddersfield, Reading, Sunderland, Swindon, Tranmere.

Won from behind: (2) Bradford C (h), Portsmouth (h).

Lost from in front: (2) Sheffield Utd (a), Swindon (h).

High spots: Early season good form.
Winning at Maine Road, Portman Road and the Riverside.
The late season emergence of Dean Crowe.

Low spots: The dismal relegation.
Being thrashed by Birmingham 0-7.
The violence after the last game against Manchester City.
The atrocious home form at the new Britannia Stadium.
Loss of form of quality players such as Sigurdsson and Kavanagh.

Player of the Year: Justin Whittle.
Ever-presents: (0).
Hat-tricks: (0).
Leading scorer: (16) Peter Thorne.

Appearances and Goals

Player	Lge	Sub	LC	Sub	FAC	Sub	Lge	LC	FAC	Tot
Angola, Zay	4	8	2							1
Crowe, Dean	10	6	1		1		4			4
Donaldson, O'Neill	2									
Forsyth, Richard	37		4			1	7	1		8
Gabbiadini, Marco	2	6				1		1		1
Griffin, Andy	23		4			1	1			1
Heath, Robert	4	2								
Holsgrove, Paul	11	1					1			1
Kavanagh, Graham	44		4	1			5	5		10
Keen, Kevin	37	3	5				1	1		2
Lightbourne, Kyle	9	4			1		2			2
Macari, Paul		3								
Mackenzie, Neil	7	5	1			1				
McKinlay, Tosh	3		1							
McMahon, Gerry	7	10	2			1				
McNally, Mark	3	1								
Muggleton, Carl	34		5		1					
Nyamah, Kofi	9	1	1			1				
Pickering, Ally	42		5				1			1
Schreuder, Dick		2								
Scully, Tony	7									
Sigurdsson, Larus	43		5			1	1			1
Sobiech, Jorg	3									
Southall, Neville	12									
Stewart, Paul	22		2			1	3			3
Sturridge, Simon		1				1				
Taaffe, Steven		3								
Thorne, Peter	33	3	4				12	4		16
Tiatto, Danny	11	4				1	1			1
Tweed, Steven	35	3	5		1					
Wallace, Ray	36	3	5		1		3			3
Whittle, Justin	15	5		4	1					
Woods, Stephen		1								
Xausa, Davide							1			1
(own-goals)										
34 players used	506	73	55	12	11	1	44	11	1	56

NATIONWIDE DIVISION 2

Manager: Brian Little

SEASON 1998-99

Match summary

(Pos = team's league position, bold; Opp = opponents' league position; Pt = points)

No	V	Opponent	Date	Att	Pos	Opp	Pt	Res	F-A	H-T	Scorers, Times, and Referees
1	A	NORTHAMPTON	8/8	6,661	—	—	3	W	3-1	1-1	Kavanagh 7p, Thorne 63, Crowe 83 / Corazzin 17. Ref: A D'Urso
2	H	MACCLESFIELD	15/8	13,981	1	24	6	W	2-0	2-0	Crowe 25, Thorne 36. Ref: B Coddington
3	A	PRESTON	22/8	11,587	1	7	9	W	4-3	0-2	Crowe 50, 85, Kavanagh 69, 72p / Nogan 6, 63, Eyres 38. Ref: T Jones
4	H	OLDHAM	29/8	12,306	1	21	12	W	2-0	1-0	Keen 22, Lightbourne 90. Ref: G Cain
5	A	COLCHESTER	31/8	4,728	1	12	15	W	1-0	0-0	Kavanagh 78. Ref: P Taylor
6	H	BOURNEMOUTH	5/9	13,443	1	4	18	W	2-0	0-0	Thorne 70, Crowe 76. Ref: P Richards
7	A	FULHAM	8/9	12,055	2	2	18	L	0-1	0-0	Brevett 60. Ref: C Wilkes
8	H	MILLWALL	12/9	12,307	1	14	21	W	1-0	0-0	Lightbourne 90. Ref: F Stretton
9	A	WREXHAM	19/9	7,290	1	13	24	W	1-0	0-0	Wallace 78. Ref: W Burns
10	H	BLACKPOOL	26/9	15,002	1	3	24	L	1-3	0-2	Crowe 69p / Carlisle 6, Aldridge 35, 86. Ref: J Kirkby
11	A	READING	3/10	13,089	1	18	24	L	1-2	0-1	Whittle 69 / Brebner 44, McIntyre 73. Ref: P Walton

Line-ups (team player / opponent)

No	1	2	3	4	5	6	7	8	9	10	11	subs used
1	Muggleton / Woodman	Robinson / Matthew*	Small / Frain	Sigurdsson / Bishop	Woods / Warburton	Whittle* / Spedding	Keen / Gibb	Kavanagh / Peel*	Thorne / Heggs^	Lightbourne^ / Corazzin	Short / Hill !	Crowe / Clarkson/Freestone/Hunt
2	Muggleton / Price	Short / Tinson	Small / Ingram	Sigurdsson / Payne	Woods / McDonald	Robinson* / Sodje	Keen / Askey	Kavanagh / Wood	Thorne / Tomlinson*	Crowe / Sorvel	Oldfield / Whittaker	Whittle/Pickering / Barclay
3	Muggleton / Moilanen	Short / Parkinson	Small / Kidd	Sigurdsson / McKenna	Woods / Jackson	Robinson* / Gregan	Keen / Appleton	Kavanagh / Rankine	Thorne / Nogan	Crowe* / Macken^	Oldfield / Eyres	Whittle/Lightbourne/Wallace / Holt
4	Muggleton / Kelly	Short / McNiven	Small / Holt	Sigurdsson / Garnett	Robinson / Graham	Woods / Duxbury	Keen / Allott	Kavanagh^ / Orlygsson	Thorne / Littlejohn	Crowe* / Whitehall	Oldfield / Reid	Lightbourne/Wallace
5	Muggleton / Emberson	Short / Haydon	Small / Betts	Sigurdsson / Williams	Robinson / Greene	Woods / Buckle^	Keen^ / Wilkins	Kavanagh / Gregory D	Thorne / Sale	Crowe* / Gregory N	Oldfield / Duguid^	Lightbourne/Wallace / Abrahams/Forbes
6	Muggleton / Ovendale	Short / Young	Small^ / Vincent	Whittle / Howe	Robinson / Berthe*	Woods / Bailey^	Keen / Cox	Wallace" / Robinson	Thorne / Stein	Lightbourne / Fletcher	Oldfield* / Hughes	Crowe/Tweed/Heath / Town^/Dean/Tindall
7	Muggleton / Taylor	Short* / Collins*	Heath / Brevett	Sigurdsson / Morgan	Robinson / Coleman	Woods / Symons	Keen / Beardsley	Kavanagh^ / Bracewell	Thorne / Moody"	Lightbourne / Hayward	Oldfield / Salako"	Whittle/Crowe / Lehmann/Uhlenbeek/Davis
8	Muggleton / Spink	Whittle / Lavin	Heath* / Ryan	Sigurdsson / Bowry	Robinson / Nethercott	Woods / Fitzgerald	Keen / Neill	Kavanagh / Cahill*	Thorne / Harris	Lightbourne / Shaw	Oldfield / Carter	Crowe / Bircham
9	Muggleton / Cartwright	Robinson* / McGregor	Woods / Brace	Sigurdsson / Russell*	Whittle / Ridler	Oldfield / Humes	Keen / Skinner	Kavanagh / Owen	Thorne / Connolly	Lightbourne / Ward	Crowe* / Spink*	Heath/Wallace / Roberts/Thomas
10	Muggleton / Banks	Robinson* / Bryan	Whittle / Shuttleworth	Sigurdsson / Bardsley^	Woods / Carlisle	Heath / Ormerod	Keen / Hughes	Kavanagh^ / Clarkson	Thorne / Aldridge"	Lightbourne / Bushell	Oldfield / Malkin^	Crowe / Brabin/Bent/Nowland
11	Muggleton / Howie	Small* / Crawford	Heath / McPherson	Sigurdsson / Parkinson	Woods / Primus	Whittle / Casper	Keen / Brayson*	Kavanagh / Caskey	Thorne / Williams	Lightbourne / Glasgow	Oldfield / Brebner	Crowe / McIntyre

Match reports

1. New boss Brian Little gets off to the best possible start as Colin Hill handles Sigurdsson's header on the line. He is sent off and Kavanagh slots the pen. Carlo Corazzin belts home a free-kick before City take control. Thorne's header and Crowe's run and shot seal an easy win. Emphatic.

2. Little's wing-back system looks impressive against Sammy McIlroy's Silkmen. Crowe heads Keen's centre home emphatically. Thorne cracks in from the edge of the box. Sodje fouls Crowe persistently and is booked but ventures upfield to fire against the crossbar deep in injury-time.

3. Kurt Nogan's cross-shot and David Eyres' drive put David Moyes' Preston in charge. Crowe belts home from an acute angle but as City press Nogan races clear to beat Muggers. Small's cross is headed in by Kav. The penalty is for handball. Crowe runs through to win it. Exhilarating.

4. Stoke attack from the off. Keen chips a brilliant goal into the far corner from 25 yards. Kelly pulls off a superb save from Keen's header. Andy Ritchie's Latics push City back. Wallace blocks Reid's shot bravely. Lightbourne converts Thorne's pass. Sheffield Utd are chasing Kavanagh.

5. City miraculously survive U's furious onslaught. 6ft 6in ex-City apprentice Mark Sale causes mayhem. Muggleton produces a string of superb saves to deny both Gregorys and Abrahams. Carl Emberson saves Thorne's header but is beaten by a 25-yard Kav volley which rockets home.

6. Stein screws a good chance wide. City rarely threaten. Little brings on Heath and Crowe who turn the game. Thorne nets amid confusion in the area. Crowe prods past Mark Ovendale. Stoke are 9-4 favs to lift the title after their best ever start to a season. Little is manager of the month.

7. Kevin Keegan's Fulham put City under heavy pressure. Robinson heads off the line. Symons hits the bar. Hayward hits the post. Rufus Brevett beats two players to drive across Muggelton. Kav slips Thorne in but he drills over. Chris Short flakes out and needs oxygen to resuscitate him.

8. Robinson nods off the line. Sigurdsson puts a free header over from six yards. Sigurdsson stands on the ball but Shaw fires straight at Muggers and then blazes high and wide from four yards. Nigel Spink lets Lightbourne's effort slip through his hands. Bolton are watching Dean Crowe.

9. A scrappy match of few chances. Crowe slices wide when well placed. Muggelton turns Peter Ward's free-kick round the post. A Lightbourne centre eludes Thorne but Ray Wallace races in to bullet a header home. A takeover bid by Derek Dougan's consortium is rejected by the board.

10. City play superbly. Blackpool ride their luck. Three out of four shots nestle in the back of the net. Kav is injured in a tackle with Steve Bushell. Martin Aldridge scores two on the break as the Tangerines withstand intense pressure. Thorne has his shirt tugged and Crowe converts the pen.

11. Kavanagh is sandwiched in the box but the ref waves play on. Tommy Burns' Royals survive as Thorne heads a great chance at Howie. Darren Caskey whips past Small to set up Grant Brebner to net. Whittle heads home a Keen cross. Jim McIntyre nods home unchallenged. Stoke wilt.

12 — H CHESTERFIELD, 12/10 — D 0-0 (HT 0-0) — Att 10,557 — Pts 25

Stoke: Muggleton, Heath, Small, Whittle, Robinson, Woods, Keen, Kavanagh, Thorne*, Lightbourne, Oldfield^ (subs Crowe/Short)
Chesterfield: Mercer, Hewitt, Nicholson, Jules, Williams, Breckin, Howard, Holland, Reeves, Ebdon, Perkins
Ref: A Hall

A turgid game with few chances. Stoke have over 70% of the possession but John Duncan's Spireites have the best chance. Jon Howard has a shot blocked point blank by Muggers. Lightbourne heads straight at Billy Mercer. Keen's flair is not matched by the rest of the team. Tedious.

13 — A LINCOLN, 17/10 — W 2-1 (HT 0-1) — Att 6,159 — Pts 28
Scorers: Robinson 49, Sigurdsson 52 / Battersby

Stoke: Muggleton, Short, Small, Sigurdsson, Robinson, Woods, Keen, Kavanagh, Thorne, Lightbourne, Oldfield (sub Gordon)
Lincoln: Richardson, Barnett, Whitney*, Fleming, Holmes, Austin, Smith, Finnigan, Battersby, Alcide, Oatway
Ref: C Foy

Lowly Imps tear into Stoke. Tony Battersby pounces after Steve Holmes heads against the bar. Lincoln pour forward. Finnigan fires wide. Half-time is timely for City, Phil Robinson nods in his first Stoke goal. Keen's next corner is headed home by Sigurdsson. Muggers denies Smith.

14 — A BRISTOL ROV, 20/10 — L 0-1 (HT 0-1) — Att 6,752 — Pts 28
Scorer: Cureton 8

Stoke: Muggleton, Short, Small, Sigurdsson, Robinson, Woods*, Keen^, Kavanagh^, Thorne, Lightbourne, Oldfield* (subs Whittle/Wallace/Crowe)
Bristol Rovers: Jones, Leoni^, Challis, Zabek, Foster, Smith, Holloway, Meaker, Ipoua*, Cureton, Hayles (subs Trees/Pennce)
Ref: A Leake

On Stoke's first visit to Rovers' Memorial Stadium, Jamie Cureton blazes a loose ball home from the edge of the box. Thorne sends a dipping 30-yarder just over and then hits the bar. Muggleton saves superbly from Barry Hayles. Crowe cuts inside but his cross evades Thorne's lunge.

15 — H WIGAN, 24/10 — W 2-1 (HT 0-0) — Att 11,480 — Pts 31
Scorers: Kavanagh 52, Griffiths 53 (og) / Barlow 74

Stoke: Muggleton, Short, Whittle, Sigurdsson, Robinson, Woods, Keen, Kavanagh*, Thorne*, Lightbourne, Oldfield* (subs Lightbourne/Wallace/Mackenzie)
Wigan: Carroll, Green, Bradshaw, Griffiths, Balmer, Rogers, Kilford, Greenall*, Haworth, O'Neill, Liddell^ (subs Lee/Barlow)
Ref: W Jordan

In monsoon conditions the balance is tipped when the referee spots a shirt tug on Crowe. Kav's spot-kick is saved but Keen picks up the pieces allowing a relieved Kavanagh to score. Gareth Griffiths nods Chris Short's cross past Roy Carroll. Stuart Barlow nets for Ray Mathias' Latics.

16 — A NOTTS CO, 31/10 — L 0-1 (HT 0-1) — Att 8,540 — Pts 31
Scorer: Farrell 35

Stoke: Muggleton, Short, Small, Sigurdsson, Robinson, Whittle, Keen^, Kavanagh, Thorne, Lightbourne, Oldfield
Notts Co: Ward, Hendon, Pearce, Redmile, Fairclough, Finnan, Owers, Farrell*, Devlin, Murray, Jones
Ref: E Lomas

Sam Allardyce's Magpies are in control from the off. Muggers saves well from Devlin, Pearce and Farrell. Robinson blocks a shot on the line. Sean Farrell nets after a static City fail to clear a corner. Stoke receive six yellow cards. Lightbourne hits a feeble shot straight at Darren Ward.

17 — H LUTON, 7/11 — W 3-1 (HT 2-0) — Att 12,964 — Pts 34
Scorers: Oldfield 3, Forsyth 37, Lightbourne 90 / Douglas 81

Stoke: Muggleton, Short*, Small, Sigurdsson, Robinson, Woods, Keen^, Forsyth, Thorne, Lightbourne, Oldfield (subs McLaren/Doherty)
Luton: Davis, Alexander/Thomas*, Spring^, Johnson, McKinnon, Evers, Garcia, Farrell, Douglas, Gray, McGowan
Ref: M Jones

David Oldfield is roundly booed by Hatters fans but retaliates by netting against his old team. Richard Forsyth volleys home from 12 yards on his first start for six months and scores. Graham Alexander is sent off for two bookings. Lightbourne heads home Steve Woods' precise centre.

18 — A BURNLEY, 10/11 — W 2-0 (HT 0-0) — Att 10,575 — Pts 37
Scorers: Lightbourne 47, Thorne 62

Stoke: Muggleton, Woods, Small, Sigurdsson, Robinson, Forsyth, Keen, Kavanagh, Thorne, Lightbourne, Oldfield
Burnley: Ward, Scott, Morgan, Windhem*, Reid, Heywood, Little, Brass, Eastwood*, Ford, O'Kane (subs Henderson/Maylett)
Ref: G Laws

Stan Ternent's Clarets miss top scorer Andy Payton. Muggers saves well from Glen Little. Lightbourne knocks in Kav's mis-hit effort. Thorne thumps in a header from Kavanagh's delicious centre. Brian Little is in the frame for the vacant job at Wolves. Kav signs a new four-year deal.

19 — H YORK, 21/11 — W 2-0 (HT 2-0) — Att 11,395 — Pts 40
Scorers: Forsyth 30, Oldfield 35

Stoke: Muggleton, Woods, Small, Sigurdsson, Robinson, Forsyth, Keen, Kavanagh, Thorne, Lightbourne*, Oldfield (subs Wallace)
York: Warrington, McMillan, Hall, Tinkler, Jones, Garratt, Connelly, Jordan, Cresswell, Rowe, Agnew* (sub Reed)
Ref: M Pike

The battle of the Little brothers sees Brian outwit Alan. Small's centre is flicked on for Forsyth to finish off at the far post. Oldfield lets loose a thunderbolt which flies past Andy Warrington. Sigurdsson subdues £1m-rated Richard Cresswell classily. Little is manager of the month again.

20 — A WYCOMBE, 28/11 — W 1-0 (HT 0-0) — Att 6,723 — Pts 43
Scorer: Kavanagh 79

Stoke: Muggleton, Petty, Small, Sigurdsson, Robinson, Woods, Keen, Kavanagh*, Thorne^, Lightbourne, Oldfield (subs Wallace/Sturridge)
Wycombe: Taylor, Lawrence, Vinnicombe*/McCarthy, Cousins, Mohan, Simpson, Brown, McSporran, Scott, Emblen, Bulman
Ref: L Cable

Sigurdsson's header crashes off the bar. Muggers produces a great save from a Michael Simpson free-kick. Woods nods McCarthy's header off the line. Kav rifles in a loose ball from the edge of the box and is booked for over-celebrating and receives a second suspension of the season.

21 — H GILLINGHAM, 12/12 — D 0-0 (HT 0-0) — Att 17,233 — Pts 44

Stoke: Muggleton, Bartram, Small, Sigurdsson, Robinson, Woods, Keen, Sturridge^, Forsyth, Lightbourne, Oldfield (subs Wallace/Crowe, Hodge)
Gillingham: Bartram, Southall, Butters, Smith, Bryant, Pennock, Patterson, Hessenthaler, Asaba, Galloway, Taylor*
Ref: T Heilbron

A bore draw. Kav and Thorne are suspended. Crowe has a close-range shot well saved by Vince Bartram. 64 Elvis look-alikes watch the match from the Sentinel Stand. Justin Whittle moves to Hull (£25k). Peter Thorne signs on until 2002. Ally Pickering joins Burnley on a free transfer.

22 — A WALSALL, 19/12 — L 0-1 (HT 0-1) — Att 9,056 — Pts 44
Scorer: Rammell 41

Stoke: Muggleton, Forsyth, Small, Sigurdsson, Robinson, Woods*, Keen, Kavanagh, Thorne, Lightbourne*, Oldfield* (subs Crowe/Wallace/Petty, Brissett)
Walsall: Walker, Marsh, Pointon, Keates, Green, Roper, Wrack, Rankine, Otta*, Larusson, Simpson (sub Rammell)
Ref: E Wolstenholme

City have plenty of possession but lack a cutting edge. Ray Graydon's Walsall soak up the pressure and break well. Andy Rammell hits the bar before heading home Neil Pointon's cross. A new attendance record is set for the Bescot Stadium. Steven Tweed signs for Dundee for £30,000.

23 — H PRESTON, 26/12 — L 0-1 (HT 0-1) — Att 23,372 — Pts 44
Scorer: Jackson 7

Stoke: Muggleton, Petty, Small, Sigurdsson, Robinson, Woods*, Keen, Kavanagh, Thorne, Lightbourne, Oldfield (sub Crowe)
Preston: Lucas, Parkinson, Kidd, Murdock, Jackson, Gregan, Cartwright, Rankine, Macken^, Byfield*, Eyres (subs Nogan/Harris)
Ref: G Frankland

A swirling wind ruins the game and contributes to an in-swinging corner finding Michael Jackson who nods in from close range. City huff and puff but Preston close down space well. David Lucas tips Thorne's overhead kick over the bar. Lack of punch up front is worrying Brian Little.

NATIONWIDE DIVISION 2 — Manager: Brian Little — SEASON 1998-99

(In each match the top line is the Stoke City line-up; the italic line below is the opponents' line-up. The figure in brackets in the "Pos" column is the opponents' league position.)

No	Date	V	Opponents	Att	Pos	Res	Pt	F-A	H-T	1	2	3	4	5	6	7	8	9	10	11	subs used
24	28/12	A	MANCHESTER C	30,478	3 (7)	L	44	1-2	1-0	Muggleton	Petty	Small	Sigurdsson	Robinson	Woods	Keen	Kavanagh	Thorne	Lightbourne*	Oldfield	Sturridge
			opponents							*Weaver*	*Crooks*	*Edghill*	*Wiekens*	*Vaughan*	*Horlock*	*Brown*	*Pollack*	*Taylor*	*Bishop^*	*Dickov*	*Goater*
25	9/1	H	NORTHAMPTON	11,180	3 (18)	W	47	3-1	0-0	Muggleton	Turley	Heath	Wallace	Robinson	Woods	Keen	Kavanagh	Thorne^	Mackenzie*	Lightbourne	Crowe/Forsyth
			opponents								*Gibb*	*Frain*	*Sampson*	*Howey*	*Parrish**	*Hunter*	*Savage"*	*Wilkinson^*	*Freestone*	*Peer*	*Corazzin/Hope*
26	23/1	H	COLCHESTER	12,507	4 (17)	D	48	3-3	3-2	Muggleton	Wallace*	Small*	Sigurdsson	Robinson	Woods	Keen	Kavanagh	Thorne	Lightbourne^	Forsyth	Crowe/Petty
			opponents							*Emberson*	*Dunne*	*Betts*	*Williams*	*Greene*	*Buckle*	*Wilkins*	*Gregory D*	*Skelton*	*Gregory N^*	*Duguid**	*Abrahams/Dozzell*
27	29/1	H	MANCHESTER C	13,679	5 (8)	L	48	0-1	0-1	Muggleton	Heath	Small	Sigurdsson	Robinson!	Woods	Keen	Kavanagh^	Crowe	Lightbourne	Forsyth^	Oldfield/Wallace
			opponents							*Weaver*	*Crooks^*	*Edghill*	*Wiekens*	*Vaughan*	*Horlock*	*Brown*	*Pollack*	*Taylor*	*Goater*	*Cooke**	*Dickov/Whitley/Jim/Bishop*
28	6/2	A	BOURNEMOUTH	7,637	6 (4)	L	48	0-4	0-2	Muggleton	Short*	Small	Sigurdsson	Robinson	Woods^	Keen	Kavanagh!	Crowe	Mackenzie*	Oldfield	Lightbourne/Forsyth/Wallace
			opponents							*Ovendale*	*Young*	*Vincent"*	*Howe*	*O'Neill!*	*Bailey*	*Cox*	*Robinson*	*Boli^*	*Fletcher*	*Hughes*	*Warren^/Hayter/Jenkins*
29	20/2	A	MILLWALL	7,855	7 (9)	L	48	0-2	0-1	Muggleton	Short	Small*	Collins	Petty	Woods^	Keen	Wallace	Crowe	Forsyth	Oldfield	Lightbourne/Mackenzie
			opponents							*Smith*	*Lavin*	*Stuart*	*Cahill*	*Nethercott*	*Dolan*	*Reid**	*Bowry!*	*Harris^*	*Sadlier!*	*Neill*	*Bircham/Hill*
30	27/2	H	WREXHAM	10,765	9 (14)	L	48	1-3	0-1	Ward	Wright	Small	Sigurdsson	Short*	Collins	Keen"	Wallace*	Lightbourne	O'Connor	Oldfield	Crowe/Forsyth/Taaffe
			opponents								*Hardy*	*Brammer*	*Ridler*	*Carey*	*Chalk*	*Russell*	*Whitley*	*Owen*	*Connolly*	*McGregor*	*Owen/Whitley*
31	6/3	A	BLACKPOOL	5,504	7 (14)	W	51	1-0	1-0	Ward	Short	Woods	Sigurdsson	Mohan	Petty*	Keen	Forsyth	Lightbourne	Crowe^	Oldfield	Small/Wallace
			opponents							*Banks*	*Bryan*	*Hills*	*Butler*	*Carlisle*	*Couzens^*	*Barnes**	*Clarkson*	*Nowland*	*Hughes*	*Ormerod*	*Bent/Aldridge*
32	10/3	H	READING	8,218	8 (10)	L	51	0-4	0-0	Ward	Howie	Gray	Robinson"	Woods	Short*	Keen^	Forsyth	Crowe	Lightbourne	Oldfield	Small/Thorne/Wallace
			opponents								*Murty"*	*Parkinson*	*Primus*	*Bernal*	*Gurney*	*Caskey*	*McKeever*	*Houghton*	*McIntyre^*	*George^*	*Brayson/McPherson/Glasgow*
33	13/3	A	LUTON	5,221	7 (14)	W	54	2-1	2-0	Ward	Short	Woods	Sigurdsson	Mohan	Robinson	Keen	Kavanagh G	Forsyth^	Crowe*	Lightbourne	Keen/Wallace
			opponents							*Davis*	*Alexander*	*Thomas*	*Spring*	*White"*	*Johnson*	*Harrison**	*McKinnon*	*Douglas*	*Gray*	*George^*	*McLaren/Doherty/Willmott*
34	16/3	H	FULHAM	12,298	8 (1)	L	54	0-1	0-1	Ward	Kavanagh J	Woods	Sigurdsson	Short	Robinson*	Keen	Kavanagh G	Lightbourne^	Oldfield	Keen	Crowe/Wallace
			opponents							*Taylor*	*Finnan*	*Brevett*	*Morgan*	*Coleman*	*Symons*	*Hayward*	*Smith*	*Horsfield*	*Trollope*	*Hayles*	

Scorers, Times and Referees — and match reports

24. Sigurdsson 31 / Dickov 47, Taylor 85. Ref: A Butler.
Sigurdsson leaps to nod Keen's cross beyond Nicky Weaver. Stoke look comfortable sitting on the lead until Joe Royle puts three up front after the break. Shaun Goater causes havoc. Dickov picks up the pieces. Gareth Taylor heads in his first goal since his £400k move from Sheff Utd.

25. Wallace 56, Thorne 74, Lightbourne 84 / Howey 90. Ref: D Pugh.
The players are booed off at the break after failing to create a chance. Billy Turley makes a mess of Robinson's effort and Wallace prods home. Thorne is gifted a tap-in after Turley fails to clear a long ball. Lightbourne heads home Keen's chip. Howey nods in a corner. First win in five.

26. Gregory D 30 (og), Lightb'rne 34, Sig 42; Betts 9, Gregory D 45, Dozzell 79. Ref: T Jones.
Simon Betts nets a cool volley. Stoke pour forward. David Gregory deflects Kav's centre past Emberson. Lightbourne powers in Keen's cross. Sigurdsson heads in Kav's cross. Gregory makes amends from close in. City sit back. Jason Dozzell nods in. Little denies he wishes to resign.

27. Wiekens 20. Ref: C Wilkes.
Stoke are totally outplayed and are lucky only to lose by one. Gerard Wiekens cracks in a loose ball. Joe Royle's Blues miss countless chances. Robinson is sent off (40 mins) for an atrocious challenge on Michael Brown. Supporters are uniting to bring together a bid to buy-out the board.

28. Fletcher 21, 39, Robinson 71, Hayter 76. Ref: S Bennett.
The wheels really come off at Dean Court. Steve Fletcher heads home and then profits when Sigurdsson nods past Muggers on the edge of the box. Kav and John O'Neill walk for fighting (44 mins). Hayter belts home a beauty from 16 yards. Little acknowledges the unrest in the camp.

29. Harris 39, Cahill 65. Ref: R Styles.
City cannot even beat nine-man Millwall – Bobby Bowry is dismissed (3 mins) for elbowing Wallace, Richard Sadlier for a second yellow (70 mins). Harris and Cahill score as the defence stands and watches. City cannot beat stand-in keeper Phil Smith. A total and utter embarrassment.

30. Sigurdsson 82 / McGregor 8, Owen 54, Connolly 67. Ref: M Messias.
Mark McGregor lobs free-transfer signing Gavin Ward. Connolly sets up Owen to finish before racing clear himself to round Ward. Sigurdsson heads home Short's corner. Stan Clarke has relinquished all interest in the club and sold his shares back to Peter Coates and Keith Humphreys.

31. Lightbourne 34. Ref: M Dean.
Nicky Mohan, free transfer from Wycombe, steadies the ship. Nigel Worthington's Blackpool put City under intense pressure. Adam Nowland forces Ward into two good saves. Lightbourne heads home Keen's corner as Stoke steal the points. 'Don't write off promotion' says Little.

32. McKeever 59, McIntyre 76, 82, Gray 87. Ref: M Cowburn.
Jason Kavanagh, another free transfer, arrives from Wycombe. His debut is a nightmare as the Royals run riot. On-loan Mark McKeever races clear to score. Crowe hits the post and Jim McIntyre is sent clear to score the first of his brace. City fall apart. The team spirit has disappeared.

33. Kavanagh G 10p, 17 / Alexander 47p. Ref: A D'Urso.
Lennie Lawrence's atrocious Hatters allow Stoke to take control. Kavanagh cracks home a spot-kick following Johnson's foul, before hitting a speculative shot which deceives Kelvin Davis. Alexander scores a pen after Woods handles. Luton have a goal disallowed for a foul on Ward.

34. Symons 10. Ref: P Danson.
Runaway leaders Fulham snatch the lead against the run of play when Kit Symons' header creeps in at the far post. Kav urges City forward but the combative Cottagers defend in depth. 10,000 red cards are displayed by disgruntled fans desperate to see money being invested in the club.

Football season results grid — matches 35–46

35 H 20/3 NOTTS CO 9,565 — "3" L 54 — 2-3 (0-0)
Oldfield 68, Keen 90
Beadle 54, Liburd 76, Stallard 85
Ref: G Cain
Lineup: Ward | Kavanagh J | Woods | Sigurdsson | Robinson | O'Connor | Keen | Kavanagh G | Wallace | Mackenzie | Oldfield
Ward | Hendon | Pearce | Liburd | Dyer | Richardson | Creaney | Redmile | Stallard | Beadle* | Tierney | Rapley
Report: A chorus of boos ends an inept first half. Magpies score with their first effort. Oldfield rounds Darren Ward. Richard Liburd waltzes through a somnambulant defence and then Mark Stallard repeats the feat. Keen's volley does not appease the protesters. Two wins in the last ten games.

36 A 27/3 WIGAN 4,133 — 8 "6 54 — W 3-2 (0-0)
Thorne 54, Kavanagh G 80, Strong 88
Liddell 49, Barlow 51
Ref: R Furnandiz
Lineup: Nixon | Kavanagh J | Small | Sigurdsson | Mohan | Strong | Keen | Kavanagh G | Thorne | Lightbourne | Oldfield
Bradshaw | Sharp | McGibbon | Balmer | Rogers | Liddell | Greenall | Jones* | Barlow | Kilford | O'Neill
Report: Wigan have won eight in a row. A much-improved performance sees City battle back from the brink. Barlow's 30-yarder sails over Muggleton before Thorne challenges Nixon and nets as the ball runs free. Kav's mazy run is ended by a superb shot. Strong scores the winner on his debut.

37 H 3/4 LINCOLN 12,845 — "22 60 — W 2-0 (1-0)
Thorne 21, 65
Ref: E Lomas
Lineup: Muggleton | Kavanagh J* | Small | Sigurdsson | Mohan | Strong | Keen | Kavanagh G | Thorne^ | Lightbourne | Oldfield*
Richardson | Barnett | Phillips | Fleming | Holmes | Brown | Wilder^ | Philpott | Battersby | Gordon* | Robinson/Crowe/Wallace | Miller | Smith/Fenn
Report: Thorne's brace arrive courtesy of a header from Keen's centre and a crisp, low drive from 25 yards. Lightbourne blazes wildly over from close range. A scrappy match peters out. Fans' organisation Save Our Stoke organise a 2,000 strong march to register their protests against the board.

38 A 5/4 CHESTERFIELD 5,296 — 3 "0 61 — D 1-1 (1-1)
Oldfield 32
Blatherwick 26
Ref: P Taylor
Lineup: Muggleton | Robinson | Small | Sigurdsson | Mohan | Strong | Keen | Kavanagh G | Thorne | Lightbourne | Oldfield
Mercer | Hewitt | Nicholson* | Blatherwick | Williams | Breckin | Lee | Beaumont | Reeves | Ebdon | Jules | Willis
Report: Steve Blatherwick heads one of a succession of corners firmly into the roof of the net. Oldfield is sent clear by Lightbourne to blast home from the edge of the area. Keen heads off the line. City fail to force a win. Little delays contract talks until May. Stoke's first away draw this season.

39 H 10/4 BRISTOL ROV 17,82? — 8 16 61 — L 1-4 (1-0)
Thorne 41
Roberts 53, Foster 81, Cureton 84, 88
Ref: M Pierce
Lineup: Muggleton | Robinson* | Small | Sigurdsson | Mohan | Strong | Keen | Kavanagh G | Thorne | Lightbourne | Oldfield
Williams | Pritchard | Challis | Foster | Thomson | Tilson | Holloway | Hillier | Penrice | Cureton | Roberts | Crowe
Report: Thorne arches his neck to nod in Kav's centre beautifully. Muggers saves Cureton's effort well but can't stop Roberts deflecting the follow-up home. Rovers take over. Kav misses from the spot after Small is tripped. Foster heads in from a free-kick. Cureton scores twice when put clear.

40 H 14/4 WYCOMBE 6,56? — 8 20 62 — D 2-2 (1-1)
Wallace 38, Oldfield 61
Devine 29, 89
Ref: R Pearson
Lineup: Muggleton | Robinson | Small | Sigurdsson | Mohan | Strong* | Keen | Kavanagh G | Crowe | Forsyth | Wallace
Taylor | Lawrence | Vinnicombe | McCarthy | Bates | Ryan | Carroll* | Simpson | Emblen^ | Devine | Baird | Oldfield | Brown/McSporran
Report: Nicky Mohan faces his old club. It appears that Stoke are heading towards a hard-earned win once Oldfield prods Crowe's pinpoint chip home to add to Wallace's cool finish. Record-signing Sean Devine turns to crack in his second goal for Wycombe from 12 yards. No play-offs now.

41 A 17/4 YORK 4,14? — 7 20 63 — D 2-2 (1-0)
Kavanagh G 10p, 85
Garratt 51, Jordan 67
Ref: J Kirkby
Lineup: Muggleton | Robinson | Small | Sigurdsson | Mohan | Wallace | Keen | Kavanagh G | Thorne | Lightbourne* | Oldfield*
Mimms | Dawson | Thompson | Jordan | Jones | Fairclough | Pouton* | Tinkler | Williams | Rowe | Garratt | Tolson | Crowe/Forsyth
Report: Thorne is felled by Bobby Mimms and Kav tucks away the penalty. Managerless York battle back. Martin Garratt intercepts Mohan's dreadful back-pass to score. Scott Jordan cracks home a beauty from a half-cleared corner. Kav fires in Forsyth's pass. No disguising the lack of quality.

42 H 24/4 BURNLEY 10,59? — 8 15 63 — L 1-4 (1-2)
Crowe 31
Pickering 5, Payton 11, Little 68, 90
Ref: D Crick
Lineup: Muggleton | Robinson | Small | Sigurdsson | Mohan | Oldfield* | Keen | Kavanagh G | Thorne | Crowe | Wallace
Crichton | Pickering | Cowan | Mellon | Davis | Brass | Little | Cook* | Payton^ | Armstrong | Branch*/Johnrose | Connor
Report: Struggling Burnley romp home. Ex-Stokie Ally Pickering nets a glorious 25-yard volley. Payton profits when Mohan sells Keen short. Crowe heads home from six yards. Glen Little robs Sigurdsson to score then outruns Mohan to fire in a long ball. City's accounts show a £3m deficit.

43 A 27/4 MACCLESFIELD 3,?75 — 8 24 66 — W 2-1 (1-1)
Oldfield 31, Crowe 50
Matias 44
Ref: E Lomas
Lineup: Muggleton | Kavanagh J* | Small | Sigurdsson | Mohan | Wallace* | Keen | Kavanagh G | Crowe | Lightbourne* | Oldfield"
Price | Tinson | Hitchen | Brown^ | Wood^ | Askey | Sadje | Sorvel | Tomlinson | Durkan" | Matias | Forsyth | Sedgemore/Davies/Bailey
Report: Condemned Macclesfield force Muggleton into two good stops. Oldfield cracks in from 15 yards. Matias heads home unmarked from a corner. Crowe lobs the keeper when put clear. The depression is temporarily lifted. Kav is called up by Ireland and scores in a friendly versus Sweden.

44 A 1/5 GILLINGHAM 8,2?9 — 8 5 66 — L 0-4 (0-3)
Taylor 30, 45, Butters 43, Smith 69
Ref: C Wilkes
Lineup: Muggleton | Robinson | Small | Sigurdsson | Mohan | Wallace* | Keen | Kavanagh G | Crowe | Oldfield | Connor
Bartram | Southall | Ashby | Smith | Butters | Pennock | Patterson" | Hessenthaler | Asaba* | Galloway^ | Taylor | Hodge/Saunders/Brown
Report: Stoke are gutless at Tony Pulis' play-off bound Gills. Robert Taylor nips past a static defence to beat Muggers twice but wastes a 44th-min pen for Sigurdsson's foul. Guy Butters nods in a free header. Paul Smith also nods in unmarked. Brian Little admits it is the worst performance so far.

45 A 4/5 OLDHAM £C15? — 8 21 66 — L 0-1 (0-0)
Beavers 50
Ref: J Robinson
Lineup: Muggleton* | Kavanagh J* | Clarke | Sigurdsson | Mohan | Oldfield* | Keen | Kavanagh G | Thorne | Oldfield | Connor
Kelly | Rickers | Holt | Garrett | Thorn | Duxbury | Innes | Sheridan | Beavers* | Reid | Allott | Tipton^/Salt
Report: Debutant Irish U-18 international Clive Clarke hits the post before Stoke's statuesque defence watches Beavers flick in a long throw. Gloom and despondency amongst Stokies at the whistle.

46 H 8/5 WALSALL 12,?91 — 8 2 69 — W 2-0 (1-0)
Connor 24, 50
Ref: K Lynch
Lineup: Muggleton* | Petty | Clarke | Sigurdsson | Mohan | Taffe | O'Connor | Kavanagh G | Crowe | Oldfield | Crowe
Walker | Marsh^ | Pointon | Larusson* | Viveash | Roper | Wrack | Steiner | Rammell | Keates | Small | Mavrak | Fraser/Wooliscroft/Heath | Ricketts/Green
Report: Youth is given its chance again and Crowe stings James Walker's fingers with a free-kick. On-loan Paul Connor (Middlesbrough) wants to stay after scoring his first senior goals. He flings himself at Crowe's cross and converts Taffe's pass for a second win in nine. Some hope perhaps?

Home 12,728
Away 7,996
Average 12,728

NATIONWIDE DIVISION 2 (CUP-TIES) Manager: Brian Little SEASON 1998-99

Worthington Cup

		Att	F-A	H-T	1	2	3	4	5	6	7	8	9	10	11	subs used	Scorers, Times, and Referees
1:1	A MACCLESFIELD 11/8	2,963	L 1-3	1-1	Muggleton	Short	Small	Sigurdsson	Robinson	Woods	Keen	Kavanagh	Thorne	Lightbourne	Oldfield		Kavanagh 19
					Price	*Tinson*	*Ingram*	*Payne*	*McDonald*	*Sodje*	*Askey*	*Wood**	*Tomlinson"*	*Sedgemore^*	*Whittaker*	*Sorvel/Durkan/Barclay*	Wood 2, Askey 76, 85 Ref: M Dean

The clubs' first meeting goes the way of Sammy McIlroy's Silkmen. Steve Wood nets before Thorne's header is inexplicably disallowed. Kav belts home a free-kick from 25 yards. John Askey runs through unchallenged to score and then cheekily back-heels a decisive third. Appalling

		Att	F-A	H-T	1	2	3	4	5	6	7	8	9	10	11	subs used	Scorers, Times, and Referees
1:2	H MACCLESFIELD 19/8	6,152 24	W 1-0	0-0	Muggleton	Short*	Small^	Whittle	Robinson	Woods	Pickering	Kavanagh !	Thorne	Crowe"	Oldfield	Tweed/Wallace/Sturridge	Thorne 78
					Price	*Tinson*	*Ingram*	*Payne*	*McDonald*	*Sodje*	*Askey**	*Wood*	*Durkan*	*Sorvel*	*Whittaker^*	*Tomlinson/Howarth*	Ref: D Pugh (Stoke lose 2-3 on aggregate)

City miss Sigurdsson, on duty with Iceland. Town storm forward looking for the killer away goal. Stoke's passing is awful. Kav is sent off for a two-footed challenge (55 mins). Sturridge appears for the first time in nearly a year. Thorne prods past Ryan Price but Macclesfield hold on.

FA Cup

		Att	F-A	H-T	1	2	3	4	5	6	7	8	9	10	11	subs used	Scorers, Times, and Referees
1	A READING 14/11	10,095 10	W 1-0	1-0	Muggleton	Woods	Small	Sigurdsson	Robinson	Forsyth	Keen	Kavanagh	Thorne	Lightbourne*	Oldfield	Wallace	Lightbourne 27
					Howie	*Bernal*	*McPherson*	*Crawford**	*Primus*	*Casper*	*Glasgow*	*Caskey*	*Williams*	*Brayson^*	*Brebner*	*Roach/Sarr*	Ref: G Barber

Thorne is robbed by Linvoy Primus in the act of scoring. Lightbourne's fierce low drive beats Scott Howie to hand Stoke a first victory against Reading since 1993 despite the Royals' heavy late pressure. Stoke's first FA Cup win against league opposition away from home for 26 years.

		Att	F-A	H-T	1	2	3	4	5	6	7	8	9	10	11	subs used	Scorers, Times, and Referees
2	A SWANSEA 5/12	7,460 3:13	L 0-1	0-1	Muggleton	Petty*	Small	Sigurdsson	Robinson	Woods	Keen	Kavanagh	Thorne	Forsyth	Oldfield	Sturridge	
					Freestone	*Jones S*	*Howard*	*Cusack*	*Smith*	*Bound*	*Price*	*Thomas*	*Alsop*	*Bird**	*Appleby*	*Jenkins*	Appleby 41 Ref: K Lynch

An open game with John Hollins' Swans' long-ball game providing Ritchie Appleby with the opening to fire past Muggers from Alsop's knock down. Thorne hits the bar. Appleby hooks off the line. Kav blazes just over. Bound nods Thorne's header off the line. Swans meet West Ham.

League Table

	Team	P	Home					Away					Pts
			W	D	L	F	A	W	D	L	F	A	
1	Fulham	46	19	3	1	50	12	12	5	6	29	20	101
2	Walsall	46	13	7	3	37	23	13	2	8	26	24	87
3	Manchester C*	46	13	6	4	38	14	9	10	4	31	19	82
4	Gillingham	46	15	5	3	45	17	7	9	7	30	27	80
5	Preston	46	12	6	5	46	23	10	7	6	32	27	79
6	Wigan	46	14	5	4	44	17	8	5	10	31	31	76
7	Bournemouth	46	12	7	2	37	11	7	6	10	26	30	76
8	STOKE	46	10	4	9	32	32	11	2	10	27	31	69
9	Chesterfield	46	14	5	4	34	16	3	8	12	12	28	64
10	Millwall	46	9	8	6	33	24	8	3	12	19	35	62
11	Reading	46	13	6	7	29	26	6	7	10	25	37	61
12	Luton	46	13	4	9	25	26	6	6	11	26	34	58
13	Bristol Rov	46	8	9	6	35	24	5	8	10	30	28	56
14	Blackpool	46	7	8	8	24	24	7	6	10	20	30	56
15	Burnley	46	8	7	8	23	33	5	9	9	31	40	55
16	Notts Co	46	8	6	9	29	27	6	6	11	23	34	54
17	Wrexham	46	8	6	9	21	28	5	8	10	22	34	53
18	Colchester	46	7	7	7	25	30	3	9	11	21	40	52
19	Wycombe	46	8	5	10	31	26	5	7	11	21	32	51
20	Oldham	46	7	4	11	26	31	6	5	12	22	35	51
21	York	46	9	8	9	28	33	7	3	13	28	47	50
22	Northampton	46	7	12	7	26	31	6	6	11	17	26	48
23	Lincoln	46	9	4	10	27	27	4	3	16	15	47	46
24	Macclesfield	46	7	4	12	24	30	4	6	13	19	33	43
		1104	263	146	163	769	589	163	146	243	589	769	1510

* promoted
after play-offs

Odds & ends

Double wins: (4) Lincoln, Luton, Macclesfield, Wigan.

Double losses: (5) Bristol Rov, Fulham, Manchester C, Notts Co, Reading.

Won from behind: (3) Preston (a), Lincoln (a), Wigan (a).

Lost from in front: (2) Manchester C (a), Bristol Rov (h).

High spots: The best start to a season in the history of the club.
Astute close season signings.
Brian Little's resignation.
The fabulous away record.
Graham Kavanagh's long-range strikes.

Low spots: Failing to even challenge for the play-offs after dominating the first half of the season.
The turn around at Maine Road which sparks the slump.
Over reliance on the club's youngsters as the squad is stretched.
Brian Little's diffidence when things go awry.
The continuation of the shocking form at the Britannia Stadium.

Player of the Year: Kevin Keen.
Ever-presents: (0).
Hat-tricks: (0).
Leading scorer: (12) Graham Kavanagh.

Appearances and Goals

Player	Appearances						Goals			
	Lge	Sub	LC	Sub	FAC	Sub	Lge	LC	FAC	Tot
Clarke, Clive	2									
Collins, Lee	4									
Connor, Paul	2	1								
Crowe, Dean	19	19	1				2			2
Forsyth, Richard	13	5			2		8			8
Fraser, Stuart		1								
Heath, Robert	7	3					2			2
Kavanagh, Graham	36		2		2		11	1		12
Kavanagh, Jason	8									
Keen, Kevin	43	1	1		2		2			2
Lightbourne, Kyle	28	8	1		1		7		1	8
Mackenzie, Neil	3	3								
Mohan, Nicky	15									
Muggleton, Carl	40		2		2					
O'Connor, James	4									
Oldfield, David	43	3	2		2		6			6
Petty, Ben	9	2	1		1					
Pickering, Ally		1	1							
Robinson, Phil	39	2	2		2		1			1
Short, Craig	19	2	2							
Sigurdsson, Larus	38		1		2		4			4
Small, Bryan	35	2	2		2					
Strong, Greg	5									
Sturridge, Simon	1	2		1	1	1	1			1
Taaffe, Steven	1	2								
Thorne, Peter	33	1	2		2		9	1		10
Tweed, Steven		1	1		1					
Wallace, Ray	11	20	1		1		3			3
Ward, Gavin	6									
Whittle, Justin	9	5	1				1			1
Woods, Stephen	33	2			2					
Wooliscroft, Ashley		1								
(own-goals)							2			2
32 Players used	506	84	22	3	22	2	59	2	1	62

NATIONWIDE DIVISION 2

Manager: Megson ⇒ Thordarson   SEASON 1999-2000

---

1   H   OXFORD   7/8
Scorers, Times, and Referees: Kavanagh 59 / Murphy 28, Anthrobus 78 / Ref: R Furnandiz
Att 11,300 | Pos — | Pt 0 | L | F-A 1:2 | H-T 0-1

	1	2	3	4	5	6	7	8	9	10	11	subs used
City	Ward	Robinson	Small	Mohan	Sigurdsson	Keen*	Oldfield*	Kavanagh G	Taaffe	Lightbourne*	Connor	Aiston/Mackenzie/Crowe
Oxford	*Arendse*	*Powell*		*Watson*	*Murphy*	*Gilchrist*	*Tait*	*Anthrobus*	*Shepherd^*	*Lilley*^*	*Beauchamp Folland*	*Aiston**

Gary Megson is in the hot seat after Brian Little's June departure. Sam Aiston, on loan from Sunderland, is the only new face. The season gets off to a terrible start when Murphy nods home in United's first attack. Kav blasts in from 20 yards but Steve Anthrobus heads home unmarked.

---

2   A   PRESTON   14/8
Scorers, Times, and Referees: Thorne 9 / Nogan 52, Murdock 80 / Ref: K Lynch
Att 11,465 | Pos 22 | Pt 0 | L | F-A 1:2 | H-T 1-0

	1	2	3	4	5	6	7	8	9	10	11	subs used
City	Ward	Robinson	Clarke	Mohan	Sigurdsson	Keen*	Oldfield	Kavanagh G	Taaffe*	Thorne	Connor"	Mackenzie/Jacobsen/Crowe
Preston	*Lucas*	*Alexander*	*Jackson*	*Murdock*	*Kidd*	*Appleton*	*Rankine*	*Gregan*	*Eyres^*	*Macken**	*Nogan*	*Basham/McKenna*

Battling Stoke grab a surprise lead at David Moyes' promotion favourites. Thorne nets whilst lying prone on the ground in a goalmouth melee. Eventually Preston's pressure tells as Kurt Nogan nips in to head past Ward. City move to three at the back but Murdock nods in from a corner.

---

3   H   MILLWALL   22/8
Scorers, Times, and Referees: Thorne 15, Connor 51, Kavanagh 84p / Bircham 75 / Ref: S Mathieson
Att 7,054 | Pos 15 | Pt 3 | W | F-A 3:1 | H-T 1-0

	1	2	3	4	5	6	7	8	9	10	11	subs used
City	Ward	Robinson	Clarke*	Mohan*	Sigurdsson	O'Connor	Oldfield*	Kavanagh G	Aiston*	Thorne	Connor	Petty/Small/Keen
Millwall	*Warner*	*Neill*	*Ryan*	*Nethercott*	*Dolan*	*Bircham*	*Cahill*	*Livermore*^*	*Moody^*	*Shaw*	*Harris*	*Reid/Hill*

City tame Alan McLeary's Lions who have not won in 10 games. Thorne nets after Joe Dolan gifts him the ball. Millwall have a goal ruled out before Connor lunges in to head Thorne's knock-back home. Kav converts after Connor is mauled over by Dolan.

---

4   A   BURNLEY   28/8
Scorers, Times, and Referees: Payton 75 / Ref: T Heilbron
Att 11,328 | Pos 19 | Pt 3 | L | F-A 0:1 | H-T 0-0

	1	2	3	4	5	6	7	8	9	10	11	subs used
City	Ward	Jacobsen	Clarke	Robinson	Sigurdsson	Short*	Keen*	Kavanagh G	O'Connor	Thorne*	Connor	Crowe/Aiston/Oldfield
Burnley	*Crichton*	*West*	*Cowan*	*Mellon^*	*Thomas*	*Armstrong*	*Smith*	*Cook**	*Lee**	*Payton*	*Johnrose*	*Branch/Little/Jepson*

Defences dominate. Anders Jacobsen organises City's back three well. Connor dwells when put through by Clarke and wastes the chance. Stan Ternent's Clarets push forward. Glen Little's direct running worries Robinson. Andy Payton breaks the deadlock with a shot which dribbles in.

---

5   H   GILLINGHAM   30/8
Scorers, Times, and Referees: Sigurdsson 87 / Taylor 90 / Ref: U Rennie
Att 8,369 | Pos 19 | Pt 4 | D | F-A 1:1 | H-T 0-0

	1	2	3	4	5	6	7	8	9	10	11	subs used
City	Ward	Short	Clarke^	Jacobsen	Sigurdsson	Oldfield*	Aiston*	Kavanagh G	O'Connor	Thorne	Connor	Keen/Small/Crowe
Gillingham	*Williams*	*Patterson*	*Smith"*	*Ashby^*	*Southall*	*Hessenthaler*	*Taylor*	*Saunders*	*Lee^*	*Pennock*	*Lewis*	*Miller/Thompson/Hodge*

A dull match is sparked into life by a nail-biting last five minutes. A dubious corner is despatched into the back of the net by Sigurdsson. Peter Taylor's Gills pour forward. Bob Taylor loops home a header from a long throw. Megson is booked for encroaching beyond the technical area.

---

6   A   CAMBRIDGE   4/9
Scorers, Times, and Referees: Connor 19, Oldfield 81, Thorne 86 / Lightbourne 47 (og) / Ref: L Cable
Att 4,007 | Pos 14 | Pt 7 | W | F-A 3:1 | H-T 1-0

	1	2	3	4	5	6	7	8	9	10	11	subs used
City	Ward	Short	Small	Mohan	Jacobsen	Oldfield	Keen	O'Connor	Thorne	Lightbourne*	Connor	Robinson
Cambridge	*V Heusden**	*Chenery*	*Ashbee*	*Duncan*	*Wanless*	*Butler*	*Benjamin*	*Russell*	*Kyd^*	*Eustace*	*Wilson*	*Marshall/Taylor*

In glorious sunshine Connor turns the ball home after Thorne's initial shot is saved. United charge forward and Stoke wobble. Eustace's shot is saved by Ward but rebounds against Lightbourne and into the net. Oldfield finishes off a brilliant free-kick routine. Thorne slams in on the run.

---

7   A   CHESTERFIELD   11/9
Scorers, Times, and Referees: Lightbourne 50, 90 / Ref: D Laws
Att 4,285 | Pos 12 | Pt 10 | W | F-A 2:0 | H-T 0-0

	1	2	3	4	5	6	7	8	9	10	11	subs used
City	Ward	Short*	Clarke	Mohan	Jacobsen	Robinson	Keen	O'Connor	Thorne	Lightbourne	Connor*	Kavanagh G/Oldfield
Chesterfield	*Leaning*	*Hewitt^*	*Blatherwick*	*Breckin*	*Woods*	*Beaumont*	*Curtis*	*Ebdon*	*Carss*	*Reeves*	*Willis*	*Dudley/Bettney*

Lowly Spireites put City under pressure. Ex-Stokie Steve Woods is prominent and the dangerous David Reeves tests Ward twice. Lightbourne nods Keen's free-kick past Andy Leaning. City grow in confidence. Lightbourne is tackled when about to tap in but then lofts home on the run.

---

8   H   WIGAN   18/9
Scorers, Times, and Referees: Lightbourne 48 / Mohan 18 (og) / Ref: S Baines
Att 11,195 | Pos 12 | Pt 11 | D | F-A 1:1 | H-T 0-1

	1	2	3	4	5	6	7	8	9	10	11	subs used
City	Ward	Short	Clarke	Mohan	Jacobsen	Robinson*	Keen^	O'Connor	Thorne	Lightbourne	Connor*	Kavanagh G Oldfield/Aiston
Wigan	*Carroll*	*Bradshaw*	*Bowen*	*Balmer*	*De Zeeuw*	*O'Neill*	*Kilford**	*Sheridan*	*Liddell**	*Haworth*	*Barlow*	*Lee/Martinez*

An ill-tempered game. Mohan deflects Liddell's shot in. Lightbourne loops a header over Roy Carroll. Robinson is scythed down and requires 24 stitches in a thigh wound. An Icelandic consortium is rumoured to want to buy the club. Larus Sigurdsson is sold to West Brom for £350k.

---

9   A   WREXHAM   25/9
Scorers, Times, and Referees: Thorne 27, Lightbourne 50, Mohan 78 / Carey 6, Lowe 83 / Ref: M Messias
Att 5,924 | Pos 6 | Pt 14 | W | F-A 3:2 | H-T 1-1

	1	2	3	4	5	6	7	8	9	10	11	subs used
City	Ward	Short	Clarke	Mohan	Jacobsen	O'Connor	Keen	Connor*	Thorne*	Lightbourne	Kavanagh G	Robinson/Heath/Oldfield
Wrexham	*Dearden*	*McGregor*	*Owen*	*Carey*	*Connolly*	*Ridler*	*Barrett^*	*Ryan^*	*Stevens^*	*Ferguson*	*F'conbridge*	*Hannon/Chalk/Lowe*

New skipper Mohan allows Brian Carey to nod Brian Flynn's men ahead. Thorne scores from 10 yards during a scramble. Lightbourne's effort is deflected past the helpless Kevin Dearden. Mohan plants a header home to make amends. David Lowe sets up a frenetic finish with a header.

---

10   H   SCUNTHORPE   2/10
Scorers, Times, and Referees: Connor 90 / Ref: R Olivier
Att 13,068 | Pos 6 | Pt 17 | W | F-A 1:0 | H-T 0-0

	1	2	3	4	5	6	7	8	9	10	11	subs used
City	Ward	Short	Clarke	Mohan	Jacobsen	O'Connor	Keen	Oldfield*	Thorne^	Lightbourne	Connor*	Kavanagh G Connor/Aiston
Scunthorpe	*Evans*	*Harsley^*	*Dawson*	*Logan*	*Wilcox*	*Hope*	*Walker*	*Hodges**	*Ipoua*	*Sparrow*	*Marshall*	*Sheldon/Gayle*

Megson is manager of the month but speculation suggests he would leave if the proposed takeover goes through. City have the better of a tight game. Kav has a shot kicked off the line. Guy Ipoua causes problems. United hit a post. Connor scores at the second attempt from Keen's pass.

---

11   H   READING   9/10
Scorers, Times, and Referees: Mohan 68, Jacobsen 89 / Forster 52 / Ref: T Jones
Att 9,621 | Pos 3 | Pt 20 | W | F-A 2:1 | H-T 0-0

	1	2	3	4	5	6	7	8	9	10	11	subs used
City	Ward	Short	Clarke	Mohan	Jacobsen	O'Connor	Robinson*	Keen^	Thorne^	Lightbourne!	Connor	Kavanagh G Connor/Oldfield/Heath
Reading	*Whitehead*	*Parkinson*	*Primus*	*Casper*	*Caskey**	*Forster*	*Williams*	*Crawford*	*Bernal*	*Hodges^*	*Smith*	*Grant/McIntyre*

A minute's silence for those killed in the Paddington rail crash. O'Connor's back-pass falls to Nicky Forster who scores. Mohan volleys home Thorne's nod down gloriously as City fight back. Jacobsen nods in his first for the club to steal the points. Lightbourne walks for two yellows.

12 A BOURNEMOUTH 16/10 5,990 21 0-1

Clarke 62
Robinson 24
Ref: A D'Urso

| Ward | Short | Small* | Mohan ! | Jacobsen | O'Connor | Robinson^ | Keen | Thorne | Lightbourne" | Kavanagh G | Clarke/Connor/**Bullock** |
| Ovendale | Young | Warren* | Howe~ | Cox | Broadhurst | Mean | Robinson | Stein | Fletcher | Jorgensen | O'Neill/**Huck** |

Stoke escape as Mel Machin's Cherries dominate. Mark Stein releases Steve Robinson to rifle past the outstanding Ward. Short and O'Connor combine to set up Clarke who skips past two challenges before cracking home. Mohan is dismissed (81 mins) for lashing out at Steve Fletcher.

---

13 A CARDIFF 19/10 6,146 24 1-1

Thorne 23, O'Connor 84
Legg 40
Ref: P Danson

| Ward | Short | Clarke | Mohan | Jacobsen | O'Connor | Keen^ | Thorne | Lightbourne" | Kavanagh G | Robinson/Petty/Connor |
| Hallworth | Faerber | Legg* | Perrett | Boland | Nugent | Hill | Eckhardt | Thomas | Vaughan | Brazier |

Thorne heads home Short's cross. Andy Legg whacks home a superb 25-yard free-kick. Stoke become disjointed but O'Connor sticks out a leg to deflect in a cross. The Icelanders, including former Bundesliga Footballer of the Year Siggy Sigurvinsson, confirm their offer to buy the club.

---

14 H WREXHAM 23/10 10,545 27 2-0

O'Connor 48, Kavanagh 58
Ref: S Lodge

Ward	Short	Clarke	Mohan	Jacobsen	O'Connor	Keen	Thorne	Connor	Kavanagh G	Robinson
Dearden	McGregor	Hardy	Owen	Carey	Chalk*	Barrett^	Spink	Connolly	Roberts	Faulconbridge/Russell
										Gibson

Ward saves brilliantly from Gareth Owen. 18-year-old Matthew Bullock drives forward down the right. O'Connor cracks a short free-kick past Dearden. Kav races on to Keen's pass to shoot inside the far post. Ward saves from Faulconbridge, who also hits a post. 12 games without loss.

---

15 H NOTTS CO 3/11 11,619 27 0-1

Dyer 23
Ref: P Richards

| Ward | Short | Clarke | Robinson | Jacobsen | **Dryden** | Bullock* | O'Connor | Keen^ | Thorne | Lightbourne Kavanagh G Crowe/Connor/Heath |
| Ward | Holmes | Fenton | Redmile | Richardson | Pearce^ | Hughes* | Owers | Bolland | Ramage | Dyer | Rapley/Liburd |

New boss Gary Brazil sees his Magpies team emerge victorious from a battering. The new fluorescent yellow ball just will not find the back of Darren Ward's net. City are on top until Alex Dyer pounces to beat Gavin Ward. Lightbourne has a drive tipped over. Best display this season.

---

16 A BURY 6/11 4,280 28 0-0

Ref: M Dean

| Ward | Short^ | Small | Robinson | Jacobsen | Dryden | Bullock | O'Connor | Keen^ | Thorne | Lightbourne" Kavanagh G Connor/Bullock/Clarke |
| Kenny | Williams | Daws | Swailes C | Billy | Barnes* | Reid | Redmond | Preece | Littlejohn | Lawson |

The consortium is to buy 66% of the shareholding from the current board. Stoke dominate but fail to convert numerous chances. Robinson fires just wide. Dryden has a header tipped round the post. Bernard Manning is dropped as an after-dinner speaker at the club's Sportsman's dinner.

---

17 H BRISTOL CITY 14/11 10,775 29 1-1

Mohan 66
Tinnion 85
Ref: R Beeby

| Ward | Short^ | Clarke | Mohan | Dryden | O'Connor | Keen" | Thorne | Lightbourne Kavanagh G Jacobsen/Robinson/Oldfield |
| Mercer | Bell | Jones S | Holland | Tinnion | Mortimer | Beadle | Murray" | Hutchings | Goodridge | Tistimetanu Millen |

The takeover is confirmed. The new board parades before the kick-off. 'We're here to win' they declare. Gary Megson's swansong is almost a victory as Mohan's header rockets in to end a 368-minute goal drought. Brian Tinnion lashes home a superb dipping volley from over 30 yards.

---

18 A WYCOMBE 23/11 4,345 32 2-0

Kavanagh 44, Danielsson 45, Thorne 62, [Mohan 71]
Ref: M Ryan

| Ward | Robinson | Clarke | Mohan | Jacobsen | O'Connor | Keen | Thorne | Lightbourne^ Kavanagh G **Danielsson**^/Oldfield/Petty |
| Taylor | Lawrence | Vinnicombe* Cousins | Bates | Carroll | Ryan | Devine | Simpson | McSporran /Emblen* | Beeton/Bulman |

Ex-Iceland international boss Gudjon Thordarson sees his new players rip Wycombe to shreds. Kav lashes in from 20 yards. Danielsson leaves two defenders and the keeper on the ground to slot a wonder goal. Thorne and Mohan head home. McSporran throws the ball at Kav in injury-time.

---

19 H COLCHESTER 27/11 14,135 33 1-1

Lightbourne 82
Skelton 71
Ref: G Frankland

| Ward | Robinson | Clarke^ | Mohan | Jacobsen* | O'Connor | Danielsson | Keen | Thorne | Lightbourne Kavanagh G Petty/Crowe |
| Vaughan | Keith | Richard | Greene | Johnson | Dazzell | Duguid^ | McGavin | Gregory D | Skelton* | White | Farley/Lock |

City are awful. Mick Wadsworth's U's score another unchallenged header as Skelton converts Duguid's cross. Crowe has a goal disallowed for a foul. Lightbourne nods in Keen's free-kick. Relief all round. Thordarson notes the difference in performance level. 'We must be consistent.'

---

20 A OXFORD 4/12 5,700 34 1-1

Thorne 79
Beauchamp 27
Ref: D Crick

| Ward | Robinson | Clarke* | Mohan | Jacobsen | O'Connor | Gislason | Keen^ | Thorne | Lightbourne Kavanagh G **Hansson**/Danielsson |
| Lundin | Folland | Weatherstone Watson^ | Whelan | McGowan | Robinson | Murphy | Beauchamp | Lilly* | Anthrobus | Lambert/Fear |

Malcolm Shotton's Oxford have the better of a poor game. Joey Beauchamp cuts in to curl home left footed. Speedy Swede Mikael Hansson is introduced and provides a spark. His right-wing centre is headed home by Thorne from six yards. Stoke's first ever point at the Manor Ground.

---

21 H BRISTOL ROV 18/12 8,3?9 34 1-2

Keen 52
Roberts 72, Walters 84
Ref: M Brandwood

| Ward | Hansson | Danielsson* Mohan | Jacobsen | O'Connor | Gislason | Keen | Thorne | Lightbourne Kavanagh G Oldfield |
| Jones | Pritchard | Foster | Thomson | Tilson | Mauge^ | Hillier | Cureton | Roberts | Pethick* | Walters^ | Challis/Ellington/Bennett |

A much better performance. In a physical match Keen is hacked down. Thorne puts himself about, flattening Jones and Thomson. The pressure tells as Keen nets Lightbourne's cross. The Pirates storm back and Roberts converts Cureton's centre. Walters powers a weak clearance home.

---

22 A BLACKPOOL 26/12 6,374 37 2-1

Robinson 21, Kavanagh 27
Nowland 57
Ref: A Kaye

| Ward | Robinson | Clarke | Mohan | Jacobsen* | O'Connor | Gislason^ | **Kippe** | Thorne^ | Lightbourne Kavanagh G Danielsson/Oldfield |
| Caig | Hills | Bardsley | Carlisle | Bent | Clarkson | Bushell | Nowland | Sh'ttlew'rth* Beesley | Lee^ | Coid/Garvey |

Frode Kippe, on loan from Liverpool, replaces the suspended Jacobsen. Robinson springs the offside trap to slot past Tony Caig. Thorne heads down for Kav to slam home. Mohan is imperious at the back. Nowland scores for Nigel Worthington's Seasiders after Ward saves Bent's shot.

---

23 H OLDHAM 28/12 13,709 38 0-0

Ref: T Parkes

| Ward | Hansson | Clarke" | Mohan | Kippe | O'Connor | Danielsson" Connor | Thorne | Lightbourne Kavanagh G Oldfield/Thorne/Gislason |
| Kelly | McNiven | Holt | Garnett | Duxbury | Rickers | Sheridan | Whitehall* Allott* | Hotte | Adams | Dudley/Tipton |

Andy Ritchie's Oldham arrive 45 mins late but it affects City more. Despite attacking constantly the Potters cannot beat Gary Kelly. He saves well from Hansson, Connor and Mohan. Ward reacts brilliantly to smother Garnett's effort on the line. Carl Muggleton is loaned to Mansfield.

NATIONWIDE DIVISION 2

Manager: Megson ⇒ Thordarson **SEASON 1999-2000**

Results

No	Date	Venue	Team	Att	Pos	Pt	F-A	H-T	Res	Scorers, Times, and Referees
24	3/1	A	BRENTFORD	6,792	9	41	1-0	0-0	W	Thorne 60. Ref: R Furnandiz
25	8/1	H	LUTON	10,016	12	44	2-1	1-0	W	Connor 24, Lighthbourne 87; Spring 59p. Ref: C Foy
26	14/1	H	PRESTON	10,285	2	47	2-1	1-0	W	Kippe 3, O'Connor 87; Alexander 84p. Ref: P Taylor
27	22/1	A	MILLWALL	11,548	4	47	0-1	0-1	L	Gilkes 33. Ref: C Wilkes
28	29/1	H	BURNLEY	15,354	5	48	2-2	0-0	D	Thorne 68, Davis 71 (og); Payton 76p, 83. Ref: M Fletcher
29	5/2	A	GILLINGHAM	7,801	7	48	0-3	0-2	L	Onuora 13, Gooden 32, Rowe 73. Ref: K Lynch
30	8/2	A	LUTON	5,396	9	48	1-2	1-0	L	O'Connor 33; Gray 62, 78. Ref: W Burns
31	12/2	H	CAMBRIDGE	9,662	24	51	1-0	1-0	W	Connor 31. Ref: M Dean
32	19/2	A	COLCHESTER	4,364	14	51	0-1	0-0	L	McGavin 86. Ref: A Hall
33	26/2	A	WIGAN	9,429	4	54	2-1	1-1	W	Kavanagh 28, O'Connor 77; Green 19. Ref: K Leach
34	4/3	H	CHESTERFIELD	11,968	24	57	5-1	3-0	W	Thorne 8, 18, 41, 61, Jacobsen 90; Reeves 70. Ref: G Cain

Line-ups (positions 1–11, subs used)

24 — BRENTFORD
- **Stoke:** 1 Ward, 2 Woodman, 3 Clarke, 4 Mohan, 5 Kippe, 6 O'Connor, 7 Petty, 8 Jacobsen, 9 Thorne^, 10 Connor*, 11 Kavanagh G — subs: Lighthbourne/Danielsson
- *Brentford:* Quinn, Powell, Marshall", Mahon, Owusu, Partridge^, Ingimarsson/Theobald, Agyemang/Clement* — subs: Anderson/Bryan/Kennedy

In torrential rain Stoke soak up pressure and play on the break. The Bees lack any sting. City look dangerous with Hansson tormenting Powell. Thorne scores when Connor is tackled six yards out. Jacobsen nods off the line. 10 away games without loss.

25 — LUTON
- **Stoke:** 1 Ward, 2 Hansson, 3 Clarke^, 4 Mohan, 5 Kippe, 6 O'Connor, 7 Petty", 8 Jacobsen, 9 Thorne^, 10 Connor, 11 Kavanagh G — subs: L'bourne/Dan'sson/Gunn'sson
- *Luton:* Abbey, Boyce^, Taylor!, Doherty, Watts, Johnson, Spring, Locke, White", Douglas^, Gray — subs: Fotiadis/George

Thorne nods down for Connor to convert. Matthew Taylor walks for striking Hansson (44 mins). The ten men win a penalty for Mohan's shove on Phil Gray. £600,000 club record signing Brynjar Gunnarsson is inspirational. Lighthbourne heads in Kavanagh's long throw at the near post.

26 — PRESTON
- **Stoke:** 1 Ward, 2 Hansson, 3 Clarke, 4 Mohan, 5 Kippe, 6 O'Connor, 7 Gunnarsson, 8 Jacobsen, 9 Thorne^, 10 Lighthbourne, 11 Kavanagh G — subs: Gislason
- *Preston:* Moilanen, Alexander, Edwards, Jackson, Murdock, Gregan, Appleton^, Rankine, Nogan, Macken, Eyres^ — subs: Gunnlaugsson/Beresford

Kippe rockets a left-footed volley into the roof of the net. Preston provide City's sternest test yet and Ward is superb in denying Appleton and Nogan. Rankine falls dramatically and the penalty is netted by Graham Alexander. O'Connor slams home in a scramble as Stoke pile forward.

27 — MILLWALL
- **Stoke:** 1 Ward, 2 Hansson^, 3 Clarke, 4 Mohan, 5 Kippe, 6 O'Connor, 7 Gunnarsson, 8 Jacobsen", 9 Thorne", 10 Lighthbourne, 11 Kavanagh G — subs: Connor/Gislason/Oldfield
- *Millwall:* Warner, Nethercott, Fitzgerald, Stuart, Newman, Hill*, Livermore, Gilkes, Cahill, Moody*, Shaw — subs: Sadler/Reid

Jacobsen's error allows Shaw to square to Michael Gilkes to score. Tackles fly in but for once the day doesn't boil over. Paul Moody misses an open goal and has a header ruled out for a foul. Clarke's shot pole-axes a Millwall defender. Other promotion challengers should be beaten.

28 — BURNLEY
- **Stoke:** 1 Ward, 2 Hansson, 3 Clarke, 4 Mohan, 5 Kippe, 6 O'Connor, 7 Gunnarsson, 8 Jacobsen, 9 Thorne, 10 Lighthbourne, 11 Kavanagh G
- *Burnley:* Crichton, West", Thomas, Armstrong, Mullin, Davis, Cook, Johnrose^, Cooke, Payton, Branch" — subs: Smith/Little/Swan

Thorne flicks home Gunnarsson's cross. Steve Davis heads past his own keeper under pressure from Lighthbourne. Andy Payton nets a penalty after Mullin is fouled and then fires past Ward from 20 yards. Swan's handball is penalised but Kav blasts the penalty straight at Paul Crichton.

29 — GILLINGHAM
- **Stoke:** 1 Ward, 2 Hansson, 3 Clarke, 4 Mohan*, 5 Kippe, 6 Petty^, 7 Gunnarsson, 8 Jacobsen, 9 Thorne", 10 Lighthbourne, 11 Connor — subs: Kavanagh G/Robinson/Connor/Bullock
- *Gillingham:* Bartram, Southall, Ashby, Butters, Edge, Hessinthal^*/Smith, Gooden, Lewis, Onuora, Thomson* — subs: Rowe/Saunders

City outplay physical Gillingham for the first half-hour but Mohan's header is cleared off the line and Thorne hits the post. Iffy Onuora nods a corner home then flicks on for Ty Gooden to beat Ward. Rowe slots in unmarked. Stoke's heads drop as the Gills squander numerous chances.

30 — LUTON
- **Stoke:** 1 Ward, 2 Hansson, 3 Clarke, 4 Mohan*, 5 Kippe, 6 O'Connor, 7 Gunnarsson, 8 Jacobsen, 9 Connor*, 10 Oldfield^, 11 Kavanagh G — subs: Petty/Lighthbourne/Thorne
- *Luton:* Abbey, Boyce^, Watts, Doherty, Johnson, George*, Locke, Spring, Taylor, Gray, Douglas — subs: McGowan/Fotiadis

Stoke are all at sea in defence but profit when Clarke beats two players before finding O'Connor who fires home. Kav screws wide when clear as City gain confidence. Kippe hits the bar. Phil Gray poaches two close-range goals as Lennie Lawrence's men fight back. One point from 12.

31 — CAMBRIDGE
- **Stoke:** 1 Ward, 2 Hansson, 3 Clarke, 4 Petty, 5 Kippe, 6 O'Connor, 7 Gunnarsson, 8 Jacobsen, 9 Connor^, 10 Lighthbourne, 11 Kavanagh G — subs: Thorne
- *Cambridge:* Marshall, Chenery, Wilson, McNeil, Eustace, Mackenzie^/Wanless, Wanless, Ashbee, Guinan*, Benjamin/Youngs" — subs: Kyd/Preece/Taylor

Roy McFarland's men have not won away all season. Ward makes a great stop from Trevor Benjamin as City struggle. Lighthbourne's header is saved by Shaun Marshall but Connor knocks home the rebound. Petty's header is tipped on to a post. Dean Crowe joins Northampton on loan.

32 — COLCHESTER
- **Stoke:** 1 Ward, 2 Hansson, 3 Clarke*, 4 Petty, 5 Kippe, 6 O'Connor^, 7 Gunnarsson, 8 Jacobsen, 9 Connor, 10 Lighthbourne, 11 Kavanagh G — subs: Gislason/Thorne
- *Colchester:* Brown, Dunne, Keith, Johnson R, Wilkins, Gregory D, Johnson G, Dozzell, Duguid^, Morralee*, McGavin — subs: Tresor Lua Lua/Lock

On a poor pitch Stoke press forward. Petty's drive is tipped over. Dozzell squanders an easy header from eight yards. The pressure builds after Tresor Lua Lua is introduced. Gislason loses Pat McGavin who nods in unmarked at the far post. An incensed Ward makes his feelings known.

33 — WIGAN
- **Stoke:** 1 Ward, 2 Hansson, 3 Clarke, 4 Mohan, 5 Kippe, 6 O'Connor, 7 Gunnarsson, 8 Petty, 9 Thorne^, 10 Kavanagh*, 11 Connor — subs: Oldfield/Robinson
- *Wigan:* Carroll, Green, Sheridan*, Balmer, De Zeeuw, McGibbon, O'Neill, Martinez, Roberts^, Peron^, Liddell — subs: Bradshaw/Haworth/Bartlow

The world's greatest player, Sir Stanley Matthews, has died aged 85. In disgraceful scenes fans of both clubs clash. The referee takes the teams off. On resumption Scott Green scores. Kav glances in a header. O'Connor cracks home from the edge of the area. Wigan eight without a win.

34 — CHESTERFIELD
- **Stoke:** 1 Ward, 2 Hansson, 3 Clarke*, 4 Mohan^, 5 Kippe, 6 O'Connor, 7 Gunnarsson*, 8 Petty, 9 Thorne, 10 Gunnlaugsson, 11 Kavanagh — subs: Jacobsen/Robinson/Small
- *Chesterfield:* Gayle, Hewitt, Pointon", Blatherwick/Breckin, Breckin, Beaumont, Curtis, Carss, Williams^, Reeves, Perkins — subs: Payne/Howard

Peter Thorne scores the first ever hat-trick at the Brit. Two headers, a tap-in and a sweet half-volley to become the first Potter to score four from open play since 1966. Jacobsen taps in from close range in a frantic scramble. John Duncan's Spireites have never beaten Stoke in 17 attempts.

Stoke City — match record (games 35–46)

No	V	Date	Opponent	HT	FT	Lg Pos	Gm	Att	Scorers / Referee
35	A	11/3	NOTTS CO	0-0	0-0	7 / 8	58	9,67?	Ref: P Danson
36	H	18/3	WYCOMBE	0-1	1-1	8 / 12	59	9,738	Gunnlaugsson 54p; McSporran 23 — Ref: F Stretton
37	H	25/3	BLACKPOOL	0-0	3-0	8 / 23	62	10,0?2	Gunnarsson 62, Mohan 69, Gudjonsson 71 — Ref: S Baines
38	A	28/3	BRISTOL CITY	2-1	2-2	7 / 9	63	8,1?3	Lightbourne 26, Kavanagh 39; Thorpe 10, 78 — Ref: B Knight
39	A	1/4	BRISTOL ROV	1-2	3-3	7 / 3	64	9,3?2	Thorne 10, 62, 79; Pethick 20, Cureton 32p, Walters 69 — Ref: R Harris
40	A	4/4	OLDHAM	1-0	1-0	7 / 11	67	4,?74	Thorne 23 — Ref: K Hill
41	H	8/4	BRENTFORD	1-0	1-0	6 / 15	70	9,?55	Thorne 8 — Ref: D Laws
42	H	22/4	BOURNEMOUTH	0-0	1-0	7 / 14	73	15,?22	Thorne 81 — Ref: M Messias
43	A	24/4	SCUNTHORPE	2-0	2-0	7 / 23	76	5,4?5	Thorne 24, 39 — Ref: R Furnandiz
44	H	30/4	CARDIFF	1-0	2-1	7 / 21	79	14,132	Gunnlaugsson 3, O'Connor 69; Young 71 — Ref: G Frankland
45	H	3/5	BURY	1-0	3-0	4 / 15	82	1?,?92	Thorne 11, 55, 81 — Ref: M Cowburn
46	A	6/5	READING	0-0	0-1	6 / 10	82	1?,?46	Caskey 81p — Ref: J Robinson

Home / Away / Average 11,426

---

35 — NOTTS CO (A)
Stoke: Ward, Hansson, Clarke, Mohan, Kippe, O'Connor, Gunnarsson, Jacobsen, Thorne*, Gunn'lgsson, Kavanagh, Lightbourne
Notts Co: Ward, Holmes*, Redmile, Richardson, Dyer, Liburd, Brough, Owers, Hughes*, Ramage, Stallard, Farrell/Bolland

Classy Arnar Gunnlaugsson, on loan from Leicester, produces a superb performance. He sends in Gunnarsson, who is fouled, but the ref waves play on. Ward pulls off a sensational save from Sean Farrell to secure a draw. Manager's son Bjarni Gudjonsson arrives from Genk for £250k.

36 — WYCOMBE (H)
Stoke: Ward, Hansson, Clarke, Mohan, Kippe, O'Connor, Gunnarsson, Jacobsen*, Thorne*, Gunn'lgsson^, Kavanagh, Gud'ss'n^/Iwelumo
Wycombe: Taylor, Cousins, Vinnicombe* Carroll, Rogers, Ryan, Simpson, Brown, Holsgrove, McSporran, Senda^, Bulman/Thompson

Lawrie Sanchez's Chairboys dig in. Thorne has an effort cleared off the line. The play-offs look a long way off now. Chris Iwelumo signs for £25k. Gunnlaugsson slams in a penalty after a handball. Frustrated Stoke cannot find the net.

37 — BLACKPOOL (H)
Stoke: Ward, Hansson, Clarke, Mohan, Dryden*, O'Connor, Gunnarsson, Gudjonsson, Thorne, Gunn'lgsson^, Kavanagh^, Lightbourne*
Blackpool: Barnes, Couzens^, Bardsley, Carlisle, Hughes, Clarkson, Newell*, Gill, Richardson", Jaszczun, Thomas, Murphy/Wellens/Hills

Stoke huff and puff but Nigel Worthington's Tangerines keep it tight. Kav urges City forward. Gunnarsson nets after Carlisle heads against his own crossbar. Mohan nods home a corner. Gudjonsson curls in spectacularly from 25 yards. Millionaire Philip Rawlins is set to join the board.

38 — BRISTOL CITY (A)
Stoke: Ward, Hansson, Clarke, Mohan, Dryden*, O'Connor, Gunnarsson, Gudjonsson, Thorne, Gunn'lgsson, Kavanagh, Lightbourne
Bristol City: Phillips, Amanwaah, Burnell, Taylor*, Bell, Murray, Holland, Clist^, Brown, Thorpe, Spencer, Hill/Tinnion

Stoke run the game but concede when Tony Thorpe heads home Shaun Murray's cross. Thorpe sets up Lightbourne to tap in and then supplies Kav who fires home. Gunnlaugsson outwits two players and cracks in but a great goal is disallowed for handball. Thorpe rounds Ward to level.

39 — BRISTOL ROV (A)
Stoke: Ward, Gunn'lgsson* Clarke, Mohan, Dryden, O'Connor, Gunnarsson, Gudjonsson* Thorne, Gunn'lgsson, Kavanagh, Lightbourne
Bristol Rov: Jones, Pethick, Thomson, Tillson, Andreasson*, Astafjevs*, Hillier, Challis, Roberts^, Cureton, Walters, Ellington/Wolleaston

Thorne nets another treble. He turns in Lightbourne's mis-hit effort, bags a great header and dummies past Jones before slotting in to complete the first away hat-trick for 5 years. Mohan gives away a soft penalty. Walters smokes in a free-kick. Two Rovers fans attempt to assault Ward.

40 — OLDHAM (A)
Stoke: Ward, Gunn'lgsson* Clarke, Mohan, Dryden, O'Connor, Gunnarsson, Gudjonsson* Thorne, Gunn'lgsson, Kavanagh, Lightbourne^
Oldham: Kelly, Garnett, Hotte*, Jones, McNiven, Holt, Rickers, Duxbury, Boshell, Sugden^, Whitehall, Tipton/Futcher

Both keepers star in an eventful match. Gary Kelly keys brilliantly from Gunnlaugsson, Thorne and Kav. Ward denies Whitehall and Sugden. Thorne heads home after Kav's long throw is allowed to bounce in the area. A glimmer of hope for the play-offs? Crowe is loaned out to Bury.

41 — BRENTFORD (H)
Stoke: Ward, Hansson* Clarke*, Mohan, Dryden, O'Connor, Gunn'lgsson Gunnarsson, Thorne, Gunn'lgsson, Kavanagh, Lightbourne
Brentford: Woodman, Theobald*, Marshall, Powell, Anderson, Quinn, Rowlands^, Evans, Scott, Owusu*, Partridge, Graham/Pinamonte/James

Thorne thumps in after Andy Woodman drops Kav's corner. City play tidy football. Right-back Steve Melton, on loan from Forest, impresses. Graham volleys just wide from thirty yards. Gunnlaugsson's free-kick hits the bar. City fans rank 9th in a national survey on supporters' fashions.

42 — BOURNEMOUTH (H)
Stoke: Ward, Hansson* Clarke*, Mohan, Dryden, O'Connor, Gunn'lgsson Gunnarsson, Thorne, Gunn'lgsson, Kavanagh, Lightbourne^
Bournemouth: Ovendale, Young*, Fenton, Howe, Warren*, Stock*, Fletcher C, Robinson, Jorgensen, Dryden/Connor, Elliott/Sheerin/Smith

City keep up the pressure on the stumbling play-off clubs by grinding out a good victory. Thorne dives full length to head past Mark Ovendale. Stoke employ American David Raney to ensure that the Feng Shui of the Britannia Stadium is maximised. Last home defeat was in December.

43 — SCUNTHORPE (A)
Stoke: Ward, Hansson, Gunn'lgsson Mohan, Dryden*, O'Connor, Gunn'lgsson Gunnarsson, Thorne, Gunn'lgsson*, Kavanagh, Lightbourne^
Scunthorpe: Evans, Harsley, Dawson, Logan, Hope, Walker, Hodges, Sheldon*, Robinson, Torpey, Stanton, Melton/Jacobsen/Clarke — Dualley/Ipoua

Thorne scores from 12 yards after Lightbourne's persistence forces an error. He then volleys in left footed. Brian Laws' Irons push forward in a bid to beat the drop. Gary Bull chips into Ward's hands when clear. Thorne has 16 goals in 13 games including the Auto Windscreen Shield.

44 — CARDIFF (H)
Stoke: Ward, Hansson, Gunn'lgsson* Mohan, Dryden, O'Connor, Gunn'lgsson Gunnarsson, Thorne, Gunn'lgsson, Kavanagh, Lightbourne
Cardiff: Kelly, Faerber, Legg, Young, Boland, Bonner, Bowen, Nugent, Brazier, Eckhardt, Brayson, Melton

Gunnlaugsson belts in a free-kick. O'Connor plays a one-two and fires past Kelly from 15 yards. Young nods home Kevin Nugent's goalbound header. Trouble as Cardiff fans run riot. A heavy police presence quells the violence. The play-offs edge even closer. Cardiff are nearly down.

45 — BURY (H)
Stoke: Ward, Hansson, Clarke, Mohan, Dryden^, O'Connor, Gunn'lgsson Gunnarsson, Thorne, Gunn'lgsson, Kavanagh, Lightbourne
Bury: Kenny, Bryan, Swailes C, Swailes D* Hill, Billy, Daws, Reid, Littlejohn*, Bhutia^, Preece, Avdiu/Barnes/Challinor

Another Thorne hat-trick sees off Neil Warnock's Bury. He nips between Chris Swailes and Kenny to slot home, swivels to fire an unstoppable shot home and heads past Paddy Kenny after Lightbourne flicks on a corner. Bury offer no resistance. Party time at the Brit. 13 without defeat.

46 — READING (A)
Stoke: Ward, Hansson, Clarke, Mohan, Dryden, O'Connor*, Gunn'lgsson Gunnarsson, Thorne, Jacobsen^, Kavanagh, Lightbourne^
Reading: Whitehead, Primus, Murty, Williams A, Igoe*, Forster, Williams M, Caskey^, Smith, Robinson, Newman, Gunnlaugsson/Connor/Keen — Henderson/Evers

City incredibly go into the final game with a chance to go up automatically if results go their way. A nervy match never looks like providing the avalanche of goals City would need. Darius Henderson hits a post before Mohan trips Caskey for the penalty. Connor nets but is given offside.

NATIONWIDE DIVISION 2 (CUP-TIES)   Manager: Megson ⇨ Thordarson   SEASON 1999-2000

Play-Offs

	Att	F-A	H-T	Scorers, Times, and Referees	1	2	3	4	5	6	7	8	9	10	11	subs used
SF H GILLINGHAM 13/5	22,124	W 3-2	2-1	Gunnlaugsson 1, Lightbourne 8, Thorne 67 / Gooden 18, Hessenthaler 90 · Ref: M Dean	Ward	Hansson	Clarke	Mohan	Dryden*	O'Connor	Gunnarsson	Gunnl'gsson^	Thorne	Lightbourne	Kavanagh	Jacobsen/Gudjonsson
					Bartram	*Southall*	*Edge*	*Ashby*	*Pennock*	*Butters*	*Smith**	*Hessenthaler*	*Gooden*	*Onoura*	*Lewis*	*Browning*

A superb game. Lightbourne tees up Gunnlaugsson after just 25 seconds before the compliment is returned. Gooden keeps Peter Taylor's team in it. Thorne taps in when Vince Bartram fails to hold O'Connor's header. Hessenthaler's fantastic effort comes as Stoke are trying to kill time.

	Att	F-A	H-T	Scorers, Times, and Referees	1	2	3	4	5	6	7	8	9	10	11	subs used
SF A GILLINGHAM 17/5	10,386	L 0-3 aet	0-0	Ashby 55, Onoura 102, Smith 118 · Ref: R Styles (Stoke lose 3-5 on aggregate)	Ward	Hansson	Clarke !	Mohan	Gudjonsson	O'Connor	Gunnarsson	Jacobsen	Gunnl'gsson^	Lightbourne*	Kavanagh !	Melton/Connor
					Bartram	*Southall*	*Edge**	*Ashby*	*Pennock*	*Butters*	*Asaba^*	*Hessenthaler*	*Gooden*	*Onoura"*	*Lewis*	*Butler/Smith/Nosworthy*

City are holding on comfortably when Clarke is sent off (43 mins) for two bookings in a minute. Kav sees red in an off the ball incident. Barry Ashby scores from the following corner. At 0-2 Connor hits the post in extra-time. Paul Smith sends the Gills to Wembley from Butler's pass.

Worthington Cup

	Att	F-A	H-T	Scorers, Times, and Referees	1	2	3	4	5	6	7	8	9	10	11	subs used
1:1 A MACCLESFIELD 10/8	2,551	D 1-1	1-0	Keen 8 / Priest 77 · Ref: M Riley	Ward	Kavanagh J	Small*	Mohan	Sigurdsson	Keen	Oldfield	Kavanagh G	Taaffe	Lightbourne*	Connor	Crowe/Clarke
					Price	*Tinson*	*Collins*	*Ingram*	*Riach*	*Sedgemore**	*Davies*	*Priest*	*Whittaker"*	*Barker*	*Tomlinson**	*Astey/Wood/Durkan*

A paltry crowd see a poor match. Kevin Keen's headed goal is eclipsed by Priest's header from yet another poorly defended set-piece. Connor beats Ryan Price but the ball is cleared off the line. Taffe misses when well placed. Durkan blazes wide as Sammy McIlroy's team end on top.

	Att	F-A	H-T	Scorers, Times, and Referees	1	2	3	4	5	6	7	8	9	10	11	subs used
1:2 H MACCLESFIELD 25/8	5,003 3:13	W 3-0 (15)	0-0	Connor 59, Thorne 69, O'Connor 75 · Ref: J Kirkby (Stoke win 4-1 on aggregate)	Ward	Jacobsen	Clarke	Robinson*	Sigurdsson	O'Connor	Oldfield*	Kavanagh G	Aiston	Thorne	Connor"	Keen/Short/Crowe
					Price	*Abbey*	*Collins*	*Riach"*	*Wood^*	*Ware**	*Priest*	*Sedgemore*	*Davies*	*Askey*	*Barker*	*Whittaker/Tomlinson/Brown*

Another low gate. City are abysmal. Luckily Macclesfield are worse. Ward pulls off a superb save from Ben Sedgemore. Confidence returns as Keen releases Connor who cracks home. Thorne nods in Kav's corner. Thorne nets his first for the club after Thorne and Connor set him up.

	Att	F-A	H-T	Scorers, Times, and Referees	1	2	3	4	5	6	7	8	9	10	11	subs used
2:1 H SHEFFIELD WED 14/9	9,313 P20	D 0-0 (12)	0-0	Ref: A Leake	Ward	Short	Clarke	Mohan	Jacobsen	Robinson	Keen*	O'Connor	Thorne	Lightbourne	Kavanagh G	Connor
					Pressman	*Nolan*	*Thorne*	*Walker*	*Briscoe*	*Alex'derson*	*Atherton^*	*Sonner*	*Rudi*	*Booth*	*De Bilde^*	*Donnelly/Carbone*

Stoke start brightly against Danny Wilson's team. Thorne hits the foot of the post as City dominate the premiership strugglers. Benito Carbone trots on to fire up Wednesday and Ward parries his 25-yard stinger. Thorne's header just drops the wrong side of the post. Much the better side.

	Att	F-A	H-T	Scorers, Times, and Referees	1	2	3	4	5	6	7	8	9	10	11	subs used
2:2 A SHEFFIELD WED 22/9	10,993 P20	L 1-3 (12)	0-2	Kavanagh G 74 / Alexandersson 5, 68, De Bilde 24 · Ref: A Butler (Stoke lose 1-3 on aggregate)	Ward	Short	Clarke	Mohan	Jacobsen	Petty*	Keen	O'Connor"	Thorne^	Lightbourne	Kavanagh G	Oldfield/Connor/Heath
					Srnicek	*Nolan*	*Briscoe**	*Donnelly*	*Emerson*	*Walker*	*Alex'dersson*	*Sonnern*	*Rudi"*	*Booth*	*De Bilde^*	*Haslam/Sibon/Cresswell*

Niclas Alexandersson volleys home on the run to settle Wednesday's nerves. Gilles de Bilde nets a carbon copy as the Owls bounce back from a 0-8 defeat at Newcastle. Alexandersson taps home after Ward saves Donnelly's effort. Kavanagh blasts in a corker left footed from 25 yards.

FA Cup

	Att	F-A	H-T	Scorers, Times, and Referees	1	2	3	4	5	6	7	8	9	10	11	subs used
1 A BLACKPOOL 30/10	4,721 23	L 0-2 (3)	0-1	Carlisle 5, Nowland 90 · Ref: D Laws	Ward	Short	Clarke	Robinson^	Jacobsen	O'Connor	Wooliscroft	Keen	Thorne^	Lightbourne	Kavanagh G	Bullock/Connor
					Caig	*Bryan^*	*Carlisle*	*Hughes*	*Hills*	*Clarkson*	*Bushell*	*Nowland*	*Robinson*	*Murphy*	*Coid**	*Forsyth/Bent*

The noon kick-off doesn't suit City. A deluge renders the pitch impossible. Clarke Carlisle lashes in after Ward parries Nowland's effort. Stoke are shocking and it is no surprise when Adam Nowland snaffles up Short's awful back-pass to score. Out of the cup before the clocks go back.

League Table

	Team	P	Home W	D	L	F	A	Away W	D	L	F	A	Pts
1	Preston	46	15	4	4	37	23	13	7	3	37	14	95
2	Burnley	46	16	3	4	42	23	9	10	4	27	24	88
3	Gillingham *	46	16	3	4	46	21	9	7	7	33	27	85
4	Wigan	46	15	3	5	37	14	7	14	2	35	24	83
5	Millwall	46	14	7	2	41	18	9	6	8	35	32	82
6	STOKE	46	13	7	3	37	18	10	6	7	31	24	82
7	Bristol Rov	46	13	7	3	34	19	10	4	9	35	26	80
8	Notts Co	46	14	6	3	32	27	5	9	9	29	28	65
9	Bristol City	46	14	2	8	31	18	5	5	10	28	39	64
10	Reading	46	10	9	4	28	18	6	5	12	29	45	62
11	Wrexham	46	9	6	8	23	24	8	5	10	29	37	62
12	Wycombe	46	11	4	8	32	24	6	9	9	24	30	61
13	Luton	46	13	7	6	41	35	3	13	9	20	30	61
14	Oldham	46	11	5	10	27	28	7	8	8	23	27	60
15	Bury	46	13	10	5	38	33	5	8	10	23	31	57
16	Bournemouth	46	11	6	6	37	19	5	3	15	22	43	57
17	Brentford	46	8	6	9	27	31	5	11	7	20	30	52
18	Colchester	46	9	4	10	36	40	6	12	5	23	42	52
19	Cambridge	46	8	6	9	38	33	4	6	13	26	32	48
20	Oxford	46	6	5	12	24	38	6	4	13	19	35	45
21	Cardiff	46	10	8	5	23	34	4	7	12	22	33	44
22	Blackpool	46	10	9	4	26	37	4	7	12	23	40	41
23	Scunthorpe	46	6	13	4	16	34	6	12	5	24	40	39
24	Chesterfield	46	5	7	11	17	25	2	8	13	17	38	36
		1104	234	155	163	770	634	163	155	234	634	770	1501

* promoted after play-offs

Appearances and Goals

Player	App Lge	Sub	LC	Sub	FAC	Sub	Goals Lge	LC	FAC	Tot
Aiston, Sam	2	4		1			1			1
Bullock, Matthew	4	3								
Clarke, Clive	39	3	3	1	1		1			1
Connor, Paul	17	11	2	2	2	1	6		1	7
Crowe, Dean		6		2						
Danielsson, Einar	3	5					1			1
Dryden, Richard	11	2								
Gislason, Sigursteinn	4	4								
Gudjonsson, Bjarni	7	1					1			1
Gunnarsson, Brynjar	21	1					1			1
Gunnlaugsson, Arnar	10	3					2			2
Hansson, Mikael	24	3								
Heath, Robert		3								
Iwelumo, Chris		3		1						
Jacobsen, Anders	29	4	3		1		2			2
Kavanagh, Graham	44	1	4		1		7		1	8
Kavanagh, Jason		1	1							
Keen, Kevin	20	3	3		1		1		1	2
Kippe, Frode	15	3					1			1
Lightbourne, Kyle	35	5	3		1		7			7
MacKenzie, Neil		2								
Melton, Stephen		6								
Mohan, Nicky	40		3				5			5
O'Connor, James	40	3	2		1		5		1	6
Oldfield, David	7	12	2	1	1		1			1
Petty, Ben	7	8	1							
Robinson, Phil	14	2	2		1		1			1
Short, Chris	14	2	2	1	1					
Sigurdsson, Larus	5		2		2					
Small, Bryan	5	3	1							
Taaffe, Steven	2	1								
Thorne, Peter	41	4	3		1		24		1	25
Ward, Gavin	46		4		1					
Wooliscroft, Ashley							1			1
(own-goals)							1			1
34 players used	506	100	44	9	11	2	68		5	73

Odds & ends

Double wins: (7) Blackpool, Brentford, Cambridge, Cardiff, Chesterfield, Scunthorpe, Wrexham.

Double losses: (0).

Won from behind: (3) Reading (h), Wigan (a), Wrexham (a).

Lost from in front: (3) Bristol Rov (h), Luton (a), Preston (a).

High spots: Making the play-offs on the back of a fabulous unbeaten run.
Having the club's future secured by the arrival of the Icelandic consortium.
Peter Thorne's fantastic form in the second half of the season.
Winning the Autoglass Trophy against Bristol City at Wembley.
Scoring in the first minute of the play-offs.

Low spots: One win in six after beating leaders Preston.
Appalling crowds at the start of the season.
Saying goodbye to the popular Gary Megson.
Andy Hessenthaler's superb late goal in the first leg of the play-offs.
Losing in controversial circumstances at Gillingham in the play-offs.

Player of the Year: James O'Connor.
Ever-presents: (1) Gavin Ward.
Hat-tricks: (3) Peter Thorne.
Leading scorer: (25) Peter Thorne.

LIST OF SUBSCRIBERS

VOTES FOR THE MOST POPULAR STOKE CITY PLAYER 1970-2000

Subscriber	Vote	Subscriber	Vote	Subscriber	Vote
Richard Adams	Garth Crooks	Dave Booth	Mark Chamberlain	Jonathan Corn	Denis Smith
John Alcock	Stanley Matthews	David Bostock	Denis Smith	Margaret Croucher	Mike Pejic
Simon Alcock	Alan Hudson	Ron Brackley	David Gregory	Norman Croucher	John Mahoney
Tom Alcock	Stanley Matthews	Robert & Bray	John Ritchie	Neil Cutcliffe	John Mahoney
Stephen Allen	Terry Conroy	Robert Brookes	Alan Hudson	Rob Davies	Mark Stein
Angela Armitt	Peter Fox	Robert Brough	Jimmy Robertson	David J Davis	Jimmy Greenhoff
Frank Armitt	Alan Hudson	Paul Bryan	Jimmy Greenhoff	Ian J Davis	Alan Hudson
Matthew Armitt	Peter Thorne	Margaret Bryant	Alan Hudson	James Devey	Mark Prudhoe
Stephen Armitt	Ian Cranson	Budge	Denis Smith	John Devlin	Vince Overson
Mr Martyn Arrowsmith	Peter Dobing	David William Burgess	Alan Hudson	Pete Divall	Alan Hudson
Paul Atkins	Jimmy Greenhoff	George Burgess	Jimmy Greenhoff	Stephen Dunn	Alan Hudson
Brian Austin	Mark Stein	Neil Burke	Alan Hudson	Alan Eardley	Terry Conroy
David J Baker	Denis Smith	Joe Byatt	Denis Smith	Rick Eastman	Gordon Banks
Russell Baker	Alan Hudson	Steve Cannon	Mickey Thomas	Daniel Edgar	Peter Fox
Karl Banford	Denis Smith	Paul Cashman	James O'Connor	Richard Edwards	Alan Hudson
Alan Banks	Alan Hudson	Stephen Mark Chaldecott	Mark Stein	Ole Egerïs	Gordon Banks
Steven Barley	Jimmy Greenhoff	Adam J Challinor	Mark Stein	Mr Malcolm Ellerton	Alan Hudson
Stephen Barlow	Denis Smith	Jane Childs	Jimmy Greenhoff	Steve Ellis	Denis Smith
John (PG) Barnes	Jimmy Greenhoff	George Clarke	John Mahoney	E William Evanson	Alan Hudson
Brian Baxendale	Denis Smith	Malcolm Clarke	Jimmy Greenhoff	Michael E Evanson	Garth Crooks
Alan Bennett	Alan Hudson	Jeff Clowes	Gordon Banks	Richard W Evanson	Jimmy Greenhoff
Chris Benmon	Mark Chamberlain	Stephen Glunn	Denis Smith	Terry Everill	Jimmy Greenhoff
Paul Bestwick	Jimmy Greenhoff	Lisa & Sara Cobden	Peter Fox	Stein Erik Finne	Denis Smith
Clive Bickley	Jimmy Greenhoff	Eric Cooper	Peter Dobing	Steve Foster	Alan Hudson
Stephen M Bloor	Jimmy Greenhoff	Paul Cooper	Mark Stein	Steve Foster	Gordon Banks
Julian Boodell	Alan Hudson	Steve & Ian Cooper	Jimmy Greenhoff	John George Garner	Alan Hudson
William Boodell	Mark Stein	Adam Cope	James O'Connor	David Gater	John Ritchie

LIST OF SUBSCRIBERS

VOTES FOR THE MOST POPULAR STOKE CITY PLAYER 1970-2000

LIST OF SUBSCRIBERS

VOTES FOR THE MOST POPULAR STOKE CITY PLAYER 1970-2000

Subscriber	Vote
Nick Nicol	Jimmy Greenhoff
Sam Norcop	Denis Smith
Mr Lars Normann	Jimmy Greenhoff
Mick O'Rourke	Alan Hudson
John Oakden	Jimmy Greenhoff
Paul & Lewis Ogle	Peter Fox
Dougie Old (Bristol)	Terry Conroy
Mark Oliver	Terry Conroy
Gillian Orrell	Gordon Banks
Willy Osby	Jimmy Greenhoff
Craig Jason Ottolini	Denis Smith
Lee & Joanne Palmer	Terry Conroy
Rachel Parkes	Terry Conroy
Andy Peck	Jimmy Greenhoff
Michael Perry	Gordon Banks
Andy Phillips	John Mahoney
Mrs Gillian Pilcher	Peter Dobing
Jim Poole	Denis Smith
Mike Preston	Calvin Palmer
Sue Prince	Jimmy Greenhoff
Ryan Procter	Vince Overson
Garry Quinn	Mark Stein
Gary M Randall	Mark Stein
John & Kath Rhodes	Jimmy Greenhoff
Gareth Richardson	Mark Stein
Michael W Richardson	Alan Hudson
Mark Rogers	Jimmy Greenhoff
Jon Rollinson	John Ritchie
Glyn Rospendowski	Jimmy Greenhoff
Gary Rowland	Peter Fox
Stuart Rowland	Peter Fox
Paul Ruane & Carolyn Jones	Mark Chamberlain
Nigel John Rushton	Alan Hudson
Phil Ryles	Jimmy Greenhoff
David Salmon	Terry Conroy
Colin Shaw	George Berry
Lee Shaw	Mark Stein
Robert Shorthouse	James O'Connor
Andy See	Denis Smith
Dan See	Mark Stein
George W E Smith	Jimmy Greenhoff
Martin Smith	Denis Smith
N J Smith	George Berry
Simon James Smith	James O'Connor
Wayne Smith	Jimmy Greenhoff
Keith Southall	Harry Burrows
Huston Spratt	Denis Smith
Jonathan Spry	Jimmy Greenhoff
Paul Stokes	Alan Hudson
Neil & Sue Surman	Jimmy Greenhoff
Tates	Alan Hudson
Mr H Taylor	Peter Dobing
C Tideswell	Jimmy Greenhoff
Nick Tindall	Alan Hudson
Philip Tomlinson	Alan Hudson
Kendall Trigg	Mickey Thomas
Lynsey Jane Unwin	Peter Fox
Mr Peter Vaughan	Jimmy Greenhoff
Roy Wakeford	Denis Smith
Graham Walker	Steve Bould
Walshy	Peter Thorne
Mr Ian M Webb	John Ritchie
Stan Whitmore	Neil Franklin
Chris Whittaker	Jimmy Greenhoff
Gary P Wilcox	Alan Hudson
Craig A Williams	Peter Fox
Robert E Wills	Jimmy Greenhoff
Kerry Winshaw	Graham Kavanagh
Steve Windsor	Jimmy Greenhoff
Neil Withington	Denis Smith
Bernard Wood	Gordon Banks
Graham Wood	Gordon Banks
Peter J Wyatt	Alan Hudson

MOST POPULAR STOKE CITY PLAYER 1970-2000
(34 different players received votes)

1st Jimmy Greenhoff	5th Gordon Banks
2nd Alan Hudson	6th Peter Fox
3rd Denis Smith	7th Terry Conroy
4th Mark Stein	